OOIS 2000

Springer-Verlag London Ltd.

Also Available:

OOIS'98
1998 International Conference on Object Oriented Information Systems,
9-11 September 1998, Paris
Edited by Colette Rolland and Georges Grosz

OOIS'97
1997 International Conference on Object Oriented Information Systems,
10-12 November 1997, Brisbane
Edited by Maria E Orlowska and Roberto Zicari

OOIS 2000

6th International Conference on
Object Oriented Information Systems
18 - 20 December 2000, London, UK

Proceedings

Edited by
Dilip Patel
South Bank University, London, UK
Islam Choudhury
London Guildhall University, London, UK
Shushma Patel
South Bank University, London, UK
Sergio de Cesare
Brunel University, London, UK

Presented by

Supported by

 Springer

Dilip Patel
School of Computing, Information Systems and Mathematics,
South Bank University, 103 Borough Road, London, UK

Islam Choudhury
School of Computing, London Guildhall University, 100 Minories, London, UK

Shushma Patel
School of Computing, Information Systems and Mathematics,
South Bank University, 103 Borough Road, London, UK

Sergio de Cesare
Department of Information Systems and Computing, Brunel University,
Uxbridge, London, UK

ISBN 978-1-85233-420-8   ISBN 978-1-4471-0299-1 (eBook)
DOI 10.1007/978-1-4471-0299-1

British Library Cataloguing in Publication Data
A catalog record for this book is available from the British Library.

Library of Congress Cataloging-in-Publication Data
A catalog record for this book is available from the Library of Congress.

© Springer-Verlag London 2001
Originally published by Springer-Verlag London Berlin Heidelberg in 2001
Softcover reprint of the hardcover 1st edition 2001

Typesetting: Camera ready by contributors

34/3830-543210 Printed on acid-free paper SPIN 10790885

Preface

New object-oriented technologies have been conceived and implemented over the past decade in order to manage complexity inherent in information systems development. Research has spanned from information systems modelling languages (UML and OML) to databases (ODMG), from programming languages (Java) to middleware technology (CORBA). A more widespread use of the Internet has led to the emergence and integration of various other technologies, such as XML and database connectivity tools, allowing businesses to access and exchange information over the Internet. The main theme of OOIS 2000 was "Object-Technology and New Business Opportunities" and focused on research conducted in the area of effective information systems development for the promotion of e-commerce. Papers were invited from academics and practitioners. The thirty-nine papers accepted for OOIS 2000 are included in these proceedings. It is nice to see this year that the shift from centralised to distributed systems and the widespread access and use of the Internet has allowed the advent of new opportunities for businesses to exploit, in the form of e-commerce.

The papers included in the proceedings embrace the above themes and have been presented in the following categories:

- Databases and Programming Issues
- Modelling and Design Issues
- Electronic Commerce
- XML and CORBA Issues
- UML and Modelling Issues
- Architectures, Patterns and Visualisation
- Measurements

During the preparation of this conference many people contributed towards the success of OOIS 2000. We would like to acknowledge the hard work of the programme committee and additional reviewers in reviewing the papers with a very short turn around time. We are indebted to the staff and research students from the Centre for Information and Organisation Studies at South Bank University who have contributed enormously in terms of time and effort. Our gratitude goes to the organising committee. Last but not least we would like to thank Rebecca Mowat at Springer-Verlag for her patience with us.

Programme Committee

Programme Committee
General Chair
Keith Jeffrey (UK)

Programme Co-Chairs
Dilip Patel (UK)
Islam Choudhury (UK)

Programme Committee

Motoei Azuma (Japan)	Brian Henderson-Sellers (Australia)
Peter Bielkowicz (UK)	Keith Jeffrey (UK)
Fang Fang Cai (UK)	Robin Laney (UK)
Francesco Capozza (Italy)	Jeff Naylor (UK)
Akmal Chaudri (UK)	Dilip Patel (UK)
Islam Choudhury (UK)	Shushma Patel (UK)
Quan Dang (UK)	D Janaki Ram (India)
Alessandro d'Atri (Italy)	Colette Rolland (France)
Sergio de Cesare (UK)	Jeff Sutherland (USA)
Tharam Dillon (Australia)	Yuan Sun (UK)
Mohamed Fayad (USA)	Bhuvan Unhelkar (Australia)
Ian Graham (UK)	Yingxu Wang (Sweden)
Jane Grimson (Ireland)	Alan Wills (UK)
Tushar Hazra (USA)	Rebecca Wirf-Brock (USA)
Gurdeep Singh Hura (USA)	Roberto Zicari (Germany)

Organising Chairs
Sergio de Cesare (UK)
Fang Fang Cai (UK)

Additional Reviewers
Costas Calcanis (UK)
Adil Dhalaboy (UK)
Maria Carmina di Camillo (ITALY
Kay Dudman (UK)
Kevin Lu (UK)
Nazmul Mannan (UK)
George Ubakanma (UK)

Contents

DATABASES AND PROGRAMMING ISSUES II

ARCHITECTURES, PATTERNS AND VISUALISATION

MEASUREMENTS

XML AND CORBA ISSUES II

DATABASES AND PROGRAMMING
ISSUES I

Definition of External Schemas in ODMG Databases

Manuel Torres [1] and José Samos [2]

[1] *Departamento de Lenguajes y Computación. Universidad de Almería.*
Carretera Sacramento S/N. 04120. Almería. Spain
mtorres@ualm.es
[2] *Departamento de Lenguajes y Sistemas Informáticos. Universidad de Granada*
Avenida Andalucía, 38. 18071. Granada. Spain
jsamos@ugr.es

ABSTRACT. *ODMG 3.0 (January 2000) does not specify how to define external schemas in object oriented databases and only offers a very basic mechanism for defining views, called named queries. In this paper, a system and a language for defining external schemas in ODMG databases are presented. Both are based on a mechanism that avoids the generation of classes that are not necessary in external schemas. The proposed language is an extension of ODMG ODL and allows the definition of external schemas using the ODMG named queries for defining derived classes. Nevertheless, the proposed language is independent of the derived classes definition mechanism used.*

KEYWORDS: *Object oriented databases, External schema definition, ODMG*

1. Introduction

Object Oriented Databases (OODB) appeared in the 80's due to the limitations of Relational Databases (RDB) for manipulating complex objects. This new generation of databases uses an object data model instead of a relational one, and should offer at least the same functionalities available in commercial RDB (Atkinson et al., 1989).

RDBs have been characterized for supporting the ANSI/SPARC architecture and for being defined on a data model widely accepted. In the ANSI/SPARC architecture, a database can be seen at three levels, known respectively as logical, internal and external. For each level, there is a schema: *conceptual*, *internal* and *external*. Due to the importance of external schema definition (logic independence, authorization, heterogeneous database integration), and the fact that OODBs did not offer external schema definition features, since the middle of the 80's numerous works were developed describing view[1] definition mechanisms as a way for supporting external schema definition in OODBs.

OODBs are not based on a data model as accepted as the relational one. Due to this fact, a group of companies built ODMG (*Object Data Management Group*). ODMG object standard[2] defines a data model for objects allowing the development of portable applications, so that applications written with different object oriented languages can use a common object base. Though in the last proposal, ODMG 3.0 (Catell, 2000), many of the issues related with OODB development are solved, in the specifications does not appear the definition of external schemas. ODMG only

---

[1] Some authors identify the term *view* with the external schema; others consider it just as a derived class. In order to avoid confusion, in this work the term view will not be used. Instead of, the terms *derived class* and *external schema* will be used.

[2] Even though ODMG is not a standard, actually is the industry standard for persistent object storage.

allows the definition of *named queries*, as a mechanism similar to relational views for defining derived classes. However, the definition of named queries does not take full advantage of the richness of the object model (Bertino, 1992; Kim et al., 1995).

Then, in this paper, a system and a language for defining external schemas in ODMG OODBs are proposed. Both are based on (Samos, 1995). Some issues for extending the ODMG named queries are also proposed, in order to take advantage of the richness of the object data models.

The remainder of this paper is organized as follows. In Section 2 the two main approaches for defining external schemas are presented. In Section 3 the ODMG named queries as a way for defining external schemas are described; an existing proposal for defining external schemas in ODMG is also discussed. Section 4 corresponds to the presentation of our external schema definition system and the steps for developing the proposed system in ODMG. In Section 5 a language for external schema definition in ODMG is presented. Finally, in Section 6 the conclusions of this paper and the future work are discussed.

2. Overview on external schemas definition in OODBs

The object oriented model is richer than the relational one. It offers features such as object identity, definition of abstract types, type and class hierarchies, not present in the relational one. However, this richness also generates new problems in the definition of derived classes and makes the definition of external schemas more difficult. The development of an OODB external schema definition mechanism entails the development of a derived class definition mechanism, the integration of the derived classes, the selection of a definition semantic, the definition of a syntax to define external schemas, and the development of external schemas generation algorithms. In this section, the main additional problems for defining external schemas in OODBs with respect to RDB are described. In addition, the most representative external schemas definition methodologies are also discussed.

External schemas in relational databases are formed by a flat list of relations, but in OODBs, external schemas must be organized in a hierarchical structure similar to the conceptual schema. This entails the integration of derived classes in the class hierarchy. This is known as the positioning problem of derived classes, and can be done manual or automatically. Another problem related to derived class definition is related to the object identity, and refers to whether instances of derived classes have the same identifier of existing objects, have a new one, or do not have an identifier and the instances are only a set of values (in the later case they are not classes strictly speaking).

The positioning problem is due to the fact that OODBs schemas are complex structures of classes interrelated with *is-a* and aggregation relationships. This means identifying the subclass/superclass relationships between derived classes and the remainder set of classes in the hierarchy, in particular with the *base classes* (the classes from which derived classes are defined). Subclass/superclass relationship entails the existence of subtype/supertype relationships between the types, and subset/superset relationships between the set of instances of derived class and the set of instances of base classes. The positioning problem appears when a derived class is neither a subclass, nor a superclass of its base classes; i.e, a derived class defined combining projection and selection operators. In such case, the type returned by the projection is a supertype of its base classes. This suggests that the derived class is a superclass of its base classes. However, the set of objects returned by the selection is a subset of the set of objects of its base classes. This suggests that the derived class is a subclass of its base classes.

Then, there is a contradiction, and different authors solve this problem generating intermediate classes in order to integrate the derived class (Rundensteiner, 1992a), or defining new relationships between the derived class and their base classes, such as the derivation relationship (Bertino, 1992), or the *may_be* relationship (Santos, 1995). In addition, different semantics (object preserving or object generating) can be used in the derived class definition. In object preserving semantic, instances of the derived class are objects of the base classes. In object generating semantic, instances of the derived class can be new objects generated from the objects of its base classes. However, there is no consensus in the functionalities, the definition mechanism, or the data model used (Motschnig-Pitrik, 1996).

Respect to the derived classes and external schema definition mechanisms, there are two main approaches, depending on the relationship existing between external and conceptual schema.

In the first approach, external schemas are subschemas of the conceptual schema (Rundensteiner, 1992a; Scholl et al., 1991), so all the classes in an external schema have to be included in the conceptual schema. Derived classes are integrated in the conceptual schema following the object oriented paradigm (only *is-a* relationships are used) and the definition semantic used is object preserving. Due to the fact that a derived class may not be a subclass/superclass of their base classes, (Rundensteiner, 1992a) generates intermediate classes for integrating derived classes in the conceptual schema, and defines *is-a* relationships between derived classes and the remainder of the classes (intermediate and already existing in the conceptual schema). Once derived and intermediate classes have been integrated in the conceptual schema, a class selection mechanism is used and a closed subset of classes of the conceptual schema corresponding to an external schema is generated.

The main advantage of this approach is that a definition repository is used, the conceptual schema, providing properties and methods reutilization. The main problem of this approach is that generation of intermediate classes and integration of intermediate and derived classes in the conceptual schema add complexity to it. Also, due to the fact that intermediate classes are generated only to integrate derived classes in the conceptual schema, they can be meaningless classes to end users, and they are added to the conceptual schema.

To illustrate the problem of generating intermediate classes, we will use an example taken from (Samos, 1995). Let us suppose an OODB with the conceptual schema of Figure 1. An external schema like the conceptual schema is wanted to be defined, but with a new class EMPLOYEES' replacing class EMPLOYEES, defined from it hiding the Salary() property and selecting objects where the Category() property returns a value different of *manager*.

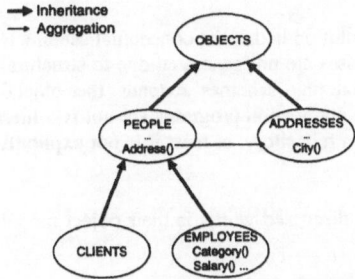

Figure 1. Conceptual schema sample

Using (Rundensteiner, 1992a) methodology for generating the external schema, the external schema of Figure 2 is obtained. In the illustration, an intermediate class (EMPLOYEES'') is generated in order to integrate the derived class (EMPLOYEES') in the conceptual schema. The external schema is bounded in Figure 2 and it is formed by the selected classes. A new *is-a* relationship between EMPLOYEES' and PEOPLE is generated.

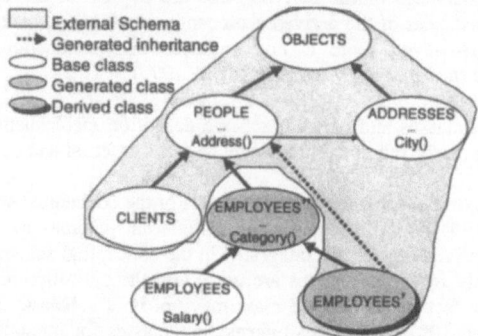

Figure 2. Conceptual schema with derived class integrated

This example shows the main problem of this kind of methodologies. An intermediate class (EMPLOYEES'') has been generated, and it is not used in the external schema. The intermediate class has been only generated to allow the integration of the derived class EMPLOYEES' in the conceptual schema.

In the other approach, external schemas have not to be subschemas of the conceptual schema, and then, external schemas can contain classes not included in the conceptual schema (Bertino, 1992; Guerrini et al., 1997; Santos, 1995). The integration is made directly in external schemas using a relationship different to the *is-a* relationship -the *derivation* relationship (Bertino, 1992), the *may_be* relationship (Santos, 1995)- without increasing the complexity of the conceptual schema. The *derivation* relationship means that instances of derived classes are *derived* or obtained from the base classes. The *may_be* relationship means that instances of the base classes *may be* instances of their derived class, depending on whether they satisfy the predicate stated through the defining query of the derived class. Then, an external schema is formed by a set of classes (base and derived) related with *is-a* relationships and *derivation* or *may_be* relationships (depending on the approach used). This approach often combines object preserving with object generating semantics.

The main advantage of this solution is that the conceptual schema is simpler than before, because intermediate meaningless classes are not generated due to structural reasons. However, using the derivation relationship in external schemas extends the object-oriented paradigm, because external schemas used by the application programs are not *is-a* hierarchies. In addition, this kind of methodologies do not use a repository, at least it is not explicitly mentioned, making difficult reusing possibilities.

Another characteristic of the discussed works is their object models. They use their own object model.

3. Definition of derived classes in ODMG

ODMG allows the definition of *named queries* since ODMG 2.0. Named queries include an OQL (*Object Query Language*) expression, and each time the named query is compiled or evaluated, the OQL expression is evaluated. Here is the syntax

define [**query**] *id* [([parameterList])] **as** *OQLexpression*

This records the definition of the function with name *id* in the database (conceptual) schema. Named queries can be used as a basic mechanism for defining derived classes similar to the one offered in relational databases for views. The function *id* can be considered as a derived class *id*. The OQL expression specifies how to calculate the extension of the derived class. As can be seen in the syntax, a list of parameters can be also included in the named query definition for defining parameterised named queries.

Even though named queries allow. the definition of derived classes at relational style, functionalities that take advantage of the richness of the object model are not offered, and are not adapted to the OODBs applications requirements (i.e. versions, schema evolution).

Figure 3 illustrates two examples of named queries. Figure 3.a represents the definition of a named query for selecting the objects with *category* "manager" in the class EMPLOYEES. Figure 3.b represents the definition of a parameterised named query.

```
define managers() as          define categories(string cat)
   select e                       select e.name
   from Employees e               from Employees e
   where e.category = "manager"   where e.category = cat
              (a)                            (b)
```

Figure 3. Named queries

Named queries are not enough as an external schema definition mechanism, and only allow the definition of a basic kind of derived classes. In addition, ODMG stores the named queries in the conceptual schema, but no mention is made about its integration. It would be interesting that ODMG named queries would be defined as a class and that allow the possibility of defining methods and attributes. Currently, we are working on a derived class definition mechanism (Garví et al., 2000) as support for the external schema definition mechanism presented in this paper.

In (Dobrovnik et al., 1994), a formalisation for defining external schemas in ODMG databases is presented. The proposed external schema definition mechanism is related only to the specification of types in the external schema and to the specification of derived classes behaviour. Defining derived classes by means of a query, as in RDBs, was proposed as a future work. Derived class types are not integrated in the conceptual schema and the positioning problem is solved specifying inheritance relationships between types. The use of a repository is not mentioned explicitly.

4. A proposal for defining external schemas in ODMG

The object model in which an external schema definition mechanism for OODB is based on, must allow to differentiate between types and classes in order to define *is-a* relationships successfully, offer support to solve the positioning problem of derived classes, and allow the selection of object semantics (Scholl et al., 1991; Motschnig-Pitrik, 1996). These issues will define the functionality of the derived class definition mechanism.

The proposed mechanism, intends to take advantage of each group of methodologies (to use of repository and to obtain easier schemas) avoiding the problems of each one (complex schemas and extension of the object oriented paradigm) in the ODMG framework. In particular, starting from (Samos, 1995), the proposed mechanism avoids the generation of intermediate meaningless classes in the conceptual schema like in (Rundensteiner, 1992a), using the derivation relationship in the *repository*. The repository includes the conceptual schema and derived classes related with the derivation relationship (Bertino, 1992). The classes to be included in the external schema are selected from the repository, and an *is-a* hierarchy for the external schema is built. Unlike in (Dobrovnik et al., 1994), it is not necessary specifying the types of the derived class. Instead of, they are inferred from the derived class definition.

In the repository, classes are related using the derivation and *is-a* relationships. To preserve the object oriented paradigm, classes in external schemas must be related exclusively with *is-a* relationships. Therefore, some transformations must be done in order to relate external schema classes using only *is-a* relationships. These transformations will be obtained from the derivation relationship and, unlike the (Rundensteiner, 1992a) methodology, only the necessary intermediate classes for building the external schema are generated. These transformations will also be stored in the repository.

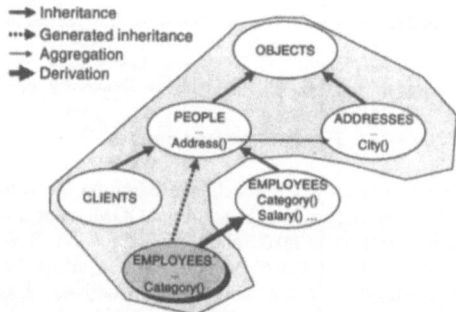

Figure 4. Repository and external schema in the proposed system

Figure 4 shows the repository and the external schema for the example we are following along this paper. This mechanism does not increase the complexity of the conceptual schema, and the set of generated classes is lower than the one generated in (Rundensteiner, 1992a), because classes are not generated to integrate derived classes in the conceptual schema, but are generated only to integrate derived classes in each external schema (Samos, 1995). Regarding to the use of the derivation relationship, it does not extend the object-oriented paradigm, because it is not used neither in the conceptual schema, nor in the external schema, like in (Bertino, 1992) and (Guerrini et al., 1997). Instead of, the derivation relationship is only used for relating derived classes with their base classes in the repository, as illustrated in Figure 4. Then, in the external schema of Figure 4, all the relationships used are *is-a* relationships, since derivation relationships were used only in the repository. Note that a new *is-a* relationship has been generated between EMPLOYEES' and PEOPLE. Despite in this example the integration has been very easy, in other situations intermediate classes must be generated, but only to integrate derived classes in external schemas, not in the conceptual schema. In (Samos et al., 1996), a mechanism to transform the derivation relationships is presented.

The tasks related to the development of the external schema definition system are the following:

- To extend the ODMG architecture to include the new concepts (external schema, derived class).
- To extend the ODMG ODL (*Object Definition Language*) to define external schemas in ODMG selecting the classes included in the external schema.
- To extend the ODMG named queries to take advantage of the possibilities of the object-oriented models.
- To develop transformation mechanisms to obtain *is-a* relationships from derivation relationship in the repository.
- To develop algorithms for generating closed external schemas from a set of classes selected in the repository.

ODMG architecture must be revisited to accommodate to the ANSI/SPARC architecture. In particular, the external schema and derived class concepts must be considered, and also their definition in the repository.

External schema definition is carried out by means of an extension of ODL. This extension allows declaration, modification and deletion of external schemas. The definition of external schemas allows the definition of derived classes and the selection of classes, subschemas and external schemas contained in the external schema.

Derived classes can be defined by ODMG named queries, or by the extension proposed in (Garví et al., 2000). This extension allows the definition of derived classes as in RDBs, but including issues related with object oriented model features.

In our proposal, derived classes are related in the repository with base classes by means of the derivation relationship. In external schemas and in the conceptual schema only the inheritance relationship is allowed. Therefore, a mechanism is needed to transform derivation relationships into inheritance relationships in order to include derived classes in external schemas preserving the object-oriented paradigm. Then, the OQL expression of the derived class must be analysed and the new type must be obtained in order to position the derived class in the external schema successfully. In (Samos et al., 1996), a mechanism for identifying the necessary transformations is presented. Once transformations are made, the repository will be updated adding the obtained classes and relationships consistently.

Closed external schemas are generated from base and derived classes selected in the external schema definition process. An external schema is closed if all the classes referenced by its classes are included into it. The closure of external schemas is assured by an algorithm based on (Rundensteiner et al., 1992b). If an external schema is not closed, the algorithm returns the minimum set of classes to close it, and these classes are added to it.

The ODL extension for external schema definition is independent of the approach used for defining derived classes. Basically, the difference between the existing approaches is given by the schema where derived classes are integrated, and by the existing relationship between derived classes and their base classes. Without loss of generality, these differences can be ignored and one can say that base and derived classes constitute a set of related classes in a schema (in our system, the repository). Next, the schema definer would use a declarative language for specifying the classes (derived or non-derived) to be included into the external schema. This selection is independent of the existing relationships between the classes and of the schema where they are integrated. In our proposal, external schema definition is not affected by the derived class definition and integration mechanisms used, and the user only selects available classes in a schema.

The derivation relationship, to be included between derived and base classes, defined explicitly in our system, exists implicitly in all derived class definition mechanisms. The difference is on the relationship used in the integration process, but not in the abstract relationship. In the examples of this paper, though the used relationships are different, the abstract relationship is the *is-derived-from* relationship, it relates a derived class with the classes that appear in the FROM clause that defines it.

5. External schema definition language in ODMG

The external schema definition language, based on (Rundensteiner et al., 1992b), is used in the repository, defining new derived classes and selecting existing classes in order to define the external schema. Derived classes can be defined by ODMG named queries, or by our extension (Garví et al., 2000). In this preliminary version, subclass relationships have to be defined manually. In future versions, specifying the classes to be included in the external schema will be enough. Then, the system, using derived class inclusion algorithms, closure algorithms and external schema generation algorithms, will do the underlying work.

Figure 5 presents the BNF syntax of the proposed external schema definition language. Next, the semantics of the defined commands in this language is informally explained.

Three commands are used at external schema level: DEFINE ES, MODIFY ES and UNDEFINE ES. DEFINE ES <es_name> initialises a new empty external schema identified by es_name, specifying the classes (base and derived) and relationships existing in the external schema. The MODIFY ES command is applied to previously defined external schemas and allows adding or deleting base o derived classes existing in other schemas. Relationships between classes have to be specified too. The UNDEFINE ES <es_name> [AND NOT USED] deletes the external schema es_name, and optionally, by means of AND NOT USED parameter, deletes from the repository the derived classes and relationships defined for es_name that are not being used by another external schemas. Derived classes that are not used by external schemas can be used as a way of shorthand in queries (Guerrini et al., 1997). However, intermediate classes and *is-a* relationships generated in the repository for building the external schema es_name, that are not being used in external schema will be eliminated, because their existence is dependent of an external schema.

Derived classes are defined with an ODMG named query, or by a richer extension like the proposed in (Garví et al., 2000). Once the derived classes to be included in our external schema have been defined, it is possible to incorporate or delete previously defined classes, base or derived, indistinctly. The ADD CLASS <class_name> command adds the base class class_name of the repository to the external schema. The ADD SUBSCHEMA ROOTED BY <class_name> command adds to the external schema all the base classes in the repository that are subclasses in the subschema rooted by class_name. The ADD DERIVED CLASS <derived_class_name> command adds the previously defined derived class derived_class_name to the external schema. Finally, the ADD ES <es_name> command adds to the external schema we are defining, all the classes belonging to the external schema *es_name*.

```
<define_es> ::= <create_es> | <modify_es> | <delete_es>

<create_es> ::= DEFINE ES <es_name> {
                <derived_classes>
                <classes_addition>
                <create_relationship> }

<modify_es> ::= MODIFY ES <es_name> {
                <derived_classes>
                <classes_operation>
                <relationship_definition> }

<derived_classes> ::= <ODMG_named_query> |
                <Extended_ODMG_named_query> |
                <derived_classes>

<classes_operation> ::= <classes_addition> |
                <classes_deletion> |
                <classes_operation>

<classes_addition> ::= ADD CLASS <class_name> |
                ADD SUBSCHEMA ROOTED BY <class_name> |
                ADD DERIVED CLASS <derived_class_name>
                ADD ES <es_name> |
                <classes_addition>

<classes_deletion> ::= REMOVE CLASS <class_name> [AND NOT USED] |
                REMOVE SUBSCHEMA ROOTED BY <class_name> [AND NOT USED] |
                REMOVE DERIVED CLASS <derived_class_name>
                REMOVE ES <es_name> |
                <classes_deletion>

<relationship_definition> ::= <create_relationship> |
                <delete_relationship> |
                <relationship_definition>

<create_relationship> ::= DEFINE RELATIONSHIP FOR <class_name>|<derived_class_name>
                AS SUBCLASS OF <list_of_names> |
                <create_relationship>

<delete_relationship> ::= UNDEFINE RELATIONSHIP BETWEEN <class_name>|<derived_class_name>
                AND <list_of_names> |
                <delete_relationship>

<delete_es> ::= UNDEFINE ES <es_name> [AND NOT USED]
```

Figure 5. BNF syntax of the proposed external schema definition language

The next four commands delete base or derived classes in existing external schemas. This can entail the deletion of these classes on the repository, but it must be indicated with the AND NOT USED parameter. By default, deleted classes from an external schema are not erased from the repository though they are not being used by another external schema. The REMOVE CLASS *<class_name>* [AND NOT USED] command deletes the base class *class_name* of the external schema. The REMOVE SUBSCHEMA ROOTED BY *<class_name>* [AND NOT USED] command deletes the subschema rooted by *<class_name>* from the external schema. The REMOVE DERIVED CLASS *<derived_class_name>* deletes the derived class *derived_class_name* from the external schema we are modifying. Finally, REMOVE ES *<es_name>* deletes the external schema *es_name* from the schema we are modifying.

Create and delete relationships are operations related to the specification of relationships, and in this preliminary version must be defined consistently by the external schema creator. Relationship creation is made by means of DEFINE RELATIONSHIP FOR <class_name>|<derived_class_name> AS SUBCLASS OF <list_of_names>. This command creates *is-a* relationships between the base class class_name or the derived class derived_class_name and the classes specified in list_of_names. These relationships are only defined in the external schema. Relationship deletion is carried out by means of UNDEFINE RELATIONSHIP BETWEEN <class_name>| <derived_class name> AND <list_of_names>. This command deletes the existing *is-a* relationship between the base class class_name or the derived class derived_class_name and list_of_names.

The definition of an external schema is only related to the definition of derived classes and to the selection of classes included in the external schema. In this preliminary version, *is-a* relationships between external schema classes must be explicitly specified. In the next version, this process will be done automatically and, once the classes to be included in the external schema are specified, a closed external schema using only *is-a* relationships will be generated. These modifications will be included in the repository.

To illustrate how this language can be used, Figure 6 shows the definition of the example external schema we are using along this paper.

```
DEFINE ES example {
define Employees' as
        select … e.category
        from Employees e
        where e.category != "manager"

ADD CLASS People
ADD CLASS Clients
ADD CLASS Addresses

DEFINE RELATIONSHIP FOR People AS SUBCLASS OF Objects
DEFINE RELATIONSHIP FOR Clients AS SUBCLASS OF People
DEFINE RELATIONSHIP FOR Employees' AS SUBCLASS OF People
DEFINE RELATIONSHIP FOR Addresses AS SUBCLASS OF Objects
}
```

Figure 6. Example of an external schema definition

6. Conclusions and future work

Due to the fact that in the specifications of ODMG 3.0 the definition of external schemas is not included, in this paper an external schema definition system for ODMG databases has been proposed. The proposed system and language for defining external schemas allow the specification of external schemas in ODMG databases, extending the ODMG architecture according to the ANSI/SPARC three-level schema architecture. In this paper, the definition of external schemas in ODMG databases uses ODMG named queries for defining derived classes.

The external schema definition language is a declarative language that extends the ODMG ODL, and allows the definition, modification and deletion of external schemas in OODBs. In this language, new derived classes can be defined and selected together with previously existing classes to be included into an external schema. It allows the addition or deletion of classes, subschemas, and external schemas. In the version proposed, relationships between external schemas classes have to be explicitly defined.

At the moment, ODMG allows the definition of derived classes by means of named queries. Named queries are defined in ODMG since ODMG 2.0 and are similar to relational views. We are working on a derived class definition mechanism which extends named queries in order to take advantage of the richness of the object model and to give support to the functionalities required by object applications. Between the functionalities required are the definition of derived classes with object preserving and object generating semantics. Nevertheless, the external schema definition language proposed in this paper can be used with named queries. Then, this proposal can be used with ODMG 2.0 and higher.

The external schema definition language proposed in this work is part of a system under development in the context of the BLOOM project (Samos et al., 1999). This system uses the derivation relationship in the repository to relate derived classes with their base classes and allows the definition of external schemas according to the object-oriented paradigm for ODMG databases, avoiding the generation of intermediate classes unnecessary for definition of the external schema. Currently, we are developing *is-a* external schema generation algorithms from derived classes defined using the derivation relationship. This implies to develop transformation mechanisms in the repository obtaining *is-a* relationships from derivation relationships. The development of closure and external schema generation algorithms is also planned.

Acknowledgements

This work has been supported by the Spanish CICYT (project TIC 1999-1078-C02-02)

7. References

(Atkinson et al., 1989):   Atkinson, M., Bancilhon, F., DeWitt, D., Dittich, K. Maier, D., Zdonik. S. The Object-Oriented Database System Manifesto. In *Proc. First International Conference on DOOD*. pp. 40-57. 1989

(Bertino, 1992):   Bertino, E. A View Mechanism for Object-Oriented Databases. In *Proc. of the Third International Conf. on EDBT*. pp. 136-151. 1992

(Catell, 2000):   Catell, R.G.G. *The Object Database Standard: ODMG 3.0*. Morgan Kaufmann Publishers. 2000

(Dobrovnik et al., 1994):   Dobrovnik, M., Eder, J. Adding View Support to ODMG-93. In *Proc. of the First International Workshop in Advances in Database and Information Systems*. pp. 62-73. 1994.

(Garví et al., 2000):   Garví, E., Torres, M., Samos, J. Extending the ODMG Named Queries. *Submitted for publication*.

(Guerrini et al., 1997):   Guerrini, G., Bertino, E., Catania, B., Garcia-Molina, J. A Formal View of Object-Oriented Database Systems. *In Theory and Practice of Object Systems*. Vol. 3(3). pp. 157-183. 1997

(Kim et al., 1995):   Kim, W., Kelley, W. On View Support in Object Oriented Database Systems. In *Modern Database Systems*. pp.108-129. 1995

(Motschnig-Pitrik, 1996):   Motschnig-Pitrik, R. Requirements and Comparison of View Mechanisms for Object-Oriented Databases. In *Information Systems*. Vol. 21(3). pp. 229-252. 1996

(Rundensteiner, 1992a):   Rundensteiner, E. Multiview: A Methodology for Supporting Multiple Views in Object-Oriented Databases. In *Proceedings of the 18th VLDB*. pp. 187-198. 1992

(Rundensteiner et al., 1992b): Rundensteiner, E.A., Bic, L. Automatic view schema generation in Object-Oriented Databases. *Tech. Report WPI-CS-TR-92-15*. 1992

(Samos, 1995):   Samos, J. Definition of External Schemas in Object Oriented Databases. In *Proceedings of 1995 OOIS*. pp. 154-166. 1995

(Samos et al, 1996):   Samos, J., Saltor, F. External Schema Generation Algorithms for Object Oriented Databases. In *Proc. of 1996 OOIS*. pp. 317-332. 1996

(Samos et al., 1999):   Samos, J. Abelló, A., Oliva, M. Rodríguez, E., Saltor, F., Sistac, J., Araque, F., Delgado, C., Garví, E., Ruiz. E. Sistema Cooperativo para la Integración de Fuentes Heterogéneas de Información y Almacenes de Datos. In *Novática*. Vol. 142. pp. 44-49. 1999

(Santos et al., 1994):   Santos, C.S, Abiteboul, S, Delobel, C. Virtual schemas and bases. In *Proc. of 4th EDBT*. pp. 81-94. 1994

(Santos, 1995):   Santos, C.S. Design and Implementation of Object-Oriented Views. In *Proceedings of DEXA, 6th Int. Conf.*. pp. 91-102. 1995

(Scholl et al., 1991):   Scholl, M.H., Laasch, C. Tresch, M. Updatable Views in Object-Oriented Databases. In *Proc. of the 2nd DOOD*. pp. 189-207. 1991

Behavioral compatibility in Concurrent Object Constructions

Michel AUGERAUD

Laboratoire L3I, Université de La Rochelle
L3i - UPRES EA 2118
Avenue Michel Crépeau,
F 17042 La Rochelle Cedex 1 (France)
E-mail:Michel.Augeraud@univ-lr.fr Fax:+33 546 513 939

ABSTRACT A formal approach using "traces" characterization is presented in order to clarify relationship between objects belonging to classes related by aggregation or inheritance.

It is well known that objects' behavior may induce anomalies if objects are related by a structural relationship mechanisms (inheritance, aggregation). A lot of studies have been done in order to explain and solve the "inheritance anomaly" problem [MTY93]. In [CSS94] J. F. Costa, A. Sernadas and C. Sernadas present a categorical semantic domain for objects in order to clarify both aggregation and specialization. In the framework of active objects, one idea is to characterize an objects behavior as a regular process [NT95].

We give a formal definition of behavioral *compatibility* in the context of structurally dependent objects. Reactive programming used as a mechanism to control objects' behavior, gives a practical technique to check compatibility. Verification takes also advantage of expression of the behavior is fully separate of expression of transformations done by methods.

KEYWORDS Concurrent object programming, model checking, reactivity, reactive controlled objects, inheritance anomalies.

1 Introduction

Inheritance and concurrency are not independent concepts. The problem has many aspects. We focus in this paper on the problem of compatibility between behaviors when instances belongs to classes related by inheritance or aggregation.

Consider a class C_2 inheriting from a class C_1. Let C_1 defines two methods m_1 and m_2 and C_2 defines an additional method m_3. During its life an object O instance of C_2 answer requests, as a C_2 object, such as $O.m_1$, or as a C_1 object, such as $(as\ C_1\ O).m_1$. As its shown in the following examples, according to C_1 and C_2 behaviors, some sequences of call may leads to dead locks.

Example 1. Let C_2 objects behavior be " a concurrent execution of methods m_1 and m_3 followed, when both are terminated, by m_2 execution ". We denote by "$(m_1||m_3); m_2$" this *behavior. And let C_1 objects behavior be " the sequential execution in this order of m_1 and m_2". This last behavior is denoted "$m_1; m_2$".*

The following incoming sequence of request may leads to a deadlock.

$$O.m_1$$
$$(as\ C_1\ O).m_2$$
$$O.m_3$$

If call 3 is received after execution requested in call 2 is completed, $O.m_3$ always wait to be executed. We say that behavior C_2 is not compatible to behavior C_1 with respect to inheritance relationship.

Example 2. *If the behavior of C_2 objects consists in " a concurrent execution of methods m_1 and m_3 followed, when both are terminated or only one has begun and is terminated, by m_2 execution ". We denote by "$(m_1|||m_3); m_2$" this behavior. Concurrency like that described between m_1 and m_3 is called weak prallelism. And let C_1 objects behavior be the same as in the preceding example.*

In this case the following incoming sequence of request may leads to a deadlock.

$$O.m_3$$
$$(as\ C_1\ O).m_2$$

If call 2 is received after execution requested in call 1 is completed, $(as\ C_1\ O).m_2$ always wait to be executed because m_1 has not been executed.

Example 3. *Let C_2 objects behavior be "a weak concurrent execution of methods m_1 and m_3 which can be preempted by m_2 execution". We denote by "$(m_1|||m_3)/m_2$" this behavior. And let C_1 objects behavior be " the execution of m_1 preempted by m_2 ". This last behavior is denoted "m_1/m_2".*

In this case considering methods as C_1 or C_2 do not change whether the request is accepted or not.

In aggregated object methods execution conditions may be constrained by components. For example in a flexible production cell a portal arm can move if an only if its head is up. So compound object behavior cannot be fully understood without considering components. Transition system of compound object behavior may have to refer to component states.

Example 4. *If an object of class C is an aggregate with two components of class C_1 and C_2. If C_1 objects have two methods m_1 and m_2 and with the iterated sequential behavior $(m_1; m_2)*$. And C_1 objects have one methods m_3. If C behavior is $(m_1/m_3; m_2)*$. It is easy to see a C object may execute m_1 then m_3 several time. This behavior does not satisfy form C_1 viewpoint the required behavioral constraint.*

The problem, in this case, is the following : "*is the behavior of a component object inside an aggregate behavior compatible with behavior of the same object considered independently of composition ?* "

This means that " *for all sequence of call, accepted by an aggregate, each call restricted to methods stated in a component, accepted by the aggregate, have to be accepted by this individual component, and this has to be applied to all components of the aggregate*".

The paper is organized as followed. In a first part we present related works on inheritance anomalies. We present also works to formally characterize behavior relationship. We present counter examples which illustrate the need of a more precise definition of behavioral relationship for an object in the context of inheritance or aggregation. In a second part we present the framework in which we consider objects. This framework include a language to specify objects' behavior. We use use it to give examples.

Reactive programming used as a mechanism to control object behavior, gives a practical technique to verify compatibility.

In a third part, after having recall trace characterization using the Arnold Nivat model, we formally define compatibility relationship. In the fourth part we present the practical way we check behavioral compatibility between objects belonging from classes related by inheritance or aggregation.

2 Related works on inheritance anomalies

To bind synchronization to the invocation of method prevents the dissemination of the controlling code on clients. In order to cope with dependency between synchronization and object structural mechanism, at least with structural aspects, many authors state that synchronization expression should be as independent as possible of the methods code. The solution consists in considering an abstract behavior. Enabled − Sets [KL89] in providing abstract states as a mechanism to represent synchronization gives a first partial answer to this problem. An abstract set is characterized by a set of enabled methods. But in this model, transitions between states are specified inside methods code. This mechanism has been implemented in Rosette [TS89].

Using similar mechanisms Matsuoka, Taura and Yonezawa [MY93] have proposed a solution minimizing inheritance anomalies. This mechanism called *method sets* have as Enabled-Sets a declarative form and gives a full separation between synchronization code and the methods code. As transitions are specified outside the methods code, it solves the problem of state changes at the end of a method execution.

Whereas Enabled Sets and Methods Sets solve the problem of structural relationships between synchronization expression and class definition, the problem we faced on is the following : "what is the relationship between behavioral abstraction of objects instance of a class C_1 and behavioral abstraction of objects instance of a class C_2 inheriting from C_1". To do so transition system and/or event models are often used as behavioral abstraction model.

Definition 1. Transition systems : Given an alphabet A of labels representing events a transition system ([AD89]) is a 5-tuple $\mathcal{A} = \langle S, T, \alpha, \beta, \lambda \rangle$ such that :

S is a finite set of states, T is a finite set of transitions,

α and β two maps $T \to S$. ($\alpha(t)$ denotes the source of t and $\beta(t)$ the target of t)

λ is a map $T \to A$ which labels every transition of T by an event name.

the map $< \alpha, \lambda, \beta >: T -> S \times A \times S$ is an injection.

Given a labeled transition system $\mathcal{A} = \langle S, T, \alpha, \beta, \lambda \rangle$ on an alphabet A, a path c is sequence of transitions $c = t_1 t_2 \ldots t_n$ where $\forall\, i < n\ \beta(t_i) = \alpha(t_{i+1})$.

The set of all finite paths is denoted by T^*.

To all state s in S is associated the set of all finite path

$$Path_\mathcal{A}(s) = \{c \in T^* | \alpha(c) = s\}$$

and the language $L_\mathcal{A}(s) = \lambda(Path_\mathcal{A}(s))$.

Définition 1. The set of traces from a state s of a transition system is

$$traces(s) \overset{def}{=} L_{\mathcal{A}}(s)$$

In order to define concepts of sub-type and aggregation, J.F. Costa, A. Sernadas and C. Sernadas use the concept of process morphism.

First, a partial map $h : A \longrightarrow B$ can be canonically extended to $h^* : A^* \longrightarrow B^*$ as follows: (i) $h^*(\epsilon) = \epsilon$ and (ii) $h^*(as) = \begin{cases} h(a)h^*(s) & \text{if } h(a) \text{ exists} \\ h^*(s) & \text{otherwise} \end{cases}$

Definition 2. A process is a couple $\langle E, \Lambda \rangle$ where E is a set of events and Λ a prefix closed subset of E^* which represents the behavior of the process.

Definition 3. A process morphism $h : \langle E_2, \Lambda_2 \rangle \longrightarrow \langle E_1, \Lambda_1 \rangle$ is a partial event map $h_E : E_2 \longrightarrow E_1$ such that $h_E^*(\Lambda_2) \subset \Lambda_1$

Concept of *Process Morphism* is just the same as *Aggregation with hiding* used by Hartmann [HJS92]. It states that the behavior of an aggregate restricted to the methods of a component object must give the behavior of this component.

But as we have seen in example 1, behavior $(m_1 \| m_3); m_2$ is not compatible with behavior $(m_1; m_2)$ whereas we have $h_E^*(\Lambda_2) \subset \Lambda_1$. So process morphism is not strong enough to ensure compatibility between behaviors for inheritance.

In the framework of active objects, one idea is to characterize an objects behavior as a regular process [NT95]. Behavior characterization appears as some kind of type—*regular type*. Compatibility consists in a relationship between these types called "request substitutability".

Let us define $Poss_{\mathcal{A}}$ which associates, for a labeled transition system $\mathcal{A}$, to each state the set of "*possible*" transition labels.

Definition 4. The set of failures from a state s of a transition system is

$$failures(s) \overset{def}{=} \{(c, R) \mid \exists s' \; \beta(c) = s' \text{ and } \alpha(c) = s \text{ and } R \cap poss(s') = \emptyset\}$$

Definition 5. The set of relative failures from a state s of a transition system is

$$failures_{s_2}(s_1) \overset{def}{=} \{(c, R) \in failures(s_1) \mid c \in traces(s_2)\}$$

Definition 6. A behavior from a state s_1 is request substitutable for the behavior from state s_2 iff

1. $traces(s_2) \subseteq traces(s_1)$

2. $failures_{s_2}(s_1) \subseteq failures(s_2)$

Request substitutability is not the relation we need. It is easy to check that initial state of $m_1; m_2$ is *request substitutable* to initial state of $(m_1 \| m_3); m_2$ whereas the example 2 shows that behaviors are not compatible with respect to inheritance.

3 Reactive Controlled Object Model

An object in a concurrent object oriented program reacts to event requests (methods call) by triggering or not called methods. Several techniques exist to compute the result of a call. Each of them being associated to an object model. Interested reader can refer to [BG96] for a complete overview.

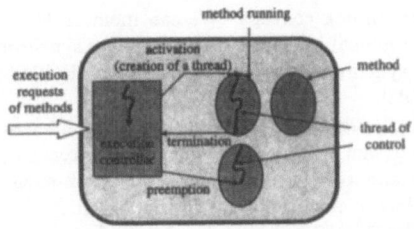

Figure 1: Architecture of a concurrent object with an execution controller.

In our model a controller is associated to each class. This controller implements a transition system which is the *"behavioral abstraction"* of objects of this class. Scheduling constraints concerning methods executions are specified using a specific domain language BDL (Behavioral Description Language) [BA99]. The following picture 1 illustrates our object model architecture.

An object controller catches requests as *arrival* events. Requests belong either from other objects or from the object itself. It must be noticed that, in our model, these events occur at distinct instants and are separately received (one by one) by the controller. This distinction allows one to model distributed objects more easily. The execution is triggered by the emission of a *start* event towards the runtime system. A *termination* event informs the controller of the end of execution. A set of events denoted $EV(C.Meth)$ is associated to each class C. It is composed for each method m of incoming events $\{arr\_m, \ term\_m\}$ and outgoing events $\{start\_m, \ done\_m, \ start\_failed\_m\}$.

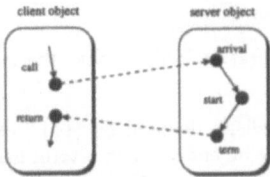

Figure 2: The events in the lifespan of a method invocation

Figure 2 describes an event sequence happening when an object (client) requests the execution of a method from another object (server).

Inside the called object, the *arrival* event is distinct from the *start* event; the controller handles the *arrival* event and emits the *start* event for the actual method only if the method execution meets the scheduling constraints. The distinction between *start* and *term* events introduces the notion of duration for an execution. This model of execution is also present in [McH94] under the name SOS (Service Object Synchronization).

In order to do not loose calls to an object, controller has to react at the input event flow speed. To cope with this kind of problem, David Harel and Amir Pnueli have designed concept of *reactive systems* [HP85]. A reactive system can be defined as a system reacting instantaneously and continuously to incoming events. Most of reactive systems have been designed for real time systems. Several programming languages have been designed to implement reactive programming concept. We can mention David Harel STATECHARTS [Har87] with a popular graphical interface, the imperative synchronous language ESTEREL [BCG86], the data-flow synchronous language LUSTRE [HCRP91] and the asynchronous language Electre [RCCE92].

For our synchronization problem, these languages present several advantages. First as they are mainly used to design critical real time systems, reactive languages have a strong mathematical semantics and tools are associated to check such systems. In our model, *Reactive Controlled Objects*, controllers have to react to incoming events (methods call or methods termination). Reaction speed is an important feature in order that objects do not miss event. At each time the controller considers only one event incoming to the object.

Reaction can be either an output event emitted to the environment or a memorization of the incoming event. Memorized events are recalled *as soon as possible*. The soonest will be when a method terminates. So each time a *terminate event* comes to the controller, memorized events are recalled.

In our model, control of incoming events is done by the reactive controller of the object. Because it reacts at event flow speed, it implements a map from accepted words of *input events* into words of *output events*. We denote this map by CTRL_output.

3.1 The Operators of the BDL Language

We do not introduce here BDL operators. The interested reader may refer to the paper [BA99]. We only mention the following :

a unary *repetition* operator, denoted by "*," indicates that the control specified by the term works indefinitely;

a binary *sequentiality* operator, denoted by ";," indicates that the left term must be executed before the right one;

two binary *parallelism* operators indicate that the two terms (left and right) can be executed at same time.

- so-called *weak* parallelism, denoted by "| | |," expressing a *possibility*: the concurrent structure may be ended when a term has achieved its execution and the other has not started yet;

- so-called *strong* parallelism, denoted by "| |," expressing a *necessity*: the concurrent structure is ended only when both terms have achieved their execution.

a binary *mutual exclusion* operator, denoted by "|," indicates that executions of both terms are mutually exclusive;

two binary *preemption* operators indicating that the execution of the left term can be stopped by the beginning of the execution of the right term. We consider both following preemption types:

- so-called *weak* preemption, denoted by "^": the execution of the preemptive structure (right term) can take place only during the execution of the preempted structure (left term);

- so-called *strong* preemption, denoted by "/": the execution of the preemptive structure is required even if the preempted structure has terminated its execution.

all these operators have the same precedence level, so parenthesis could be used to modify this precedence.

3.2 Examples of BDL Programs

The control of the behavior of a group of objects (or *aggregate*) is achieved by using the behavior control for each object as a pattern. The following example illustrates how the behavior control of an aggregate can be defined. The *microwave oven* following example pictures this construction. An object *microwave oven* belonging to a class `MWOven` is composed of a `MWGenerator` and a `MWDoor`.

BDL specification for `MWGenerator` is (on / off)*

And BDL specification for `MWDoor` is (open ; close)*

And BDL specification for `MWOven` ((on / off) | (open ; close))*

In our model control of component object is done by unique controller of compound object. Because of independence between control structure and object structure it is easy to do in our model. Semantics of BDL have been presented in [BA99].

4 Specification on setting compatibility between behaviors of classes related by inheritance or aggregation

During its life an object instance of a class C_2 which inherits or contains of a class C_1 answers to method requests. But this request can be on the object as a C_2 or as a C_1.

4.1 Example to the contrary for inheritance relationship

Let us consider anew example 1. Processes $P_2 = \langle C_2.Meth, traces((m_1\|m_3); m_2)\rangle$ and $P_1 = \langle C_1.Meth, traces(m_1; m_2)\rangle$ are homomorphic processes. So an object instance of C_2 may have the following behavior,

$$arr\_m_1 \rightarrow term\_m_1 \rightarrow arr\_m_3 \rightarrow term\_m_3 \rightarrow arr\_m_2 \rightarrow term\_m_2.$$

Its homomorphic image by h^* of the behavior is,

$$arr\_m_1 \rightarrow term\_m_1 \rightarrow arr\_m_2 \rightarrow term\_m_2.$$

But such behaviors are not compatible with respect to inheritance as we have shown in example 1.

The following picture 3 represents by a transition system the behavior of the object. (It has been generated by FC2tools from the Esterel code produced by our tool applied to BDL expression $(m1\|m3); m2$. Symbol "?" means an event reception and "!" an event emission. A "+" symbol in a label means an exclusive choice among several transitions. Initial state is tag by a double circle. To make the picture more readable transition labels for loops have been hidden.)

On this picture it can be seen that m_1 execution leads to a state 2 which do not allows m_2 execution.

The problem is that partial event map does not separate states in C_2 behavior according to events the object may accept. That is, arr_m_1 $term\_m_1$ sequence of events leads the object behavior in a state 2 where possible events set it may accept is not the same set it may accept in state 8. Following formalization will explain this problem.

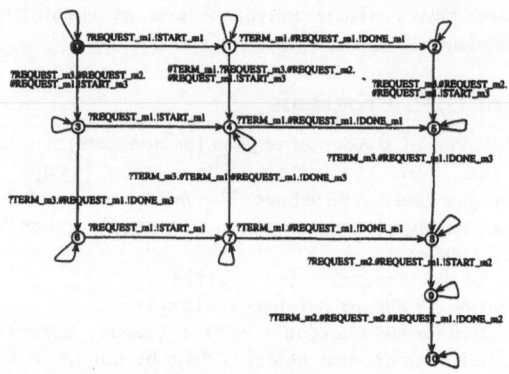

Figure 3: C_2 behavior of specification: "$(m1\|m3); m2$"

4.2 Behavior compatibility problem

An object instance of a class C_2 which inherits from a class C_1 can be considered according to different viewpoints (as a C_2 or as a C_1). For each viewpoint, a transition system represents the behavioral abstraction of the object. Namely A_1 for class C_1 and A_2 for class C_2.

Let b be an instance of a class C_2. As C_2 inherits C_1 at each time b is in a state s_1 or s_1' according to the viewpoint (i.e. respectively b is a C_2 or b is a C_1). At this point an accepted call to a method belonging to C_1, when the object is view as a C_1, produces a transition in A_1 but also in A_2. Conversely an accepted call to a method belonging to C_2 produces a transition in A_2 but also in A_1. But in this case if the method does not belong to C_1 transition in A_1 is unobservable (an ϵ-transition).

For the object be still coherent according to both viewpoints, we should have the following property : *for each trace c accepted by A_2, an event belonging to A_1 alphabet A_1 and accepted by A_2 have to be accepted by A_1. And also each trace c accepted by A_1 have to be accepted by A_2.*

The following aims to characterize formally this property.

4.3 Theoretical aspects of behavioral compatibility in inheritance relationship

As we have seen characterization needs both traces and states. In [Arn94] A. Arnold gives a characterization of trace equivalences. He points out that *readiness semantics* [OH83] defined by Hoare is strictly stronger than *failure semantics* [BHR84] defined by Brookes, Hoare and Roscoe.

A state s of a transition system A is reachable if it exists a path $c \in Path_A(initial_A)$ such that $\beta(c) = s$.

Definition 7. A transition system A is deterministic if for all $t \in T$ and $t' \in T$,

$$(\alpha(t) = \alpha(t')) \wedge (\lambda(t) = \lambda(t')) \Rightarrow t = t'$$

Proposition 1. Let $\mathcal{A}$ be a deterministic transition system. If c and c' are two paths in $Path_{\mathcal{A}}(s)$ $\lambda(c) = \lambda(c') \Rightarrow c = c'$.

In the following we suppose that behaviors $\mathcal{A}$ are deterministic.

Definition 8. If $\mathcal{A}$ and $\mathcal{B}$ are deterministic transition systems with respective initial states $initial_{\mathcal{A}}$ and $initial_{\mathcal{B}}$ and h a partial event map from respective label sets $Ev_{\mathcal{A}}$ into $Ev_{\mathcal{B}}$. We define $\hat{h}^* : Path_{\mathcal{A}}(initial_{\mathcal{A}}) \longrightarrow Path_{\mathcal{B}}(initial_{\mathcal{B}})$ by :

$$\hat{h}^*(c) = \lambda_{\mathcal{B}}^{-1}(h^*(\lambda_{\mathcal{A}}(c))) \bigcap Path_{\mathcal{B}}(initial_{\mathcal{B}})$$

Proposition 2. If $\mathcal{B}$ is a deterministic transition system, $\hat{h}^*$ maps $Path_{\mathcal{A}}(initial_{\mathcal{A}})$ into $Path_{\mathcal{B}}(initial_{\mathcal{B}})$

In the example 4.1, calling h the canonical surjection from $Ev(\mathcal{C}_2.Meth)$ into $Ev(\mathcal{C}_1.Meth)$. Process morphism defines in §3 is just the same as
$h^*(L_{\mathcal{A}_2}(initial_{\mathcal{A}_2})) = L_{\mathcal{A}_1}(initial_{\mathcal{A}_1})$ where $initial_{\mathcal{A}_1}$ and $initial_{\mathcal{A}_2}$ are respectively initial states of $\mathcal{A}_1$ and $\mathcal{A}_2$.

If we look at the example §4.1 the problem is that

$$arr\_m_1 term\_m_1 arr\_m_2 term\_m_2 \in traces_{\mathcal{A}_1}(initial_{\mathcal{A}_1})$$
$$\text{but } arr\_m_1 term\_m_1 arr\_m_2 term\_m_2 \notin traces_{\mathcal{A}_2}(initial_{\mathcal{A}_2}) \quad (1)$$

It is also needed for all states s of $\mathcal{A}_2$, reached from initial states after executing a sequence of events w_2 of $Ev(\mathcal{C}_2.Meth)$ which satisfy $h^*(w_2) = w_1 \in Ev(\mathcal{C}_1.Meth)^*$ with respect to $\mathcal{C}_2$ behavior, the following property holds.

$$Poss_{\mathcal{A}_2}(s) \bigcap Ev(\mathcal{C}_1.Meth) \subset Poss_{\mathcal{A}_1}(\beta_1(\lambda^{-1}(w_1) \bigcap \mathcal{C}_{\mathcal{A}_1}(initial_{\mathcal{A}_1})))$$

So we need the following property to be satisfied:

$$\forall c \in Path_{\mathcal{A}_2}(initial_{\mathcal{A}_2}) \; h(Poss_{\mathcal{A}_2}(\beta_2(c))) \subset Poss_{\mathcal{A}_1}(\beta_1(\hat{h}^*(c)))"$$

To cope with this constraint we consider "parameterized transition systems".

Definition 9 (Parameterized transition system). A transition system of sort $\mathcal{X}$ where $\mathcal{X} = \{X_1, \ldots, X_n\}$ is a finite set of parameters names
is a transition system $\mathcal{A} = \langle S, T, \alpha, \beta, \lambda \rangle$ where subsets $S_{X_1}, \ldots, S_{X_n}$ of S are distinguished for each $X_i \in \mathcal{X}$

In order to separate states in sets satisfying the same property, André Arnold defines parameterized transition systems [Arn94]. Using parameterized transition systems an equivalence relationship between states (*Multitrace equivalence*) may be defined.

Definition 10 (Multitrace equivalence). Let $\mathcal{X} = \{X_1, X_2, \ldots, X_n\}$ a finite set of state parameters' name. $\mathcal{A}$ being a labeled transition system with state parameters S_X for $X \in \mathcal{X}$. $L_{\mathcal{A}}^X(s) = \{\lambda(c) | \alpha(c) = s, \; \beta(c) \in S_X\}$. Two states s and s' are multitrace equivalent if for all $X \in \mathcal{X}$, $L_{\mathcal{A}}^X(s) = L_{\mathcal{A}}^X(s')$.

Readiness semantics is multitrace equivalence with parameters X which are

$$\mathcal{X} = \{X | \exists s \in S_1 \; Poss_{\mathcal{A}_1}(s) = X\}$$

whereas failure semantics is multitrace equivalence with parameters X which are $\mathcal{X} = \{X | \exists s \in S_1 \; Poss_{\mathcal{A}_1}(s) \bigcap X = \emptyset\}$.

One can notice for failure semantics, the following property : for a transition system $\mathcal{A}$ $(c, R) \in failure_{\mathcal{A}}(initial_{\mathcal{A}}) \iff c \in L_{\mathcal{A}}^R(initial_{\mathcal{A}})$

We are going to show that readiness semantics is too strong to characterize behavioral compatibility with respect to inheritance.

Let $\mathcal{C}_2$ be a class inheriting from $\mathcal{C}_1$. Let $\mathcal{A}_2 = \langle S_2, T_2, \alpha_2, \beta_2, \lambda_2 \rangle$ and $\mathcal{A}_1 = \langle S_1, T_1, \alpha_1, \beta_1, \lambda_1 \rangle$ their respective behaviors. In order to cope with compatibility we consider the set of parameters name induced by $\mathcal{A}_1$. We define the set $\mathcal{X}$ by : $\mathcal{X} = \{X | \exists s \in S_1 \; Poss_{\mathcal{A}_1}(s) = X\}$

As transition systems are finite, $\mathcal{X}$ is a finite set. For each parameter's name $X \in \mathcal{X}$ we define a partition of the set of states S_2 of the $\mathcal{C}_2$ behavior. $S_X \subset S_2$ by

$$S_X = \{s \in S_2 | Poss_{\mathcal{A}_2}(s) \bigcap Ev(\mathcal{C}_1.Meth) = X\}$$

Example 5. *Let us consider example 3 again. The behavior* $(m1|||m3)/m2$ *of* $\mathcal{C}_2$ *is represented by the transition system on figure 4.*

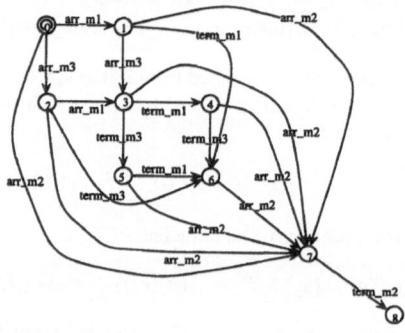

Figure 4: $\mathcal{C}_2$ behavior of specification: "$(m1|||m3)/m2$"

The set of parameters name is $\mathcal{X}$.
$$\mathcal{X} = \begin{cases} \{arr\_m1, arr\_m2\} = X_0 & \{term\_m1, arr\_m2\} = X_1 & \{arr\_m2\} = X_2 \\ \{term\_m2\} = X_3 & \emptyset = X_4 \end{cases}$$
$S_{X_0} = \{0, 2\} \quad S_{X_1} = \{1, 3, 5\}$
$S_{X_2} = \{4, 6\} \quad \dots$

We can see on this example that initial states $0 \in \mathcal{A}_1$ *and* $0 \in \mathcal{A}_2$ *are not "Multitrace equivalents"*.

$h^*(L_{\mathcal{C}_2}^{X_2}(0)) = h^*(\{arr\_m1 \; term\_m1, \; arr\_m3 \; arr\_m1 \; term\_m3 \; term\_m1,$

$arr\_m3 \; arr\_m1 \; term\_m1 \; term\_m3, \; arr\_m1 \; arr\_m3 \; term\_m3 \; term\_m1,$

$arr\_m1 \; arr\_m3 \; term\_m1 \; term\_m3, \; arr\_m3 \; term\_m3\})$

$= \{\epsilon, arr\_m1 \; term\_m1\} \quad (2)$

whereas $L_{C_1}^{X_2}(0) = \{arr\_m1 \; term\_m1\}$
So initial states of C_2 and C_1 behaviors are not equivalent for readiness semantics.

Property 1. For two behaviors A_1 and A_2 such that
$$traces_{A_1}(initial_{A_1}) \subset traces_{A_2}(initial_{A_2}),$$
let $\mathcal{X} = \{X | \exists s \in S_1 \; Poss_{A_1}(s) \bigcap X = \emptyset\}$,
if we have the following property,

$$\forall c \in Path_{A_2}(initial_{A_2}) \mid h(Poss_{A_2}(\beta_2(c))) \subset Poss_{A_1}(\beta_1(\hat{h}^*(c)))"$$

then $\forall R \in \mathcal{X} \; L_{A_1}^R \subset h^*(L_{A_2}^R)$

Proof. $\forall s \in L_{A_1}^R$ as $traces_{A_1}(initial_{A_1}) \subset traces_{A_2}(initial_{A_2})$ then $s \in L_{A_2}^R$
if $ev \in R$ and if $ev \in Poss_{A_2}(\beta_2(c))$ as $h(Poss_{A_2}(\beta_2(c))) \subset Poss_{A_1}(\beta_1(\hat{h}^*(c)))$ there is
contradiction because $Poss_{A_1}(\beta_1(h^*(c))) \bigcap R = \emptyset$ □

Définition 2. Let a class C_2 with behavior A_2 which inherit a class C_1 with behavior A_1. A behavior A_1 is compatible with the behavior A_2 with respect to inheritance if the following relationship holds :

$$traces_{A_1}(initial_{A_1}) \subset traces_{A_2}(initial_{A_2}) \tag{3}$$

$$\forall c \in traces_{A_2}(initial_{A_2})$$
$$\forall (h^*(c), R) \in failures(initial_{A_1}) \Rightarrow (c, R) \in failures(initial_{A_2}) \tag{4}$$

And for this property $(m1|||m3); m2$ and $m1; m2$ behaviors are not compatible because :
$(arr\_m_3 \; term\_m_3, \{arr\_m_2\}) \notin failures(initial_{A_2})$
and $(\epsilon, \{arr\_m_2\}) \in failures(initial_{A_1})$.

Property 2. Compatibility is less stronger than failure equivalence. If for two behaviors A_1 and A_2, such that $traces_{A_1}(initial_{A_1}) \subset traces_{A_2}(initial_{A_2})$, initial states $initial_{A_1}$ and $initial_{A_2}$ are failure equivalent then the following property holds,

$$\forall c \in traces_{A_2}(initial_{A_2}) \forall (h^*(c), R) \in failures(initial_{A_1}) \Rightarrow (c, R) \in failures(initial_{A_2})$$

Proof. $(h^*(c), R) \in failures(initial_{A_1}) \Leftrightarrow h^*(c) \in L_{A_1}^R(initial_{A_1})$.
If $c \notin L_{A_2}^R(initial_{A_2})$ because of failure equivalence, $h^*(c) \notin L_{A_1}^R(initial_{A_1})$ which is a contradiction. □

5 Practical verification of behavioral compatibility

We present in this section the practical technique used with our model to verify behavior compatibility in an inheritance or aggregation relationship.

Used technique is based on the use of observers [HLR93]. Thanks to reactive programming of controllers which allows an easy use of observers. Figure 5 shows architecture devoted to this technique. An observer verifies out going events restricted to $C_1.Meth$ flows,

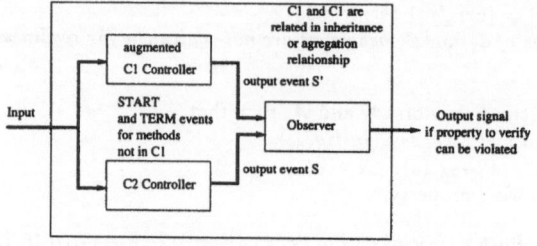

Figure 5: Architecture of compatibility verification system

for the same input, out of C_1 and C_2 controllers with respect to a property. This property characterizes behavior compatibility either for inheritance or for aggregation.

Properties to check on Esterel modules are : in an inheritance and aggregation construct : at each instant,

$$\forall output\_event \in EV(C_2.Meth) \bigcap EV(C_1.Meth) \mid$$
$$\mathbf{present}(C_2.output\_event) \Rightarrow \mathbf{present}(C_1.output\_event) \quad (5)$$

5.1 This technique implements compatibility

Proposition 3. For Given C_2 which inherits from a class C_1 of respective behaviors $\mathcal{A}_2$ and $\mathcal{A}_1$. Temporal property

$$\mathcal{P}(C_1, C_2) \equiv \square(\forall m \in C_1 \; (start_{C_2}\_m \longrightarrow start_{C_1}\_m) \; \wedge \; (done_{C_2}\_m \longrightarrow done_{C_1}\_m))$$

is true for C_2 and C_1 if and only if $\mathcal{A}_2$ and $\mathcal{A}_1$ are compatible.

Proof. First of all in our model for each accepted input event an output event is produced, namely $start\_m$ for arr_m and $done\_m$ for $term\_m$.

If $\mathcal{P}(C_1, C_2)$ holds, $(f^*(c), R) \in failures_{\mathcal{A}_1}(initial_{\mathcal{A}_1})$ for each $ev \in R$, if $(c, \{ev\}) \notin failures_{\mathcal{A}_2}(initial_{\mathcal{A}_2})$ because of temporal property, $(f^*(c), \{ev\}) \notin failures_{\mathcal{A}_1}(initial_{\mathcal{A}_1})$ which is a contradiction.

Conversely, if compatibility holds, after a path c of transitions, for all $ev \in \mathcal{A}_1$ accepted by $\mathcal{A}_1$. It is true $(c, \{ev\}) \notin failures_{\mathcal{A}_1}(initial_{\mathcal{A}_1})$. As compatibility holds, $(c, ev) \notin failures_{\mathcal{A}_2}(initial_{\mathcal{A}_2})$. So ev is not accepted by $\mathcal{A}_2$ which means $CTRL\_output_{\mathcal{A}_2}(ev) \longrightarrow CTRL\_output_{\mathcal{A}_1}(ev)$ where $CTRL\_output_{\mathcal{A}}(ev)$ is the corresponding output event to accepted event ev.

$\square$

5.2 Examples

In order to illustrate our verification technique when object structure use inheritance, let us consider the previously presented example 3 :

Verification ensures that each time presence of an outgoing event of sort *start_m* or *done_m* is detected ("present" statement in Esterel) at the C_2 controller module output presence of the same event is equivalently detected at the C_1 controller module output and this for all method $m \in \{m_1, m_2\}$.

The observer code in reactive language Esterel [BG92] consists in parallel composition of modules such as :

```
present [ ( C2_output_ev_m and not C1_output_ev_m )
        ]
then
    emit PROBLEM_output_ev_m
end present
```

The elementary module structure presented here results of equivalence rewriting.

$$\neg(p \Rightarrow q) \Leftrightarrow (p \wedge \neg q)$$

Verification succeed when no event of sort PROBLEM_*output_ ev_ m* is emitted.

Let us consider the previously introduced microwave oven example. Its behavior is given by the following BDL expression :

$$(\text{on} \ / \ (\text{off} \ | \ (\text{open} \ ; \ \text{close} \ )) \ )*$$

The property we have to check is the following : " *behavior of a MWOven object with such a behavior is it compatible with behaviors of its components MWGenerator and MWDoor considered as individual objects.*"

Property can be checked using observer technique previously presented. Use of FC2Tools [BRRdS96] allows :

1. transition system synchronized product of MWOven aggregated object behavior $\mathcal{A}_{MWOven}$ and MWDoor object behavior $\mathcal{A}_{MWDoor}$.

2. to check adding an observer the property

$$\forall output\_event \in EV(MWOven.Meth) \bigcap EV(MWDoor.Meth) \ | $$
$$MWOven.output\_event \Rightarrow MWDoor.output\_event$$

The observer checks this property for all output events in $EV(MWOven.Meth) \bigcap EV(MWDoor.Meth)$ and emits a violation event if for some event s in $EV(MWOven.Meth) \bigcap EV(MWDoor.Meth)$ presence of the same event is not detected as an output event of $MWDoor$ controller. The Esterel observer code is written using the logical property $(p \Rightarrow q) \Leftrightarrow (\neg p \vee q)$.

```
[
    present [MWOven_START_open and not MWDoor_START_open] then
        emit VIOLATION_START_open
    end present
||  present [MWOven_START_close and not MWDoor_START_close] then
        emit VIOLATION_START_close
```

```
    end present
||  present [MWOven_END_open and not MWDoor_END_open] then
        emit VIOLATION_END_open
    end present
||  present [MWOven_END_close and not MWDoor_END_close] then
        emit VIOLATION_END_close
    end present
]
```

6 Conclusion

We have presented here a formal definition of compatibility between behaviors for objects related by inheritance or aggregation relationship. Using our reactive controlled object model, these definition allows us to automatically verify compatibility between behaviors.

Aggregation and inheritance compatibility is an aspect of possibilities offer by our model "*reactive controlled object*". This model allows concurrent programming without having to explicitly use threads. In this area Junior Reactive Kernel [HSB99] presents a reactive model for concurrent programming without threads. Our model splits, as required by first works on inheritance anomalies, concurrency control and expression of transformations as expressed in objects methods.

Using a reactive language for expressing synchronizations allows to use associated tools to visualize behavioral or check properties. In this paper we have characterized the properties to check in order to have classes which have compatible behaviors when one inherit from the other or one is an aggregate containing the other.

The main difficulty in this characterization results of state changing in an object considered on one point of view whereas event is received by the object considered according the other. Our work uses similar technique as A. Arnold but consider properties up to an abstraction criteria (events belonging to $EV(C_1.Meth)$). Using an automaton as target code enables us to dispose of a mathematical model upon a certain number of properties can be verified. Proofs enable us to control that the initial specification have been correctly translated.

Nowdays, BDL cannot express conditions of activation related to object attributes. This restriction is a constraint imposed by versions prior than 5_21 of ESTEREL and associated verification tools. We are now working towards this way be using Toupie [CR94] a constraint language working on finite domains instead of Esterel. Our now days work aims to realize an integrated tool enabling all verification aspects—properties verification, compatibility with inheritance or aggregation—and production code.

References

[AD89]   A. Arnold and A. Dicky. An algebraic characterisation of transition system equivalences. *Information and Computation*, 82:198–229, 1989.

[Arn94]   A. Arnold. *Finite transition systems. Semantics of communicating sytems.* Prentice-Hall, 1994.

[BA99]   F. Bertrand and M. Augeraud. Bdl: A specialized language for per-object reactive control. In *IEEE Software Engineering*, pages pp 347–362, May/June 1999.

[BCG86]   G. Berry, P. Couronné, and G. Gonthier. Synchronous programming of reactive systems. *France-Japan Artificial Intelligence and Computer Science Symposium*, 86, 1986.

[Ber96]   F. Bertrand. *Un Modèle de Contrôle Réactif pour les langages à Objets Concurrents*. PhD thesis, Université de La Rochelle, Janvier 1996.

[BG92]   G. Berry and G. Gonthier. The esterel synchronous programming language: design, semantics, implementation. *Science of Computer Programming*, 19(2):87–152, 1992.

[BG96]   J.P. Briot and R. Guerraoui. Objets, parallélisme et répartition. *Technique et science informatique*, 15(6):765–800, 1996.

[BHR84]   S.D. Brookes, C.A.R. Hoare, and A.W. Roscoe. A theory of communicating sequential processes. Number 31, pages 560–599, 1984.

[BRRdS96]   A. Bouali, A. Ressouche, V. Roy, and R de Simonne. The fctools user manual. Technical Report 191, INRIA, Avril 1996.

[CR94]   M.-M Corsini and A. Rauzy. Symbolic model checking and constraint logic programming: a cross-fertilization. *Proc. of the European Symposium on Programming ESOP'94*, 1994.

[CSS94]   J.F. Costa, A. Sernadas, and C. Sernadas. Object inheritance beyond subtyping. *Acta Informatica*, 31:5–26, 1994.

[Har87]   D. Harel. Statecharts: A visual formalism for complex systems. *Science of Computer Programming*, 8:231–274, 1987.

[HCRP91]   N. Halbwachs, P. Caspi, P. Raymond, and D. Pilaud. The synchronous dataflow programming language lustre. *Proceedings of IEEE*, 79(9):1305–1320, 1991.

[HJS92]   T. Hartmann, R. Jungclaus, and G. Saake. Aggregation in a Behavior Oriented Object Model. In O. L. Madsen, editor, *Proceedings of ECOOP'92*, volume 615 of *Lecture Notes in Computer Science*, pages 57–77. Springer Verlag, 1992.

[HLR93]   N. Halbwachs, F. Lagnier, and P. Raymond. Synchronous observers and the verification of reactive systems. In M. Nivat, C. Rattray, T. Rus, and G. Scollo, editors, *Third Int. Conf. on Algebraic Methodology and Software Technology, AMAST'93*, Twente, June 1993. Workshops in Computing, Springer Verlag.

[HP85]   D. Harel and A. Pnueli. On the development of reactive systems: logic and models of concurrent systems. *Proceedings of NATO Advanced Study Institute on Logic and Models for Verification and Specification of Concurrent Systems*, 13:477–498, 1985.

[HSB99]   Laurent Hazard, Jean-Ferdinand Susini, and Frédéric Boussinot.   The junior reactive kernel.   Rapport de recherche, INRIA, Juillet 1999. http://www.inria.fr/meije/rc/RRInria-3732.ps.

[KL89]   D.G. Kafura and K.H. Lee. Inheritance in actor based concurrent object-oriented languages. In S. Cook, editor, *Proceedings of ECOOP'89*, pages 131–145, 1989.

[McH94]   Ciaran McHale. *Synchronisation in Concurrent Object-Oriented Languages: Expressive Power, Genericity and Inheritance.* PhD thesis, University of Dublin, Trinity College, 1994. http://www.dsg.cs.tcd.ie.

[MTY93]   S. Matsuoka, K. Taura, and A. Yonezawa. Highly efficient and encapsulated re-use of synchronization code in concurrent object-oriented languages. In *Proceedings of OOPSLA'93*, pages 109–126, 1993.

[MY93]   S. Matsuoka and A. Yonezawa. Analysis of inheritance anomaly in object-oriented concurrent programming languages. In P. Wegner et A. Yonezawa G. Agha, editor, *Research Directions in Concurrent Object-Oriented programming*, pages 107–150, 1993.

[NT95]   O. Nierstrasz and D. Tsichritzis. Object-oriented software composition, 1995.

[OH83]   E.R. Olderog and C.A.R. Hoare. Specification-oriented semantics for communication processes. In J. Diaz, editor, *Automata, Languages and Programming*, number 154, pages 561–572, 1983.

[RC95]   O. Roux and F. Cassez. Compilation of electre reactive language into finite transition systems. *Theorical Computer Science*, (142):109–143, 1995.

[RCCE92]   O. Roux, D. Creusot, F. Cassez, and J.P. Elloy. Le langage réactif asynchrone electre. *Technique et Science Informatiques*, 11(5), 1992.

[TS89]   C. Tomlison and V. Singh. Inheritance and synchronisation with enabled sets. In *Proccedings of the OOPSLA'89*, volume 24 of *SIGPLAN Notices*, pages 103–112, 1989.

A Formal Dynamic Schema Evolution Model for Hypermedia Databases

Bing Wang

Computer Science Department

University of Hull

Hull, HU6 7RX

United Kingdom

E-Mail: B.Wang@dcs.hull.ac.uk

Abstract

A hypermedia database schema is a meta-information which defines the structures of applications and objects. A dynamic schema evolution model is an abstract machine which describes changes of schemata. Unfortunately, because of the lack of formal data structures of hypermedia databases, it is very difficult to describe the dynamic changes of a hypermedia schema. The research presented in this paper proposes a formal approach to define the model of dynamic schema information. That is, a complete formal structure of a hypermedia database on the basis of previous research[WH93, WH95, Wan96, Wan97], and the schema operations defined for the schema evolution. The significant features of this research are, firstly, a formalized model to define the dynamic schema structure, secondly, a theoretical approach to manage the global schema of a distributed system, and finally, a design strategy to integrate the Web databases to support a wide range of application areas.

Keyword Formal Data Model, Multimedia, Dynamic Schema, Distributed Databases and Object Orientation.

1 Introduction

When a hypermedia application involves a large amounts of different types of multimedia information, it becomes more and more difficult to maintain the complex object types due to the lack of a powerful mechanism to define and maintain the structure of nodes and links. Consequently, a well-known problem in hypermedia, *the disorientation of hypermedia navigation*, appeared[Hal88, Hal91]. The essence of the disorientation is that the multimedia information types are unstructurally organized. The solution to this problem relies on the way of how to store information and how to describe relationships among nodes. Databases can be naturally chosen as the most suitable candidates for supporting complex hypermedia applications. This is because databases themselves are well structured for modelling a complex application structures. Since 90's, the author has focused on the data structure of linking databases with hypermedia to support complex application environments[HW92, Wan93, WH93, WH95]. Several enhanced hypermedia data models are developed[Wan96, Wan97]. In this paper, a further study of the dynamic hypermedia schema based on an extended hypermedia model[WH95] is discussed. In particular, we will illustrate the mechanisms of how to maintain the semantics of hypermedia application schemata in order to keep the consistency the node and link structures.

This paper is organized as follows. Section 2 reviews the semantic constructors of an extended hypermedia data model in order to illustrate the hypermedia schema structure which is described in section 3. Section 4 describes some related works and we conclude our discussion in section 5.

2   A Hypermedia Model

The dynamic hypermedia schema evolution model is set up on the basis of an existing extended hypermedia data model which is an object oriented data model capturing both semantics of hypermedia and object databases.[1] There three basic constructors in this model. They are *node constructor, composite node constructor* and *schema constructor*. These constructors are used as essential semantic building blocks for constructing a hypermedia application structure on the basis of object oriented databases. In the following review of this model, we will focus on the semantic aspects of these constructors and show how these constructors can formally present a hypermedia application.[2]

2.1   Relationships

The main problem of the current hypermedia systems to model an application structure is that they lack a powerful facility to reveal relationships among node. Thus, our extended hypermedia model focus on this aspect and reveal how the node structure can easily capture those semantic relationships among nodes.

In the conventional hypermedia approach, components of an application are stored in nodes and the nodes are connected by links. Because links are used simply to represent a fact that there exists a connection among nodes. It is very difficult for both designers and users to know the exact semantic relationship between nodes. Thus, it depends heavily on the human beings abilities to reveal relevant information behind nodes and links. It is therefore useful if a hypermedia node can automatically represent some semantic meanings of application structures.

There are two major relationship types between hypermedia components. They are part-of and inheritance relationships. In the extended hypermedia data model we developed, we define two node constructors to reveal such internal structure of a node.

Component Node Constructor

This is the first node constructor which reveals the part-of relationship between nodes. In general, a conventional hypermedia node is constructed by multimedia information. The multimedia data types within a node can be used as a either the destination or target of links. Thus, a node structure can be described by figure 1.

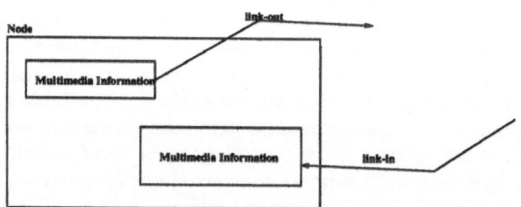

Figure 1: A conventional node structure

In the conventional approach, we cannot find out the exact semantic relationship between the node and its multimedia components. The node is a virtual object. It is only used as a concept to describe an information container. However, if we impose the part-of relationship between components and its container, we can modify the above picture into a more semantic node type as described in figure 2.

---

[1]This is a unified data model called HyperDB which was developed by the author in 1997[Wan97].

[2]A formal specification language Z is used to describe these constructors. Z is the formal specification language developed by the Oxford University in the late seventies. Now, it is widely used both in industry and academia.

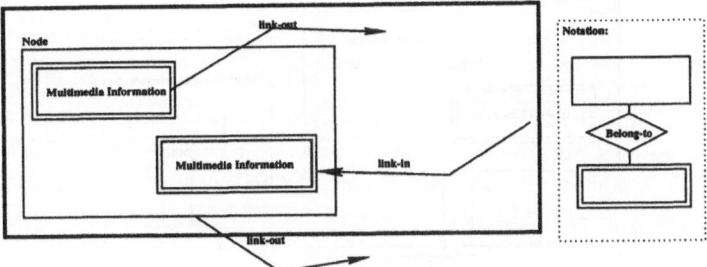

Figure 2: A semantic node structure

In figure 2, a significant difference between the conventional node (figure 1) and the new node is that a component is explicitly expressed as the *part* of a node. The node itself can be used not only as a container to group components but also a component for another node. The following Z schema exactly represents such semantic meaning.

$$\begin{array}{|l}
\underline{\quad Composite\_Node\_Constructor \quad\rule{8cm}{0pt}} \\
Node\_Constructor \\
composite\_parts : \mathbb{P}\ Multimedia \\
\hline
\exists\, n : Node \mid n = node \bullet composite\_parts = n.source.media\_part \cup n.destination.media\_part
\end{array}$$

By using the above definition, a conventional hypermedia node is a special case of our definition. More importantly, using the Z schema definition to capture semantics of the node structure, we can further define the dynamic schema evolution model which can automatically maintain consistency of nodes and links.

Inheritance Node Structure

The inheritance property is the second important characteristic of existing applications. It reveals potential links between nodes. Most importantly, it organizes nodes in a structural way. From software engineering point of view, it reuses the sources of some software components. In the hypermedia design point of view, it imposes a semantic constraint between nodes. That is, the node A is a *super node* of the node B. By defining such semantic constraint among nodes, it guarantees that semantic operations such as *delete nodes, change nodes* and *create nodes* can be correctly executed when a defined application structure is evolved. The following picture illustrates the inheritance relationship between nodes.

The inheritance property defined above is different from that of object oriented model. An inheritance node inherits not only attributes of its super objects but also link structures defined within its super nodes. The following Z schema defines such scenario.

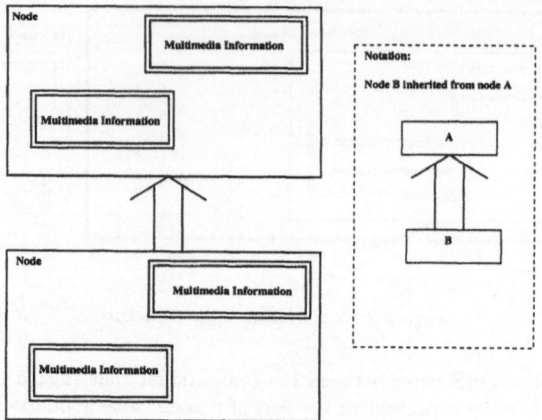

Figure 3: A semantic node structure

$$
\begin{array}{l}
\rule{0pt}{0pt} \\
\textit{Node\_Constructor} \\
\hline
\textit{node : Node} \\
\textit{new\_media\_part : Components} \\
\textit{new\_id' : ComponentID} \\
\textit{super\_sub : } \mathbb{P}(\textit{Components} \times \mathbb{P}\ \textit{Components}) \\
\hline
\textit{dom super\_sub} = 1 \\
\\
\textit{ran super\_sub} = \{\textit{node.source.id}\} \cup \{\textit{node.destination.id}\} \\
\\
\exists\, c : \textit{Components} \mid c = \textit{new\_media\_part} \bullet (c.\textit{media\_part} = \{\} \Rightarrow \\
(c.\textit{id} = \textit{node.source.id} \vee c.\textit{id} = \textit{node.destination.id}) \wedge \\
(\textit{new\_media\_part} = (c.\textit{media\_part} \cup \textit{node.source.media\_part}) \vee \\
\textit{new\_media\_part} = (c.\textit{media\_part} \cup \textit{node.destination.media\_part}))) \\
\vee \\
(c.\textit{media\_part} \neq \{\} \Rightarrow \textit{new\_media\_part.media\_part} = c.\textit{media\_part} \wedge \\
\textit{new\_id'} = \textit{new\_media\_part.id} \cup \textit{ComponentID}) \\
\hline
\end{array}
$$

2.2 Schema

A hypermedia application is constructed on the basis of the above node constructors. The application is abstracted by the general purpose schema definition in the proposed approach. This is defined as follows.

```
__ Scheme__Constructor _____
  Node__Constructor
  Composite__Node__Constructor
  node_object : Node__Type ↦ ObjectType
 _____
  ∀ nodes : ℙ Node__Type • ∀ n : nodes • ∃ o : ObjectType; N₁ : Node__Constructor;
  N₂ : Composite__Node__Constructor | n = InheritableNode N₁ ∨ n = CompositeNode N₂
  • o = node_object n
 _____
```

The above schema specifies that all defined nodes must belong to the existing node types that have the corresponding object types supported by a database system. Since the purpose of the extended hypermedia data model is to use database facilities to model a hypermedia application structure, the above schema constructor provides users both database's and hypermedia's view to analyse and model an application structure. Figure 4 illustrates the relationships between a hypermedia node and a database schema.

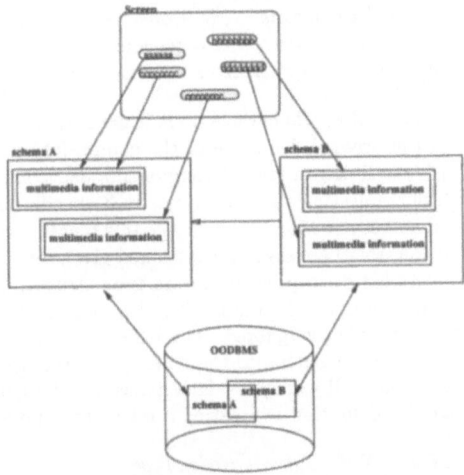

Figure 4: The relationships between nodes and schema

The schema of the extended hypermedia data model plays a role of structurally organize hypermedia information. The database is used as object store to maintain multimedia information. Thus, in order to get more semantics of an application schema, we need to define and use schema operators to combine or integrate different schemata which will discussed in the next section.

3 The Schema Operators

The dynamic evolution of a hypermedia database schema is a facility of managing hypermedia schema information when the hypermedia database is in operation. When a hypermedia application structure is defined, its semantic components and relationships among objects are automatically captured by the database. The dynamic schema evolution facility will use the information captured by the database to define a new application structure on the basis of the existing one. In order to formally describe such evolution, it is important to formalize a schema structure at the first stage as we have done in the previous section. In the second stage, what we need to do is to define schema operators which are essential for the dynamic schema evolution.

We have four basic operators for the schema evolution. In this paper, due to the limited length of the paper, we omit the discussion of the schema refinement. A complete description of the schema refinement will appear in the paper entitled *A dynamic Schema Structure for a Hypermedia Database.*[3]

3.1 Creating a Hypermedia Node

A node cannot be created without any semantic meanings. This means a hypermedia node can only be created as either a composite or an inheritance node. This is the potential constraint defined in HyperDB. In order to avoid creating an isolated node, we need two different functions to describe how to create a hypermedia node in HyperDB.

$$
\begin{array}{l}
Create\_Composite\_Node : \mathbb{P}\, Components \nrightarrow Composit\_Node\_Constructor \\[4pt]
\forall\, c : \mathbb{P}\, Components;\ s : Schema\_Constructor \bullet \\
\exists\, new\_composite\_node : Composite\_Node\_Constructor;\ new\_id : ComponentID; \\
s' : Schema\_Constructor \mid s'.Composite\_Node\_Constructor.composite\_parts = \\
new\_composite\_node.composite\_parts \wedge c.id = new\_id \\
\wedge\ new\_composite\_node = s.Node\_Constructor \vee s.Composite\_Node\_Constructor
\end{array}
$$

In the above function, it guarantees that whenever a node is created its components must be the one of existing nodes. This meets the original definition of the composite node constructor. The partial function is defined to establish the linkage between components and composite node type. This is a typical mathematic approach of connecting two object sets in Z specification. Its main purpose is to explicitly express the output of an action. More importantly, this function can be used to construct and refine a schema. In this definition, there are several pre-defined given sets. A given set is a mechanism used in Z in order to ignore detailed description of a data type structure. By using this facility, we can focus on the fundamental design issue of a model. The ComponentID is a given set which means the structure of the component identifier is ignored. The Node_Type is a free type structure defined in [Wan96]. This definition allows us to generalize the node type structure in our model. The second given set used in the above function is ObjectType which describes all possible object types supported by an object oriented. The similar definition of creating a inheritance node is defined as follows.

$$
\begin{array}{l}
Create\_Inheritance\_Node : Node\_Type \nrightarrow Node\_Type \\[4pt]
\forall\, n : Node\_Constructor;\ c : Composite\_Node\_Constructor;\ s : Schema\_Constructor \bullet \\
\exists\, new\_inheritance\_node : Node\_Type;\ new\_obj : ObjectType;\ s' : Schema\ constructor \bullet \\
s'.node\_object = s.node\_object \cup \{new\_inheritance\_node \mapsto new\_obj\} \\
\Rightarrow\ new\_inheritance\_node = CompositeNode\ c \vee new\_inheritance\_node = InheritableNode\ n
\end{array}
$$

The above function specifies that an inheritance node is such a node that is generated from the existing node, which is a node with the type of either Composite_Node_Constructor or Node_Constructor.

By using these two function definitions, the first schema operator of creating a hypermedia node which has the semantics defined in HyperDB is defined as follows:

---

[3] A paper submitted to th Journal of Information Science

```
┌─ Creating_Node ─────────────────────────────────────────────────
│ Δ Schema_Constructor
│ node? : Node_Type
│ components? : ℙ Components
├─────────────────────────────────────────────────────────────────
│ ∀ new_node : Node_Type • new_node = Create_Inheritance_Node node? ∨
│ new_node = Create_Composite_Node components?
└─────────────────────────────────────────────────────────────────
```

3.2 Finding a Hypermedia Node

Before a schema is evolved, we need to know if a node is existed. This means that we need to find out a specific node according to our needs. First, we specify the existence status of a node. A set is defined to represent two different status.

$$Existence\_Status ::= Existence \mid Nonexistence$$

On the basis of this set, a schema operator to indicate if a node is existed is defined as follows:

```
┌─ Report_Node_Status ───────────────────────────────────────────
│ node_status! : Existence_Status
├────────────────────────────────────────────────────────────────
│ node_status = Existence
└────────────────────────────────────────────────────────────────
```

Furthermore, we define a schema operator to check if a node is absolutely existed in the information basis. This is:

```
┌─ Examining_Node ───────────────────────────────────────────────
│ Schema_Constructor
│ found_node! : Node_Type
├────────────────────────────────────────────────────────────────
│ found_node! ∈ dom node_object
│ ∃ I_node : Node_Constructor; c_node : Composite_Node_Constructor •
│ found_node! = InheritableNode I_node ∨ found_node! = CompositeNode c_node
└────────────────────────────────────────────────────────────────
```

The above schema operator guarantees that the found node must be a node defined in the corresponding application structure and it is a valid node by imposed the node type constructor (Node_Type)[Wan96].

In a more general situation, an evolution of a hypermedia application schema of successfully finding a node can be described as:

$$Find\_Hypermedia\_Node \triangleq Examining\_Node \wedge Report\_Node\_Status$$

In this schema operator definition, we have shown the simple way of how to define a schema evolution by using the first order logic connectives. However, in most object oriented schema evolution approaches, there are many complex operators are defined in order to check or change an existing object. The advantage of our approach is that we rely only on the first order logic to connect schema and to infer a new schema operator such as Find_a_Hypermedia_Node defined above. That is why we only need to define four basic schema operators in our approach.

3.3 Add Operator

The third general schema operator in the hypermedia schema evolution is the add operator. When a schema is changed, it implies that either a new node is inserted into the new application structure or a node is deleted from the existing application structure in order to keep semantic consistency between node types defined in the new application structure. Thus, we need to consider two different situation. They are, adding a node according to the need and delete a node according to the requirements. We first discuss how to add a node when a schema is changed. Next section will illustrate the situation of deletion.

- *A complete new node is inserted*

  In this situation, a new node is created without any input information such as Creating_Node schema defined above. This is because a node is created due to the specific requirements of a application structure. Such schema operator is defined as follows.

  ┌─ *Insert_New_Node* ─────────────────────────────
  │ $\Delta Schema\_Constructor$
  │
  │ $\forall a\_new\_node, n : Node\_Type \bullet \exists c : \mathbb{P}\ Components \bullet$
  │ $a\_new\_node = Create\_Composite\_Node\ c$
  │ $\lor a\_new\_node = Create\_Inheritance\_Node\ n$
  └──

  This schema says that all newly inserted nodes are automatically inserted into the new application schema without any input information. That means, if it a composite node, a corresponding components are generated. Otherwise, a inheritance node is generated.

- *A new node is inserted on the basis of the existing one*

  In the second situation, the new generated node is based on an existing node. This means that the new node will inherit all link structures defined in the old node. We re-define link definitions defined in HyperDB in order to define this schema. All the predicate parts of link schema remain the same, but they are defined as generic definition.

  1. *Navigation Link Type*

     A navigation link type is a functional link to link instances of a node type. In the HyperDB approach, an instance link is a non-semantic link. That means it only physically links two instances. This is just a browsing function defined on the source and the target of nodes. Its generic form is defined as follows.

     ┌─ *Navigation_Link*$[M_1, M_2]$ ──────────────────
     │ $target_1, target_2 : Node\_Type$
     │ $navigation\_link : \mathbb{P}(M_1 \times M_2)$
     │
     │ $\forall nodes : \mathbb{P}\ Node\_Type \bullet \exists n_1, n_2 : nodes;\ N_1 : Node\_Constructor;$
     │ $N_2 : Composite\_Node\_Constructor \mid n_1 = InheritableNode\ N_1 \lor$
     │ $n_1 = CompositeNode\ N_2 \lor n_2 = InheritableNode\ N_1 \lor$
     │ $n_2 = CompositeNode\ N_2 \bullet N_1.node.source.media\_part = target_1 \land$
     │ $N_2.node.destination.media\_part = target_2$
     │ $\Rightarrow target_1 = navigation\_link\ target_2$
     └──

     This schema says that whatever nodes they are, a navigation link is a connection between the source and the target of a node.

  2. *Connection Type*

     A connection between node types is a high level relationship type which specifies a user's defined semantics between node types. The *generalization/specialization* and *part-of* relationships are already revealed by the definitions of node constructors themselves. However, it is difficult to represent the following semantics between two entities:

Figure 5: A *written-by* relationship between two entities

We need a specified relationship exactly represent a semantic meaning between two node types. This is achieved by the connection type defined by the following schema.

$$
\begin{array}{l}
\underline{\quad Node\_Type\_Connection[Node_1, Node_2]\quad\rule{3cm}{0pt}} \\
connection : \mathbb{P}(Node_1 \times Node_2) \\
\rule{10cm}{0.4pt} \\
\forall\, node\_types : \mathbb{P}\, Node\_Type \bullet \exists\, n_1, n_2 : node\_types;\; N_1 : Node\_Constructor; \\
N_2 : Composite\_Node\_Constructor \mid n_1 \neq InheritableNode\; N_1 \vee \\
n_2 \neq CompositeNode\; N_2 \bullet n_1 \mapsto n_2
\end{array}
$$

The above schema expresses that if two node types are not inheritable and composite node types, there must be a named semantic relationship defined between them. This further implies that no isolated node types exist in the hyper-space. Thus, a complete schema operator of adding a new node on the basis of existing nodes can be defined as follows.

$$
\begin{array}{l}
\underline{\quad Insert\_Based\_Node\quad\rule{5cm}{0pt}} \\
nodes : Node\_Type \rightarrowtail ObjectType \\
link_1 : Navigation\_Link_{[Multimedia, Multimedia]} \rightarrowtail ObjectType \\
link_2 : Node\_Type\_Connection_{[Node\_Type, Node\_Type]} \rightarrowtail ObjectType \\
\rule{10cm}{0.4pt} \\
\mathrm{dom}\; nodes \in \mathbb{P}\, Node\_Type \\
\mathrm{dom}\; link_1 \in \mathbb{P}\, Navigation\_Link_{[Multimedia, Multimedia]} \\
\mathrm{dom}\; link_2 \in \mathbb{P}\, Node\_Type\_Connection_{[Node\_Type, Node\_Type]} \\
\langle \mathrm{ran}\; nodes, \mathrm{ran}\; link_1, \mathrm{ran}\; link_2 \rangle\; \text{partition}\; ObjectType
\end{array}
$$

Finally, as we illustrate before, we use the basic logical connectives to describe the add schema operator as follows.

$$Add\_Node \triangleq Insert\_New\_Node \vee Insert\_Based\_Node$$

3.4 Delete Operator

This the final schema operator for evolution purpose. It is a complex issue to delete a node. This is because a deleted node may have relationships with other nodes. In most cases, the deletion operation is executed on the basis of the assumption that all the related nodes are automatically deleted as well. The following delete operator schema expresses such situation.

```
┌─ Delete_Node ──────────────────────────────────────────────
│ △ Schema_Constructor
│ Examining_Node
│ Report_Node_Statusdeleted_node? : Node_Type
├────────────────────────────────────────────────────────────
│ ∀ s : Schema_Constructor •
│ ∃ results : Node_Type; relevantnodes : ℙ Node_Type; s' : Schema_Constructor |
│ results = found_nodes ∧
│ results = InheritableNode deleted_node? ∪ CompositeNode deleted_node? ∧
│ node' = (relevantnodes ∪ results) ⊲ node
└────────────────────────────────────────────────────────────
```

This schema says that, firstly, if a node will be deleted, we find out all its relevant nodes; secondly, all the relevant nodes are automatically deleted without any conditions.

By using the above schema operators, can finally describe how a a new hypermedia application schema is defined by the following definition.

$$Define\_a\_New\_Schema \; \hat{=} \; Creating\_Node \lor (Finding\_Hypermedia\_Node \land Add\_Node) \lor (Delete\_Node \land Add\_Node)$$

This simple algorithm illustrates a complex situation of the schema evolution. It abstracts a complex evolution strategy and provides a simple way to modify an existing application structure. This is the main advantage of this research.

4   Related Work

Orion[JKso87] is the earliest research of using invariants and rules to structurally organize the database schema information. A invariant is a constraint to maintain schemata consistency and rules are used to control invariants if a schema is changed. The schema propagation of Orion is through screening. A similar approach is used in the GemStone system design[PS87]. In later 80's, Zdonik proposed a framework for object version type[SZ86]. In this approach, their focus is on the object types' propagation. The schema operations are still similar to Orion.

In general, there are three methods used to deal with semantics of schema changes. They are screening, conversion and filtering. In the screen approach, a conversion program is automatically generated when evolving a database schema. Old object types are monitored and converted into the new types of new or changed schema. In the conversion approach, old object types are immediately changed according to the new schema definition. Finally, in the filtering approach, a set of new definitions are defined as filters to deal with the consistency between old and new object types, that is, object types belonging to the old schema are becoming a specific version types of the defined schema. Orion, GemStone and Zdonik's approaches use the combination of these techniques to explicitly enforce objects to coincide with the new definition of the schema. Because there is not a universal definition of object databases, it is difficult to say which technique is best. On the other hand, since the hypermedia node types are organized by using links, it is impossible to use the above techniques to coerce nodes to coincide with the new or updated application structures. The reason is that node types are pre-connected by unstructured links. Thus, when we use a general purpose object oriented database as the information base for supporting hypermedia, it is very difficult for us to keep consistency of both links and node types. The proposed research avoids the complex definition of hypermedia application structures by introducing two basic node types. These two node types plays two roles. First, they are the only existing object types. This means no other isolated node types will be allowed to exist. Secondly, they are used as abstract templets to represent all possible objects. Thus, it simplifies the complex definition of application structures. More importantly, this allows us to use limited schema operators to specify all the possible change among a schema.

Formal methods are currently being increasingly introduced and frequently y used in hypertext research. When compared with other research areas, studies on the formal specification of hypertext structures only began a few years ago. From 1988 onwards, several research results have been published. The earliest person to use mathematical methods to define formally the structure of a hypertext system was Garg[Gar89], The important contribution of Garg's work is the definition of the abstraction mechanisms — *aggregation* and *generalization* — which were constructed on the basis of the mathematical definitions of nodes and links. Garg's work shows that we are able to define the hypertext structure using set theory and first-order logic. In the 90's, formal specification languages such as VDM and Z have been introduced into hypertext research. Lange[Lan90] used VDM to define the hypertext structure. His work experiments with the use of an OODBMS to build a hypertext system, and he formally defines his hypertext data model in an object oriented way. Halasz and Schwartz[HM90] used Z to formalize the Dexter hypertext reference model. The Dexter model divides a hypertext system into three layers, these being the runtime, storage and within-component layers[HM90]. Dexter's specification focuses mainly on the storage layer, which is used to model the basic hypertext node/link structure. Dexter model defines hypertext operations clearly and unambiguously, and guarantees addressing for any hypertext component. It is also beneficial to us when defining operations, constraints and relationship types. From these approaches, we see that the formal specification of hypertext structures can provide the foundation for understanding the essentials of hypertext systems.

5 Conclusion

The dynamic schema evolution of a hypermedia database is a new research area in the hymerpedia area. The importance of this research is to reveal formally the linkage between a database and hypermedia, and in particular the schema facilities of a database to maintain complex relationships among application schemata. The significant contribution of this research are, firstly, it is the first time of using formal notations to describe a hypermedia schema structure and corresponding schema operations; secondly, it provides a sound basis of how to use object oriented databases to integrate hypermedia and multimedia; and finally, it offers a mechanism of how to automatically support schema generation and maintenance. Furthermore, the research presented in this paper can be used as one of fundamental data structures for integrating Web with object oriented databases. We need a global supporting tool to control and maintain thousands of Web information. The proposed data model meets such requirements and it can be used to precisely define the data structure of the new generation Web systems. To explore the potential power of this data model, a research project entitled the design of Web meta-information search engine is being done by the database research team at the University of Hull, U.K.

References

[Gar89] P. K. Garg. *Information Management in Software Engineering: A Hypertext Based Approach.* PhD thesis, Computer Science Department, University of Southern California, USA, 1989.

[Hal88] F. G. Halasz. Reflections on notecards: Seven issues for the next generation of hypermedia systems. *Communications of the ACM*, 7(7):836–862, July 1988.

[Hal91] F. G. Halasz. Seven issues: Revisited. *Hypertext'91 Keynote Talk*, December 18, 1991.

[HM90] F. G. Halasz and S. Maye. The dexter hypertext reference model. *Proceedings of the Hypertext Standardization Workshop*, pages 95–131, January 16-18, 1990.

[HW92]   P. Hitchcock and B. Wang. Formal approach to hypertext system based on object oriented database systyem. *Information and Software Technology*, 34(9):573–592, September 1992.

[JKso87]   J.Banerjee, W. Kim, and so on. Semantics and implementation of schema evolution in object oriented databases. In *Proceedings of the ACM SIGMOD International Conference on Management of Data*, pages 311–322, San Francisco, May 1987.

[Lan90]   D B Lange. A formal approach to hypertext using post-prototype formal specification. *Lecture Notes in Computer Science*, (428):99–121, April 17-21 1990.

[PS87]   D.J. Penney and J. Stein. Class modification in the gemstone object oriented dbms. In *Proceedings of the International Conference on Object Oriented Programming: System, Language and Applications*, pages 111–117, Orland, FL, October 1987.

[SZ86]   A.H. Skarra and S.B. Zdonik. The management of changing types in an object oriented database. In *Proceedings of the International Conference on Object Oriented Programming: System, Language and Applications*, pages 483–495, Portland, OR, September 1986.

[Wan93]   B Wang. *Integrating Database and Hypertext to Support Documentation Environments*. PhD thesis, Computer Science Department, University of York, Heslington, York, Y01 5DD, U.K, 1993.

[Wan96]   B. Wang. The design of an integrated information system. In Roland R. Wagner and Helmut Thomas, editors, *Database and Expert System Applications (DEXA'96), Lecture Notes in Computer Science No. 685*, pages 479–488, Zurich, Switzerland, September 1996. Springer-Verlag.

[Wan97]   B. Wang. Toward a unified data model for large hypermedia applications. In Ab delkader Hameurlain and A Ming Tjoa, editors, *Database and Expert System Applications (DEXA'97), Lecture Notes in Computer Science No. 1308*, pages 142–152, Toulouse, France, September 1997. Springer-Verlag.

[WH93]   B. Wang and P. Hitchcock. An object oriented database approach for supporting hypertext. In Colette Rolland, Francois Bodart, and Corine Cauvet, editors, *Advanced Information Systems Engineering (CAiSE'93), Lecture Notes in Computer Science No. 685*, pages 601–628, Paris, France, June 1993. Springer-Verlag.

[WH95]   B. Wang and P. Hitchcock. *InterSect_DM*: a hypertext data model based on oodbms. *Information and Software Technology*, 37(3):573–592, March 1995.

MODELLING AND DESIGN
ISSUES I

Towards a Building Methodology for Software Agents

Xiaocong Fan

Turku Centre for Computer Science (TUCS)
Lemminkäisenkatu 14
FIN-20520 Turku, Finland
E-mail: fan.xc@abo.fi Fax: +358 2 241 0154

ABSTRACT. *The importance of agent-oriented methodology can't be more emphasized, and AOM is becoming the most promising research area in agent field. In this paper, we propose a component-role-agent model, formally define the concepts and dependency relations used in agent-oriented analysis and design. Based on such formalization and the mental hierarchy theory(Fan, 2000), an agent-oriented methodology is introduced, and a case study is given to show how to analyze and design an electronic library.*

KEY WORDS: *Software Agent, Inheritance, Agent-oriented Methodology*

---

1. Introduction

Agent-based computing is emerging as a powerful new paradigm (Wooldridge,1997,1998), and will be the backbones for the next generation of mainstream software systems. However, it is essential to have complexity management mechanism and design methodology to support the development of large embedded systems. Lack of them is the main reason why many projects trying to apply agent technique ended with failure (Kinny, et al.,1996; Wooldridge, et al.,1998a). For this reason, agent-oriented methodology was highly emphasized, and is becoming the most promising research area in agent field.

Much work has been done in this area, from formal specification (Brazier, et al.,1995; d'Inverno, et al.,1997) to analysis and design (Ferber, et al.,1998; Iglesias et al.,1999; Kinny et al.,1996; Wooldridge et al.,1998b), which can be classified into two camps. The first kind is component-based methodology, where agents are modeled as composite components built up from lower level components. The other kind is BDI-based (Kinny et al.,1996), which combines BDI architecture with object-oriented technique and has been shown to be a feasible solution.

From the viewpoint of traditional software engineering, the modeling concepts used in analysis and design should be formalized, the interactions between different agents should also be characterized in an appropriate way. Moreover, to support the analysis and design, especially for the reason that the design can be understood easily by programmers, some auxiliary diagrams (such as data flow diagram in SA/SD) are needed as well. However, such effort was neglected in the previous work.

Agent-oriented methodology has just been driving out of its starting point. There is much work to do and a long way to go before agent-oriented methodology can evolve into its maturity. Based on the previous research in this field, the work in this paper is just trying to go a step forward toward this goal.

We proceed as follows. In section 2 we introduce the framework of ARC method. Activities that should be carried out during analysis and design phases are provided in section 3, and section 4 gives a case study to show how to use ARC to analyze and design an agent systems in the electronic library domain. We compare with the other work and conclude the paper in section 5.

2. Building Shells– From Components to Roles and Agents

Roles and components are not at all new concepts used in analysing and modeling agent systems (Brazier et al.,1995; Kinny et al.,1996; Wooldridge et al.,1998b), but there has been no effort to show they can be geared together smoothly. We try to combine components with roles and use them as adobe to build agents. Here the name ARC (Agent-Role-Component) comes.

In ARC, primitive components are rudimental function units. Generally, a role consists of a few different components, which can cooperate with each other in problem solving. The functions or services a role can provide depend on the components it comprises. An Agent is composed of roles, and provides control over the roles to embody the beliefs, goals, intentions or interests of its own.

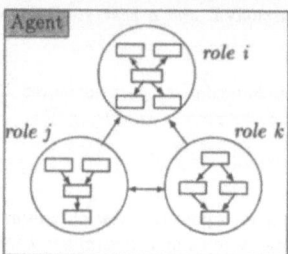

Fig.1. The relations between agents, roles, and components

Definition 1 *A primitive component c is a tuple $< \mathcal{I}_c, \mathcal{O}_c, \mathcal{P}_c, \mathcal{L}_c >$, where predicate set $\mathcal{I}_c$ specifies invocation conditions, reaction strategies, and constraints about incoming data stream; $\mathcal{O}_c$ is a predicate set which specifies the side-effects of c to its environment, and constraints about the outgoing data stream. $\mathcal{P}_c$ is a set of patterns of primitive procedures, and $\mathcal{L}_c$ is the native language used to negotiate and cooperate with the other primitive components, which includes definitions of the ontology and translation mechanisms.*

There may have more than one feasible implementations in $\mathcal{P}_c$ defined for a single non-trivial function, since the more behavior patterns we provide, the more robust the system will be. $\mathcal{P}_c$ circumscribes what types of tasks c can commit to, and determines how a role (c belongs to) decomposes a problem into smaller parts which are the instantiated versions of some procedures in $\mathcal{P}_c$. Compared with primitive components, which can only handle simple tasks, composite components, which can be built from primitive components by connecting their input and output interfaces, can deal with even more complex tasks in more effective ways.

Definition 2 *A role r is a tuple $< \Theta_r, H_r, S_r, \pi_r >$, where Θ_r is the set of all the primitive components in r, H_r is a set of task hierarchy diagrams, set S_r is composed of all the initial plans of r, and set $\pi_r \subseteq \Theta_r$ comprises all the controlling components in r.*

Divide-and-conquer is a common used technique in different areas of computer science to deal with complex problems and systems. A complex task can be divided into many sub-tasks again and again until primitive operations to which we have more efficient and effective solutions. In this paper, we model the decomposing of complex tasks by hierarchy diagrams, where each node of the diagram keeps track three kinds of information about decomposition: its parent nodes which have itself as a sub-part; its sibling nodes from which one of its parents builds up; and children nodes from which it can be reconstructed logically.

A task node n is a structure $< PC_n, SC_n, CC_n >$, where PC_n, SC_n, and CC_n are chains of parents, siblings and children of n respectively. For convenience, three projection functions are thus defined: $PC(n) = PC_n, SC(n) = SC_n, CC(n) = CC_n$. n is a root node (which corresponds to a top level task) if $PC(n) = \emptyset$; while, if $CC(n) = \emptyset$, n is a leaf node (a bottom level task), which corresponds to a primitive operation in set $\mathcal{P}$ of some component it belongs to.

Definition 3 *A task hierarchy diagram $\mathcal{G} =< N, \angle >$, where N is a set of task nodes, $\forall t_1, t_2 \in N, t_1 \angle t_2$ iff $t_2 \in CC(t_1)$. Let $root(\mathcal{G}) = \{t \in N | PC(t) = \emptyset\}$, and $node(\mathcal{G}) = N$. $t \angle^j t'$ is used to denote $t \angle_1 \cdots \angle_j t'$.*

Definition 4 *(sub-task sharing) For a task hierarchy diagram $\mathcal{G}$, $\forall t_1, t_2, t_3 \in N$, t_1 and t_2 are sub-task sharing at node t_3 iff $\exists i, j$, such that $t_1 \angle^i t_3$ and $t_2 \angle^j t_3$ hold.*

For example, in Fig.4(b), *returning* and *fining* have shared sub-task *lifting/lowering*.

A plan $p \in S_r$ is of the same form as (Kinny et al.,1996), which has an invocation event, a context condition, and plan body statements. A plan p is usually rendered as a graph $< N_p, E_p, root_p >$, where $root_p$ is the initial node, node set $N_p \subseteq 2^T$ ($T = \bigcup \mathcal{P}_c$, where $c \in \Theta_r$), edge $(n_i, l_k, n_j) \in E_p$ if the execution of the plan statement represented by n_j is activated upon the completion of n_i(invocation event) and the condition l_k holds.

When an agent intends to achieve some initial or dynamically created goal g in his goal set, a responsible role, say r_1, will be activated. r_1 then tries to invoke a plan pl from its plan set S_{r_1} or create one dynamically. The plan body of pl may include sub-plans or complex tasks. After substituting corresponding primitive procedures for the sub-plans and complex tasks according to the task hierarchy diagrams in H_{r_1}, the goal g can be carried out by dispatching each primitive procedure to the responsible components in Θ_{r_1}.

Definition 5 *(Agent Class) Agent class A is a tuple $< \Xi_A, \Re_A, \mathcal{B}_A >$, where set Ξ_A is composed of all the mental attributes, such as beliefs, goals, interests, etc. of A, $\Re_A$ and $\mathcal{B}_A$ are A's role set and behavior set, respectively.*

Let $\mathcal{B}_0 = \bigcup_{r \in \Re_A} S_r$. $\mathcal{B}_A$ is closed under composition $\circ$ in the meaning that $\mathcal{B}_0 \subset \mathcal{B}_A$, and if $f_1 \in \mathcal{B}_A, f_2 \in \mathcal{B}_A$ then $f_1 \circ f_2 \in \mathcal{B}_A$. i.e. $\mathcal{B}_A$ is composed of all the possible compositions of initial plans in S_r, where $r \in \Re_A$.

2.1. Dependency Relations

There exist different kinds of relations between different ingredients of our building methodology. For example, the task-subtask relations embodied in task hierarchy diagrams also specify a kind of dependency relations: the execution of a complex task is dependent on the executions of its sub-tasks, or in other word, there exists controls from a task to its sub-tasks to ensure the overall execution be carried out correctly.

The sequence of plan statements (sub-plan) predefined in a plan body is another kind of dependency relations. The result of a plan depends on its sub-plans, The paths and branches in a plan graph reflect the control flow during the execution of the plan.

In cooperative problem solving (CPS), the agent initiated a high-level task has control over the agents who have committed to some sub-tasks of the high-level task. Inside an agent, the behaviors of each role must depend on the current mental states of its controlling agent. Likewise, inside a role, the components which are responsible for the concurrence controlling or load balancing are also relied on by the other components.

Definition 6 *(Controlling dependencies) Given a set* **A** *of agent classes, let* $\mathcal{A} = \{a | \exists A \in \mathbf{A} \cdot instance of(a, A)\}$, $\mathbf{R} = \bigcup_{A \in \mathbf{A}} \Re_A$, $\mathbf{C} = \bigcup_{r \in \mathbf{R}} \Theta_r$, $\mathbf{T} = \bigcup_{\mathcal{G} \in H_r, r \in \mathbf{R}} node(\mathcal{G})$.

(i) $\xrightarrow{T} \subset \mathbf{T} \times \mathbf{T}$, *where* $(t_i, t_j) \in \xrightarrow{T}$ *iff* $t_i \angle^+ t_j$. t_j *is controlled directly by* t_i *when* $t_i \angle t_j$;

(ii) $\xrightarrow{A} \subset \mathcal{A} \times \mathbf{R}$, *where* $(a, r) \in \xrightarrow{A}$ *iff* $r \in \Re_a$;

(iii) $\xrightarrow{R} \subset \mathbf{R} \times \mathbf{C}$, *where* $(r, c) \in \xrightarrow{R}$ *iff* $c \in \Theta_r$;

(iv) $\xrightarrow{C} \subset \mathbf{C} \times \mathbf{C}$, *where* $(c_i, c_j) \in \xrightarrow{C}$ *iff* $\exists r \in \mathbf{R} \cdot c_i \in H_r \wedge c_j \in H_r \wedge c_i \in \pi_r$;

(v) $\xrightarrow{A^+} \subset \mathcal{A} \times \mathcal{A}$, *where* $(a_i, a_j) \in \xrightarrow{A^+} \Rightarrow \exists t \in \mathbf{T} \cdot (\exists r \in \Re_{a_j}, \exists \mathcal{G} \in H_r \cdot t \in root(\mathcal{G})) \wedge (\exists r \in \Re_{a_i}, \exists \mathcal{G} \in H_r \cdot t \in node(\mathcal{G}))$.

For example, in Fig.3, $Librarian \xrightarrow{A} r_1$, $r_1 \xrightarrow{R} c_1$, $c_1 \xrightarrow{C} c_4$, and $c_1 \xrightarrow{C} c_5$. In Fig.4(b), $returning \xrightarrow{T} receiving$.

In multi-agent society, an agent can entrust his tasks to the other credible agents, as well as helping voluntarily the other agents implement their tasks, depending on whether he is in spare or not at that very time. We call such relations binding two agents loosely together by credibility friendship dependency. Although different designers of multi-agent systems have definitely different viewpoint on the concrete structure of Ξ_A during implementation, we would like to introduce a specific component $Friend$ to Ξ_A. For $a \in \mathcal{A}$, $Friend_a = \{b \in \mathcal{A} | is friend(a, b)\}$.

Definition 7 *(Friendship dependency) Friendship dependency* $\xrightarrow{F} \subset \mathcal{A} \times \mathcal{A}$, $a \xrightarrow{F} b \Rightarrow b \in Friend_a$.

Symmetry and transitivity can also be added to friendship dependency. In (Wooldridge et al.,1998b) they happened to use acquaintance model to define the communication links between different agent types. While, here we use friendship dependency just to describe the possible cooperations between different instances of the same agent class or different classes. Such relation will be embedded into agent model without introduce another new model in design stage.

3. Towards a Building Methodology

3.1. Analysis Phase

The activities involved in analysis phase include the following (shown in Fig.2):

1. Goals identifying: Why this is emphasized is for three reasons. First, different goals may conduce to different solutions. A goal can make a problem domain scale down into a manageable one. It's nonsense trying to identify agents from an application domain without a deterministic goal or goals. Second, goals are more stable than behaviors in an application domain(Kinny et al.,1996). Goal-oriented analysis can conduce to much more robust system designs, if the goals of the concerned domain can be identified correctly. Third, Goal-oriented analysis distinguishes itself from traditional procedure-oriented methods in that users often have much clearer cognition about their (high level) abstract goals of the expected system, even though they don't quite clear the concrete functions the future system will include, which is a drawback for procedure-oriented methods.

2. Roles identifying: There are domain independent roles and domain specific ones. Domain independent roles, such as concurrent control, information maintenance, can be reused. However, the major task in this step is to identify domain specific roles, which needs simulate the business activities in different situations. Use case diagram of UML can be used here as a convenient tools to obtain correct roles from an application domain.

3. Agents identifying: Agents are carriers of roles, which are the actual executors of tasks. In this step, determine what kinds of agents should be covered in the system, what subordinate roles each agent should have, by considering geography, organization, resource sharing, etc..

4. Components identifying: Identify the possible components for each role. Generally, the leaf nodes of task hierarchy diagrams correspond to primitive components.

5. Interactions identifying: Identify the possible interactions between different components of a role, between different roles of an agent, between different agent classes, and between different instances of a certain agent class, specify them in the forms of controlling dependency, or friendship dependency.

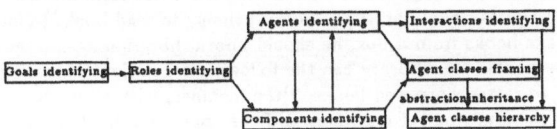

Fig.2. The analysis phase of ARC

6. Agent class framing: Obtain the framework for each agent class (as Fig.1), where the compositions of each role and the relations between components and roles are depicted.

7. Agent classes hierarchy: By means of generalization, association, and aggregation, organize the identified agent classes in a concise hierarchical way.

The above activities are not carried out in sequence, but conform to fountain development model, where analyzers can go backward and forward iteratively to add new information, and refine blurred cognitions.

3.2. Design Phase

In design phase, we should refine the abstract structures of components, roles, and agents identified in the analysis phase into more concrete ones, by using the same concepts as that in analysis phase. New modules may be embedded to make the constructions more robust and problem-oriented. The mental states, inter-agent (role, component) relations, kernel plans, and complex tasks should be designed and depicted in some appropriate forms (such as diagrams, patterns, etc.), even some implemention details can be involved, owing to the features of incremental development model. In detail, in design phase we should

1). For each component, specify each primitive procedure in some specification language, give the pre- and post- conditions, and the possible side-effects.

2). For each role, design and refine task hierarchy diagrams for each complex task; work out feasible plan graphs in detail for each non-trivial plan.

3). Design the mental hierarchy structure for each mental set of each agent class. Design appropriate lifting/lowering rules and scheduling algorithms(Fan,2000).

In this way, the component model, role model, and agent model can be constructed by a bottom-up design method.

Inter-agent relations should also be kept in mind in design phase in order to be embodied in implementations. There are four interaction models should be built in this stage. Three of them are used to specify inter-component, inter-role, and inter-agent class interactions, respectively. The other one is concerned about interactions between different agent instances of the same agent class. Inter-agent interaction model can be depicted by sequence-like diagrams borrowed from UML(Booch et al.,1998), with the extension that there may be more than one thread (each role has one) drawn away from an agent class (refer to Fig.4(c) as an example for inter-agent model). Inter-role and inter-component model can be expressed in the same way.

As for the relations between agent instances of the same agent class, such as friendship, it's most appropriate to record them in their individual belief sets. For example, in agent m's belief hierarchy structure, $frd(n)$ $(frds(n))$ can be used to express m has a (strong) friendship relation with n.

4. A Case Study—An Electronic Library

On the internet there is an electronic library, where its members can borrow books in hardcopy or electronic forms through the agent programs running on their computers. Each member has been allocated a box in the library to hold borrowed or returned books. A member can go directly to the box to take the books just borrowed by his agent, or leave books he want to return after negotiation between his agent and librarian agent (fine should be paid in the form of electronic checks in case of delay). Librarian agents signal librarians (person) timely to send books to members' boxes, and when a librarian take books from a box, he should inform librarian agents by means of scanning the bar code of the books. The library has the following regulations: 1)new books can't be lent to those who used to ratten borrowed books, 2)the members who return books in time are prior to those who used to return out of deadlines, 3)if the count of a book is less than 3, it can't be lent to those who used to lose books, 4) a member can't hold more than 3 books at the same time, 5)the members who pay their fine in time are prior to those who used to defer their payment. In addition, there is an odeum in the ground floor of the library, agents can also book tickets for their owners to a concert held in the odeum. We see how to analyze and design such an application by ARC method.

4.1. Analysis Phase

The goal of the problem domain is to facilitate the interaction process between library and members, and free people from the time-consuming task of searching for a certain book. To meet this goal, at least two kinds of roles should be identified: a role (r_a) which can borrow and return books for his host, a service provider (r') which, being a proxy of librarians, interacts with its clients r_a. If we take the other requirement (booking tickets) into account, a role (r_b) which is responsible for booking tickets is also needed. In addition, It's better to divide the work of r' in case that it would make r' overloaded. A possible devision is one role (r_1) takes charge of interacting with clients, and the other (r_2) runs at the background to signal librarians (persons) timely or receive feedbacks from librarians. So, we get four roles: r_a, r_b, r_1 and r_2. In this scenario, it's feasible to integrate the four roles into two agents, Client (r_a, r_b) and Librarian (r_1, r_2), even though one can only inherit r_1 or r_2 or both roles of Librarian during implementations.

Now we zoom in to analyze the constructs of roles of librarian agent. By means of use case diagrams in identifying components of r_1, the following cases exist: client agent may borrow, or return books; if there isn't some book needed by some member, librarian agent should order such book from a bookstore. So r_1 is composed of at least three components: returning, in the case that members want to return a book; lending, in the case that members intend to borrow a book; and buying, in the case that a new book is needed to order. In the same way, we identify two components for r_2: sending, signal a librarian to send books to a member's box; receiving: scan the bar code of returned books, or create new records for new books received from a bookstore.

As far as interactions inside Librarian are concerned, there exist work flows between the components of r_1 and those of r_2: after lending, sending will be stimulated to signal a librarian to do the action $(lending \overset{C}{\to} sending)$; after returning, receiving will be stimulated to signal a person to check corresponding boxes and wait for feedbacks $(returning \overset{C}{\to} receiving)$; after buying, receiving will be activated $(buying \overset{C}{\to} receiving)$ periodically to signal a person to check that until a feedback is arrived (in Fig.3).

The coarsely constructing of agent classes and class hierarchies is trivial and is omitted.

4.2. Design Phase

We consider the refinement of librarian agent. Generally, there maybe many Librarian agents working in a library, which form an agent society. In common sense, one book can not be lent to two members at the same time. Moreover, if a member has initiated two *Client* agents, who interact with two *Librarian* agents at the same time, respectively. The two *Librarian* agents should guarantee the member can't borrow more than 3 books. In such cases, we should add a new role into *Librarian* to coordinate (concurrent control) the behaviors of different *Librarian* agents in CPS.

Also, when a member returns a book, maybe he would like to renew it, maybe he should be fined in case of breaking the deadlines, losing or blurring a book. So two new components, *renewing* and *fining* should be added into r_1 of *Librarian*.

We take *Librarian* for example to show how to model the mental hierarchy structures of an agent. Let α be the set of members, β be the set of books, $hold(m,x), blur(m), late(m), defer(m)$ and $lost(m)$ means member m holds x books currently, m blurred a book, m returned books out of deadlines, m deferred his payment, and m lost a book, $new(b), null(b), out(b), lend(b,m), left(b,y)$ means b is a new book, there is no b in the library, all books titled b have been lent, b will be lent to m, and the left count of b is y. According to the scenario, in *Librarian*'s knowledge base we have: $\forall m \in \alpha \cdot hold(m,x) \rightarrow x \leq 3$, $\forall m \in \alpha, b \in \beta \cdot < blur(m), i > \wedge new(b) \wedge i \leq k_1 \rightarrow \neg lend(b,m)$, $\forall m \in \alpha \cdot < lost(m), i > \wedge i \leq k_2 \rightarrow \forall b \in \beta \cdot left(b,y) \wedge y \leq 3 \rightarrow \neg lend(b,m)$, where constants k_1, k_2 are water marks predefined in the system, and i in $< p, i >$ is the net applying times of lifting and lowering rules for p.

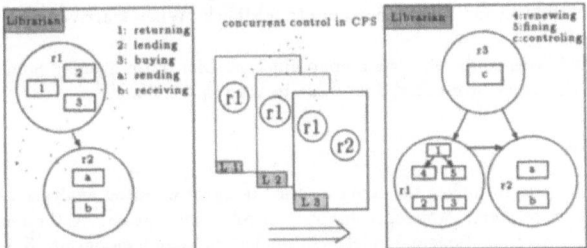

Fig.3. Refinment of Librarian during design phase

In *Librarian*'s belief set, there are predicates of $blur(m), lost(m), defer(m)$ and $late(m)$, which are hierarchized in the following ways: initially, all such predicates are indexed by the maximal element, say v, of some finite well-founded set W, i.e. $< blur(m)_v, k_1 >, < lost(m)_v, k_2 >, < defer(m)_v, 0 >$, and $< late(m)_v, 0 >$. When a member has lost (blurred) a book, deferred their payment, or been late to return, the corresponding predicates will be lowered. If, for example, a member has not lost (blurred) a book, defer their payment, or been late to return in the recent four times, then corresponding predicates will be lifted. Two predicates at the same level, say, $< blur(m)_v, x >$ and $< blur(m)_v, y >$, $< blur(m)_v, x >$ will be prior to $< blur(m)_v, y >$, provided $x > y$ (refer to (Fan,2000) for details about mental hierarchy theory).

As an example, one of the plan graphs of r_2, which corresponds to the *receiving* component, is shown in Fig.4(a). r_2 keeps sensing the triggering events from r_1, then it signals a person to bring books from appropriate boxes, depending on the triggering event was sent by *returning* or *buying*. After scanning the bar code of a book, it can judge whether it is a new book. If it is a returned book, some information about this book and the member who had just returned it will be modified. If it is a new book, a new record will be created and added into the database, and *buying* will be signaled about the completion of an ordering procedure.

One of the task hierarchical diagrams is shown in Fig.4(b), where the complex task "return a book out of deadline" was decomposed into two parts, which were dispatched to components *returning* and *fining*. *returning* has two sub-tasks: signal *receiving*, and apply lowering rules to the concerned member m ($late(m)$ will be re-indexed). *fining* also has two sub-tasks: interact with electronic bank agent, and apply lifting/lowering rules to the concerned member $(defer(m)$ will be re-indexed).

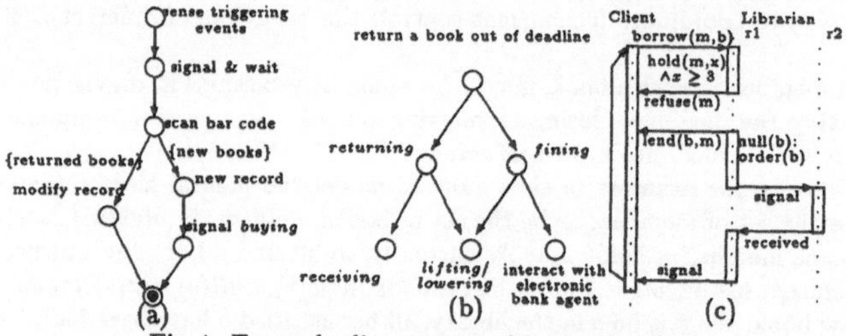

Fig.4. Example diagrams used in design phase

One of the interactions between *Librarian* and *Client* is shown in Fig.4(c), where "borrow a book" is illustrated by means of a sequence diagram. Initially, *Client* sends a message $borrow(m, b)$, m wants to borrow b, to *Librarian*. *Librarian* first checks whether m holds more than 3 books currently, if so, refuse m. Then it will check whether there are books titled b, if so, lend it to m. Otherwise, it will order b and signal *receiving* to feedback. When b arrived, it will signal m about the availability of b.

There may exist friendship relations among different *Librarian* agents. Some *Librarians* may help voluntarily the other overloaded *Librarian* in their spare time.

5. Conclusions

In this paper, we try to formalize the concepts used in agent-oriented analysis and design, identify different interaction relations between components, roles and agents. A three-level methodology, ARC, is evolved, where component model, role model and agent model are built from bottom to top, and appropriate diagrams (task hierarchy diagram, plan graph, extended sequence diagram, use case, etc.) are used to specify and document analysis and design results to make them more understandable.

Other methodologies proposed so far in the literature, e.g. (Brazier et al.,1995; Kinny et al.,1996; Wooldridge et al.,1998b), either didn't give formalization for the stages of analysis and design, or lacked appropriated mechanisms to support the documentation of analysis and design results.

Inheritance and reuse of agents have been studied only recently(Crnogorac et al.,1997; Fan et al.,1999). In our building methodology, there exist three levels of reuse. In component level, primitive procedures can be reused by different components. In role level, a component can be reused by many roles. There also exist sub-task sharing between complex tasks. In agent level, mental hierarchy structure (lifting/lowering rules) can be reused in other applications of the same problem domain, as well as some behaviors can be shared by different agent classes.

References

(Booch et al.,1998): G. Booch, J. Rumbaugh, and I. Jacobson. The unified modeling Language User Guide, Addison–Wesley, 1998.

(Brazier et al.,1995): F. Brazier, B. Dunin Keplicz, N. R. Jennings, and J. Treur. Formal specification of multi-agent systems: a real-world case. In Proceedings of the First International Conference on Multi-Agent Systems (ICMAS95), pages 25–32, San Francisco, CA, June 1995.

(Crnogorac et al.,1997): L. Crnogorac, A. S. Rao and K. Ramamohanarao. Analysis of Inheritance mechanism in agent-oriented programming. In Proc. of IJCAI-97, pages 647-652, Japan, 1997.

(d'Inverno et al.,1997): M. d'Inverno, D. Kinny, M. Luck, and M. Wooldridge. A formal specification of dMARS. In M. P. Singh, A. Rao, and M. J. Wooldridge, eds, Intelligent Agents IV (LNAI Volume 1365), pages 155–176. Springer-Verlag: Berlin, Germany, 1997.

(Fan et al.,1999): X. Fan, D. Xu, and G. Zheng. Reasoning about Inheritance and Cloning Behaviors of Software Agents. In C. Jian, L. Jian, and M. Bertrand, eds: Proceedings of Technology of Object–oriented Languages and Systems (TOOLS 31), pages 77–82, Nanjing, China, September 1999.

(Fan,2000): X. Fan. Towards a Building Methodology for Software Agents. TUCS Technical Report, Turku Centre for Computer Science, No 351, June 2000.

(Ferber et al.,1998): J. Ferber and O. Gutknecht. A meta-model for the analysis and design of organizations in multi-agent systems. In Proceedings of the Third International Conference on Multi-Agent Systems (ICMAS- 98), pages 128–135, Paris, France, 1998.

(Iglesias et al.,1999): C. A. Iglesias, M. Garijo, and J. C. Gonzalez. A survey of agent- oriented methodologies. In J. P. Müller, M. P. Singh, and A. S. Rao, eds, Intelligent Agents V-Proceedings of the Fifth International Workshop on Agent Theories, Architectures, and Languages (ATAL 98), Lecture Notes in Artificial Intelligence. Springer-Verlag, Heidelberg, 1999.

(Kinny et al.,1996): D. Kinny, M. Georgeff, and A. Rao. A methodology and modelling technique for systems of BDI agents. In W. Van de Velde and J. W. Perram, eds, Agents Breaking Away: Proceedings of the Seventh European Workshop on Modelling Autonomous Agents in a Multi- Agent World, (LNAI Volume 1038), pages 56–71. Springer-Verlag: Berlin, Germany, 1996.

(Wooldridge,1997): M. Wooldridge. Agent-based software engineering. IEE Proceedings on Software Engineering, 144(1):26–37, February 1997.

(Wooldridge et al.,1998a): M. Wooldridge and N. R. Jennings. Pitfalls of agent-oriented development. In Proceedings of the Second International Conference on Autonomous Agents (Agents 98), pages 385–391, Minneapolis/St Paul, MN, May 1998.

(Wooldridge et al.,1998b): M. Wooldridge, N. R. Jennings, and D. Kinny. A Methodology for Agent–Oriented Analysis and Design. In O. Etzioni, J. P. Muller, and J. Bradshaw, eds: Agents '99: Proceedings of the Third International Conference on Autonomous Agents, Seattle, WA, May 1998.

(Wooldridge,1998): M. Wooldridge. Agent-based computing. In Interoperable Communication Networks. 1(1), pages 71-97. January 1998.

Design Units - A Framework for Design Driven Software Development

Jaehyoun Kim and C. Robert Carlson

Department of Computer Science
Illinois Institute of Technology
201 East Loop Road, Wheaton, Illinois 60187, USA
Email: *kimjaeh@charlie.cns.iit.edu* | *carlson@iit.edu*

ABSTRACT. *As· software systems get more complicated, the task of the system developer becomes increasingly difficult and time consuming. The focus of this paper is on the development of a well-designed framework that supports code generation in the context of a use case design methodology. Its foundation is the use case based approach that partitions the design schemata into a layered architecture of functional components called design units. Our approach provides the basis for the generation of modular, well-structured code and a means of keeping a high-level design and its implementation consistent. Such properties as traceability, reusability, modularity and change management are achieved by applying design unit concepts to the design and code generation process.*

KEY WORDS: *object-oriented, use case methodology, design unit, traceability, code generation.*

1. Introduction

In the past few years, various software development methodologies (Booch, 1991; Coleman et al., 1994; Jacobson et al., 1992; Rumbaugh, 1991; Shlaer, 1992) have been introduced that could lead to the development of application source code from graphical models of application behavior. However, most methodologies do not sufficiently describe how to generate code from high-level design artifacts such as interaction diagrams and event state diagrams. Some methods (Booch, 1991; OMG, 1999; Rumbaugh, 1991; Shlaer, 1992) support structural code generation that is based on models of object structure (static relationship). UML (OMG, 1999) and Fusion method (Coleman et al., 1994) support behavioral code generation that verify system behavior based on the state models before code is generated and then implemented in a target language. However, they offer weak behavioral code generation capabilities.

Even if the code generation tool generates code automatically or the programmer writes code manually, subsequent changes will be made to the generated code without corresponding changes being made to the design models. Eventually, the analysis and design models will be seen as irrelevant and will be thrown away. As a result, an important issue in software development is how to maintain consistency between the graphical design models and the code generated to support the design. Thus, the key is to develop a modular, integrated approach with traceability property.

Currently, use case driven approach has become popular as an effective software development technique used in leading methodologies such as UML because of its capacity for capturing functional requirements. UML provides a visual modeling language that utilizes three famous methods – the Booch Method (Booch, 1991), the Object-Modeling Technique (OMT) (Rumbaugh, 1991) and the Object-Oriented Software Engineering (OOSE) (Jacobson et al., 1992). However, it does not sufficiently describe the stepwise systematic development process. It will be effective if it is used with a well-designed software development process. Carlson (Carlson, 1999) and Hurlbut (Hurlbut, 1998) introduced an adaptive use case methodology for software development that creates an algorithmic coupling between the design processes. An important aspect of this methodology is the deployment of design techniques that lead to semi-automatic processes for code generation and test plan generation.

This paper focuses on the framework for object-oriented design with the development of a code generation technique that achieves several quality control properties supported by the use case methodology. Thus, we provide an integrated traceable approach from the high-level design model through to code generation. Our code generation process starts from interaction diagrams because we want to get control over the quality of code and establish a manageable relationship between design and code. This code generation technique preserves such properties as traceability and modularization from the high-level design model to the source code, i.e., the partition of design artifacts (interaction diagrams and event-state tables) based on design units is uniquely identified by the code segments/components. It also provides a means of keeping a high-level design and its implementation consistent. When a change is needed, the change is made in the high-level design rather than in the source code. The code is then simply regenerated from the high-level design.

This paper is organized as follows. In section 2, we describe the design of an automated teller machine application using an interaction diagram and event-state table. In section 3, design units are identified and later used to generate code. In section 4, design unit tracking process from the use case model to the event-state table is described. And a code generation technique based on the design unit is introduced in section 5.

2. Use Case High-Level Design

In the use case based approaches to software development, analyzing the use case model produces interaction diagrams and event-state tables/diagrams. In this section, we describe an interaction diagram and an event-state table using a *Withdraw Money* use case drawn from an automated teller machine application.

2.1 Interaction Diagram

Interaction diagrams correspond to the high-level use case scenarios identified during requirements analysis. An interaction diagram shows the sequence of messages passed among the participating objects in a use case. The functionality of the use case is captured in its flow of events. Objects belong to one of three different object types - interface, control, and service object as mentioned (Jacobson et al., 1992). Existing interaction diagrams – called sequence diagrams in Unified Modeling Language (OMG, 1999), event trace diagrams in Object Modeling Technique (Rumbaugh, 1991) – capture only limited information such as sequential object interaction with a single use case scenario. Thus, we use an extended interaction diagram (Byun, 1999) that supports multiple use case scenarios in one interaction diagram and different types of external event.

The interaction diagram shown in Figure 1 represents multiple use case scenarios in one interaction diagram and different types of external event. The interaction between the system and a customer combines four separate dialogues, *Insert Card, Enter Pin Number, Enter Amount and Receipt*. Each external event starts a particular dialogue with the system that, in some cases, is repeated. After receiving a response from the system, the actor decides whether that dialogue with the system is to be repeated or different dialogue with the system is to be initiated. The label at the left side of the interaction diagram indicates that a dialogue may be repeated. For example, the label A means that the customer can be subsequent initiate an *Enter Pin Number* external event (associated with label A) again.

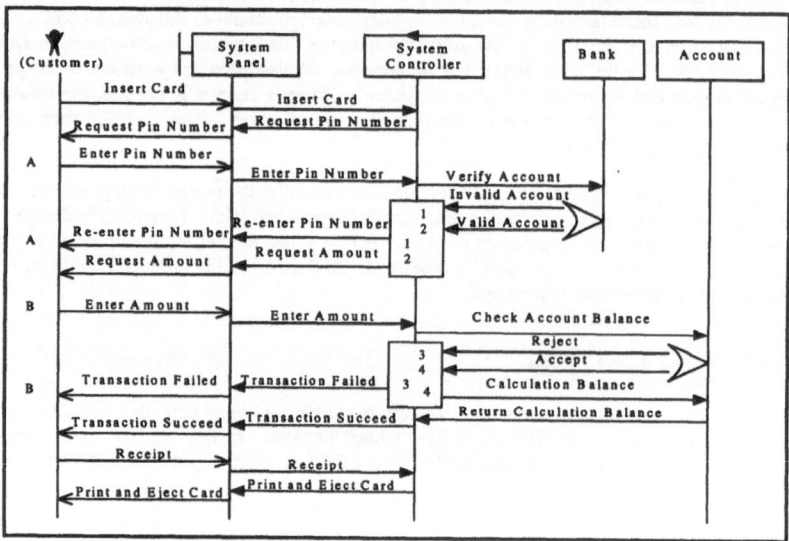

Figure 1. *Withdraw Money* Use Case Interaction Diagram

An analysis of the *Enter Amount* scenario yields two different use case scenarios, *Transaction Failed* and *Transaction Succeed*. In the *Transaction Failed* scenario, when a customer enters the amount, it is verified by the system. If the balance is smaller than the amount requested, the *Transaction Failed* scenario follows. Otherwise, the *Transaction Succeed* scenario follows. In order to describe multiple use case scenarios we use the graphical notation where numbers are used to relate distinctive in-message to their corresponding out-message. For example, the *System* Controller sends the *Transaction Failed* to the actor when receiving a *Reject* message while the *System* Controller sends the *calculation Balance* to the *Account* object when receiving an *Accept* message. The interaction diagram for the use case *Withdraw Money* is shown in Figure 1.

2.2 Event-State Table

Most object-oriented methodologies (Jacobson et al., 1992; OMG, 1999; Rumbaugh, 1991; Shlaer et al., 1992) use a state-based formalism to describe system behavior. This formalism helps developers analyze and understand system behavior through graphical notation and makes it possible to generate code that implements the structure, communication, and behavior of the object model. Thus, at this stage we describe the behavior of a system using an event-state table that is automatically generated from the interaction diagram (Byun, 1999).

The event-state table describes all the possible states that an object can get into and how it transits from one state to another. When an object receives an event, an object may change state and send out an action that is received as an event by another object or by an external actor. Our event-state table uses the Moore form of state machine (Shlaer, 1992), which means activity is associated with each state and not each transition. In the event-state table, each row represents one of the possible states, and each column represents an event. The cell is filled in with the name of the next state of the object. The event-state table is used to generate a CASE statement that abstracts, or factors out commonality during the code generation stage.

In our use case approach, the event-state table is produced automatically from the interaction diagram (Byun, 1999). In this paper, we build an event-state table only for the control object *System Controller* because it controls the event flow in a use case and describes system behavior. An event-state table for the *System Controller* control object based on the interaction diagram for the use case *Withdraw Money* is shown in Figure 2.

S \ E	E1	E2	E3	E4	E5	E6	E7	E8	E9
0	1								
1		2							
2			3	4					
3		2							
4					5				
5						6	7		
6					5				
7								8	
8									0

E1: Insert Card
E2: Enter Pin Number
E3: Invalid Account
E4: Valid Account
E5: Enter Amount
E6: Reject
E7: Accept
E8: Return Current Balance
E9: Receipt

Figure 2. Event-State Table for a System Controller

3. Design Unit

In this section, we define the design unit concept, which provides the key to maintainability, traceability, and modularization. The interaction diagram and event-state table can be partitioned into a sequence of design units. Several partitioning strategies are possible, each providing different properties at the boundary points between adjacent design units which can be exploited by our test generation strategies (Carlson, 1999). Subsequent discussion will be focus on the method, state, maximal linear, dialogue and use case units. These design units provide the designer and test engineer with different options to choose from at design time. Each design unit is described as follows:

Method Unit: Method executed by an object in response to a message.

The simplest choice is to let each method be a design unit. . Figure 2 has twenty-eight method units, as listed in the left column of Table 1. Each method represents a distinctive method unit in the interaction diagram such as *Insert Card, Request Pin Number, Enter Pin Number, Verify Account, Invalid Account, Re-enter Pin* Number, *Valid Account, Request Amount, Enter Amount, Accept,* etc. Method units provide a good choice during unit testing.

State Unit: Sequence of methods executed bounded by consecutive states.

State units are algorithmically identified (Byun, 1999) based on the message received by a control object and the messages sent from the control objects. We can identify each state for a particular object, that is, the control objects. A state unit can be characterized by a state pair [Si, Sj], where Si is a current state and Sj is a subsequent state. Each state pair can be enhanced at design time by predicate conditions associated with each of these states. Such information is useful when state based testing techniques are applied later. A state unit consists of multiple method units. In the interaction diagram shown in Figure 2, eleven state units have been algorithmically identified. For example, when receiving the event *Insert Card* in state S0, the state of control object is changed to state S1 and the action *Request Pin Number* is initiated.

Maximal Linear Unit: Sequence of methods executed during interval bounded by consecutive choices, either actor or object choices.

A maximal linear unit consists of one or more state units. A maximal linear unit is the same as a dialogue unit if no choice/branch nodes exist. In the interaction diagram shown in Figure 2, a choice node for the control object occurs when it receives either the *Invalid Account* or *Valid Account* message from the *Bank* object and either *Reject* or *Accept* message from the *Account* object. Thus, the maximal linear units for the *Withdraw Money* use case are [*Insert Card, Request Pin Number*], [*Enter Pin Number, Verify Account*], [*Invalid Account, Re-enter Pin Number*], [*Valid Account, Request Amount*], [*Enter Amount, Check Account Balance*], [*Reject, Transaction Failed*], [*Accept, Calculate Balance, Return Current Balance, Transaction Succeed*], and [*Receipt, Print and Eject Card*]. Maximal linear units have significance for referencing straight line testing techniques.

Dialogue Unit: Sequence of methods bounded by input from an actor and the response to that actor.

A dialogue unit consists of one or more maximal linear units. In the interaction diagram shown in Figure 2, we can identify all possible paths from the actor and the response to the actor. The dialogue units include [*Insert Card, Request Pin Number*], [*Enter Pin Number, Verify Account, Invalid Account, Re-enter Pin Number*], [*Enter Pin Number, Verify Account, Valid Account, Request Amount*], [*Enter Amount, Check Account Balance, Reject, Transaction Failed*], [*Enter Amount, Check Account Balance, Accept, Calculate Balance, Return Current Balance, Transaction Succeed*], and [*Receipt, Print and Eject Card*]. Dialogue units are useful for establishing user acceptance test specification.

Use Case Unit: Sequence of method executions defined by a use case scenario.

Each use case unit corresponds to the interaction diagram. In Figure 1, we can identify all possible paths from Dialogue 1 to Dialogue 4.

Table 1. Enumeration of Design Units

Method Unit	State Unit	MLU	Dialogue Unit		
Insert Card [2]	S0, S1	MLU1	DU1		
Request Pin Number [2]					
Enter Pin Number [2]	S1/S3, S2	MLU2	DU2	DU2.1	DU2.2
Verify Account					
Invalid Account	S2, S3	MLU3			
Re-enter Pin Number [2]					
Valid Account	S2, S4	MLU4			DU2.2
Request Amount [2]					
Enter Amount [2]	S4/S6, S5	MLU5	DU3	DU3.1	DU3.2
Check Account Balance					
Reject	S5, S6	MLU6			
Transaction Failed [2]					
Accept	S5, S7	MLU7			DU3.2
Calculate Balance					
Return Current Balance	S7, S8				
Transaction Succeed [2]					
Receipt [2]	S8, S0	MLU8	DU4		
Print and Eject Card [2]					

Table 1 summaries the different design units that can be obtained from the interaction diagram and the event-state table for the *Withdraw Money* use case. Each column represents one of the above design units. Each event in the interaction diagram is represented by a method unit. Each cell in the event-state table (Figure 2) defines one boundary point of a state unit. For example, when an object receives an event *Enter Amount* at state 4, current state 4 is changed to state 5 as shown in Figure 2. Thus, the method sequence (*Enter Amount* and *Check Account Balance*) bound by states 4 and 5 define a state unit. Dialogue units DU1, DU2, DU3, and DU4 shown in Table 1 represent a basic interaction between an actor and the system. Dialogue units can be further decomposed. For example, DU2 consists of two subdialogues DU2.1 and DU2.2.

4. Design Unit Tracking Process

In this section, we determine the architectural layers of each use case based on the design unit concept. Each use case consists of four layers which are method unit layer, state unit layer, maximal linear unit layer, and dialogue unit layer (Figure 3). It is up to the designer and test engineer to use the architectural framework for integrating design, implementation and testing techniques.

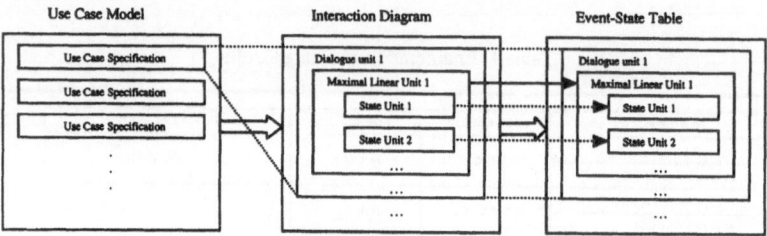

Figure 3. Design Unit Tracking Process

4.1 Partitioning Use Case Model

The tracking process begins with the assumption that a requirements specification has been developed based, in part, on the use case model. Further, the use case model is partitioned into specific use case scenarios.

4.2 Partitioning Interaction Diagram

For each use case specification, the designer develops an interaction diagram. Each interaction diagram consists of multiple dialogues between actor and the system. Thus, it is partitioned into multiple dialogue units based on external events. Each interaction diagram based dialogue unit is produced from the use case specification based dialogue unit. These dialogue units are further decomposed into low layered design units such as maximal linear units and state units.

4.3 Two-Level Event-State Table Architecture

For each interaction diagram, an event-state table is automatically produced. In the event state model, state transitions depend on the current state and either an internal or external event. An external event triggers internal system behavior. Thus, we develop a two-level architectural approach in which a high-level event-state table provides an abstraction of detailed event state behavior defined by low-level units. This approach provides a behavioral approach to code infrastructure specification where ultimately the method units act as stubs in this infrastructure framework. A high-level event-state table shows the integration of dialogue units, each represented by a low-level event-state table (see Figure 4). Each low-level event-state table shows the internal state changes of the system initiated by an external event in a dialogue unit.

Let's consider an event-state table for the use case *Withdraw Money* shown in Figure 2. An event-state table describes the behavior of the use case unit. This use case unit consists of four dialogue units. Thus, the event-state table is partitioned into four event-state tables based on these dialogue units as shown in Figure 4. Each table is named DU1, DU2, DU3, and DU4. DU1 is followed by DU2 and DU2 is followed by DU3. Also, DU3 is followed by DU4. The final state of each dialogue unit determines another dialogue unit in the event-state table. Therefore, the initial state of each dialogue unit must be equal to the final state of previous dialogue unit. For example, the final state 1 in DU1 determines the initial state 1 in DU2. We call this dependency a state dependency. The state dependencies between dialogue units are defined as follows:

(1) DU1.State 1 -> DU2.State 1
(2) DU2.State 4 -> DU3.State 4
(3) DU3.State 8 -> DU4.State 8

DU1

S\E	E1
0	1
1	

DU2

S\E	E2	E3	E4
1	2		
2		3	4
3	2		
4			

DU3

S\E	E5	E6	E7	E8
4	5			
5		6	7	
6	5			
7				8
8				

DU4

S\E	E9
8	0
0	

Figure 4. Low-Level Event-State Table based on Dialogue Unit

In general, each low-level event-state table shown in Figure 4 can have any one of the input and output characteristics – namely SISO (Single-In-Single-Out), SIMO (Single-In-Multiple-Out), MISO (Multiple-In-Single-Out), and MIMO (Multiple-In-Multiple-Out). DU1 and DU4 are SISO while DU2 and DU3 are SIMO. For example, the system responds with either *Re-enter Pin Number* or *Request Amount* to the actor when it receives an *Enter Pin Number* (see Figure 1).

Figure 5 shows a high-level event-state table that is the integration of the dialogue units defined by the low-level event-state tables. The high-level event-state table deals with external events that we map to the high-level CASE structure in the code skeleton. Each cell represents the dialogue unit defined by a low-level event-state table. For example, when an external event

E2 occurs during state 1 or state 3, it initiates dialogue DU2 defined by the low-level event-state table. Thus, each cell represents the abstraction of a dialogue unit in the low-level event-state table. The number 3 and 4 in this case (i.e., DU2/(3, 4)) represents the end states defined by the low-level event-state table. The end state 3 of DU2 waits for an external event E2 that initiates dialogue DU2 again while the end state 4 of DU2 waits for an external event E5 that initiates next dialogue unit DU3. This high-level event-state table may be used for integration testing.

S\E	E1	E2	E5	E9
0	DU1 / 1			
1		DU2 / (3, 4)		
3		DU2 / (3, 4)	DU3 / (6, 8)	
4			DU3 / (6, 8)	
8				DU4 / 0

Legend:

E1: Insert Card
E2: Enter Pin Number
E5: Enter Amount
E9: Receipt

Figure 5. High-Level Event-State Table

5. Code Generation

In the previous section, we described the design units found in the interaction diagrams and event-state tables. The artifacts created during the design phase – interaction diagrams and event-state tables – will be used as input to the code generation process. Our code generation technique suggests a way to produce design unit based skeletal code from interaction diagrams and event-state tables. Each component of a design unit in the interaction diagram and the event-state table is translated into a corresponding code segment in our code skeleton.

We standardize the code skeleton format for code generation based on the interaction diagram and the event-state table from the design stage. Our code skeleton is represented through a collection of event-condition-action statements. The format used in our code skeleton is a "CASE statement" based on external events. Externally, an event-state table is implemented as a collection of external events and their current states because each external event determines the behavior of the system. Thus, each CASE statement corresponds to a dialogue unit based on a single external event. When a control object receives an external event from the actor, a state of the control object is changed. Then the control object carries out all actions in that state until another message arrives. When the control object sends a message to the actor, it waits for a response from the actor. We call this a wait-state. The code segment for wait-state is represented as *wait (state)*. This code framework provides a direct translation of the event-state table into a code skeleton. Each transition's action can be obtained from the interaction diagram. The skeletal code of the control object *System Controller* in the use case *Withdraw Money* is shown in Figure 6.

Let's consider the event-state tables in Figure 4 and 5 for the use case *Withdraw Money*. Figure 5 defines the six external event/state combinations that initiate the four dialogue units described in Figure 4. Note that the CASE code in Figure 6 is organized into four "cases" representing the six "conditions" under which the four dialogue units are externally triggered. The code segments associated with each CASE condition represent the "internal" action/behavior defined in the low-level event-state tables shown in Figure 4. The modularity of the code is further illustrated by the hierarchical bracketing, shown at the right side of Figure 6, based on the four identified dialogue units. This approach can be subsequently applied at lower levels of the design. Further, our code skeletons can be easily mapped to specific languages such as Java and C++, as has been demonstrated in (Kim, 2000). For example, each message received by an object corresponds to the member function of classes.

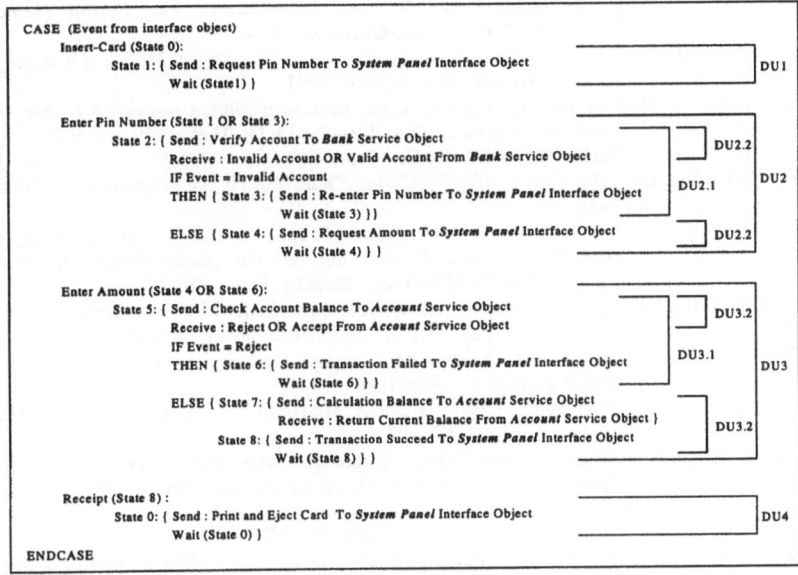

Figure 6. Code Skeleton

6. Conclusion

This paper describes how the properties of modularity, standardization, reusability and traceability can be established throughout all phases of the software development process. A hierarchy of design unit concepts is applied to achieve these properties, as illustrated in this paper. This approach has the additional benefit that the team of designers and developers employ a consistent approach to software development. This improves team communication and productivity and enhances the prospects for effective change management.

64

References:

(Booch, 1991): G. Booch. *Object-Oriented Design with Applications*. Benjamin/Cummings, Redwood City, CA, 1991.

(Byun, 1999): K. Byun. *A Use Case Approach to Algorithmic Event-State Table Generation*. Ph.D. Thesis Dissertation, Illinois Institute of Technology, Chicago, IL 1999.

(Carlson, 1999): C. R. Carlson. *Object Oriented Modeling and Design*. Lecture Notes, Illinois Institute of Technology, Chicago, IL. 1999.

(Coleman et al., 1994): D. Coleman, P. Arnold, S. Bodoff, C. Dollin, H. Gilchrist, F. Hayes and P. Jeremaes. *Object-Oriented Development: The Fusion Method*. Prentice Hall, Englewood Cliffs, NJ, 1994.

(Fowler, 1997): M. Fowler. *UML Distilled: Applying the Standard Object Modeling Language*. Addison-Wesley, Reading, MA, 1997.

(Hurlbut, 1998): R. Hurlbut. *Managing Domain Architecture Evolution through Adaptive Use Case and Business Rule Models*. Ph.D. Thesis, Illinois Institute of Technology, Chicago, IL. 1998.

(Jaaksi, 1998): A. Jaaksi. *Our Cases with Use Cases*. JOOP, Vol.10, No.9, pp. 58-65, February 1998.

(Jacobson et al., 1992): Ivar Jacobson, M. Christerson, P. Jonsson, and G. Övergaard. *Object-Oriented Software Engineering: A Use Case Driven Approach*. Addison-Wesley/ACM Press, Reading, MA, 1992.

(Kim, 2000): J. Kim, *A Layered Approach to Automatic Code Generation and Testing based on Design Units*, Ph.D. Thesis, Illinois Institute of Technology, 2000.

(OMG, 1999): Object Management Group, *OMG Unified Modeling Language Specification (draft)* Version 1.3, June 1999.

(Rumbaugh, 1991): J. Rumbaugh. *Object-Oriented Modeling and Design*. Prentice Hall, Englewood Cliffs, NJ, 1991.

(Rumbaugh, 1996): J. Rumbaugh. *Layered Additive Models: Design as a Process of Recording Decisions*. JOOP, Vol.9, No.1, pp. 21-24, March/April, 1996.

(Shlaer et al., 1992): S. Shlaer and S. J. Mellor. *Object Lifecycles: Modeling the World in States*. Prentice Hall, Englewood Cliffs, NJ, 1992.

(Wolber, 1997): D. Wolber. *Reviving Functional Decomposition in Object-Oriented Design*. JOOP, Vol.10, No. 6, pp. 31-38, October 1997.

Perspectives and Complex Aggregates*

Lars Kirkegaard Bækdal   Bent Bruun Kristensen

The Maersk Mc-Kinney Moller Institute for Production Technology
University of Southern Denmark/Odense University, DK 5230 Odense M, Denmark
e-mail: {lkb, bbkristensen}@mip.sdu.dk

ABSTRACT. *When we model a phenomenon we apply a perspective on the phenomenon. The perspective decides which properties we include in the model. It also decides how we conceive a phenomenon in terms of its constituent parts. Several perspectives on the same phenomenon create several distinct, but overlapping models. The models of the phenomenon use potentially shared parts. Their combination is a complex aggregate. The objective of this article is to investigate a conceptual model behind several perspectives and the resulting complex aggregate, and to illustrate various techniques for representing perspectives and complex aggregates as usual object models. We present a number of extensions to common modeling techniques at the conceptual level, and we discuss shortcomings and weaknesses of implementation techniques based on the object model.*
KEYWORDS: *Conceptual Modeling, Aggregation, Perspective, Shared Parts, Object Model*

1   Introduction

We distinguish between a referent system and a model system. The referent system is the domain that we observe. It can either be a real or an imaginary system. A model system expresses our comprehension of a referent system. Phenomena, which we observe, belong to a referent system. Concepts, which we form by abstraction processes, also belong to a referent system.

A number of more or less well-defined notions regarding abstraction are available for formation of concepts in the referent system. These include classification, generalization and aggregation among others. Also the notion of perspective is available for the concept formation process in the referent system. An objective of this article is to develop the notion of perspective from a loose and informal notion to a well-defined, though still informal, notion. We define the meaning of perspectives on phenomena. A concept covering a phenomenon directly reflects

---

*This research was supported in part by the Danish Academy of Technical Sciences, EF627.

perspectives on the phenomenon as a specific collection of properties extending the concept. Different perspectives cause different conceptions of aggregates. By observation of a phenomenon in a referent system, a perspective may lead to a particular conception of parts constituting the phenomenon. This collection of aggregated parts can be partially unique for the perspective, and partially shared between perspectives. The notion *complex aggregate* refer to the combination of different aggregates making up *a* phenomenon due to several perspectives. Figure 1(a) illustrates two developers, each with their own understanding and model of the same phenomenon at the conceptual level.

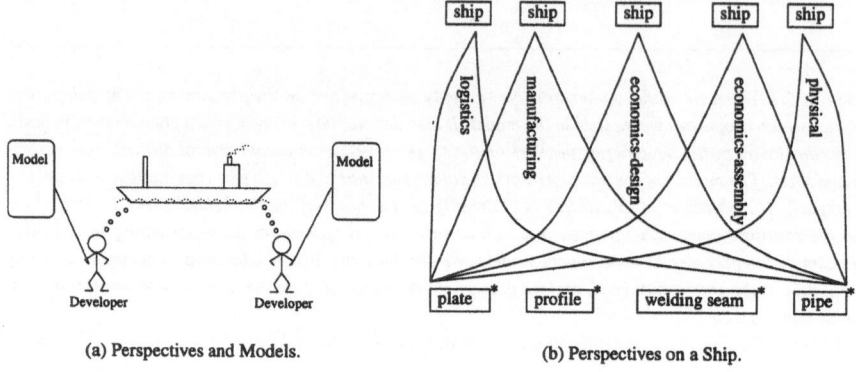

(a) Perspectives and Models. (b) Perspectives on a Ship.

Figure 1: Perspectives

A model system models the referent system. It is the universe supported by our available language or notation — be it formal or partially informal, for example object-oriented programming languages and UML. Systems described by such notations form model systems. A model system explicitly represents phenomena and concepts conceived in the referent system.

Objects and classes are fundamental mechanisms in a model system. Other mechanisms such as references, subclassing, etc. are used to model the notions from the referent system. In general, a transformation is necessary from a referent system to a model system. Common languages and notations do not provide mechanisms for explicit representation of perspectives and complex aggregates. Thus, the result of a transformation must simulate these. Understandable and efficient representations of such notions in the common object paradigm are important to ease the task of design and implementation.

The Shipyard Example. For exemplification we look at an integrated software system for a shipyard [Bækdal 97] as it contains a variety of principal problems, among others various perspectives on ships.

Building large ships, e.g. super tankers and container carriers, involves design, manufacturing, economics, logistics, etc. Each of these tasks regards the ship from a particular point of view — a perspective. For each perspective we focus on structure and properties relevant to it. Figure 1(b) illustrates some of the perspectives and related structures which we find in a shipyard application.

Paper Organization. In section 2 we discuss the problem of perspectives and complex aggregates at the conceptual level. The notions phenomenon, concept and perspective are described. We present the notion of complex aggregates as well as indications of the complications at the implementation level. Also the dynamics of complex aggregates is briefly discussed. In section 3 we discuss the implementation of notions from the conceptual level in terms of objects. For the support of shared parts we discuss the use of shared aggregation, association as well as design patterns, and an advanced language mechanism, the role mechanism. We also describe problems and solutions to shared properties in terms of methods and attributes. In section 4 we briefly discuss related work, and in section 5 we briefly summarize our approach to modeling of perspectives and complex aggregates.

2 Conceptual Model

This section presents a conceptual understanding of perspectives and aggregates. First, we describe a foundation based on our comprehension of phenomena/concepts and perspectives. Then a discussion of complex aggregates based on the described foundation follows.

2.1 Foundation

The foundation presented is based on understandings presented in [Abiteboul et al. 1991], [Bækdal 1999], [Carré et al. 1990], [Carré et al. 1988], [Bardou et al. 1996], [Harrison et al. 1993], [Henderson-Sellers 1997], [Kiczales et al. 1997], [Kristensen 1995], [Kristensen et al. 1996], [Reenskaug et al. 1992].

Phenomena & Concepts. Concepts describe phenomena. We can think of a phenomenon as an instance of a concept. *Identity* follows from the phenomenon. The meaning or substance of a phenomenon follows from the concept as it sees the phenomenon in a perspective [Madsen et al. 1993]. We assume that *properties* can describe any phenomenon/concept by enumeration and description of relevant properties. Properties are essential for the relations between concepts. The notions of generalization and aggregation are defined in terms of relations between properties of concepts [Kristensen et al. 1994].

Identity means that a phenomenon can be distinguished from all other phenomena — identity implies uniqueness. Thus, two distinct phenomena can never have the same identity [Reenskaug et al. 1992]. Identity is an inherent characteristic of all phenomena. The very existence of a phenomenon implies an identity. It exists and it remains preserved throughout a phenomenon's lifetime, independently of perspective and properties of the phenomenon.

At an object-oriented implementation level the notion of identity is well-known. For instance object-oriented databases operates with object IDs. Brokers supporting distribution have naming services. Object-oriented languages, however, are more focused on references and the support for identity is less direct.

A *property* describes a certain aspect or characteristic of a phenomenon. Thus, a phenomenon usually consists of a collection of properties, each realizing a particular aspect. A phenomenon without properties only has identity. We express properties in terms of state and behavior. They may be elementary as well as composite. That is, properties, state and behavior are all potential building blocks with respect to description of a property.

A property is only relevant as belonging to a phenomenon/concept. It cannot exist on its own, though it is possible to talk about properties in general. Thus a property has no independent identity which also applies to the state and behavior realizing it. A phenomenon must qualify access to properties. Properties do not provide encapsulation, but rather organization/clustering in terms of coupling between state, behavior and perspectives. The contents of a property become part of the containing phenomenon. Encapsulation/visibility of these, or the property in general, is relatively to the containing phenomenon.

Properties may be independent or (partly) shared. Independent properties have nothing in common. Use of such properties is without problems. Contradicting modifications cannot occur since independent properties are only visible in the perspective they belong to. Shared properties may imply that the complete property, that is, all state and behavior defining it, appear in two or more perspectives. It may also imply that some perspectives just share a part of a property, typically a fraction of its state [Bardou et al. 1996].

At the implementation level we find mixin classes (e.g. [Booch 1994]), multiple inheritance (e.g. [Stroustrup 1991]) and roles (e.g. [Kristensen et al. 1996]) which support the definition of relations between properties as described above and thus may support implementation. The major difference originates from the missing coupling to perspectives. Moreover, mixin classes and multiple inheritance are static[1]. Object-oriented languages in general provide means for expressing the contents of a property using methods and attributes of various kinds, but not the clustering. We can only refer to methods and attributes by use of an object reference as qualifier.

Perspectives. This paragraph discuss the nature of perspectives and the strong coupling of properties to perspectives.

As analysts we always engage perspectives, though often unconsciously as the context decides them. More constructively, we may apply perspectives to simplify inherent complexity of a domain since perspectives let us consider one aspect at a time, assuming that we can synthesize our observations later on.

We characterize a perspective as an external view imposed on a phenomenon. A perspective may be elementary or composite depending on whether or not it can be subdivided. Conversely, we may form larger (broader) perspectives by composition of more specific part perspectives where the properties of a part perspective form a subset of the properties of the composite perspective.

Application of a particular perspective to a phenomenon causes a specific collection of properties, possibly just one, at the concept to match (implement) the perspective. We say that

---

[1]It is commonly impossible to change class of objects dynamically (at runtime).

properties are a phenomenon's response to imposed perspectives. A strong coupling between perspectives and properties exists — a specific set of properties realize a perspective.

Furthermore, perspectives qualify access to properties (state or behavior) of phenomena, either explicitly or implicitly. Without specification of phenomenon and perspective, we exclude access to a property, its state or behavior, because of the strong coupling between property and perspective.

Figure 2 illustrates the a phenomenon, perspectives on these, and properties.

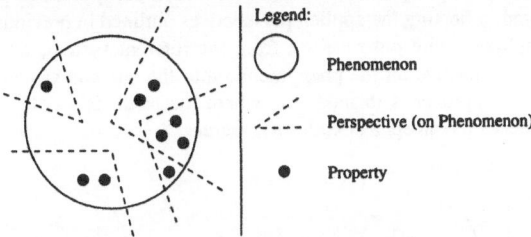

Figure 2: Phenomena, Properties and Perspectives

Perspectives on a phenomenon may overlap. As a consequence, properties realizing these are shared correspondingly. If perspectives are independent, realizing properties also are independent.

In a referent system a shared property has the same value in all its overlapping perspectives. A change from one perspective is instantaneously reflected in all overlapping perspectives. Some problems regarding overlapping perspectives are rooted at a conceptual level. For instance, a change of a shared property from one perspective may be forbidden or cause inconsistency in other overlapping perspectives, and changes from different perspectives may be contradicting. Separation of concern tells us to solve these problems at a conceptual level, too. To our experience, however, clear separations are rare.

At the implementation level there is little explicit support for perspectives and consequently also no coupling to properties. We suggest to objectify the notion of perspective. Among other things, that may imply an object representing each perspective. Section 3 discusses and compares possible representations of perspectives and properties while next section discusses complex aggregates.

2.2 Complex Aggregates

We discuss two aspects of complex aggregates. First static issues are subject to illumination. Based on that, considerations regarding dynamics follow.

Static Aspects. This paragraph considers the structure of aggregates in the light of several perspectives.

A phenomenon may be elementary or composite, depending on the particular perspective. An elementary phenomenon has no constituent parts while a composite phenomenon has a number of aggregated parts — it is an aggregate. Each perspective dictates its own decomposition of a phenomenon into parts. As a part itself may be an aggregate the model of a phenomenon in a particular perspective may form a hierarchic structure.

For each perspective applied to a phenomenon we potentially end up with a hierarchy of parts making up the very same phenomenon. A part can be unique for a perspective or it can be shared among a number of perspectives. Besides that, each part possesses properties, possibly independent or shared, reflecting the applied perspectives outlined in previous section.

To stay in compliance with observations from the referent system, we combine each aggregate reflecting a perspective on the phenomenon into the one and same concept. This is in contrast to traditional approaches to modeling where the result is a collection of uncoupled[2] aggregates. We name such concept a *complex aggregate*.

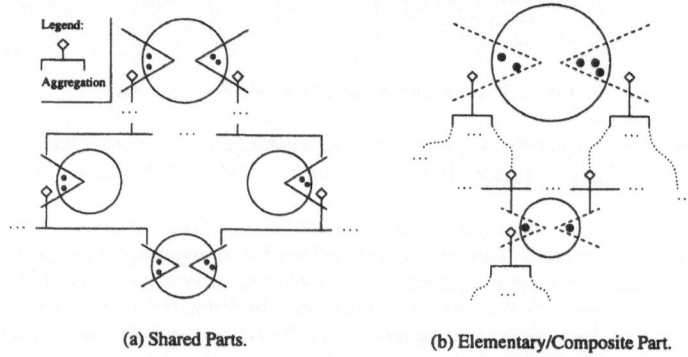

(a) Shared Parts.   (b) Elementary/Composite Part.

Figure 3: Complex Aggregates and Shared Parts

Parts of a composite phenomenon reflect the perspective. Properties of the composite phenomenon and its parts may be mutually dependent. Certain more or less well-defined relations between properties of the composite phenomenon and the property of a part define that the relation actually is what we consider to be aggregation.

Structurally, a phenomenon forms a hierarchy if the applied perspectives cause only unique parts. If not, the structure is a directed graph. We restrict our discussion to the case where the models actually have shared parts and thus form a directed graph as a hierarchic structure just is a special case. Figure 3(a) outlines a complex aggregate with shared parts.

A shared part in a complex aggregate may appear at any level (besides the root) in a hierarchy realizing a perspective of a complex aggregate. In one perspective a shared part may be

---

[2]Often, an implicit coupling in terms of code or rules exists. This is, however, not satisfying from the viewpoint of modeling.

elementary while being a composite in another — it is completely the decision of the concrete perspective. That is, being elementary the part ends the hierarchy while forming an intermediate part if being a composite. Figure 3(b) illustrates a complex aggregate including independent and shared parts at varying levels. The shared part is a composite in the perspective to the left and an element in the perspective to the right.

Two conformations of perspectives on complex aggregates are particularly important: Overlapping perspectives and composite perspectives. These may of cause be combined. Figure 4(a) depicts a common situation where some overlapping perspectives applies to a complex aggregate. The result is a collection of hierarchies of unique as well as shared parts.

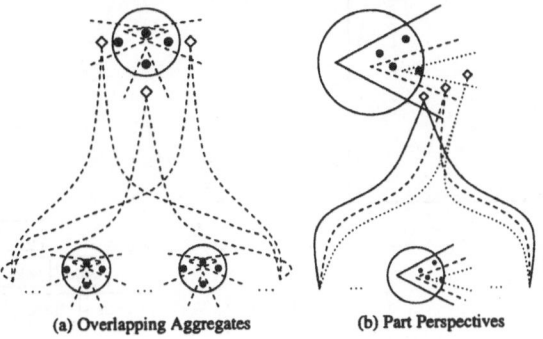

(a) Overlapping Aggregates   (b) Part Perspectives

Figure 4: Complex Hierarchies

So far we have assumed that perspectives recursively apply to all parts, but the conception of a referent system is more sophisticated. A perspective may enter the scene at any level of a hierarchy making up a phenomenon. Likewise, it may also end before the bottom of a hierarchy or it may introduce a further decomposition. It may also introduce its very own decomposition, possibly building on top of shared parts. The constellations are evidently unrestricted, even for part-perspectives (essentially a special case of overlapping perspectives), cf. Figure 4(b).

Dynamics Aspects. In this paragraph we consider the dynamics of complex aggregates, i.e. we assume that a complex aggregate is given, and then discuss 1) how to add a part, and 2) how to add an additional perspective. Since removal of parts and perspectives can be derived from observations regarding addition, the paragraph does not discuss these aspects. Dynamics of complex aggregates also include copying and cloning. The approach is similar to copying and cloning of simple[3] aggregates and is thus out of scope of this article.

Adding a part to a complex aggregate introduces some complications, seen in relation to simple aggregates. Assume that we must add a (perspective of a) phenomenon as a coming part of some complex aggregate in a particular perspective. As for ordinary aggregates, assume that

---

[3]Simple in the sense that only one, possibly implicit, perspective apply.

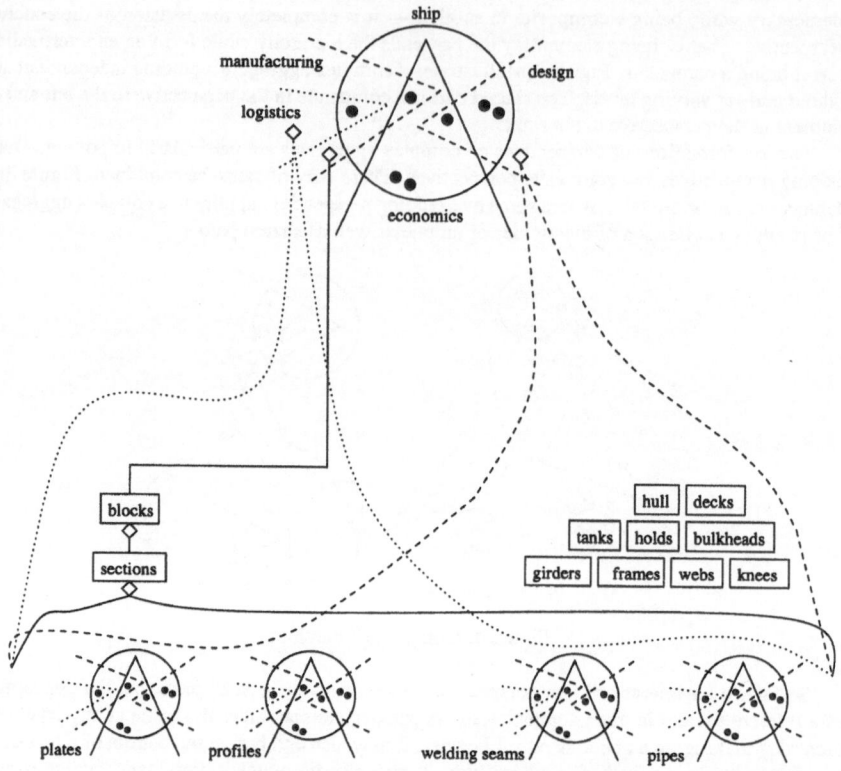

Figure 5: Perspectives Added to the Shipyard Example.

the properties of the complex aggregate and the coming part fits together. That is, necessary relations[4] can be established between properties of given perspectives. Then the coming part can be added as a part of several perspectives, if and only if the relevant perspectives exist for the coming part. The coming part can then be added subsequently to relevant perspectives, making it shared.

Adding a perspective to a complex aggregate also requires some comments. To add an elementary perspective, we select among the existing properties and we supply additional properties. During this operation an existing property may become a shared property, if not shared already. A property, added during this operation is an independent property, at least until we add

---

[4]According to [Kristensen et al. 1994] possible relations/dependencies include *hereditary*, *emerging* and *concealed* properties for aggregates.

another perspective relying on the property. Adding a perspective to a composite phenomenon is essentially the same as adding a perspective to an elementary phenomenon — addition of perspective just has to be applied recursively. That is, the perspective must be added to every part of the composite phenomenon, down till the perspective's elementary parts.

The addition of a composite perspective is similar to the addition of an elementary perspective, except that a number of part perspectives must be added in order to complete the construction.

2.3   The Shipyard Example (cont.)

During design activities naval architects, designers, engineers, draughtsmen and others first decide the general arrangement (overall aspects satisfying functional requirements to the ship) and later on the concrete implementation of it. They carry out a logical decomposition of the ship. The result is a complete specification of the steel structure (hull, decks, tanks, holds, bulkheads, girders, frames, webs, knees, plates, profiles, welding seam, etc.), outfitting (engines, winches, cranes, pumps, pipes, etc.) and electricity (cabling, light, instrumentation, etc.). To achieve their goal they use various simulations (e.g. sea keeping, maneuverability and impact) and evaluations (of stress, deformation, bending, buckling, fatigue, resonance, center of gravity, mass, hydrodynamics and many others).

Manufacturing impose another view of the ship. We are now interested in the assembly (composition) process rather than the decomposition process. Here, welders assembles plates, profiles, etc. into sections, sections into blocks and blocks into ships. Thus, manufacturing engineers break up the ship into a hierarchy of manageable components having no logical or functional meaning.

Logistics take care of "things to the right place at the right time", in principle from ordering of materials to delivery of the ship. Essentially, logistics does not care much about the logical components of the ship. The manufacturing hierarchy, however, documents important information as sections and blocks make up units of elements that have a strong timely connection.

Economic analyses evaluate the price of various parts to ensure profitability. Both logical parts and assembly parts are subject to such analyses. Moreover, both estimated and actual price of each element are important to make budgets and find the final costs.

Even from this superficial introduction we observe at least[5] four alternative perspectives: design, manufacturing, logistic and economics. At least two structurally distinct aggregation hierarchies originating from design and manufacturing exist. Logistics impose a hierarchy similar to the assembly hierarchy, but with different properties of components. The economics perspective adapts to any perspective we might construct. That is, the economic perspective adapts the structure and attaches properties relevant to the economics. We regard these as part perspectives. Figure 5 adds perspectives to the shipyard example. It is limited to the hull and it shows a ship consisting of a (huge) collection plates, profiles, pipes and welding seams.

---

[5]It would possibly make sense to split the design perspective into several part perspectives. These could be perspectives for simulations, evaluations, compartments, structural system taking up loads, etc.

2.4   Summary: Conceptual Model

In brief, we summarize conceptual characteristics as follows:

- A *complex aggregate* is a composite phenomenon subjected to two or more perspectives. It contains *unique parts* as well as *shared parts*, cf. Figure 6. A part may be composite as well. A unique part occurs in one perspective only. A shared part occurs in two or more perspectives.

- A phenomenon — elementary or composite — may be subject to *overlapping perspectives*. Consequently, it may contain *independent properties* as well as *shared properties*, cf. Figure 6. An independent property occurs in a related independent perspective only. It has no relations to properties of other perspectives. A shared property (partly) occurs in related overlapping perspectives. Either perspectives share a complete property (not depicted) or different properties share common state and/or behavior.

Shared parts may be subject to overlapping perspectives, implying shared properties too. Conceptually, this causes no further complications since sharing of parts is orthogonal to sharing of (part of) properties.

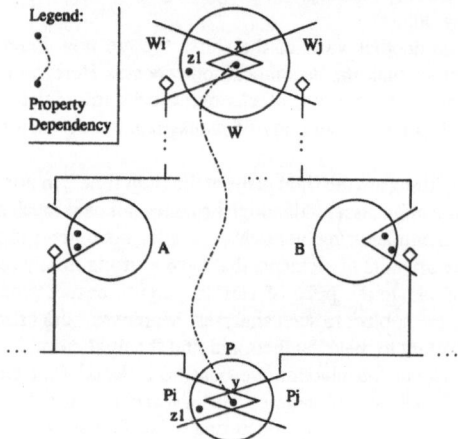

Figure 6: Shared Parts and Shared Properties

3   Implementation with Objects

In this section we discuss the support of the perspective-oriented approach to modeling. We discuss the implementation by means of objects. The following subsections discuss 1) potential alternatives to the implementation of shared parts of complex aggregates, and 2) the consistency problem with the use of shared properties of several perspectives.

3.1 Support of Shared Parts

Objectifying Perspectives. Simple aggregation where a part can only appear in one aggregate [Booch 1994], [Rumbaugh et al. 1991] is inadequate for modeling of complex aggregates, because the result is a collection of completely uncoupled aggregates as opposed to a whole. The notion of identity is violated and we cannot explicitly relate objects from different perspectives. Moreover, consistency issues remain untreated during analysis/modeling, and also unsupported with respect to implementation. Information is duplicated which in itself invites to inconsistency. The object's interface, however, is fine as it is tailored for the perspective. Consequently, simple aggregation is an insufficiently expressive alternative. Thus we discuss other approaches supporting complex aggregates.

As basis for the discussion of approaches, we evaluate the result of each of the alternative approaches with respect to object identity, interface and modeling. Preferably, 1) the identity of an object is always the same regardless of the perspective, 2) the object's interface matches the perspective, and 3) the model is expressive and simple.

To simulate a complex aggregate, the following approaches objectify perspectives, i.e. objects represent perspectives whereas aggregation, association etc. express relations between perspectives. Figure 6 schematically illustrates the essence of the problem. A complex aggregate W with two perspectives Wi and Wj, has a shared part P with the perspectives Pi and Pj. $Wi.z1$[6] and $P.z1$ are both independent properties. Wi and Wj share the property $W.x$ and Pi and Pj share $P.y$.

Shared Aggregation. Shared aggregation expresses the composition of parts into one aggregate where a part can appear in several aggregates [Rational 1997]. Figure 7(a) schematically illustrates how we would use shared aggregation to model a complex aggregate.

The result is a collection of coupled aggregates. Object identity is partly supported. The comparison of references to perspective objects (Wi and Wj) will fail. The inclusion of perspectives pollutes W's interface with properties concerning manipulation of perspective objects. Interfaces of perspective objects (Wi and Wj) are fine as long as the perspective is not further divided. Consistency of shared properties is still a problem that must be maintained explicitly by the programmer. The model is complicated, but still not satisfying, though more expressive. We can relate objects from different perspectives, but properties of perspective objects (Wi and Wj) cannot be related to one another or properties of the object W. Moreover, a technical issue (the modeling of perspectives) confuses the description of the problem domain. A problem is that programmers must explicitly decide with which object (Wi or Wj) to qualify method invocations.

Associations. Associations model relationships among mutually independent objects [Rumbaugh 1987]. Figure 7(b) schematically illustrates how we would use associations to model

---

[6]Here we use $Wi.z1$ as a simple and yet precise notion for telling that we speak of method $z1$ of Wi.

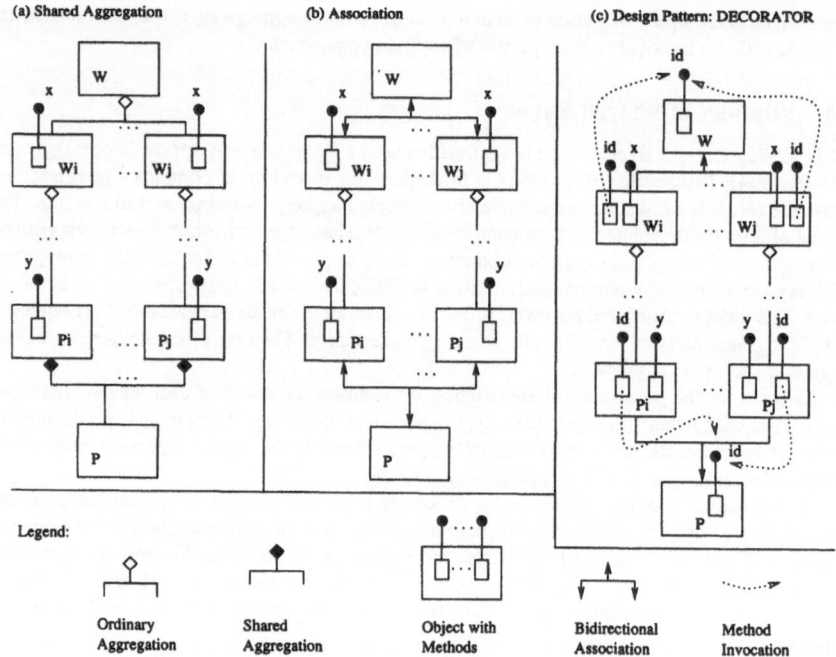

(a) Shared Aggregation   (b) Association   (c) Design Pattern: DECORATOR

Legend:

| Ordinary Aggregation | Shared Aggregation | Object with Methods | Bidirectional Association | Method Invocation |

Figure 7: Shared Aggregation, Association, Design Pattern

a complex aggregate.

The result is a collection of related aggregates. We can now simulate object identity as perspective objects are aware of the object W. Thus to compare two objects we just have to use the object W associated to the perspective object. This can be achieved by addition of an identity property that must be used instead of the object reference. As for shared aggregation interfaces of perspective objects (Wi and Wj) are fine as long as no part perspectives exists. Note, that perspective objects can use properties of the object W. Thus programmers do not need to distinguish explicitly between these objects when using properties. Consistency of shared properties is still a problem that must be maintained explicitly by the programmer. With respect to modeling the same remarks as for shared aggregation apply — it is still imperfect.

Design Patterns. The DECORATOR pattern [Gamma et al. 1994] lets us attach additional responsibilities to objects dynamically. A concrete decorator simulates a concrete perspective, i.e. a decorator implements object properties for a particular perspective (Figure 7(c)).

The result is a collection of coupled aggregates. As for associations we can simulate object identity. This can be achieved by addition of an identity property, id, to the DECORATOR and COMPONENT classes. The identity property of a decorator must forward the decision of identity to its component which then decides upon identity. Then, by convention, we can obtain object identity. The interface matches the perspective quite well. As for other techniques, modeling tends to reveal irrelevant technical aspects, namely how decorators are implemented. Moreover, the object is still scattered over a number of separate objects. That is, we lose information about the purpose of the decorator. In UML we might repair this using stereotypes. The DECORATOR pattern is very similar to the solution with associations.

The ADAPTER pattern [Gamma et al. 1994] is another option. It aims at interface conversion. Pure interface conversion, however, is not sufficient — it must be possible to attach additional properties. A modified version of the ADAPTER enabling additional properties is similar to the decorator pattern without any significant advantages. In this situation, the remarks to the DECORATOR also applies to the ADAPTER.

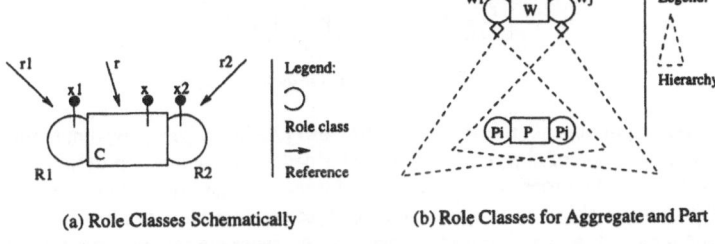

(a) Role Classes Schematically   (b) Role Classes for Aggregate and Part

Figure 8: Role Classes

Roles. We discuss the use of *role* classes, [Kristensen et al. 1996], [Kristensen 1995], to support additional perspectives on objects, and the dynamic change of roles of an object. A role can be instantiated and glued onto the *intrinsic* object (the object playing the role) and later removed from the object. Generalization and aggregation hierarchies model relations of role classes. Properties (instance variables and methods) of a role are additions to properties of the intrinsic object's class — in the description of the role class properties of the intrinsic class/object are directly accessible. An object and its currently available roles are seen as a *subject* with one identity. However, other objects can access this subject through it roles — by references that are typed by the role classes — to obtain different interfaces and behavior from the subject.

Figure 8(a) illustrates access of role classes by means of the references r, $r1$ and $r2$. We assume that class c and Ri qualifies r and ri, respectively. An object of class c can have one or several instances of role classes Ri as its roles. Through the reference r of class c only method c.x is accessible — but not the Ri.xi methods. The reference r1 of role class R1 gives access to the methods R1.x1 and x — but not R2.x2. The implementation of method R1.x1 may invoke c.x.

Figure 8(b) illustrates a principal model using roles. A given perspective is used in construction of a role class for the aggregate w. For each perspective on the aggregate we add a role to each shared part. The role includes properties needed to support a particular perspective for a part. Properties of a role are described as part of the role and in relation to properties of the part. The result is a structure very similar to the conceptual understanding of perspectives and complex aggregates. Identity is supported, the interfaces of the roles classes match the perspectives, and the model is expressive and relatively simple.

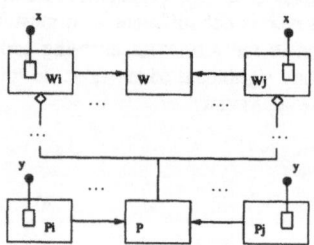

Figure 9: Split Objects

Split Objects. Split objects [Bardou et al. 1996] also provides a per-viewpoint (similar to perspectives) representation of objects. A split object is defined as a collection of pieces (similar to properties), carrying the properties of the object. Pieces are organized within a delegation hierarchy and forming an object. As opposed to split objects, pieces have no identity. Pieces can be added to and removed from split objects as needed. Messages are sent on a per-viewpoint basis by giving an identifier of a piece. It is also possible to send messages without any viewpoint. Using split objects to model complex aggregates principally results in Figure 9. Note that the arrows denotes delegation rather than association. We conclude that the support provided by split objects is essentially similar to that of roles.

3.2 Support of Shared Properties

This section discusses how to maintain consistency of shared properties. We outline two approaches. The discussion treats the alternatives from the previous subsection as one case because the consistency problem applies generally to all alternatives. The role alternative provides basis of our discussion.

Figure 10(a) indicates the principal solution to the representation of shared properties. Methods and attributes in some combination represent properties of perspective objects. Notice that in case of independent properties no special consistency problems occur. In Figure 10(a) the method $z1$ represents independent properties, that use — and are used by — other methods in the aggregation structure. Figure 6 indicates that the shared properties x and y are mutually dependent. The consistency problem due to shared properties also involves shared parts with shared

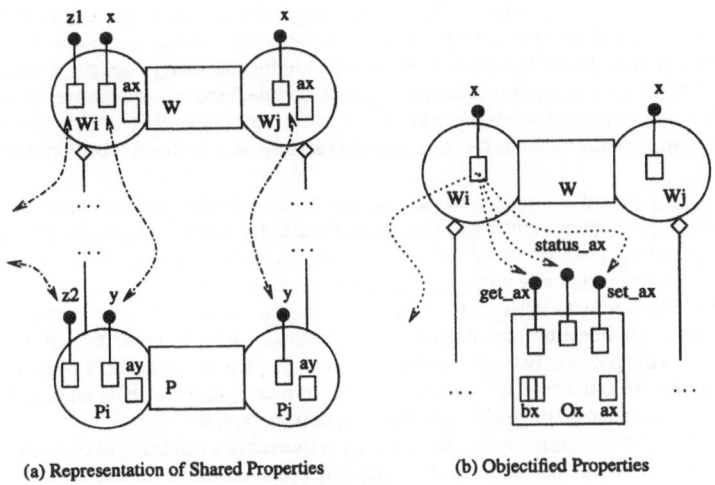

(a) Representation of Shared Properties   (b) Objectified Properties

Figure 10: Perspectives

properties. We distinguish between *measurable properties* and *transformations*. According to [Madsen et al. 1993] a measurable property calculates a result based on some substance, whereas a transformation changes the substance. In practice, properties (and their representations in terms of methods and attributes) are combinations of these. The representation of a measurable property causes no consistency problems, because the method does not update any attributes. For methods representing transformations the consistency problem is that a transformation to a property of the entire complex aggregate may cause several updates of the representation in the shared parts and properties.

Duplicating Shared Properties. This approach simply duplicates attributes realizing shared properties. In Figure 10(a) the methods x and y and the attributes ax and ay illustrate the approach. Both the attribute ax and the attribute ay have been duplicated in respectively Wi, Wj and Pi, Pj. The method Wi.x updates only its own attribute, namely Wi.ax. When the transformation x is to be applied to the composite object W both Wi.x and Wj.x must be invoked in order to ensure that the entire complex aggregate is updated appropriately. At a shared part object (like for example P with a shared property y) only the y method belonging to the perspective is invoked — the invocation chain from Wi.x only includes Pi.y (and not Pj.y). Note that the message initiating the method invocations only spread out between shared properties at the root of the complex aggregate.

Objectifying Shared Properties. This approach objectifies shared properties. In order to control the update of a shared property we objectify the shared property, i.e. an object implements the shared part of the property, and let methods representing different perspectives access the objectified part[7]. Figure 10(b) illustrates this approach based on the role alternative. Ox objectifies the attribute ax, and the methods Wi.x and Wj.x access this object. Use of or update of Ox.ax takes place through the methods Ox.get_ax and Ox.set_ax. A similar objectification is done for P.y.

The major problem lies in the control of updates of the complex aggregate. Not only one, but several, overlapping perspectives and thus hierarchies in the complex aggregate may share and thus depend on the property being updated. If one perspective modifies such shared property, several hierarchies potentially must be updated to stay consistent.

To ensure that, we let a message to a complex aggregate spread out to all overlapping perspectives and penetrate down through its parts — for example we let an invocation of Wi.x invoke tts Wj.x too. This potentially implies multiple updates to properties of shared parts, coming via different paths. To avoid that, we associate identity to messages (essentially an objectification). Then a shared part can distinguish original messages from replicas.

State and behavior implementing this invocation mechanism resides in two places. The message must be able to invoke methods of overlapping properties of an object, and the objectified shared property must be able to filter out replica invocations. Ox.bx and Ox.status_ax symbolize state and behavior supplied by objectified property.

3.3   The Shipyard Example (cont.)

For each perspective — design, manufacturing, logistics and economics — we identify properties relevant to it. If a property exists for more perspectives we also consider whether these are independent or overlapping.

It should be noted, that a perspective may apply for a limited time. For instance, we would possibly discard a logistics perspective when delivering the ship as the information becomes useless. Figure 11 shows a first draft of intuitive properties, their relevance to concrete perspectives and whether they are independent (I) or shared (S). The table does not picture lifetime (transient or persistent) as the information is considered premature at current stage. For instance, we expect that the division of the design perspective into more fine-grained perspectives will show persistent as well as transient perspectives.

Figure 11 illustrates the model after addition of properties. It is not complete, it only shows selected properties for two perspectives (design and manufacturing), but nevertheless it covers the situations where a property is shared or independent. The property mass is an independent (and measurable) property, whereas move (design.move and manufacturing.move) is an example of a shared property. The property move is also an example of a transformation. That implies that moving a component in a design perspective also must affect the components position in a manufacturing perspective. The solution in Figure 11 duplicates the representa-

---

[7]Note that we cannot simply place Ox in W since this would make Ox permanent while it may only be relevant to a subset of possibly temporary perspectives applying to W.

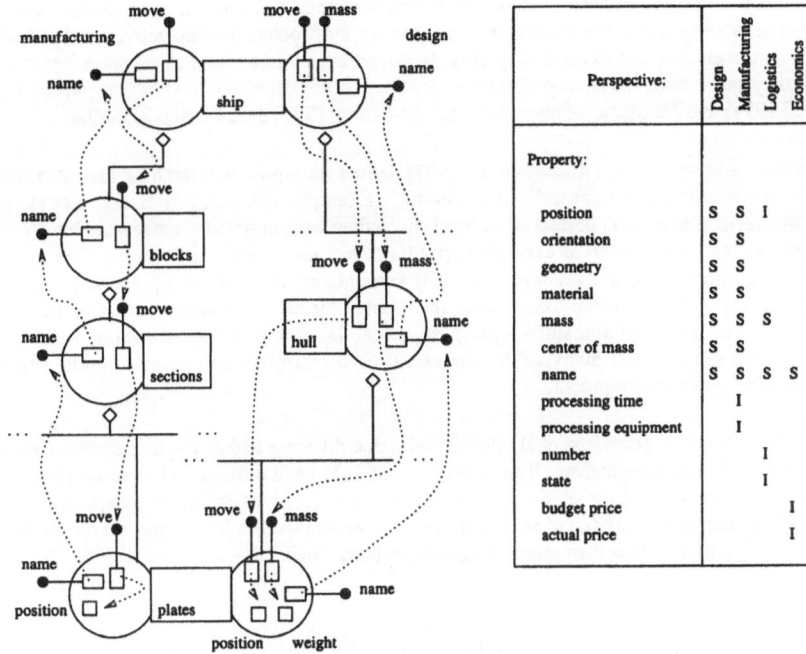

Figure 11: The Shipyard Example

tion in relation to the move property, namely the position attribute of the perspective objects of plates. Figure 11 also shows an example of another kind of property, name, which is a combination of perspective-dependent names of parents, e.g. ship.block.section.plate.

4 Related Work

In the literature we have seen neither an analysis of the problems of applying perspectives to aggregated (hierarchic) phenomena nor a conceptual description integrating perspectives, properties and aggregates. However, many ([Abiteboul et al. 1991], [Carré et al. 1990], [Carré et al. 1988], [Bardou et al. 1996], [Harrison et al. 1993], [Henderson-Sellers 1997], [Kiczales et al. 1997], [Kristensen 1995], [Kristensen et al. 1996], [Reenskaug et al. 1992]) do provide a (larger) part of the picture. In particular, section 2.1 draws upon previous work.

Other Kinds of Aggregation. Winston et al. [Winston et al. 1987] provides a taxonomy of meronymic relations (aggregations). The classification results in six categories of aggregations which are distinguished on functional, homeomerous and separation properties: component/integral object, member/collection, portion/mass, stuff/object, feature/activity and place/area. These are irrelevant in this context as they do not address the problem of complex aggregates. Thus they suffer from the same problems as ordinary aggregation. For later refinements by Odell [Odell 1994] and Henderson-Sellers [Henderson-Sellers 1997] the situation is similar.

Aspects. Kiczales et al. [Kiczales et al. 1997] defines an aspect as something that "can not be cleanly encapsulated in a generalized procedure". Examples discussed by Kiczales et al. suggest that aspects operate at objects meta-level, since they were targeted at design/implementation issues such as optimization of execution speed and memory usage. Essentially, aspects serve the same purpose as meta-level objects, namely computation about the computation (reflection). However, aspects seem more fine-grained than meta-objects. Perspectives address the understanding of the problem domain[8] — perspectives can be seen as a way of slicing the problem domain into relevant and manageable chunks. Thus perspectives and aspects aim at different phases of program development.

Subjects. Subjects [Harrison et al. 1993] model that different agents might view the same object from different perspectives. The agents do not only have a filtered view of an object, but some of the methods of the object may be there only because of the given perspectives of an agent. The theme in [Harrison et al. 1993] relates to generalization hierarchies according to different perspectives, rather than related aggregation hierarchies.

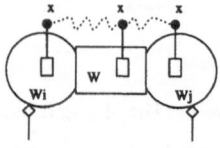

Figure 12: Subject Methods

[Kristensen et al. 1996] allows a *subject method* as a combination of methods of the intrinsic class and role classes to behave like one method. The methods $Wi.x$, $Wj.x$ and $W.x$ — Figure 12 illustrate a subject method. Whenever any of these methods is invoked both bodies are executed (options include execution order, input/output parameters, etc.).

5 Summary

We conclude that perspectives, (shared) properties and complex aggregates are powerful and natural notions during modeling at the conceptual level. In practical applications the notions seem to be expressive and necessary for complex problem domains.

---

[8]We note, that perspectives also can be applied to design issues. For instance, analysis of a technical domain — an issue typically considered a design task — makes completely sense.

At the implementation level objects, methods and attributes related in various ways support perspectives and complex aggregates to some extent. In many situations, more powerful modeling abstractions and mechanisms supporting these are preferable. Though object identity can be resolved it relies on programming by convention, i.e. we cannot assure it. The problem lies in the inability to model the "wholeness" of an aggregate. Moreover, objects are scattered over numerous objects which is unfortunate as modeling of property dependencies between these objects is largely unsupported. Finally, expressing and ensuring consistency of shared properties is complicated.

Based on our work on perspectives and complex aggregates at the conceptual and the implementation level we note that:

1) The notions of perspective and complex aggregates are natural and expressive. Current modeling notations however do not support the expression of these notions. That is, we can only use perspectives, properties, and complex aggregates with parts reflecting several perspectives informally during the modeling process.

2) In the implementation of these notions by means of objects, consistency is the major problem for shared properties. When updating in one perspective, the change must be verified with and then updated in other perspectives. We have discussed various mechanisms for that purpose, where the programmer manually must maintain consistency. Identity, interface and naturalness cause various kinds of problems in the implementation.

Acknowledgments. We thank Bob Basu, Kåre Groes Christiansen, Henning Kierkegaard, Kjell Harr, Nepper Larsen, Claus Risager, Gunnar Schønfeldt, Carl Erik Skjølstrup and other employees at Odense Stell Shipyard for their contribution to the shipyard example.

References

[Abiteboul et al. 1991] S. Abiteboul, A. Bonner. Objects and Views. Proceedings of SIGMOD, Denver, 1991 (SIGMOD Record 20(2):239-247)

[Bardou et al. 1996] D. Bardou, C. Dony. Split Objects: a Disciplined Use of Delegation within Objects. Proceedings of Conference on Object-Oriented Programming Systems, Languages and Applications, 1996.

[Booch 1994] G. Booch. Object Oriented Analysis and Design with Applications. Benjamin/Cummings, 1994.

[Booch et al. 1999] G. Booch, J. Rumbaugh, I. Jacobson. The Unified Modeling Language User Guide. Addison-Wesley, 1999.

[Bækdal 97] L. K. Bækdal. ShipDesign Requirements. Odense Steel Shipyard, August 1997.

[Bækdal 1999] L. K. Bækdal. Configurable Autonomous Objects: Constraint and Framework Modelling. Ph.D. dissertation, University of Southern Denmark, Odense University, 1999.

[Carré et al. 1988] B. Carré, G. Comyn. On Multiple Classification, Points of View and Object Evolution. In Artificial Intelligence and Cognitive Sciences, Manchester University Press, 1988.

[Carré et al. 1990] B. Carré, J. M. Geib. The Point of View notion for Multiple Inheritance. Proceedings of European Conference on Object-Oriented Programming/ Proceedings of Conference on Object-Oriented Programming Systems, Languages and Applications, 1990.

[Gamma et al. 1994] E. Gamma, R. Helm, R. Johnson, J. Vlissides. Design Patterns: Elements of Reusable Object-Oriented Software. Addison Wesley, 1994.

[Harrison et al. 1993] W. Harrison, H. Ossher. Subject-Oriented Programming (A Critique of Pure Objects). Proceedings of the Conference on Object-Oriented Programming Systems, Languages and Applications, 1993.

[Henderson-Sellers 1997] B. Henderson-Sellers. Open Relationships — Compositions an Containments. Journal of Object-Oriented Programming, 1997.

[Kiczales et al. 1997] G. Kiczales, J. Lamping, A. Mendhekar, C. Maeda, C. Lopez, J. Loingtier, J. Irwin. Aspect-Oriented Programming. Proceedings of European Conference on Object-Oriented Programming, Lecture Notes in Computer Science, vol. 1241, Springer Verlag, 1997.

[Kristensen 1995] B. B. Kristensen. Object-Oriented Modeling with Roles. Proceedings of the 2nd International Conference on Object-Oriented Information Systems, 1995.

[Kristensen et al. 1994] B. B. Kristensen, K. Østerbye. Conceptual Modeling and Programming Languages. Sigplan Notices, 29 (9), 1994.

[Kristensen et al. 1996] B. B. Kristensen, K. Østerbye. Roles: Conceptual Abstraction Theory & Practical Language Issues. Special Issue of Theory and Practice of Object Systems on Subjectivity in Object-Oriented Systems, 1996.

[Madsen et al. 1993] O. L. Madsen, B. Møller-Pedersen, K. Nygaard: Object Oriented Programming in the Beta Programming Language. Addison Wesley 1993.

[Odell 1994] J. J. Odell. Six Different Kinds of Composition. Journal of Object-Oriented Programming, 1994.

[Rational 1997] Rational. UML v.1.1. http://www.rational.com.

[Reenskaug et al. 1992] T. Reenskaug, E. P. Andersen, A. J. Berre, A. Hurlen, A. Landmark, O. A. Lehne, E. Nordhagen, E. Ness-Ulseth, G. Oftedal, A. L. Skar, P. Stenslet. OORASS: Seamless Support for the Creation and Maintenance of Object Oriented Systems. Journal of Object-Oriented Programming, 1992.

[Rumbaugh 1987] J. Rumbaugh. Relations as Semantic Constructs in an Object–Oriented Language. Proceedings of the Object-Oriented Programming Systems, Languages and Applications Conference, 1987.

[Rumbaugh et al. 1991] J. Rumbaugh, M. Blaha, W. Premerlani, F. Eddy, W. Lorensen. Object-Oriented Modeling and Design. Prentice Hall 1991.

[Stroustrup 1991] B. Stroustrup: The C++ Programming Language. 2/E, Addison-Wesley 1991.

[Winston et al. 1987] M. E. Winston, R. Chaffin, D. Herrmann. A Taxonomy of Part-Whole Relations. Cognitive Science, 1987.

Achieving Workflow Flexibility through Taming the Chaos

Maxim Khomyakov

Magnificent Seven, 1-st Baltiyskiy per. 6/21-3, Moscow, Russian Federation
E-mail: maxim@mag7.ulter.msk.su   Fax: +7 095 155 81 73

Ilia Bider

IbisSoft, Box 19567, S-10432, Stockholm, Sweden
E-mail: ilia@ibissoft.se Fax: +46 8 15 10 10

ABSTRACT. Traditionally, flexibility in workflow is introduced by moving from the rigid predefined control flow to permitting alternative patterns. The paper propose a reverse approach to achieving flexibility, namely to start with chaos and then impose restrictions. This approach employs an untraditional view on business process which is regarded not as a "flow of work", but as a trajectory in the space of all possible states. The execution control in the proposed approach is realized via the notion of valid state, were a state includes activities currently planned for the given process. The flexibility is achieved by breaking the rules of planning into three categories: obligations, prohibitions, and recommendations.

KEY WORDS: workflow, business process, dynamical system

1. Introduction

Workflow management systems (WFMS) are now coming to the forefront of business application development. However, the field of workflow still have a number of unsolved problems, see for example (Trammel, 1996). One of the main problems with current WMFS is their lack of flexibility, i.e. means of handling business processes that deviate from the standard pattern.

To illustrate the flexibility problem, consider an example from (Kim&Pike, 1998) that discusses the issues of using WFMS for supporting the hiring (recruiting) process. In this example, the process of hiring is designed in the way that background checking and medical screening is done after actual hiring. The question is what happens if "for some applicants, a hiring manager would perform at first the background checking and medical before the decision" (on hiring). The paper's answer runs as "based on the current workflow management systems, the hiring process has to be redesigned."

Obviously, redesigning the process is not a proper way to handle deviations that can be numerous. By making an "experiment of thought", we can easily create a long list of deviations for the hiring process. For example, what happens if directly after the interview with the department manager, he/she (the manager) is replaced? Would the new manager accept the opinion of the previous one, or would he/she prefer to form his/her own opinion?

The above case can not be considered as an example of wrong definition of the business process. The problem is much deeper than that. When a modeling technique is focused on defining the order of activities, it is only natural that process description would reflect the standard way of doing things. Considering all possible ways the business process can develop is not practical. Besides, the number of ways may be too great to consider each of them separately. In a business process like in the example above, almost any thinkable sequence of activities can occur.

The problem of flexibility is widely discussed in research papers. Several approaches to combining the predefined flow of activities with ad-hoc planning were proposed to solve this problem, see for example, (Aalst, 1999, Blumenthal&Natt, 1995, Bogia&Kaplan, 1995). The most commonly used way of introducing flexibility is by moving from the rigid predefined control flow to allowing deviations. This, for example, can be done via introducing alternative patterns of behavior, by permitting the process to deviate on particular paths, etc.

In the current paper, we try to introduce flexibility starting from the opposite end. We begin with full chaos, and then introduce some means to restrict it. To be able to do that, we use an untraditional view on business process. Traditionally, a business process is viewed as a flow of activities, i.e. "work flow." We view it as a trajectory in the space of all possible states, i.e. "state flow".

The rest of the paper is structured in the following way. In section 2, we introduce a state-oriented view on business process. In section 3, we introduce a way of imposing restrictions on the set of all possible trajectories. This is done via the notion of valid state, were the state includes activities currently planned for the given process. Section 4 explains how we propose to deal with unsolicited events. Finally, section 5 clarifies the relationships between the proposed model and other approaches, and outlines the directions for future research. The approach is discussed on the conceptual level to make the paper understandable for the people outside the academic world. The readers interested in the underlying formal logic are referred to the formal paper (Bider et al., 2000).

2. State flow view on business processes

A WFMS is a software system that supports business processes (Workflow, 1999a). The most general definition of business process, see for example (Hammer&Champy, 1994), defines it as a set of partially ordered activities aimed at reaching a well-defined goal. Some examples of goals are as follows:

- Reaching an agreement in business negotiations.
- Discharging the patient from the hospital in a (relatively) healthy state.
- Closing a sale.

The goal is a core notion of the business process definition. Having a goal presumes that at any moment of a process's lifetime, we can tell whether the process's goal is achieved or not. If it is not achieved, it is desirable to know how far we are from the goal. This leads us to the concept of process's *state*. The state can be *final*, i.e. the goal has been reached, or *intermediate*, i.e. the goal has not been reached yet. As an example, various states of a "house building" process are illustrated on figure 1.

To be able to analyze the process's state, we need to have some way of representing it on a piece of paper, in the computer, etc. This leads us to the notion of *state representation*. For example, for the house building process from Figure 1, a state may be represented as a snapshot of the house under construction and everything around it. Where it does not cause confusion, it is possible to refer to state representation as to state. This is especially applicable to the processes that do not deal with manufacturing physical objects, e.g., a sale process aimed at closing a sale. For this kind of processes, the state is always an abstract construct that is difficult to differentiate from the state representation.

The notion of state allows us to consider a business process as a dynamical system that moves in the space of all possible states until it reaches the final state (the goal). Movement forward (to the goal) is done via activities execution, e.g. build a wall. However, activities are not the only possible source of movement. An unpredictable external event can move the process backward in the state space, e.g., the wall has been destroyed (by an earthquake). The behavior of a business process resembles the behavior of a hybrid dynamical system for which a gradual movement in one direction can be interpolated with jumps that can move the system in the opposite directions (Schaft, 2000).

The presence of the external influence makes it impossible to define the process's goal just as a point in the space of all possible states. The goal should rather be defined as a set of final states with a criterion of which final states are reachable, and which ones can be considered as nearest to the given intermediate state. If the unpredicted external event moves the process backwards or sidewards, the initially projected final state might become unreachable, but another one can become reachable instead. (Compare, for example, the first and the last slides in fig. 1.)

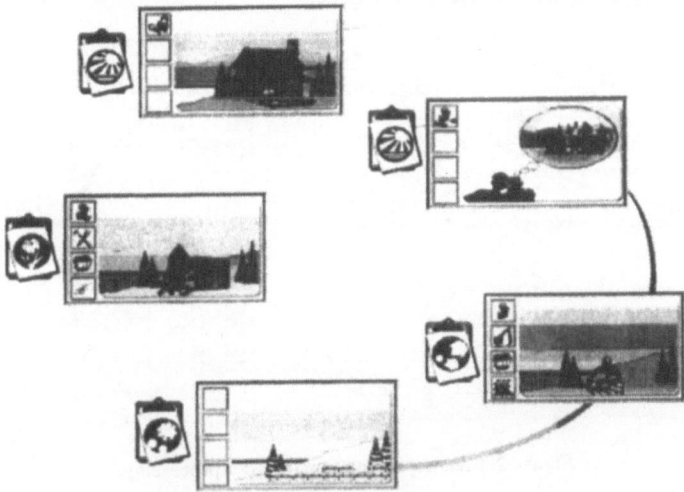

Fig. 1. States in a house building process.

3. Taming the chaos

The concept of state has been introduced in the mathematical system theory (Calman et al., 1969) in order to reduce the need of considering the history of inputs when calculating the outputs. The input changes the state, and the output is fully determined by the new state.

The same principle can be applied to business processes. The current state of a process normally contains enough information to determine what activities need to be executed to move the process forward. Consider, for example, the state of order processing in a retail store on fig. 2. The set of final states for this process can be defined as follows:

- For each ordered item *Ordered = Delivered*
- *To pay = Total + Freight + Tax*
- *Invoiced = To pay*
- *Paid = Invoiced*

The set of activities that should be executed depends on how the current state differs from the projected final one. Examples:

- If for some item *Ordered > Delivered*, shipment should be performed.
- If *To pay > Invoiced*, an invoice should be sent.
- If *Invoiced > Paid*, steps should be undertaken to get money from the customer.
- If, on the other hand, *Invoiced < Paid*, money should be returned to the customer.

Execution of an activity changes the state of the process, moving it nearer to the final state. For example, when shipping is completed, *Ordered* may become equal to *Delivered*, at least for some items. Obviously, the activities required for reaching the goal can't be executed in an arbitrary order. Some way of imposing restrictions is required.

```
┌─ F1 ══════════════════ O R D E R ══════════════════
│                         ┌────────────┐          Ibis:HRS
│   Deal Category:travel  │ 50331651   │          Deal # :00002
│                         └────────────┘
│                      ───────CUSTOMER───────
│ Company                        Reference:IvP   Job:Manager
│ Name: Travelshop               Firstname:Ivar
│ Tel :(___)00__-5809090_        Lastname :Petersson
├──────────────────────────────────────────────────────────
│Pos  Article#  Article name              Ordered  Deliv      Sum
│
│ 1   CS6000GR  Suitcase 60x80 green          9      9   10800.00
│ 2   CB4030BL  Computer bag 40x30 black     20     20    6000.00
│ 3
│ 4
│   Mark            Way of del.          Weight
│                                              ┌────────────────────
│  Notes          •Closed deals•               │Disc.    %
│          F3                    Payment in 15 days │Total      16800.00
│ •Events•         •Plans•       VAT(y/n)y   25.00 %│Freight
│                                Invoiced           │Tax         4200.00
│                                Paid               │
│                                                   │To pay     21000.00
└─00-05-23══22:55══════════════════════════════════════
```

Figure 2. State representation of order processing.

In business practice, activities are planned first and executed later. Planning can be used as a tool of execution control. Let us create for a particular process's state a list of activities that *should* and are *allowed to* be executed in this state. Obviously, this list can't include two activities such that the presence or/and execution of one of them is based on the outcome of the other. The list constitutes an immediate plan of the current process.

As soon as an activity from the process's plan has been completed, new activities can be planned based on the new state of the process. Thus, the restriction on the order of execution can be defined through the rules of *dynamic planning*. To formulate these rules, we use the following method. We regard the process's plan as being an integral part of the process's state (more precisely, state representation). This allows us to define a notion of *valid* state in addition to the notion of final state. To be valid, the state should include all activities *required* and *allowed* for moving the process to the next stipulated state. See, for example, plan on fig. 3 that complements the process state from fig. 2 and makes it valid.

Based on the notion of valid state, the order of execution can be defined in the form of rules that given an invalid state, correct it in a way that it becomes valid. The state is corrected by changing the plan, i.e. via adding and/or removing activities. The correction can be done by one general rule that observes the whole complex state, or with the help of many local rules, each of which watches a limited part of the state structure. The last option allows introducing the notion of sub-process, but in a *declarative* way.

Depending on what kinds of rules are introduced for controlling the processes, we can get full range from predefined control to almost full chaos. The latter occurs when all activities are planned manually, the rules requiring not more than "something is planned" when the process is not in a final state. If the plan is empty, the general activity *plan something* is added.

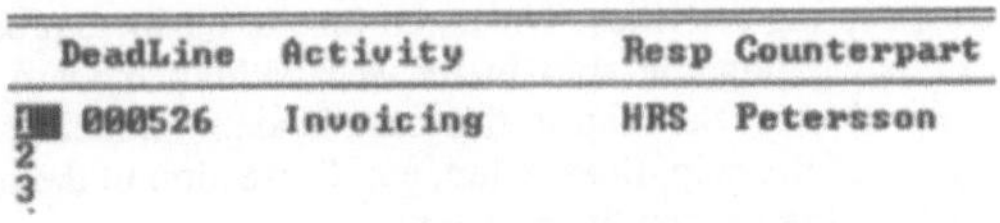

DeadLine	Activity	Resp	Counterpart
000526	Invoicing	HRS	Petersson

Figure 3. Process's plan that complements the state from fig. 2 and makes it valid.

To get some order while allowing a certain degree of deviation, we need to structure the rules of planning in some way. We choose to structure the rules according to the idea of policies, as defined, for example, in ODP reference model (ISO/IEC, 1995), or in (Lipu&Sloman, 1997). Policies are usually divided into three groups: obligations, prohibitions, and permissions. However, when applying the concept of policies to the idea of dynamic planning, we group the policies in a slightly different way. We also divide them in three categories. The first two run as usual:

1. *Obligations.* Based on the current state and possibly the process's history some activities must be present in the process's plan. In case of absence, they are added. For example, suppose all the goods have been delivered, but not all money has been invoiced. Then the *invoice* activity should be in the plan.
2. *Prohibitions.* Based on the current state and possibly the process's history some activities can't be present in the process's plan. In case of presence, they are removed.

In respect to execution control, the concept of permission does not make much sense. Everything that is not dictated by obligations and is not prevented by prohibitions is permitted. However, another type of policies could be useful here, i.e.:

3. *Recommendations.* Based on the current state and possibly the process's history some activities are normally present in the process's plan. In case of absence, they are suggested (strongly or weekly) for inclusion.

Classification of rules into three groups above implies the two steps scheme of planning after executing an activity. First, the state is corrected automatically using all rules, the suggested activities being marked in a special way. Then, the responsible person may change the resulting plan, but without breaking any obligations or prohibitions.

4. Dealing with unsolicited events

As was pointed in section 2, the trajectory of a business process in the state space is affected not only by activities aimed at reaching the goal, but also by unpredictable external events. As soon as such event is detected, the state representation of the process should be corrected.

Consider an example of order processing being in the state defined by fig. 2 and fig. 3. Suppose customer Travelshop rings and informs the store that the situation in his market place has changed, and he won't be able to sell all 20 computer bags. He then asks permission to reduce his order from 20 to 10 bags. Granted the permission has been obtained, the number of bags ordered should be changed from 20 to 10. As all 20 bags have already been delivered, activities aimed at getting the excessive bags back should be completed. These activities can be added to the plan by standard rules of dynamic planning based on the process state emerged after correction.

The need to correct the state can arise not only due to an external event, but also due to human errors in executing and registering activities. The conditions of business process management are very similar to those of navigating the ship in the sea without modern systems of position recognition. The ship's position on the map in this case is approximated via calculations based on the current course, speed of the ship, tides, wind, etc. Correction in the position is made from time to time when the meteorological conditions allow it.

Consider one more experiment of thought. Let 9 black suitcases where sent to Travelshop instead of 9 green ones as is indicated in fig. 2, which can be attributed to a human mistake. The mismatch can be discovered when Travelshop makes a complaint, or when a responsible worker from the store checks whether all deliveries reached their destination. As soon as a mismatch has been detected, the state representation should be corrected. The first item in Fig. 2 gets the *Delivered* quantity set to zero. A new item is added to the list that corresponds to the green suitcase with the *Ordered* quantity set to 0, and the *Delivered* quantity set to nine. The corrected state will require new activities added to the plan, like delivering the right goods, and getting back the wrong ones.

Let us continue the experiment, and suppose that the customer is willing to accept the black suitcases instead of the green ones but at a lower price. Then the state representation should be corrected as shown in fig. 4. In this case, the plan in fig. 3 will remain consistent with the state of the affairs.

5. Concluding remarks

When formulating our approach, we use many notions and concepts that are present in many other research works on workflow, and the workflow standards (Workflow, 1995, 1999a,b). Many features of our model can be found in other papers, in some commercial or experimental WFMS, or are in the air. Detailed comparison of our approach with those of others is beyond the frame of this paper (an exception has been made for the field of hybrid dynamical systems which is considered below). Generally speaking, the essence of our approach is not the features themselves, rather the way we are trying to obtain them from one consistent view on business process. This view considers only one flow in the process, the flow of states. The flow of activities is derived from the process's plan that is an integral part of the process's state. Each activity finds information needed for its execution directly in the relevant parts of the state, thus no explicit information flow is defined. Our view presents also an attempt of a declarative description of the business process dynamics.

Conceptually, our approach to describing processes is similar to the idea of hybrid automata (see, for example (Schaft, 2000). In the theory of hybrid automata, the state of the system consists of two different constituents: a set of values assigned to the state variables, and a location to which one or more activities are assigned. Each activity is specified as a set of differential equations showing how the state variables are being changed in time. The main difference of this presentation from ours (on the conceptual level, of course) is as follows. In the theory of hybrid automata, the number of locations is finite. In our approach, we add activities directly to the state, and thus we do not have an explicit notion of location. Potentially the number of "locations" in our approach may be infinite.

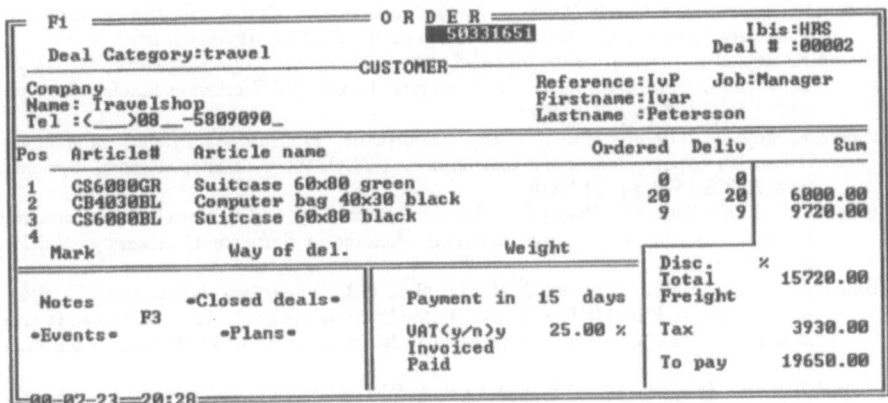

Figure 4. Corrected state of the order processing.

Historically, the proposed view on the business processes is derived from our general framework for modeling discrete dynamic systems. We call it CHAOS, where the acronym stands for Concurrent Human-Assisted Object Systems. In this framework, which is presented in (Bider et al., 2000), we view the system as consisting of:

- a set of *objects*,
- a code of *laws*,
- a set of *connectors*, each connector hanging on a group of objects that must obey a certain law.

Both, rules of dynamic planning, and activities represent special types of laws. A planning engine(s), and planned activities (activities included in the process's plan) are connectors that ensure that those laws hold.

The current paper summarizes also the results of our practical work on business process analysis, and building systems to support business processes. The results of our practical work are presented in (Bider, 1997a,b), and shortly reviewed in (Bider&Khomyakov, 1998a,b)

The paper is focused on the issues related to flexible execution control of business processes. Other issues, like resource distribution and management, are left outside. These issues are relatively independent from the execution control, and we hope that the results already achieved in these fields can be connected to our approach with minor modifications. This area is currently under investigation. Another direction in the future research is creating a formal language for rules of planning. (In our practical work, we more or less used hard coding.)

References:

(Aalst, 1999): Aalst, W.M.P. van der. *How to Handle Dynamic Change and Capture Management Information? An Approach Based on Generic Workflow Models.* http://wwwis.win.tue.nl/~wsinwa/genwf.ps, 1999.

(Bider, 1997a): Bider, I. *Developing Tool Support for Process Oriented Management.* Data Base Management 26-01-30, Auerbach, 1997.

(Bider, 1997b): Bider, I. *Object Driver: A Method for Analysis, Design, and Implementation of Interactive Applications.* Data Base Management. 32-10-25, Auerbach, 1997. 4

(Bider&Khomyakov, 1998a): Bider, I. and Khomyakov, M. *Object-Oriented Model for Representing Software Production Processes.* ECOOP'97 Workshop Reader, Springer, 1998. LNCS 1357, pp. 319-322.

(Bider&Khomyakov, 1998b): Bider, I. and Khomyakov, M. *Business Process Modeling – Motivation, Requirements, Implementation.* ECOOP'98 Workshop Reader, Springer, 1998. LNCS 1543, pp. 217-218.

(Bider et al., 2000): Bider, I., Khomyakov, M. and Pushchinsky, E. *Logic of Change: Semantics of Object Systems with Active Relations.* Automated Software Engineering. Vol.7:1, 2000, pp. 9-37.

(Blumenthal&Natt, 1995): Blumenthal, R. and Nutt, G.J. *Supporting Unstructured Workflow Activities in the Bramble ICN System.* In the Proceedings of the 1995 ACM Conference on Organizational Computing Systems (COOCS'95), pp. 130-137, Milpitas, California, 1995.

(Bogia&Kaplan, 1995): Bogia, D.P. and Kaplan, S.M. *Flexibility and Control for Dynamic Workflows in the wOrlds Environment.* In the Proceedings of the 1995 ACM Conference on Organizational Computing Systems (COOCS'95), pp 148-159. Milpitas, California, 1995.

(Hammer&Champy, 1994): Hammer, M., and Champy, J. *Reengineering the Corporation – A Manifesto for Business Revolution,* Nicholas Brealey Publishing, London, 1994.

(ISO/IEC, 1995): ISO/IEC 10746-2. *Open Distributed Processing – Reference Model – Part 2: Foundations.* 1995.

(Kalman et al, 1969): Kalman R.E., Falb P.L., and Arbib, M.A. *Topics in Mathematical System Theory.* McGraw-Hill, 1969.

(Kim&Pike, 1998): Kim, K. and Paik, S. *Practical Experience and Requirements on Workflow.* In Coordination Technology for Collaborative Applications. LNCS 1364, pp. 145 –160. Springer, 1998.

(Lipu&Sloman, 1997): Lupu E., and Sloman M. *A Policy Based Role Object Model.* In the Proceedings of EDOC'97, pp. 36-47. Gold Cost, Australia, October 1997.

(Schaft, 2000): Schaft A. Van der, and Schumacher H. *An introduction to Hybrid Dynamical Systems.* Springer 2000.

(Trammel, 1996): Trammel K. *Workflow without fear.* Byte, April 1996.

(Workflow, 1995): Workflow Management Coalition. *Reference Model - The Workflow Reference Model.* WFMC-TC-1003, 19-Jan-95.

(Workflow, 1999a): Workflow Management Coalition. *Terminology & Glossary.* WFMC-TC-1011, Feb-1999.

(Workflow, 1999b): Workflow Management Coalition. *Interface 1 - Process Definition Interchange.* WfMC-TC-1016-P, Oct-1999.

ELECTRONIC COMMERCE

HotFlow: E-Commerce processes from a language/action perspective

Daniela Handl

Darmstadt University of Technology
Programming Languages and Compilers
Alexanderstrasse 10, D-64283 Darmstadt
E-mail: handl@pu.informatik.tu-darmstadt.de   Fax: +49 6151 16 6648

ABSTRACT. *HotFlow can help you through a sophisticated business process in E-Commerce, starting with the contact, guiding you and your partner(s) through negotiation and contracting until the item is delivered or the service rendered, and the bill is paid.*
This workflow control is based on the language/action perspective, which allows the process definition to be adapted even during run-time.

KEY WORDS: *language/action theory, speech acts, dynamic workflow, E-Commerce.*

1. Introduction

Electronic Commerce (E-Commerce) is currently developing, especially the business-to-business (b-to-b) area is growing.

The common approaches, based on filling order forms, are suitable for business processes which can be characterized as:

find supplier • fill order form • receive products/services • pay bill

There are many areas for which this way of trading is not suitable, e. g., craftsmen, artisans, and small enterprises in general with their often sophisticated negotiation procedures actually lack profitable access possibilities to E-Commerce.

Imagine an American software company, let's call it NanoSoft, with about 100 software developers. The average software developer drinks a whole lot of coffee during each workday. For the convenience of their staff — and in order to save working time — NanoSoft managers decide to buy a fully automated coffee machine. The only thing to do for someone longing for a fresh-brewed coffee made of fresh-grinded coffee beans would be to put a cup under the delivery outlet and press the button for either coffee or espresso.

For corporate identity reasons, the coffee machine should have the typical sky-blue colour of NanoSoft and the NanoSoft logo printed on its front. Swiss coffee machines seem to have the best grinders.

So what NanoSoft managers wanted would be: a Swiss coffee machine, colour sky-blue, with the NanoSoft logo printed upon, and robust enough for continuous use as in catering area.

International contact via phone or letter has the well-known disadvantages. NanoSoft people search the Internet and find a wholesaler who offers blue coffee machines made in Switzerland, but the online order form gives no hint which shade of blue it is and whether the printing of the NanoSoft-logo would be possible.

NanoSoft also finds the name and address of a coffee machine manufacturer in Switzerland, but their homepage just gives sample pictures and some technical data of their products.

So what now?

Since there are some details to be negotiated upon, communication via email would probably get quite mixed up or run out before details could be settled. And what about delivery and payment? Even if the supplier is trustworthy, there might be problems coming up when the coffee machine is shipped to the United States.

This paper introduces HotFlow, a system for the dynamic control of individual business processes like the (simple) one described above. (For a more sophisticated example of a negotiation among multiple partners, see (Handl, 1999)).

HotFlow supports business processes in their entirety:

contacting • negotiating • contracting • settling

The paper is structured as follows. In section 2, the specification of HotFlow and the relevant parts of the environment in which it is developed is followed by a description of the adapted language/action paradigm of HotFlow. Then, the introductory business example is revisited, this time describing the course of business it would take using HotFlow. Section 3 shows how the workflow definition changes during a business and describes the basic speech acts a business conversation can consist of. Section 4 concludes the paper.

2. Language/action negotiation processes with HotFlow

With HotFlow, extended E-Commerce business processes can be controlled as workflow processes, the negotiation is handled from an adapted language/action perspective.

2.1 The HotFlow system

HotFlow is a system for document-based b-to-b E-Commerce, currently developed in the scope of the project MALL2000 (sponsored by European Union: INCO Copernicus no. 977041). Its target group are small and medium sized enterprises (SMEs).

MALL2000 will enable them to establish international contacts and to do business with partners from all over the world. In the scope of this paper the focus is on the possibility for and the handling of document-based negotiations (Hoffmann, Handl, 1999) within MALL2000.

Negotiations in E-Commerce include more sophisticated procedures than bargaining for a price. E-Commerce enables trading among partners who wouldn't even have known about the existence of each other. This is especially significant for SMEs who are more easily handicapped by distances, national regulations for trading, and language barriers than big enterprises which often have branch offices in many countries.

The conduct of a business consists of many steps ranging from getting in touch with (former unknown) partners, checking whether one partner can supply something the other one wants, up to concluding a contract. Maybe even multiple partners are involved.

The organization and control of the steps is important in our context, because communication might be complicated by several factors:

- There can be multiple partners involved,
- partners might be from distant countries
- in maybe different time zones,
- speaking different languages.

Within the scope of MALL2000, HotFlow has been architectured as a specialized Workflow Management System (WfMS) to meet these requirements. With its paradigm of enabling peer-to-peer relationships of participating enterprises, HotFlow provides the possibility for negotiations and E-Commerce more sophisticated than based on filling order forms.

2.2 Workflow based on speech acts

Austin (Austin, 1962) and Searle (Searle, 1969) developed the idea of speech acts: many utterances are not true or false statements, but by uttering, the speaker does exactly what he or she is saying. For example: a judge saying "I sentence you to..." or, in our context: a supplier saying "I offer you ...", a customer saying "I order ..." .

Winograd and Flores (Winograd, Flores, 1999) transferred the work of Austin and Searle into the context of computer systems. Conversation phases in speech act theory are closely related to the sophisticated kind of business process supported by HotFlow (as described in the introduction).

The modelling of workflows under the language/action perspective proceeds on the assumption that the conversation of the involved partners consists of four phases:

initiating • negotiating • executing • confirming

Several conversations can be combined and constitute a workflow (Böhm et al.1997).

The phases for a simple and straightforward business process would be:

demand-driven process		offer-driven process	
phase	actor	phase	actor
1. ask for a product/service	customer	1. offer a product/service	supplier
2. agree to supply/do it	supplier	2. accept offer	customer
3. fulfill work + report it	supplier	3. fulfill work + report it	supplier
4. accept report + declare satisfaction	customer	4. accept report + declare satisfaction	customer

Business process definitions used in HotFlow have to be highly adaptable. Each step can change the further proceeding of the course of business. So the user must be able to adapt the workflow definition during runtime.

This can be achieved by the language/action approach. At each state of the communication cycle, a certain set of further steps is possible. For example, a client cannot declare satisfaction before he or she actually accepted an offer.

HotFlow internally provides the set of possible graphs and the set of paths inside each graph. So what for the user appears to be a change in the workflow definition, in fact is a switch between or a combination of predefined graphs or a chosing of an alternative path inside a graph.

Since there is such a strong coherence of negotiations and speech acts, any course of business can be mapped onto a graph. If necessary, supporting parties can be involved (such as consultants, or translators in case of international business), and related processes can be combined (e. g., one process with a supplier and another one with a shipping agency, in the case that a customer will only buy an item if a shipping agency can be found to transport it, and of course vice versa).

Additionally, HotFlow provides mechanisms for easy specification of constraints such as time limits.

2.3 Applying HotFlow

The first step for someone to initiate a deal as decribed in the introduction is to start the HotFlow system.

The user is prompted whether the intended business procedure is (among others) an offer, a request, or a request without obligation.

Processing this information, HotFlow prepares the business process document ("MALLdoc"), which is a hierarchically structurable document based on the HotDoc system (Buchner, 1998). A MALLdoc initially contains a specialized document part, in our example for a request without obligation.

Additionally, HotFlow provides the graphical representation of a plain workflow definition, based on the kind of business process intended by the user.

At any time the user has the possibility to modify the workflow definition, e. g., to add time constraints for some step, to define access restrictions for a particular document part, or to change the supposed course of business by returning to a former step or by introducing further partners. Depending on additional constraints, a supplier might even turn a business process which might have been started by a customer as a request without obligation into an offer.

A customer has the possibility to ask several suppliers for their offers or to treat related business processes combined.

3. The HotFlow negotiation system

As mentioned above, the flexibility of HotFlow is based on an all-embracing graph. For reasons of clearness, during the course of business only the most likely and straightforward part of the graph is presented to the user as a template for individual adjustment. For example: If you start a business conversation by supplying a product, you proceed on the assumption that your offer will be either refused or accepted, and in case of acceptance the product will have to be delivered and finally payed by the customer. You wouldn't want to look at all the possible ways the conversation might take, many of which are merely theoretical.

3.1 Some speech acts of the HotFlow-system

The graph presented to a supplier of a product would be (see section 3.2 for a detailed description of the single speech acts):

offer (supplier) • acceptance (customer) • realization (supplier) • consent (customer)

This is the (preliminary) workflow definition. As mentioned above, several possibilities are omitted in the presentation to the users, e. g. the breaking of the conversation. The workflow definition can be modified by the supplier, and it is sent to the customer, together with the MALLdoc containing the text of the offer. When sending the MALLdoc, HotFlow marks the offer phase as settled and internally prepares the possible actions of the next step.

The customer opens the MALLdoc, reads the text, and chooses to react. There are several possibilities which make sense in this situation. Apart from disrupting or settling actions like "breaking" and "demanding", the most likely ones are:

- accept offer,
- refuse offer (and break communication),
- inquire (ask for another/similar product),
- ask for further information,
- talking.

Choosing the accept-option is equivalent to the utterance "I accept ...", the customer formally accepts the offer. In case of acceptance, HotFlow marks the acceptance phase as settled and again internally prepares the actions which are possible at this point of the conversation. The workflow definition is maintained, since it is the most straightforward course, and again, for reasons of clearness several possibilities are omitted in the graph as presented to the user.

Should the customer refuse the offer, the workflow definition would be modified to:

offer (supplier) • refusal (customer)

and the conversation would end at this point.

The customer might be interested in a modified version of what was offered initially (e. g., in case of an offered computer, the customer might prefer another monitor). If the customer exactly knows what she/he wants and orders it, the workflow definition is modified:

[offer (supplier)] •
order (customer) • confirmation (supplier) • realization (supplier) • consent (customer)

Maybe the customer wants to know without obligation whether the supplier's range comprises this somehow modified product. Then workflow definition would be turned to that of an inquiry, which is a prefix for the order-workflow above:

inquiry (customer) • confirmation (supplier) • order (customer) • ...

There are some situations, in which the reaction cannot be put in one of the listed categories. For those cases, the option "talking" is provided.

3.2 HotFlow-Speech acts in detail

In spite of the wide range of situations which might occur in a negotiation handled by the HotFlow-system, the workflow definition consists of just a few basic speech acts.

- *offer:*
  A binding offer is made by the supplier of a service/product. A special usage of an offer occurs in cases of complaints by the customer: the supplier offers e. g., to reduce the price (see below: *demand*).
- *acceptance:*
  The customer accepts an offer, which is either a usual offer of some product/service, or an offer by way of compensation for a complaint.
- *realization:*
  The service is rendered or the product manufactured and/or delivered by the supplier, usually preceded by *acceptance* of an offer or by *confirmation* of an order.
- *consent:*
  The customer gives his/her consent, usually implicitly by paying the bill.
- *order:*
  The customer gives a binding order for some item/service, e. g. out of some catalogue.
- *confirmation:*
  The supplier confirms that the product will be delivered / the service rendered, usually as a consequence of an *order*.
- *inquiry:*
  The customer sends an inquiry without obligation, often to multiple suppliers in order to compare prices/quality..., usually answered by the supplier with an *offer*, an *advertising*, or a counter-*inquiry*. An inquiry by the supplier could be answered by the customer with an *order*, or again with an inquiry.
- *refusal:*
  The customer refuses an *offer* or the supplier refuses an *order/inquiry*. This could be followed by a counter-*inquiry/order* or an counter-*offer*, respectively. Otherwise, it leads to the end of the conversation. If the customer receives another offer or the supplier another order, this would (technically) be the start of a new conversation.
- *advertising:*
  As the *inquiry* is a non-binding version of an *order* by the customer, an advertising is a non-binding version of an *offer*.
- *break:*
  A break can either be explicit, or implicit, e. g. by not reacting during a given time-limit. It ends a conversation.
- *demand:*
  The customer demands some touching up or complains, e. g., about some defect of the product, or the supplier sends a (further) request for payment or a remainder to the customer. A complaint should ideally be followed by an *offer*, a demand made by a supplier should result in a *consent* (i. e.: making a payment). It might as well be followed by a negotiation, consisting of sequences of *offers/demands* (and/or others).
- *talking:*
  Talking does not proceed the course of business. Nevertheless, it has several application areas: It might be used for translation purposes – in this case, the partners would modify the in general horizontal workflow definition such that vertical lines with talking are added. Another application area is some clarifying, informal conversation, e. g., in case of transmission errors or other cases of uncertainty.

4. Conclusion

Due to the close coherence of business processes in E-Commerce and speech acts, HotFlow enables easy and intuitive handling of extended negotiations.

Process definitions are highly adaptable even during run-time, multiple partners can be involved. HotFlow can be applied to areas not yet opened up for E-Commerce.

References:

(Austin 1962) J. L. Austin. *How to Do Things with Words.* Cambridge, MA, 1962.

(Böhm et al, 1997) M. Böhm, C. Bussler, R. Kaschek, W. Liebhart, B. Paech, and K. Stein. Modellierung von Workflows. In S. Jablonski, M. Böhm, and W. Schulze, editors, *Workflow Management; Entwicklung von Anwendungen und Systemen; Facetten einer neuen Technologie,* chapter 8, pages 65-130. Heidelberg, 1997.

(Buchner, 1998) J. Buchner. *HotDoc — Ein flexibles System für den kooperativen Aufbau zusammengesetzter Dokumentstrukturen.* PhD thesis, Darmstadt University of Technology, Germany, 1998.

(Handl, 1999) D. Handl. HotFlow — A Visual Language for Workflow Applications in E-Commerce. In D. C. Martin, editor, *Proceedings of 1999 IEEE Symposium on Visual Languages,* pages 185-186, Los Alamitos, CA, 1999.

(Hoffmann, Handl, 1999) H.-J. Hoffmann and D. Handl. Document exchange as a basis for business-to-business co-operation. In J. Y. Roger et al., editor, *Business and Work in the Information Society,* pages 325-331, Amsterdam, 1999.

(Searle 1969) *Speech acts.* Cambridge, 1969.

(Winograd, Flores, 1999) T. Winograd and F. Flores. *Understanding Computers and Cognition.* Reading, Mass, 14th edition, 1999.

Situation-based Approach for E-Business Functional Modeling

El-Sayed Abou-Zeid

Department of Decision Sciences and MIS
Faculty of Commerce and Administration
Concordia University
Montreal (Quebec), Canada
1550, de Maisonneuve Blvd. W.,
Montreal, Canada, H3G 1M8

Fax: (514) 8482824
Email: elsayed@vax2.concordia.ca

ABSTRACT. *Several reference models have been developed for e-business systems. In spite of their differences the deep structure underlying them is identified with its three layers, namely, business, functional and resource layers. However, despite the importance of the functional layer little attention has been paid to the problem of which proper conceptual construct can be used for modeling it. Viewing e-business as a semiotic phenomenon, in which all the interactions among the involving parties aim at changing the state of an e-thing in both its visibility state space and its lifetime state space, the concepts of the "semiotic communicative situation" is introduced as the required modeling construct. It is defined as a dynamic construct that is composed of collection of interacting actors that are configured and re-configured to actualize certain semiotic actions that affect the states of e-things (e.g., e-order). The application of the proposed conceptual construct is illustrated by using it to build a simple functional model for an e-broker. The implications of the proposed conceptual construct are discussed.*

KEYWORDS: E-Business, E-Broker Model, UML, Conceptual Modeling, Communication.

----

1. Introduction

With the proliferation of E-Business Systems (EBSs), the necessity of developing a "Reference Model" that answers the question "How can an EBS be developed, operated and assessed?" is becoming evident. Following are some of the objectives of the EBS reference model:

- To provide basis for defining conceptual activities in the E-Business and for identifying improvement opportunities,
- To provide basis for a systematic approach for developing EBSs,
- To provide a framework for the creation of application-related models,
- To create a framework for a quantitative approach to understanding and analyzing e-business scalability,

In order to meet one or more of these objectives, several reference models have been proposed (Menasce et al, 2000, Schmid et al, 1998, Zwass, 1996, 2000). Among the common characteristics of these models is their layered structure where the components of the higher level set the functional requirements and constraints for those in the lower level while the latter deliver the functional support for the higher-level components. Moreover, despite the variation of the number of layers and their definitions from one model to another, one can recognize their underlying deep structure. Such deep structure is composed of three main layers (or perspectives), namely (See table 1):

- **Business Layer**
  The possible E-business models such as E-shop, E-auction and E-mall   (Julta et al, 1999, Menasce et al, 2000, Timmer, 1998)
- **Functional (Business infrastructure) Layer**
  The EB processes and transactions that realize a specific EB model together with customer behavior characteristics.

- **Resource Layer**
  The specialized EB services that support EB transactions such as enabling services, e.g., E-catalogs, E-money and secure messaging services together with their supporting IT infrastructure.

It is evident that the constituents of the middle layer play crucial role in developing, operating and assessing EB systems, as they actualize the means of realizing the business objectives through the utilization of IT infrastructure. Nevertheless, it is the least structured one. This is partially due to the absence of a structuring conceptual construct similar to "entity" in data-oriented paradigm or "object" in object-oriented paradigm.

To this end the main objective of this work is to introduce a conceptual construct, i.e., the "semiotic communicative situation" that can be used to model the constituents of the functional layer in e-business reference model.

The paper is organized as follows. In section 2 the definition, the characteristics, and the modeling requirements of the e-business functional layer will be discussed. Then the proposed conceptual construct will be introduced in section 3. In section 4 the application of the proposed conceptual construct is illustrated by using it to build the functional model of a simple e-business model, i.e., e-broker. Section 5 concludes the paper by discussing the implications of the proposed conceptual construct.

Table (1): Comparison between the different EC reference models

	(Menasce & Almeida, 2000)	(Schmid & Lindermann, 1998)	(Zwass 1996, 2000)
Business Layer	**Business Model** [An architecture for product, service, and information flow, including a description of business players, their roles, and revenue sources]	**Business View** [Business model]	**Products and Structures** 7. Electronic Marketplaces and Electronic Hierarchies, e.g., E-Auction, E-Brokerage.
Functional Layer	**Functional Model** [The trading processes that deliver services to customers of an electronic business company]	**Transaction View** [The way of doing business, i.e., E-business processes and transactions]	6. Products and Systems, e.g., Remote consumer services, On-line marketing.
	Customer Model [The navigational pattern of a customer during a visit to a e-business site]		
Resource Layer		**Services View** [The specialized EC services that support EC transactions, e.g., electronic product catalog, electronic contracting tools, computer integrated logistics together with their interfaces]	**Services** [The services that enable the finding and delivery of information] 5. Enabling Services, e.g., E-catalogs, E-money.
	Resource Model [A representation of the various resources of a site that captures the effects of the workload model on theses resources]		
		Infrastructure View [The necessary IT processes for EC services, e.g., EDI]	4. Secure Messaging, e.g., EDI, E-mail, ETF.
			Infrastructure 3. Hypermedia/ Multimedia Object Management 2. Public and Private Communication Utilities 1. Wide-Area Telecommunications Infrastructure

2. E-Business Functional Model: Definition and Modeling Requirements

E-business functional model is defined as the configuration of e-business processes and transactions that provides the user of e-business system with the supporting functions s/he needs to achieve her/his goal(s). Moreover, this configuration has to

- Conform with and support a specific e-business model;
- Provide a blueprint for modeling user (e.g., customer) behavior; and
- Provide a blueprint for the necessary implementation (technology) model

In order to meet these conditions the conceptual construct needed to build the e-business functional model has to satisfy the following requirements:

i. Since e-business systems are communication-intensive ones, the required construct must have the capability of modeling the interactions among the involving parties whether being human, individual or collective (e.g., customer, organizational functional unit, organization), or artifact (e.g., IT-based system).

ii. Communication, in the context of e-business system, is understood as coordinated behavior and mutual co-adaptation not just as exchange of information. This can be achieved through the ongoing process of building agreed-upon representations of the relevant e-things (e.g., e-order), their contents, their meanings and their states. Therefore, the required construct has to explicitly represent the actions that realize the dynamics of their changes.

iii. In order to describe the dynamics of e-things' changes, one has to first determine which states an e-thing can have along with what actions cause the state to change. For the purpose of this work two-dimensional state space of e-things will be assumed. The first dimension is the visibility dimension that determines the visibility of an e-thing to one or more of the interacting parties. Along this dimension one can recognize three different visibility spaces, namely, Buyer Visibility Space, BVS, (e.g. buyer's browser), Seller Visibility Space, SVS, (e.g. seller's web server) and Virtual Visibility Space, VVS, which plays the role of buffer between the latter spaces. The second dimension is the lifecycle dimension that represents the possible sequence of states an e-thing has in its lifetime. For example, figure (1) shows e-order state space. The change of the state of an e-thing is a result of at least one situated action performed by one or more of e-business involving parties.

Visibility Dimension

	Being Created	Being Visible to the Seller	Captured	Completed	Confirmed	Fulfilled	Being Shipped	Archived
Buyer Visibility Space								
Virtual Visibility Space								
Seller Visibility Space								

Order Life-Cycle Dimension

Figure (1): E-order state space

iv. E-business is, by its very nature, a semiotic phenomenon where the physical activities, if any, are driven by the semiotic activities such as information presentation, manipulation and exchange. Therefore, the e-business situated actions are the semiotic actions that handle the semiotic constructs, e.g., an object, representing e-things.

3. A Conceptual Construct for E-Business Functional Modeling

In order to model the dynamics of e-business the concept of situation will be used to represent the basic building block of e-business functional layer, i.e. e-transaction. In general, a situation can be thought as a configuration of some aspect of the world. It may have spacio-temporal extent or it may be more abstract. It may also include people and things with their actions and speeches (Devlin et al, 1996, Sowa, 2000). For the purpose of this work a more specific type of situations will be used, namely, *semiotic communicative situation*. It is defined as *a dynamic construct that is composed of collection of interacting actors that are configured and re-configured to actualize certain semiotic actions that affect the states of e-things* (Abou-Zeid, 1999). Moreover, in this context, an **actor** is the concept of an active or responsive agent that can play a role in relation to e-things. It could be human, individual or collective (e.g., customer, functional unit, enterprise), or artifact (e.g., search engine, web server, order processing system). Within e-business an actor can play several roles such as a *doer* of certain activities, a *governor (decision maker)* of their execution or as a *provider/requester* (or *recipient*) of information.

In order to meet the modeling requirements of e-business functional layer, the structure of a situation is represented as follows

$$<(K, S), T (D), \{R (A)\}, O>$$

where

K	is an e-thing, e.g. e-order;
S	is the current state of the e-thing
T (D)	is a semiotic action T needed to manipulate some information D about the pertinent e-thing, e.g., generate, notify, update, determine, collect, send, and store;
R (A)	is the role **R** played by an actor A; and
O	is an e-thing, e.g. e-order;

Moreover, e-business situations can be classified into two main categories: buyer e-business situations (BESs), which are initiated by the buyer, and seller e-business situations (SESs), which are initiated by the seller. In general, each BES activates at least one SES. Figure (2) shows UML class representation of the deep structure of e-business reference model with emphasis on its functional layer.

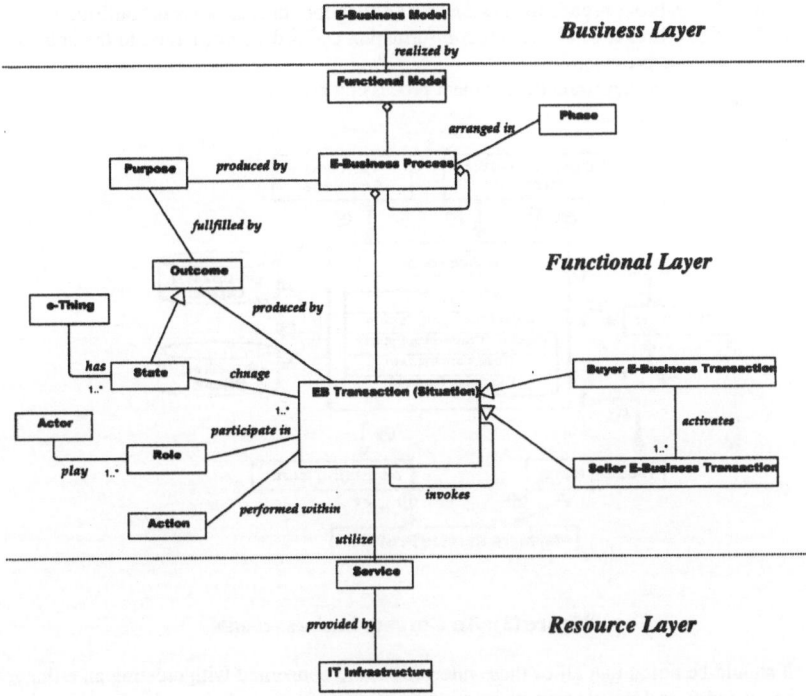

Figure (2): UML class representation of the deep structure of e-business reference model

4. Case Study

In this section a simplified version of a business model for an e-broker will be used to illustrate how the concept of situation can be used to develop an e-business functional model. The e-broker business model is characterized by an intermediary between suppliers of goods and/or services and the customer (Julta et al, 1999). Figure (3) shows the architecture for an e-broker business model described in terms of interactions among the business parties. In this model an e-broker X has access to external databases of the suppliers. The suppliers are viewed as partner companies-companies with which the broker conducts business transactions and holds trusted relationships. Moreover, this business model supports shipping the product from supplier to the consumer directly through another delivery service provider, such a Federal Express or UPS. The architectural model consists of querying multiple online supplier databases, requesting service from third party businesses, and responding to the consumer. As shown in figure (2) the interactions among the involving parties can be summarized as follow:

1. The customer creates an order and makes it visible to e-broker X.
2. The e-broker X responds by collecting customer and payment information.
3. The e-broker verifies items' availability.
4. The e-broker verifies payment information.
5. The e-broker determines taxes and shipping costs.
6. The e-broker sends the customer a notification that the order is confirmed.
7. The e-broker sends customer information and order information to the delivery service provider.
8. The e-broker starts the payment processing process.

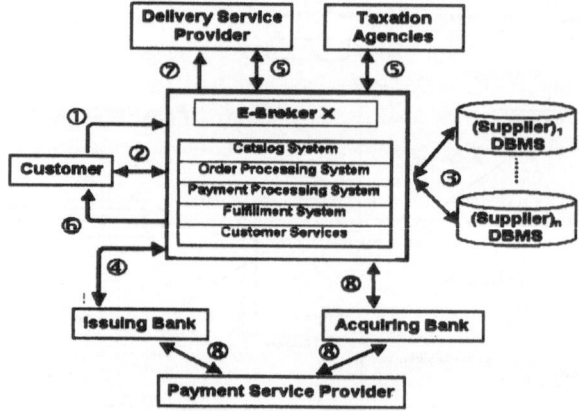

Figure (3): An e-broker business model

It should be noted that all of these interactions are concerned with creating an e-thing, i.e., e-order, and developing its informational content progressively through changing its states in both visibility state space and lifetime state space. Therefore, each interaction can be represented by one or more situations. In tables (2) and (3) the e-order states together with partial description of their associated situations are shown. In table (4) the mappings between e-business interactions and situations are listed.

Table (2): Examples of e-order lifetime states and their associated situations

Outcome State (O)	Situation (s)		
	Name	**Action (D)**	**Role (Actor)**
Being Created	Search (**B1**)	Find (Item specifications)	Governor (Customer) Doer (Search engine)
	Decide (**B2**)	Select (Item)	Governor (Customer) Provider (Catalog)
	Build (**B3**)	Add (Item)	Governor (Customer) Doer (Shopping Cart)
Captured	Customer information (**Cap1**)	Collect (Customer Information)	Provider (Customer) Requester (X)
	Payment information (**Cap2**)	Collect (Payment Information)	Provider (Customer) Requester (X)
Completed	Verification of item availability (**Com1**)	Verify (Item Availability)	Requester (X) Provider ((Supplier)'s DBMS)
	Verification of payment information (**Com2**)	Verify (Payment Information)	Requester (X) Provider (Issuing Bank)
	Calculation tax & shipping costs (**Com3**)	Determine (Tax/Shipping Costs)	Doer (X) Provider (Delivery Service Provide) Provider (Taxation Agencies)

Fulfilled	Transmission of order information (Ful1)	Send (Order Information, Customer Information)	Provider (X) Recipient (Delivery Service Provider)
	Payment processing (Ful2)	Exchange (Order Payment Information, Customer Information)	Requester/Doer/ Provider (Issuing Bank) Requester/Doer/ Provider (Acquiring Bank) Requester/Doer/ Provider (Payment Service Provider)

Table (3): E-order visibility states and their associated situations

Outcome State	Situation(s)		
	Name	Action (D)	Role (Actor)
Being Visible to the Seller	Inform (V1)	Send (Order information)	Provider (Customer) Recipient (X)
Confirmed	Confirm (Con1)	Send (Verified order information)	Provider (X) Recipient (Customer)

Table (4): The mappings between e-business interactions and e-business situations

Business Interaction	Corresponding Situation (s)	
	Buyer e-business situations	Seller e-business situations
1	Search (B1), Decide (B2), Build (B3), Inform (V1)	
2		Customer information (Cap1), Payment information (Cap2)
3		Verification of item availability (Com1)
4		Verification of payment information (Com2)
5		Calculation tax & shipping costs (Com3)
6		Confirm (Con1)
7		Transmission of order information (Ful1)
8		Payment processing (Ful2)

5. Conclusions

The proposed approach introduces the concept of "semiotic communicative situation" as the fundamental conceptual construct for e-business functional modeling. The concept that modularizes the communication requirements as it encapsulates the communication content, the action to be performed and the actors involved. Moreover, based on the type and the nature of the actors involved, the proposed construct can be applied at different levels of granularity. These levels extend from the macro level, e.g. the whole enterprise level, to the micro level, e.g. secure web server, payment server, through an intermediate level that includes functional systems such as payment system. For example, the seller e-business situation "Payment Information" can be rewritten as follows:

<(E-order, Being Created), Collect (Payment information), {Provider (Customer), Requester (Payment System)}, Captured}

or

<(E-order, Being Created), Collect (Payment information), {Provider (Customer), Requester/Provider (Web Server), Requester/Provider (Secure Web Server), Requester/Doer/Provider (Payment server)}, Captured}

Therefore, it provides a blueprint for the implementation (technology) model. Similarly, the fine-grained buyer e-business situations provide blueprints for modeling customer behavior (Menasce et al, 2000).

As the structure of proposed construct includes the outcome states, which are related to business goals (Eriksson et al, 2000), and actors, which at micro level represent the IT-based services, it represents the logical link between the business layer and the resource layer of the e-business reference model.

Finally, a situation dependency diagram (modified version of UML activity diagram) can used to depict the dynamic interdependence among situations (Abou-Zeid, 1999).

References

(Abou-Zeid, 1999)   E. Abou-Zeid, *An Autopoietic View of the Concept "Information System"*, Proceedings of IFIP WG8.1 International Conference on Information Systems Concepts: An Integrated Discipline Emerging, Ed. Falkenberg E., Lyytinen K. and Verrijn-Stuart A., Kluwer Academic Publishers, 1999, pp. 165-186.

(Devlin et al, 1996)   K. Devlin and D. Rosenberg, *Language at Work*, CSLI Publications, Lecture Notes No. 66, 1996.

(Eriksson et al, 2000)   Eriksson H. and Penker M., *Business Modeling with UML: Business Patterns at Work*, John Wiley, 2000.

(Julta et al, 1999)   D. Julta, P. Bodorik, C. Hajnal and C. Davis, *Making Business Senses of Electronic Commerce*, IEEE Computer, March 1999, pp. 67-75.

(Julta et al, 1999)   D. Jutla, P. Bodorik and Y. Wang, *Developing Internet E-Commerce Benchmarks, Information Systems*, Vol. 24, No. 6, 1999, pp. 475-493.

(Menasce et al, 2000)   D. Menasce and V. Almeida, *Scaling for E-Business*, Prentice Hall, 2000

112

(Schmid et al, 1998)   B. Schmid and M. Lindermann, *Elements of a Reference Model for Electronic Markets*, Proc. 31st Hawaii International Conference on Systems Sciences, HICCS98, January 1998.

(Sowa, 2000)   J. Sowa, *Knowledge Representation*, Brooks/Cole, 2000.

(Timmer, 1998)   P. Timmer, *Business Models for Electronic Markets*, International J. Electronic Commerce, Vol. 8, No. 2, July 1998.

(Zwass, 1996)   V. Zwass, *Electronic Commerce: Structure and Issues*, International Journal of Electronic Commerce, Vol. 1, No. 1, 1996, pp. 3-23.

(Zwass, 2000)   V. Zwass, *Structure and Macro-Level Impacts of Electronic Commerce: From Technological Infrastructure to Electronic Marketplaces*, http://www.mhhe.com/business/mis/zwass/ecpaper.html, retrieved June 2000.

An Architecture for the Support of Knowledge-intensive e-Business Processes

Ingrid Slembek and Valérie Gay

Faculty of Information Technology
University of Technology, Sydney, Australia
{ingrid, valerie}@it.uts.edu.au

In many industries, e-business practices are increasingly being adopted in a bid to improve the inter-organisational efficiency of integrated business processes, resulting in a shift towards a higher degree of complexity than previously experienced. Some of these business processes are knowledge-intensive (KI), often characterised by an emergent nature and the lack of a pre-defined organisational goal. We define a functional architecture for the support of KI business processes, employing principles similar to those in risk management: measurement, analysis, assessment and feedback. The architecture makes use of organisational process experience preserved in the form of historical analyses, as well as organisational targets, in formulating assessments that can be used to support the business process instance. We illustrate the operation of our architecture with a KI business process for the preparation of customer proposals.

Keywords: Information systems, e-business, business process management, continuous process improvement, architecture, workflow.

1. Introduction

Advances in information technology have facilitated the spread of e-business practices in many industries. Such practices are being increasingly adopted in a bid to improve the inter-organisational efficiency of integrated business processes that deliver value to the end customer (Kalakota et al., 1999), (Yang, 2000), with a resulting shift towards a higher degree of complexity than previously experienced. Further complexity is introduced to an e-business process when it is knowledge-intensive (KI), since this type of process may not have a precise organisational goal nor follow a set of predefined steps towards an organisational goal as would a production process. An important aspect of KI business processes, a term that we will use throughout this paper to include KI e-business processes, is that they emerge dynamically and sometimes rapidly as new insights are gained during the interpretation and social interaction required for the creation of knowledge (Hawryskiewycz, 2000). Although they are frequently opportunistic in nature (Dourish, 1999), and may result in islands of disconnected work, they nevertheless must be supported (Debenham, 2000) towards some common organisational goal. We feel that, despite their complexity and lack of predictability, these KI business processes can be successfully supported by applying principles from risk management within a continuous process improvement (CPI) framework.

A modern enterprise engaged in KI business practices probably uses some form of IT to support their business processes. Each business process can be represented by a model, or a description of the elements involved in the process and how they interact to achieve the process goal. Process elements may include roles, artefacts and activities, among others (Hawryskiewycz, 2000). Each case in which a business process model is applied to a particular set of parameters is an instance of the process, also known as a business case (Kueng, 1997). The example described later in this paper concerns the business process for customer proposal generation, an instance of which is the generation of the proposal for Sydney Telecommunications Company (SydTel). A business process implementation system, hereafter referred to as implementation system, such as a workflow management or collaborative support system, may be provided to support the KI business process instance (BPI).

The continuous and incremental aspects of a CPI approach are particularly suitable to the emergent nature of a KI business process, providing frequent feedback to stakeholders throughout the process as it may be changing. (Kueng, 2000) characterises the functionality of his process performance measurement system, based on business process improvement principles, among others, to include the collection of identified process data, its evaluation against existing targets, and the provision of the resulting assessment to process participants. These steps are similar to those that occur in the risk management process (Standards Australia, 1999), starting with the initial establishment of the context in which the process will take place, followed by the identification, analysis and evaluation of risks, and finishing with the remediation of risks. At all stages of this cycle, outcomes are monitored, reviewed and reported to the organisation. The risk management process is designed to be applied iteratively, providing periodic feedback on the status of the organisational risks under consideration, which is consistent with the aim of steady, incremental progress under CPI.

In response to the identification of the need to support KI business processes we propose a functional architecture that applies a risk management methodology within a CPI framework to make use of organisational experience by these processes. Our architecture incorporates the high-level aspects of risk management paradigms (Greenstein et al., 1999), (Standards Australia, 1999), (Karolak, 1996) with the aim to increase the awareness of potential weaknesses in KI business processes, as well as facilitate their treatment. This proactive approach to KI business process support incorporates lessons from past experience and provides feedback on process performance compared with organisational expectations. Our architecture is designed to be applied in an iterative manner, periodically cycling through the steps of data collection, analysis and assessment in order to provide current progress information about the business process instance.

We have addressed the need for quality management in our architecture by supporting recognised standards to promote a clear understanding of the architecture, as well as to allow seamless integration with ancillary applications. These include the implementation system supporting the KI BPI, and applications for analysis and assessment. The adoption of the administration and monitoring interface of the Object Management Group's (OMG) Workflow Reference Model as explained in (OMG, 1998) would facilitate standard data collection from similarly-compliant implementation systems. Communication of the architecture and its functions within the software development community is facilitated by the use of object-oriented (OO) modelling techniques. OO techniques are a flexible means of expressing the architecture in business terms, while later translating smoothly into a software implementation (Sutherland, 1998), (OMG, 2000). For example, the use of an industry standard such as UML would allow the description of the business process and the meta-model in common terms.

The following section of this paper introduces the business process support architecture at a high level and provides an example of a KI business process for proposal generation used throughout the remainder of the paper as a means of illustrating the architecture's application. Functional detail about the architecture is then described. Our paper concludes with a discussion on future research and conclusions drawn from our work to date on this architecture.

2. Business Process Support Architecture

This section describes the functionality of our business process support architecture. An overview of its design and operation is provided, and a knowledge-intensive business process for proposal generation is introduced. Finally, each functional area of the architecture is discussed in detail, and illustrated within the context of the proposal generation process.

In selecting a paradigm after which to model the business process support architecture, those employed in the field of risk management were found to offer a common sequence of steps that address our goal of establishing status and suggesting changes to increase the success potential of the BPI. Our architecture must support the following steps: the collection of audit and performance data from the BPI; the derivation of information, through analysis of the collected data, about the BPI; the assessment of the resulting analysis; and the provision of analysis and assessment information to the implementation system.

Our resultant architecture, depicted in Figure 1, defines three major components: the business process object (BPO), which encompasses the BPI; the business process data analyser (BPDA); and the business process assessor (BPA). Data is collected about the BPI by the BPO and supplied to the BPDA, where it is processed to produce a current analysis. The BPA uses this analysis in a comparison against historical analyses of a BPI of the same process and an organisational performance target for the business process to generate an assessment. Through the BPO, the analysis and assessment are supplied to the implementation system.

It is intended that our architecture and the implementation system are tightly integrated through computerisation. This would allow the implementation system to use the analysis and assessment information to update workflow status and to make adjustments in the workflow management of the business process instance. It would automatically update process milestone dates based on analysis information, and make resource adjustments to activities based on recommendations in the assessment. However, this architecture was designed to be useful even if the technological factor is low, producing readable analyses and assessments that may be acted upon manually.

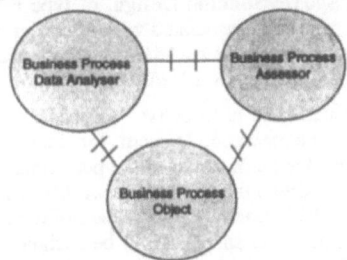

Figure 1 - Business Process Manager Architecture

To illustrate the architecture's operation, we use a KI business process for generating a customer proposal, which is described in more detail in (Slembek et al., 2000). In this process, each request for proposal (RFP) received by an organisation is evaluated by a small team of managers. If the decision is taken to submit a proposal in response to the RFP, four high-level activities must be undertaken. These include the assessment of the business opportunity, identification of the risks associated with the development and delivery of the proposed customer solution, costing and pricing of this solution, and the preparation and final review of the proposal. A cross-functional project team is formed, comprised of a bid manager, experts from relevant parts of the organisation, and any subcontractors required to develop and deliver the solution. Our example specifically concentrates on an activity from the proposal generation process instance for SydTel in which the proposed solution is designed.

2.1. Business Process Object

The BPO communicates directly with the implementation system to collect data about the BPI and to supply it with feedback upon completion of the analysis and assessment stages. The BPI may represent a single business process or a chain of business processes working together towards the same organisational goal. Our architecture allows for one instance of the BPO for each BPI. The BPO collects data about a BPI based on the process meta-model that defines the structure of the relationship between process elements as depicted in (Biuk-Aghai, 2000).

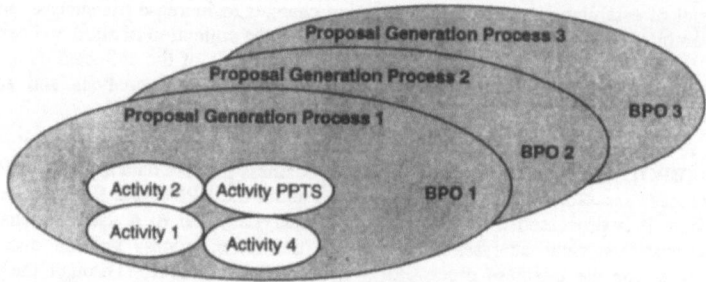

Figure 2 – Business Process Example

Our example is based on the activity "Prepare Proposal Technical Section" (PPTS), shown in Figure 2 as an activity of the Proposal Generation Process (PGP) 1. BPO 1 collects data about PPTS using the process model and organisationally-supplied communication requirements, defining the type of data to collect. Data collected may include role names and the participants assigned to them as well as audit information, such as their commencement and completion dates in the activity. Table 1 shows a sample of the data collected from PGP 1. From the Proposal Generation Process (Data) column, we see that the activity SydTel Solution Design, of type PPTS, began work on 10/8/00, completing on 1/9/00. It has one milestone associated with it, Design Complete, which had a target completion date of 30/8/00 but was completed on 28/8/00. Participant Julia has taken the role of Bid Manager, starting on 10/8/00 and finishing on 1/9/00, and so on. Dates are in dd/mm/yy format.

The other function that the BPO performs is to deliver feedback in the form of the analysis and assessment information to the implementation system for incorporation into the BPI. The implementation system may use this feedback to adjust the performance or report on the progress of the BPI. The analysis information may be used to update workflow status, while assessment may be used to make adjustments to the BPI's structure. In the case of the SydTel project, the assessment (refer to Table 3) suggests that a business analyst (BA) be assigned to the PPTS activity, as the combination of two solution architects, one bid manager and a BA proved to be the most successful instance of this activity type in the generation of the Perth Telecommunications proposal.

Data Collected	Proposal Generation Process (*Data*)
Activity Name	SydTel Solution Design
Type	PPTS
(Commencement date, Completion date)	(10/8/00, 01/9/00)
Milestone (Target date, Actual date)	Design Complete (30/8/00,28/8/00)
List of Role : participant assigned to it (creation date, completion date)	Bid Manager (BM): Julia (10/8/00, 01/9/00) Solution Architect (SA): Joanne (10/8/00, 25/8/00), Greg (14/8/00, 25/8/00)
List of Artefact name; type[1]; (creation date, completion date), role assignments [1]BKGD = background PLAN = plan WDOC = working document	Bid Proposal Template; BKGD; (03/03/00,-); BM, SA. RFP Tracking Information; BKGD; (01/8/00,-); BM, SA. Customer RFP; BKGD; (01/8/00,-); BM, SA. Bid Proposal Project Plan; PLAN; (03/8/00, 01/9/00); BM, SA. Proposal Risks; WDOC; (04/8/00, 01/9/00); BM, SA. Bid Proposal Technical; WDOC; (10/8/00, 28/8/00); BM, SA.

Table 1 - Sample of Data Collected for Proposal Generation Process (PGP)

2.2. Business Process Data Analyser

The BPDA has the primary role of creating an analysis model of the BPI. Organisationally-supplied communication requirements, defining information of interest to process stakeholders, is derived from the collected process data, using the meta-model to define the relationship between process elements. The commencement and completion dates of an activity are used to derive the duration of that activity. Similarly, the difference between the completion date and commencement date of a participant on an activity results in the duration of the actual resource assignment.

Table 2 describes some of the communication information derived during an analysis of the SydTel PGP instance, as well as that derived previously about the Perth Telecommunications PGP instance, which we will discuss during the assessment stage. The analysis yields information that establishes the duration of the SydTel PPTS activity as 17 days, and confirms that the key milestone date was achieved two days ahead of schedule. The participant assigned to the bid manager role is identified, along with the information that she has been working since the start date of the activity for a total of 17 days, and for a 12-day period prior to the completion of the key milestone date. Similar information is derived for the other two participants assigned to the activity.

Analysis	SydTel	PerTel
Activity Name Type Duration (in days) Milestone Name, Milestone Accuracy (in days)	SydTel Solution Design PPTS 17 Design Complete, -2	PerTel Solution Design PPTS 12 Design Complete, 0
List of role, participant: relative start to activity start date, relative start to key milestone, duration of participation in activity (in days)	BM, Julia: 0, 12, 17 SA, Joanne: 0, 12, 12 SA, Greg: 2, 10, 10	BM, Constantine: 0, 10, 12 SA, Anna: 0, 10, 10 SA, Anton: 0, 10, 10 BA, Theodora: 0, 10, 10

Table 2 - Sample Business Process Data Analysis

2.3. Business Process Assessor

The BPA receives the current analysis and stores it in a database with previous analyses, representing a pool of business process experience within the organisation. The BPA assesses process performance by comparing the analysis model produced by the BPDA against both historical analyses of previous process instances and an organisational performance target for the business process. A comparison of the current analysis against historical analyses aims to identify business process success factors at the activity and process levels. The second component of the assessment is carried out against an organisational performance target for the process, as defined by the organisation. The organisational performance target provides an organisationally-defined benchmark for the purposes of assessment, and is provided in the same format as a process analysis. A similar comparison is carried out against the organisational performance target for the process, with the results of the two comparisons forming the assessment for the BPI.

Using the SydTel PGP analysis, the historical portion of the assessment commences with a comparison of activities comprising the SydTel BPI with activities of the same type from the historical pool of analyses. The SydTel PPTS activity is compared against previous analyses for the same activity type, hence the importance of adherence to standard naming conventions within process models, communication requirements and organisational target performance models. The historical comparison identifies the most successful instance of the PPTS activity type as having occurred within the PerTel PGP instance.

Assessment Detail	Assessment against Historical Analyses	Assessment against Organisational Target
Activity Name	SydTel Solution Design	Solution Design Target Activity
Type	PPTS	PPTS
Assessed against	PerTel Solution Design	Proposal Generation Process Target
Date Completed	11/12/99	--
Duration delta (in days)	-3	+7
Milestone	Design Complete	Design Complete
Milestone accuracy delta (in days)	-2	+2
Delta Roles	BA lacking	BA lacking
Delta participants per role	-1 BA	-1 BA
Delta participant start dates: List of role, milestone, duration	BM, +2, +5 SA1, +2, +2 SA2, 0, 0	BM, +2, +7 SA1, +2, +2 SA2, 0, 0 BA, -10, -10
Actual, delta cost (in person-days)	39, -3	-, -1

Table 3 - Sample of Business Process Assessment Outcome

The success criteria for selecting the best match during the comparison are set by the organisation. In our SydTel example, the criteria used for activity selection was based on a successful outcome (proposal accepted by the customer) and a short duration, with a cap on resource effort of no more than 10% greater than that of the organisational target activity. The PerTel PPTS activity best matched this selection criteria, having been accomplished with a total of three roles, including bid manager (BM), solution architect (SA) and BA (refer to Table 2). The number of participants assigned to the roles of BM and SA for each activity was the same, however the SydTel PPTS did not have a participant filling the role of BA (refer to Table 3). The duration of the PerTel PPTS was five days shorter than that for SydTel, with all participants starting at the commencement of the activity. The PerTel PPTS cost 42 person-days, compared with SydTel PPTS' 39 days and falls within the 10% resource effort cap on the organisational target, which was 40 days.

The comparison of the current analysis for the SydTel PGP against the organisational performance target proceeds in a similar manner. Once the comparisons are complete, conclusions in the form of recommendations for adjustment at the activity level, in terms of process elements such as resource assignment, and at the process level, in terms of workflow, may be drawn. The SydTel PPTS activity took 7 elapsed days longer than the target although it completed with a cost of two fewer person-days. The additional duration might be attributed to the lack of the BA role, which was expected to participate for a duration of 10 days. Instead, the lack of BA was made up in effort between the BM and SA1, contributing 9 additional days between them.

The extent of the assessment will map to the level of detail specified by the communication requirements. The assessment is stored by the BPA for later use as a comparison of ongoing progress. That is, if assessments are performed weekly, a subsequent assessment may be compared with the one from the previous week to determine the remediation has been made in the intervening period. Ad hoc reports may be generated to present this information to management.

2.4. Operations of the Business Process Support Architecture

In this section, we illustrate the interaction between the three objects by a walkthrough of the two possible functional paths available through the architecture, as shown in Figure 3. We present the functions available from each object, and explain the structure and content of their arguments.

An assessment of the business process can be initiated in two ways, either from the BPO or the BPA, which is the main distinction between the two functional paths. The first path (illustrated in figure 3 as operations 1-3), is initiated by the BPO function Check_Me(*Analysis*, *Assessment*), where an argument in italics indicates the returned argument, which requests the BPA to provide the current analysis and corresponding assessment of the BPI's performance to the BPO. Upon receipt of this request, the BPA initiates the request Check(Business_Process, *Analysis*) to the BPDA to analyse the business process and to return the analysis as an argument to the function.

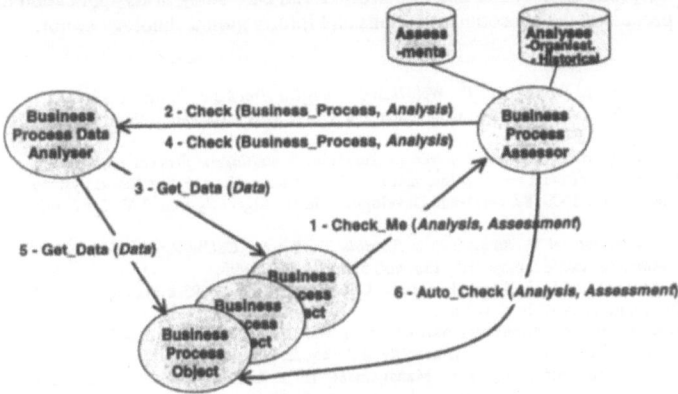

Figure 3 - Interactions between the objects

The BPDA reacts by initiating a collection of data from the BPO corresponding to the business process named in the argument Business_Process. It does this by initiating the function Get_Data(*Data*). The BPO returns the data in the argument. The BPDA performs its analysis and returns the Analysis to the BPA, at which point the BPA creates an assessment of the BPI. To close the loop, the BPA returns both analysis and assessment to the BPO, where action to incorporate information gained about the process may be initiated by the implementation system.

The second way in which an assessment can be initiated is by the BPA, rather than from the BPO, illustrated in Figure 3 by functions labelled 4-6. It may be desirable to set up a periodic assessment of the BPI from the BPA. A check of the BPI is initiated with the BPDA, which collects the appropriate data from the appropriate BPO. Once the assessment has been completed, it is provided to the BPO with the Auto_Check(*Analysis*, *Assessment*) function.

3. Conclusions and Future Directions

KI business processes are difficult to support when compared with pre-defined processes, as the path to achievement of their goal(s) depends on the outcomes of intermediate activities and is therefore not predictable. Motivated by the need to support such business processes, we have described a functional architecture that facilitates their support, drawing its operational paradigm from the area of risk management and applying it within the framework of CPI. By analysing process instance data and comparing it with analyses taken from instances of the same business process, it may be possible to formulate recommendations in the assessment that will provide useful feedback to the implementation system in terms of workflow and process structure. Throughout the paper, we employed a concrete example from e-business to illustrate the suitability of our chosen paradigm to the problem of KI business process support.

We recognise that a great deal of work needs to be done to complete our architecture. Critical to the value of the architecture to support KI business processes is the identification of valid communication requirements by process stakeholders, extending to the definition of sensitivity values for use during analysis comparison in the formulation of the assessment. Interface requirements for data collection and the importation of the meta-model, process model, and organisational performance target analysis from the implementation system, as well as the exportation of the analysis and assessment information to the implementation system must be formulated and confirmed. Finally, an approach to gaining maximum value from the organisational process memory is required.

We plan to continue to develop this architecture and to perform a full case study of its application to an integrated, KI business process in the telecommunications and information technology sector.

4. References

(Biuk-Aghai, 2000): R. Biuk-Aghai. *Virtual Workspaces for Web-Based Emergent Processes.* In the Fourth Pacific Asia Conference on Information Systems: Electronic Commerce and Web-Based Information Systems, pages 864-880, Hong Kong China, 1-3 June 2000.

(Debenham, 2000): J. Debenham. *Supporting knowledge-driven processes in a multiagent process management system.* To appear in the Proceedings of the Twentieth International Conference on Knowledge Based Systems and Applied Artificial Intelligence, ESf2000: Research and Development in Intelligent Systems XV, Cambridge UK, December 2000.

(Dourish, 1998): P. Dourish. *Using Metalevel Techniques in a Flexible Toolkit for CSCW Applications.* ACM Transactions on Computer-Human Interaction, pages 109-155, vol. 5, no. 2, June, 1998.

(Greenstein et al., 1999): M. Greenstein and T. Feinman. Electronic Commerce: Security Risk Management and Control (pre-publication edition), McGraw-Hill, New York.

(Hawryszkiewycz, 2000): I.T. Hawryszkiewycz. *Knowledge Networks in Administrative Systems* Proceedings of the Working Conference of the IFIP WG 8.5, pages 59-76, University of Zaragoza, February, 2000.

(Karolak, 1996): D. Karolak. Software Engineering Risk Management, IEEE Computer Society Press, Los Alamitos.

(Kueng, 1997): P. Kueng. *Goal-based business process models: creation and evaluation.* Business Process Management Journal, pages 17-38, vol. 3, no. 1, 1997.

(Kueng, 2000): P. Kueng. *Process performance measurement system: A tool to support process-based organizations.* Total Quality Management, pages 67-85, vol. 11, no. 1, January 2000.

(OMG, 1998): OMG. OMG BODTR RFP #2 Submission on Workflow Management Facility, document bom/98-06-07.

(OMG, 2000): OMG. *E-Business: Success on a Sound Software Architecture* in Software Magazine (http://www.omg.org/attachments/pdf/OMG.pdf)

(Kalakota, 1999): R. Kalakota and M. Robinson. e-Business: Roadmap for Success, Addison-Wesley, Reading, Massachusetts.

(Slembek et al., 2000): I.M. Slembek and I.T. Hawryszkiewycz. *The Application of a Knowledge-sharing Workspace Paradigm to e-Business Processes,* http://witiko.ifs.uni-linz.ac.at/workshop/, June 2000.

(Standards Australia, 1999): Standards Australia. AS/NZS 4360: Risk Management, Standards Association of Australia, Strathfield, NSW.

(Sutherland, 1998): J. Sutherland. *Why I Love the OMG: Emergence of a Business Object Component Architecture.* StandardView, pages 4-13, vol. 6, no. 1, March 1998.

(Yang, 2000): J. Yang and M. P. Papazoglou. *Interoperation Support for Electronic Business.* Communications of the ACM, pages 39-47, vol. 43, no. 6, June 2000.

An Anytime MultiAgent System to manage Electronic Commerce Transactions

Claude Duvallet, Bruno Sadeg and Alain Cardon

LIH, Université du Havre
Faculté des Sciences et Techniques
25, Rue Philippe Lebon
76058 Le Havre Cedex, France
E-mail:{duvallet, sadeg}@univ-lehavre.fr, cardon@iut.univ-lehavre.fr

ABSTRACT. *Electronic commerce applications are inherently distributed. They must allow actors (sellers and buyers) to trade products thanks to computer systems. These systems must be designed so as to manage distributed information systems and to allow timely negotiation between the actors. That is why decisions must be taken timely in spite of the lack of information. Furthermore, these systems use a lot of information which may be complex and difficult to analyze. So, a promizing approach is to use a multiagent system in which anytime techniques are added. In this paper, we present ANYMAS, a model of real-time multiagent systems applied to the judicious extraction of information from distributed information systems. Then, we give experimental results that show how the system may help sellers and buyers to take good decisions. We particularly show how in anytime techniques, more the time allowed to the computer system is important, more accurate are the results.*

KEY WORDS: *MultiAgents Systems, Real-Time Systems, Anytime Algorithms, Electronic Commerce.*

1. Introduction

In several applications, computer systems are used to help the decision-maker. These systems are often based on information systems which are used to extract some information about a current situation. For example, in an electronic marketplace, if we want to buy or to sell some products, we need to gather some information about the state of the market, the product stock and so on. We need also some information about the actor who proposes the transaction. All this information must be available in a simple manner in order to permit to the decision-maker to understand the situation quickly. The management of marketplaces (electronic commerce) is complex. A promised approach to manage them is to use multiagent systems [Wooldridge and Jennings, 1994] where are added real-time aspects in order to deal with the needs of the market, that is to take decisions timely about selling or buying something. These real-time aspects are often taken into account by techniques called anytime techniques. Indeed, anytime techniques allow to provide query results at any time. For example, the analysis of the criteria to determine the price of a product can take a day, a week, etc. According to each analysis duration, the result is different: more we have time to analyze the information, more the result is accurate.

The design of anytime MultiAgent System (MAS) is not so easy because we must take into account real-time aspect at both the agent level and the multiagent level. Some works have been done about anytime techniques [Dean and Boddy, 1998] [Horvitz, 1987] [Grass and Zilberstein, 1995] but few works have been done about anytime multiagent systems [Salvant and Brunessaux, 1997] [Mouaddib, 1999]. In this paper, after a brief description in section 2 of the related works, we describe, in section 3, ANYMAS model (ANYtime MultiAgent System), a model we design to take into account real-time aspects in MAS. In section 4, we illustrate ANYMAS implementation in the area of electronic commerce and we conclude by describing ANYMAS future extensions.

2. Anytime MultiAgent Systems

Real-time multiagent systems is a new domain of research which merge multiagent systems and real-time systems. These two domains are usually studied separately whereas it is needed to study them together in order to build an efficient decision aid-based system, notably in the domain of electronic marketplace management. In this section, we begin to present some features of real-time systems and anytime techniques. Then, we give a state of the art of real-time multiagent systems.

2.1 Real-Time Systems and Anytime techniques

Real-time systems are systems which are submitted to temporal constraints (deadlines, periods,...). They must be able to react timely facing the environment which they control [Stankovic and Ramamritham, 1988]. Indeed, in many computer systems tasks must be executed before certain deadlines. These tasks are called real-time tasks. One can classify these tasks according to the type of deadlines they must respect:

- soft deadlines: if a deadline is not met, the task can still continue to execute but the quality of service (QoS) offered by the system is deteriorated,
- firm deadlines: if a deadline is missed, the task associated becomes useless for the system, and it is aborted,
- hard or critical deadlines: missing a deadline leads to catastrophic consequences.

We note that transactions in electronic commerce belongs to the two last categories according to the economical consequences led by the transaction deadline missing. Classical real-time systems [Stankovic and Ramamritham, 1988] are not suited to manage some real-time applications where approximate responses obtained timely may be more useful than complete responses obtained late [Duvallet et al., 1999]. For example, in a market management application, a buyer or a seller must take a decision as earlier as possible even if he/she has not the complete information. So, a new approach, called anytime [Zilberstein, 1996] [Haddawy, 1996], has appeared which allow to build progressive solutions according to the time allowed. Indeed, anytime techniques allow the system to provide useful partial results at any time.

2.2 Real-time in MultiAgent Systems

Anytime approach is widely used to take into account real-time in MAS [Salvant and Brunessaux, 1997] [Duvallet et al., 1999] because in a lot of applications managed by MAS the timeliness of a result is privileged, whereas the quality of the result may be altered. Indeed, in applications like market management or process control, we have not always enough time to wait for a complete result in order to take a decision. This kind of applications can be qualified as hard real-time applications. In classical hard real-time applications, we need to know the worst case execution time if we want to design it. In applications based on multiagent systems, it is difficult to know the execution's time of a task. That is why we have chosen anytime techniques to design our system. Some works exist about real-time multiagent systems using anytime techniques. Salvant et al. [Salvant and Brunessaux, 1997] designed an anytime agent architecture composed of four components: tasks monitor, domain tasks, real-time clock and computing resources. However, the real-time aspect is not taken into account at the system level.

Occello et al. [Occello and Demazeau, 1994] use an architecture based on a blackboard system in order to build real-time agents. This approach seems to be too restrictive in comparison with possibilities of agent architectures [Wooldridge and Jennings, 1994]. Most of current works are concentrated on real-time implementation at agent level. The model we present, ANYMAS, deals with implementation both at the agent level and at the interaction one and at the organization one.

In the next section, we present ANYMAS, a MAS model where anytime approach is used to implement real-time aspects in order to manage applications where partial results obtained timely may be more useful that complete results obtained late, i.e., decisions taking in electronic commerce [Duvallet et al., 1999].

3. ANYMAS model

ANYMAS architecture is composed of anytime agents which belong partially to a component-based architecture [Guessoum and Briot, 1997] where some improvements are done. We add an introspection component to the initial agent architecture in order to allow agents to predict the time needed to execute tasks. This component may modify dynamically previous predictions if necessary (if there is not enough time to terminate execution). A task being composed of subtasks, an agent's celerity compute subtasks necessary-time. To this purpose, agents can create temporal co-ordination agents, called reification of a temporal co-ordination agent, used to reduce communications between agents since the MAS execution is tightly dependent on the communications between agents. Furthermore, according to the available time, it might be interesting to influence the behaviour of agents so that the system can provide useful partial results. Therefore, in ANYMAS, we discard some groups of agents and we encourage other groups that are well-suited to get an exploitable result. In summary, to control the duration of system's execution, it is necessary to control the interactions between groups of agents. This control is done by temporal co-ordination agents.

3.1 Anytime techniques

The term "anytime" was coined by Dean et al. in the late 1980s [Dean and Boddy, 1998] in the context of his work on time-dependant planning. Anytime algorithms are algorithms whose quality of results improve gradually as computational time increases, hence they offer a trade-off between resource consumption and output quality. This technique is particularly appropriated in the context of artificial intelligence in order to take into account the real-time aspect of computer-aid based systems. The quality of a result is represented by performance profiles as it is shown in figure 1 where x axis represent the time and y axis represent the quality of the result.

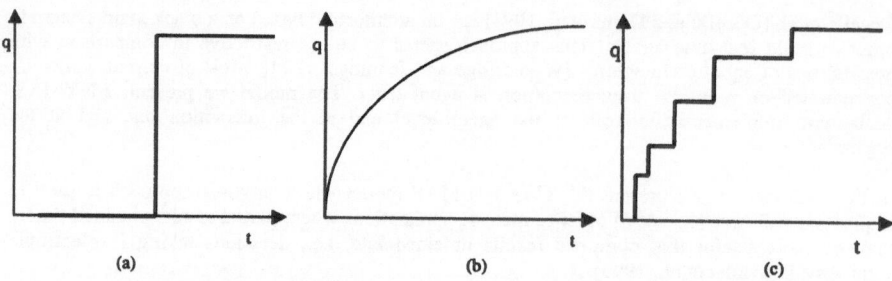

Figure 1: Typical performance profile (quality of result q according to the time allowed t): (a) classical algorithm (b) Idealized anytime algorithm (c) Actual anytime algorithm

We apply anytime techniques in the design of agents and multiagent systems in order to build Anytime MultiAgent Systems.

3.2 The proposed model

ANYMAS model is composed of anytime agents based on an Augmented Transition Network (ATN) which is used to allow the system to stabilise agents in different states. Each ATN's state corresponds to a step of the anytime algorithm (executed by the anytime agent) where an exploitable partial result may be provided. An anytime agent execute a transaction with initial global deadline, which is then subdivided into steps where partial results may be provided. In an anytime agent, we define agent's celerity as its capacity and its speed to build a result. These notions allow to measure agent performances (see section 4). In the multiagent system where ANYMAS is implemented, we consider two modes of execution: training mode and working mode. During the training mode, agent's speed is constantly computed in order to get an average value of successive speeds, whereas in working mode it only uses these values to compute the necessary-time to execute the next transaction. These average time values computed during training mode are discretized in a unit of time at the end of this mode. This construction is made in the following way:

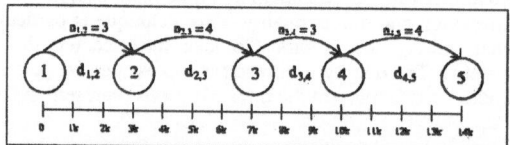

Figure 2: Example of discretization of time in ANYMAS

Given an ATN with n states (see figure 2, where n is set to 5), $d_{i,i+1}$ ($1 \leq i \leq n-1$) is the transition duration between state i and state i+1; Let a variable k be the time subdivision and $n_{i,i+1}$ the number of k subdivisions between states i and i+1.
Therefore, we obtain the following equation:

$$d_{i,i+1} = k * n_{i,i+1}, where\ i = 1,2,3,... \Rightarrow k = \frac{d_{i,i+1}}{n_{i,i+1}}$$

For example, in figure 2, we obtain:

$$k = \frac{d_{1,2}}{n_{1,2}} = \frac{d_{2,3}}{n_{2,3}} = \frac{d_{3,4}}{n_{3,4}} = \frac{d_{4,5}}{n_{4,5}}$$

The number of subdivisions for the first interval being set, an algorithm (see figure 3) allows to determine (1) the value of the k variable and (2) the time subdivisions between states. ε is a variable providing a degree of time precision allowed. K value represents the computed unit value which measures the transition time between two successive states of the ATN.

```
Input: N = number of states ;
       the values d_{i,i+1} where 1 ≤ i ≤ N
Output: K the value of a computed unit of time
        the values n_{i,i+1} where 1 ≤ i ≤ N

n_{1,2} ←1
i ←1
K ← 0
Last_State ← false
WHILE ( (|d_{i,i+1} - K * n_{i,i+1}|> ε ) AND NOT(Last_State))
      i ←1
      n_{1,2} ← n_{1,2} + 1
      K ← round (d_{i,i+1} / n_{i,i+1})
      WHILE ( (|d_{i,i+1} - K * n_{i,i+1}| < ε ) AND NOT(Last_State))
            i ← i + 1
            IF (i = N) THEN
                  Last_State ← true
            ELSE
                  d_{i,i+1} ← d_{i,i+1}+ d_{i-1,i} - K * n_{i-1,i}
                  n_{i,i+1} ← round (d_{i,i+1} / k)
            END IF
      END WHILE
END WHILE
```

Figure 3: Discretization time algorithm

The algorithm is implemented in Java. Simulation results (see figure 4) illustrate how the algorithm determines the K value (during the training mode) which is used as a unit of time during execution mode in order to go from step i (where a partial result is available) to step i+1 (where a better partial result is available) (see Figure 5). These experimentation show that the algorithm behaviour is compliant to our expectations. In summary, based on slack time's execution, the goal of the algorithm is to evaluate agent's celerity in order to determine whether or not the execution will be terminated before deadline. This outlines the ANYMAS predictive aspect.

State i	State i+1	Time (ms)	Time (K units)
1	2	10556	2640
2	3	20173	5043
3	4	54043	1361
4	5	34256	8564
5	6	29654	7413
=>Value of K : 4			

Figure 4: Simulation of the algorithms ATN's states

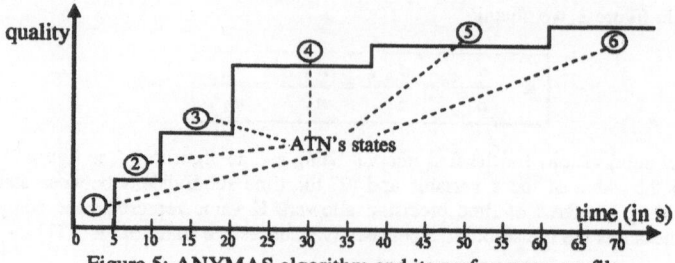

Figure 5: ANYMAS algorithm and its performance profile

4. Anytime extraction of information in a marketplace

In order to validate ANYMAS model, an application of marketplace management is used (cf. figure 6). In an electronic marketplace, actors use a computer system to buy and sell objects, say firms. When a seller wants to sell a firm, he proposes his price to the other actors of the electronic marketplace.

In order to know the moment to buy the firm, a buyer need to have some information about the firm (for example its number of employees, its economic situation) and about the seller (seriousness, ...). To help the buyer to take his/her decision, we have designed a computer system (electronic marketplace) which has to extract the information needed by the buyer to take the good decision. The concurrency of the other actors require the buyer to take the decision as earlier as possible even if he/she does not have the whole information needed to take the best decision. So, the computer system must be able to give him/her the maximum amount of information as possible in a minimum amount of time.

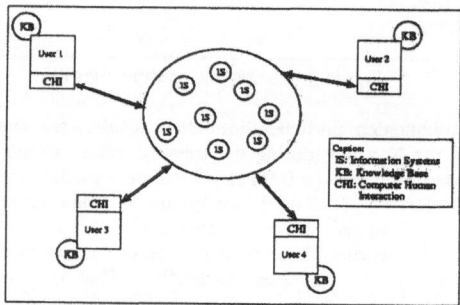

Figure 6: Multi-users marketplace management

In our electronic marketplace (see figure 6), we use several information systems to store information about firms (employees, financial aspects, position on the marketplace, geographical situation), and information about actors, in the form of Oracle databases. Users use a computer system (which is based on ANYMAS model) which communicates with the distributed information systems through the JDBC (Java DataBase Connectivity) interface. Moreover, our computer system is based on a multiagent system in order to extract, analyse and filter the information which are available in the information systems. The user sends a query to the information systems represented by a distributed Oracle database. This query is taken into account by ANYMAS algorithm which provides an answer whose quality depends on the time specified by the user. For example, the user receives only few tuples at time t and he receives more tuples at time t+Δ. This application was implemented using the MadKit platform [Gutknecht and Ferber,1997] where we have had to increase agent functionalities. As we can see in the figure 7, an ATN, a clock and a function of discretization are added to the initial structure of the agent. We note that the instropection component was implemented with an ATN and a discretization function.

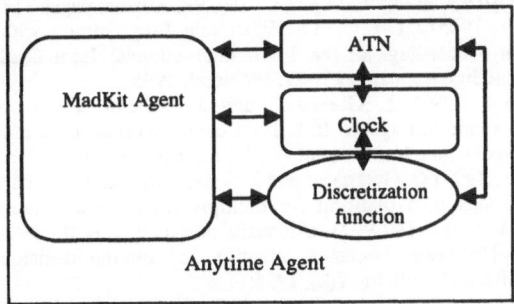

Figure 7. Construction of an anytime agent with MadKit

The anytime agents are used to extract information from distributed information systems. More the time allowed to the query, more precise the results or more quantities of information we can retrieve. The anytime agents of ANYMAS are used to extract intelligently information from distributed information systems.

5. Conclusion and future work

In this paper, we have presented ANYMAS model designed to take into account real-time aspects in multiagent systems. This model based on anytime techniques allows to construct real-time complex applications. We have chosen to implement ANYMAS model an electronic marketplace application.

This application has allowed to validate a part of the ANYMAS model. An extended version of the marketplace is being currently implemented in the context of a system used to help users to make their transactions (sell and buy products) in the best conditions. Our perspective is to implement ANYMAS model in hard real-time application [Stankovic and Ramamritham, 1988], that is, in sirens'manager system of a town (Le Havre, France).

Indeed, ANYMAS needs to be completed in order to take into account emergence aspects in anytime component of multiagent systems. Other aspects need to be detailed or completed (anytime query manager, RT-MAS design methodologies, time constraints specification, ...).

An other aspect of our work is to use distributed multiagent systems in order to build a computer aid based system working on either wired or wireless networks. Therefore, in wireline networks we can use the CORBA norm [OMG, 1995] to distribute ANYMAS multiagent system. In wireless networks, one may use system's agents with adapted anytime algorithms in order to alleviate the problem of frequent disconnection of the network. Indeed, each agent must define steps where it may provide useful partial results according to the network disconnection frequency and duration.

128

References:

[Dean and Boddy, 1998] T. Dean and M. Boddy. Solving time-dependant planning problems. In Proceedings of the 7 th National Conference of Arti_cial Intelligence, pages 419_454, Minneapolis, Minnesota, 1988.

[Duvallet and al., 1999] C. Duvallet, B. Sadeg, and A. Cardon. Real-time in multi-agents systems. In Proceeding of CAINE'99, Atlanta, pages 212_215, 1999.

[Grass and Zilberstein, 1995] J. Grass and S. Zilberstein. Programming with anytime algorithms. In Proceedings of the 14 th Internationnal Joint Conference on Artificial Intelligence, pages 22--27, Montreal, 1995.

[Guessoum and Briot, 1997] Z. Guessoum and J.-P. Briot. From concurrent objects to autonomous agents. In 8 th European Workshop on Modelling Autonomous Agents in a Multi-Agent World, Ronneby, 1997.

[Gutknecht and Ferber,1997] O. Gutknecht and J. Ferber. Madkit: Organizing heterogeneity with groups in a platform for multiple multi-agent systems. Technical report, LIRMM, UMR 9928, Université de Montpellier II, 1997.

[Haddawy, 1996]P. Haddawy. Focusing attention in anytime decision-theoretic planning. SIGART Bulletin, 7(2), 1996.

[Horvitz, 1987]E. Horvitz. Reasonning about beliefs and actions under computational resource constraints. In Proceedings of the Workshop on Uncertainty in Artificial Intelligence, Seattle, Washington, 1987.

[Mouaddib, 1999]A. Mouaddib. Anytime coordination for progressive planning agents. In Proceedings of the Sixteenth National Conference on Arti_cial Intelligence and Eleventh Conference on Innovative Applications of Artificial Intelligence, pages 564--569, Orlando, Florida, 1999. AAAI Press / The MIT Press.

[Occello and Demazeau, 1994] M. Occello and Y. Demazeau. Building real time agent using parallel blackboards and its use for mobile robotics. In IEEE International Conference on Systems, Man and Cybernetics, San Antonio, 1994.

[OMG, 1995] OMG. The common object request broker: Architecture and specification. In OMG TC Document 95-7-X, July 1995.

[Salvant and Brunessaux, 1997] T. Salvant and S. Brunessaux. Multi-agent based time-critical decision support for c31 systems. In Practical Applications of Intelligent Agents and Multi-Agents, PAAM, London, 1997, 1997.

[Stankovic and Ramamritham, 1988] J. Stankovic and K. Ramamritham. Hard real-time systems: a tutorial. IEEE Computer Society Press, 1988.

[Wooldridge and Jennings, 1994] M. Wooldridge and N. Jennings. Agent theories, architectures and language : A survey. In M. Wooldridge and N. Jennings, editors, Intelligent Agents, ECAI 1994, volume LNAI 890, pages 1--32. Springer Verlag, 1994.

[Zilberstein, 1996] S. Zilberstein. Resource-bounded sensing and planning in autonomous systems. Autonomous Robots, 3:31--48, 1996.

MODELLING AND DESIGN
ISSUES II

TINA-ODL and Component Based Design

J. Fischer, O. Kath

Humboldt University Berlin, Dept. of Computer Science
Rudower Chaussee 5, 10099 Berlin, Germany
kath@informatik.hu-berlin.de

M. Born

GMD Fokus
Kaiserin-Augusta-Allee 31, 10589 Berlin, Germany
born@fokus.gmd.de

Abstract - Advanced design methods are needed to fulfill the increasing requirements of telecommunication service development. For a design method the relevant concepts for the application domain have to be defined, a supporting notation has to be declared and finally rules have to be developed to map design models to supporting runtime environments.
The TINA-Consortium has made the attempt to define a concept space for the design of distributed telecommunication applications (Computational Modelling Concepts) and a supporting notation for these concepts (TINA-ODL). In this contribution we will show how ODL can serve as a starting point for the definition of a component-based design method which overcomes limitations and restrictions of the ODL language. Furthermore, a language mapping to the SDL-2000 language is presented.

Keywords: Service Design, Computational Object, Component, Interaction, Behavior Specification, Language Mapping

1. Introduction

A dedicated and efficient design methodology contributes significantly to a reduction of the time to market distributed applications and telecommunication services. An appropriate treatment of all kinds of communication aspects lies in the very nature of the targeted application domain. These aspects span from functional requirements (e.g. transactionality) on object interactions over quality of service issues to security properties. Taking into account the broad acceptance of object middleware technology, middleware platforms provide an ideal implementation environment for such designs, so the design method should take this into account.

A design method normally consists of 3 separate parts:

- A concept space which contains all relevant entities, the information needed to describe them and relations between these entities,

• A notation in order to specify models using the elements of the concept space and
• Rules how models can be mapped onto target middleware technology.

The TINA community has taken up this general concept with the definition of its computational modelling concepts [15] and the supporting notation Object Definition Language (ODL) [16]. By doing so, it has defined key concepts necessary for the design of distributed telecommunication applications which are Computational Objects (COs) communicating via well defined interfaces. Interfaces are described in terms of signatures which define the interaction elements for the possible interactions an CO instance may participate in. ODL distinguishes between operational and stream interactions. However, ODL was designed to be technology independent and therefore no language mappings to implementation languages have been defined. This fact together with the absence of supporting tools prevented a broad usage of ODL outside the TINA community.

In 1996 the International Telecommunication Union (ITU) started a standardization process to define an own Object Definition Language based on the TINA-ODL concepts. This initiative resulted in recommendation Z.130, published in 1999 [10]. Part of this recommendation are language mappings to C++ and to the ITU language SDL [12] which can be used to specify the behavior of COs based on the concept of extended finite state machines. However, the SDL language version available at this time did not allow a straightforward mapping and many proposals for SDL improvement have been issued to the ITU. Since March 2000 a new SDL version is available.

In this paper we concentrate on two major contributions:
• Definition of a language mapping from ODL to SDL-2000 which overcomes the restrictions of the mapping defined in [10].
• Proposal for a design method based on ODL but with significant extensions of the concept space and with the introduction of a complete graphical notation.

It is expected, that the ITU in the ongoing development of ODL will update the language mapping to SDL as proposed here and possibly also take the new concepts of the design method into account for the next generation of ODL.

As the result of these two contributions the situation would be as depicted in Fig. 1:

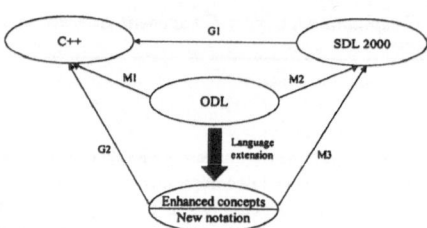

Fig. 1   Mapping and code generation scheme for ODL

2. ODL and Behavior Descriptions

Since ODL describes structures and signatures of the application only, there are two ways to cover the semantics of them. The traditional one is to step directly into the implementation. In order to support this, there is a need for a language mapping from ODL into the used implementation language in order to make use of the specified structure and signature information. Such a language mapping to C++ has been developed and is part of Z.130 (M1 in Fig. 1).

Though the way of directly mapping of ODL to the implementation language is the most common method, another approach is needed in order to allow validation of the applications behavior before its implementation and to perform automated code generation and testing. That is to provide a computational behavior description for the COs. This behavior description should be an abstract one since in most cases only the externally visible behavior should be specified, without prescribing any implementation details. SDL is a convenient candidate language to do that, if the behavior of the COs can be expressed with state machines. If the behavior cannot adequately expressed with state machines, other languages should be selected.

As already mentioned, Z.130 already contains a mapping to SDL-92, but the application of this mapping is not straightforward. This is due to the following SDL- 92 restrictions:

• No nested package concept to support nested namespaces.
• No interface concept.
• No exception definition and exception handling concept.
• Insufficient data concept which implies the need for ASN.1 usage.
• Insufficient structural concepts for behavior providing entities.

These restrictions are overcome with the SDL-2000 version. In the following, we present mapping rules from ODL to SDL-2000 which apply new concepts of the SDL language (M2 in Fig. 1). We concentrate on those aspects which differ from the language mapping defined in Z.130.

Name scopes in ODL are provided by the definition of modules. Modules are mapped to packages in SDL where nested modules become nested packages. Entities defined in the packages can be referred from the outside by use package declarations and qualified names. There is no need to use full names in identifiers as it was necessary before. Since interfaces in ODL can contain local definitions, there is a package definition in SDL which contains all local defined entities of the ODL interface definition and that is defined in the same scope as the interface itself with the same name as the interface definition. This is allowed in SDL since interfaces and packages are not of the same entity kind.

Data types of ODL can be mapped to SDL data types as follows:

• Simple types are defined in an SDL package named ODL as SDL data types inheriting from predefined SDL types like Integer or Boolean.
• Constructed data types (structs, unions) are defined as SDL types containing structs or choices.
• Sequences are mapped to SDL vector types (if bounded) or Powersets (if unbounded).
• Arrays are mapped to SDL vector types.
• Typdefs are mapped to syntypes in SDL.

Exceptions are directly mapped to SDL exception definitions. The only difference is, that the names of the exception members are not relevant in SDL and are omitted.

Operational interface definitions in ODL are mapped to SDL interface definitions containing the interaction elements as defined in the ODL interface signature. Operations are mapped to remote procedures at the SDL interface, exceptions can be declared as raised by the remote procedure. Explicit remote declarations are not necessary. Oneway operations are just defined as signals at the SDL interface. Attributes are mapped to a pair of get- and set-remote procedures, where the set-remote procedure is only present, if the attribute is not declared as being read only.

As already mentioned, local definitions (data types, exceptions and constants) in the interface are mapped onto appropriate definitions in a package with the interface name in the same scope as the interface definition itself.

In SDL-2000 interfaces define a sort of type PId which is used as references for the interface. There is no need to map interfaces to a special PId sort explicitly.

COs are defined as capsules for state and behavior. For that reason, CO definitions in ODL are mapped to SDL agent types of kind block, which are behavior providing entities in SDL. However, SDL allows only single inheritance for agents. So, if the ODL specification contains multiple inheritance for contained COs, this inheritance must be flattened beforehand.

It is assumed, that the ITU will prohibit local definitions for COs, so there is no need to map them to SDL. The block type definition contains three gate definitions: One gate is named „initial" and is defined with the initial interface, the second is named „supported" and is defined with all supported interfaces of the CO and the third is named „required" and is defined with all required interfaces of the CO. The SDL block type definition contains already a state machine which is bound to the gate providing the initial interface of the CO. An important factor for the application of the ODL SDL combination is the presence of tools. In the past tools for a realization of the mapping have been developed and applied in different projects.

Currently, the development of a tool which realizes the mapping is on the way. Tools supporting SDL-2000 itself and the code generation to C++ will be available soon (G1 in Fig. 1) [11].

3. From ODL to Components

Component-oriented design of distributed applications is a non-trivial task. Many different aspects of applications have to be considered in the design phase. ODL is a suitable starting point to describe the structure and signatures of these applications but there are a lot of aspects which are not covered by ODL and need further study. Besides the non-presence of behavioral features, for which a possible solution was presented in section 2., missing concepts further include but are not restricted to:

- Instances of interfaces and how they are accessible at instances of COs,
- Structures of implementations of COs and association of elements of interface signatures to the implementations which realize them,
- Bindings between interfaces of COs and rules for those bindings,
- Quality of services (QoS) description types and QoS requirements as part of binding rules,
- Requirements components may have on the environment into which they will be deployed.

To cover these aspects we have developed a design method which is based on the concepts of ODL but overcomes the restrictions mentioned above. The concepts of this design method are structured into views to ease its application.

The *structural view* focuses on the modeling of the types forming a distributed application. These are mainly types of COs which have relations to interfaces. Interfaces can be supported or required by COs. Interfaces define the signature of possible interactions a CO may involved in. There are three relevant interaction kinds: operational, signal and continuos media interaction which consists of interaction elements operations, attributes, signals and exchangeable media sets. All interaction kinds can be combined at one interface from a modeling perspective. In addition data types, types to express Quality of Service (QoS) constraints and media types can be specified. The structural view concepts are known from ODL except for signals, QoS-types, media types and the fact, that all three interaction kinds can be defined in the scope

Instances of COs support instances of interfaces at well defined named ports (similar to the CORBA Component Model (CCM)) [5]. This is modeled in the *instance view*. A definition of a port results in operations which allow to obtain or to store interface references at runtime. In contrast to CCM, the ports can be declared either as single ports or multiple ports where at a multiple port multiple references to interfaces can be registered or obtained.

To support the developer of the application components, the *implementation view* allows to specify which artifacts (classes in object-oriented implementation languages) are responsible for certain interaction elements of interfaces supported by a CO. This specification is similar to a Component Implementation Definition Language (CIDL) [5] specification of CCM, but it is allowed to have interaction elements of a single interface realized by different artifacts. In addition, the association between interaction elements and artifacts realizing them also indicates the part of the state information of the CO which is necessary for the implementation of the interaction element by the artifact.

COs can be bound together via their interfaces. Those bindings can be specified and rules for the interactions which occur via the binding can be declared. Such rules allow to specify security or transaction policies as well as performance or reliability requirements. The *interaction view* specification allows to distinguish certain conditions under which bindings are established., e.g. the security policy may be different if a client connects to a server from the intranet or the internet.

The artifacts which realize the behavior of a CO are physically contained by components. Hence, such components may have certain requirements on the environment into which they will be deployed. The *deployment view* supports the definition of those requirements. Examples are the required co-location with other components or the specification of necessary main storage on the target host.

The concepts above form the concept space of our design method. However, to be used by application developers there must be a suitable notation supporting the concepts. From the experiences made with ODL, there is also the requirement to have:

- A graphical syntax for the notation since this increases the acceptance of the design method by the users and decreases their learning curve,
- Rules for generation of implementation language code out of the design models, and tools which support the design method as well as the code generation.

The Unified Modeling Language (UML) [6] seems to be powerful enough to express all concepts introduced. This is mainly due to the fact, that the UML Core Model can be extended by restrictions on the use of modeling elements for a specific purpose. This mechanism is named profiling. The Object Management Group as the standardization body

for UML and for the Common Object Request Broker Architecture (CORBA) [7] currently makes use of this mechanism in order to standardize a UML profile for CORBA. However, this profile will be not sufficient for all required design information of distributed applications, because
- it obviously does not abstract from the concrete platform technology the application will be running on, i.e. CORBA,
- it only covers structural aspects of COs and interfaces the application is being made of, and
- it is restricted to the interaction kinds supported by CORBA.

To provide a notation for our concept space we have developed a UML profile which goes beyond the OMG CORBA profile and supports all necessary design concepts. This profile and the notation which is defined by it can be seen as a direct successor of ODL. Furthermore, we have also defined mapping rules to show, how design models can be transformed into code fragments for specific target middleware platforms (G2 in Fig. 1). The profile and the code generation rules are explained in [4]. A tool supporting the profile is under development, the first prototype based on the commercial UML tool Rational Rose is up and running.

3.1 Example Specification

Models, that were built using the design principles presented above, include a set of information regarding external and internal view on COs structure and their behavior, that can be considered to form a complete CO definition. Most design tools, that support a design method for distributed objects based software development end up supporting the developer at this stage. Our approach includes mapping strategies to component aware as well as component unaware middleware platform technologies. Component awareness here addresses the platform capabilities to support aggregation and deployment of software pieces that form building blocks for distributed applications. The CORBA Component Model (CCM) [5] forms one candidate for such a platform. Component unawareness on the other hand means, that the platform technology supports a number of transparencies with regard to interactions between distributed objects, but doesn't provide a model of aggregating such distributed objects to deployable, identifiable components with implementation composition support. A platform that is made of CORBA 2.3 compliant products is an example for such a technology. Due to its most advanced state of realization, we focus here on the task to represent concepts of our design method in a purely CORBA 2.3 based environment.

The aspects of notation and code generation according to the design method we present here will be introduced using a hypothetical task which has to be fulfilled by a service designer summarized as follows:

„An Interactive TV Service component shall be developed which provides a number of channels to clients. The channels combine audio and video data. The are two special channels, an advertisement channel and an initial channel, where all programs are for free. The service component shall be able to receive input from its clients in form of joystick and mouse events. The client component for this station shall also be designed, it must be able to receive the channels and to provide the mouse and joystick events which trigger some changes in the received channel. There has to be a possibility to obtain the actual costs for an ongoing connection of a channel. If the client and the server are not in the same domain, security to get this information is to be ensured."

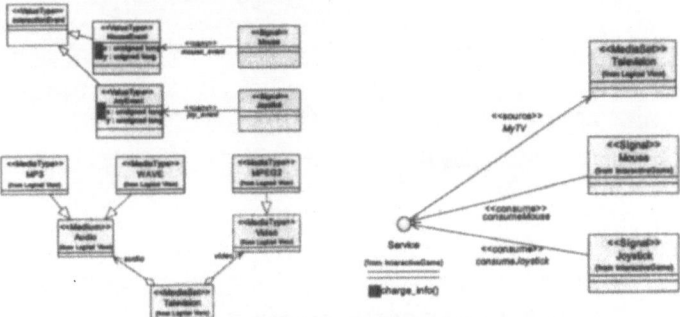

Fig. 2   Interaction elements for interface Service

Fig. 2 shows the interface service, which is defined for the TV example. This interface defines the concrete set of interaction elements for that example. As to be seen, the interaction elements are defined using some elementary definitions like data types or media types. It is the intension that those elementary definitions will be part of predefined packages which can be used for a particular design model. Especially for signal and continuous media communication those packages will be shipped together with supporting hardware, e.g. a Joystick comes together with a design model containing a description of the events it generates.

Given the definition of the interface service, the structural view onto COs can be defined. Fig. 3 specifies two CO types, one representing a client object, that may require the services provided at interfaces of type service, while the other provides such services.

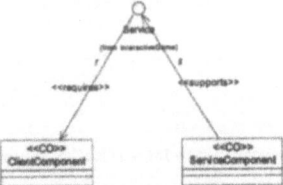

Fig. 3   Requires and supports relations

The concepts of the structural view define, *which* services a CO may provide via its interfaces or which services it may use at interfaces of other COs. The concepts of the instance view define, *how* instances of a CO provide such services via instances of its supported interfaces or *how* a CO instance makes use of the services provided by another component instance. The corresponding term within the concept space is port of a CO, which may be either single port or multiple port.

In order to identify the ports of a component, they must have unique names in the scope of the component. In Fig. 4, ports for the serviceComponent of the TV Service example are declared.

138

One port (channels) is a multiple port, the others are single ports. Similar declarations are done on the client side for the required interface.

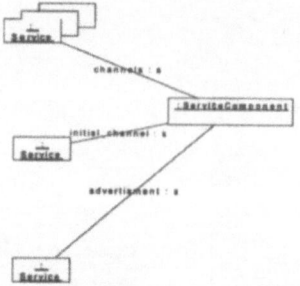

Fig. 4   Instance view for ServiceComponent

From the perspective of "black box modeling" the structural and instance view would form a sufficient minimal set of definitions of a CO. However, as motivated before, the design method leads to an implementation and therefore some internal aspects of a component implementation are covered that realizes a COs behavior. In the TV Service example, the implementation of the ServiceComponent is structured into artifacts as to be seen in Fig. 5:

Fig. 5   Implementation view for ServiceComponent

As already mentioned, there is an implicit interface for each CO were attributes and operations are provided. To implement those interaction elements, there shall be an artifact (a1) which is associated with the component directly. This special case is also to be seen in the figure.

3.2 Code Generation Aspects

Generally, concepts of the design method not only map to definitions of interfaces that are supported by a particular component, but also to implementation language specific code skeletons of implementation artifacts, descriptions of the state of such artifacts and programming language specific code that form the runtime environment for a component instance. In particular, the CORBA Interface Definition Language (IDL) is used as a platform specific mapping target for the concepts of the structural view. An interface that is required or supported by a component of the design model maps to a set of IDL-interfaces, that support the different interaction kinds defined for the interface in the model. The resulting IDL interface definitions for a component's supported or required interfaces are referred to as implied interfaces. Beside the mapping to IDL interfaces, model elements are added to the design model, that are refined during the definition of the component implementation. The definitions of the instance view extend the implied interfaces definition by a platform view onto the CO itself, i.e. interfaces are generated that represent the CO and its ports. Also these definitions are provided through code generation as IDL interface definitions.

The concepts of the implementation view provide a model of a composition of artifacts that implement the services provided by a component via its interfaces. The platform specific mapping targets to implementation language definitions that represent the defined composition. To support this representation, the delegation design pattern [17] is applied to the mapping, and realized by delegating classes that couple the CORBA runtime system and the implementation artifacts. Through this approach, the realization of the component behavior is de-coupled from the actual activation procedures for the implementation artifacts. The flexibility of this approach also allows the implementation class definition to be independent from the implied interface definition, in a way that an implementation artifact can implement only parts of the services that are provided through the defined interfaces. The implementation view also allows to assign persistency information to implementation artifacts. To represent this, the recently adopted Persistent State Service specification [8] is applied, and the Persistent State Description Language (PSDL) defined there is used to represent persistent state information of implementation artifacts.

The concepts of the binding view describe specific binding cases between component instances. A platform that is based on CORBA doesn't provide a view on the binding of objects, but provides hooks, were a so called ORB service can be plugged into, that e.g. may provide a binding negotiation service integrated with the ORB. The Portable Interceptors (PI) specification [9] defines such hooks in a portable way, i.e. interceptor implementations can be integrated with different ORB products in a portable manner. The PI technology, together with servant management capabilities of the Portable Object Adaptor (POA), is used to negotiate the binding case as specified by the binding view, and to negotiate the actual binding policies according to the constraints given by the model.

Whereas for the operational and signal based interaction kinds, standard CORBA mechanisms are used as a platform mapping target, the elements of the design model, that regard continuous media interactions, are mapped onto a proprietary multimedia content composition and delivery platform. Within the scope of that platform, multimedia content composition is treated as a process of describing a structure, how media are presented to a consumer. This process is modeled as a composition of meta information on media (content description), were the media data themselves may be distributed over a network. Such meta information regard the content of the medium itself as well as the properties of its physical representation. Such a content description is taken as input to the content delivery task of the platform, that calculates a plan for the delivery of referenced media (content schedule) and delivers media data according to it in a quality of delivery adoptive way. The platform architecture conceptually supports the distinction between logical media flows and physical media data transmission as well as the openness to specific network and media presentation technologies. The platform concepts are prototypically implemented in a CORBA 2.3 environment and are presented in more detail in [2].

4. Conclusion and the Future

By the introduction of refined modelling concepts for structural, instantiation, interaction and implementation aspects, ODL originally defined by TINA-C can be extended to a language which can be used for a component-oriented design of distributed applications. The practical importance of that approach results from its orientation to existing technologies like CORBA and EJB. The concrete syntactic representation of the extended ODL concepts can be easily expressed in UML. To support this an UML profile was developed. This and also a mapping to SDL-2000 was already contributed to the further ITU-T standardization process of ODL.

Further we found that the existing recommendation Z.109 [13] which defines an UML profile for SDL is not convenient for the mapping of the enhanced ODL (syntactically expressed in UML) to SDL-2000. The reason for that are differences in the main goals. Z.109 recommends a definition of the UML to SDL mapping for the use in the combination of UML and SDL and for a two-way transformation. Our new ideas of an ODL-SDL mapping, which are focused on a structural equivalent mapping use the new concepts of SDL-2000 (like interface, nested packages and exceptions). Our proposals were already warmly accepted by ITU-experts.

Smooth transition from the design models to a concrete implementation environment are presented. Although being not yet conform to the UML standard the extensibility mechanism of Rational Rose can be applied for the implementation of our profile and of the transformation rules thereby ensuring the applicability of the methodology for real-life development projects.

References

[1]   Born, Hoffmann, Li, Schieferdecker: *"Combining Design Methods for Services Development"*; Proc. of FMOODS '99
[2]   Kath, Takita: *"OMG A/V Streams and TINA NRA: An integrative Approach"*; Proc. of TINA '99
[3]   Fischbeck, Fischer, Holz, Kath, v. Löwis, Schröder: *Improving the Development and Validation of Viewpoint Specifications*; Proc. of FMOODS '97
[4]   Born, Kath: *„Code Generation for Component based Telecommunication Service Development"*, Proceedings of SoftCom2000
[5]   BEA Systems et. al.: *"CORBA Components - Volume I"*; OMG doc. orbos/99-07-01
[6]   OMG: *"OMG Unified Modeling Language Specification, Version 1.3"*; OMG doc. ad/99-06-08
[7]   OMG: *"The Common Object Request Broker: Architecture and Specification, Revision 2.3.1"*; OMG doc. formal/99-10-07
[8]   OMG: *Persistent State Service 2.0*; OMG doc. orbos/99-07-07
[9]   BEA Systems et. al.: *Portable Interceptors*, OMG doc. orbos/99-12-02
[10] ITU-T: *Recommendation Z.130: The ITU-T Object Definition Language*, 1999
[11] http://www.informatik.hu-berlin.de/SITE
[12] ITU-T: *Recommendation Z.100*, 2000
[13] ITU-T: *Recommendation Z.109*, 2000
[14] ITU-T: Rec. X.903/X.904 | ISO/IEC 10746-3/-4: 1995, Open Distributed Processing - Reference Model Part 3/4.
[15] TINA-C: *„Computational Modelling Concepts"*, Version 3.3.0, 1997
[16] TINA-C: *„Object Definition Language"*, Version 2.3, 1997
[17] Gamma, Helm, Johnson, Vlissides: *Elements of Reusable Object-Oriented Software*; Addison-Wesley '99
[18] Szyperski: *„Component Software"*, Addison Wesley, 1999

Objects@Work

- An Activity Theoretical Framework for OO Modelling of Computer Mediated Cooperative Activities

Ole Smørdal

Department of Informatics
University of Oslo
PO Box 1080, Blindern N-0316 OSLO
E-mail: ole.smordal@ifi.uio.no

ABSTRACT: *The roles of computer systems in modern organisations are addressed in this paper, and three modelling metaphors are proposed in order to address human activities that are mediated by computer systems: Physical modelling to address production (how people orient in and change the world they live and work in), theatrical performances (how the work is divided in the work community), and flow (how people interact and communicate). Several metaphors may be combined in order to address the activity as a whole.*

1. Introduction

Is object orientation (OO) suited as a means for systems developers to understand the complexity of human work in modern organisations in which computers are used heavily? Several authors of OO methods argues it is (e.g., Høydalsvik et al. 1993; Jacobson et al. 1994; Bürkle et al. 1995). However, there are several weaknesses in OO when analysing and designing systems involving a complex interaction between people using computers (Carstensen et al. 1995; Krogh 1996; Smørdal 1997).

Carstensen et al. (1995) reports that OO analysis was useful for specifying the structural properties of coordination mechanisms as classes and objects. However, the dynamic properties of coordination mechanisms reflecting interaction between actors [humans] are not easily expressed (ibid. p. 115). Krogh (1996) reports: «The strengths of the object oriented analysis approach lies in the structural powerful techniques, but the means for capturing dynamics are weak; mainly the support for modelling the application domains needs strengthening.» (ibid. p. 337).

Smørdal (1997) has reviewed six OO modelling approaches in an activity theoretical perspective, and concludes that none of these OO approaches addresses all the relevant aspects of work. There is weak support for addressing the role of the computer in work practices, except for regarding the computer as a tool or as a computational or storage resource in work. The challenge is to view the computer as an incorporated part of human activity, merging the dichotomy of non-technological and technological aspects in a unified whole (Dahlbom 1996). There is also a tendency in OO approaches to regard human action as a prescribed sequence of tasks to be performed by a user, thus failing to regard the important dynamic interactions between the planned actions and the unforeseen contingencies that are present in any work (Suchman 1987), and thus require reflection and unpremeditated actions by the workers to get the work done.

This paper introduces a conceptual framework for object oriented modelling of computer mediated activities. The conceptual framework is based on an interpretation of activity theory in Fjuk and Smørdal (1998), and lends itself to basic concepts in the physical modelling and role modelling school of OO as identified in Smørdal (1997). This paper distinguishes between conceptual frameworks and notation/languages, and puts the main emphasis on basic concepts. According to Madsen (1995) this distinction is important, because the conceptual framework should not be restricted to what can be expressed in a formal language. Also, the IS developer has a conceptual framework that is richer than the formal language being used in order to have the best means for understanding and organising knowledge about the real world.

In Section 2 basic concepts addressing computer mediated activities are described. In Section 3 I map *aspects* of an activity onto OO modelling concepts, using *metaphors*, and, in order to address an activity as a whole, intersect these metaphors. Illustrations of using the framework are provided. The illustrations are based on a case study where a group of researchers performed a needs assessment in a municipal agency. Section 4 concludes the paper.

2. Understanding Computer Mediated Cooperative Work

This section presents the first part of the OO framework, which is a theoretical foundation for OO modelling, based on an interpretation of activity theory within the field of information systems.

2.1. Empirical background

The theoretical foundation presented here has been developed with a grounding in practice (Kaasbøll and Smørdal 1996). A case study has been conducted at a municipal agency in Norway dealing with town planning, building permits, and geodata (Smørdal 1996). The agency has three main responsibilities: Keeping new and changed buildings complying with current building standards and plans; making overall and detailed plans for the city areas; and keeping geodata for the city up to date. The agency faced problems in using a central journal, archive and case application (JAC) because it in several respects did not fit the current work practice, and the management of the agency wanted to improve or replace this computer system. I have provided illustrations based on this case study when proposing OO modelling concepts, referred to below as JAC example.

2.2. Basic Unit of Discourse: the Activity

Activity theory originated as a psychological theory providing notions of a context for human actions in their environment, in the sense that an activity *orients a subject in an objective world* (Leontjev 1983). The concept of activity serves as a basic unit of analysis (Kuutti 1991; Fjuk and Smørdal 1998). The process of delineation is based on a common object of work shared by a community, because an activity is given by its object. This principle is known as object-orientation in activity theory (Leontjev 1983) (and should not be confused with OO in programming or information systems development).

The concept of artefact mediation is particularly interesting for information systems development. The computer is an artefact that may mediate several aspects of an activity, and this is the background for proposing the concept of computers incorporated into work (Fjuk and Smørdal 1998). One of the claims of activity theory is that the nature of any artefact can be understood only within the context of human activity – by identifying the ways people use this artefact, the needs it serves, and the history of its development (Kaptelinin 1996a).

2.3. The Driving Forces within Activities

An activity constitutes a hierarchical structure with inner dynamics, transformations and its own development. (Leontjev 1983). The driving force behind activity, action and operation is different, as can be seen in Figure 1.

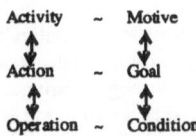

Figure 1. The internal side of an activity, along with corresponding driving forces (ibid.).

An activity is realised through goal-oriented processes, termed actions. An action can realise different activities as the given action may fulfil different motives. Actions are realized through operations, that face conditions in the world. There is often a need for automatisation, in turning routinesed actions into operations, and thus qualify them for computerisation (Leontjev 1983).

2.4. Multiple Activity Systems

There is an increasing attention paid to interactions between multiple activity systems. However this work is only in its initial stage within the activity theory community (Engeström et al. 1995). In my context, there has been a need for regarding the various objects of work in an organisation both as separate and as being connected. An example is how the mail handling office in the municipal agency (that are in charge of opening, registering and routing incoming mail) is connected to other activities in the agency, and to the agency as a whole. Obviously the object of the mail handling office is mail handling, but this activity is also a part of and linked to more overall objects of the agency, such as just treatment of cases, quick case handling, traceability of documents, etc.

Within this background, I have interpreted activities as *sharing* part of their objects with other activities. The separate activities considered may thus be similar in terms of their object and community, but still be regarded as a whole.

According to Leontjev (1978), actions are usually polymotivated; two or more activities can temporarily merge, motivating the same action, if the goal of one action is a prerequisite for reaching the motives for all the activities simultaneously (Kaptelinin 1996b). Thus, the subjects may have different (even conflicting) motives for the collective action.

2.5. The Tool/Sign Duality

Vygotsky (1978) distinguished between two interrelated types of instruments [mediating artefacts]: tools and signs. According to Vygotsky, the function of a tool «(...) is to serve as the conductor of human influence on the object of activity; it is external oriented; it must lead to changes in objects.» (ibid., p. 55). The signs have a different character and are means of thought, and reflective and conscious actions. A sign «(...) is a means of internal activity aimed at mastering oneself; the sign is internally oriented.» (ibid., p. 55].

2.6. *Aspects of an Activity*

Engeström (1987) has developed four different perspectives on an activity, see Figure 2. In my framework each of these is used as a point of departure for defining a metaphor that provide modelling concepts addressing the relevant phenomena and concepts of the activity when regarded in this perspective. A metaphor is in this paper regarded as a perspective that provide a scope, structure and concepts from one domain, in order to refer to another domain.

The upper triangle of the model illustrates Leontjev's basic interpretation of human activity (termed *production* by Engeström), and denotes the relationship between subject and object. This relation is mediated through instruments. The computer may be regarded as an instrument, as it may be used as a tool to change the object, or as a sign orienting the subject in the objective world. The two other aspects represent the collective aspects of human activity: *Distribution* denotes the relationship between community (e.g. the workgroup or the employees in the organisation) and an object. This relation is mediated through the division of labour. The computer may be regarded a mediator of this division of labour, e.g. that coordination of work, or distribution of tasks, may be done by means of the computer. *Exchange* denotes the relationship between the a subject and the community. This relation is mediated through rules of social behaviour and communication. The computer may be regarded as a communication channel in this relation. E- mail and conferencing software are examples of this role in the work context. *Consumption* denotes a *meta level aspect,* the consumption of the outcome of an activity (such as using a service or a product). Consumption is not used in this framework, because it focus on customer and client relationship with the information system. Future research will explore an extension to this framework to include customer/client concerns in models.

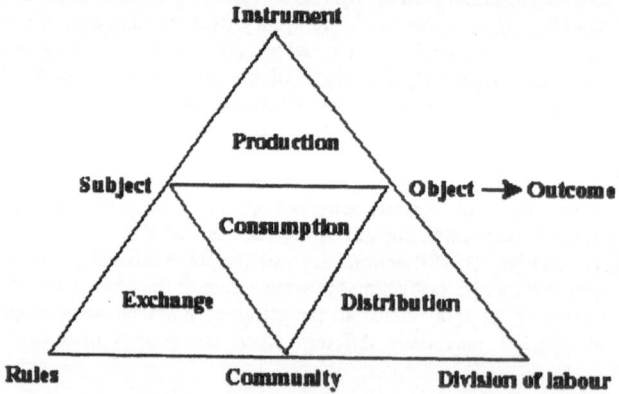

Figure 2. The aspects of a human activity (Engeström 1987).

The pyramid in Figure 3 is a conceptualisation of the instrument's role in the web of human actions embedded in production, exchange and distribution, which is the aspects that is selected for this framework. See Fjuk and Smørdal (1998) for details.

The dialectics between these three aspects is crucial in understanding collective work. In any collective work arrangement, neither of these aspects can be considered separately, because they all influence each other continuously. Rules mediated interpersonal interactions influence the course of individual and collective actions. Moreover, individual and collective actions may influence and change the whole work organisation, and the work organization influences these actions. The work organisation also influence what kind of instruments that is used in the web of actions, and the instruments may in turn influence the work organisation and division of labour.

Figure 3. The idea of integrating the aspects of an activity (Fjuk and Smørdal 1998).

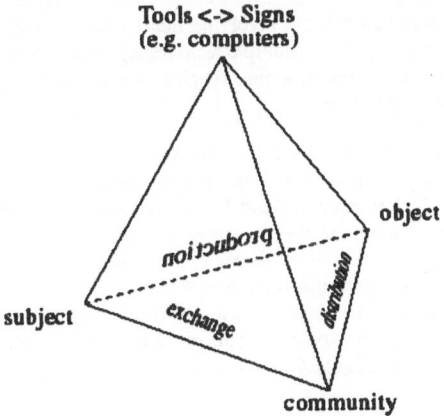

3. OO Modelling Revisited
This section presents the second part of the OO framework, and presents modelling concepts and metaphors.

3.1. Shift from the Problem Domain to the Application Domain
OO modelling traditionally relate to the *problem domain* of a computer system, which is the part of the world that the computer system is supposed to handle, control or monitor, while the *application domain* of a computer system consists of the users, the organisational context, and the work in which the computer system is used (Mathiassen et al. 1993). OO is an universal modelling approach, hence it could be argued that work and organisational concerns is just another problem domain to be modelled. In my view, this is a too simplistic approach, because analysing and designing systems involving people using computers require a framework witch address the role of the computer in work.

The concept of a *system* is basic in OO approaches in order to model a part of the world (a problem domain) that, for some purpose, is regarded as a whole (Dahl et al. 1967; Holbæk-Hanssen et al. 1975; Nygaard et al. 1987; Mathiassen et al. 1993).

The concept of activity has similarities to the system concept, because both regard a whole as a *perspective*. In this paper, the concept of activity is regarded as a specialisation of the system concept, due to the richer theory behind the activity concept, explaining relationships and dynamics within activities (the application domain).

JAC example: *JAC contains a model of the building permit process, the Norwegian archive standard (NOARK), and the physical archive in the agency (the problem domain). Many departments are involved in the building permit handling, such as the building permit department, the archive, the citizen relations office, the planning department, geodata department etc. (the application domain).*

Comment: The organisational units are divided according to function, and it was natural for people at the agency to regard an organisational unit as a whole (an activity), e.g. archiving could be regarded as an object, and the people at the archive department as the community sharing that activity. However, the work was divided between units (and in many cases individuals), and the units/individuals had to cooperate. Building permit handling is an example of an activity involving many organisational units. This made it useful to regard the agency as a multiple activity system, where activities could be delineated according to individuals, groups (such as professions), organisational units or across such organisational borders.

3.2. Models for Reflection and Models in Action

A model has two interpretations in this framework: Models may be regarded as signs (c.f. Section 2.5) in IS development, and hence mediate the object of a development project (such as improvements to the fit between current work practices and computer systems). This interpretation *-models as means in a reflection process* - is obviously useful for analysis and design of information systems.

Object oriented models may in addition be a tool (c.f. Section 2.5) because OO models may be realised as a computer execution. This gives another interpretation, as a *model in action*. This is illustrated in Figure 4.

Figure 4. Two interpretations of models

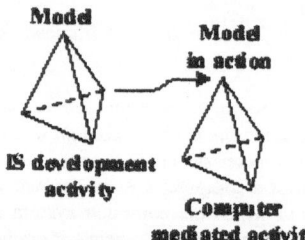

This dual interpretation of models could be used as a bridge between development concerns and actual use of computer systems. In this conceptual framework the property of OO models to be realised by a computer is an important bridge between technical concerns and work/organisational concerns, because models are interpreted in both in a technical perspective in IS development and interpreted within a work practice that is mediated by the OO model.

Bertelsen (1997) points to the possibility of object oriented models to «secure the sanity between design and domain, by allowing all involved parties to perceive, use and recreate the models in their own professional terms not fully understandable for the other involved groups» (p. 319).

This duality of models is similar to the idea of a boundary object (Star 1989), which can be given an interpretation of heterogene groups that have different backgrounds and languages. «Boundary objects are objects that are both plastic enough to adapt to local needs and constraints of the several parties employing them, yet robust enough to maintain a common identity across sites» (p. 46).

3.3. Three Basic Metaphors for Modelling Activities

The choice of metaphors is related to basic concepts in different schools of OO modelling. The metaphors primary address the *role of the computer* in the various aspects of an activity, see Figure 5.

Figure 5. Three metaphors corresponding to the aspects of an activity

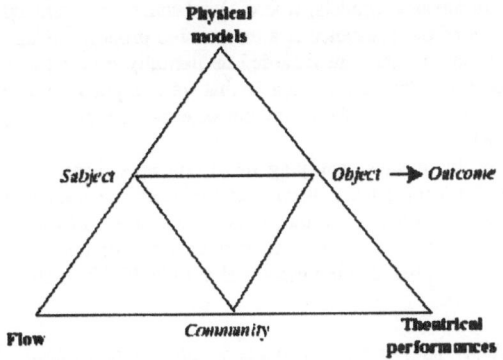

In Table 1 the basic concepts in each metaphor is aligned with basic concepts in activity theory.

Table 1. Three metaphors corresponding to the aspects of an activity

Basic concepts in Activity Theory	Physical model	Theatrical performance	Flow
Activity	The application domain	Performance	N/A
Object	The problem domain	Play	The problem domain
Subject	Human observer	Actor	Node
Community	N/A	Ensemble	Set of nodes
Instrument	Object (physical matter)	Props	Message
Rules	N/A	see comment (1)	Protocol
Division of labour	N/A	Roles	Connectors

---

1 In classical theatre, such as Commedia Dell'Arte, the actors improvised the performance, based on fixed role characters and a general idea about the play. Hence, there was a need for communication between actors in order to interpret their roles. In modern theatre, the need for communication among actors are reduced due to the use of scripts, however some communication regarding cueing etc. is needed. In post-modern theatre, improvisation and thus communication is again more important.

A Metaphor for Production: Physical Models

Engeström's aspect of production comprises the individual worker's relation to her work (the subject - object relation). The computer mediates the problem domain (object), as a *sign*, giving the worker clues about the structures and states of the object of work, thus enabling planning, selection of tools and procedures and giving context of the work in the total work arrangement, and as a *tool*, providing means of transforming the object.

I use the conceptual framework developed in the BETA project[2] as a point of departure when mapping the production aspect of activities onto OO concepts. According to the BETA conceptual framework (Madsen et al. 1993), there are several perspectives to modelling, e.g. physical modelling, mathematical modelling and transition modelling. A physical model has substance (since it is built out of physical material), the substance has properties (which can be measured, producing values), and the substance can be transformed, thus changing its measurable properties. Object oriented models are physical models, where 1) substance is organised by objects, 2) A measurable property of the substance is a measurable property of one or more objects, and 3) transformations of state are regarded as partially ordered sequences of actions associated with objects. The central idea is that «a computer execution is regarded a physical model, thus simulating the behaviour of either a real or imaginary part of the world» (ibid, p. 290).

There is a problem when applying these concepts directly, due to the idea of *simulation* in the BETA framework. A computer execution is not a simulation of a work practice in this context, rather it is a mediation of the object of the work practice. This implies that the model should be open to various ways of articulating the work. For physical models, this implies that the models should be highly malleable (Simone et al. 1995).

IAC Example: *Jenny uses a word processor (object) to produce building permits (object). In her judgement of applications, she consults the city-maps (object), and the regulations for the area in question (object). After a permit is written, Jenny updates the workflow sheet (object) and mark the building permit case (object) as closed in JAC (object).*

Comment: In Jennys work environment there are many artefacts, some are tools (such as the word processor and JAC), others are signs (such as various documents and the registrations in JAC). The tools consist of a set of operations (c.f. Section 2.3), which Jenny can select in order to realise her actions, and thus meet her goals. The challenge in modelling is to make the *model in action* fit with Jennys work practice. One interesting approach is to regard the artefacts in the workplace as tools and materials (Bürkle et al. 1995; Wulf et al. 1996). Artefacts in a work environment may be classified as either a tool or a material, a tool is an object which can refine another object, the material.

A metaphor for distribution: Theatrical performances

The aspect of distribution contains the division of labour among the members of the community (the object - community relation). Division of labour is necessary to

---

2 The conceptual framework for BETA is based on earlier frameworks for Simula (Nygaard 1970) and DELTA (Holbæk-Hanssen et al. 1975).

organise and coordinate the different actions of the individuals. Distribution is usually operationalised using a role concept, in the sense that the work is divided among roles, and that each role has some responsibility for a part of the whole job to be done. Note that distribution in this context has a different meaning than what is usual in the OO literature, where distribution is the physical organisation of objects on different computers, and the means to connect and organise them.

I am introducing a theatre metaphor developed in the GOODS project (see also earlier work in Nygaard 1992; Nygaard 1997) as a point of departure when mapping the distribution aspect of activities onto OO concepts. This metaphor is developed with software organisation in mind, as is the case for the role modelling approaches (Smørdal 1997). In my context however, the metaphor should be understood as addressing the relationship between the community and the object of work.

A subject is regarded as an actor, and only subjects qualify as actors, since the computer only execute operations in order to realise subjects' actions (c.f. Section 2.3). The community is regarded as an ensemble. The division of labour is reflected in roles, each having a set of scripts which explain the role. A script could be interpreted as a routine that has to be strictly applied in a particular work situation, or a loose work description that needs to be creatively handled (interpreted) by a subject. An activity is regarded as a performance, and the object of work is regarded as the play itself. The assignment of actors to roles is termed *casting*.

JAC example: *Linda and Knut (ensemble) opens mail (prop) at 10 o'clock every day (script), and register (perform) the dates and headlines of each document in JAC (prop). Linda (actor) assign each document to one of the departments in the agency (script), using JAC. She's responsible for correct registration and routing of documents (role), during the years she has become very skilled in determining (performing) the case context for newly arrived documents.*

Comment: One of the instruments in this example (JAC) can be interpreted as a shared tool for the community to conduct changes in the object of the activity, while the scripts and roles are signs mediating the division of labour. The shared tool is a set of operations for realisation of the subjects' goals, and the challenge in modelling is to make the *model in action* fit with the roles and scripts of the actors.

A metaphor for exchange: Flow

This aspect contains the communication between workers (the subject - community relation). Signs mediate thoughts, knowledge and perspectives among subjects in a community.

I will use a simple flow metaphor when mapping the exchange aspect onto OO concepts. A node is capable of processing input from other nodes, and producing output which is sent to other nodes. Nodes may send data or physical material to other nodes by means of connectors between nodes.

Representing the communication patterns is an important part of approaches in the role modelling school (Smørdal 1997), however these approaches (see e.g. Reenskaug et al. (1996)) use rather formalised notations, such as the IDEF0 standard (IDEF0 1993). This may be a problem because communication is fixed at the operations level (c.f. Section 2.3).

150

JAC example: Linda (node) sends (flow) the newly arrived documents (material) to Jens (node), who is the leader of the building case department (node). Jens decides who to handle the case, and register (data) the assignment in JAC (flow).

<u>Comment:</u> The computerised connectors between the nodes in this example are partly realised by JAC, and partly by e-mail. JAC has a parallel non-computerised connector, due to the flow of material (documents, maps etc.) that ideally should be in synchronisation with the registrations in JAC, e.g. that the physical building application is located in the office of the registered case handler for that application. The agency had severe problems in this respect.

3.4.   Intersecting the perspectives

The systemic whole of an activity is handled by intersecting the metaphors. When intersecting the metaphors, similar concepts in two metaphors is related and explained in a way that is meaningful for both metaphors. I regard metaphors as perspectives, and Nygaard and Sørgard (1987) propose that perspectives can be combined using union and intersection.

Figure 6. Intersecting the perspectives

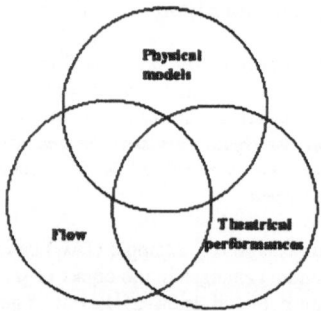

Physical modelling ∩ Theatrical performances

The first step in addressing the activity as a whole (c.f. Figure 6) is to intersect the metaphors which address production and distribution. Production is individually oriented, while distribution is collectively oriented. Both these aspects mediate the object of the activity. A physical model mediates production, and a theatrical performance mediates distribution. The intersection of these is interpreted here as a web of physical models (that orient actors in the performance) that are organised according to the roles (for the actors to interpret) in that performance. The web of physical models allows mediation of coworkers' actions within the individual work environments.

An interesting consequence of this interpretation is that objects in various physical models may be interconnected in order to mediate the division of labour. I propose therefore that a set of objects in a physical model may be regarded as a role, for some actor to interpret. In this way physical models may contain within them objects that are realised by other subjects that share a part of the object of work. There is also the possibility that several subjects must cooperate in realising one object in a physical model. Thus there could be a many to many object-role relationship.

I will also propose an actor-object relationship. This is because the actions of one subject in some production aspect may result in changes of the physical model of another production aspect. Hence, a set of objects may be regarded as an actor, if the objects are reflecting actions of some other subject in the community. There is also the possibility that the actions of several subjects are reflected in one object in a physical model. Thus there is a many to many relationship between objects and actors.

JAC example: *Henry (actor) is working at the accounting department, and he is responsible for the production of invoices (role) at the agency. He has (by means of the IT-department at the agency) made an invoice application (object) consisting of a set of operations (scripts) that could realise his goals. Ann (actor) is working at the front office in the building application department and she is responsible for all mail exchange with applicants, neighbours and other citizens (role). She use JAC (object) when an building permit is accepted, in order to produce a letter and an invoice for the application fee and sends these documents to the applicant.*

Comment: In this example Henry and Ann have different physical models mediating their work environments, Henry's model accounting, while Ann's mediate customer relations (c.f. Multiple Activity Systems, Section 2.4). Still, Ann is the actor for a role that is placed in her work environment by Henry, and this role has a relation to objects in Ann's physical model that through tools and signs mediate the registration of an invoice.

Physical modelling ∩ Flow
The second step in addressing the activity as a whole is to intersect the metaphors which address production and exchange. Production is individually oriented, while exchange is inherently collectively oriented. Both these aspects orients a subject, the first aspect in relation to the object of the activity, the second aspect in relation to the community of the activity. Above it was proposed that a physical model mediates production, and flow mediates exchange. The intersection of these is interpreted here as a web of physical models that are organised in order to be a means for exchange in the community.

From a modelling point of view, this web of physical models is accomplished by defining connectors between physical models, and thus have the means for moving objects between physical models (material flow) and by message sending between objects (data flow).

JAC example: *Linda (node) register the dates and headlines of each document in JAC (physical model) and sends (flow) the newly arrived documents (objects) to Jens (node), who decides who to handle the case, and register (data flow) the assignment in JAC (object).*

Comment: In this example Linda and Jens have different physical models, but still they are able to handle and understand documents that are moved between these physical models. Communication between the two workers are mediated by their physical models.

Theatrical performances ∩ Flow
The third step in addressing the activity as a whole is to intersect the metaphors which address distribution and exchange. Both are collectively oriented, and orients a

community in its activity. Distribution mediate the object of the activity, while exchange mediate rules of communication.

Theatrical performances and flow are proposed as metaphors for these aspects, and the intersection of these is interpreted here as a means of communication between the actors of a performance. The communication thus reflect the division of labour, e.g. regarded as a means for actors to interpret their roles.

From a modelling point of view, this is accomplished by defining connectors between roles, in order for the actors to communicate.

JAC example: *Horst (actor) is working at the customer service, and he is responsible for giving correct information about building cases to the public (role). When asked about some building project, he finds the case handler in JAC (actor), and sends an e-mail (flow) requesting information.*

Comment: In this example Horst initiates an exchange based on the division of labour, i.e. the case handler that is assigned to a building case.

4. Conclusions and Future Work

In this paper I have developed an object oriented framework which is based on an activity theoretical perspective. The framework provides a general approach to model computer mediated cooperative work. The basic abstraction is a human activity. An activity denotes individual or collective work in a social context, and is mediated by artefacts. When analysing and designing computer artefacts, three aspects of an activity, and therefore three perspectives in modelling are needed. This paper propose three modelling metaphors to address activities: *Physical modelling* to address production (how subjects orient in and change the objective world), *theatrical performances* (how the work is divided in the community), and *flow* (how the subjects interact and communicate). Several metaphors may be combined in order to address the activity as a whole.

The object oriented model has two interpretations in this framework: As a *sign*, meaning that the models orient people in the world (both problem domain and application domain), and as a *tool*, meaning that the models are regarded as program executions, which may change the real world.

Future work will include development of a notation in line with the basic concepts and metaphors in this framework, expressing the intersections of the metaphors.

Acknowledgements

Jens Kaasbøll, Ole Lehrman Madsen, Birger Møller-Pedersen and Kristen Nygaard gave useful comments to this paper.

References

Bertelsen OW (1997) Understanding objects in use-oriented design. In *Proceedings of The 20th Information Systems Research Seminar in Scandinavia (IRIS'20)* Braa K and Monteiro E (eds.), Hankø, Norway, Department of Informatics, University of Oslo, Conf. Proc. No. 1: 311-23.

Bürkle U, Gryczan G and Züllighoven H (1995) Object-Oriented System Development in a Banking Project: Methodology, Experiences and Conclusions *Human-Computer Interaction* 10: 293-336.

Carstensen PH, Krogh B and Sørensen C (1995) Object oriented Modelling of Coordination Mechanisms. In *Proceedings of The 18th Information Systems Research*

Seminar in Scandinavia (IRIS'18) Dahlbom B, Kämmerer F, Ljungberg F, Stage J and Sørensen C (eds.), Gjern, Denmark, Gothenburg Studies in Informatics, Report 7.

Dahl O-J, Myhrhaug B and Nygaard K (1967) *SIMULA 67 Common Base Language*, Norwegian Computing Center.

Dahlbom B (1996) The New Informatics *Scandinavian Journal of Information Systems* 8(22): 29-48.

Engeström Y (1987) *Learning by Expanding. An Activity-theoretical approach to developmental research*, Orienta-Konsultit Oy. Helsinki.

Engeström Y and Escalanta V (1995) Mundane Tool or Object of Affection? The Rise and Fall of the Postal Buddy. In *Context and consciousness: activity theory and human- computer interaction* Nardi B (ed.), MIT Press.

Fjuk A and Smørdal O (1998) The Computer's Incorporated Role in Work. In *Proceedings of The 21st Information Systems Research Seminar in Scandinavia (IRIS'21)* Buch NJ, Damsgaard J, Eriksen LB, Iversen JH and Nielsen PA (eds.), Sæby Søbad, Denmark, Department of Computer Science. Aalborg University.

Holbæk-Hanssen E, Håndlykken P and Nygaard K (1975) *System description and the DELTA language*, Norwegian Computing Centre (Norsk Regnesentral).

Høydalsvik GM and Sindre G (1993) Object-Oriented Role Modelling for the Analysis and Design of Organisational Information Systems. In *Proceedings of 26'th HICSS*: 159-68.

IDEF0 (1993) *Software Standard Integration Definition for Function Modelling (IDEF0)*, Federal Information Processing Standards Publication 183.

Jacobson I, Ericsson M and Jacobson A (1994) *The Object Advantage - Business process reengineering with object technology*, Addison-Wesley.

Kaptelinin V (1996a) Activity Theory: Implications for Human-Computer Interaction. In *Context and Consciousness. Activity Theory and Human-Computer Interaction* Nardi BA (ed.). Cambridge, The MIT Press: 103-16.

Kaptelinin V (1996b) Computer-Mediated Activity: Functional Organs in Social and Developmental Contexts. In *Context and Consciousness. Activity Theory and Human-Computer Interaction* Nardi BA (ed.). Cambridge, The MIT Press: 45-68.

Krogh B (1996) Object Oriented Analysis of Groupware Applications. In *Proceedings of The Fifth International Conference Information Systems Development (ISD'96)* Wrycza S and Zupancic J (eds.), Gda´nsk, Poland.

Kuutti K (1991) The concept of activity as a basic unit of analysis for CSCW research. In *Proceedings of the ECSCW'91* Bannon L, Robinson and Schmidt K (eds.), Kluwer Academic Publishers: 249-64.

Kaasbøll JJ and Smørdal O (1996) Human Work as Context for Development of OO-Modeling Techniques. In *IFIP WG 8.1/8.2 working conference on principles of method construction and tool support (Method Engineering' 96)* Brinkkemper S (ed.), Atlanta, USA, Chapman & Hall: 111-25.

Leontjev AN (1978) *Activity. Consciousness. Personality*, Englewood Cliffs, Prentice Hall. New York.

Leontjev AN (1983) *Virksomhed, bevidsthed, personlighed (In Danish)*, Forlaget Progress. Denmark.

Madsen OL (1995) Open Issues in Object-Oriented Programming *Software Practice and Experience* 25(S4).

Madsen OL, Møller-Pedersen B and Nygaard K (1993) *Object Oriented Programming in the BETA Programming Language*, Addison Wesley.

Mathiassen L, Munk-Madsen A, Nielsen PA and Stage J (1993) *Objektorienteret analyse (in Danish)*, Marko. Aalborg.

Nygaard K (1970) *System Description by SIMULA - An Introduction.* Publication S-35, Norwegian Computing Center.

Nygaard K (1992) *Information Processes, Programming Languages and Perspectives · on Reality*, Lecture notes from a talk at the 25th Newcastle Conference.

Nygaard K (1997) GOODS to Appear on the Stage (Invited Speech). In *ECOOP'97* Magnusson B (ed.), Jyvaskala, Finland.

Nygaard K and Sørgaard P (1987) The Perspective Concept in Informatics. In *Computers and Democracy: A Scandinavian Challenge* Bjerknes G, Ehn P and Kyng M (eds.). Aldershot, Avebury Gower Publ. Comp. Ltd: 371-93.

Reenskaug T, Wold P and Lehne OA (1996) *Working With Objects: the OOram Software Engineering Method*, Manning. Greenwich.

Simone C, Divitini M and Schmidt K (1995) A notation for malleable and interoperable coordination mechanisms for CSCW systems. In *Conference on Organizational Computing Systems* Comstock N, Clarence E, Kling R, Mylopoulos and Kaplan S (eds.), California.

Smørdal O (1996) Soft Objects Analysis, A modelling approach for analysis of interdependent work practices. In *3rd International Conference on Object-Oriented Information Systems (OOIS'96)* Patel D and Sun Y (eds.), London, UK, Springer-Verlag: 195-208.

Smørdal O (1997) Classifying Object Oriented Analysis Approaches with Activity Theory. In *4th International Conference on Object-Oriented Information Systems (OOIS'97)* Orlowska ME and Zicari R (eds.), Brisbane, Australia, Springer-Verlag.

Star SL (1989) *The Structure of Ill-Structured Solutions: Boundary Objects and Heterogeneous Distributed Problem Solving.* Distributed artificial intelligence (Research notes in artificial intelligence), Pitman. London.

Suchman LA (1987) *Plans and Situated Actions*, Cambridge University Press.

Vygotsky LS (1978) Mind in Society. The Development of Higher Psychological Processes. In Cole M, John-Steiner V, Scribner S and Souberman E (eds.). London, England, Harvard University Press.

Wulf M, Gryczan G and Züllighoven H (1996) Process Patterns: Supporting Cooperative Work in the Tools & Materials Approach. In *Proceedings of The 19th Information Systems Research Seminar in Scandinavia (IRIS'19)* Dahlbom B, Ljungberg F, Nuldén U, Simon J, Stage J and Sørensen C (eds.), Lökeberg, Sweden, Gothenburg Studies in Informatics, Report 8: 445-59.

Establishing the Framework for Business Object Analysis and Design Models

Ying Liang

Department of Computing and Information Systems
University of Paisley
High Street, Paisley PA1 2BE - UK
E-mail: lian-ci0@paisley.ac.uk Fax: +44 141 848 3542

ABSTRACT. *There were frameworks established for analysis and design models of conventional information systems (IS). They showed the common features of the models on the common aspects of IS, and provided general strategies for developing IS. Now we need to establish similar frameworks for business object analysis and design models of object-oriented information systems (OOIS), because object technology is becoming more mature and is widely used in developing e-commerce and web applications. Also the promotion and use of industry standard such as UML (Unified Modelling Language) notation have provided the possibility and basis for establishing the frameworks. This paper first shows the analysis and design strategies used by current object-oriented methods in building the two models. It then introduces a framework that was established for business object analysis and design models of OOIS. UML notation is fitted into the framework also for the purpose of representing the models using standard notation.* Finally, it shows part of the results of applying the framework in analysing and designing a small business system.

KEY WORDS: *business domain object, OOIS object, business object analysis and design models*

1. Introduction

Business object analysis and design are two important stages of object-oriented information systems (OOIS) development. In them, identifying the right objects is one of the main skills of object-oriented (OO) development (Stevens, 2000). This involves both discovery from a problem domain as part of analysis and invention as part of the design (Booch, 1994). Developers discover business domain objects by analysing system requirements and invent OOIS objects by designing system structures. This must be done under the guidelines that assist in identifying and inventing appropriate objects in business object analysis and design models. Unfortunately, many of existing guidelines are often inexact and insufficient (Prins, 1996). I think that the lack of useful frameworks for business object analysis and design object models in OOIS development have affected the provision of useful and sufficient guidelines required.

In conventional IS development, there were frameworks, such as the one shown in (Olle et al., 1988), for traditional analysis and design models with processes and data. The frameworks included common features of the models on common aspects of the business system and IS. Based on them, exact and sufficient guidelines were defined and provided for helping to identify and invent right processes and data during analysis and design. However, until now we still do not have a similar framework for business object analysis and design models in OOIS development, which enables to finding and defining exact and sufficient guidelines for identifying and inventing right objects for OOIS. Now object technology has been widely used in OOIS development, in particular, in e-commerce and web systems development. The lack of the framework for OOIS will seriously affect the efficiency of OOIS development in future.

This paper introduces a framework that I established for the business object analysis and design models of OOIS as an attempt to find a general strategy to building the models in OOIS development. Section 2 will discuss about analysis strategies and design strategies available to build the business object analysis and design models, and the objects that are identified and invented in terms of the strategies. Section 3 will show the details of the framework. Section 4 will show part of the results of applying the framework in analysing and designing a small business system.

2. Business Object Analysis and Design Models

Business object analysis and design models of OOIS are built in terms of analysis strategies and design strategies provided by OO methods. Current object-oriented methods provide different strategies for building the two models because of their specific interests and emphasis on the aspects of OOIS, although the process of development is thought seamless.

2.1 The Business Object Analysis Model

The business object analysis model describes the business domain objects identified from the problem domain and the links between objects. Table 1 shows the analysis strategies that I found from current OO methods after assessing and comparing the methods in terms of approach shown in (Liang, 2000). These strategies produce different types of business objects, as shown in Table 1, for the same system. The business object analysis models built in terms of the strategies are therefore different because of the difference between the strategies.

Table 1 Analysis Strategies and Business Domain Objects in the Analysis Model

Analysis Strategy	Objects to Be Considered
Class categories	Tangible things, roles, incidents, interactions, and specifications (Shlaer et al., 1988; Rumbaugh et al., 1991; Booch, 1994)
Business elements	Resources, processes, organization units (Taylor, 1995) Structures, other systems, devices, things, events, roles, processes, sites, organizational units (Coad et al., 1991)
Problem domain	Concepts in the domain (Booch, 1994; Fowler, 2000)
Business objects	Entities, processes, events (Estrin, 1998)
Scenarios, use cases, responsibilities	Interfaces, controls, entities (Jacobson et al., 1995) Things which business processes involve (Kristen, 1994; Booch, 1994; Graham, 1994) Physical objects or conceptual entities having responsibilities (Wirfs-Brock et al., 1990)
Object types	Concrete and abstract things (Cook et al., 1994)
Object interactions specification	Objects required to communicate with the system (Carmichael, 1994)
Soft system thinking	Purposeful activities, actors, owners, customers (Liang et al., 1998)
Development stages	Objects in analysis model (entities), object in design model (device objects, folder object, workplace object, document object, view object, control object, model object) (Prins, 1996)

2.2 The Business Object Design Model

The business object design model shows OOIS objects that implement the business domain objects and their links in an OOIS. They are designed and invented based on the need of software architecture of the OOIS. However, most of OO methods provide similar design strategies for building business object design model based on the similar OOIS software architecture such as the one supported by Microsoft Visual InterDev 6 (Microsoft, 1999) shown in Figure 1. Therefore the design strategies are often similar in different OO methods, as summarised in Table 2.

Figure 1 A Software Architecture of OOIS

Table 2 Design Strategies and OOIS Objects in the Design Model

Designing strategy	Objects to Be Considered
User services	Specific application objects on the user machine such as windows, HTML pages, specific transactions, etc.
Web services	Control objects on the web server such as scripts, etc.
Business services	Common application objects on the business server such as common transaction components, COM or CORBA components, etc.
Data services	Objects on the database server such as business data objects (e.g., documents and images), multimedia objects (e.g., vision, sound, videos), etc.

The business domain objects in the business object analysis model are accommodated to the architecture by either becoming OOIS objects without change or by being converted into OOIS objects with some change, expanding, mergence, and/or splitting. In addition, new OOIS objects may be invented and added to the model during design because of needs of implementing the architecture. Each stage of OOIS development in fact contributes new properties to the business object model of OOIS (Prins, 1996).

3. The Framework

The framework to be established for business object analysis and design models should provide the general analysis and design strategy for building the models with common features in respect of common aspects of the business system and OOIS. OO analysis and design can become a truly seamless in OOIS development with the common aspects focused. The strategies shown in Table 1 and Table 2 cannot be regarded as the general analysis and design strategies required because they build the models with different kinds of features and without focusing on common aspects of the business system and OOIS. After assessing and comparing the strategies and the objects show in the two tables, it was found that, no matter which strategies are used in building the models in analysis and design, an object identified and invented always describes either something existing in the systems, or something taking a responsibility in the systems, or something triggering the systems, or something placing other things in the systems, or something monitoring other things in the systems. This commonality shows that objects can be identified and invented based on the five common aspects of the business system and OOI: *what, how, when, where*, and *who*. Then the common features of the two models can be defined in respect of the five aspects. I established a framework based on these five common aspects.

3.1 Definition of the Framework

The definition of the framework for business object analysis and design is shown Table 3 in which there are four parts: strategy, common types of objects, subtypes of common types, and representation in UML (Unified Modelling Language (Booch et al., 1999)) that is industry standard defined by OMG (Object Management Group). The common features of the two models are defined in the framework in respect of the five common aspects of the business system and OOIS, as shown in Table 4-7.

Table 3 The Framework for Business Object Analysis and Design Models

Aspect of System	Strategy	Common Types of Objects	Subtypes of Common Types	Representation in UML
What, how, when, where, who.	It shows strategy of building the models.	It shows the object categories for the models. Figure 2 and 3 show the links of common types of objects in the systems. The object models can be built based on the categories and links.	It shows potential important objects in the categories. They should be considered and identified in analysis, or invented in design. They are identified or invented in the five views referred to the five aspects of the systems. Each view focuses on a set of specific objects with a common type.	This part shows representation of the five aspects in UML.

Table 4 *Part 1*: Strategy of Building Business Object Analysis and Design Models

Aspect of system	Strategy	
	Analysis Model	Design Model
What	What exist and are important in business system/problem domain	What are needed for OOIS
How	How business system works	How OOIS works
When	When business system works	When OOIS works
Where	Where organization units locate	Where OOIS objects place
Who	Who manages business processes	Who controls OOIS functions

Table 5 *Part 2*: Common Types of Objects in the Models

Aspect of system	Common Types of Objects	
	Analysis Model	Design Model
What	Business entities	OOIS objects
How	Business processes	OOIS transactions
When	Scenarios of business processes	OOIS object interactions with transactions
Where	Business sites	OOIS deployed objects
Who	Organisation units	OOIS controllers of transactions

Table 6 *Part 3*: Subtypes of Common Types

Aspect of system	Subtypes of Common Types	
	Analysis Model	Design Model
What	*Business entities*: entities, resources, tangible things, roles, devices	*OOIS objects*: business data objects, multimedia objects, user interface objects
How	*Business processes*: processes	*OOIS transactions*: transaction objects
When	*Business scenarios*: events, interactions	*OOIS object interactions with transaction*: event objects
Where	*Business sites*: countries, cities, headquarters, branches	*OOIS deployed objects*: local objects on user machine, remote objects on servers
Who	*Organisation units*: companies, departments, divisions	*OOIS controllers*: control objects

Business Rule

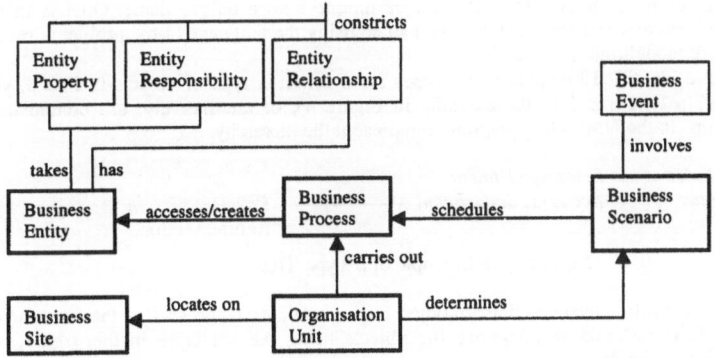

Figure 2 Links of Common Types of Objects in the Business Object Analysis Model

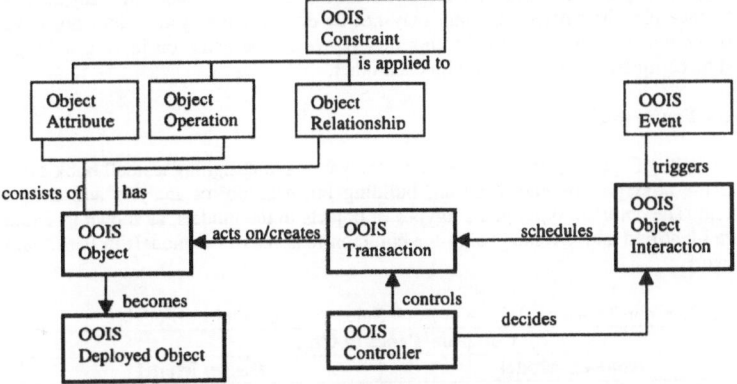

Figure 3 Links of Common Types of Objects in the Business Object Design Model

Table 7 *Part 4*: Representation of the Models

Aspect of system	Representation in UML	
	Analysis Model	**Design Model**
What	Class diagram	Class diagram, component diagram
How	Use case diagram, activity diagram	Activity diagram
When	Interaction diagram, statechart	Interaction diagrams, statechart
Where	Class diagram	Deployment diagram
Who	Class diagram	Class diagram, component diagram

3.2 Rules of the Framework

The framework should be used based on the following rules:

Rule 1. There is no order of rows in the four parts of the framework. You can start the analysis and design from any of the rows.

Rule 2. Objects in each of the two models must be unique with a unique name. Objects in the business object analysis model should be named using the language of the problem domain that you are modelling.

Rule 3. If you have identified hierarchical subtypes for a common type of objects in Part 3, you should use a type-tree (see the example in Figure 4), or alternatively, use composition relationships in the UML class diagram to represent the hierarchy.

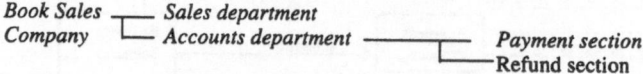

Figure 4 An Example of a Type-Tree

Rule 4. If you have identified business domain objects using other strategies such as the ones shown in Table 1, you should re-categorise the objects using the strategies in this framework before building the design model.

Rule 5. Converting from business domain objects into OOIS objects must be carried out with consistent meanings.

Rule 6. Not all of UML diagrams in Table 7 have to be drawn for every system in analysis and design. For example, the activity diagram may not be drawn if the system does not have complex states and behaviour. All diagrams that represent the same business system or OOIS must be complete and consistent with each other.

4. Application of the Framework

Here shows part of results of applying the framework in analysing and designing a small book sales system. I followed the strategies in Part 1 during building business object analysis and design models for the system. The common types and subtypes of objects in the models, as shown in Table 8 and Table 9, were identified and invented using the common features of the models in Part 2 and Part 3 of the framework.

Table 8 Common Types of Objects in Book Sales Business Object Models

Aspect of system	Common Types of Objects	
	Analysis Model	Design Model
What	Book sales entities	Book sales OOIS objects
How	Book sales processes	Book sales OOIS transactions
When	Book sales scenarios	Book sales OOIS object interactions
Where	Book sales sites	Book sales OOIS deployed objects
Who	Book sales units	Book sales OOIS controllers

Table 9 Subtypes of the Common Types in Book Sales Business Object Models

Aspect of system	Subtypes of Common Types	
	Business domain objects in Analysis Model	OOIS objects in Design Model
What	Book, customer, order, fax, printer, etc.	Booklist, Orderlist, FaxDevice, PrinterDevice, BookView, OrderView, PaymentView, etc.
How	Place order, check payment, etc.	AddOrder, PayforOrder, etc.
When	Receive order, receive payment, etc.	OrderEvent, PayEvent, etc.
Where	Sales branch in London, Finance branch in Manchester, etc.	OrderView (on the user machine), AddOrder (on the application server), etc.
Who	Sales dept, accounts dept, etc.	OrderController, PayController, etc.

I also produced the UML diagrams as the representation of the models, in terms of Part 4 of the framework. The diagrams are not shown here because of limited size of the paper.

5. Conclusions

In the past, there were frameworks that provided general strategies for building analysis and design models for conventional IS. They also show the common features of the two models in respect of common aspects of the systems. However, no such a framework was found so far in OOIS development. The lack of the framework can delay the process of standardising business objects, the evolution of business object models, and the production of business object analysis and design patterns.

In order to overcome the lack, I established a framework for business object analysis and design models of OOIS, which provides a general strategy for building the models using common features of the models in respect of common aspects of the business system and OOIS. This paper shows the framework. The framework may be also helpful in the following aspects:

- Getting rid of confusions existing in analysing and designing business objects in OOIS development.
- Converting business domain objects into OOIS objects in a seamless process of analysis and design.
- Finding a way of standardising business domain objects and OOIS objects, and recognising analysis and design patterns in the business system and OOIS.
- Using common features of the models to compare and evaluate the features of business objects analysis and design models that are built by different OO methods.
- Finding more efficient and useful strategies of building business object analysis and design models.

This framework will be extended to covering all stages of OOIS development in future.

References:

(Booch, 1994): G. Booch. Object-Oriented Analysis and Design with Applications. (2nd Edition) The Benjamin/Cummings, Redwood City, California, 1994.
(Booch et al., 1999): G. Booch, J. Rumbaugh and I. Jacobson. The Unified Modeling Language User Guide. Addison-Wesley, Reading, Massachusetts, 1999.
(Carmichael, 1994): A. Carmichael. Object Development Methods. SIGS Books, New York, 1994.
(Coad et al., 1991): P. Coad and E. Yourdon. Object-Oriented Analysis. (2nd Edition), Prentice-Hall, Englewood Cliffs, New Jersey, 1991.
(Cook et al., 1994): S. Cook and J. Daniels. Design Object Systems-Object-Oriented Modelling with Syntrophy. Prentice-Hall, New York, 1994.
(Estrin, 1998): L. Estrin. *Business Object Transitioning.* In the Proceedings of OOPSLA'98. 1998.
(Fowler, 2000): M. Fowler. UML Distilled: A Brief Guide to the Standard Object Modelling Language, (2nd Edition) Addison-Wesley, Reading, Massachusetts, 2000.
(Graham, 1994): I. Graham. Object Oriented Methods. (2nd Edition) Addison-Wesley, Wokingham, England, 1994.
(Jacobson et al., 1995): I. Jacobson, M. Ericsson and A. Jacobson. The Object Advantage: Business Process Reengineering with Object Technology. Addison-Wesley, Wokingham, England, 1995.
(Kristen, 1994): G. Kristen. Object Orientation: The KISS Method. Addison-Wesley, Wokingham, England, 1994.
(Liang et al., 1998): Y. Liang, D. West and F. A. Stowell. *An Approach to Object Identification, Selection and Specification in Object-Oriented Analysis.* In the Information Systems Journal, 8(2), pages163--180, 1998.

(Liang, 2000): Y. Liang. *An Approach to Assessing and Comparing OOA Methods.* In the Journal of Object-Oriented Programming, pages 27--33, June 2000.

(Microsoft, 1999): Microsoft Official Curriculum Product. Mastering Web Application Development Using Visual InterDev 6. Material NO: 1017ACP, 1999.

(Olle et al., 1988): T. W. Olle, J. Hagelstein, I. G. Macdonald, C. Rolland, H.H. Sol, F. J. M. Van Assche and A. A. Verrijn-Stuart. Information Systems Methodologies—A Framework for Understanding. Addison-Wesley, 1988.

(Prins, 1996): R. Prins. Developing Business Objects, McGraw-Hill, London, 1996.

(Rumbaugh et al., 1991): J. Rumbaugh, M. Blaha, W. Premerlani, F. Eddy and W. Lorensen. Object-Oriented Modeling and Design. Prentice-Hall, Englewood Cliffs, New Jersey, 1991.

(Shlare et al., 1988): S. Shlare and S. Mellor. Object-Oriented Systems Analysis: Modeling the World in Data. Prentice Hall, Englewood Cliffs, New Jersey, 1988.

(Stevens et al., 2000): P. Stevens and R. Pooley. Using UML: Software Engineering with Objects and Components. (Updated Edition) Addison-Wesley, Harlow, England, 2000.

(Taylor, 1995): D. Taylor. Business Engineering with Object Technology. John Wiley & Sons Inc. New York, 1995.

(Wirfs-Brock et al., 1990): R.J. Wirfs-Brock, B. Wilkerson and L. Wiener. Designing Object-Oriented Software. Prentice Hall, Englewood Cliffs, New Jersey, 1990.

XML AND CORBA
ISSUES I

Towards an Auto-Adaptive Model to Compose Multimedia Telecom Services

Zièd Choukair, Guy Leonhard and Safouane Sfar

ENST Bretagne – Département Informatique

Technopôle de l'Iroise

29285 Brest cedex France

FirstName.LastName@ enst-bretagne.fr

August 2000

Abstract

The upcoming 3rd telecommunication telephony generation is setting forth a new set of challenges in the development and deployment of numerous telecom services which follow the requirements and expectations of end-users. This paper describes our approach to provide the user with an environment to set up his own preferences when using such multimedia telecom services. Our purpose is to keep services, profiles and behaviors unchanged and just compose them in a safe way in purpose to generate added value services that answer to the end user expectations. The first implementation is provided and tested on e-commerce applications where we integrate the user profiles with no modification on the XML document. In particular we describe how we adapt the representation according to the end-user requirements. Then we extend our approach to a more flexible system. Our purpose was to provide an environment for end-user QoS control of multimedia telecom services that integrate behaviors as well as profiles. We also present our evaluation of the approach that has been realized and the future study.

1. Introduction

In addition to classical services, the increase in service providers are seeking to add behavioral aspects. The purpose of this work is to adapt the telecom services to the profile of each end-user and to help him to set up his own preferences. The underlying system will be in charge of this combination of a service and its associated behavior.

Traditional telecom services used to be developed from scratch following a development, validation and deployment cycle which is not a judicious line to take for the next multimedia generation as it does not allow any flexibility or adaptation on line. In the future, we expect complex and composed telecom services to be widely available. These services may be composed of simple services affected by presentation preferences as well as the contextual preferences, or otherwise composed of the combination of elementary on-the-shelf services to set up the expected service.

We developed a primary model which deals with the adaptation to the presentation and are still working on a more generic model to compose services in a simple and correct way whether they are classical or non-functional. Non-functional services add to the classical services behavior and then provide them with an added value. Our model named *ACTES* for

"Auto-adaptive model for Composition of TElecommunication Services" is intended to provide an environment in which to compose telecommunication services with their non-functional aspects.

The delicate problem of service interaction is still a major issue encountered by the developers of new services. Although much effort has been focused on providing a widely useful solution for service interaction which may have impacts in the near future, there are no concrete and definitive solutions as these problems occur as a result of events which are unpredictable a priori [5]. However, software engineering provides interesting solutions to assemble software components according to proven methodologies and technologies.

In the first chapter we briefly present the need to integrate QoS into the next generation telecom service and will introduce major interesting approaches. In the second chapter, we present the ACTES model as well as a the first implementation to access electronic portals and how this makes it possible to meet behavioral expectations and increase semantical compliancy with the user's profile according to his preferences. Then we develop our perspectives and the work to be done in term of providing a model to cope with added value services. We will finish with a conclusion.

2. QoS Requirement for Telecom

Multimedia telecom services are intended to be useful for a wide range of users in an open and free way. The characteristics of open systems are rather unpredictable : they consist of a group of users who share the same resources, their requests being neither predictable nor schedulable a priori. The underlying system should then do its best to decrease the suffering due to resource unavailability as much as possible. Moreover, the display of the data should be managed so that it is adapted to the hardware characteristics and optionally to the final user preferences. The composition of the basic classical services with the additional behavior to handle this openness and hardware availability variation will help the evolution of new services as a response to the hyper-competitiveness between operators. New multiservice adaptive architectures should then be specified to support the structuring of these new services.

Adapting the behavior of a service to its environment and to the users' preferences differentiates the classical services and is an important competitiveness factor. For example, customizing a particular service according to geographical position such as weather broadcasting is an appreciated added value for such a usual service.

Beyond the object oriented approach, which usually starts at design level, aspect separation aims at resituating the starting stage at analysis level. The gap which usually separates analysis of the problem from its design is then reduced. Once again it is from the problem analysis that a design is deduced. Moreover, the aspect oriented approach makes it possible to treat the different facets of a problem in a separate way. This decomposition should be nominal so that we only manipulate simple and reusable entities. The extracted entities should be orthogonal to limit side effects and cross influences which we may not master. [Aksit et al.] develop the advantages of this aspect oriented programming (AOP) concept and propose a methodology for a nominal separation of aspects.

However, aspect extraction following those principles and this methodology do not guarantee a dependable recomposition. In addition, this recomposition would be better automated as aspects are by nature composable with basic services or entities. This aspect of the problem has, to our knowledge, no known solution .

Introducing this approach will help to developing a composition service environment based upon AOP. This environment will provide two main advantages : a basis for the analysis support of the problem to decompose clearly the aspects and a composition platform. This way classical services can be reused and available adequate behavior also.

QoS and the telecom service architecture

The access to the Web through mobile telephony systems is a major concern for the operators. Web data as well as a wide range of various services should be accessible through a plethora of handsets (cellular phones, PDA, embedded computers ...). This hardware has limited resources (displays, connection bandwidth, memory size, ...). Some efforts are being made at W3C (World Wide Web Consortium) and 3GPP (3rd Generation Partnership Project) to provide a normalized protocol for the compliancy of the data from the Web to the terminal. However, this provision will not be rich or flexible enough to be sufficient for the operators. The user profile seems to be a better solution as it also integrates hardware profile as well as additional personal preferences and contextual information. A user who owns many profiles may activate them dynamically based on rules stored at set-up time. These rules may concern time, place, hardware, required service, etc.

The 3GPP User Service Profile (USP) includes a list of the subscribed services and the references to appropriate preferences applicable to each service. The description of the profile of a user is based upon the specification of Composite Capability/Preference Profiles (CC/PP) introduced by W3C [3]. This profile may also include QoS parameters and specific information concerning the targeted services. QoS is defined according to the IUT-T N° E-800 recommendation [1], as being the effect of the execution of services which determine its user satisfaction. Generally speaking, we may say that QoS is related to the respect of the contract established with the user whether concerning functional or behavioral aspects.

The QoS in an UMTS network is a major factor in the decision to adopt it universally [4]. A sine qua non condition for efficient deployment and better management of an UMTS network is to provide a QoS support for final users comparable to the one with fixed networks (PSTN, RNIS, B-RNIS....). An UMTS network has many levels represented in the next figure at which to define the QoS [4]. Each type of service presented in this architecture has an associated QoS with parameters and attributes related to the support and to the application class.

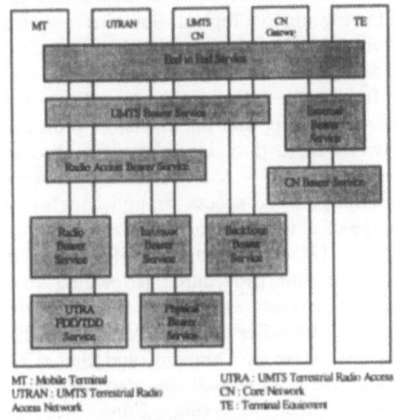

MT : Mobile Terminal
UTRAN : UMTS Terrestrial Radio Access Network
UTRA : UMTS Terrestrial Radio Access
CN : Core Network
TE : Terminal Equipment

Fig : UMTS QoS architecture

The QoS at the internal levels of the UMTS architecture depends closely on the software functionality of each layer and on the service capabilities it implements. For example, at the application level, the parameters which manage end to end QoS are mandatory. 3GPP defined 4 classes of service for UMTS which vary according to the nature of the service and its characteristics : Conversational Class, Streaming Class, Interactive Class, Background Class. The QoS attributes at the user level are composed mainly of the following characteristics : Service or traffic class (Conversation, Streaming, Interactive, base), Maximum throughput with or without guarantee, delivery order, format size and error rate of an SDU, etc.

Software Engineering Support

An UMTS network is expected to support a wide range of applications with QoS expectations which vary according to the service profile [4]. Hence, the telecommunication service architecture of UMTS is designed to help manage telecommunication services in a flexible way taking advantage of interesting paradigms of software engineering. This short presentation of its architecture will help us discover its openness and flexibility. UMTS architecture is decomposed into the following major logical domains : «User Equipment Domain», «USIM Domain», «Core Network Domain» and «Infrastructure Domain» [6] [8]. The interfunctioning and the exchange protocols between these domains take place through communication stratum. We focus especially on the access stratum which is in charge of developing access strategies to the services [7]. It is composed of a group of protocols and procedures associated to a class of services as well as functionalities provided by «Serving Network Domain», «Access Network Domain» and the «User Equipment Domain».It is also the node between the « Serving Core Network Domain » and the « MT (Mobile Terminal) ».The «Access Stratum» take charge of the monitoring and the management of the resources and the access to the radio interface. Its functionalities also express the need of the user in terms of QoS.

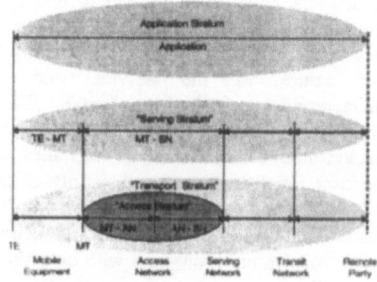

Fig : UMTS logical domain architecture

The 3GPP defined a structure of service capabilities at the service management layer for the UMTS. This provision helps to create a collection of services and to develop and deploy new services. This structure takes advantage of technologies such as Customized Applications for Mobile Network Enhanced Logic (CAMEL), SIM tools, WAP protocol, mobile agent, java, CORBA and RM-ODP. The service management layer at the Personal Service Environment (PSE) level is based upon Mobile Station Execution Environment (MExE) which contains service capabilities. This layer is influenced by the operator parameters, the server network and the VHE environment.

The management mechanisms consist of adapting the user profile to his real use. Their role is also to discover services, to configure them, to control their execution and to act on their functioning, for example through pre-emption or canceling. The interaction between the modules of the service management layer rely upon the provision of a distribution platform which may be CORBA compliant.

In another respect, as we stated before, components are the most adequate software entity to implement added value services and make them interact together. They are, from the software perspective, the most interesting entities required to develop autonomous units which may constitute units of collaboration or interaction as well as units of distribution. Their compositional facets as well as their event flow communication support make them the best candidates to implement the future 3rd generation services which are expected to be composable and to interact without an a priori interaction schema. Using such component composition support will reduce the time-to-market period as the proper positive characteristics of component based architectures are configuration, multiple interfaces, abstraction, reuse, and assembly [23].

There are now three major architectural models to develop components : JavaBeans from Sun Microsystems [9], the CORBA Component Model (CCM) from OMG [10] [11] [12] [13] [14] [15] and Component Object Model (COM)+ from Microsoft. Next, we will focus only on composition and QoS provision. The JavaBeans in particular offer roles to developers, assemblers and deployers. They provide interaction interfaces between clients and containers and components and concentrators. The JavaBeans also possess the advantage that they integrate a deployment descriptor for each component to help set up its system prerequisite. The CCM offers three points of view; the construction, assembling and deployment mechanisms.

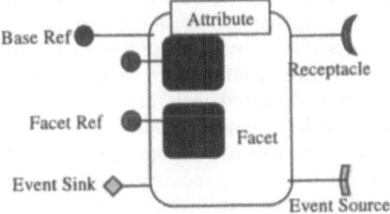

Fig CCM abstract model

Although they are more or less comparable, the CCM model offers a better support for the composition: it provides many facets, receptacles and connector descriptors useful for composition. The CCM model has the advantage of possessing CORBA paradigms and services from which the event service, management of transactions, security, persistency as well as specific extensions such as filtering, lifecycle management etc. Construction and assembling functionalities may rely upon stored descriptions at XML format such as CORBA software descriptor, component descriptor (task model, transactional system, QoS, ...), component property file and component assembly descriptor (localization, connection, etc.).

The CCM model is based upon four nominal models which constitute as many points of view for the analysis and design of such systems : "abstract model", "programming model" , "deployment model" and "execution model". The "abstract model" describes the way to express interfaces and component properties. The IDL language was extended to this purpose. Facets provide a synchronous communication support whereas event sinks/source support the asynchronous mode. The configurable properties belong to the component attributes. The "programming model" uses the Component Implementation Definition Language (CIDL) which describes the implementation structure of the component. It makes it possible to generate the skeleton of the component to be extended with functional scripts using Component Implementation Framework (CIF) which describes the interactions between the functional and non functional parts of the component implementation. This is particularly interesting for our own needs. The "deployment model" is supported by the use of component packages which are the unit of distribution and configuration for open heterogeneous systems. The "execution model" is based upon component container mechanisms. The container intercepts the incoming requests and plays a similar role than the POA and the transaction management. In the next section we will develop the architectural issues and show how multiservice architectures of the next generation can benefit from distributed systems paradigms to answer the expected auto-adaptivity requirement.

3. Auto-adaptive Architectures

The next generation of multiservice architectures needs to be auto-adaptive so that they may integrate evolutive services as well as new ones on the fly. This requirement will be the cornerstone for the operators to remain competitive and attractive to subscribers. In addition, service applications are becoming more and more complex and need additional support from outside the network it self. The architectures have then to be open and inter-operable with external systems. The UMTS service architecture integrates constraints such as openness and flexibility to comply with the requirements of service providers in terms of the richness of their offers as well as the adaptivity of the behavior of services to the final user profile. Virtual Home Environment Specifications (VHE) makes it possible to adapt the service to its use context and execution environment by providing API to manage the users (authentification, profiles and QoS parameters), to introduce generic users, to standardize the API independently of the terminal and to manage and monitor the subscribed contract (tax, credit,...), to manage the session...

From the service management perspective, a distributed architecture should provide common services to UMTS service developers as if they were local. Distribution issues should be transparent so that the attention focus is only on the service management issues. The common services expected to be provided by these architectures are mainly : mediation, storage, notification, security, transactional, performance monitoring, non-functional aspects.

Platforms of services

Telecom services must be accessed through wide area networks and also internet. Service providers look forward to gaining the loyalty of customers by providing new offers and updating old ones. Their applications are usually developed according to the n-tiers architecture model. The terminal puts up a thin client software and is in charge of accessing the diverse services of its application. Most of the application is on the server side and the network is used in an optimized way to deliver the service. The telecom services are then spread through the network to improve system performance and dependability. Moreover, the mobility of the user and the change of his use context and preferences lead him to adopt an application model compliant with the following recommendations.

To implement no-functional properties, a CORBA compliant platform which supports the CCM component model will guarantee the adaptability of the applications as the containers provide mechanisms to integrate non-functional properties. The interception and control of requests will help interpose a behavioral code between the service and the caller. The benefits will be explained at the behavioral filter approach section which we studied using the SINA [22] prototype developed by the TRESE team of Twente University [16]. For example, real-time aspects may then be integrated to a service through these interceptors specifying for instance the required minimum duration for the execution of this service. In this case, real-time constraints are not programmed but only configured to be integrated as an aspect. Service providers will then be able to rely on this platform to combine new services and extend their offer. They will also be able to develop applications which compose services according to the selection done by the user at connection time. For critical composition which may induce interaction problems, out-of-line specification should be used based on languages such as Architectural Description Language (ADL) to help specify the composition of services safely.

Elementary functionalities should be stored inside a component library with a description stored inside a repository to help find out adequate required functionalities. This description should contain three levels : a semantical level for the first search (role of the component), a functional level for more a precise search (which facet may convene) and finally technical information to verify whether or not this component can be used in the specific context.

To try out the proposed approach we developed a model which adapts the services to the profile of each user [21]. This study targets the e-commerce document access services through mobile phones and according to final users 'preferences. At subscription time , the user specifies his own absolute preferences and then when connecting to a site his preferences are taken into account. Moreover, when navigating through a server site, the server may use the choices of the client to setup a "relative profile". This session profile will be combined with his absolute profiles to provide the best service at the best rate. The adopted approach does not induce any change in the server code neither in the XML document nor in the XSL sheets. Only a configuration sheet is generated to reference the choices retained by the client. The standard to define documents is XML (eXtensible Markup Language) which uses a presentation language called XSL (eXtensible Stylesheet Language) to apply styles on different elements declared inside the XML document. XSL styles are independent of the XML data to which they apply. However, XML documents have to be marked to be adapted according to XSL styles. The strength of XSL is that it distributes one data source towards multiple display sources as the next figures show.

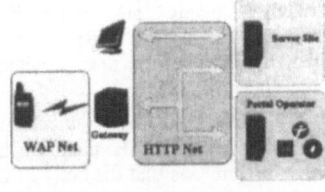

Fig XML document dynamic adaptation schema

The same data is displayed on the wire line PC and the wireless phone. The XML is processed with XSL to output HTML data or WML (Wireless Markup Language) data.

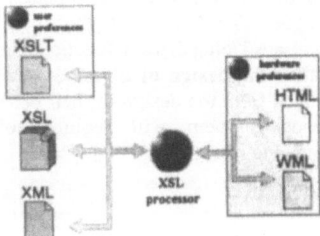

Fig XML document processing

In addition, we offer an environment to the final user to set up his own profile. At subscription, he may select specific profiles to be considered unless he modifies them. These absolute profiles are referenced on the client side and then sent whenever a request is processed to an electronic commerce site. At the server side, the absolute profile is combined with the local profiles (selected by the user during his navigation inside the site) and then the service is processed according to these preferences. Our approach consisted in limiting the creation of new services to none. Only one profile reference file is created and then there is no addition of any new service or document. This approach seems to us very interesting for the operators as the obtained system does not involve any interaction with newly created services.

This study may be extended for example to the case where the use environment changes (from VHE to another kind of network). This change will be modeled by a new data schema which determines new resources and service use characteristics (functionalities, technical attributes, QoS, available service, etc.). Hence, XML generic documents will adapt dynamically to the new circumstances of service environment. Next, we will discuss the extension of this approach to generic telecom services.

Behavioral filters approach

To go further in this auto-adaptivity approach, we considered the behavioral filter model which separates the aspects and then recomposes them manually by integrating them inside precise places inside the code. The benefit is that behavioral aspects are isolated from functional aspects and then the design of nominal services is separated from the design of their behaviors. Composing them will require software engineering rules.

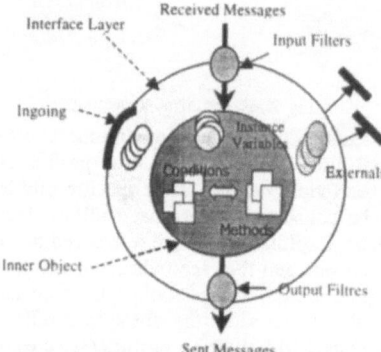

Behavioral filters are composed from a core (implementation part) close to the object oriented model and an extension (interface part) implementing mainly the filters. The interface part is in charge of intercepting messages and treating them according to acceptability patterns. Filters match the incoming messages to check whether or not they may be retained and sent to the next filter. Before passing or rejecting the message, the filter may execute some action [16].

Behavioral filters allowed us to develop aspects such as synchronization, real-time, delegation as well as other examples using SINA [22]. The following example shows the implementation of a synchronization Bounded Buffer filter :

```
Class BoundedBuffer interface
comment        "boundedbuffer;"
conditions     Empty; Partial; Full;
methods
       put(Any) returns Nil;
       get returns Any;
inputfilters
       bufferSync : Wait = {Vide=>put,
```

```
                          Partiel=>{put, get},
                          Plein=>get ;
       execute : Dispatch = { inner.* };
end
```

This approach is simple to handle and offers numerous benefits for static approaches. However, the integration of these behavioral aspects is to be done manually. This will not be a judicious line to take for the 3rd telecom generation to provide such a static compositional approach, which is tributary of the developer skills. The interaction problem may then raise many problems. Next, we will describe our current work to provide a dynamic compositional support for telecom services.

AOP and ASPECTJ

"Aspect oriented programming" (AOP) [20] is intended to factorize systemic and cross-cutting concerns. The separation of these concerns, in addition to the analysis and design benefits we developed, will help to improve the expressiveness of programs and their maintainability. AspectJ was developed by Xerox Palo Alto Research Center as a general purpose extension to Java. Other teams are working on developing models to cope with the expected flexibility of the next architecture generation [17][18][19].

We retrieve the mechanisms developed by the TRESE team such as "before" which means that the body of these weaves are to be executed before the body of the method, "after", "catch" and finally "crosscutting", "advice" and "introduce" which affect a cross-cutting aspect to methods of a class. AspectJ is the most general purpose aspect oriented programming language (AOP) [23]. After testing this language, we retained it for our own purposes. AspectJ, even if it provides many advantages and mechanisms, is still a static approach.

As an example, here is the classical bank account for which we define a generic transactional aspect. The developer will set up his application without thinking about transactional concerns. Afterwards, he will decide that some methods will be transactional and some object servers will be recoverable. The example focuses on the withdrawal calls which need to be cancelled if the balance is negative and is inspired from [24].

```
Public Class Account {
public void deposit (float amount)
        { _balance += value; }
public void withdraw (float amount)
  throws AccountnotAvailableException
        {
if (_balance – value < 0)
        { AccountnotAvailableException e =
        New (AccountnotAvailableException
        ("_balance < 0");
        throw e;
  }
        else
        _balance -= value;
        }
}
```

```
public Class Client
{
public static void main  (String args[])
  {
        try { transferAmount ();}
        catch (AccountnotAvailableException e)  { }
  }
private void transferAmount ()
  throws AccountnotAvailableException
  {       consumer.deposit (amount);
        supplier.withdraw (amount);}
  }
```

```
import java.lang.reflect.*;
public Class transactionaspect
{
  // CLIENT SECTION
  crosscut concernedclientclasses() : Client;
  crosscut starttransactionaspect () :
```

```
concernedclientclasses () & * transferamount (..);
  static advice() : starttransactionaspect () {
            before {transactionservice.begin();}
            after { transactionservice.commit();}
            catch      (exception      e)            {
transactionservice.rollback();}
}
  // SERVER SECTION
  crosscut concernedserverclasses() : Account;
  crosscut backupaspect (account ac) :
ac & (*deposit (..) I *withdraw (..));
    introduction concernedserverclasses ()
    {
            Void commit () {// save the new account
status}
            Void Rollback () {// rollback}
            Void backup () {// backup to the previous
status }
    }
    static advice (account ac): backupaspect (ac) {
            before                  {            if
(transactionservice.pendingtransaction())
            ac.backup();}
}
```

In the previous example, to transfer an amount, the client will deposit the amount in the consumer account and withdraw it from the supplier account. The integration of the transactional aspect is based upon the use of a classical transaction service called *transactionservice*. Two crosscuts are defined, one for the clients concerned and the other one for the recoverable server classes. *starttransactionaspect* crosscut concerns the *transferamount* methods of the classes concerned. Backupaspect crosscut concerns the deposit or withdraw methods of the recoverable server classes. The advice applied for *starttransactionaspect* makes it possible to execute some instructions *before*, *after* or in the event of an exception. For example, the *before* action will initiate the beginning of a classical ACID transaction. From the server side, the advice applied for *backupaspect* makes it possible to execute the instructions *before*. These instructions check whether a transaction is pending and then launches the backup service defined through the introduction of *concernedserverclasses*.

The previous example shows that we can introduce crosscuts to classes with or without being specific about the targeted methods. These crosscuts define advices which contain methods to be executed before (resp. after, resp. in the event of an exception etc.) the execution of the original method. The crosscuts may also introduce new classes and their associated methods. Actually, we defined a transactional aspect based upon the usual transactional server. The use of such an aspect instead of the use of a classical server presents the advantage that the crosscuts can target specific methods as well as a buried code but keep separate from the simple version of the client. This way, we may factorize the actions related to this concern and offer a good level of specialization of behavioral aspects. Nevertheless, this separation of concerns does not resolve the composition aspects between a server and many aspects (think about transaction and real-time, two aspects which do not cohabitate without some arrangements).

Perspectives

We are using AspectJ with JavaOrb to develop a new model to compose telecom services online. We started working on this model and are developing a platform which supports an environment to develop applications compliant with this model. The idea consists in providing an *OffersRepository* in which to register the profiles of the ingoing facets of the components and a *Requirements* introspection method which will give information about the required characteristics of the components to be coupled with. An intermediate agent will then look for such an aspect, check whether it is fully compliant with the requirements of the requester and then, in the event that the aspect is not active, set up the system with this aspect preparing it to collaborate with the requester. As stated in the transaction example, the client classes concerned as well as the server classes concerned have to be updated unless they are kept generic using asterisks. To remain sufficiently generic, clients and servers have to be developed in such a way that they are useful for the major uses of final users. We are developing some services inspired directly from OMG COSS as well as from our experiments with the adaptation of the documents to the final user's profile. Concerning the services (transaction, security and real-time), our approach differs from the OMG approach as the services will not be designed as objects and so. will not face object oriented programming anomalies. The intermediate agent will base his work upon matching information between the client and its aspect section and the server and its aspect section. This matching information has to be specified in common terms so that requested concerns and provided concerns can be matched. A hierarchical information system is being specified to help find the requested aspect according to the specified characteristics on behalf of the caller. The callee will then be updated by the agent which will register the caller and specify the affected methods. This modification is safe as it does only extend the list of the client classes concerned as well as the methods concerned on which the advice will act.

The update of the system will take place at connection time and the aspect compiled again to take this modification into account. The same will be done for the server side part of the aspect which affects the calls processed towards the aspect. This way, we are able to develop aspects and to check whether they are orthogonal and may be combined together by final users. For example, a final user may ask for a classical bank service with transactional service and security aspects. In addition, he may like to retain only classical services and the ones which correspond to his trader profile. The provision of services and aspects will offer the opportunity to select a service as well as some required behaviors and to set up his own profile according to his subscription class.

This model is being specified in detail and our approach will be developed as soon as we get our preliminary results. This study is being done with the hopefully funding of Bouygues Telecom as a research activity tied to the deployment of the next generation telecom services. The complete model will be provided as soon as the first experimentation results become available, by the end of October. We are still working specifically on the data model and the lookup model which will be in charge of matching the requested and the provided information. Two main examples will be developed to demonstrate the feasibility and the interest of our approach. The first one deals with bank account management and the second one concerns free phone calls.

Conclusion

Most of the related work in the area of multiservice architectures does not provide any auto-adaptivity to support a dynamic set up for the users' preferences whether they concern QoS or more general behaviors patterns to affect to telecom services so that they gain an added value. In this paper, we described how we managed to provide the final user with an environment to integrate his profile in electronic documents. Our purpose was to provide this feature without creating any service or changing the code. Afterwards, based on the first learned lessons, we developed the general ideas of our approach to develop a model which will auto-adapt the telecom services to the user's requirements at connection stage without adding any new service. This model is being developed and our previous experience using SINA and AspectJ will be invaluable in coping with its provision.

References

[1] IUT-T Recommandation E-800

[2] World Wide Web Consortium W3C, http://www.w3.org/

[3] "CC/PP exchange protocol based on HTTP" Extension Framework, http://www.w3.org/TR/NOTE-CCPPexchange

[4] 3rd Generation Partnership Project ; Technical Specification Group Services and System Aspects ; QoS Concept and Architecture ; Release 1999.

[5] Dirk O. Keck and Paul J.Kuehn, Fellow, IEEE; The Feature and Service Interaction Problem in Telecommunications Systems : A survey; IEEE Transactions on Software Engineering; VOL. 24, NO. 10, October 1998.

[6] Safouane SFAR, "UMTS Architecture" Technical Report, ENST-Bretagne, April 2000.

[7] 3rd Generation Partnership Project ; Technical Specification Group Services and System Aspects; UMTS Access Stratum Services and Functions ; Release 1999.

[8] UMTS forum; http://www.umts-forum.org.

[9] A. Thomas, "Enterprise Javabeans Technology, Server Component Model for the Java Platform"; December 1998; http://java.sun.com/products/ejb/white_paper.html

[10] OMG; "CORBA Component Model, Request For Proposal"; OMG Document : orbos/96-06-12; Submissions due : November 10, 1997.

[11] OMG, "CORBA Components - Volume I"; Joint Revised Submission; OMG TC Document orbos/99-07-01; August 2, 1999

[12] OMG, "CORBA Components - Volume II, MOF-based Metamodels"; Joint Revised Submission; OMG TC Document orbos/99-07-02; August 2, 1999

[13] OMG, "CORBA Components - Volume III, Interface Repository"; Joint Revised Submission; OMG TC Document orbos/99-07-03; August 2, 1999.

[14] R. Marvie, P. Merle, J.M. Geib; "A Dynamic Platform for CORBA Component Based Applications"; SNPD'00 - International Conference on Software Engineering Applied to Networking and Parallel/Distributed Computing - (Reims, France - May 18-21, 2000).

[15] N. Wang, D. Levine, D.C. Schmidt; "Optimizing the CORBA Component Model for High-performance and Real-time Applications"; The Middleware 2000 Conference, IFIP/ACM, Palisades, New York, April 3-7, 2000.

[16] "The composition filters object model"; CS Departement, University of Twente, Netherlands; http://trese.cs.utwente.nl/tresepapers/trese.html

[17] The Parlay Group ; http://www.parlay.org/.

[18] INRIA COMPOSE Project; "Design and Development of Adaptive Programs and Systems"; http://www.inria.fr/Equipes/COMPOSE-fra.html.

[19] INRIA PAMPA Project; "Models and tools for programming distributed parallel architectures"; http://www.inria.fr/Equipes/PAMPA-eng.html.

[20] C.V. Lopez and G. Kiczales; "Recent Developments in AspectJ"; Workshop on Aspect and Dimensions of Concerns, ECOOP2000.

[21] A. behedi, G. Bonnefoy, S. carini, Z. Choukair, A. Fafin, R. Ogor and A. tafer; "Adaptation Dynamique de Pages XML Selon le Modèle de Profil"; Technical Report, ENST Bretagne, june 2000.

[22] B. Benali and Z. Choukair; "Intégration de la QoS aux Services Télécom"; Technical Report, ENST Bretagne, december 1999.

[23] B. Traverson; "Panorama des Architectures Réparties à Composants"; TOOLS 2000.

[24] L. Bussard; "Towards a Pragmatic Conception of CORBA Services Based on AspectJ"; Workshop on Aspect and Dimensions of Concerns, ECOOP2000.

Component-Based Web Page Composition

Grant Holland
Senior Java Architect
Sun Microsystems, Inc.
Atlanta, GA, USA
grant.holland@sun.com

And

Kishore Kumar
Senior Software Engineer
SDK Software
Minneapolis, MN, USA
kishorekollam@hotmail.com

ABSTRACT. *This paper develops a component model for entities that are comprised of markup language (HTML, XML) elements. This model will explain how these components can be constructed, nested to any level, laid out and rendered – all of these dynamically. The need for such components to accompany and extend Java Server Pages technology is discussed and exemplified. An object model for dynamic construction, nesting, layout management and rendering of these markup language components is presented, and a framework based upon certain design patterns is described.*

KEYWORDS: *Page composition, page rendering, Java, J2EE, JSP, Servlets, design patterns, Composite, markup languages*

1. Introduction: Web Page Composition - Prevailing Practices

Current standard practices for composing web-based visual presentation is based on the standard markup languages HTML and (increasingly) XML.

The use of markup languages for visual presentation has conspicuously displaced the pure use of standard third- and fourth-generation programming languages for such purposes. Prior to this trend, programming languages that achieved critical acceptance in the production of graphical user interfaces were Smalltalk, C, Visual Basic, PowerBuilder, C++ and Java.

However, almost from the outset, the limitations of using markup languages for visual presentation began to emerge. The use of programming languages in support of markup languages began early and has enjoyed a steady increase.

The full-fledged adoption of programming languages for the construction markup-based web pages has evolved into a modern industry. The Common Gateway Interface (CGI) has steadily evolved from using PERL, Visual Basic and C to the increasing use of full-fledged object-oriented languages – mostly Java. Page composition technologies such as Servlet and Java Server Pages (JSP) have emerged to dominate web page composition practices (J2EE ref).

2. Limitations of JSPs

As well as process-related improvements, Servlet and JSP technologies (JSP spec) have improved the CGI programming model by introducing three major innovations: 1) component technology, 2) improved server-side scripting and 3) the replacement of placeholder tags with object-oriented component references. Servlet and JSP technology have brought more power of object-orientation to web page composition and have improved the integration between markup language and programming languages. This paper emphasizes JSPs over Servlets since JSPs are emerging as the preferred source-level format. (Although JSPs are compiled to Servlets for execution.)

JSP provides the ability to develop an HTML-style template that contains object references (to JavaBeans) as placeholders for dynamically generated data. This means that a JavaBean component can dynamically calculate the values of certain data, and that the placeholder tags within the JSP can obtain the dynamic content at runtime and insert it into the static HTML content of the template.

However, the nesting of dynamic content within large container elements, such as HTML lists and tables, can become cumbersome to code using the simple JavaBean references within JSPs, as described above. To overcome this difficulty, JSP provides for placing Java code within "scriptlets" within the JSP template HTML code. This provides for writing Java constructs such as "for loops" to facilitate the rendering of large or nested container elements. Indeed, JSP scriptlets support virtually any kind of Java programming.

JSPs are very good for simple dynamic content. However, if the number or level of nested elements becomes large or dynamically defined, then the sophistication of Java coding required increases until it becomes more manageable if placed within a pure Java class - rather than in a JSP.

Moreover, placing such code in one or more Java classes provides the opportunity to bring the power of Java and object-oriented design patterns (Gamma, 1995) to the problem. Design patterns exploit techniques and concepts that involve the use of multiple classes - such as interfaces, inheritance and polymorphism. Thus, placing code outside of JSPs and into possibly multiple classes can avail the applications of power of object-oriented design patterns. JSPs can then reference these classes in a variety of ways.

3. The Need for a Nested Web Page Component Architecture

Graphical User Interface frameworks, such as Java Abstract Window Toolkit, Java Foundation Classes and Motif, have support for graphical components that can be nested to any reasonable level. For example, a display panel can contain multiple frames, one of which displays a calendar component which contains multiple day entries. Panel, frames, calendar and days are all components that involve nesting.

These components can be defined either statically (prior to runtime) or dynamically - or a mixture of the two. Also, these components are rendered utilizing basic elements of the underlying graphical system that supports the framework. These include such elements as points, lines, rectangles and bitmaps - which can also be nested within each other.

We have a similar situation with utilizing markup languages to render web pages. There are both static and dynamic requirements to define and render components that can be nested.

If we consider HTML to be the underlying "graphical system" for web page rendering, then it also contains elements, most of which can be nested - including text, lists, tables and forms.

However, these elements do not, of themselves, generally constitute component types any more than points and lines constitute component types. A component needs to be an application-defined assemblage of elements.

But a component is more than an individual assemblage of elements. We need to create categories of components by named type. And these types need be able to be nested to any level - and to allow a mixture of component type within the nesting. This nesting structure is generally extended to the enclosing container itself. That is, for the sake of generality, the enclosing container itself should be defined as a component. For example, a web page should be considered a component that nests sub-components.

Often it is sufficient to create and compose these nested component assemblages with an editing tool (or manually) prior to runtime. Other times, these components need to be instantiated and nested at runtime. Frequently, the requirement is a combination of static and dynamic composition.

The need for dynamic generation of web component nested relationships is emphasized, since this must be programmatically generated.

Another capability that GUI frameworks offer is that of layout management. For any visual component that can contain sub-components, there must be a mechanism to determine and control the location of each of the sub-components within the drawing area of the super-component. Such is the purpose of layout managers. A layout manager provides a way to identify the visual placement of sub-components within the 2-dimensional drawing area of the super-component. HTML doesn't present the notion of a layout managers. An HTML frame element can be used to provide a clipping region with content scrolling, but it is not a layout manager.

We have identified two needs of dynamically-generated web page components: 1) nesting to many levels and 2) layout managers. This paper shall propose an approach to providing both a nest-able component entity together with an associated layout manager entity that allows for nesting of components and that applies to web page composition.

4. An Example of Dynamically-Nested Web Page Components

The authors were principle architects of an e-commerce framework that developed the model presented below. This framework, named Portal Framework, was developed on the Java 2 Enterprise Edition (J2EE) platform (J2EE ref). The purpose the Portal Framework is to form a "kit" from which multiple community portals are built. The example below is a simplified version of the Portal Framework.

Consider, then, a community-oriented portal web site. This portal periodically connects to several external information providers and imports data feeds that are of interest to community members. Examples of these feeds are local news, national news, topical news, weather, sports, and financial news from a variety of sources.

These information feeds are then packaged individually as Enterprise JavaBeans ("Content Entities") where they are made accessible to any web pages on the portal web site that are interested in displaying them.

This portal defines several Content Entities, among which are:
News
Weather
Sports
Financial.

What has been described above is the "Content Tier" of the portal web site. A separate tier is the "Page Composition Tier". The responsibility of the Page Composition Tier is to compose various types of web pages that are supported by the portal and to display them on user's web browsers.

In order to render one of these pages, the Page Composition Tier will reference the associated Content Entities and supply their data as dynamic content to the page composition mechanism - such as JSPs. However, as we shall see, it will be difficult and cumbersome to design JSPs that alone can support the web pages that this portal defines. The portal defines web pages for each of its user "interest groups". These interests groups are various civic clubs that subscribe to the portal. The permutations and combinations of interest in News, Weather, Sports and Financials are large. As a consequence, the Page Composition Tier will define various "web components" according to the needs of its subscriber population.

The defined component types are:

Component Type Name	Content Entity types referenced
News	News
Weather	Weather
Sports	Sports
Financial	Financial
NewsRoom	News, Weather, Sports, Financial
NewsRoomLite	News, Weather, Sports
SportsExtra	Sports, Weather
NewsLite	News, Weather

Many web pages are defined to accommodate the various subscriber clubs. These consolidate various combinations of the basic component types listed in the above table. Some of these web pages collect multiple instances of these components in tabular or list form.

Other "components" need to be defined for the portal that consolidate multiple of the basic component types into a single component with a particular layout. An example of this might be a "SportingClub" component that features the Sports component at the top and the NewsLite component at the bottom. This SportingClub component might, for example, appear on the web pages of the NFL Fan Club and the Minnesota Hockey Fan Club.

Obviously, it would be quite cumbersome to program simple nested "for loops" within (JSP spec) scriptlets to accommodate this portal. Rather the considerable power and extensibility of certain object-oriented design patterns (Gamma, 1995) should be brought to bear to devise a solution.

Lets add an additional requirement to this portal that specifies a high level of dynamism – or decision making about page composition at runtime.

Personalization Requirement: The portal web site must provide an online interface that allows any end user of this portal to interactively design his/her own web pages. The user's ability to design personalized web pages on this portal will be limited to defining a layout that consists of the components defined in the table in the previous section. These components may be nested within each other according to the user's declaration. (An assembly tool will be provided through the portal for this purpose.)

This Personalization Requirement means that the portal web site designers cannot statically define all pages. The "personalized" ones will be defined by the user and need to be dynamically constructed at runtime by the portal software.

5. Frameworks and Roles

This paper will present an object model with multiple levels of reusability. The design patterns (Gamma, 1995) presented below could be implemented in such a way as to be reusable by multiple Web sites. We shall refer to such an implementation as the framework, and its implementers as the framework providers.

Subsequently, particular Portal sites could take the framework and customize it to develop a particular Web site. We shall refer to the results of this enterprise as the extended framework, and as its implementers as the framework extenders.
But, who would implement such a framework as this? Application Server vendors could extend their Web containers to provide such a framework as an extension to JSP (JSP spec).

6. Dynamic Composition of Web Page Components – an Object Model

This section considers an object model that can be used to develop a dynamic component architecture for web page composition.

By component, we mean an independently constructed software entity that can be composed of other independently constructed software entities. By our recursive definition, you can see that we mean to emphasize the nested nature of components.

In addition, we are focusing on dynamic composition. That is, we are interested in situations wherein not enough information is known until runtime to be able to design the layout and aggregation relationships among the components.

Specifically, this paper is interested in any combination of the following situations:
Which types of components are to be composed is not known until runtime.
How many components of various types are to be composed is not known until runtime.
How the components are nested within each other is not known until runtime.

Normally, components that fit this description are mingled on a web page with components that are statically defined. The design patterns discussed below embrace this mixture of static and dynamic components.

This paper does not focus on statically defined visual "compound document" component technologies, such as JavaBeans, that are assembled and deployed prior to runtime. (Although the design patterns discussed can be applicable to them as well.)

6.1. Framework Overview

We shall develop a framework to model nested web page components. This framework shall consist of four collaborating class hierarchies whose responsibilities are variously described as follows:

PresentationComponent. This class hierarchy will represent the components themselves.

LayoutManager. This class hierarchy is responsible for the layout of components that have sub-components.

Renderers. This class hierarchy is responsible for composing a component. For a web page, this consists of generating a String of markup language (HTML) that will constitute the visual representation of the component in its web page.
Dynamic Content. Variable information that is required for rendering a web page that is not available at design time, which can change at runtime.

We shall now overview each of these.

PresentationComponents. Any specific layout of nested components on a web page can be modeled as a containment hierarchy. The page itself is the root. Any sub-components that, themselves, have no sub-components are leaves of the hierarchy.
So, web page components fall into two categories:
Simple components: those that have no sub-components. These are the "leaves".
Composite components: those that have sub-components. These are all of the non-leaves, and include the web page itself.

Note that composite components can contain a mixture of simple and composite components. Also, they can be nested to any level. Any leaf components are simple components.

LayoutManagers. Any component that has sub-components needs to specify how those sub-components are visually laid out when they are rendered. In other words, a composite component needs to have a LayoutManager.

Renderers. Ultimately, the only components that actually need to render themselves directly are simple components. This is because composite components can be entirely composed by having each of their sub-components compose themselves in the correct location. (That is, according to the composite component's layout manager.)

Consequently, any simple component needs to have a Renderer that knows how to "draw" it. And, no composite component needs a Renderer.

(Note: This design requires that any visual portion of a composite component must itself be another component. We could have allowed composite components to have renders in order to have relaxed this restriction. But the present design is simpler to describe. However, you are free to make this change in your implementation.)

Dynamic Content. Any component that has runtime-determined content will own a business object that generates and supplies this content. A class hierarchy is defined to accommodate this responsibility.

Classes. So, we shall define a class hierarchy for components that have two subclasses: one for simple components and one for composite components. The super-class of this hierarchy shall be named PresentationComponent. The class PresentationItem shall represent simple components, and the class PresentationItemGroup shall represent composite components. Further we shall define a class hierarchy for layout managers (LayoutManager) and a class hierarchy for Renderers (Renderer). PresentationItem objects shall "own" a Renderer object, and PresentationItemGroup objects shall "own" a LayoutManager object. Additionally, the dynamic content classes that are owned by PresentationItem objects shall be of type DynamicContent.

Design Patterns. This framework uses many of the design patterns that are described in (Gamma, 1995). These will be referenced in the course of defining these class hierarchies.

Class Diagram. The following (incomplete) summary class diagram models what we have defined so far. The remainder of this paper will develop and expand this diagram.

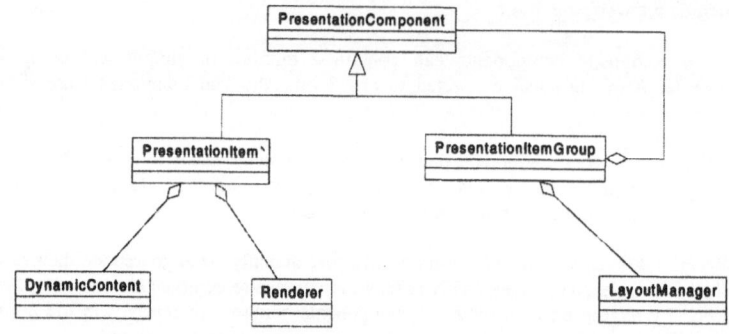

6.2. Presentation Components

Classes of this hierarchy represent components. They are responsible for defining the constitution of a component as well as its layout and rendering.

The PresentationComponent class hierarchy implements the "Composite" design pattern (Gamma, 1995). The following defines the responsibilities of the classes in the PresentationComponent class hierarchy.

PresentationComponent

Responsibility. Abstract super-class of hierarchy. Defines any sub-components and controls the layout and drawing of the component.

Any logical element that is presentable to the client is a presentation component. Company Logo, Footer information etc are all Presentation components. All of the components from the Portal example above, including News, Weather, NewsRoomLite, are object of class PresentationComponent.

Interface. This class defines an abstract compose() method which implies a contract to draw the components. All concrete sub-classes must implement this method.

Implementation. PresentationComponent is a pure abstract class and has no implementation.

PresentationItem

Responsibility. Represents a "simple" component that has no sub-components. Is responsible for drawing the component.

PresentionItem is a very basic and irreducible presentation component. This means that it is a logically complete and separate presentation component. The PresentionItem promotes reusability. A PresentionItem object may or may not contain dynamic content.

Example. A News presentation item may be responsible for getting news headlines and showing them in a tabular form. A company logo presentation item may be responsible for showing a static logo image.

Interface. This class implements the compose() method which implies a contract to draw the components.

Implementation. A PresentionItem object aggregates a Renderer object of its own particular type. For example, a PresentionItem of sub-type ReutersNewsItem will "own" a Renderer object of type ReutersRenderer. If it has any dynamic content, then it will own an object of type DynamicContent. For example, it may aggregate an item of class ReutersContent.

This class's implementation of the compose() method will delegate to the aggregated Renderer object in order to draw the component.

PresentationItemGroup

Responsibility. Represents a "composite" component that contains sub-components. Is responsible for drawing the component.

Interface. This class implements the compose() method which implies a contract to draw the composite component.

Example. A NewsRoom component may be represented by a PresentationItemGroup containing a News PresentationItem , company logo PresentationItem, and company footer Presentation Item.

Implementation. A PresentionItemGroup object aggregates a collection of objects of type PresentationComponent that make up a presentable page or group. This collection may be a mixture of simple (PresentionItem) and other composite (PresentationItemGroup) components.

Also, a PresentationItemGroup object always owns (aggregates) a LayoutManger object that decides how to use the associated collection of components and lay them out to produce a visual component.

This class's implementation of the compose() method will invoke it's LayoutManager, which will determine the layout of this component's sub-components – and will compose those sub-components into that layout. The PresentationItemGroup class's compose() method does this by invoking the layout() method of its LayoutManager and passing its collection of sub-components as a parameter. In turn, the layout()method will invoke the compose()methods of all of the sub-components in the collection passed to it.
So, when composite components are nested to many levels, there will be alternation going on in which compose() calls layout() which calls compose(), and so on. This will continue until a simple sub-component is reached. Then, it's compose() method will invoke the render() method of its Renderer object – and some markup will finally be produced.

Consequently, a single call to the compose() method of a PresentationItemGroup object can produce a cascade of calls which results in the rendering of the entire composite object. Note that a web page is represented by a PresentationItemGroup object. Therefore, an entire web page can be rendered by a single call to its compose() method.

6.2.1. Design of Presentation Components as Java Classes

The following class diagram defines the design of the PresentationComponent class hierarchy. Design pattern fans will recognize the Composite design pattern (Gamma, 1995) in the diagram.

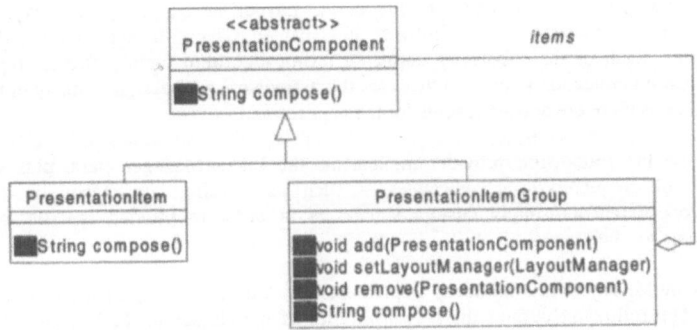

The above figure shows the design of the presentation component system. It is modeled around the composite design pattern. Thus, this structure is capable of nesting presentation components to any depth and flexibility to produce the desired page. A top-level PresentationItemGroup object will always correspond to a page. A PresentationItemGroup object maintains a list of PresentationComponent objects that represent its sub-components. Its compose() method iterates through this list and calls the individual compose() methods of each component in order to compose a whole page. Each PresentationItemGroup will be associated with a layout algorithm, which lays out the presentation components, and build the final page. The compose() method of a PresentationItem object returns a String. This String contains the HTML presentation information needed by a client browser to render this component.

6.3. Layout Managers

Classes of this hierarchy control the layout of various categories of components. They are responsible for determining various layout configurations. For example, "Grid Bag" or "Border" layouts can be defined.

In our Portal example, we may wish to define a particular layout manager for any "Newsroom" components. ("Newsroom" components consist of News, Weather, Sports and Financial sub-components.) We may wish to have News rendered at the top of the display, and the Weather, Sports and Financial info displayed in columns immediately below the News. Therefore, we would define a Layout Manager to implement such a layout.

These various layouts are distinguished by their algorithms – which are implemented as polymorphic methods. A typical approach taken by layout algorithms is to use the HTML table element in creative ways. For example, by use of the rowspan and colspan attributes of the table HTML elements, one can create tables with combined rows and columns – resulting in tables containing variously sized cells.

Layout management is the responsibility of the LayoutManager class hierarchy. This class hierarchy consists of one abstract class, named LayoutManager, with multiple subclasses. Each of the subclasses defines a layout algorithm for a particular type of layout. Each application (web site) that uses this framework will design as many of these subclasses as there are desired layouts for the application.

Generally, the framework provider implements the LayoutManager class, plus some number of frequently-used subclasses – such as GridBagLayoutManager. Then, framework extenders supply custom subclasses in order to provide specific layout algorithms for their portal.

The LayoutManager class hierarchy implements the "Strategy" design pattern (Gamma, 1995). The following defines the responsibilities of the classes in the LayoutManager class hierarchy.

LayoutManager

Responsibility. Abstract super-class of hierarchy.

Interface. This class defines the abstract method layout(). This method implies a contract to implement a layout algorithm. All concrete sub-classes must implement this method. This method's signature is
layout(PresentationComponent[]);

This method is intended to be called by the compose()method of a PresentationItemGroup object. Such object, you will recall, owns a collection of PresentationComponent objects – which represent its sub-components. When layout()is called, this collection will be passed as a parameter.

Implementation. LayoutManager is a pure abstract class and has no implementation.

LayoutManager Subclasses

Responsibility. These classes are responsible for implementing a layout algorithm. Each such algorithm should be implemented in its own such subclass. There may be any number of these layout algorithms, and thus, any number of subclasses. The names of these subclasses are application-dependent and are chosen, or implemented, by the framework extenders.

Interface. These subclasses must implement method layout(), which overrides the abstract method of the same signature of the LayoutManager class. The signature is:
layout(PresentationComponent[]);

Implementation. This method must implement the layout algorithm for its subclass. In doing so, it will lay out the components of PresentationComponent[] collection according to the layout algorithm that is it implements. As described above, such algorithms typically make heavy reliance on the HTML table elements and its related attributes.

6.3.1. Design of LayoutManagers as Java Classes

The following class diagram defines the design of the LayoutManager class hierarchy. Design pattern fans will recognize the Strategy design pattern (Gamma, 1995) in the diagram.

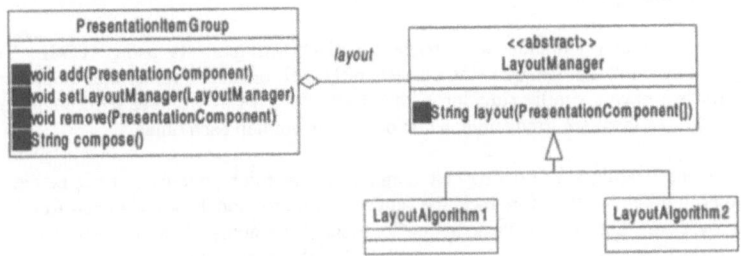

The above figure shows the design of a layout manager. Every presentation item group has a layout algorithm associated with it. The layout manager is modeled around the strategy pattern. This gives the flexibility to add any number of layouts at design time. Then, single presentation item components can be laid out in multiple ways. Also, multiple presentation item data can share the same layout. Moreover, layout can even be assigned at runtime to various components.

This allows maximum flexibility in client personalization of pages. It is exactly this capability to dynamically associate composite components with layout managers that satisfies the personalization requirement of our portal example web site.

6.4. Renderers

Classes of this hierarchy control the visual rendering ("drawing") of simple (non-composite) components. Such components are instances of the class PresentationItem , or subclasses thereof.

(Of course, strictly speaking, the web browser performs the actual "drawing". But since the generation of HTML code is the closest the application developer gets to "drawing", we shall take the liberty applying the term here.)
In other words, all instances of type PresentationItem aggregate an object of class Renderer.

Composite components - instances of the type PresentationItemGroup - do not have renders. Rather, they delegate their rendering to their non-composite sub-components.

The visual representation of even simple components is made up of complex elements. For example, in a graphical system such as the Java Abstract Windowing toolkit (AWT), a component such as a CheckBox is actually constructed of simpler drawing elements such as points, lines and rectangles.

However, these drawing elements have relationships to each other that are similar to the relationships that components have to each other. That is, some of these elements are constructed from ("contain") others of these elements. Some of these elements are irreducible. For example, a point is irreducible. But a line is not irreducible because it contains multiple points.

We have a similar situation with rendering visual components using HTML. The "graphical system" that we are using consists of HTML elements, rather than points and lines. But we have a similar situation with HTML elements as we have with points and lines – some of them are irreducible, while others can contain each other.

Since we are dealing with both reducible and irreducible components that can be nested within each other, we therefore have the same situation to model for the a class Renderer hierarchy as we had for the PresentationComponent hierarchy. Consequently, we shall also use the Composite design pattern (Gamma, 1995) for this subsystem.

The Renderer class hierarchy has one abstract superclass (Renderer) and two immediate subclasses (SimpleElementRenderer and ComplexRenderer). These three form the Composite pattern, with ComplexRenderer being the composite subclass.

The class SimpleElementRenderer represents irreducible HTML elements – that is, elements that cannot contain any other elements inside of them. (Examples of this are HorizontalRule, Text, LineBreak, and Image.) These are few in number.
The class ComplexRender is responsible for rendering reducible entiities. These are of two kinds: 1) reducible HTML elements, and 2) simple components (of type PresentationItem).

Reducible HTML elements include almost all HTML elements – since they can have other HTML elements coded inside of them. The Renderer class ComplexElementRenderer will represent these. SimpleComponentRender will render any simple component (of type PresentationItem) that cannot be reduced to a single HTML element.

In general, every PresentationItem component will create and "own" an object of one of these three subtypes of class Renderer that knows how to draw it.
In order to facilitate the construction of such a class by the PresentationItem component, we shall create a factory class named RendererCreator. This class will use the Factory Method design pattern (Gamma, 1995).

The following class diagram shows the relationship between the PresentationItem class and the Renderer hierarchy. A PresentationItem object will invoke the createRenderer()

method of the RenderCreator, which will produce (and return) the correct type of SimpleComponentRenderer object for the PresentationItem object.

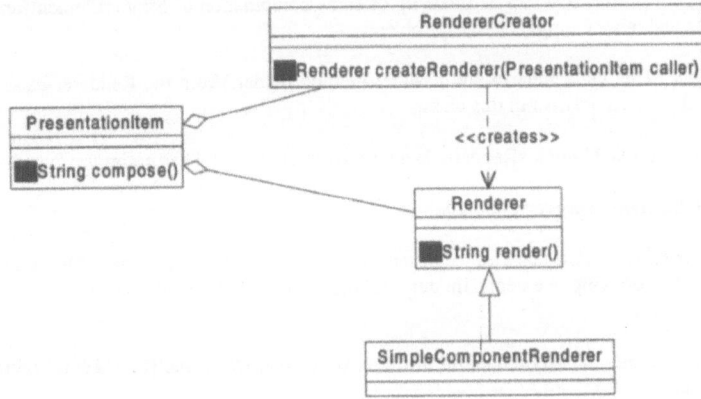

The following defines the responsibilities of the classes in the Renderer class hierarchy.

Renderer

Responsibility. Abstract super-class of this class hierarchy.

Interface. This class defines the abstract method render(). This method implies a contract to draw an irreducible component. All concrete sub-classes must implement this method. This method's signature is
String render();

This method is intended to be called by the compose()method of a PresentationItem object. The return String will contain the HTML code that will be capable of directing a web browser to draw the element or component.

Implementation. Renderer is a pure abstract class and has no implementation.

SimpleElementRenderer

Responsibility. This class is an abstract superclass for a set of subclasses that represent irreducible HTML elements. Interface. This class inherits the abstract method render()from the Renderer class. This method remains abstract in this class.

Implementation. SimpleElementRenderer is a pure abstract class and has no implementation.

ComplexRenderer

Responsibility. This class is an abstract superclass for a set of subclasses that represent "drawable entities that can be made up of some combination of SimpleElementRenderer objects and other ComplexRenderer objects.

Interface. This class inherits the abstract method render()from the Renderer class. This method remains abstract in this class.

Implementation. ComplexRenderer is a pure abstract class and has no implementation.

SimpleElementRenderer Subclasses

Responsibility. These classes represent irreducible HTML elements. These are the irreducible drawing elements in our "HTML graphical system". They correspond to Points in AWT.

Example. There are only a handful of these, which are: HorizontalRule, Text, LineBreak, Image etc.

Interface. These class must implement the render()method.

Implementation. The render()methods of these classes will generally generate and return a String that contains the HTML code to render the element.

ComplexRenderer Subclasses

Responsibility. These classes represent "drawable" entities that can be made up of some combination of SimpleElementRenderer objects and other ComplexRenderer objects. These are the reducible drawing elements in our "HTML graphical system".

Complex entities are of two types: ComplexElementRenderer and SimpleComponentRenderer.

ComplexElementRenderer objects are "reducible" HTML elements (e.g. paragraphs and tables). ComplexElementRenderer objects can be defined in terms of a single composite HTML elements that constitute ComplexElementRenderer objects.

SimpleComponentRenderer objects, on the other hand, require more than one single HTML element to constitute. These lie outside of our "HTML graphical system". Most PresentationItem (simple) components will aggregate a SimpleComponentRenderer object that knows how to render it.

ComplexElementRenderer and SimpleComponentRenderer are both made up of collections of objects of type SimpleElementRenderer. The distinction between these two is that the first type is enumerable. There are exactly as many of them as there are "reducible" HTML elements. Consequently, a Framework could provide implementations of these. However, the extender of the framework, who is defining the simple components, must provide the implementations of the SimpleComponentRenderer classes – one per simple component.

Interface. This class inherits the abstract method render()from the Renderer class. This method remains abstract in this class.

Implementation. Each of these classes aggregates a collection of other Render objects. These may be a mixture of ComplexRenderer objects and SimpleElementRenderer objects.

The render()method of a ComplexRenderer class must invoke the render()method of each of object in its aggregate collection.

RendererCreator

Responsibility. To construct instances of subclasses of the class Renderer. This class shall implement the Factory Method design pattern (Gamma, 1995). In particular, it will implement the parameterized variation of the Factory Method.

Interface. This class defines the method createRenderer(). This method implies a contract to create an instance of the correct subclass or Renderer that knows how to draw the PresentationItem (simple) component that invokes the method. This method's signature is Renderer createRenderer (PresentationItem caller);

This method is intended to be called by the constructor of a PresentationItem object in order to obtain an instance of its Renderer.
Additionally, the framework extender must define the pairings between the PresentationItem classes their corresponding Renderer classes. To provide for this, the following method is provided:
void addRenderer (Class presentationItem, Class renderer);

During application initialization, the framework extender must instantiate a RendererCreator object and invoke its addRenderer method for every PresentationItem class defined in his extended framework.

Implementation. Normally, a PresentationItem component object will invoke the createRenderer() method in order to obtain the correct kind of a object that knows how to render it. And, the createRenderer() method will expect to receive a reference to this object that has called it. The implementation of the createRenderer() method will use this reference to figure out the class of the calling component. It will then use this knowledge to figure out what kind of Renderer subclass knows how to render it. It will then obtain an instance of such subclass and return it to the caller.

The addRenderer method will have placed its pair of Class objects in the a Hashtable. The createRenderer() method will use this Hashtable to ascertain the correct Renderer class and return it to the caller.

6.4.1. Design of Renderer as Java Classes

The following class diagram defines the design of the Renderer class hierarchy. Design pattern fans will recognize the Composite and the (parameterized) Factory Method design patterns (Gamma, 1995) in the diagram.

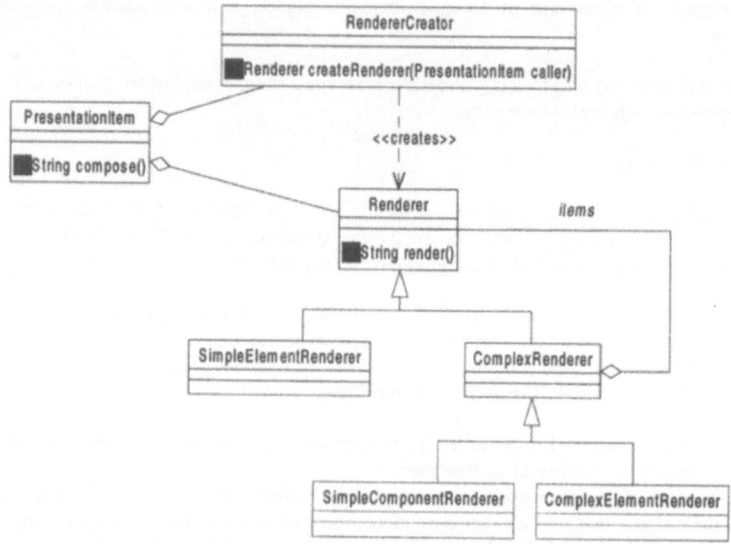

7. Retrieving Dynamic Content

When composing itself, each object of type PresentationItem must be able to accept both static and dynamic component content in the process of constructing the component and rendering it. For example, a table element must be able to be constructed with specific column headers. It must also be able to populate the table cells with variable data before rendering it. The column headers may stay constant while the cell data is changing across renderings.

In order to accommodate this we shall create a specific class hierarchy, named DynamicContent, and give it the responsibility of generating and managing dynamic information for PresentationItem components.

Then, in the same way that a PresentationItem object owns a Renderer, it will also own an DynamicContent object which is responsible for it dynamic information.

DynamicContent objects expose data values that are used by a PresentationItem component to populate itself with variable data when it is rendering itself by calling its Renderer.

A DynamicContent class can be any class that exposes data, including full-fledged business objects such as JavaBeans. In a distributed environment, these may include value objects, SessionBeans, EntityBeans and CORBA services. We implemented a system in which DynamicContent objects were web-tier proxies for EntityBeans.

DynamicContent is actually a "marker" interface that represent the business classes at a site that provide dynamic data to web components. For pedagogical reasons, this paper assumes that these business classes can be organized into a class hierarchy and that each PresentationItem class is associated with an DynamicContent class. We shall adopt the conventional of giving the DynamicContent classes the same name as their associated PresentationItem class, but with the addition of the letters "DynamicContent". For example, the News presentation item class may have a DynamicContent class named NewsDynamicContent.

The following represents this interface hierarchy.

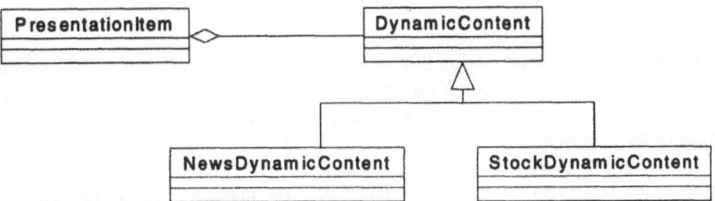

8. Calling the Framework from JSPs

There are many ways that JSPs (JSP spec) can use the components of the framework presented above. We shall discuss two approaches.

Lite. In this approach, JSPs are defined for site web pages, and framework components (e.g. PresentationItem classes) are defined for web page "sub-components", such as News, Weather and NewsLite. Then JSPs for each web page would define a UseBean scriptlet tag for each component that it uses. Then, each JSP would invoke, using scriptlet syntax, the compose() methods of each of its sub-components.

Complete. The problem with the "Lite" approach is that it fails to take advantage of the component framework's layout capability for the web page itself - although, each composite sub-component will have layout.

This is accomplished by creating a PresentationItemGroup class to represent an entire JSP. Then the entire JSP will have layout capability as well as its composite sub-components.

In this case, the JSP for each web page would define a UseBean scriptlet tag (JSP spec) for its corresponding PresentationItemGroup class only. Then, the JSP would invoke, using scriptlet syntax, only the compose() method of its PresentationItemGroup object.

9. Reuse Issues

A component model is expected to provide a mechanism for packaging components in such a way that they can be independently developed, distributed, stored and assembled. Framework extenders who are providing Web components must be able to package and distribute the components that they have developed. Framework extenders who are re-using the provided components need to be able to store and interconnect them into an assembly.While many of these issues are beyond the scope of this article, packaging must be described and the other subjects must be introduced.

10. Packaging

The Web components described in this paper are defined as Java classes. As such the use of the Java package mechanism is sufficient for organizing code modules and namespace management. The Java Archive (JAR) file mechanism is adequate for packaging and delivery of these components.

Simple (non-composite) components consist of three classes – one from each of three types: PresentationItem, Renderer and DynamicContent. Composite components consist of two classes – one from each of two types: PresentationItemGroup and LayoutManager. In addition, the component developer may include "helper classes" to collaborate with the component classes.

These component types can be organized in many possible ways using Java packages and JAR files. These, in turn, can be distributed, stored and interconnected.

11. Development

It is certainly true that the development of the components discussed in this paper requires knowledge of both Java and object-oriented programming. This implies that this component model is beyond the reach of the non-programmers who are developing Web site content - whereas straight HTML development is accessible to non-programmers.

However, few Web site developers are currently coding HTML elements directly. Rather, they have become highly dependent on the use of HTML editors, such as the DreamWeaver product from Macromedia.

Consequently, there is little loss of accessibility by using Java in our component model. Accessibility can be maintained by providing an HTML Component editor that generates the Web components discussed above.

Of course, few component models actually support a graphical tool for generating its components. However, graphical tools abound (HTML editors) for generating whole web pages. Consequently, it will be expected that graphical tools exist for generating the Web components that we have described in this paper.

Such tools are the logical extension of HTML editors. However, rather than generating simple streams of HTML code, these tools would need to generate code for the Java component classes described by this paper as well as any static HTML that these components generate at runtime. The development of these tools is beyond the scope of this paper.

12. Storage

The Java packages or JAR files described above can be stored in any persistent system and can be exposed at runtime to a JVM.

13. Application Assembly

Modern GUI component models often support visual interconnect tools for assembling components into an application. This type of tool can also be developed for this component model, but is also beyond the scope of this paper.

14. Performance Considerations

14.1. The Cost of Recursion

The rendering of nested components that was described above involves recursive calls to the rendering methods of sub-components. This recursion is a direct result of the generous application of the Composite design pattern (Gamma, 1995). A reasonable objection is that this rendering process can consume a lot of processor cycles. We shall discuss this objection at this time.

If you want to support nested Web components with layout, you must either do it inline, or use recursion. For a specific amount of component nesting, either approach will generally require the same amount of processor cycles. Of course, the recursive approach recommended by this paper will require additional loop management and function call cycles. However, this should be minimal as compared to the overall latency of a distributed web transaction. It is the view of the authors that the manageability, extensibility and scalability provided by the Composite design pattern approach that is recommended by this paper more than compensates for any difference.

14.2. Total Overhead

Another reasonable objection pertains to the total overhead at a Web site that could be required if every reference to a Web page requires nested rendering.

Hereagain, this resource consumption would be essentially the same whether the recursive Composite design pattern (Gamma, 1995) were applied, or whether in-line rendering were implemented. The essential cost is due to the nesting of components.

It important to realize that there is no reason to re-render a component if its underlying dynamic content (object of type DynamicContent) has not changed - and the rendered (HTML) component can be cached.

Thus, if you can cache the rendered version of the component, then 1) all requests for the component are taken directly from the cache, and 2) rendering occurs only when the underlying DynamicContent object changes.

In other words, the rendering methods only need to be called whenever the underlying dynamic content changes – never at the time that the component is requested.
This works well whenever the component is being viewed more rapidly than it's dynamic content is changing.

Of course, this requires two other mechanisms: 1) component caching and 2) change event registration and notification. Although we have implemented both of these mechanisms in conjunction with nested web page components, a discussion of these is beyond the scope of this paper.

15. Extending the Framework Beyond HTML Components

This paper confined the application of its object model to that of markup language components. However, the framework can be extended to include multiple kinds of graphical systems (e.g. Swing). A principle alteration requires the replacement of the Factory Method design pattern (Gamma, 1995) within the Renderer class hierarchy with the Abstract Factory. Further development of this issue is beyond the scope of this paper.

16. Conclusions

Prevailing web page rendering practices make use of markup languages such as HTML and XML. However, these approaches fail to provide recursive component rendering. That is, markup languages are not component-oriented.

By developing an object-oriented framework utilizing the Composite design pattern (Gamma, 1995), we demonstrated that componentization derives naturally from standard best practices of contemporary object-oriented design. In order to see widespread application, this framework should be incorporated into popular HTML editors.

This framework is also capable of supporting future client-side object-oriented page rendering systems that may or may not use markup languages.

References:

(Gamma, 1995): Erich Gamma, Richard Helm, Ralph Johnson and John Vlissides [Gang of Four]. Design Patterns: Elements of Reusable Object-Oriented Software. Addison-Wesley.

(J2EE ref): J2EE specification from Sun Microsystems, inc.

(JSP spec): Java Server Pages 1.2 specification, Sun Microsystems, Inc.

Ubiquitous Computing Environments through Open Systems

Arno Puder

Deutsche Telekom AG
400 South El Camino Real, Suite 1550
San Mateo, CA 94402
E–mail: arno.puder@telekom.de

Abstract: *With the growing trend of making information and services available online, one of the challenges for ubiquitous computing environments will be to provide access through handheld devices. The complexities involved can best be met by an open system. This paper provides a novel approach to interpret an open system. We then present an open platform based on CORBA which bridges the gap between handheld devices and online services. The architecture of a prototype is described where an open source implementation of CORBA has been ported to 3Com's Palm.*

Keywords: *Open System, Open Source, CORBA, Handheld Devices.*

1   Introduction

One trend of a modern information society is that information and services for everyday users is coming online. The World–Wide Web (WWW) serves as an enabling technology to provide easy access to the information and services. With the growing success of handheld devices, the demand to have access through these devices increases. Some of these devices, such as the Palm 7, already include a wireless modem which underlines this trend. This makes it increasingly attractive to provide online access for legacy applications such as SAP/R3 as well, e.g. to allow sales persons with immediate access to cooperate services independant from their current location.

The challenge for an ubiquitous computing environment will be to connect handheld devices with legacy applications (see Figure 1). Currently there is a gap which makes it difficult to access online information from handheld devices. First of all handheld devices are often still missing wireless capabilities which will change in the near future. But even with appropriate wireless add–ons, access to online information from handheld devices is limited to web content. This is usually done using a *micro–browser* approach which simply shrinks the well–known web browser interface to fit on a handheld device.

We believe that the user interface for handheld devices has to follow different paradigms than those for the desktop simply because the user behaviour patterns for handhelds and

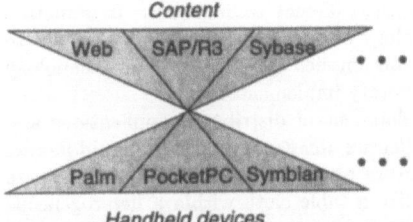

Figure 1: Ubiquitous computing environment.

desktops are very different as are their I/O capabilities. Especially access to legacy applications demand native interfaces which follow the user interface paradigm of a handheld device. The web was also meant for providing access to information, not for operational interaction with services. Operational interaction is already poorly supported from a desktop browser; from a handheld device using micro–browsers it will become infeasible.

Bridging the gap between handheld devices and online information to create an ubiquitous computing environment requires new approaches through what we call an *open system*. An open system manifests itself on different levels, ranging from standardization adoption processes to software development. It is important to acknowledge the diversity and complexity of existing technologies and legacy applications when seeking new solutions.

This paper is divided in two major sections. Section 2 provides a characterization of an open system from different perspectives. Based on the analysis, Section 3 describes an open platform to support ubiquitous computing environments including handheld devices. Finally, Section 4 concludes this paper with a brief summary and an outlook.

2 Characterization of Open Systems

Ubiquitous computing environments which embrace a diversity of technologies introduce new levels of complexity. No single vendor can solve the problems which have to be faced because the nature of ubiquitous computing demands cross platform solutions. The central claim of this paper is that this requires a paradigm shift from closed to open systems. This section establishes the term open system as used for the remainder of this paper. When reasoning about open systems, different perspectives have to be considered. In the following sections a discussion on technologies with respect to standards (Section 2.1) and software development (Section 2.2) is presented for the context of open systems.

2.1 Technological perspective

Coping with the complexities of ubiquitous computing at a technical level requires to accept the heterogeneous nature of todays systems. Legacy applications need to be integrated and made accessible through handheld devices employing different technologies. It is neither feasible nor possible to prescribe a specific technology and for that reason any attempt to build a homogeneous system is bound to fail. This implies the promotion of technology through open standards and not by pushing proprietary implementations.

A popular solution which facilitates the development of distributed applications and which honours the de–facto heterogeneity is a *middleware architecture*. The term middleware derives from the fact that it is a software architecture which resides between the hardware and the application. A middleware spreads out like a table cloth within a heterogeneous environment, offering the same *Application Programming Interface* (API) at each location of the network, yet embracing different kinds of technologies.

A popular specification of a middleware architecture is CORBA (*Common Object Request Broker Architecture*, (see [1]). It is issued by the *Object Management Group* (OMG), an international, non–profit organization with over 800 information software vendors, software developers, and users. The goal of the OMG is the establishment of industry guidelines and object management specifications to provide a common framework for application development. There are several dozen vendors which provide CORBA technology for different market segments.

CORBA as a standard is derived through an open, technology driven adaptation process. If a need for a standard in a certain domain is recognized, a *Request For Information* (RFI) is issued which helps to determine the scope of the problem. Members and non–members of the OMG can contribute to a RFI. The next step is to issue a *Request For Proposals* (RFP). Only members can make contributions for RFPs and through discussions and a final vote the standard is derived. It is important to note that every member has exactly one vote. This prevents "political" decisions and guarantees that only good technical solutions are adapted as standards.

With respect to the characterization of an open system we propose to employ open standards which have been derived through a transparent, technology driven, open discussion. The general availability of the standard promotes a multiplicity of implementations, tailored for different technological domains.

2.2 Software development perspective

With the increasing popularity of Linux, the term *open source* has become a synonym for a new software development process. The origin of open source is attributed to Richard Stallman, who opposed in the early eighties the growing trend of making Unix proprietary. He started the GNU (GNU's Not Unix) initiative with the intention to write a free Unix operating system, which eventually let into the Linux operating system.

The essense of open source is that the source code of a project is released to the public, allowing independant peer review. One often used definition of open source was given by Eric Raymond (see [6]):

> *"Open source promotes software reliability and quality by supporting independent peer review and rapid evolution of source code. To be certified as open source, the*

license of a program must guarantee the right to read, redistribute, modify, and use it freely."

The essense of the open source model is that it allows independant peer review by other programmers throughout the Internet which greatly enhances the quality of the code. This has also coined the phrase *debugging is parallizable*. Open source projects have an impressive record when it comes to fixing problems. Programmers who report problems with an open source project often not only provide a problem description but also contribute a so–called software patch which solves the problem. The turnaround time from identification to correction of a problem is usually much shorter than with any commercial product (hours/days vs. months).

Open source projects typically have a much shorter release cycle than compared to commercial software. It is not unusual to have several new releases of a project per month. This can only work by using the web as a media to distribute the source code of the project. Commercial vendors have a rigorous and lengthy release cycle to assure the highest possible quality. But beta programs and quality assurance in the commercial world only expose a future product to a subset of all potential customers. The amount of testing is therefore limited. This distinction of beta test and final release is not made with open source projects where problems are usually fixed immediately once they are identified. Commercial product development leads to a slower innovation cycle than compared to an open source project.

It is also argued that open source increases security and reliability because the blue–print of a program is available through the source code. This allows independant inspection and decreases the possibility of "unwanted features" such as Trojan Horses. These unwanted features are much harder to detect in a compiled version of a program. For example, many users of Microsoft's Outlook are not aware that this program contains a hidden game (a complete flight simulator) which can be activated by a certain sequence of key strokes. Especially with the increasing need for security with the rise of ECommerce applications, supporters of open source argue that the availability of source code to the general public make it more difficult for governements to force vendors to include hidden trapdoors.

2.3   Comparison

The essense of an open system is that in order to cope with todays infrastructure problems one must employ a collaborate effort to achieve a common goal. As argued in the previous subsections, it seems unfeasable and probably impossible for one company to solve all problems. In summary, the following attributes are essential for an open system:

- decentralized organization: members are distributed over various physical locations

- distribution channel: in order to cope with the decentralization, an efficient communication media is required.

- open membership: membership is open to anyone who wishes to contribute, independant of their affiliation

- equality: each contribution is evaluated only for its content, not by the member making the contribution

- transparency: no information is kept proprietary; all information is freely available

With respect to this characterization we see similarities between the way the OMG is organized and open source projects. For the scope of this paper we consider both as examples of an open system.

3 Towards an Open Platform

In the remainder of this paper we make a proposal for an open platform which enables next generation ubiquitous computing. This proposal evolves around the issues of open systems as explained in the previous section. We explain how the middleware platform as specified by the CORBA standard (see [1]) can be used to embrace handheld devices. The realization of the middleware platform is based on the open source CORBA implementation called MICO (see [5]). Section 3.1 will first provide an overview of CORBA. Section 3.2 then explains how CORBA supports ubiquitous computing environments. In Section 3.3 some deficiencies of the current CORBA standard with respect to ubiquitous computing environments are discussed and Section 3.4 finally gives an overview of MICO and the current status quo of the port of MICO to 3Com's Palm.

3.1 Overview of CORBA

One important aspect of CORBA is that it is a *specification* and not an *implementation*. CORBA just provides a framework allowing applications to interoperate in a distributed and heterogeneous environment. But it does not prescribe any specific technology for how to implement the CORBA standard and different vendors can target different markets. The following principles summarize the goals of CORBA:

Object orientation: Objects are the basic building blocks of CORBA applications.

Distribution transparency: A caller uses the same mechanisms to invoke an object whether it is located in the same address space, on the same machine, or on a remote machine.

Hardware, operating system, and language independence: CORBA components can be implemented using different programming languages on different hardware architectures running different operating systems.

Vendor independence: CORBA compliant implementations from different vendors interoperate.

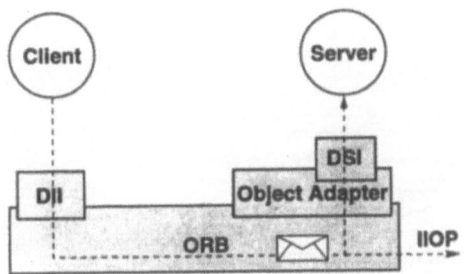

Figure 2: Components of a CORBA platform.

The basic building blocks of a CORBA platform are depicted in Figure 2. The central piece of the architecture is the *Object Request Broker* (ORB) which serves as a "software bus" connecting different objects over the network. At the client side the ORB offers a generic API to send operation invocations called the *Dynamic Invocation Interface* (DII). The ORB's task is to locate an appropriate server and to deliver the operation invocation to the server via an *Object Adapter* (OA). The purpose of the OA is to support the life cycle and management of server objects. The OA delivers an operation invocation via the *Dynamic Skeleton Interface* (DSI) which mirrors the behaviour of the DII for the server side.

The CORBA standard also includes an inter–ORB protocol called *Internet Inter-ORB Protocol* (IIOP) which describes the on–the–wire representations of basic and constructed IDL types as well as *Protocol Data Units* (PDU) needed for the protocol. The design of IIOP was driven by the goal to keep it simple, scalable, and general. IIOP uses TCP/IP for transporting operation invocations and their parameters between different ORBs.

3.2   CORBA and ubiquitous computing environments

In CORBA, the *Interface Definition Language* (IDL) describes the interface of an object. Given an IDL specification, a programmer knows how to implement the client or server side of an application based only on the interface specification. In fact, the programmer does not even need to know how operation invocations are handled by the underlying ORB or in which programming language client or server are implemented. For the scope of this paper this interface between application programs and an ORB is called the *horizontal interface* (see Figure 3). The corresponding *vertical interface* is defined through the IIOP protocol (see [4]).

Whereas the horizontal interface guarantees *portability* (i.e., ease portability of applications), the vertical interface guarantees *interoperability* among applications. A compliant ORB must conform to both the horizontal and vertical interface. Under the premise of compliance, it should be possible to distribute an application across different ORBs, exploiting specific features of each ORB implementation. This independence in the choice of

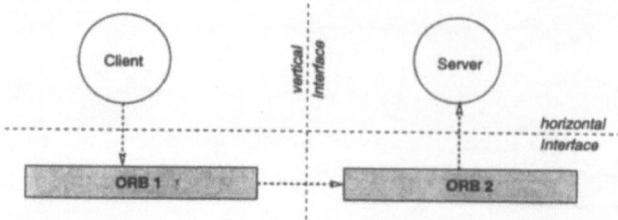

Figure 3: Horizontal and vertical interfaces in a CORBA environment.

implementation is a necessary prerequisit of an open platform. The separation of horizontal and vertical interfaces in a distribution platform supports ubiquitous computing by allowing different vendors to focus on different market segments while guaranteeing interoperability between these segments.

With respect to Figure 3 it is important to point out that ORB₁ and ORB₂ can be from different vendors and can run on completely different kinds of hardware platforms. In one of the next sections this will be shown for the case that ORB₁ runs on a handheld device and ORB₂ on a fixed network. If the domain of ORB₂ is identical with an operator network, one can draw a comparison to the electrical power system. The power outlet defines a standard with respect to physical dimensions and electrical characteristics. This corresponds to a vertical interface. Through plug–and–play different kinds of "information appliances" can be connected to the "information outlet" in the same way IIOP serves as the glue between an operator, retailer and end user. An operator can even offer value added services without having to worry which kind of technology is used on the client side (e.g., desktop running a web browser or a handheld device with a native user interface).

3.3   Deficiencies of CORBA

This section discusses some shortcomings of the current CORBA 2.3 standard with respect to ubiquitous computing environments. While providing an open platform for heterogeneous systems there are some issues which make it difficult to support CORBA on handheld devices. The first issue relates to the limited resources of a handheld device. CORBA in is entirety does not make any assumptions concerning resource restrictions. This clearly is not the case of handheld devices where memory, computing power, external communication bandwith are usually scarce resources. These problems have been recognized by the OMG and a future CORBA standard will include a MinimumCORBA specification (see [2]).

The current draft of MinimumCORBA defines a true subset of CORBA 2.3. It removes some components from the architecture which are not needed for embedded systems, e.g., such as the dynamic components (DII, DSI). There are no restrictions to IDL or IIOP in order to guarantee interoperability with existing CORBA applications. One drawback of the current MinimumCORBA standard is that it does not have separate compliance points for client and server side functionality. For many applications having only client side functionality on a handheld device is sufficient.

Another deficiency of the CORBA 2.3 standard is that is has no support for asynchronous operation invocations. IIOP as defined by CORBA makes the assumption of a reliable, end-to-end connection between client and server object. This is clearly not the case for handheld devices. Frequent disconnects are common because of wireless network disruptions or power shutdowns of the handheld device. Especially the latter is common when a user for example decides to turn off his or her handheld device in the middle of a long running operation and to view the results at a later time.

A proposed standard which could help here is the messaging service (see [3]). The basic idea of the messaging service is to get rid of the constraining assumption of having a reliable end-to-end connection. This is achieved by introducing a store and forward mechanism on the IIOP level. Message routers located on the handheld device as well as the network can temporarily buffer operation invocations and their actual parameters. Once a network connection is established, the previously buffered operations are forwarded to the next message router.

Both the MinimumCORBA specification and the messaging service are still in draft mode and are subject to revisions. It is expected that they will be included in an upcoming version of the CORBA standard. With these two additional specifications CORBA from our point of view is a viable solution as an open platform for ubiquitous computing environments.

3.4 Prototype

In early 1997 a free implementation of the CORBA standard called MICO (Mico Is COrba) was started at the University of Frankfurt, Germany. Although the implementation was done for academic purposes, the authors decided nevertheless to release the source code under the GNU general public license. Soon afterwards the first people interested in CORBA downloaded MICO and started using it. Bug reports as well as new contributions were made which lead to a thorough re-design of the distribution process as well as lead to a mailing list to support the increasing number of users.

Individuals and organization who were using MICO were pushing the implementation when at the middle of 1998 MICO was fully compliant to the CORBA 2.0 standard. The development still continues and the developers were able to catch up with changes made to the CORBA standard. The MICO developer mailing list counts more than 2000 subscribers world-wide who use MICO for both research projects and commercial products. In recognition of the open source movement, The Open Group branded MICO as CORBA compliant.

MICO's architecture is based on a micro kernel approach. Its ORB is designed to be small and efficient. Any extra functionality is moved outside the ORB. MICO's ORB can only transport operation invocations within one address space. Any Inter-Process Communication (IPC) support resides outside the ORB. Special purpose adapters which can register with the ORB give it its full functionality. The IIOP protocol for example is implemented

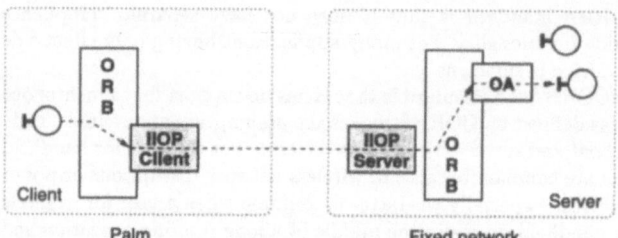

Figure 4: Extending the CORBA platform to handheld devices.

as a pair of special purpose adapters.

Figure 4 depicts the architecture of MICO in a scenario, where the client runs on a Palm and the server runs in the fixed network. Due to resource restrictions only client side functionality is available on the Palm. This accounts for the fact that there is no Object Adapter (OA) inside the Palm. The IIOP protocol is implemented through a pair of special purpose adapters which are depicted in gray in Figure 4.

An operation invocation takes the following path: originating from an application on the Palm, the client invokes the operation via a stub object. The ORB, unaware of objects residing outside its own address space, forwards the operation to the special purpose IIOP client adapter. This adapter, which implements the client side of the IIOP protocol, establishes a TCP connection to its counter part: the IIOP server adapter. After the operation invocation has been received by the IIOP server, it is again send to the remote ORB. While the IIOP client is perceived as the "receiving end" (i.e. a server object), the IIOP server acts as an ordinary client object towards its ORB. As the final step, the operation is delivered to the target object by the remote ORB via the object adapter.

The prototype was developed in the spirit of the open source movement in a distributed manner, exploiting expertise of various people on the Internet. The MICO group was the first to deliver an ORB for a PDA, demonstrating the moving force behind open source projects in general. The result is an early prototype that can be downloaded from the web at http://www.mico.org/pilot. The prototype was implemented using the commercial development environment CodeWarrior from MetroWerks. One interesting conclusion of the project is that reducing the complexity of a C++ ORB to make it fit on an resource limited device does not necessarily mean to reduce its size. More often problems arose with the C++ compilers and reducing the complexity on a pragmatic level meant to restrict the kind of C++ language features used in the implementation.

3.5 Benchmark

A simple IDL specification was chosen for the benchmark test. The IDL specification consists of one interface with four operations. Beside an operation with no input and return

	Request	Reply	Colocated	TCP	PDA
m1	68	24	0.0059	0.9683	180.1
m2	72	24	0.0059	1.0034	191.0
m3	68	28	0.0060	0.9981	184.2
m4	72	28	0.0060	1.0030	194.7

Table 1: Performance of operation invocation in different scenarios (average time in milliseconds).

parameters, there are various permutations of one argument input/output parameters. The complete IDL specification looks as follows:

```
interface Benchmark {
  void m1 ();
  void m2 (in long x);
  long m3 ();
  long m4 (in long x);
};
```

The benchmark was conducted in three different scenarios. In each scenario, the above IDL specification was implemented on the server side using the *Portable Object Adapter* (POA) and running on an Intel Pentium 266 MHz PC with Linux 2.0.35 as the operating system. The three scenarios differ in the way the client is implemented. For the first scenario, the client is colocated with the server (i.e. client and server reside in the same address space). In this case, a CORBA operation invocation decays to a normal C++ method call and no marshalling of parameters is necessary.

For the second scenario the client is moved to a different process, but still on the same machine. Here, IIOP version 1.0 is used to connect the client and the server over the loopback device. The third scenario finally moves the client to the Palm. In this configuration, the client (memory footprint 48 kBytes) runs on a Palm III and is connected via a cradle to the Linux PC. The connection between the Palm and the PC uses a 19.200 baud serial link, running PPP on top. As with the second scenario, the client and server use standard IIOP version 1.0 for their interactions.

Note the server is exactly the same in all three scenarios. From the server's point of view it is transparent from where the client is located, under which operating system the client runs and in what language it is implemented. Table 1 gives the result of the benchmark. For each of the four operations, the size of the IIOP request and reply packets in octets is given (one operation invocation first sends a request from the client to the server; the server then returns the results via a reply in the other direction). Since IIOP is used when client and server are not colocated, the amount of data transmitted between the client and the server is the same, independant of the location of the client.

4 Conclusion and Outlook

The claim of this paper is that ubiquitous computing requires an open system. Open systems manifest themselfs in different ways and are a necessary prerequisit to achieve a consensus in a heterogeneous environment. With respect to standardization, an open system is characterized by a transparent, technology driven adaption process where all members of the standardization body have equal rights. With respect to the software development process, we believe that open source models have benefits regarding the quality and reliability of software.

CORBA seems to be a good candidate for a middleware architecture because it is an open standard with many different implementations, both in the commercial and open source domain. The IIOP protocol separates the concerns between provider, retailer and end users, thus enabling interoperability. A telecommunication company can for example focus on integrating value added services into their networks which can be used through IIOP. Other vendors on the other hand can focus on domain specific applications which can make use of the generic services offered by an operator.

A prototype demonstrating the feasibility to have CORBA on handheld devices is available based on the open source project MICO. The prototype runs on a Palm and currently relies on a fixed connection to the network due to restrictions of IIOP. It is planned to evaluate the messaging service for its suitability of supporting the offline characteristics of handheld devices.

References

[1] Object Management Group (OMG), The Common Object Request Broker: Architecure and Specification, Revision 2.3, June 1999.

[2] Object Management Group. Draft Specification of MinimumCORBA. ftp://ftp.omg.-org/pub/docs/orbos/98-08-04.ps, 1998.

[3] Object Management Group. Draft Specification of the Messaging Service. ftp://ftp.-omg.org/pub/docs/orbos/98-05-06.ps, 1998.

[4] A. Puder and M. Moscarda. Native ATM Support for CORBA Platforms. In *International Conference on ATM (ICATM'98)*, Colmar, France, 1998. Institute for Electrical and Electronics Engineers.

[5] A. Puder and K. Römer. *MICO — a free CORBA compliant implementation.* dpunkt Verlag, 1998.

[6] E. Raymond. The Principles of OpenSource Projects. http://www.opensource.org/, 1998.

The Devil is in the Detail: A Comparison of CORBA Object Transaction Services

Ian Gorton[1], Anna Liu, Phong Tran

Software Architectures and Component Technologies Group,
CSIRO Mathematical and Information Sciences, Locked Bag 17, North Ryde
NSW 2113, Australia
{ian.gorton, anna.liu, phong.tran}@cmis.csiro.au

ABSTRACT. *The CORBA Object Transaction Service (OTS) is a key component in many enterprise information systems built using distributed object technology. The Object Management Group (OMG) defines the OTS through a set of standard interfaces and services that a CORBA-compliant OTS must adhere to. Product vendors then implement a realization of the OTS in their CORBA technology. This level of standardization in theory allows application designers to architect their systems in a product-neutral manner, using a standard set of interfaces that all the various OTS implementations support. This paper examines three concrete OTS products from different vendors. The underlying approaches and architectures are compared, and their strengths and weaknesses analyzed. The analysis clearly shows that major differences exist in the behavior of the different products, and these have profound effects on application design and implementation.*

KEY WORDS: CORBA, Object Transaction Service, middleware

1. Introduction

Until relatively recently, distributed transaction processing (TP) technology was only supported by TP monitor systems (e.g. TUXEDO, Encina) that were largely procedural in nature. TP systems were typically written in C, and the products offered mainly C-based programming interfaces for constructing applications and coordinating transactions. The procedural nature of TP monitors betrayed their heritage as products developed in the late 1980's and early 1990's when C was the predominant systems programming language.

However, reflecting trends in software technology during the 1990's, object-oriented distributed TP technology has recently blossomed. Over a number of years, the Object Management Group (OMG) has been working to define the Object Transaction Service (OTS) as part of the Common Object Request Broker Architecture (CORBA) standard. This work has now reached maturity and a number of complete implementations of the OTS are now available from TP monitor and middleware product vendors. These systems can coordinate transactions that involve multiple objects residing in various processes in a distributed system, and combine the architectural advantages of distributed systems with the programming benefits of object-oriented design and implementation.

Importantly, the OTS service only specifies the interfaces that a transaction service must support in a CORBA environment. Product vendors are consequently free to support the mandated OTS interfaces in any way they see fit. This deliberately gives the vendors a fair degree of latitude in

---

[1] Adjunct Professor, Basser Dept of Computer Science, University of Sydney, Sydney, Australia

how they architect and build an OTS service. At one extreme, a vendor can design and build a brand new transaction service from the ground up, which is custom designed to support the OTS interfaces. At the other extreme, a vendor can provide a simple wrapper that maps the OTS interface services to the features provided in an existing transaction service API from an existing TP monitor product. Hence, while different transaction services should appear identical at a high-level interface level, they may be structured radically different internally, and perform very differently in applications.

In this paper, we describe the architectures of three CORBA transaction services that are provided by three product vendors. The paper firstly gives a brief overview of the CORBA OTS. It then explains the architectures of IONA's OrbixOTS, Inprise's ITS, and BEA's WLE when used in a C++ application. The major strengths and weaknesses of the transaction services are then clearly explained, and illustrated in some cases with example performance figures. This analysis of the three technologies clearly highlights the need for software architects and engineers to gain a deep understanding of the specific services they are using, or intend to use in their enterprise applications.

2. Overview of the CORBA OTS

As ORB applications grow in scale and provide mission-critical functionality, the need to reduce the effort in constructing reliable, high integrity systems becomes paramount. To this end, the CORBA OTS brings the transactional model, so successfully utilised in traditional TP monitors, to the CORBA environment. OTS-enabled CORBA applications acquire the ability to access and update multiple data sources and ensure they remain in a consistent state.

Figure 1 illustrates where the OTS fits in to the CORBA application architecture. As a CORBAService, it supplements the ORB's capability by providing transaction management for distributed objects. Objects can begin a transaction, and then perform one or many operations on remote objects within the context of that transaction. When complete, the object can attempt to commit the transaction. The OTS will then drive the commit protocol and complete the transaction accordingly.

In addition, the OTS design has been conceived to satisfy a number of specific requirements:

* Portability, supported through specifying standard interfaces for interaction between the ORB and OTS
* Support for both single and multithreaded implementations at both the client and server
* Avoid OTS-specific extensions to CORBA IDL
* Achieve comparable performance with transaction services that implement the X/Open procedural model. In this context, performance is measured in terms of the number of network messages and disk accesses required, and the amount of data logged

The OTS provides a number of interfaces in an IDL module known as `CosTransactions` for applications to use. These interfaces represent the set of abstractions that cooperate to support a transaction service, namely:
* `TransactionFactory`
* `Control`
* `Terminator`
* `Coordinator`
* `Resource`
* `Current`

The most widely used interface for transaction coordination in application code is the Current interface. It is shown in Figure 2, and contains a set of services that make it easy to begin, commit and rollback transactions.

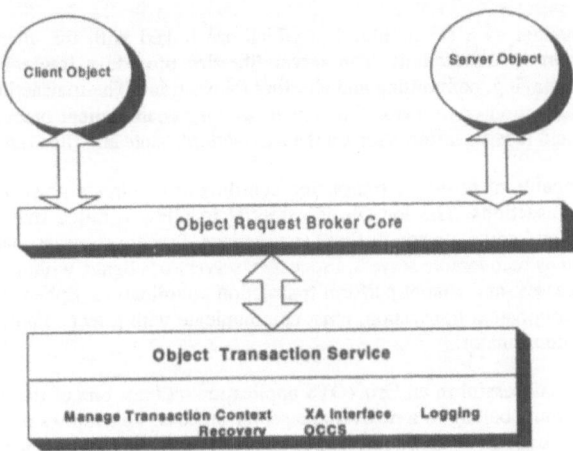

FIGURE 1: The CORBA Object Transaction Service

```
interface Current {
      void begin()
      raises(SubtransactionsUnavailable);
      void commit(in boolean report_heuristics)
            raises(
            NoTransaction,
            HeuristicMixed,
            HeuristicHazard
            );
      void rollback()
            raises(NoTransaction);
      void rollback_only()
            raises(NoTransaction);

      Status get_status();
      string get_transaction_name();
      void set_timeout(in unsigned long seconds);

      Control get_control();
      Control suspend();
      void resume(in Control which)
            raises(InvalidControl);
};
```

FIGURE 2: The OTS Current Interface

The OTS is a reasonably complex CORBA service. Interested readers can find more information on the service in at www.omg.org or in [GORTON00].

3. OrbixOTS

IONA's OrbixOTM product contains IONA's implementation of the CORBA OTS service. OrbixOTS provides distributed transaction management capabilities predominantly to C++

applications, and fully supports the OMG's Object Transaction Service. IONA licensed IBM Transarc's Encina transaction engine and has integrated this with their product suite. This approach attempts to leverage the proven capabilities of the Encina code, and brings it to the CORBA world through the use of IIOP. Hence OrbixOTS has the Encina TP libraries at its core.

OrbixOTS is implemented as a set of libraries, which are linked with the client and server processes that take part in transactions. The server libraries provide a transaction manager, capable of creating, managing, committing and aborting transactions. The transaction manager is also known as the transaction coordinator. The client libraries enable client processes to begin and end transactions, and receive information on the transaction's state and final outcome.

Any server process capable of hosting a transaction coordinator requires a persistent log file to record the state of transactions. The log file is essential to allow a failed transaction server process to be restarted and complete any in-flight transactions. Server processes that have access to a log file are known as recoverable servers. Processes, servers or clients, without a log file are called ephemeral processes, and cannot perform transaction coordination. Ephemeral processes, typically clients who originate a transaction, must communicate with a recoverable process that will act as transaction coordinator.

For a transaction to be successful in an OrbixOTS application, at least one of the objects taking part in the transaction must belong to a recoverable server process. This allows the transaction's state to be logged and a commit or abort outcome to be reached. When a transaction commences, the first recoverable server process that the transaction touches takes the responsibility of coordinating that transaction. This means the OTS service is effectively distributed amongst all the recoverable servers in an application, with no single point of system failure. This basic scheme for a single server process is shown in Figure 3.

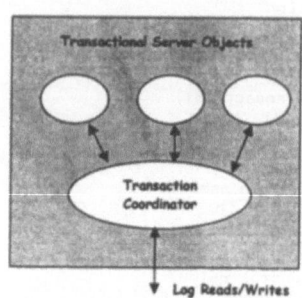

Figure 3 OrbixOTS Server

The OrbixOTS architecture has two main deployment configurations for recoverable server processes. The first, illustrated in Figure 4, allocates a log file to each server process. Log files are typically a minimum size of 4-8MB, and the OTS reuses old records in the log to ensure the log doesn't need to grow. This configuration provides the highest possible performance for an OrbixOTS application, as each transaction coordinator has its own log file to record transaction state. The trade-off against better performance is one of increased disk usage.

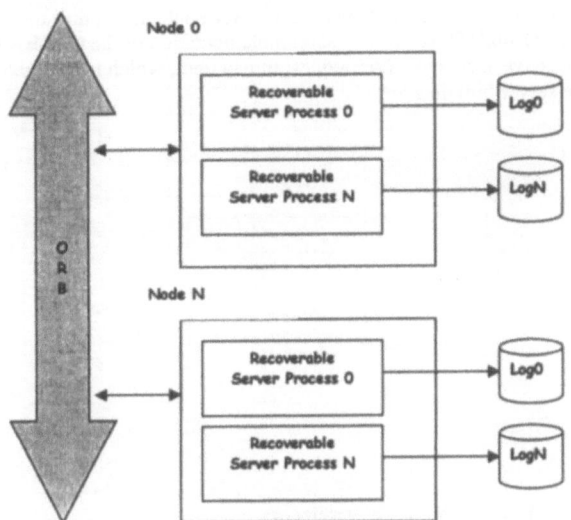

**Figure 4 OrbixOTS Architecture –
Separate Transaction Logs per Process**

Figure 5 depicts the alternative configuration. This utilizes another OrbixOTS server process as a logging process for all the other server processes on the node. This scheme minimizes disk space usage, but will increase the cost of writing log records, as they now include the time to issue a remote call to the logging server. OrbixOTS provides a simple API to achieve this, as shown below:

```
OrbixOTS::Server_var ots = OrbixOTS::Server::IT_create();
ots->logServer("Log_Server");
```

To reduce the overheads of the configuration in Figure 5, the logging server should not have any application server objects, and only support server processes on the same node. It's sole aim is to receive log read and write requests from other local transactional server processes.

In addition, on operating systems such as Solaris and HP-UX, OrbixOTS supports the use of raw disk partitions. This allows the log read and write operations to by-pass the operating system's file system functions, and can provide a significant speed up in server performance. OrbixOTS also allows transaction logs to be mirrored. In a mirrored configuration, the transaction state is logged to two (or potentially more) log files, and the log write operations are performed serially to ensure that one of the logs contains the correct state information. The advantage of mirroring is that, provided the two log files are physically located on different disks, it insulates the application against the failure of one of the volumes that a log resides on. It does however come with a performance penalty.

The implementation of OrbixOTS utilizes a number of internal threads to improve performance of the commit, rollback and recovery protocols. There are separate thread pools for handling administration, logging and transaction protocol messages. These thread pools are dynamic in size, and are set to have a minimum of 5 threads and a maximum of 50: these settings are not configurable. In addition, transactional client and server applications may themselves create multiple threads, as OrbixOTS is a thread-safe implementation of the CORBA OTS. OrbixOTS server applications have access to a user request thread pool, which is automatically created upon completion of the server initialization.

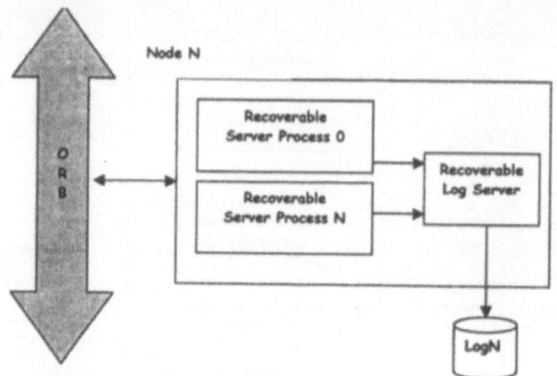

Figure 5 OrbixOTS Architecture –
Transaction Logging Server per Node

Other OrbixOTS features worthy of note are:

- Full support for subtransactions, and a defined mapping from OrbixOTS subtransactions to XA resource manger transactions (which do not understand subtransactions).

- Support for transactional Java clients and servers. Java clients can use a set of Java classes that support the client-side OrbixOTS libraries. This means Java clients can make calls to C++ or Java transactional server objects. On the server, there is an equivalent Java OrbixOTS API. This however does not support interactions with XA resource managers, and hence distributed transactions are not supported. Also, as the OTS service is not written in Java, Java servers must use a remote OrbixOTS process called the *transaction factory*. This means that Java transactional servers must issue a remote method invocation in order to access OrbixOTS, and pay the accompanying performance penalty.

4. Visibroker ITS

The Inprise Integrated Transaction Service (ITS) forms part of Inprise's CORBA-based technology for enterprise information systems. ITS v1.2 conforms to the OMG Transaction Service specification version 1.1. The core ITS functionality can be deployed in C++ applications as a shared library, or as a stand-alone, potentially replicated process. In addition to the transaction service, Inprise provide a number of components that are tightly coupled with the ITS to provide database integration and XA compliant distributed transactions.

The basic server side architecture of an ITS application is shown in Figure 6. This shows three example server processes on two machines, one with an embedded ITS instance, and the others sharing a standalone ITS. Each ITS instance can have its own transaction log, or a log can be shared between multiple ITSs.

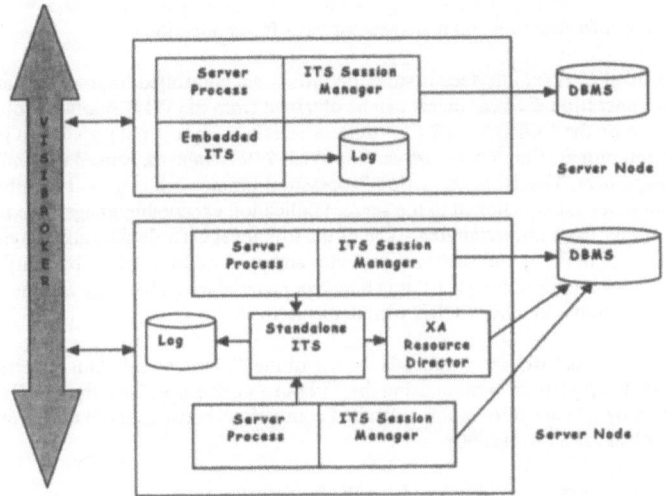

Figure 6: Visibroker ITS example

The ITS Session Manager (SM) component provides services for an application to obtain an ITS-enabled database connection. SM's provide a consistent class interface for applications to obtain a database connection for different database products[2]. They also automatically perform database connection pooling, which is particularly useful in performance terms for multi-threaded server processes. There are two specific types of SM, namely DirectConnect and XA.

The DirectConnect SM is designed to operate with a single database, and therefore performs a one-phase commit for ITS transactions with the database. The XA SM is required to manage XA-compliant resources (normally databases) that will participate in distributed transactions. The SM is responsible for coordinating with the ITS to start an XA transaction with the resource manager on a particular connection. When an attempt is made to commit the XA transaction, the coordinating ITS uses the XA Resource Director (RD) to perform the two-phase commit using the XA protocol. Each resource manager needs to be associated with a single standalone RD process. In a distributed transaction, the ITS will ask the RD for each participating resource in the transaction to prepare, and subsequently commit or rollback. In addition, the RD participates in the recovery of transactions after a failure has occurred

5. WebLogic Enterprise

WebLogic Enterprise (WLE) from BEA Systems provides distributed transaction management capabilities with XA-compliant resource managers. WLE contains an implementation of the CORBA OTS. However, BEA's OTS is only partially compliant to the OMG's Object Transaction Service, as not all CORBA OTS defined interfaces are implemented.

The WLE transaction service is built on TUXEDO's transaction management engine, which is encapsulated by the CORBA OTS interface. This means that the underlying TP functionality is

---

[2] Currently Sybase and Oracle

actually provided by TUXEDO. This leverages a proven technology for WLE, and provides ready-made system infrastructure and management tools for applications.

The CORBA defined *Current* interface is supported for client controlled transactions, and a reference to the transaction *Current* object can be obtained from the WLE *Bootstrap* object. WLE does not expose the CORBA OTS *Coordinator* interface, so it is not possible to perform explicit transaction propagation. On the server, the WLE *TPFramework* is used to handle transaction management. The TP (Transaction Processing) Framework is a run-time library of default implementations that is linked to the server application executable image. The framework frees the programmer from understanding some of the low-level OTS details, and provides a declarative method of defining transactional behavior and policies for a server by using an Implementation Configuration File (ICF). It is however proprietary technology and the resulting server code is not portable to other CORBA implementations.

It is interesting to note that BEA recommends the use of the TPFramework. Our experience with WLE indicates that applications written using the TPFramework outperform the CORBA OTS compliant method by a factor of two. For a detailed comparison between these two approaches and test results, please refer to [Liu00].

Figure 7 illustrates the typical architecture for a WLE application.

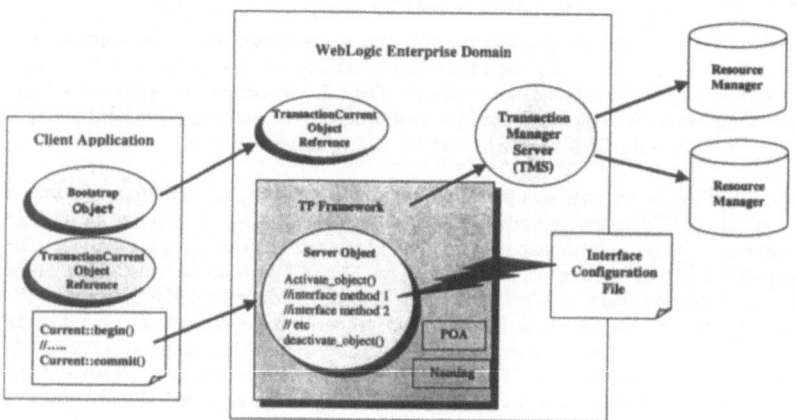

Figure 7 WLE Architecture

The WLE Transaction Manager Server (TMS) process provides global transaction coordination. The TMS is generated at the server compilation stage, when the resource manager XA library and its corresponding open string are supplied as configuration parameters. The TMS process is started on a per WLE application *group* basis, where the group acts as a logical unit for interaction with the resource manager. For performance reasons, at least two TMS processes are started at boot up time. This also ensures no single point of failure. Associated with the TMS is a persistent log file called TLOG for recording the state of transactions. TLOG needs to be set up by the administrator on a per machine basis, and can exploit raw disk partitions to improve performance.

During the two-phase commit, the transaction initiator is normally blocked waiting for the outcome of the commit process. WLE exploits the underlying TUXEDO capabilities to allow control to be passed back to the initiator after the transaction outcome is logged at the end of the prepare phase. The TM then has the responsibility to ensure the returned value is secured. If a fault occurs in the second phase, the TM would perform recovery using the logged information. It does so by prompting RMs to supply their latest status of open transactions and compares the result with what has been logged. Commits or rollbacks can then be issued accordingly to bring the system back to a consistent state.

The following are some other features and constraints of WLE's OTS implementation:
- WLE supports multithreaded non-transactional clients. For transactional clients, WLE supports only single-threaded client implementations. Clients cannot make transaction requests concurrently in multiple threads. Only single-threaded server processes can be built.
- In WLE, clients using third-party implementations of the OTS or the Java Transaction API (for Java applications) are not supported.
- WLE supports both C++ and Java transactional clients and servers.

6. Analysis

It should be clear from the above descriptions that the three transaction services differ dramatically in their underlying architectures. These differences manifest themselves in a number of ways that can have a dramatic effect on application design and performance. Some of these issues are briefly addressed below:

6.1 Programming Model

One of the promises of using standards like the CORBA OTS is code portability between products. However, with the three products we have examined, this is certainly not easy to achieve. OrbixOTS is probably the most true to the standard, but this is achieved by adopting a fairly minimalist approach and not providing any enhancements to ease programming. The Inprise ITS takes a very different view, and provides Session Manager components which provide an abstraction layer to hide some of the difficulties of access resource managers. This requires code that is ITS-specific. BEA's WLE also provides tools to ease OTS programming with its TP Framework. Again, this requires the application to be closely coupled to WLE features. With both the Inprise and WLE OTSs, we are unaware of simple and effective ways to build systems that are highly portable across other OTS-compliant products.

6.2 Multithreading and Database Connections

Inprise ITS has database connection pooling capabilities in the Session Manager components. This is particularly useful in multi-threaded servers, which Visibroker supports through a simple API call. Neither of the other two products provides any support for connection pooling. OrbixOTS servers can be multi-threaded, but the designer must decide how multiple threads get access to a database connection. This typically requires a simple, thread-safe database connection pool handler to be handcrafted. WLE servers are inherently single-threaded due to their TUXEDO heritage, and hence database connection pooling in a single server is not an issue.

6.3 Overheads of Transaction Creation

A standard design decision in applications is which process should start the transaction. In most systems, this is done by using the *begin()* method of the *Current* interface (see Figure 2) in either the client or server process. In both cases, the transaction originator must get a reference to the *Current* object. We have found that the cost of calling the *begin()* method varies dramatically between products, especially when called from an OTS client.

In OrbixOTS, the *begin()* method is a local call in a client, and hence extremely fast (substantially less than a millisecond). This is due to the underlying Encina architecture, which does not designate a transaction coordinator at the transaction creation stage, but instead waits until a transactional call is made to a recoverable server process that is linked with the transaction service.

This is not the case with the ITS and WLE. A *begin()* call in an ITS client results in a remote method invocation to an object in the transaction service that supports the *Current* interface. This is typically on a different machine, and hence costly. As an example, in a sample ITS application with 300 concurrent clients, we found the cost of starting a transaction on the client was on average 21 milliseconds [TRAN00]. We have also seen similar overheads with WLE, where again the *begin()* method requires a remote call. Consequently both the ITS and WLE suffer considerably in terms of their scalability when client-side transaction coordination is needed.

6.4 Transaction Commit Performance

The cost of transaction completion is mainly determined by the number of remote calls required, transaction log accesses, and the commit protocol used (ie one-phase or two-phase commit). With OrbixOTS, the transaction service is linked with the resource manager's XA library, and hence *prepare* and *commit* calls travel directly to resource manager. If only a single resource is participating in a transaction, it is also possible using an API call to configure OrbixOTS to perform a faster single-phase commit.

WLE automatically uses a single-phase commit protocol with a single resource. The TMS process knows how many resource managers there are in a system, as this is specified in a system-wide configuration file called *UBBConfig*. Using this information, the TMS process automatically uses a one phase commit when appropriate.

With the ITS, the designer must decide at build time whether two-phase commit should be used. The DirectConnect SM is designed to handle single-phase commits with a single resource manager, and the XA SM performs two-phase commits. In addition, the XA transactions require the involvement of an XA RD process that is responsible for managing the XA protocol for the particular resource manager. This again requires an extra remote call during the commit, and introduces a performance penalty. As an example, Figure 8 shows the comparative performance of calls to the ITS Current interface *begin()* and *commit()* methods when called from an ITS server process with an embedded ITS instance[3]. The application was using Oracle as a resource manger, and had 10 server threads servicing 300 simultaneous clients. The overheads of the two-phase commit process and XA RD are extremely evident.

---

[3] As the ITS instance was embedded, *begin()* calls for the DirectConnect SM were in-process, and hence averaged less than a millisecond.

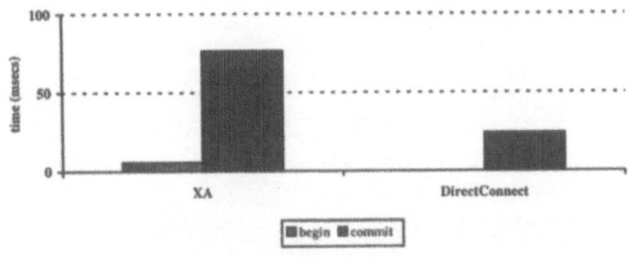

Figure 8: Comparing ITS Transaction Demarcation Performance

7. Conclusions

This paper aims to expose some of the key differences of three implementations of the CORBA OTS service. This has been achieved by illustrating the differing architectures of three OTS services, and explaining how architectural influences effect application design, programming and performance. This is particularly apparent in the areas of product-specific features and extensions, provision of database connection pooling and multi-threaded servers, and the performance of transaction creation and completion operations. There are also many other points of differentiation in terms of features and performance, but these are beyond the scope of this paper.

It should be apparent that architects and designers need to thoroughly understand the implications of an OTS technology before selecting a particular product to implement their mission-critical enterprise systems. Superficially minor differences in OTS features can have high downstream engineering and performance costs when the application scales to handle large numbers of clients in a highly distributed environment. As the old saying goes, the devil, truly, is in the detail.

References:

(Gorton, 2000)   Ian Gorton, *Enterprise Transaction Processing Systems: Putting the CORBA OTS, Encina++ and Orbix OTM to Work* (The Addison-Wesley Object Technology Series), Addison-Wesley, January 2000

(Liu, 2000)   Anna Liu, Ian Gorton, *Evaluating WebLogic Enterprise*, CSIRO Publishing, September 2000

(Tran, 2000)   Phong Tran, Ian Gorton, *Evaluating Inprise ITS v1.2*, CSIRO Publishing, August 2000

UML AND MODELLING
ISSUES I

A Reference Architecture for Component Based Development

Mark Collins-Cope (markcc@ratio.co.uk) and Hubert Matthews (hubert@ratio.co.uk)
Ratio Group Ltd.

Abstract. This paper proposes a reference architecture for object-oriented/component based systems consisting of five layers. Our purpose is to show how this model helps us to understand the overall structure of a system, how layering helps to clarify our thoughts, and how it encourages the separation of concerns such as the technical v. the problem domain, policy v. mechanism, and the buy-or-build decision.

Assuming an application is made up of a number of components, the layering we propose is based on how specific to the particular requirements of an application each component is. More specific (and therefore less reusable) components are placed in the higher layers, and the more general, reusable components are in the lower layers. Since general non-application components are less likely to change than application specific ones, this leads to a stable system as all dependencies are downward in the direction of stability, and so changes tend not to propagate across the system as a whole.

As well as presenting the reference model, this paper also discusses and clarifies in concrete terms the *meaning* of one architectural layer being above another. Perhaps surprisingly, our background research has shown that the meaning of the layering metaphor is the subject of some confusion. Specific examples of this are given in the paper.

The model presented contains five layers, which are as follows: the interface layer; the application layer; the domain layer; the infrastructure layer; and the platform layer.

Keywords: Architectural layering, OO design, component based design, UML, packages, re-use.

1.   Introduction

Architectural layering is a visual metaphor whereby the software that makes up a system is divided into bands (layers) in an architectural diagram. Many such diagrams have been used, and by way of introduction we show two of these.

Apps
LIBS
O/S
Device Drivers
Hardware

Figure 1 – Layered architecture – Example from [Szyperski98]

Szyperski [Szperski98] presents a view of a strictly layered architecture as can be seen in figure 1. Note that this model has the device drivers below the operating system - a topic we will return to discuss later in this paper.

Figure 2 shows a type of ad-hoc architecture diagram [Carlson99] that is not uncommon in modern technical documentation. The example shown describes the architecture of the IBM San Fransisco product.

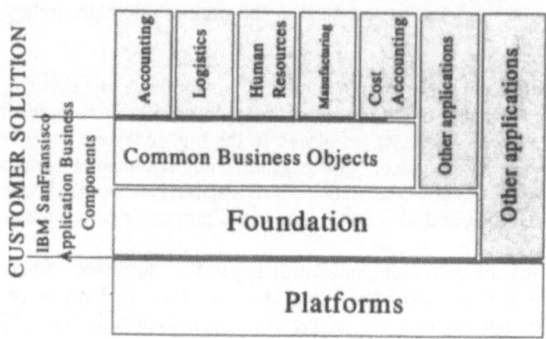

Figure 2 - Typical 'ad-hoc' architectural layering diagram

Some common themes run through these diagrams:

- that it is possible to identify a number of layers in the construction of pieces of software,
- that some layers sit on top of others (although there may be some question as to what one layer being above another actually means – see section 3.4), and
- that one may broadly categorise layers as being either horizontal (applicable across many, if not all business domains), and vertical (applicable across a subset or only one domain);

Turning to UML class diagrams (a younger notation), we notice that common convention usually place subclasses, which are more specialised, below their parents, which are more general purpose. This convention is the exact opposite of the architectural convention *highest is most specific*, and the cause of a undoubtedly confusing visual metaphor mismatch which we discuss further in our article *The Topsy Turvy World of UML* [Collins-Cope+00].

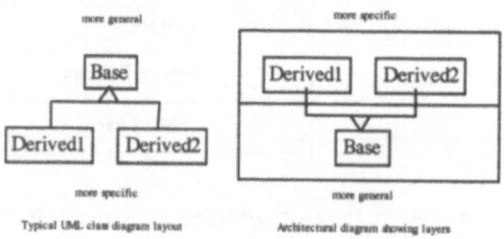

Figure 3 - Class diagrams and architectural views

This paper takes a revised look at application layering, with a particular focus on clarifying the unstated assumptions in such diagrams, and proposes a five layer architectural reference model for component based OO applications that can be used to assist in the design of component based systems.

2. Proposed model

2.1. Motivation

The objectives behind the architectural reference model presented in this paper are as follows:
- to provide a framework for decision making during the design of components,
- to support and re-enforce the appropriate application of good OO design principles, in particular those concerned with stability and dependency management,
- to provide an architectural framework to encourage re-use,
- to encourage re-use of business specific (not just technology) components,
- to position components as the unifying concept that tie together different architectural views of a system, and
- to provide clarification on the meaning of layering in a component context.

We come back to these motivations in the conclusions section of this paper.

2.2. Reference Model

We define the architecture of a system as *the structural relationship between the individual components that together create an application as a whole[1]*. We define a component as *an (object-oriented) software development deliverable implementing a well defined interface that is released at the binary (or equivalent) level[2], which may have a number of well-defined extension points to enable it to be customised.*

Examples of components conforming to this definition might include '.o' or '.a' files on a Unix system, '.obj', '.dll' or '.ocx' files on a Windows based system. Components developed within a COM or EJB type environment are, of course, equally within this definition[3]. Note, however, that in most of the following discussion we consider the *design view* of components, which we represent as packages in UML notation.

Figure 4 shows our proposed reference model. Figure 5 shows the same model populated with a number of classes, components and relationships between them, taken from an example banking

---

[1] We accept there are other defintions!

[2] Three points here:
a) Framework is a term for a software deliverable which is generally assumed to 'drive' an application, leaving hooks for customisation. As can be seen in figure 6 - in which certain components 'drive' higher layers, whilst also being 'driven' by them, we do not see a clear distinction between components and frameworks, but rather view them as a continuum. We use the term 'component' generically across this continuum.
b) For the purposes of this paper, we discuss components as an extension of object technology, but note that we accept that components can be written in non-OO languages.
c) This definition presented does not preclude source parameterised components: in this case one would generate the binary file having instantiated the parameters in order to fit it into the framework described.

[3] We see technologies such as CORBA, COM and Java Beans as *component inter-operability support technologies*, which may or may not be present in a 'component based system.' In the example shown in figure 6, they are not present.

application. Two external *actors* [Jacobson+94] interact with the system: a bank clerk (using a debit dialog box), and an external banking system (using an intermediate file format).

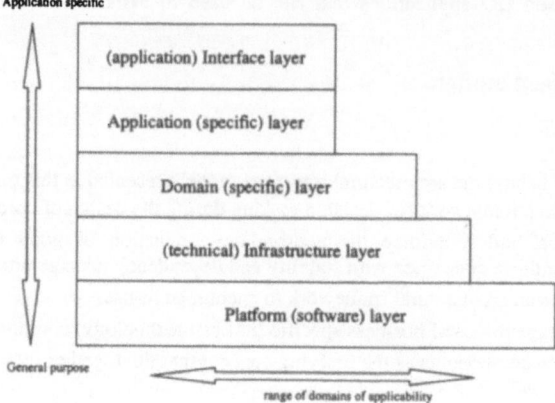

Figure 4 - Layered architecture reference model

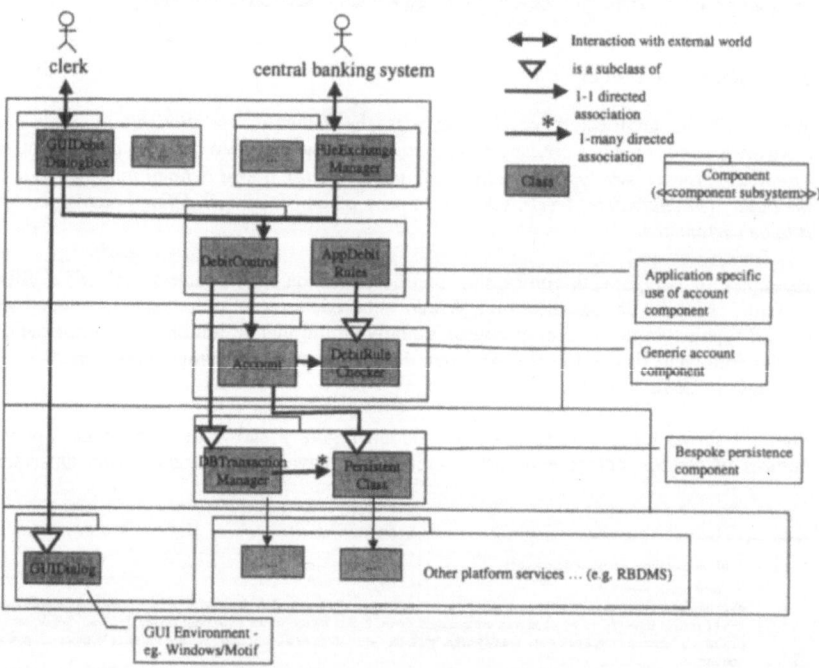

Figure 5 - Layered architecture populated with an example

The layers presented in this model may be summarised as follows:

- Highest (and most specific) in the layering is the application *interface*[4] layer. This layer is responsible for managing the interaction between the 'outside world' and the lower layers within the application. It typically consists of components providing GUI interface functionality - managing the interface to human users, and/or components providing external system interfaces - managing the interface to external systems. This layer often contains what Jacobson et al. call *boundary* classes [Jacobson+94].

  In the example application shown in figure 6, we can see two classes packaged within this layer. The *GUIDebitDialogBox* class implements an application specific dialog (to enter a debit). The *FileExchangeManager* class reads an external file format. Both classes use the application specific *DebitControl* class to process the information they receive from the outside world.

- Below this is the *application* specific layer. This layer is comprised of objects and components that encapsulate the major business processes and associated business rules automated within an application. Typically it will contain many objects akin to Jacobson's (use case) 'control' objects [Jacobson+94]; and often also acts as the 'knowledge' layer in Fowler's operational/knowledge split [Fowler98] (another description of this is separating policy from mechanism.) It may also contain specialised subclasses implementing interfaces left 'open' (as in Open Closed Principle [Meyer97][Martin96]) by the more general purpose components in the layer below, and typically does not contain persistent business classes. Most importantly, this layer contains the "glue" to tie together components within the domain layer below.

  In the example application shown in figure 6, we can see two classes packaged within an application specific debit component. The *DebitControl* class takes over application control when asked to do so by one of the higher level interface classes. It then drives the domain level *account* class to implement its functionality (which may involve several method calls on *account*). Note that the *DebitControl* class is derived from a database transaction management class defined in the bespoke persistence component in the infrastructure layer[5]. The other class - *App. debit rules* - implements the debit-rule checker interface (derived from the lower level *account* component) to customise the debit checking rules as required by this application.

- Next is the business *domain* specific layer. This layer is comprised of components which encapsulate the interface to one or more business classes, which are specific to the domain (area of business) of the application, and are generally used from multiple places within the application. They might also be used by a family of related applications - a software product line. This layer typically contains the 'entity' classes discussed by Jacobson et al in [Jacobson+94].

  The example application shown in figure 6 shows an *account* component in this layer. The *account* class is driven by higher level components to undertake account related activities such as debiting and crediting of monies. As part of this, it uses a *DebitRuleChecker* interface (abstract class) to enable individual applications to customise the particular debit checking rules that may be applied (e.g. can go overdrawn, can't go overdrawn, etc.) This is an example of the open/closed principle [Meyer97][Martin96] being used to implement an operational/knowledge

---

[4] We chose the term interface rather than 'presentation', as some application interfaces are to external systems, and the term presentation tends to imply a user-interface.

[5] This will implement database transaction begin and end commands, and manage the rollback of database changes if necessary.

split [Fowler98]. Note also that, being persistent, the *account* class is derived from the *persistence* class in the infrastructure layer[6].

- Then comes the technical *infrastructure* layer. This layer is made up of *bespoke* components that are potentially re-usable across any domain, providing general purpose 'technical' services such as persistence infrastructure, general programming infrastructure (e.g. lists, collections).

  The example application shown in figure 6 shows a general purpose persistence component being present in this layer. In this component, a *DBTransactionManager* class keeps tabs on a number of *PersistentClasses*[7], which provide the hook by which higher level domain classes many be made persistent.

- Finally, most re-usable of all, is the *platform* software layer. This is comprised of standard or common-place pieces of software that are *brought in* to underpin the application (e.g. operating systems, distribution infrastructure (CORBA\COM), etc.) The example application shown in figure 6 shows a relational database and a GUI class library being used to build the application.

2.3. Associated rules

Some simple rules are associated with this model:
- there should be a clear and simple mapping between component structure and source code structure (the simplest being a 1-1 mapping), and between the component structure any other analysis and design artefacts produced during the development process (e.g. the design view of a component, as shown in a package diagram, or the use case view of a component, as shown using packages of use cases);
- the level of a component is the highest level of any of its constituent classes;
- components should not (and by the above definition, cannot) cross layers[8];
- the compile time dependencies between components within any particular layer should be to components in either the same or a lower layer;
- the application and domain layers should be technology free in the interface components within them present to the outside world;

2.4. Layering Semantics

Most layering diagrams omit to discuss the meaning of one layer appearing on top of another, or any description of the axis of the diagram. Earlier reviews of this paper, and the example shown in figure 1 have lead us to believe some further discussion of these aspects of the layering model presented here is desirable:
- *Vertical axis semantics*. The vertical axis of figure 5 indicates the *specificity* (how specific it is to a particular application/environment) of a component in the application. The higher it appears in the layering of the reference model, the more specific it is. The lower it appears, the more general purpose it is. This has lead us to coin the phrase *the centre of gravity of the application* - essentially a way of classifying the overall architectural feel of a system as being either 'high'

---

[6] Since the original draft of this paper was written, Sun have released their EJB product. It is particularly interesting to note that the session bean/entity bean separation in EJBs mirrors the application/domain layer separation in this paper.

[7] Transactions encapsulate a group of related operations which business logic dictates must be either completed in their entirety, or not executed at all. The DBTransaction class is used to encapsulate this type of transaction. If the transaction succeeds, it can then automatically write all modified objects back to an underlying database – hence the need for tabs to be kept on all objects that may be modified.

[8] Here we ignore issues of 'convenience' packaging for customers (e.g. an account component that provides an GUI interface and some business logic may be packaged as a single component on release, following the RREP [Martin96-3]).

(very application specific, difficult to extend without substantial modification to existing components), or 'low' (good layering applied, likely to have hooks for extension without any modification to existing components).

Layer ordering (highest to lowest) is based on component compile time dependencies. In figure 1, Szyperski shows a layering model in which the device driver layer is shown below the O/S layer. Whilst this seems appropriate at first glance, a deeper examination reveals the ordering in Szyperski's example is not based on the same criteria as the layering presented in our model. In our model, layer ordering is based on the compile time dependencies between the components that reside within the layer. In the terms presented in this paper, the device driver interface of an operating system is an *extension point* to enable customisation of the operating system "component" to a piece of particular hardware. The operating system is *more* generic (general purpose) than the device drivers it uses (which are tied to particular hardware). The device drivers are also dependent *upon* the operating system for their definition – their interface must conform to the calling interface used by the operating system (they will use the function prototypes defined in an operating system header file) – not the other way round. For this reason, we would present the middle three layers of figure 1 in the following manner (with additional detail to show interface definitions and instantiation of interface)[9]:

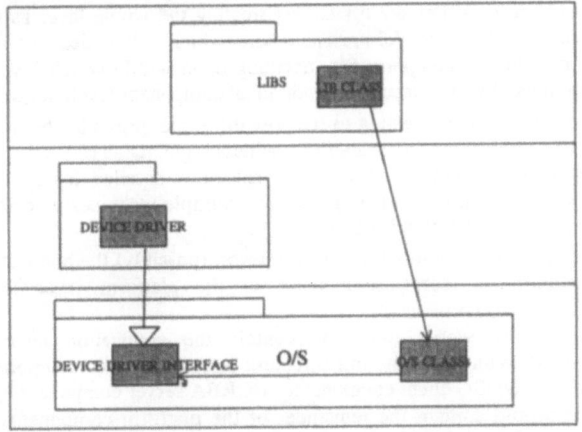

Figure 6 – Szyperski's example using our layering rules

Summarising, the layering semantics presented here tie together the concept of the specificity of a component (how much detail is filled in, how specific it is) with the notion of compile time dependencies. The higher a component in the model, the more specific it is likely to be, and the more dependent it is likely to be on other components, and *vice versa*.

---

[9] Note, however, that using our classification scheme, the bottom two layers of figure 7 would both reside at the platform layer – see section 7 for further discussion of this. Note also, in a non-OO operating system, pointers to functions would be used instead of abstract interface instantiation. The dependency implications of this are, however, identical.

2.5.   Further notes

A number of additional points are worthy of brief discussion:

- *A component oriented approach.* We have defined our view of architecture as one being based on the structural inter-relationships between the binary components that are used to make up a system. We adopt this focus because at the end of the software development process we would like to have a number of well-defined and well-structured, loosely coupled, internally cohesive binary components that we may, without modification, use again in extending the current application (or possibly another application).
- *GUI components.* All GUI components do *not* reside at the interface level. The interface level may contain application specific refinements of general purpose GUI components (e.g. an application specific dialog box), however the *general purpose* elements themselves (e.g. the generic dialog box from which the application specific one is derived) live at the platform level. The same is true for any general purpose GUI component without application specific customisation (e.g. a graph drawing widget).
- *Substitutability.* Many discussions of architectural layering focus on being able to replace one *whole layer* with another – they are effectively treating the whole layer as a single component. This is *not* the purpose of the model presented here, which is intended as a guide to determining the contents of a particular component by deciding upon within which layer it is appropriate it reside. Substitution would take place at the individual component level, not on a per layer basis.
- *Three-tier architecture.* It is interesting to see how the model presented here maps to the classical view of a three-tier architecture (presentation, business logic, database). The model presented here can be viewed at a conceptual level as being independent of detailed deployment issues. However, it can also be used for applications deployed across multiple machines/processes – for example as in the classic three-tier model. In this case:
- the *presentation tier* would contain the interface layer, (possibly) the application layer (in a thick client configuration), and some components of the platform layer (e.g. CORBA client components, generic GUI components).
- the *business logic tier* would (possibly) contain the application layer (in a thin client configuration), the domain layer, the infrastructure layer, and some components of the platform layer (e.g. distributed ODBC client components , CORBA server components), and
- the *database* tier would contain the remainder of the platform components (e.g. the RDBMS, ODBC server components, etc.);

The net result being that the higher layers are deployed in one particular machines/process, and that the lower two layers are often present on multiple processes/machines.

3.   How the layering helps us understand design

To see how layers and particularly our visual metaphor help us, let's examine the Adapter pattern from the Gang of Four's book [Gamma+95].

Figure 7 shows an adapter being used to allow two components with incompatible interfaces to be used together (a common problem in component design).   The billing adapter implements the Account component's outward billing interface and passes on any messages to the credit card billing component's inward billing interface, with possibly modified parameters.   Since both of the components are reusable and not specific to this application they belong in the domain layer.   The adapter, on the other hand, is very specific to this particular configuration and so it is not in general reusable and so belongs in the application layer instead – it is acting as application-level "glue" for the other components. Note here that the two component dependencies point downwards – one being caused by an inheritance relationship, the other by a directed association.

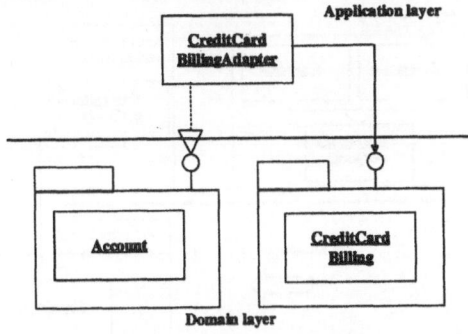

Figure 7 - Getting an account paid by credit card

For a second example, we show in figure 8 one of the refactoring patterns from Martin Fowler's book [Fowler+99]: Separate Domain from Presentation.

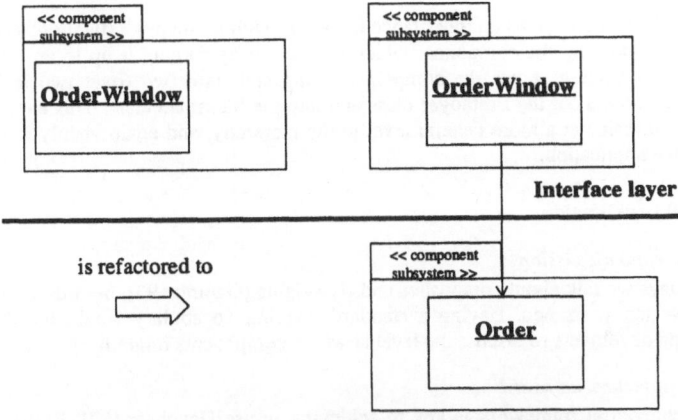

Figure 8 - Separate Domain from Presentation

Here we see a GUI dialog class containing business logic being split into two. Our architectural overlays add context to this, showing that in doing so what was previously an interface layer component has now been split into two components: one still in the interface layer, and one in the application specific (or possibly domain) layer. The refactoring visibly lowers the centre of gravity of the application. Two more benefits are that we have separated the usage of the Order component from its implementation (in other words we have separated policy from mechanism), and that we have separated the technology-free Order component from the inherently technology-based

OrderWindow, thereby giving us more portable code and allowing us more freedom in deployment (for example in a three-tier system).

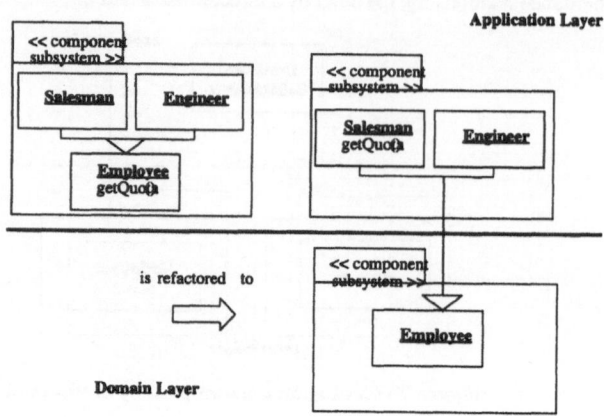

Figure 9 - Push Down Method (reworked by us as Pull Up Method!)

In figure 9, Fowler shows us an inheritance hierarchy with an inappropriately placed method, which is effectively *polluting* the component which contains it by forcing it up to an inappropriate level. The refactored version shows the component being split into two (over two levels), the method having being moved out the Employee class and into the Salesman class. This enables the Employee component to reside at a more general level in the hierarchy, and again visibly lowers the centre of gravity of the application.

4. Broader issues

- *No name, no discussion*

  Nowadays we talk about composites and flyweights [Gamma+95], but this would not have been possible ten years ago. Having a standard layering vocabulary would be of clear benefit in enabling developers to discuss the level at which components might lie.

- *No architecture, no re-use*

  An architectural framework is key to achieving re-use [Jacobson+97]. Re-use requires a clear understanding of what is specific and what is general in designing a set of related components. The reference model assists in understanding these separations, whilst also adding clarity to the layering semantics.

- *Architecture adds context*

  An architectural view adds additional context to many design patterns. Take the observer pattern [Gamma+95]. If packaged together in a single component, the base classes Subject and Observer can be seen as providing a low level (infrastructural) flexible component from which higher level (domain, application or interface) concrete observation mechanisms can be built. The derived ConcreteSubject and ConcreteObserver can be seen as application, domain or interface specific extensions to a general purpose mechanism.

- *Architecture aids (good) design*

  The layering presented also supports a number of OO design principles: the open closed principle [Meyer97][Martin96] – the idea being that lower layer components are closed against modification, and higher layer components extend the open aspects of them; the stable dependencies principle [Martin97] - the layers are organised based on expected stability of their contents – the lower layer components being more stable; and the acyclic dependency principle[Martin97] - the depend downwards rule supports this principle.

- *Invariants*

  One important part of the design of component based systems is the identification and allocatiion of responsibility for maintaining invariants *across* (possibly bought in) components. It may be necessary for two components in the domain layer to maintain an invariant relationship - e.g. customer address must be maintained in both components. The responsibility for maintaining invaritants across components resides in a layer *above* that in which the components reside. So in the case of our customer address invarient, it would be the responsibility of a component within the application layer to ensure it was not violated (perhaps using a change event generated when the customer address was changed in either domain layer component).

5.   A brief philosophical aside

Many classification systems are blurred around the edges, and our layer classification is no exception. In his excellent book *Darwin's Dangerous Idea* [Dennet96] Dennet describes how examining the characteristics of a particular species of gull, starting in Britain and moving west to east around the globe, yields a set of gradually evolving changes until, as the loop closes and the examiner returns to Britain, a *different* species of gull is finally found next to the original! Species clearly have blurred edges, so we're in good company!

6.   Compromises

The model presented here is not perfect, but a compromise between simplicity and meeting the stated set of objectives. Some potential shortcomings of the model are as follows:

- It would have been superficially pleasing to have a rule that said: *you can only depend on the layer below you.* However, upon deeper consideration we believe that the reason for this is an emphasis in previous discussions of layered architectures on complete substitutability of layers. As discussed in section 3.5 (*substitutability*) this is not the motivation behind the model presented here.
- There are clearly times when there will be sub-layerings within the layers presented, and we could have made these explicit. However, we feel the price would have been too high in terms of additional complexity. Instead, we prefer to allow the option of discussing the 'lower application' layer to resolve such issues.
- We have chosen to separate the infrastructure and platform layers based on a buy versus build criteria. Architectural purists may object to this - why should the layer in which a particular component resides be dependent on whether you buy or build it? Our motivation is simple: we wanted to put the focus clearly on the *aspects of the application being developed*. For similar reasons we have been unconcerned with sub-layerings within the platform layer.

7.   Conclusions

Summarising, in this paper we have proposed a simple five layered reference model and a number of associated rules to assist the software designer. We have noted that, by convention, *UML class diagrams are upside down*, at least when considered in parallel with architectural layering conventions, and that this is a block to visualising one aspect of what happens during refactoring. We have shown that once this is addressed, UML and the architectural model complement and re-enforce each other.

We have identified examples from Gamma et al's Design Patterns book, and Fowler's refactoring book that show the reference model adds context to well known design (and refactoring) paradigms.

We have discussed how the model supports good OO design principles, in particular those concerned with ensuring stable dependency management, and have emphasised and clarified the rules on which our layering model is based (specificity/generality and compile time dependency).

Coming back to the objectives detailed in section 3.1, we believe the architectural reference model presented here:

- *provides a framework for decision making during component design* by providing a number of layers within which the developer can position their components,

- *supports and re-enforces the appropriate application of good OO design principles*, by encouraging components to be extended (customised) by other components in higher layers, and by imposing a downwards only dependency rule,

- *encourages re-use* by providing a layering system and associated set of rules that puts the focus of design on the specificity/generality of components, encouraging components contents to be seperated on the basis of the layering provided,

- *provides clarification on the meaning of layering in a component context*, by putting the emphasis on compile time dependency management,

- *encourages re-use of business specific (not just technology) components* by presenting two layers within which business components may reside. This encourages more generic functionality to be in the domain layer, and application specific customisation/glue type functionity to be in the application layer, and

- *positions components as the unifying concept that tie together different architectural views of a system*, by stating that the package structure of the system (and associated specification, design or use case views) should be based on the target component structure.

8.   References and credits

[Carlson99]   Brent Carlson, Design Patterns for Business Applications, the IBM SanFransisco Approach, ObjectiveView Issue 3, available at www.ratio.co.uk/ObjectiveView.htm, 1999.

[Collins-Cope+00] The Topsy Turvy World of UML, Hubert Matthews and Mark Colllins-Cope, ObjectiveView Issue 4, available at www.ratio.co.uk/ObjectiveView.htm, 2000.

[Dennet96] Daniel C. Dennet, Darwin's Dangerous Idea: Evolution and the Meanings of Life, Touchstone Books, 1996.

[Fowler+99] Martin Fowler with contributions from Kent Beck, John Brant, William Opdyke, and Don Roberts, Refactoring - Improving the Design of Existing Code, Addison Wesley, 1999.

[Fowler98] Martin Fowler, Analysis Patterns - Reusable Object Models, Addison Wesley, 1998.

[Gamma+95] Erich Gamma, Richard Helm, Ralph Johnson and John Vlissides, Design Patterns - Elements of Reusable Object-Oriented Software, Addison-Wesley, 1995.

[Jacobson+94] Ivar Jacobson, Magnus Christerson, Partrik Jonsson, Gunnar Övergaard, Object Oriented Software Engineering - A Use Case Driven Approach, Addison-Wesley, 1994.

[Jacobson+97] Ivar Jacobson, Martin Griss, Patrik Johsson, Software Reuse - Architecture, Process and Organization for Business Success, Addison Wesley Longman, 1997.

[Martin96] Robert C. Martin, The Open Closed Principle, C++ Report, Jan 1996.

[Martin97] Robert C. Martin, Stability, C++ Report, Feb 1997.

[Meyer97] Bertrand Meyer, Object Oriented Software Engineering (second edition) - Prentice Hall Professional Technical Reference, Published 1997.

[Szperski98] Clemens Szyperski, Component Software: Beyond Object-Oriented Programming, January, Addison Wesley Longman, 1998.

Particular thanks are due to Andy Vautier, Nigel Barnes and Keith Haviland of Andersen Consulting, upon whose 1 million line+ C++ project many of the underlying concepts presented in this paper were formulated. Further detailed technical discussion this project can be found at www.ratio.co.uk/techlibrary.html.

Version Management in Unified Modeling Language

D.Janaki Ram, M.Sreekanth and A.Ananda Rao

Distributed Object Systems Lab
Department of Computer Science and Engineering
Indian Institute of Technology, Madras
Chennai-600036
INDIA
PH: 91-044-4458343
FAX: 91-044-4458352
URL: http://lotus.iitm.ac.in
Email: {janaki,kanthms,anand}@lotus.iitm.ernet.in

ABSTRACT: *Change in requirements leads to evolution of software systems. Evolution of software projects can be captured using version management mechanisms. Unified Modeling Language (UML) is a well known modeling language for software projects. One of the limitations of the UML is lack of support for version management. The paper suggests semantics based version management for projects represented using UML. Class diagrams of UML are used for representing the project as a semantic entity called Unified Representation of Artifacts (URA) graph. Version propagation can be captured with class diagrams. Also, the paper considers the Object Oriented (OO) issues like inheritance, aggregation, association etc. for propagating a change in software system. Various cases of change propagation have been explored depending upon the attributes that participate in the change. Also, the role of accessibility of attributes such as private, public and protected in version management is discussed. Different versions of a project have been considered to present the scenario of the change management.*

KEYWORDS: *Change propagation, class diagrams, unified modeling language, unified representation of artifacts and version management.*

1. Introduction

One of the major concerns of software development is change in requirements. User requirements of a software system will keep changing. This leads to evolution of the software system. As the requirements of users keep changing, software has to support the evolution easily. This is extendibility issue of the software system. Though, a software is extendable it is required to capture a clear picture of how the changes are affecting the system. Understandability of the system will be clear if and only if the system is properly documented. Also, capturing the evolution of software project is a major issue in the software maintenance phase. The concept of version management is used for managing the evolutions of the software projects.

UML is well known modeling language for specifying, visualizing and documenting the artifacts of a software system [UML Site]. As per the Object Management Group (OMG) specifications of the UML it does not provide support for documenting the version management mechanism of software projects represented using UML [UML Spec 2000].

The contribution of the paper is to incorporate the version management mechanism for UML and to present a semantics-based version management mechanism based on URA model [Srinath 2000]. The model also addresses the version propagation rules. The paper presents version management issues regarding OO concepts namely aggregation, inheritance and association. Also, the role of accessibility of attributes in version management is discussed.

The rest of the paper is organized as follows. Section 2 discusses the related work on version management. URA model for representing an artifact is presented in section 3. Also, a brief introduction to generic model of semantics based versioning in projects is presented in the section. Section 4 gives a brief introduction of the UML and the representation mechanisms in UML. In section 5 the contribution of the paper and version management in UML is presented. Section 6 explains the version management of UML diagrams using a case study. Finally, section 7 concludes the paper and provides directions for future work.

2. Related Work

Maintenance phase is a crucial phase in software development process [Roger 1997]. Configuration Management (CM) plays an important role in development/maintenance process [Ivica]. The purpose of the CM is to identify and manage different versions of source code, configure the components and control the changes. Version management is a part of CM, and it includes managing revisions and versions. A component version will change due to added functionality or behavior change. There exist many issues in controlling the versions such as granularity of versions, version selection and propagation etc. [CSCW 1995].

A unified version model for CM is presented by Zeller [Zeller 1995]. It unifies modeling, realizing and integrating tasks of the CM. Central CM models are encompassed and combined by version set model. Version sets are sets of software components that denote common and individual version properties. A general model for version management in databases is introduced based on the concepts of version environments [Peter 1986]. Version environment offers graphs and partitions for structuring the version sets of objects. Also they can be tailored to specific user requirements based on the views, constraints and transactions. Version management of composite objects in CAD (Computer Aided Design) databases is presented in [Rafi 1991]. It presents various version management issues starting from the changes that are due to artifact changes to the states of version objects, which determine the update ability of composite objects. Version change at runtime using artifact's state transfer is discussed in [Jalote 1993].

A generic model for semantics based versioning in projects is proposed in [Srinath 2000]. This is the basic model for the paper to incorporate the version management in UML. It addresses the changes as well as the change propagations. Basically the model is developed based on the URA mechanism. Introduction to the generic model is presented in the next section. The model as it addresses the version management at the required level of granularity authors opted for version management in UML. But the model won't address the role of attribute accessibility and the OO concepts in version management. Role of accessibility of attributes and OO concepts in version management are presented in the paper. Also, the paper addresses incorporation of the version management in UML.

3. Introduction to URA Model

In this section first the representation model URA is explained. Next, semantics based version management using URA graph is presented briefly. Detailed versioning model in the perspective of the UML version management is presented in section 5.

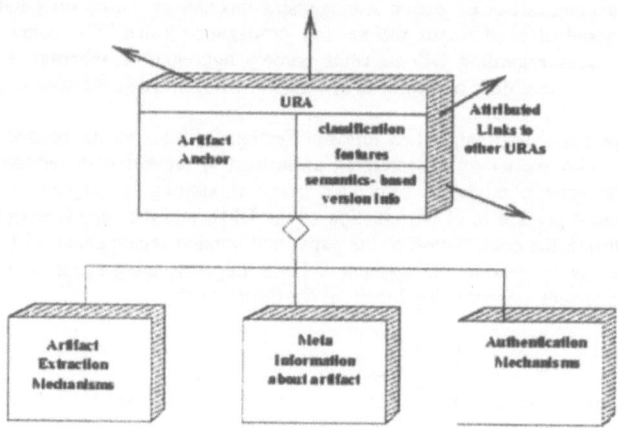

Figure 1: Structure of an URA

A meta level entity called a Unified Representation of Artifacts (URA) which represents an artifact of any type or granularity is presented in [Srinath 2000] [Srinath 1998]. Any logical entity of interest is an artifact. Artifacts map to physical entities in different ways like classes, sets of classes, subsystems, documents etc. The structure of URA is shown in figure 1. URA mainly consists of three components - first one for extracting the artifact from the information system, second one contains the information about the artifact, third and the last one enforces authentication mechanisms. A set of features is associated with the URA, which allows it to be classified and queried. These features can be either attributes or functionalities of the artifact. Semantic based version information set keeps track of the evolution of the artifact. In addition to these, there are labeled links pointing to other URAs, which reflect the relationship between the artifacts that the URAs represent.

A project is represented as a directed graph of URAs. The graph will evolve as changes occur in the project. An artifact in the project is represented as an URA, that is a node in the URA graph. Directed edges in the graph are labeled. These labels are the relationships between the artifacts that correspond to the URA nodes in the graph. Features of a node are classified either versioning or non-versioning. If a change of an attribute leads to other changes of the artifact then it is a versioning attribute, otherwise non-versioning attribute. In this paper, the term attribute is used to mean a feature of an artifact. The labeled links indicate the dependencies between the nodes of the graph and the need to propagate the changes. A pivot node in the graph stands for the whole project. Changes are propagated to this node also. The version of this node is nothing but the version of the project.

4. Introduction to UML

UML represents a unification of the concepts and notations of Booch, Rumbaugh and Jacobson [RJB 1999]. Notation plays an important role in modeling. The goal of the UML is to provide notations for creating models of OO software. It is a general purpose visual modeling language that is used to specify, visualize, construct and document the artifacts of the software system. There exist various concepts and constructs in UML. Basically, they are of two types i.e views and diagrams. Class diagram, use case views, activity diagram and sequence diagram etc. are the various notational constructs in UML. It is out of the scope to present about UML in detail. Only the class diagram and sequence diagrams are introduced in this section.

Class diagrams represent the static structure of the classes and their relationships (e.g., inheritance, aggregation) in a system. A class icon is divided into three components-class name, attributes and operations. In version management, as attributes and operations together are treated as features the paper uses only two components in a class icon. A Sequence diagram is typically used to show object interactions in a single use case. The emphasis of sequence diagrams is on the order of message invocation. These diagrams will be useful in finding the number of messages invoked from an object to another object. This calculation is required to estimate the amount of dependency between the classes that is used in version propagations.

UML is intended to incorporate current software best practices into a standard approach. As per the latest OMG specifications it does not facilitate version management of software systems[UML Spec 2000]. Various versions of a project are organizable in UML suite, but the changes of artifacts and their change propagations are not considered in it [Telelogic Suite]. Next section presents a version management mechanism for projects represented in UML.

5. Version Management in UML

This section presents the version management of projects represented in UML using the URA generic model of version management. UML class diagrams are used to capture version management of projects represented in UML. UML class diagrams depict the attributes and the methods in a class and relationship between classes. As they are the major components in the version management, it is easy to trace the version changes through this diagram. Hence, the authors selected class diagrams for version management of projects represented in UML.

The process of version management is as follows. Initially, the class diagram is converted to a URA graph. Each class is treated as an artifact and represented as a URA. Links between the URAs depict the relationship between the classes such as aggregation, association and inheritance. In a URA graph it is easy to manage the versions. This section elaborates the generic model for semantics-based version management in the perspective of UML class diagrams. The distinction of the model comes from the attributes' accessibility. The paper presents the importance of the private, public and protected attributes roles in version management. Also, the paper considers the OO concepts aggregation, association and inheritance in version management. These concepts have not been explored before in the perspective of version management.

The two basic issues of version management are version change and version propagation. These are addressed below. Whenever a version change occurs to an artifact then there will be a need to propagate the change to other dependent artifacts.

5.1 Version Changes

Version changes of a software project are of two types. One is change in version and the other one is equivalent change. If the changes in software are considerable and affect the project functionality then it is a version change. Otherwise, if the changes of the software are due to minor improvements and the system functionality is not affected much, then it is an equivalent change. In most advanced version management techniques, there will be three version or change levels [TPC 1998]. The third tier change indicates insignificant changes. As conventionally versions are expressed in two levels of changes, this paper considers only version and equivalent changes.

Changes can also be differentiated as follows. One is internal change of artifact and the other is change propagated from related artifacts. Internal change of an artifact can occur through versioning or non-versioning attributes.

Versioning attributes or non-versioning attributes decide the type of the change of an artifact. Change of an artifact can occur in two ways. One is change in attributes and the other is addition of new attributes to the artifact. In the context of the UML version management a class is an artifact. Thus, the term class and artifact are used interchangeably. If the attribute that is changing or getting added to a class is a versioning attribute then the type of change occuring in the class is called as version change (V-Change). Otherwise, if the attribute is non-versioning attribute then the type of change occuring in the class is called as equivalent change (E-Change).

5.2 Version Propagations

Incremental development of a project can be done by creating new versions of it's artifacts [Telelogic Suite]. Creating new versions of artifacts in a project is a critical problem, as the changes of the artifact will cause changes to other related artifacts. Thus, change propagation mechanism is a major issue in version management. This paper presents various cases of change propagations depending on the attributes that participate in the change.

Version change of an artifact will affect the change of the related artifacts that are having accessibility to the artifact's attributes and functionality. In a class there will be three types of attributes in the perspective of accessibility. They are public, private and protected attributes. Attributes can also be of versioning or non-versioning type.

The main aspects of the version propagation are *focus* and *cdegree* (degree of cohesion) [Srinath 1998]. The *focus* is with respect to a change in a URA. Whereas, the *cdegree* is with respect to a link between the related URAs. Each URA in URA graph corresponds to an artifact of the project. A change in the URA has a value called *focus*. The *focus* of a change is the amount of the attention to the particular artifact. In other words, the *focus* of a change is the probability that the change does not necessitate similar changes in other related URAs. Related URAs means that there exist some link between those URAs that reflect the dependency between the corresponding artifacts. The estimation of the focus of the change pertaining to an attribute depending on the accessibility is tabulated in figure 2. It is obvious that if an attribute is private attribute of the artifact then the changes of that attribute may not necessitate changes in related artifacts. Thus, the *focus* of this attribute is HIGH. Similarly, public attribute's *focus* is LOW. In case of protected attribute the change may affect the related artifacts depending on link between the URAs. If the link is inheritance link then the *focus* is LOW, otherwise *focus* is HIGH.

Attributes	FOCUS
Private	HIGH
Public	LOW

Protected	If (Link == Inheritance)
	LOW
	else
	HIGH

If (Attribute is Versioning attribute)
    Version–Focus = FOCUS
else   /* non–versioning attribute */
    Equivalent–focus = FOCUS

Figure 2: Focus evaluation table

Degree of cohesion (*cdegree*) of a link is the indicator of the amount of dependency that exist between the two artifacts represented by the URAs. This is indicated by an optional weight to the corresponding link between the URAs. The value of the *cdegree* has a range [0,1]. Though the calculation of *cdegree* is a major issue in software paradigm and it is out of the scope of this paper, a simple way of calculating *cdegree* is presented later in section 5.5.3. If the *cdegree* value is more than the threshold then the link is said to be ``strong" and this link is called as *cohesive* link. Otherwise, if the value is less than the threshold then the link is ``weak" and called as *non-cohesive* link. These are the possible properties and labels of the links between URAs. Assigning a value for threshold is the choice of software developers, as they have the knowledge about the system and its cohesiveness. The cohesiveness of the link is decided based on the type of relation between the artifacts. This is elaborated later in section 5.3, while presenting the version propagations between classes through the various links namely inheritance, aggregation and association.

5.3 Various cases of change propagations

In UML class diagram, classes are artifacts and the relations between the classes such as inheritance, aggregation and association are the links between the classes. Correspondingly URA graph of the class diagram contains the URAs and links between them. These links are labeled either *cohesive* or *non-cohesive*. Change of an artifact is propagated to related artifacts based on the *focus* of the change and the property of the link between the artifacts. These change propagations are divided into two categories, one is propagation of version change and the other is propagation of equivalent change. The two cases are tabulated in figures 3 and 4 respectively. While propagating a change, the recommended changes to the related URAs are shown in those figures.

Whenever a change of an artifact occurs, it will be indicated in the corresponding URA node. Change is indicated using the notion [m,n]. Where `m' indicates version change and 'n' indicates the equivalent change. Related artifacts will be affected by these changes. This can be captured in URA graph. Depending on the link between the URAs changes are propagated to URAs, which corresponds to related artifacts.

	Version Focus	
	LOW	HIGH
Cohesive Link	V-Change	E-Change
Non Cohesive Link	E-Change	E-Change / *N-Change

Figure 3: Change propagation table I

Change propagations in case of version change of an artifact is as follows (figure 3):

- When there is a version change of an URA and the *focus* of the change is LOW, then a version change (v-change) is recommended to related URAs which are connected by *cohesive* links.

- An equivalent change (e-change) is recommended to related URAs, which are connected by *cohesive* links if the version *focus* is HIGH.

- An equivalent change is recommended to related URAs which are connected by *non-cohesive* links if the version *focus* is LOW.

- If the link is *non-cohesive* and *focus* of the change is HIGH then also equivalent change is recommended to related URAs. If the value of the *cdegree* is too less and the *focus* of the change is too HIGH then no change (n-change) is recommended. Assigning the too HIGH value for the *focus* of a change is up to the person who is responsible for the maintenance of the project.

Change propagations in case of equivalent change of an artifact is as follows (figure 4):

- When there is an equivalent change of a URA and the *focus* is LOW, then an equivalent change is recommended to related URAs which are connected by *cohesive* links.

- If the *focus* is HIGH and the link is *cohesive* then an equivalent change is recommended.

- If the *focus* is LOW and the link is *non-cohesive* then an equivalent change is recommended.

- No change is recommended to related URAs, which are connected by *non-cohesive* links if the *focus* is HIGH.

	Equivalent Focus	
	LOW	HIGH
Cohesive Link	E–Change	E–Change
Non Cohesive Link	E–Change	N–Change

Figure 4: Change propagation table II

5.4 Causes of change propagation

Version propagation can occur because of two reasons:

		Direction of the link		
		To the new artifact	From the new artifact	Bi–directional
Property of the link	Cohesive	N–change	V–change	V–change
	Non–cohesive	N–change	E–change	E–change

Figure 5: New artifacts cause changes to existing artifacts

- An artifact has changed. Related artifacts that are connected from the artifact will also change. Various cases of this cause have been explained in the above subsection.

- A new artifact is added to a system. That will add new dependency links, which causes changes to the existing artifacts in the system. These link's directions can be *to* or *from* the new artifact. Depending on the direction as well as the cohesiveness of the link recommended changes of the artifacts are tabulated in figure 5.

Whenever an artifact changes, it moves into a *transient* state. Before the changes the artifact will be in *normal* state. Changes will lead to a chain of change propagations. It may also form a cycle. This leads to infinite change recommendations. To avoid this situation, the state of an artifact that is already changed is marked as *transient* state. That is the use of the states of an artifact in version propagation. There exist various set of states for change management of an artifact [Srinath 2000] [Rafi 1991] [Telelogic Suite]. Currently, for the sake of simplicity, only three states are considered. These are *transient*, *normal* and *replace* states. Whenever a defective version of an artifact is replaced then there is no need to propagate the changes. By marking the state of the replacing artifact as *replace* state change propagation can be avoided.

5.5 Change propagation in class diagrams

The three different links between the classes in UML class diagrams namely inheritance, aggregation and association are mapped to URA labeled links i.e *cohesive* and *non-cohesive* links. These mappings as well as change propagations are discussed in this section.

5.5.1 Inheritance

Inheritance is a unidirectional dependency link. Representation of UML class diagram with inheritance structure as a URA graph is shown in figure 6. It is a *cohesive* link because the changes of base class will affect the derived class. Changing a public or protected attribute leads to a change with LOW *focus* and changing a private attribute leads to a change with HIGH *focus*. The changing attribute can be either versioning attribute or non-versioning attribute. Correspondingly the *focus* of the change will become version *focus* or equivalent *focus*. Thus, the recommendation of the change propagated to derived class is obtained from the figures 3 and 4.

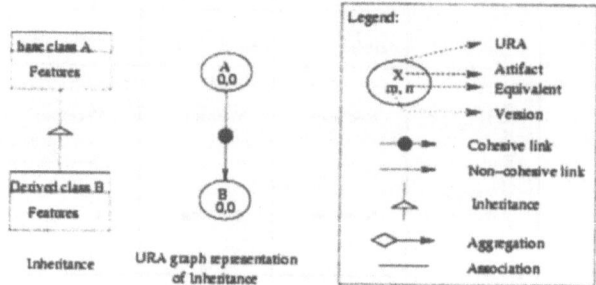

Figure 6: Inheritance and URA graph

5.5.2 Aggregation

Aggregation is also a unidirectional dependency link. Corresponding, URA graph for aggregation structure is shown in figure 7. It is a *cohesive* link because the changes made to part classes leads to changes of the whole class. Changing a public attribute leads to a change with LOW *focus* and changing a private or protected attribute leads to a change with HIGH *focus*. Version changes and propagations will be as described in sections 5.1 and 5.2.

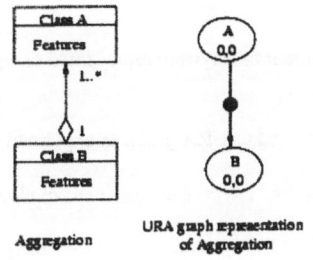

Figure 7: Aggregation and URA graph

5.5.3 Association

Association will be a bidirectional dependency link. Its representation as a URA graph is shown in figure 8. It can be *cohesive* or *non-cohesive* link depending on the inter-connection between the two associated classes. The property of the link can be found by calculating the *cdegree* value. That can be estimated from the messages invoked between the classes. Estimating the *cdegree* value for the association link is given in equation (1).

Cdegree of the link from A to B

$$CD_{A\text{->}B} = (\text{No.of } Msg_{A\text{->}B}) \, / \, (\text{Total no.of } Msg_{A\text{->}all}) \quad\text{--- (1)}$$

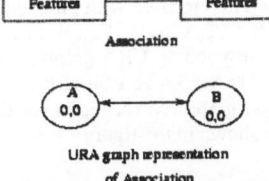

Figure 8: Association and URA graph

Thus the *cdegree* is the ratio of the messages sent from instance of class A to instance of class B and the messages sent from instance of class A to each instance of the related classes. Similarly, the value of the *cdegree* for the link from B to A can be calculated. It may be required to consider the sequence diagrams in order to know the number of messages invoked from a class to another class. From *cdegree*, the cohesiveness of the link i.e *cohesive* or *non-cohesive* can be found by putting a threshold cut-off. In a class, changing a public attribute leads to a change with LOW *focus* and changing a private or protected attribute leads to a change with HIGH *focus*. Thus, the version changes and propagations will apply as explained in sections 5.1 and 5.2.

6. Example

Process of the version management of a system represented using UML is as follows:

- UML class diagram is converted to URA graph as explained in the paper.

- Links are labeled and if required *cdegree* of the links are also calculated.

- Whenever there is a change in the system, *focus* of the change is calculated using the figure 2.

- Then, change propagations are applied as presented in the paper.

- Thus, the new URA graph represents the evolved version of the project.

- If an old version of any part of the system is required then it is possible to keep track of the various versions using URA graphs. It will be required when users are acquainted to specific versions. It will be useful even in the case of a module failure of the new version in the project.

Different versions of nachos [Christopher] [Nachos] system have been taken as the case study to present the version management mechanism in UML. Initially, the available code of the system is converted into UML diagrams using the Rational Rose tool [Rational Rose]. Then by applying the above mechanism various versions of the nachos are managed. The changes propagated in the file system module in nachos system are discussed below.

Figure 9 shows class diagram for version 3.4 of the file system. The corresponding URA graph representaion of the module is shown in Figure 10. As the *SynchDisk* class does not has inheritance or aggregation or association relation with other classes, authors did not represent any URA with respect to this class in the URA graph. Figure 11 shows class diagram for version 4.0 of the file system module. The corresponding URA graph is shown in Figure 12. Thus, an extra class *PersistBitmap* has been added to the 3.4 version of the file system. That leads to the change propagations as shown in the URA graph representation of the file system version 4.0 (Figure 12). The updated versions are also shown in the figure.

Initially, *PersistBitmap* URA version is assigned as 4.0 and it's state is changed from *normal* to *transient*. As there is a *cohesive* link from this new class to *Fileheader* class, the version of the *Fileheader* class is changed from 3.4 to 4.0 and it's state to *transient*. Then these changes are propagated to other related classes (artifacts represented as URAs). Also, the change propagation is not affecting the already changed artifact's versions, because their states are in *transient* (Thus, the change is not propagated from *Openfile* to *PersistBitmap*). Finally, the latest version of an artifact in the graph is assigned for the file system module, which can be represented using a pivot node. Similarly for all modules this mechanism is applied if any change is occurred in the system. Finally, the version changes are propagated to the pivot node ie. nachos system. After the change process and before the change process all the URAs will be in *normal* state.

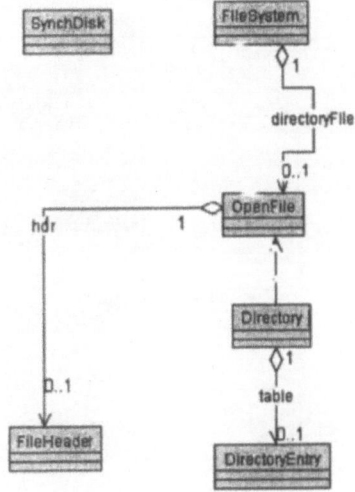

Figure 9: Nachos 3.4 file system module class diagram

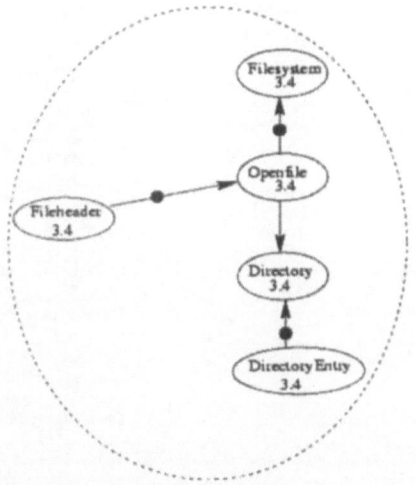

Figure 10: Nachos 3.4 file system module represented as URA hyper graph

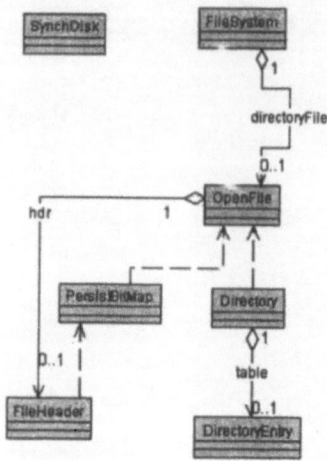

Figure 11: Nachos 4.0 file system module class diagram

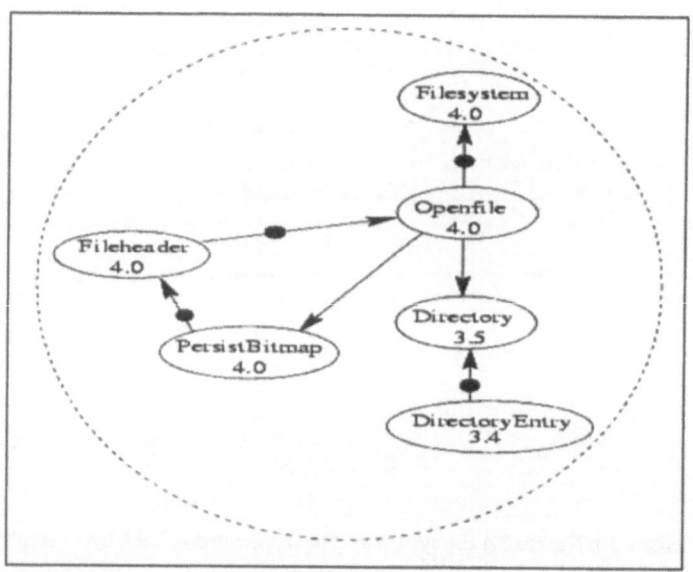

Figure 12: Nachos 4.0 file system module represented as URA hyper graph

7. Conclusions and Future Work

Version management is one of the issues of software maintenance. It will be easy to maintain if the software is properly documented. If the modeling languages like UML could not support the documentation of versioning it will be a deficiency. The paper explored the mechanism of incorporating version management in UML using semantic-based URA model. Software version change is estimated depending on the attributes that are participating in change. In the paper, accessibility of the attributes is also considered while changes take place. Various cases of change propagations are captured and tabulated. Version management in the perspective of OO concepts like inheritance, aggregation and association is also presented. A case study of the version management from different versions of the nachos project is presented.

In version management perspective, there exist various set of states regarding the artifacts changes. A standard set of states for artifacts to manage changes can be worked out. Representation of software projects is supported in UML through various diagrams like class diagram, sequence diagram, component diagram etc. Though they are related artifacts of the software UML has no mechanism to inter-relate the different diagrams. It will be possible to inter-relate these diagrams through URA graph representation. For instance, to know the method invocations done in a method of a class it will be useful to have inter-link between the class diagram and the sequence diagram.

References:

[CSCW 1995]: Workshop Summary, *Proceedings of the ECSCW'95: Workshop on the Role of Version Control in CSCW (Computer Supported Cooperative Work) Applications*, September 10, 1995, Stockholm, Sweden.

[Christopher]: Christopher. W. A., S. J. Procter and T. E. Anderson, *The Nachos Instructional Operating System*, Technical report, University of California, Berkeley, California.

[Ivica]: Crnkovic. I and M. Larsson, *Managing Standard Components in Large software Systems*, Position paper, Malardalen University, Vasteras, Sweden.

[Jalote 1993]: Gupta. D and P. Jalote, *On-Line Software Version Change Using State Transfer Between Processes*, Software - Practice and Experience, Vol.23, No. 9, pp. 949-964, September 1993.

[Nachos]: General Nachos Documentation, *The University of Washington*, <http://www.cs.washington.edu/homes/tom/nachos>.

[Peter 1986]: Klahold. P, G. Schlageter and W. Wilkes, *A General Model for Version Management in Databases*, pp. 319-327, Proceedings of Twelfth International Conference on Very Large Data Bases, Kyoto, Japan, August 25-28, 1986.

[RJB 1999]: Rumbaugh. J., I. Jacobson and G. Booch, *The Unified Modeling Language Reference Manual*, Addison Wesley Longman, Inc., USA, 1999.

[Rafi 1991]: Ahmed. R and S. B. Navathe, *Version management of composite objects in CAD databases*, Proceedings of ACM SIGMOD international conference on Management of data, pp. 218 - 227, Denver, Colorado, May 29-31, 1991.

[Rational Rose]: Rational Rose-The visual modeling tool, *Rational Software Corporation*, <http://www.rational.com/products/rose/index.jsp>.

[Roger 1997]: Pressman. R. S., *Software Engineering - A Practitioner's Approach*, Fourth Edition, McGraw-Hill International Editions, Software Engineering Series, New York, 1997.

[Srinath 1998]: Srinath, S., *URA: A Paradigm for Context Sensitive Reuse*, A Thesis of Master of Science by Research submitted to Department of computer Science & Engineering, Indian Institute of Technology, India, April 1998.

[Srinath 2000]: Srinath, S., R. Ramakrishna and D. Janaki Ram, *A Generic Model for Semantics Based Versioning in Projects*, IEEE Transactions on Systems, Man and Cybernetics, Part A, March 2000, Vol. 30, No. 2, pp. 108-123.

[TPC 1998]: TPC Policies and Guidelines, *Transaction Processing Performance Council*, Version [4.12], 28-September-98, Changes Made at 55th General Meeting in Portland, Oregon.

[Telelogic Suite]: Telelogic Tau UML Suite 4.3 Tutorial, *Telelogic Internatioal Ltd.*, <http://www.telelogic.com>.

[UML Site]: Unified Modeling Language (UML), *Rational's resource center*, Available at <http://www.rational.com/uml/index.jsp>.

[UML Spec 2000]: OMG Unified Modeling Language Specification, Version 1.3, First Edition: March 2000, Available at <http://cgi.omg.org/cgi-bin/doc?formal/00-03-01>.

[Zeller 1995]: Zeller. A, *A Unified Version Model for Configuration Management*, Proceedings of the third ACM SIGSOFT symposium on The foundations of software engineering, October 12 - 15, 1995, Washington United States, pp.151-160.

Requirements-Based UML

Joseph D. Schulz
Technical Director, International Channels

Technology Builders, Inc.
400 Interstate North Parkway, Suite 1090
Atlanta, Georgia 30339
USA
Fax: (815) 333-0160
Email: joes@tbi.com

Abstract

The purpose of this paper is to describe the "Requirements-Based UML" (RBU) development technique. RBU is a straightforward, pragmatic methodology for integrating structured requirements analysis into a UML-based analysis and design effort. It involves a very high degree of customer participation and involves the creation of measurable requirement definitions before each stage of modeling and/or coding. RBU includes only the essential tasks and is designed to be highly communicative and easily understood by both customers and professional development staff. Most often developed in direct cooperation with customers via a "Joint Application Design" (JAD) approach, the requirements are used to both design and validate the application functionality.

This paper only includes a brief description of the RBU process. Accordingly, it is not meant as a complete implementation guide for a professional development organization. RBU's major tasks and techniques are described here, but there has been no attempt to include all of the necessary components of a robust methodology (e.g., standards, procedures, forms, etc.). In addition, the examples contained within are merely illustrative of the overall approach.

Keywords:

Requirements; Object-Oriented; JAD, UML; Quality Assurance; Application Development; Coding; Collaboration

Requirements-Based UML

Introduction

The Dreaded "M" Word

Every project needs one and every developer follows one, whether formal or informal, prescribed or ad-hoc. Unfortunately, for most IS professionals the word *"Methodology"* invokes dreadful images of the worst kind. It often implies reams of unnecessary work, impossibly rigid standards, and lots of wasted time. When the average developer hears the dreaded word, they usually assume that the related project is doomed.

Of course, just the opposite is true. A development project that doesn't actively use some sort of methodology has relatively little chance of success. If such a project does succeed, it is merely through coincidence or sheer dumb luck. These are the kinds of projects that ramble about generating lots of paperwork but relatively few measurable results. They miss every major deadline because they change directions so frequently, and usually require large quantities of rework to "fix" previous mistakes. In a project without a methodology, there is usually no such thing as a *frozen* deliverable, so consequently there are *no* deliverables.

So, then what exactly is a methodology? In its simplest form, a methodology is a set of steps to accomplish a task. That's it. No fancy buzzwords or expensive terminology, just a set of steps. It is a plan that describes each task and its sequence relative to the others. After all, any job worth doing is worth planning for. As the old military adage goes, "If you fail to plan, you are planning to fail."

Of course, a robust methodology can also include many other components. Strictly speaking, a complete methodology includes not only task descriptions but also supporting components like task standards, technique guidelines, deliverable outlines, and quality metrics. These items, though, are merely present to supplement the basic purpose of the methodology, which is to identify and prioritize the work to be done. That is, to describe the set of steps needed to accomplish the goal.

Unified Modeling Language

The latest emerging industry-standard in the object-oriented methodology arena is the *Unified Modeling Language*, commonly referred to as "UML". UML is a collaborative effort between the "Three Amigos" of the object-oriented analysis and design (OOAD) industry, i.e., Grady Booch, Ivar Jacobson, and Jim Rumbaugh. Each of these three had previously authored their own competing methodologies and realized the significant benefits of a truly global standard for (OOAD). By combining much of their previous work, the UML standard was born.

Of course, UML is not actually a methodology. Rather, it is a notational standard that can be used to implement the tasks within a methodology. By having a common notation, methodology and tool vendors can easily develop complementary solutions without requiring retraining of the workforce. UML-based methodologies define differing sets of tasks, but the techniques all employ the standard graphical symbologies.

One such example is the "Rational Unified Process" (RUP) from Rational Software. RUP is a complete methodology developed by the "Three Amigos" which uses the UML notation to represent all of its deliverables. It includes suggested task plans and also defines guidelines and metrics that can be used to manage and measure the development process.

Use Case Models

The UML specification includes graphical notations for many different diagram types, with most being optional steps based on the complexity of the application being developed. Relatively speaking, the "first" deliverable described in the UML notation is the Use Case Diagram. A Use Case Diagram graphically depicts the interaction between system users (i.e., "actors") and system functions (i.e., "use cases"). Subsequent UML diagrams build on this basic information to identify the system components, methods, and packages necessary.

Unfortunately, this focus on beginning with use cases creates a glaring deficiency in most UML-based methodologies, that is, they don't address the business-oriented application requirements. Instead of first defining the purpose and objectives for the development effort, UML methods begin by jumping directly to the software functions. This presupposes that the use case participants already know why they need a system and what the optimal solution should look like.

In reality, the most important part of any systems development effort is to first establish a firm understanding of the problem so that potential solutions can be effectively weighed. To do this, the key business requirements must be defined, including the return-on-investment justification for each. Once this *Objective Baseline* is established, proposed alternatives can then be measured to determine which best solves the stated problem. Without this requirements analysis, a UML-based approach may only help to deliver the *wrong* application faster and cheaper.

Requirements-Based UML

One possible solution to this problem is the use of *"Requirements-Based UML"* (RBU). RBU is a structured approach for incorporating business-oriented requirements analysis into a UML-centric development method. It balances the need for non-technical business analysis against the need for the structured technical approach defined in UML. Furthermore, it identifies business requirements analysis as a precursor to software-centric use case modeling efforts.

RBU also relies on a more natural, textual format for requirements deliverables. Non-technical staff members are generally more comfortable with words than diagrams, so RBU business requirements are defined in sentences and paragraphs. These textual descriptions are then related to the graphical objects defined in the UML deliverables.

After the first level of UML diagrams is completed (use case models, collaboration diagrams, etc.), the requirements are refined into more detailed textual technical specifications. In turn, these specifications are then related to the next round of UML diagram objects. This process of textual requirements leading UML modeling can continue to whatever level of detail is appropriate for the specific project.

By using this alternating approach with requirements and diagram objects, a more complete analysis and design model is produced. This provides a clearer picture of the application environment, including not only answering the "How?" questions for the application but also clarifying the "Why?" and "What?" as well. All too often development teams are eager to rush into coding and the latter two questions remained unvisited. It is these types of projects that are most often cancelled or rejected by the customers because they provide little business value.

UML Overview

What is UML?

The Unified Modeling Process (UML) is a common notation for structured modeling within an Object-Oriented Analysis and Design (OOAD) framework. It was originally developed by several of the leading OOAD methodologists as a means to help standardize the types and format of deliverables produced by the competing OOAD methods. While not strictly a methodology itself, UML describes the notation that methodology outputs employ.

The current UML notational standard addresses the system analysis, design, and deployment steps in a development lifecycle. This version of the UML, v1.3, was approved in June 1999 by the Object Management Group (OMG). A new draft standard, v2.0, is currently in RFI review and will extend the current standard to include a range of other activities. The most notable addition expected in v2.0 is a common notation for business process redesign.

A Typical UML Process

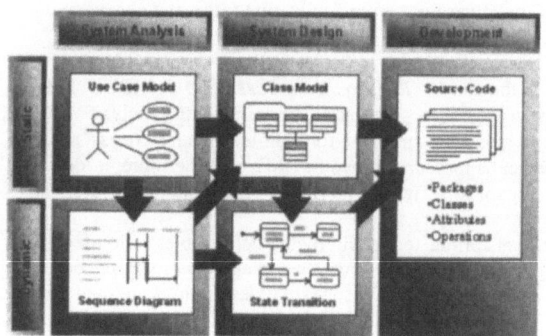

A UML-based development methodology usually involves a series of graphical models which are used to define the functional and technical aspects of an application system. Each model depicts a diagrammatic representation of one aspect of the application and is integrated with the other model objects. These models are then used as the component specifications for the construction phase of the project.

As shown in the graphic, the first and primary model developed in most UML-based methods is the Use Case diagram. Use Case diagrams are used to identify the external system boundary for an application by depicting the system functions ("use cases") that external entities ("actors") are able to interact with. Use Case diagrams are generally developed in very close collaboration with the application's ultimate customers or sponsors.

These Use Case diagrams are often then more fully described by the creation of either Object Sequence diagrams and/or Object Collaboration diagrams. Both of these diagram types serve to more fully describe the Use Case by including the nature and order of each of the major work steps within the Use Case. Together, some combination of these three diagrams provide the functional application requirements for a system.

At the beginning of the system design, then, the system analysis models are used as input to create the relevant Class diagrams and/or State Transition diagrams. These design models describe the technical structure of the application. Any of several deployment models (e.g., Package Deployment diagrams, etc.) may also be defined in order to complete the technical specification before code development begins.

UML Requirements

In the context of a UML-based method as outlined above, the term "requirements" generally refers to a set of technical specifications that describe the software features in an application. These requirements are imperative statements of functionality that must exist in the developed code and are written as "Plain Language" textual sentences or paragraphs. This deliverable is often named the "System Requirement Specification" (SRS).

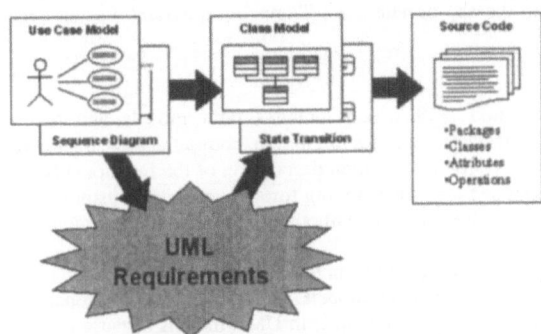

Most often, these "UML requirements" included in the SRS are developed as extensions of a Use Case diagram. For each Use Case defined, the complete set of mandatory characteristics is identified and documented in clear, concise language. Modelers will then use these requirement definitions to help complete and validate the systems design models, ensuring coverage of all required functionality.

The SRS generally includes both functional and non-functional requirements. Functional requirements state a capability that invokes or performs an actor-oriented transaction. Non-functional requirements, on the other hand, state a characteristic of the application which limits or bound a designer's ability to develop a solution. Non-functional requirements usually include information about traits like performance and capacity limits, security rules and responsibilities, and/or technological considerations.

UML Requirements Example

In the example pictured below, a Use Case has been defined named "Enter Product Order". This Use Case would exist on one or more Use Case diagrams and would be detailed with the inclusion of a Use Case narrative (e.g., pre-conditions, post-conditions, etc.). In the diagram, the appropriate actor(s) would also be associated to the Use Case.

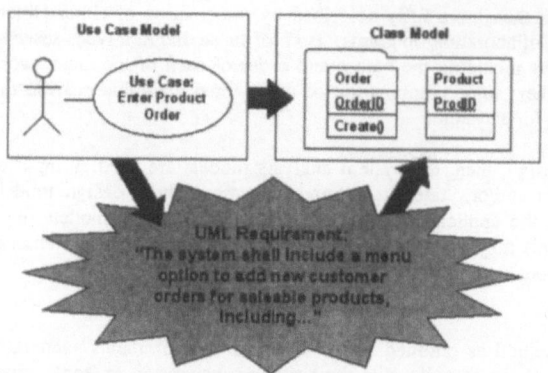

As part of the transition from system analysis to system design, UML requirements would then be defined for this Use Case. These requirements would itemize the specific features necessary in the software in order to fully accomplish the "Enter Product Order" Use Case. As mentioned above, this might include both functional requirements and non-functional requirements.

One such UML requirement for the "Enter Product Order" Use Case might be the statement that "The system shall include a menu option to add new customer orders for saleable products...". As a result of this requirement, when the user interface class is developed in the Class diagram the system designer will know to include a method to invoke this process. This may also be reflected in the appropriate State Transition diagram(s) as an event which triggers a change in state.

Benefits of UML Requirements
The advantage of developing a structured SRS which includes both models and textual requirements is twofold. Firstly, the textual statements are often more communicative than UML notation to non-technical customers as they provide a written description of the functionality that anyone can read. The graphical notations can often be daunting for an uneducated customer, and so the textual descriptions are more comfortable for those without any previous UML training.

Secondly, the textual requirements provide a place to document software features that may not be readily apparent or do not exist in the graphical models. For example, non-functional characteristics like hardware constraints are difficult to include in UML models because they are typically global issues that cannot be incorporated into the description of just one model object.

So, UML requirements become the document-centric "bridge" between the graphical system analysis deliverables (Use Case diagrams, etc.) and the graphical system design deliverables (Class diagrams, etc.). Most often these requirements are managed with a word processing application and reviewed and approved in document format. This comfortable paradigm mimics traditional document-oriented analysis techniques.

Drawbacks to UML Requirements
However, there are also disadvantages to limiting the requirements process to technical feature descriptions. First and foremost, by beginning the analysis process with Use Case definitions, the focus is immediately on the design of the software. Since Use Cases describe systemic

solutions to problems, the derived UML requirements will address only the systemic characteristics as well.

With this approach, the only solution that can be developed will be one that can be automated with an application. This virtually ignores the relevant business issues that may be all or part of the problem as well. Often a minor business process redesign (like job function reorganization) can facilitate a more efficient application or even eliminate the need for an application at all.

Also, UML requirements tend to include a lot of technical language since they are describing technical features. This is typically because they are written for the development organization to use as an input to the system design process. However, another goal of a structured requirements analysis is to validate the system analysis deliverables and the customers needed to do this are often non-technical. So, the personnel with the appropriate business knowledge may not be able to adequately understand the requirements definitions.

Finally, another problem with UML requirements is that they tend to focus on one business transaction at a time. Since they are most often derived from Use Cases, the requirements are documented with an eye toward that one transaction and often ignore the business workflow surrounding it. Without a highly structured reuse analysis, it is often possible to end up with highly efficient transactions that contain a lot of business redundancy between them.

Requirements-Based UML (RBU) Overview

What is RBU?
Requirement-Based UML (RBU) is a structured approach for integrating formal requirements analysis into a UML-based analysis and design effort. It balances the need for non-technical business analysis against the need for the system-oriented approach defined in UML by including a multi-level requirements definition. Instead of just the technical feature descriptions captured in traditional UML requirements (see previous chapter), RBU defines multiple requirements deliverables with a specific focus for each. Simply put, requirements management becomes a lifecycle task that runs in parallel with the OOAD tasks.

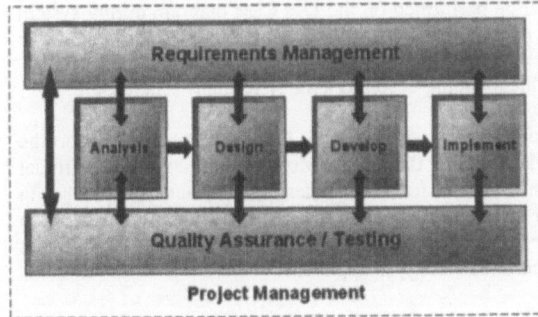

As with UML requirements, RBU requirements deliverables are defined in a natural, textual format. This allows non-technical customers to more comfortably review and understand the requirements information. These textual descriptions are then related to the relevant graphical objects defined in the UML-based deliverables.

Often, development teams

prematurely rush into the development of the application solution and ignore the larger business issues. This can easily lead to inappropriate or expensive technological solutions. By using alternating "rounds" of modeling and textual specifications, the RBU approach helps to temper that tendency and delivers a richer, more complete picture of the business problem. In this manner, it helps to ensure a higher quality, more cost-effective solution.

In addition, the RBU approach addresses Quality Assurance as a lifecycle task as well. Requirements are thoroughly tested before any development is performed, detecting conflicts and omissions that would stall later development. At each stage, the QA/Testing plan is refined and more detail is added until specific test cases have been identified. By developing the test cases from the requirements rather than the code, a more complete test harness is be established.

Typical RBU Process

The RBU technique begins with a textual specification of all of the requirements for any solution to the business problem. These requirement statements define both the functionality required in the solution as well as the boundaries the solution must operate within. All of these requirement statements should be specified in a non-technical, "plain language" format. Ideally, the customers will define these textual requirements themselves without restatement by the development staff.

These requirements, usually referred to as "Business Requirements", should be defined without regard to how the application will look. Specifically, they should not reference menu options or screen formats. The intent is to capture a definition of the business process needed to completely solve the business problem. In essence, they answer the question of "What?" not "How?".

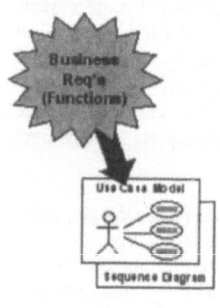

Once the Business Requirements are defined, they can then be used as the basis for developing the Use Case diagrams. Specifically, each functional requirement identified in the Business Requirements will initially correspond to one Use Case if it can be automated. If it can't be automated, then a manual transition plan will need to be developed.

While it may appear redundant to develop a 1:1 correspondence between Business Requirements and Use Cases, it isn't because further refinement will be performed on the Use Case diagram during system analysis. The mapping is only 1:1 at the beginning of this stage. Once the Use Case diagram is refined with "Extends" and "Uses" relationships, the mapping becomes a many-to-many relationship.

It is important, though, that this reuse analysis be performed on the Use Cases and not on the Business Requirements. This is to avoid corrupting the real business requirements with artificial technological constraints. All too often users are forced to redesign their business process in order to accommodate technology rather than the reverse. As the saying goes, "Just because you know how to use a hammer, not every problem is a nail". That is, define the business requirements for a solution before a specific technology is applied.

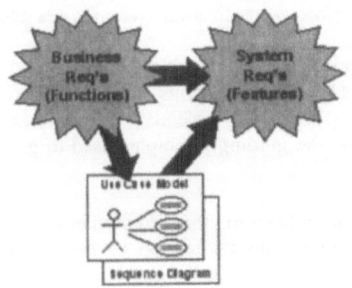

As part of the transition to system design, both the Business Requirements and the system analysis models are used to develop System Requirements. As with the Business Requirements, the System Requirements are stated in a textual format. However, unlike the Business Requirements, the System Requirements define the technical features of the application rather than the business needs. They are used to define the "How?" for the application.

At this point, relationships should be established between the System Requirements and the previous deliverables. For example, each System Requirement should be an implementation of at least one Business Requirement and at least one Use Case. These relationships are then analyzed to look for inconsistencies in the model. For example, if any Business Requirement does not have at least one "child" System Requirement, there is a gap somewhere in the Use Case model. On the other hand, if there are System Requirements without at least one "parent" Business Requirement, then the scope of the original project has been increased, either intentionally or unintentionally.

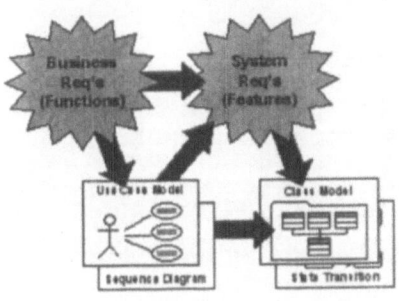

Once the System Requirements have been fully defined and quality checked, they are used in conjunction with the Use Case model to develop the Class model. As with the System Requirements, relationships should be established to the "parent" objects in the previous deliverables and used to look for inconsistencies and omissions in the Class model.

Finally, the system design and implementation models are then used to develop the application code itself. By using this "matrix" approach to building the UML deliverables, the resulting application is more complete and of higher quality.

If a formal business process model is desired, the RBU process can be extended to support this work as well. Although the UML specification does not include notation for business process models, there are many popular methodologies which do. For example, the CSC Lynx method is used by many modeling tools to implement this work.

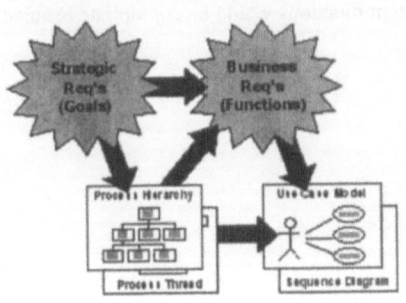

In these cases, additional diagrams are developed before the UML deliverables listed above are created. These might include models like a Process Hierarchy diagram and/or a Process Thread diagram. Both of these diagrams show the flow of work through an organization without regard for job titles and application boundaries.

Their purpose is to optimize the organizational process before an application system is designed.

Using the RBU approach, the Process Hierarchy and Process Thread diagrams would be preceded by a set of requirement definitions. These requirements, called "Strategic Requirements" define the goals of the organization, including the objective metrics used to measure success. These Strategic Requirements become the guiding principles used to govern which possible business process is the most desirable.

As with previous requirements, Strategic Requirements are related to other requirements and the modeling objects. Specifically, Strategic Requirements should be related to the Business Requirements necessary to accomplish the goals and to the processes in the business models that implement them. Again, these relationships can be inspected for inconsistencies before moving forward in the development lifecycle.

Finally, as mentioned earlier, the RBU method includes a third parallel activity for Quality Assurance and Testing. This set of work is performed by the QA organization and is used to detect flaws in the requirements and models deliverables and to develop the test harness used for verification of the application code. By deriving the test cases from the requirements in a progressive manner, the resulting test plan will be more complete and should validate both functional and operational performance.

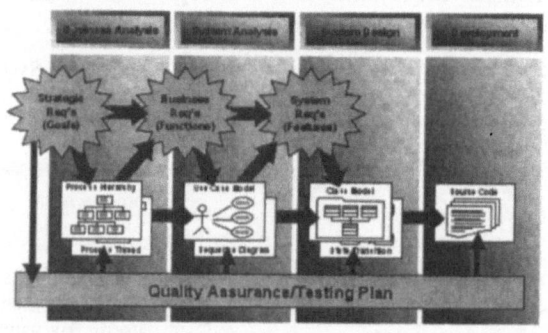

At first glance, the RBU approach may seem to introduce additional work on the project team because there are more steps than in a traditional UML-based method. However, in the opinion of this author, the work that RBU dictates is not additional work, but rather it is a matter of formalizing work that is already being done with informal methods. By purposefully addressing these steps, the quality of the work will increase and productivity may actually improve. At the very least, the quality of the software product itself will be measurably higher.

RBU Example

To demonstrate the RBU technique, consider the example of the "Enter Product Order" Use Case shown in the previous chapter. How did the user and/or development staff conclude that this Use Case was necessary? How did they know which system functions would be appropriate to solve the business problem?

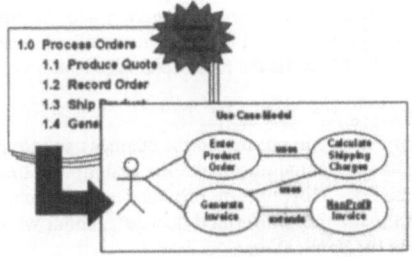

Most often, the answer to these questions is that the Information Systems staff asked the customer what the solution should be. This assumes, however, that the customer has the information and expertise necessary to make this decision. Very often that is not the case and dangerous assumptions are introduced into the development effort before a single line of code is written.

In an RBU-based project, the Use Case model would be preceded by a set of Business Requirements which document the business solution to the problem. In our example, the Business Requirements would include information about not only the two automated tasks ("Record Order" and "Generate Invoice") but also the two manual tasks that surround them ("Produce Quote" and "Ship Product"). Together, these four tasks identified in the Business Requirements describe the complete business solution necessary to solve the stated problem. Now the development team has sufficient information to make an informed decision about which tasks can be automated and how best to implement them.

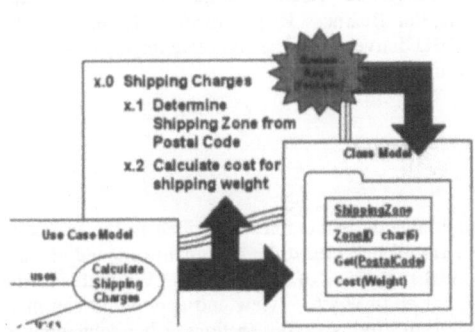

Initially, only two Use Cases are defined. These would be named "Enter Product Order" and "Generate Invoice" and would be related to the two Business Requirements that are being automated. During the course of the system analysis, however, additional Use Cases might be identified in order to encapsulate reusable logic (e.g., "Calculate Shipping Charges") or to extend the model for alternate courses (e.g., "Non-Profit Invoices"). These additional Use Cases would not be directly related to Business Requirements but would instead derive their relationships through other Use Cases.

Once the Use Case model was completed, the System Requirements would then identify the functional and non-functional software features needed to automate the Use Case definitions. These System Requirements would then, in turn, be used to help define the objects in the system design models (e.g., Class diagram, State Transition diagram, etc.).

Benefits of the RBU Approach
There are many benefits to using the RBU approach instead of traditional UML-based methods that treat requirement as "features". The most important is that a structured requirements-based approach to development will dramatically improve the level of communication between end-users and the development staff. By providing a non-threatening textual format for

deliverables, customers without training in UML notation are able to participate in the application specification. The requirements documents produced will be easier to read and more likely to be reviewed by the appropriate customers. All of this means more feedback which will lead to higher quality deliverables.

Another major benefit is that RBU provides a facility to document the entire business solution, not just the automated subset of it. Where UML modeling techniques make the assumption that a systemic solution is available, RBU requirements do not. This, in turn, provides a much richer picture of the solution and allows the project team to make more informed decisions about what automated functionality can and should be included in the application.

In fact, business improvements are often suggested as a result of the RBU requirements analysis that have nothing to do with application development. These solutions would typically not even be discussed during a UML-based project. Just as often, applications cannot efficiently solve the root cause of the business problem being solved because it is not an automated problem. It is important to understand this before an expensive development project is launched and then later cancelled due to lack of substantive results.

Finally, a third major benefit of RBU is that the scope of the application can be managed based on customer needs rather than on software features. By using the requirements as an integral part of the change control process, change requests can be evaluated on the basis of the business improvement in the Strategic Requirements and/or Business Requirements. Then, using the relationships established between the various RBU deliverables, the complete impact of a change can be determined before the change is approved.

Advanced Topics

Requirement Hierarchies

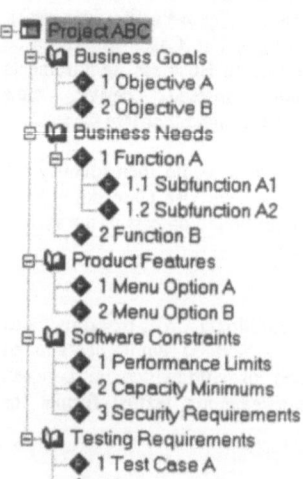

The requirements deliverables described in the preceding chapters are all intended to be document-oriented artifacts with textual statements of requirements. While this format is easier for end-users to review and approve, it can make it difficult to find specific sections when changing or searching the requirement information. To help resolve this problem, most requirement deliverables are organized in requirement hierarchies.

A requirement hierarchy is simply a "tree-like" structure of requirements with similar requirements grouped into common "branches". The major branches of the tree correspond to the requirements deliverables listed above (Strategic Requirements, Business Requirements, etc.). The subordinate branches are defined based on the business area or organizational structure most appropriate to the project under development.

For example, in the Strategic Requirements analysis, the goals are most often subdivided by the organizational unit(s) being analyzed. Within each unit, then, the specific objectives might be identified and listed in priority order. However, during Business Requirements analysis, it may be more convenient to organize the sub-branches by business area or logical transaction.

No matter how the requirements hierarchy is organized, the most important aspect of the hierarchy is to understand and manage each requirement as an individual object within the set. Rather than treating a requirements document as a single block of text, each requirement should be treated as a separate entity and uniquely identified. In this manner, attribute identification, historical tracking, and object traceability can all be managed at the requirement level.

Requirement Traceability

Once the requirement hierarchy has been established, the rules for relationships between the requirements and the UML objects can be defined. These relationships, usually referred to as "traces", identify the dependencies between the various development objects. Typically, these traces are used to understand the impact of a request during the change control process as well as ensuring that changes are completely propagated throughout the development model.

For traces between requirements, relationships can either be established between two requirements on the same branch of the hierarchy or across branches. Most often, traces within one branch of the hierarchy are established to show a logical precedence between the two requirements.

For example, in the picture on the right there are two primary business goals that have been identified for *Project ABC*. These are named *Objective A* and *Objective B*. However, in addition to the textual definition of each, there is business rule that must be defined in the requirements document. Specifically, *Objective A* must be met before *Objective B* can be attempted. This precedence relationship is modeled as with traceability link between the two requirements, shown as a blue arrow in the graphic. It indicates that *Objective A* is the "logical parent" of *Objective B* and that any changes to *Objective A* must be reviewed to determine their impact on *Objective B* as well.

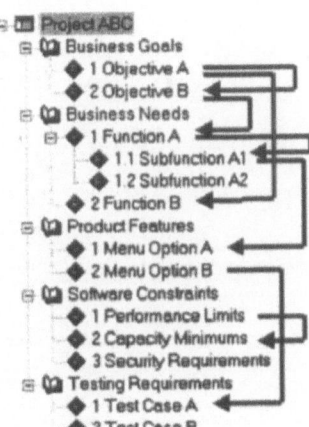

Traces between major branches in the requirements hierarchy, however, generally indicate a developmental dependency. That is, requirements in earlier stages of development should have traces to requirements in later stages of development in order to show the progression of the development effort.

In our example, *Objective A* is one of the business goals that must be met by the project. In order to show the development dependency to the business functions, a traceability link is established between *Objective A* and

Function B. This indicates that *Function B* is necessary in order to accomplish *Objective A.* This relationship is shown on the graphic with a red arrow. Any changes to *Function B* must be reviewed to determine their effect on the project's ability to accomplish *Objective A.*

Generally, only "direct" traces are modeled between requirements. "Indirect" traces can then be implied by following the chain of the parent-child relationships. For example, in the *Project ABC* tree, *Objective B* has an indirect relationship to *Menu Option A* by following the chain through the intermediate nodes of *Function A* and *Subfunction A1.*

Traces are also established between the requirements and UML objects in much the same way. For example, if *Function A* was implemented by *Use Case 1,* a dependency trace would be defined between the two to show this relationship. Subsequent impact analysis could then be performed by following the trace from the requirement to the UML model or vice versa.

Without these traces, proposing changes during the development lifecycle becomes a subjective effort depending entirely on the memory of the requirements analyst(s). While this may occasionally be effective, most often it leads to understated estimates and inconsistencies in the software design. Requirements traceability makes change control an objective, rational process

References

[1] Grady Booch, Ivar Jacobsen, James Rumbaugh. *The Unified Modeling Language Reference Manual.* Addison Wesley Longman Inc., Reading, MA USA. 1999.

[2] Bernd Oesteriech. *Developing Software with UML.* Addison Wesley Longman Ltd., Harlow, England UK. 1997.

[3] Paul Allen, Stuart Frost. *Component-Based Development for Enterprise Systems: Applying the SELECT Perspective.* Cambridge University Press, Cambridge, UK. 1998.

[4] Pierre-Alain Muller. *Instant UML, English Translation.* Wrox Press Ltd., Olton, Birmingham, Canada. 1997.

[5] Martin Fowler, Kendall Scott. *UML Distilled: Applying the Standard Object Modeling Language.* Addison Wesley Longman Inc., Reading, MA USA. 1997.

[6] James Martin. *An Information Systems Manifesto.* Prentice-Hall International, London, England UK. 1984.

[7] Geri Schneider, Jason P. Winters. *Applying Use Cases: A Practical Guide.* Addison Wesley Longman Inc., Reading, MA USA. 1998.

UML AND MODELLING
ISSUES II

Conceptual Analysis of Flexibility Concepts in Object-Orientation and UML

Feroz A. Siddiqui and Guy Fitzgerald

Department of Information Systems & Computing
Brunel University
Uxbridge, Middlesex UB8 3PH - UK
Fax: +44 (0)1895 251686
E-mail: feroz.siddiqui@brunel.ac.uk, guy.fitzgerald@brunel.ac.uk

ABSTRACT. *The paper discusses the issue of flexibility in information systems and its implications in the Object-Oriented paradigm including the Unified Modelling Language (UML). Object-orientation is considered a remedy for many problems of information systems development including that of rigidity and the handling of change due to its flexible nature. An analysis and design technique like UML could help to achieve more flexibility in the object-oriented systems. The paper examines the concepts of flexibility and derives a set of features that characterise flexibility. The Objected-Oriented paradigm and UML technique are examined and discussed in relation to the flexibility features. Finally, a figure summarising the findings is presented which shows the relationship of the identified flexibility concepts and the Object-Oriented domain and UML.*

KEY WORDS: *Object-Orientation, Unified Modelling Language (UML), Flexibility and Adaptability.*

1. Introduction

Information systems are built with the intent of supporting businesses and organisations, the systems usually automate some set of business operations for greater efficiency, effectiveness and control. However, increasingly information systems are seen as barriers to change and as limiting the ability of organisations to be effective in a rapidly changing and turbulent organisational environment (Allen and Boynton, 1991). Flexibility, i.e. the ability to accommodate change easily, is becoming one of the key features of an effective information system. The concept of flexibility is not a new one and its importance has been well known in business since the 1960s but it has only recently become an issue in information systems. When the business rules and requirements that a system supports are frequently changing it means that the system should be capable of itself changing to reflect these changing needs and to remain relevant. The maintenance and enhancement of systems has always been costly and a slow process but with increasing turbulence information systems are proving unequal to the task of keeping up with the changing demands of business.

The use of systems development methodologies and modelling techniques to analyse and design a system, play a vital role in the system outcome and whether it is deemed a success or not. Recently the object-oriented systems development approach and the Unified Modelling Language (UML) have become popular and it is argued that they solve many of the problems of systems development including that of producing more flexible systems. The purpose of this paper is to examine in more detail the different concepts relating to flexibility and to show the relationship of those concepts to the object-oriented characteristics and UML features. Thus the next section discusses some of the general concepts associated with flexibility and what they mean. This is then followed by an examination of the characteristics of object-orientation and features of the UML, and whether they meet or support the flexibility concepts. Finally a table of 'which flexibility concepts' are found in 'which object-oriented and UML features' is produced.

2. Concepts of Flexibility

The concept of flexibility, and what it really means, is rather ill-defined especially in the general, non-IS/IT, literature. Terms are used loosely and similar terms are frequently used for the same concept and vice versa. In general terms flexibility is usually defined simply as the ability to adjust or adapt to change (e.g. Scott, 1965). Some authors go a little further (e.g. Hees & Monhemius, 1970) and introduce the notion of speed of change as being an important part of flexibility. Veld (1978) states that flexibility is the ability to recognise changes in goals and make rapid alterations to achieve these new goals but additionally suggests that flexibility is achieved by anticipating change rather than reacting to it.

Many other terms are used in discussions of flexibility and we use some of these to help further define the concepts of flexibility. The most frequent term used is probably *'adaptability'*, which usually refers to the ease of making modification, adjustment or (making) suitable for a particular situation. A distinction that is sometimes made between flexibility and adaptability, where they are not used simply as synonyms, is that adaptability implies relatively small changes within a domain whereas flexibility is concerned with more major change that alters 'the original intention' (Duffy, 1992). Stigler (1939) further suggests that adaptability implies a singular and permanent adjustment to a newly transformed environment, whereas flexibility enables successive but temporary approximations to this state of affairs. It also involves repositioning to deal with the imperatives of a new environment.

Other terms that are used in connection with flexibility are, for example, *robustness* (Rosenhead et al., 1986), which literally refers to a system's ability to absorb, deflect, or endure the impacts of unanticipated changes, it also reflects the strength and firmly built nature of the system. *Versatility* is said to be achieved by either installing a capability to respond to a wide range of scenarios ahead of time, or by affecting a rapid modification once a change has occurred (Bonder, 1976). *Pliability* is sometimes used to denote the degree to which something can be bent, bowed or twisted without breaking; thus implying that whatever is being manipulated will yield to pressure (Evans, 1991), it also reflect the quality to influence by argument or easily persuade. *Manoeuvrability* is about managing skilfully or the capability to manage in many dimensions, while *corrigibility* is used to reflect the facility for making corrections in a system.

These above terms we use as a starting point to define elements that constitute flexibility. This will then provide a more systematic means of analysing methods and approaches for developing information systems as to their degree of flexibility. In this paper we have chosen to examine the Object-Oriented paradigm and the Unified Modelling Language in terms of the flexibility concepts that they support.

3. Object Orientation

As indicated above information systems have frequently been criticised for being difficult to change and lacking flexibility. However, it is suggested that the object-oriented (OO) approach is inherently much more flexible than other development approaches and capable of dealing with uncertain futures (Prager, 1996). Further OO is also considered suitable for managing complexity, as the more complex a system is the more difficult it is to maintain. We test out these claims by identifying which features of the OO approach support which features or concepts of flexibility. Six concepts of flexibility were identified above and these are highlighted in italics in the analysis below as they are identified.

3.1. Encapsulation

The principle of binding data and methods into an object is called encapsulation, which is similar to information hiding (Parnas, 1972) and helps to build secure systems. The internal structure of an object is hidden from the other objects and can only be accessed by the methods of the object itself. Encapsulation deals with the issue of how we intend to modularise a system, it is basically a design issue that deals with how functionality is compartmentalised within a system (Ambler, 1995). This provides certain advantages in terms of facilitating reusability and maintenance, which makes system easily modifiable and open to make any corrections and changes. E.g. if there are two classes A and B, 'class A' have a static functionality while 'class B' just stores the data without knowing the functionality of 'class A'. Tomorrow, if we decided to change the functionality of 'class A' from static to dynamic, it will not effect on the data of 'class B'. As the functionality of 'class A' is encapsulated, it is much easier to make any alteration in the system. This is argued to provide the flexibility concept of *corrigibility* in a system. System evolution and maintenance problems are mitigated by the strong partitioning, resulting from encapsulation and uniform object interfaces, which makes a system *robust*.

3.2. Modularity

One of the unique features of the object-oriented approach is that it supports both composability and decomposability (Graham, 1995). Composability refers to the property of modules to be freely combined even in systems for which they were not developed, and this provides the foundation for reusability (also supported by the concept of encapsulation). It also relates to the notion of extensibility, which is the ability to add functions to a system without radical surgery, as it manages modification and adjustment intelligently. This reflects the characteristic of *adaptability* in the system. On the other hand, decomposability is related to the concept of decentralisation. It is based on the principles of encapsulation and simple object interfaces. Each module in a system needs to know only about its own implementation rather than that of its servers, thus its code can be more readily extended or modified internally.

3.3. Inheritance

The facility that models common behaviour between objects is called class (Pressman, 1994), and the items created using the class are called instances. The value of the class concept arises from the facility of inheritance where instances usually inherit all the features of the classes to which they belong. It allows objects or sub-classes of a parent class or super-class to inherit the common data and methods of the parent class. When specifying an object, it is only necessary to consider the differences between the object and its parent class, as the common data and methods can be inherited automatically. E.g. if we have a 'class A' and two subclasses B and C, which obviously inherit the common data from 'class A'. Later on, if we decided to add another 'subclass D' of same category on the system, we will not have to write the whole code for 'subclass D', as it will inherit the common code from 'class A', which helps to increase the *adaptability* in system design for changing requirements.

3.4. Polymorphism (Coupling & Cohesion)

Coupling describes the degree of interrelationships among the objects that make up a system, and cohesion is a measure of how logically related the components of the external view of an object are to each other (Berard, 1996). The features that make up an object-oriented system flexible are low coupling and high cohesion. This phenomenon is known as polymorphism or dynamic binding. It provides the ability to use the same expression to denote different operations (Graham, 1995), that is a generic message can be sent to several different objects, without needing to specify any implementation details. The objects can all respond differently to the same message, this reflects the concept of *versatility*. The idea behind polymorphism is that a group of heterogeneous objects can be made to look homogeneous, but can be distinguished based on their own specific type (Riel, 1996) resulting in *pliability* in system design. E.g. if 'class A' have 'method 1', and subclasses B and C have to perform different operations in the response of a single message from 'class A', as both subclasses are inherited by 'class A', they will perform the same operation. If we define 'method 1' in 'subclass B', it will override the 'method 1' defined in 'class A', and will perform different operation than 'subclass C' for the same message. Thus, polymorphic behaviour allows change to be accommodated more transparently, which provides the facility of *adaptability* and *manoeuvrability* in a system.

4. Unified Modelling Language (UML)

The UML is recognised as a modelling language, and is more of a vocabulary or a mostly graphical notation for expressing underlying object-oriented analysis and design ideas. As UML does not have any process or method it is not considered to be a methodology. A method or process consists of recommendations or advice on how to perform object-oriented analysis and design (Ambler, 1997). Essentially UML defines a number of diagrams (Fowler & Scott, 1997, Stevens & Pooley, 2000) that are used to describe a system. These diagrams relate to the following modelling types:

4.1. Static Modelling

Static modelling is uses *Use Case diagrams* and *Class diagrams*. A use case describes a way in which a real-world actor (a person, organisation or external system) interacts with an organisation. Use case models are important inputs for the development of class diagrams. Class diagrams show the classes of the system and their interrelationships including, inheritance, aggregation and associations. These are the mainstays of object-oriented modelling and are used to show both what the system can do (analysis) and how the system will be built (design). The information contained in a class diagram directly maps to the source code that will be written to implement the application. As a result of using these diagrams a system could be said to be *adaptable* and *corrigible*.

4.2. Dynamic Modelling

Dynamic modelling uses *Interaction diagrams*, *State diagrams* and *Activity diagrams*. Interaction diagrams records in detail how objects interact to perform a task and show the types of objects involved in the use case, the massages they send each other, and any return values associated with the massages. These diagrams are used to look at the behaviour of several objects within a single use case. Apart from use cases, interaction diagrams also describes other behaviours as well, i.e. how a 'class provides an operation', 'how design patterns works' and 'how components can be used'. This multi-use nature of interaction diagrams reflects the quality of *versatility* in its use. As objects have both behaviour and state; in other words, they do things and they know things, some objects do and know more things, or at least more complicated things, than other objects. State-chart or state-transition diagrams are drawn to describe how complex objects work across several use cases. Activity diagrams are like a graphical pseudo code, these describes the flow of activities or tasks within an operation. They can be used for everything from showing the sequencing of use cases to flow charting an individual method. Activity diagrams can handle parallel processes with concurrency, which reflects the facility of *manoeuvrability*.

4.3. Architectural Modelling

Architectural modelling uses *Component diagrams* and *Deployment diagrams*. One of the main role of component diagrams in architectural modelling is to partition a system into cohesive components that have stable interfaces, creating a core that need not change in response to subsystem-level changes, which increase the systems *adaptability*. Deployment diagrams show the configuration of run-time processing units, and are reasonably simple models that are used to show how the hardware and software units will be configured and deployed for an application. As it provides ease of modification in a system, it can be said to reflect the flavour of *adaptability* and *corrigibility* in system design.

Finally, the UML notation is big and flexible enough to accommodate the needs of a wide range of projects (Rosenberg, 1997), as it is a method-independent modelling language, which reflects its *versatile* nature in use. The main advantage of using UML is that it enhances communication between the various parties and that the diagrams can be levelled according to need, which is argued to provide the concept of *pliability* in UML. As the whole system could be described in a single and easily comprehensible diagram, presenting a particular view of a system, abstracting or hiding particular details as necessary (Hunt, 2000). This also helps the modification of a system in future and reflects the feature of *adaptability* in the overall system. The identification of these features of flexibility (concepts) in UML makes the case that UML is indeed flexible.

Thus well designed objects in Object-Oriented systems are the basis for systems to be assembled largely from reusable and extensible modules; leading to flexibility in a system, as the more extensible and reusable a system is the easier it is to change and maintain. Similarly UML, as an analysis and design technique, helps to achieve that flexibility during the development of an object-oriented information system.

More formally the following figure draws together and summarises the above analysis and shows the relationship between the identified elements of flexibility for each of the major concepts in the object-oriented domain and the UML modelling techniques. The figure shows which OO/UML concepts provide the flexibility and helps substantiate the proposition that object-orientation and UML does indeed embody characteristics of flexibility. Specifically object-orientation is argued to be a flexible approach because it embodies reusability and extensibility.

		Object-Orientation				UML			
		Encapsulation	Modularity	Inheritance	Polymorphism	Static Modelling	Dynamic Modelling	Architectural Modelling	In-use
Flexibility Concepts	Adaptability		X	X	X	X		X	X
	Robustness	X							
	Versatility				X		X		X
	Pliability				X				X
	Manoeuvrability				X		X		
	Corrigibility	X				X		X	

Figure -1 Relationship between Flexibility concepts, Object-Orientation and UML

5. Conclusion

Flexibility, it is argued, is an increasingly important element of information systems. Without flexibility systems are unable to respond to the increasingly rapid changes demanded of them. Indeed information systems have been described as barriers to change rather than enablers of change. For this reason the authors have investigated many aspects of information systems flexibility (Fitzgerald, 1990, Fitzgerald et. al., 1999). Within these studies they discovered that the use of the term flexibility is very variable and imprecise so this paper has identified a set of lower level concepts that together are argued to define flexibility. These have then been used to assess whether the object-oriented approach and UML are indeed flexible as claimed by their proponents. The analysis indicates which features provide what kind of flexibility and in conclusion it is argued that indeed they can be said to be flexible in that they do support some of the flexibility concepts as depicted in the figure.

The research on which this paper is ongoing thus the findings are necessarily early. However, it is hoped that the paper makes a number of contributions. Firstly, it has clarified various concepts that together build the notion of flexibility, i.e. it has moved forward the previously very ad-hoc and imprecise use of the term. Secondly, it has used this clarification to analyse two related areas (OO and UML) to see if they exhibit flexibility as claimed by their advocates, and thirdly it suggests that indeed in specific ways they do support these claims. Further work is required in this context but, as far as we can ascertain, this is the first attempt to address these issues in an analytical way. Hopefully, in due course, the work will help to make the information systems we develop more maintainable and flexible in the future and reduce the 'barriers to change' identified earlier.

References:

(Allen & Boynton, 1991):   B. R. Allen and A. C. Boynton. *Information Architecture: In Search of Efficient Flexibility*, MIS Quarterly, pages 435--445, December 1991.

(Ambler, 1995):   S. W. Ambler. *The Object Primer: The Application Developer's Guide to Object-Orientation*, SIGS Books, New York, 1995.

(Ambler, 1997):   S. W. Ambler. *How the UML Models Fit Together*, (Online document), Software Development Magazine, 1997.

(Berard, 1996):   E. V. Berard. *Basic Object-Oriented Concepts*, (Online document), The Object Technology, Inc, 1996.

(Bonder, 1976):   S. Bonder. *Versatility: An Objective for Military Planning*, Keynote Address Presented at the 37th Military Operations Research Symposium, Fort Bliss, Texas, 1976.

(Duffy, 1992): F. Duffy. *Arguing Useful Research, The Changing Workplace*, Phaidon Press Limited, 1992.

(Evans, 1991): J. S. Evans. *Strategic Flexibility for High Technology Manoeuvres: A Conceptual Framework*, Journal of Management Studies, Vol. 28, No. 1, pages 69--89, 1991.

(Fitzgerald, 1990): G. Fitzgerald. *Achieving Flexible Information Systems: The Case for Improved Analysis*, Journal of Information Technology, Vol. 5, pages 5--11, 199-.

(Fitzgerald et al., 1998): G. Fitzgerald, A. Philippides and S. Probert. *Information Systems Development Maintenance and Flexibility: Findings From a UK Survey*, International Journal of Information Management, Vol. 40, No. 2, pages 319--329, 1998.

(Fowler & Scott, 1997): M. Fowler and K. Scott. *UML Distilled: Applying the Standard Object Modelling Language*, Addison Wesley Longman, Inc, 1997.

(Graham, 1995): I. Graham. *Object-Oriented Methods*, 2nd Edition, Addison-Wesley Publishing Company, Inc., 1995.

(Hees & Monhemius, 1970): R. N. van Hees and W. Monhemius. *Produkiebesturing en Voorraadbeheer: Theoretische Achtergronden*, Deventer: Kluwer, 1970, (In Dutch).

(Hunt, 2000): J. Hunt. *The Unified Process for Practitioners; Object Oriented Design, UML and Java*, Springer-Verlag, London, 2000.

(Parnas, 1972): D. Parnas. *On the Criteria to be Used in Decomposing Systems into Modules*, Communications of the ACM, Vol. 15, No. 12, pages 1053--1058, 1972.

(Prager, 1996): K. P. Prager. *Managing for Flexibility: The New Role of the Aligned IT Organisation*, Information Management, pages 41--46, Fall 1996.

(Pressman, 1994): R. S. Pressman. *Software Engineering: A Practitioner's Approach*, European Edition, McGraw-Hill, Maidenhead, 1994.

(Riel, 1996): A. J. Riel. *Object-Oriented Design Heuristics*, Addison-Wesley Publishing Company, Inc., 1996.

(Rosenberg, 1997): D. Rosenberg. *UML Applied: Nine Tips to Incorporating UML into Your Project*, (Online document), Software Development Magazine, 1997.

(Rosenhead et al., 1986):   J. Rosenhead, G. Best and G. Parston. *Robustness in Practice*, Journal of the Operational Research Society, Vol. 37, No. 5, pages 463--478, 1986.

(Scott, 1965):   B. W. Scott. *Long-Range Planning in American Industry*, New York: American Management Association, 1965.

(Stevens & Pooley, 2000):   P. Stevens and R. Pooley. *Using UML; Software Engineering with Objects and Components*, Addison Wesley Longman Limited, 2000.

(Stigler, 1939):   G. J. Stigler. *Production and Distribution in The Short Run*, Journal of Political Economy, Vol. 47, pages 305--327, 1939.

(Veld, 1978):   J. in't Veld. *Analyze van Organisatieproblemen*, Elsevier, 1978, (In Dutch).

UML2Z: An UML-Based Modeling Tool for an Internet Integrated Formalization Process

Emanuel Grant, Robert B. France, Ramchander Varadarajan, and Adam Carheden

Colorado State University, Fort Collins CO 80523, USA
E-mail: france@cs.colostate.edu Fax: 970.491.2466

Jean-Michel Bruel

Université de Pau et des Pays de l'Adour, 64000 Pau, France
E-mail: Jean-Michel.Bruel@univ-pau.fr

Abstract: An approach to making informal OO models semantics precise and thus amenable to rigorous analysis is by integrating them with a suitable formal notation. Such work has been carried out in the development of a CASE tool (FuZE) for formalizing UML class diagrams. Two major drawbacks with the current approach are that it is CASE tool specific, and the models developed are not portable across multiple hardware and software platforms. In this paper we propose an UML XMI interchange tool (UML2Z) for transforming UML class diagrams to the Z notation. With this approach the integration process, will be CASE tool and platform independent. This makes it available to a larger sphere of usage in terms of available CASE tools, and diverse development teams.

Keyword: UML, XML, Internet, rigorous analysis, formal notation.

1. Introduction

The *Unified Modeling Language* (UML) [OMG, 2000] provides good support for developing concise, well-structured models of software systems. The UML is based on some of the best object modeling experience known, and consists of a rich set of structuring and abstraction mechanisms. Though the UML syntax is well-defined, the underlining semantics are loosely described via a mixture of natural language text, and meta-model diagrams. This lack of precise semantics in the modeling constructs limits support for rigorous analysis, and often lead to multiple interpretations of the same construct.

If the UML is to be used effectively in the development of large, complex systems then it is necessary that a mechanism for determining a precise interpretation of the modeling constructs be devised, along with a common communication representation that can be used on different types of platforms. One approach to making informal OO models semantics precise, and thus amenable to rigorous analysis is to integrate them with a suitable formal notation. There are several studies published in this area (e.g. see [Evans et al., 1999 and France et al., 1997]. Though the word *integration* is used to describe the work of going from the informal OO models to a formal specification of these models, our approach may best be described as providing a *bridge* between the informal OO models and the corresponding formal representation. This bridge takes the form of a set of *transformation rules* that specify how UML CD models may be translated into a formal notation.

The use of an *interchange format* is exploited in developing a solution to the problem of communicating OO graphical models between different teams of developers, who are conducting their work with a diverse mix of CASE (*computer aided software engineering*) and analysis tools. This solution is based on an interchange language, namely the UML XMI (*XML Metadata Interchange*) [OMG, 2000]. This concept is graphically captured in Figure1, where multiple users, using a variety of CASE tools are able to exchange their models over the Internet, as web-based files, by use of the XML (*eXtensible Markup Language*}) [Maruyama et al., 1999] notation.

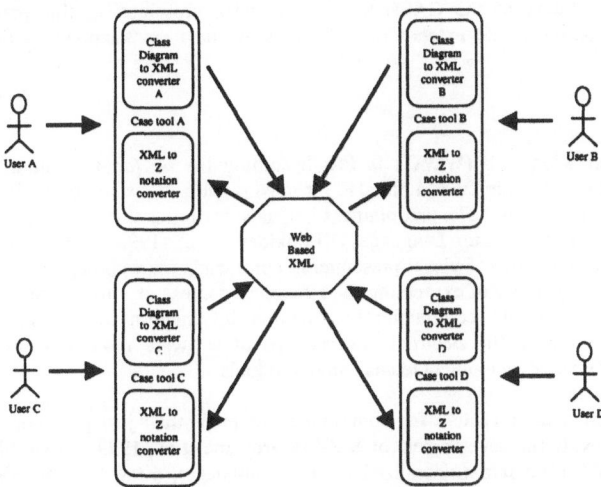

Figure 1. XML interchange environment

The focus of our work is the generation of formal specifications from the UML class diagrams (CD). CASE tool specific representations of UML CD are converted to XML (using the UML XMI specification), and then transformed to a formal specification notation in preparation for rigorous analysis. The use of a common representation notation for the OO models, and the use of transformations expressed in Java [Maruyama et al., 1999] (a platform independent programming language) results in a formalization process that is portable across heterogeneous platforms.

In Section 2 we outline the background and motivation for the work presented in this paper. In Section 3 we describe the architecture, operation and programs of our tool UML2Z (*Unified Modeling Language* class diagram to *Z* notation}), along with a small example that has been developed with UML2Z, and we conclude in Section 4 with a short summary.

2. Background

Our early work (see [France et al, 1997 and Bruel et al. 1997]) resulted in the derivation of a set of formalization rules, which were incorporated into the commercial CASE tool, Paradigm®, via its application programming interface (API) language. The result was a prototype tool called FuZE. A developer using FuZE, can create UML CDs then invoke the API modules that execute the formalization rules, to produce a set of Z schemata. The API modules are able to detect some CD syntax errors. Once an error-free set of Z schemata is obtained, the developer can then invoke additional API modules to call a Z type checker (ZTC [Jai, 1995]), and a Z analysis tool (ZANS [Jai, 1995a]). The outputs of FuZE are the Z schemata in an ASCII formatted L^{A}T$_E$X [Lamport, 1994] file, and a postscript version.

Building FuZE on top of Paradigm Plus® has the advantage of leveraging an industrial-strength commercial tool environment, but it has the disadvantage that many developers and researchers may not have access to this specific CASE tool. An alternate approach is to use a representation that is independent of the CASE tool. The work presented in this paper implements this alternate approach, and extends on it by making the formalization program platform independent.

2.1 XML and XMI

The Internet, via the world wide web (WWW) is fast becoming the *de facto* medium of communication in not just the computing world but also for most organizations and individuals that interact with computer technology. The predominant language for Internet communication has been the HTML (*HyperText Markup Language*}) [Loukides et al., 1998]. While this language offers an extensive repertoire of visual presentation commands for web page data, in the form of tags, it lacks the capability of expressing the structured context of information sent over the Internet. This inability to communicate structured information makes HTML unsuitable as a candidate language for electronic interchange of software models between geographically dispersed software development teams and individuals.

The goal of using the Internet as a vehicle for communicating more than just presentation information about data has led to the development of XML [Maruyama et al., 1999]. XML like HTML is a subset of SGML (*Standard Generalized Markup Language*), a tag language that separates the view and the description of data from its content. XML has been designed specifically to bring structured information to the WWW via tags that express this structure, as well as the rules for expressing the structure of the document containing the data. Unlike an HTML document, a XML document does not contain information specific to its presentation. By applying layout style information with XSL (*eXtensible Style Language*) technology, a XML document may be rendered for visual presentation. A number of WWW browser developers are now adding XML and XSL functionality to their products.

XML documents all have a tree-based structure of matched nested tag-pairs with encapsulated data. XML facilitates the encoding of a variety of data structures via structuring rules for tags called *Document Type Declaration* (DTD). A DTD allows a developer to define the structure of a XML document. While a XML document is valid and usable without a corresponding DTD, the DTD is essential in checking the validity of the XML document. A graphical description of a XML document, in the form of an UML CD, is presented in Figure 2A. An *internal* DTD is included in the file that contains the data whose structure is defined by the DTD. An *external* DTD is stored in a separate file from that of its corresponding data file, and is referenced in the file that contains the date.

The Object Management Group (see *http://www.omg.org*) (OMG) has defined a standard specification for interchanging UML models using XML called XMI (*XML-based Metadata*

Interchange}) {OMG, 2000]. XMI is a specification for the generation of XML DTD that conforms to the UML meta-model descriptions (see [Maruyama et al., 1999 and OMG, 2000] for detail descriptions of XML and XMI.). The DTD generated for the description of the abstract syntax of the UML meta models is called XMI DTD. This DTD is recommended when interchanging UML model files over the Internet. One of the primary goals of using XML XMI format is to facilitate development tool inter-operability. Figure 2B presents the UML XMI file architecture, as an UML CD.

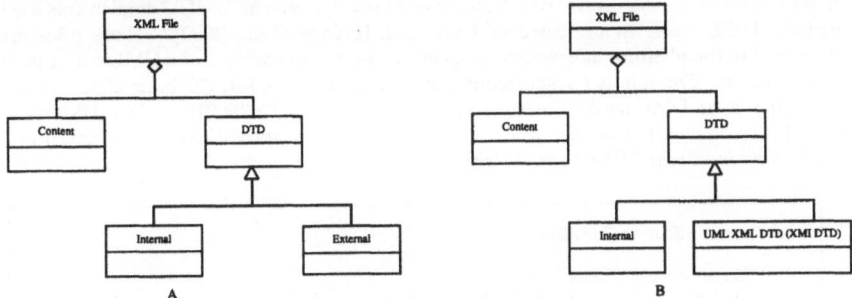

Figure 2. XML file description

3. Description of UML2Z

An architectural model of our UML2Z tool is presented in Figure 3. From any CASE tool the *class diagram to XML converter* generates a XML version of the UML CD, which is in compliance with the UML XMI specification. The converter is usually a program module, written in the API of the particular CASE tool. The XML representation of the CD is then converted to the formal notation, Z. The *XML to Z converter* is written in the Java programming language so as to make it platform independent. The Java program generates an ASCII formatted L^AT_EX file of the Z schemata along with a postscript version. The broken line region of Figure 3 bound the scope of our work. The main benefits of this approach is that the core of UML2Z, the *encoded formalization rules*, exist as the same Java program on any platform, and the interchange language XML is CASE tool independent.

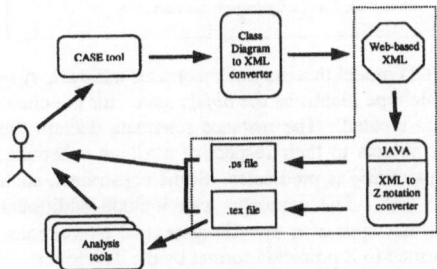

Figure 3. Architectural model of UML2Z

The goal of UML2Z is the representation of a UML CD in a tool neutral format, which may be translated into Z using the FuZE process. By converting the UML CD models to XML, the models may be accessed over the Internet. This facilitates the display of documents over the Internet by use of existing browsers that supports XSL technology.

The purpose of developing UML2Z is to take the work of France *et al.* on FuZE [France et al., 1997 and Bruel et al., 1997] to a level where it has a larger sphere of usage, both in terms of available CASE tools, and diverse development team configurations. UML2Z implements a set of updated FuZE rules, as presented in UMLtranZ [France et al., 2000]. These rules are implemented in the platform independent language of Java. An example of a UMLtranZ rule is presented below. The rule is for generating a Z schema from a UML CD basic class (see the full description of UMLtranZ formalization rules [France et al., 2000]). In the UMLtranZ report a {\it basic class} is defined as, ``...*a class that is not a specialization* [(subclass)] *in a generalization hierarchy.*" [France et al., 2000].

Basic Instance Schema (BIS) Rule

A basic class, *Cl*, with:
- a multiplicity *m..p*, where *m* is a natural number and *p* is a natural numbers or `*',
- an attribute schema *Cl_Attrs*
- an user-supplied invariant on configuration sets of the class, `objs_invariant`,
is transformed to the following Z specification

$$[CL]; [\text{Object space of Cl}]$$

Instance Schema

$$
\begin{array}{l}
\hline
Cl \\
\hline
cl : \mathbb{P}\ CL \\
cl\_attribs : CL \nrightarrow Cl\_Attrs \\
\hline
m \leq \#\ cl \leq p \\
\text{dom } cl\_attribs = cl \\
objs\_invariant \\
\hline
\end{array}
$$

The variable *cl* in the *Cl* schema given in the BIS rule is called a *configuration set variable*.

The BIS rule specifies that for all classes, in the CD model that are not subclasses a Z *basic type* (given set) is created for those classes. This basic type identifies the *object space* for the class. An *instance schema* for each basic class is next created. The instance schemata declare the configuration sets of the classes, and maps the objects to their respective attribute schemata. The instance schemata also specify the class constraints, as predicates. Some constraints, such as multiplicity, are directly obtained from the CD. The developer can include additional constraints (`objs_invariant`), in the schemata that appear in the CD as textual annotations. These annotated constraints must first be transformed to Z predicate format by the developer.

3.1 Description of XML2Z

Translating XML to Z is accomplished by a Java application called XML2Z. The program interface is simple: It reads an a XML file (that complies with the UML XMI DTD specification) containing a UML class diagram content, and creates a L^{A}T$_E$X text file with the Z specifications for that diagram, (see Figure 4). This program will produce a Z specification in accordance with the *UMLtranZ* formalization rules, from a correct UML XMI document.

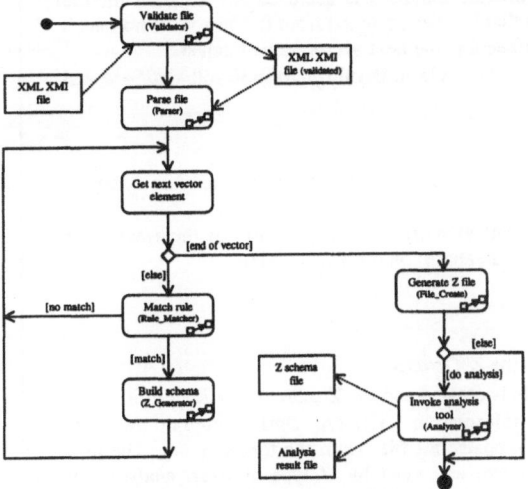

Figure 4. Activity Diagram of UML2Z Java program

Figure 4 shows that the Java program in UML2Z has six sub-activities whose descriptions are as follows:

Validator
- **input**: The XML file down-loaded via the Internet.
- **process**: Validates the contents of the XML file against the UML XMI DTD specification. This ensures that the *Parser* will not halt because of a syntax error.
- **output**: The validated file along with a message stating whether the validation was successful or not.

Parser
- **input**: An XML file, which has been validated against the UML XMI DTD specification.
- **process**: Parses the XML file extracting the *content* of all XML elements that are related to UML analysis CD constructs, i.e. *CD name, classes, class attributes, generalization/specialization, associations,* and *constraints* (inclusive of multiplicity). These *content* values are stored in a Java *vector* for later processing.
- **output**: The Java vector.

Rule_Matcher
- **input**: A Java vector that has been created by the *Parser*.
- **process**: The formalization rule database is searched for a match for the value of the CD construct that has been fetched from the vector. If no match is found the value is discarded and the next vector value fetched.
- **output**: Pointers to the matched rule in the formalization rule database and the vector value.

Z_Generator
- **input**: Pointers to a Java vector value and a formalization rule database entry.
- **process**: A Z schema is generated from the application of the *UMLtranZ* formalization rule (from the database) on the vector value.
- **output**: The Z schemata.

File_Create
- **input**: The schemata from the *Z_Generator*
- **process**: A L^{A}T$_E$X text file is created and the Z schemata written to it, along with standard file header information. The type-setting program `latex` is then invoked to generate a postscript file, from the text version. The user then has the option to invoke any available Z type checker, analyzer, or animation tool (example *ZTC, ZANS, Z/EVES* etc.), on the text file.
- **output**: L^{A}T$_E$X text, and postscript files.

Analyzer
- **input**: The L^{A}T$_E$X text file from *File_Create*
- **process**: The available Z analysis tool, i.e. *ZTC, ZANS, or Z/EVES*, is invoked on the file.
- **output**: Analysis results files.

The rigorous analysis that can be carried out on the Z representations provides a mechanism for detecting errors in the CDs. The main drawback to the UML2Z approach is that the developer is restricted to using the semantics of the UML CD constructs that are encoded in the *transformation rules*. This semantics may not be appropriate for all usage of the UML.

3.2 An example

We illustrate the UML2Z technique by applying it to a simple UML CD as shown in Figure 5. Figure 5 shows a class diagram that is made up of three classes where: **Class1** is a specialization of **class0** with an association, **assocret,** between **Class1** and **Class2**, and association ends **role1** and **role2**, whose multiplicity are given by **0..1** and **1..n** respectively.

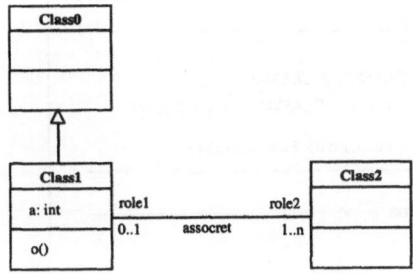

Figure 5. Three Class CD example

Listed below is an abridged listing of the XML file for the CD that was generated by an IBM XMI toolset, (see *www.alphaworks.ibm.com/tech/xmitoolkit*).

```
<Foundation.Core.ModelElement.name>threeClasses</Foundation.Core.ModelElement
.name>
<Foundation.Core.ModelElement.name>int</Foundation.Core.ModelElement.name>
<Foundation.Core.ModelElement.name>class1</Foundation.Core.ModelElement.name>
<Foundation.Core.ModelElement.name>o</Foundation.Core.ModelElement.name>
<Foundation.Core.ModelElement.name>a</Foundation.Core.ModelElement.name>
<Foundation.Core.ModelElement.name>class2</Foundation.Core.ModelElement.name>
<Foundation.Core.ModelElement.name>assocret</Foundation.Core.ModelElement.
name>
<Foundation.Core.ModelElement.name>role2</Foundation.Core.ModelElement.name>
<Foundation.Core.AssociationEnd.multiplicity>1..n</Foundation.Core.
AssociationEnd.multiplicity>
<Foundation.Core.ModelElement.name>role1</Foundation.Core.ModelElement.name>
<Foundation.Core.AssociationEnd.multiplicity>0..1</Foundation.Core.
AssociationEnd.multiplicity>
<Foundation.Core.ModelElement.name>class0</Foundation.Core.ModelElement.name>
```

The *Parser* activity, of Figure 4, reads this file and extracts the '*content*' (data) that represents class diagram of Figure 5. The *File_Create* activity of Figure 4 produces the Z schemata representation of the Figure 5 CD, which given below:

[*CLASS0*][*CLASS2*]

⌐ *Class0* ───────────────
 Class0 : ℙ *CLASS0*
 ───────────────

⌐ *Class2* ───────────────
 class2 : ℙ *CLASS2*
 ───────────────

$$\begin{array}{|ll|}
\hline
\end{array}$$

┌─ *Class1 Attrs* ──────── a: int	┌─ *Class1* ──────────── *Class0* *Class1, CLASS1* : P *CLASS0* *Class1_attribute : CLASS0* ⇸ *Class1_Attrs*
┌─ *Class0Config* ──────── *Class1*	*Class1* = {*x* : *Class0* | *x* ∈ *CLASS1*}
CLASS1 ∩ = ∅ *class1* ∪ = *class0*	┌─ *Assocret* ──────────── *Class1* *Class2* *assocret : CLASS2* ⇸ *CLASS1*
┌─ *ThreeClassConfig* ──── Assocret	*assocret* ∈ *1..n* ↔ *0..1*[*class2, class1*]

4. Conclusion

The lack of precise semantics for the UML notations hinders rigorous analysis of the UML models, particularly the class diagrams. Our approach to tackling this problem is the same as that proposed by France *et al.* in their work [France et al., 2000]. However, we have extended this process so that it has an *interchange format* for communicating UML CD models between geographically dispersed software development teams who are working on heterogeneous platforms, in a seamless manner. The tool (UML2Z) that implements our new process is made CASE tool independent by use of the UML specification (XMI) for electronic data interchange on the Internet. In addition the UML2Z tool is rendered platform independent by being written in the programming language Java.

References

[Bruel et al., 1997] R. France, J-M. Bruel, G. Raghavan. *Towards Rigorous Analysis of Fusion Models: The MIRG Experience*. Proceedings of the 2nd Northern Formal Methods Workshop. Springer-Verlag. 1997

[Evans et al., 1999] A. Evans, R. France, E. Grant. *Towards Formal Reasoning with UML Models*. Proceedings of the 8th OOPSLA Workshop on Behavioral Semantics, 1999

[France et al., 1997] R. France, J-M. Bruel, M. Larrondo-Petrie, E. Grant. *Rigorous Object-Oriented Modeling: Integrating Formal and Informal Notations*. Proceedings of the 6th AMAST Conference, 1997.

[France et al., 2000] R. France, E. Grant, J-M. Bruel. *UMLtranZ: An UML-based Rigorous Requirements Modeling Technique*. Technical report, Colorado State University, Colorado, USA. January 2000.

[Jai, 1995a] X. Jai. *An Approach to Animating Z Specifications*. DePaul University, Illinois, USA. 1995.

[Jai, 1995]   X. Jai. *ZTC: A Z Type Checker, User's Guide, version 2.01*. DePaul University, Illinois, USA. 1995.

[Lamport, 1994]   L. Lamport. *L^ATEX A Document Preparation System*. Addison-Wesley Publishing Co., second edition. 1994.

[Loukides et al., 1998]   M. Loukides, C. Musciano, B. Kennedy (Editors). *HTML: The Definitive Guide*. O'Reilly and Associates, 1998.

[Maruyama et al., 1999]   H. Maruyama, K. Tamura, N. Uramoto (editors). *XML and Java: Developing Web Applications*. . Addison-Wesley Publishing Co. 1999

[UML, 2000]   Object Management Group (OMG). *Unified Modeling Language Specification, version 1.4alpha*. Massachusetts, USA. 2000.

Intelligent Object-Oriented Software Systems Development with OMT/UML Methodology for Airportuary Environments

Adilson Marques da Cunha, Walter Strafacci Jr, Lineu Fernando Stege Mialaret

Instituto Tecnológico de Aeronáutica - ITA, São José dos Campos, São Paulo, Brazil.
E-mail:{cunha@comp.ita.cta.br, strafaci@infra.cta.br, lineu@comp.ita.cta.br}
ATECH, BRAZIL, and TELELOGIC AB, USA sponsors this research.

ABSTRACT. *One of the main problems in airport environments is the lack of an appropriate information system systematic to improve operational efficiency, resource allocation wastefulness and quality service and delays, to reduce customer's dissatisfaction. A solution for this airportuary environment problem is the development of an Intelligent Software Systems for airportuary environments. This paper describes an investigation for a new methodology tailored from the OMT methodology and extended to meet the UML standard, using I-CASE-E and RAD tools. This new hybrid methodology for Object Oriented Software System is applied for developing Intelligent Airportuary Resource Allocation Software - IARAS prototype. This article also points some major trends in the use of intelligent objects technique, as an important ingredient to integrate Intelligent Systems, enabling Intelligent Software Components - ISC encapsulation and reusability.*

KEY WORDS: Airport, OMT, UML and I-CASE-E.

1. Introduction

As an essential part of air transportation systems, airports represent resource transfer sites (Ashford et al., 1984). A proper planning, allowing these airportuary resources in terms of right times and places, involving hundreds aircrafts and thousands of passengers simultaneously processed, requires special cares, mainly, concerning time pressures and delays of any kind.

Handy made airportuary operational resources management have been responsible for resource allocation waste, causing services quality losses, delays and customer's dissatisfaction.

Currently, one of the main airports problem has been the lack of an appropriate systematic for the information management system, aiming to improve operational efficiency and supplied quality services, in order to reduce resource allocation waste, delays and the customer's dissatisfaction.

The supplied services improvement is directly concerned with the development of Intelligent Software Systems to aid appropriate managements, using the Information Technology (Hamzawi, 1992).

In this context, methods, tools and techniques for Information Engineering, Software Engineering and Knowledge Engineering must be used to develop quality software for both Process and Product level.

2. Proposed software system methodology

Software Engineering is a field of computer science applying technologies in different layers (Pressman, 1997). Layers contain own processes, methods and tools. Processes combine methods and tools to economically produce reliable software within quality patterns. Methods provide "how to's" for building software. And tools allow automated support for processes and methods. Inside to layers, there are programming languages, linking software and hardware.

Nowadays, there are more than 50 methodologies for Object-Oriented software system development. Each one having its notation and emphasizing its aspects for software construction. The Unified Modeling Language – UML (Booch, et al., 1999) is a Grady Booch, James Rumbaugh, Ivar Jacobson and other's work consolidation and has represented lately a "de facto" standard in the Software System modeling.

The Object Modeling Technique – OMT was developed by James Rumbaugh et al. and has been considered an Object-Oriented Methodology for Software Development (Rumbaugh et al., 1991). It is a well-known methodology for analysis and design and actually has been applied by scientific community. It is also a backbone for others methods such as OMT++ (Aalto et al., 1994), OMT* (Holz et al., 1995) and Unified Software Development Process (Jacobson et al., 1999), (Pons et al., 2000). Eventhough it does not provide much support for requirements elicitation (Hasselbring et al., 1998). Requirements are one the most important factor in the Software Engineering development, because then expresses the customer's needs. The OMT could be tailored to cover this deficiency.

The proposed OMT / UML Methodology consists of the tailoring of the traditional OMT Methodology and UML standard comprising of 06 (six) Stages: Pre-Analysis, Analysis, System Design, Object Design, Implementation and Tests and Reengineering, emphasizing the quality aspects for Software Systems Development. A first stage was added to OMT/UML methodology, named Pre-Analysis, describing the system aspects that would facilitate its modeling in the Analysis stage.

This Pre-Analysis stage involves the development of the following steps:
- Context Description – this step describes the temporal and situational aspects involving the System in a textual narrative;
- System Objective – this step states the problem to be solved by System that will be develop and alternative chosen solution;
- Title – this step chooses the most appropriate title for the System. At this time a trade name and a acronyms for the System is recommended to be chosen to facilitate the its future references; and
- Requirements Specification – this step specifies the initial functional, not functional and quality requirements for the System.

It is good to remember that the four steps above were considered consistence amongst themselves.

Together with Integrated Computer Aided Software Engineering Environment I-CASE-E and Rapid Application Development - RAD tools new methodologies and standards represent, nowadays, the state of the art for complex and critical Software Systems development. Figure 1 shows the proposed OMT / UML Methodology.

292

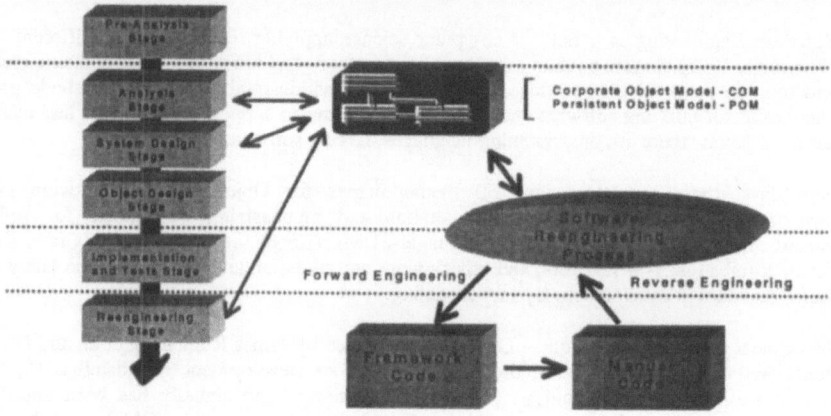

Figure 1: The Proposed Methodology.

The following sections describe the airport system features and some fragments of the application of the proposed OMT / UML Methodology tailored to the UML standard and the use of I-CASE-E and RAD tools. A short airport study case is presented in order to show the modeling technique foreseen by the methodology, looking forward Intelligent Airportuary Resource Allocation Software - IARAS.

3. The airport system features

The airport features resource allocation is defined as follows. There are a master timetable of flights and a resource's collection of the airport facilities, including gates (or ramp parking). Every arriving and departing flight must be assigned to gates satisfying various demands. The timetable of flights and resources are not fixed and experienced additions, cancellations and unexpected events may occur. The goal in solving this problem is to produce a schedule of gate's assignments, times processings and resource allocations to all flights, satisfying relevant constraints. These features allocations characterizes scheduling problems, which also include job-shop, project management and crew scheduling (Jo et al., 1997). The airport system features could be found in other similar transportation systems such as bus, train and docks terminals.

In practice, professional schedulers manually make the schedules everyday. This requires domain-specific knowledge, experience, heuristics, considerable amount of time, and tedious paperwork to complete the scheduling. Gate allocation is subject to numerous operational constraints, as for example:
- No two aircraft can be allocated to the same gate simultaneously;
- Particular gates can be restricted to admit only certain aircraft types; and
- Airlines and ground handlers prefer to use particular gates or terminals (Henz et al., 2000).

Researchers have been using mathematics and operations research techniques to solve this kind of problem. However, it is very difficult to model constraints and domain knowledge with only mathematical variables. Serious difficulties related with large-scale practical systems due to real-time operations support had been reported (Gosling, 1990), (Jo et al., 1997).

Many researchers have proposed the use of Artificial Intelligence to solve these problem (Brazile et al., 1988), (Gosling, 1990), (Jo et al., 1997). The implemented artificial intelligence systems are developed using software shells and appropriated specialized languages such as PROLOG and LISP. However, the object-oriented modeling aspects stressed on this paper are not approached in these systems.

4. Describing intelligent software system modeling

The Pre-Analysis Stage describes the main System aspects in order to reduce modeling efforts. The main intermediate software product produced was a Requirement Specifications, including also a Context Description, and the System Objective and Title. The identification of Macro-Functions or Global Use Cases heuristic representing main System functionalities has been also included in the Requirement Specifications work.

In the Analysis Stage, after defining Macro-Functions, the specialization process has continued by inserting Specific Use Cases into each Macro-Function, and by identifying possible Scenarios. In this Stage, the Use Cases involving the Intelligent System functionalities have been also mapped. Figure 2 shows a Use Case Diagram with its Macro-Functions and also those functions involving the Intelligent System behaviors.

In the System context, the more important Conceptual Elements have been used to create Business Class or Objects Prototypes that represent the basic abstractions. They have been identified with the aid of Sequence and Collaboration Diagrams, mapped later on into a Class Diagram to outlook and specify the System static structure.

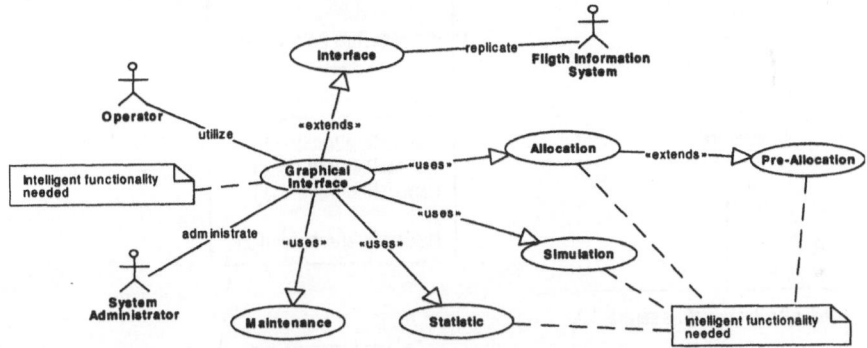

Figure 2: The IARAS System Macro-Functions.

After this point, the Objects' dynamic behavior has been mapped, with their non-trivial aspects, normally described in Activity and State Diagrams.

In the System Design Stage, the Physical Architecture mapping has been carried out by means of the Component Diagram distributing objects in physic containers. The distribution of these

containers among processors (hardware) was modeled by means of the Deployment Diagram.
In the Object Design Stage, the same Objects have been specified in terms of its attributes and operations, getting close to the Implementation Language chosen.

Later on, in the Implementation and Tests Stage, Objects for code mapping has occurred. Then, within the Reengineering Stage, a refining cycle between framework or synchronized code generated for I-CASE-E tools has successfully performed, by using the TELELOGIC TAU 4.0 UML Suite, from TELELOGIC AB Enterprise, and the handy made code generated by using RAD tools.

4.1 Intelligent software component

The Object-Oriented Software Engineering Paradigm has provided the mapping of reality by means of Objects. The extension of this Paradigm has enabled Business Objects creation, which has captured and incorporated Business Rules. The mapping of these Rules and its intelligent processing have taken advantage of Intelligent Object using aggregation, by creating Business Intelligent Objects.

For example, an Object representing an airport gate has been mapped together with its Intelligent Object aggregated. These Objects later on have been mapped into a logical and physic structure of an Intelligent Software Component, which could be reused in other applications, encapsulating its Business intelligence processing. This type of Component was very similar to the JavaBeans type of Java Components. This mapping is shown in Figure 3.

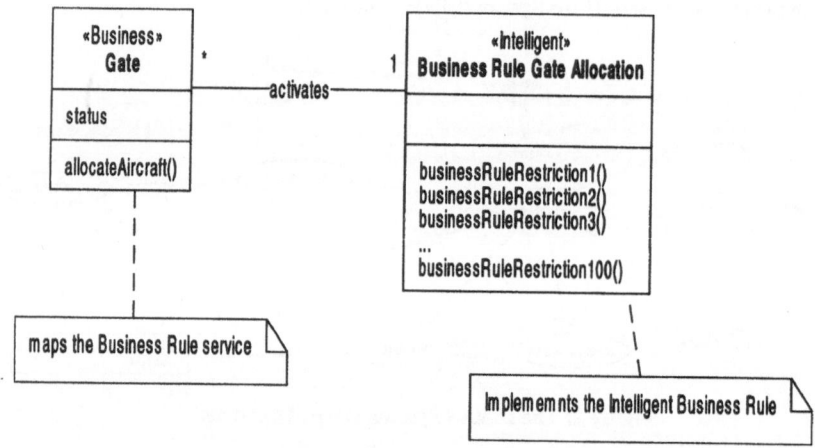

Figure 3: The Intelligent Software Component Mapping.

5. Conclusion

As it is well known, information management for local airportuary resources needs a more appropriate systematic for its evaluation to improve operational decision effectiveness.

This improvement directly relates to the development of a management tool that incorporates the operational necessities of airports into an Intelligent Software System.

The development of this System has followed modern standards of Information Engineering, Software Engineering and Knowledge Engineering, aiming to magnify the system reliability and quality, minimizing errors and faults occurrence probability.

The major finding of this article was the proposed tailoring of OMT Methodology to UML standard. This tailoring has been added two new Stages to the development process. The first one, right at the beginning, named Pre-Analysis, and the second one, right at the end, named Reengineering. The Pre-Analysis Stage has simplified the Requirements Specification work and the Reengineering Stage has also simplified the reusability and synchronization of legacy codes, by means of I-CASE-E and RAD tools. Mainly due to this contribution, the proposed Methodology extends its application potential.

Another important contribution from this article was the introduction of Intelligent Software Components as Business Rules intelligent processors, extending Components reusability.

The continuity of this research work points out to the incorporation of Dynamic Intelligent Software Components, applying the Intelligent Agents Paradigm.

References:

(Aalto et al., 1994): J. M. Aalto, A. Jaaksi. *Object-Oriented Development of Interactive Systems with OMT++*. R. Ege, M. Singh, B. Meyer, editors, TOOLS 14, Technology of Object-Oriented Languages & Systems, Prentice Hall, 1994.

(Ashford et al., 1984): N. Ashford, H. P. M. and C. A. Moore. *Airport Operation*. John Wiley & Sons, Inc, 1984.

(Brazile et al., 1988): Robert P. Brazile, K. M. Swigger. *GATES: An airline gate assignment and tracking expert system*. IEEE Expert, 3(2):33-39, 1988.

(Booch et al., 1999): Booch, Grady; Rumbaugh, James; Jacobson, Ivar. *The Unified Modeling Language User Guide*. Addison-Wesley object technology series, Addison-Wesley Longman, Inc, Massachusetts, 1999.

(Gosling, 1990): Gosling, G. D. *Design of an Expert System for Aircraft Gate Assignment*. Transp. Res.-A, Vol. 24^a, No. 1, 1990.

(Hamzawi, 1992): Hamzawi, S. G. *Lack of airport capacity: exploration of alternative solutions*. Transp. Res.-A, Vol. 26^a, No. 1, 1992.

(Hasselbring et al., 1998): W. Hasselbring, A. Kröber. *Combining OMT with a prototyping approach*. The Journal of Systems and Software, 43 pp. 177-185, 1998.

(Henz et al., 2000): Yun Fong Lim, Seet Chong Lua, Xiao Ping Shi, J. Paul Walser and Roland H. C. Yap. *Solving Hierarchical Constraints over Finite Domains*. AMAI 2000.

(Holz et al., 1995): E. Holz, M. Wasowski, D. Witaszek, S. Lau, J. Fischer, B. Algayres, T. Courtiade, L. Cuypers, J. Heirbaut, K. Verschaeve, V. Jonckers, N.

Kyrloglou, V. Mariatos, P. Roques, B. Wydaeghe, J.-L. Roux, and J.-P. Delpiroux. *The insyde methodology -- report.* Report INSYDE/WP1/HUB/200/v3, ESPRIT Ref: P8641, April 1995.

(Jacobson et al., 1999): Jacobson, Ivar, Booch, Grady; Rumbaugh, James, Ivar. *The Unified Software Development Process.* Addison-Wesley object technology series, Addison-Wesley Longman, Inc, Massachusetts, 1999.

(Jo et al., 1997): Geun-Sik Jo, Jong-Jin Jung, Chang-Yoon Yang. *Expert System for Scheduling in an Airline Gate Allocation.* Expert Systems With Applications, Vol. 13 No 4, 1997.

(Pressman, 1997): Roger S. Pressman. Software Engineering in *Software Engineering Project Management.* 2nd ed., Richard H. Thayer, ed., IEEE Computer Soc. Press, USA, 1997.

(Pons et al., 2000): Claudia Pons, Gabriel Baum. *Formal foundations of object-oriented modeling notations.* 3rd International Conference on Formal Engineering Methods, IEEE ICFEM 2000 IEEE Computer Society Press, University of York, York, UK 4-7 September 2000.

(Rumbaugh et al., 1991): Rumbaugh, J., Michel B., Premerlani, W., Eddy, F. & Lorensen, F. *Object-Oriented Modeling and Design.* Prentice-Hall, 1991.

DATABASES AND PROGRAMMING
ISSUES II

Using Object-Oriented Databases to Preserve Integrity and Improve Performance - But at What Cost?

Abdulaziz Al-kandari and Ray Dawson

Dept. of Computer Science, Loughborough University,
Loughborough, Leics. LE11 3TU, UK
E-mail:A.AlKandari@Lboro.ac.UK, R.J.Dawson@Lboro.ac.UK   Fax: +44 1509 211586

ABSTRACT. *Two alternatives to using object-oriented databases to improve performance of complex relational databases are, firstly de-normalisation which improves performance but at a cost of additional errors and/or code to be maintained, and secondly, obtaining a bigger and faster computer though this may not give the same improvement. This paper identifies a need to properly cost the reported performance advantages of object-oriented databases and to compare these costs with alternative performance improvement methods.*

KEY WORDS: Object-oriented, database, integrity, cost.

1. Improving performance of relational databases

The innovation of normalisation concepts in database systems helped to achieve such desirable features as safty, consistency and maintainability (Delobel, 1995). The DBMS guarantees reliable data definitions and manipulations when data are properly modelled. In the case of a relational database, the data must be well normalised to attain reliability. However, the normalised model for complex data usually suffer from many side effects concerning performance and response time. For this reason many working databases are often not fully normalised (Elmasri, 1994).

A problem area for normalised databases concerns many to many relationships, where an additional table (intersection entity) is required for each relationship to ensure consistency, and reduce maintenace cost but the number of table joins for data retrieval increases performance cost (Douglas, 1996).

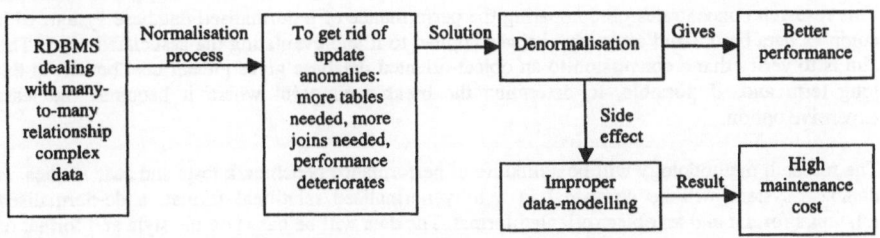

Figure 1. Steps that a RDBMS application developer may take to improve performance.

RDBMS performance improvments may be achieved through "de-normalisation" which is moving away from intersection entities (Douglas, 1996). In other words the system returns back to its improper model phase which then requires extra code to prevent any anomalies which might occur. As a result, the database system may face higher maintenance cost and would be vulnerable to errors. However, the authors determined from informal enquiries to a number of companies that companies were prepared to accept the extra development and error risk to achieve a gain performance. (See figure 1).

Another method for improving performance of a complex normalised database system is to convert it to an object-oriented system. Douglas (1996) has shown that an object-oriented database can run 7 to 100 times faster than a relational database. The advantage of this method is that proper data modelling is preserved as well as improving the overall performance. This leads to further advantages of fewer errors, easier extension and reduced maintenance costs. This is the opposite of the effect of de-normalisation.

Published papers on methodologies for converting relational to object-oriented databases assume the relational database is based on a proper, normalised data model. However, many working databases in the real world are not normalised for performance reasons or for reasons of convenience or simply because the developers did not fully understand how to normalise the database in the first place! However, this need not prevent direct convesion to an object-oriented database because, as previously reported by the authors (Al-Kandari, 1999), the conversion process will itself informally normalise the data.

2. The impact of performance on the cost of a system.

Normally, the better quality the merchandise usually means the greater the cost or value. For database systems the cost savings from improving the performance has to be measured against the cost incurred as a result of the improvement to determine the best quality solution. These improvement costs for a de-normalised system would include the cost of writing and maintaining the extra code to prevent anomolies plus the cost of additional errors incurred. For a move to an object-orientated database the costs could include the database management system, the cost of converting the data plus possible costs to train employees in object-oriented methods. Costs need to be determined over time as the de-normalisation method may give short term gains but the object-oriented system's greater integrity and resulting reliability is likely to give longer term gains. (See figure 2.)

This research concentrates on comparing the performance of a normalised database system with complex data before and after any changes applied to it and evaulating the associated costs. The aim is to verify that a conversion to an object-oriented database gives greater cost benefit in the long term and, if possible, to determine the break-even point where it becomes the least expensive option.

The research methodology will be a mixture of performance benchmark tests and case studies. A database system will be compared in a fully normalised relational format, a de-normalised relational format and an object-oriented format. The data will be based on the style and format of real databases at a large engineering company in Derby, UK. Benchmark tests will be made using a number of database management systems. For example, non-normalised data systems will be compared with normalised systems using available databases such as Microsoft Access and MySQL. Relational data modelling will be compared with object-oriented data modelling using

Java programs with systems such as POET. This benchmark data will be compared with other published data where such data is available such as provided in the report by STR (STR 1997).

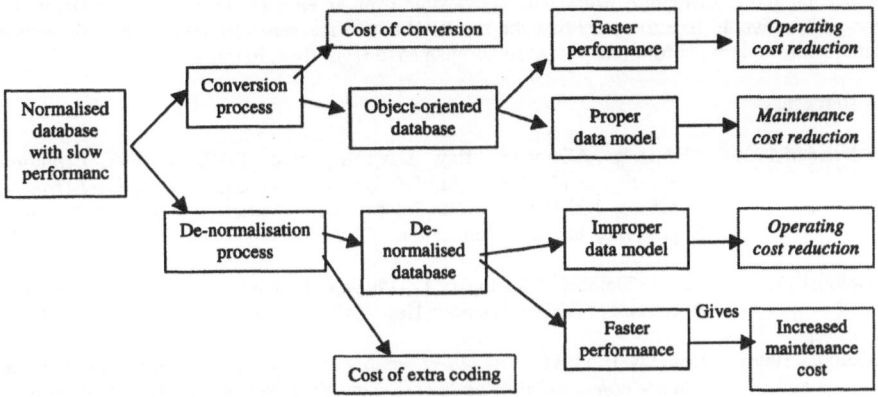

Figure 2 : Cost comparison for performance improvement alternatives

Both paths in figure 2 would improve the performance but the question is which will give the greater cost savings. The authors will examine case study data to provide the costs of maintaining de-normalised and object-oriented databases. Data will come from employee timesheet records for employees involved in creating and maintaining the systems. Other company data that will be analysed will be the fault reports for the database systems. The faults attributable to integrity errors resulting from table de-normalisation will be identified and the associated costs to correct the errors will be calculated. Some data will be provided by the company in Derby, the authors will then seek to verify the findings with data provided from other sources.

Finally a third, and perhaps even more significant alternative method of improving performance needs to be considered. Could the same level of improvement be achieved simply by getting a bigger and faster computer? As one industrial employee reported to us, *"Once I had to make changes to 3 forms to add various triggers to get the update/insert things to work properly after the affected tables were de-normalised. The performance gain was a response below 3 seconds compared to 15 seconds. It took about 3 days of coding on the forms (working 18-hour each day!). If the database was on a slightly better machine (more RAM, disk, etc.) I wonder if there would have been any need to do the de-normalisation."* Clearly this alternate must be costed and compared with the de-normalised and object-oriented database methods of improving performance.

3. Conclusion

This paper has identified two alternatives to moving to an object-oriented databases to improve performance. De-normalisation will also improve performance but at a cost of increasing the number of errors and/or increasing the code to be maintained. The second, simpler alternative is to obtain a bigger and faster computer but it is uncertain whether this can give the same improvement or cost benefits. This identifies a need to properly cost the reported advantages of speed and low maintenance of object-oriented databases and to compare these costs with the alternative methods of improving performance.

The paper outlines the methodology to be undertaken to establish the costs of creating, operating, and maintaining databases in normalised and non-normalised relational systems and also in object-oriented systems. This data will be taken from company records of employee time allocation and error reports. Some data is available from an engineering company in Derby, but the authors would like to verify that the results obtained are generally applicable. The authors are, therefore, looking for other volunteer companies to assist them in this research.

4. References

(Alkandari 1999)   Abdulaziz Alkandari, Ray Dawson. (Dec 1999). *System Evolution: Converting a Non-Normalised Relational Database to an Object-Oriented Database*. ICSSEA '99 12th International Conference Software &Systems Engineering and their Applications, CNAM - Paris, France.

(Delobel 1995)   Claude Delobel, Christophe. L., Philippe Richard (1995). *Databases: From Relational to Object-Oriented*, New York, International Thomson Publishing.

(Douglas 1996)   Douglas, B. (1996). *The object database handbook: how to select, implement, and use object-oriented databases*. New York, Wiley Computer Publishing.

(Elmasri 1994)   Ramez Elmasri, S., B. Navathe (1994). *Fundamentals of Database Systems*. Redwood city, California, The Benamin/Cummings Publishing Company, Inc.

(STR 1997)   Strategic Technology Resources, *Java Data Management : Comparing ODBMS and RDBMS Implementations of Quantum Objects*, STR Company Report, Chicago, Illinois 60606

Reconfigurability in Object Database Management Systems: An Aspect-Oriented Approach

Awais Rashid[†] and Ruzanna Chitchyan[‡]

[†]*Computing Department, Lancaster University, Lancaster LA1 4YR, UK*
E-mail: marash@comp.lancs.ac.uk   Fax: +44 1524 593608

[‡]*The Open University, UK & Open College of the North West, Storey Institute,*
Lancaster LA1 1TH, UK
Email: r.chitchyan@lancaster.ac.uk   Fax: +44 1524 388467

ABSTRACT. *Cost-effective reconfiguration in ODBMSs is difficult to achieve due to the trade-off between modularity and efficiency. Existing ODBMS designs offer limited reconfigurability because reconfigurable features are closely woven with the components to improve efficiency. This paper proposes the use of aspects - entities used by Aspect-Oriented Programming to localise cross-cutting concerns - to separate reconfigurable features from the components regardless of their granularity. This provides a cost-effective solution for both static and dynamic reconfiguration. The effectiveness of the approach is demonstrated by discussing dynamically reconfigurable instance adaptation in the SADES evolution system.*

KEY WORDS: Reconfigurability, Object Database Management Systems, Aspect-Oriented Programming, Aspect-Oriented Databases, Static Reconfiguration, Dynamic Reconfiguration, Evolution

1. Introduction

Like any other software product reconfigurability is an essential requirement in object database management systems (McCann 2000). An effective reconfiguration mechanism is one which localises the impact of changes and automatically propagates them to the rest of the system without compromising consistency. This reduces maintenance and upgrade costs and makes it possible to customise (with minimal effort) the object database management system to the specific needs of an organisation. An example of the latter is instance adaptation during object database evolution[1]. For one organisation it might be sufficient that objects simulate a conversion to a compatible type interface (similar to error handlers employed by ENCORE (Skarra et al. 1986)) while for another organisation it might be essential to actually convert objects between historical type definitions (similar to update/backdate methods employed by CLOSQL (Monk et al. 1993)). Such customisations may even be application specific (this implies dynamic reconfiguration using more than one instance adaptation strategy). An effective reconfiguration mechanism localising changes to the instance adaptation strategy and the associated adaptation routines can provide such customisation in a cost-effective fashion.

Existing approaches e.g. (Guzenda 2000, McCann 2000) employ a component-based architecture for the ODBMS to achieve reconfigurability. However, there exists a trade-off between

---

[1] Evolution case studies at Open College of the North West where day-to-day activities revolve around the databases.

modularity and performance (Kiczales et al. 1997). As a result reconfigurability is available only at a coarse granularity. For example, the transaction manager component can be exchanged with the ripple effect limited to the glue code for the various components[2]. However, similar functionality is not available at a finer granularity. Relatively minor changes to the individual components are expensive as their modularity is compromised to preserve both modularity and performance of the ODBMS. Code handling any cross-cutting features in these components is spread across them (Kiczales et al. 1997). Consequently changes to these cross-cutting features are not localised making reconfiguration an expensive task.

This paper proposes the use of aspects - entities used by Aspect-Oriented Programming (AOP) (Kiczales et al. 1997) to localise cross-cutting concerns - to separate reconfigurable features at both coarse and fine granularity. This allows cost-effective reconfiguration as changes are localised. The aspects encapsulating reconfigurable features can be modified at compile-time (static reconfiguration) or run-time (dynamic reconfiguration). The performance of the system is not compromised due to the modularity as aspects are merged with the entities cross-cut by them (at compile-time or run-time) to produce efficient code. The next section takes a closer look at the reconfigurability problem in ODBMSs. Section 3 provides an overview of Aspect-Oriented Programming. The aspect-oriented reconfiguration approach is discussed in section 4. Section 5 identifies some open issues while section 6 concludes the paper and discusses future directions.

2. Reconfigurability: The Problem

(Kiczales et al. 1997) demonstrates that a highly modular system is not necessarily the most efficient. Efficient implementations tend to be less modular with the various components closely woven. This is termed as *code tangling* (Kiczales et al. 1997). There is a trade-off between modularity/maintainability and efficiency/performance. This trade-off has a strong bearing on the reconfigurability of an ODBMS as shown in fig. 1.

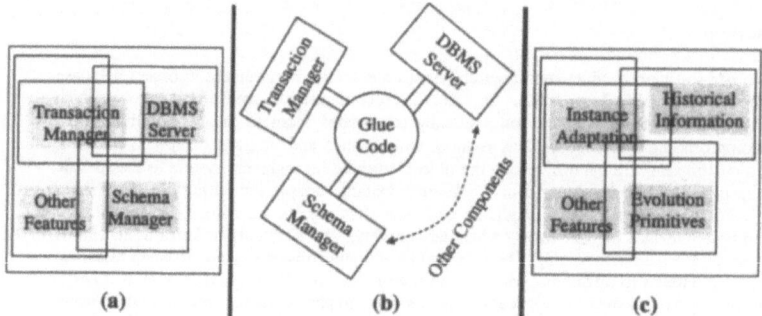

Fig. 1: Reconfigurability issues in (a) a monolithic ODBMS (b) a component-based ODBMS (c) a component (schema manager) in a component-based ODBMS

---

[2] Such an exchange might also introduce erroneous behaviour into the system (Brown et al. 1996). However, for the purpose of this discussion it is assumed that consistency is maintained.

Fig. 1(a) shows the structure of a monolithic ODBMS. Only three key components: the DBMS server, the transaction manager and the schema manager are shown. Other components such as the storage manager, etc. have been omitted for simplification. As shown in the figure the various components are tangled in a monolithic system. While such a closely woven implementation provides good performance/efficiency, reconfigurability is an expensive and difficult task as changes to the various components are not localised (due to code tangling). Changing the transaction model employed by the transaction manager, for example, at either compile-time or run-time can have a large ripple effect on the whole system.

Fig. 1(b) shows a modular, component-based implementation of an ODBMS similar to the one proposed by (McCann 2000). Again, only three key components: the DBMS server, the transaction manager and the schema manager are shown for simplification. Such a design provides effective reconfigurability. For example, the transaction manager (or any other component) can be exchanged with the ripple effect mainly limited to the glue code. However, in order to strike the right balance between modularity and efficiency the design of the individual components is not highly modular. As shown in fig. 1(c) the modularity of the individual components is compromised to preserve both modularity and efficiency of the ODBMS. As a result the coarse-grained component, the OODBMS, is reconfigurable. However, reconfigurability at a finer granularity (i.e. the components forming the OODBMS) is expensive as design at this level is largely monolithic. Reconfiguring the instance adaptation strategy in such a system, for example, requires exchanging the whole schema manager component as changes to the instance adaptation strategy are not localised (cf. fig. 1(c)). The reconfigurability problem simply moves to a different granularity. This also limits possibilities for dynamic reconfiguration. Application specific reconfiguration of the instance adaptation strategy, for example, requires dynamically exchanging the whole schema manager component which is an expensive task. Such reconfiguration would be cost-effective if changes at the fine granularity were localised without compromising the system performance obtained through closely woven components i.e. both modularity and efficiency need to be preserved.

3. Aspect-Oriented Programming

Aspect-oriented programming (Kiczales et al. 1997) aims at easing software development by providing further support for modularisation. *Aspects* are abstractions which serve to localise any cross-cutting concerns e.g. code which cannot be encapsulated within one class but is tangled over many classes. A few examples of aspects are memory management, failure handling, communication, real-time constraints, resource sharing, performance optimisation, debugging and synchronisation. Although patterns (Gamma et al. 1995) can help to deal with such cross-cutting code by providing guidelines for a good structure, they are not available or suitable for all cases and mostly provide only partial solutions to the code tangling problem. With AOP, such cross-cutting code is encapsulated into separate constructs: the aspects. As shown in fig. 2 classes are designed and coded separately from code that cross-cuts them (in this case debugging and synchronisation code). The links between classes and aspects are expressed by explicit or implicit *join points*. An *aspect weaver* is responsible for merging the classes and the aspects with respect to the join points. This can be done statically as a phase at compile-time or dynamically at run-time (Kenens et al. 1998, Kiczales et al. 1997).

Different AOP techniques and research directions can be identified. They all share the common goal of providing an improved separation of concerns. AspectJ (Xerox 2000) is an aspect-oriented extension to Java. The environment offers an aspect language to formulate the aspect code separately from Java class code, a weaver and additional development support. AOP extensions to other languages have also been developed. (Boellert 1999), for example, describes an aspect language and a weaver for Smalltalk.

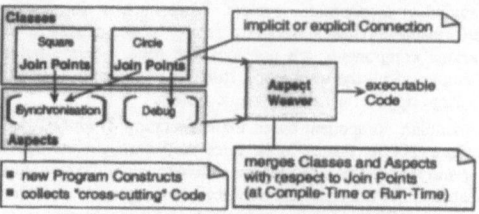

Fig. 2: Aspect-Oriented Programming

Other AOP approaches aiming at achieving a similar separation of concerns include subject-oriented programming (Harrison et al. 1993), composition filters (Aksit et al. 1998), adaptive programming (Lieberherr 2000, Mezini et al. 1998) and Hyperspaces (IBM 2000). In subject-oriented programming different subjective perspectives on a single object model are captured. Applications are composed of "subjects" (i.e. partial object models) by means of declarative composition rules. The composition filters approach extends an object with input and output filters. These filters are used to localise non-functional code. Adaptive programming is a special case of AOP where one of the building blocks is expressible in terms of graphs. The other building blocks refer to the graphs using traversal strategies. A traversal strategy can be viewed as a partial specification of a class diagram. This traversal strategy cross-cuts the class graphs. Instead of hard-wiring structural knowledge paths within the classes, this knowledge is separated. Hyperspaces introduce the notion of *multi-dimensional separation of concerns* by permitting clean separation of multiple, potentially overlapping and interacting concerns simultaneously with support for on-demand remodularisation to encapsulate new concerns at any time.

Experience reports and assessment of AOP can be found in (Kersten et al. 1999, Pulvermueller et al. 1999).

4. Reconfigurability: The Aspect-Oriented Solution

Since reconfigurability is a cross-cutting concern (as discussed in section 2), we propose separating reconfigurable features from components using aspects. This applies to both coarse and fine-grained components. As a result the approach can be employed for cost-effective reconfiguration in monolithic ODBMSs (cf. fig. 1(a)), individual components in component-based ODBMSs (cf. fig. 1(b) & (c)) or components at finer granularities.

As shown in fig. 3 aspects are used to separate reconfigurable features from the core functionality and other non-configurable features of a component. Changes to the features encapsulated by aspects are localised making it possible to achieve a high degree of reconfigurability. Both minor and major reconfigurations can be carried out in a cost-effective fashion. It also makes it possible to exchange fine-grained reconfigurable features without a ripple effect on the rest of the component. Changes are automatically propagated during weaving (at compile-time or run-time) or reweaving (at run-time). It might be argued that the proposed approach simply shifts the complexity of the reconfiguration process to the aspect weaver. This might be true if for each reconfigurable feature a specifically designed aspect language and weaver were being used. Since most ODBMSs are developed using general-purpose programming languages, a general-purpose aspect language similar to AspectJ (Xerox 2000) and its associated weaver will be sufficient to provide a woven solution which is both performance optimised and correct. Understandably the correctness of the code produced by the weaver and efficiency of the weaver (especially during dynamic weaving) will be crucial to the process. In case one or a few reconfigurable features require specific aspect languages and weavers the effort to develop these will pay-off in terms of reduced reconfiguration and maintenance costs.

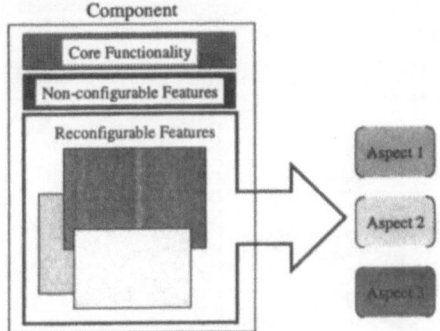

Fig. 3: Using aspects to separate reconfigurable features from a component (whether coarse-grained or fine-grained)

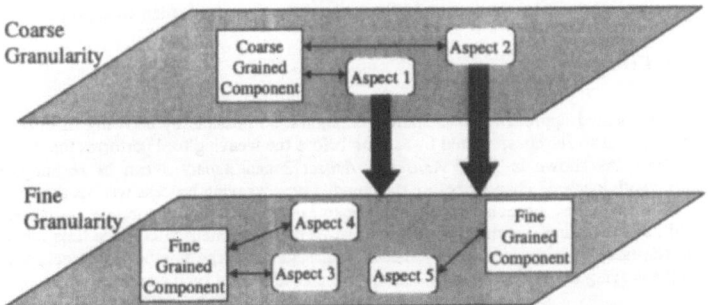

Fig. 4: Propagating reconfigurability aspects at coarse granularity to fine granularity

It should be noted that although fig. 3 shows reconfigurability aspects associated with one particular component, one such aspect can serve more than one component if the same reconfigurable feature exists in all of them. These semantics make it possible to separate common reconfigurable features at a coarse granularity and transparently propagate them to finer granularities as shown in fig. 4. One example of such reconfigurable aspects is error-handling. Although the specific error-handling routines for various components considerably vary, the ODBMS normally has a uniform error-handling strategy. The error-handling strategy can exist at the coarse granularity (the ODBMS level) as a reconfigurable aspect while the error-handling routines specific to the finer-grained components can exist at their particular granularities. The reconfigurable error-handling strategy is automatically propagated to the finer-grained components when it is woven into the ODBMS.

The aspect-oriented solution also provides support for both static and dynamic reconfiguration as discussed in the following sections.

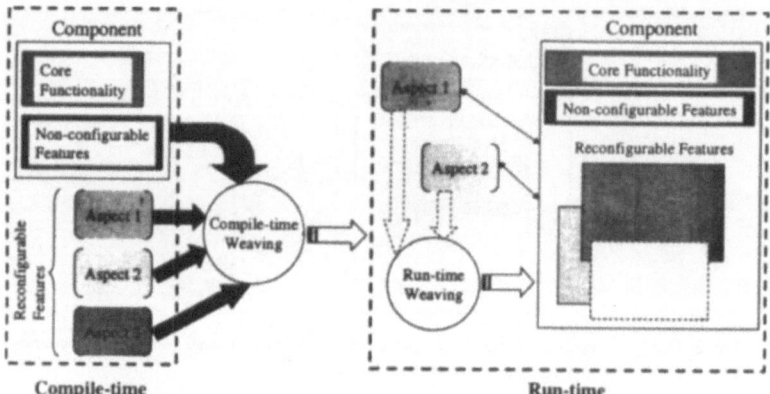

Fig. 5: Static and dynamic reconfiguration using the aspect-oriented approach

4.1 Static Reconfiguration

The aspect-oriented approach makes static reconfiguration possible by allowing reconfiguration or exchange of features encapsulated by aspects before the weaving tool performs the weaving at compile-time. As shown in fig. 5 *Aspect 1*, *Aspect 2* and *Aspect 3* can be reconfigured or exchanged with localised changes before the compile-time weaving process weaves them with the rest of the component. Aspects encapsulating features that need reconfiguration at compile-time only and not at run-time are merged with the rest of the component at compile-time and do not exist at run-time. This reduces the overhead of managing a large number of aspects and their weaving/reweaving at run-time. *Aspect 3* in fig. 5 is an example of such an aspect.

4.2 Dynamic Reconfiguration

Aspects encapsulating features which require reconfiguration at run-time have a lifetime extended beyond compile-time. They exist at run-time and may even outlive the program execution (Rashid 2000a). *Aspect 1* and *Aspect 2* in fig. 5 are examples of such aspects. As shown in fig. 5 such aspects fall into two categories:

- Aspects encapsulating features less frequently reconfigured at run-time
- Aspects encapsulating features frequently reconfigured at run-time

Aspect 1 in fig. 5 is an example of the former while *Aspect 2* is an example of the latter. In the example *Aspect 1* is woven at compile-time and rewoven at run-time only when it is reconfigured (rarely). The weaving of *Aspect 2* on the other hand is left to run-time. As shown by the dotted line around the woven feature (encapsulated by *Aspect 2*) *Aspect 2* is woven and rewoven at run-time frequently due to extensive dynamic reconfiguration. It should be noted that the scenario in fig. 5 is just an example. *Aspect 2* could have been woven at compile-time and still frequently reconfigured at run-time. The example simply demonstrates that it is not necessary to weave all the dynamically reconfigurable features at compile-time and vice versa.

4.3 Implementation

The aspect-oriented approach has been employed to provide a dynamically reconfigurable instance adaptation strategy in the SADES evolution system (Rashid et al. 1998, Rashid et al. 1999a, Rashid et al. 1999b, Rashid 2000b). It has also been applied to achieve reconfigurable versioning, clustering and inheritance in object-oriented databases (Rashid et al. 2000b). Due to space limitations the following discussion focuses on reconfigurable instance adaptation in SADES only. Interested readers are referred to (Rashid et al. 2000b) for a description of other reconfigurable features mentioned above.

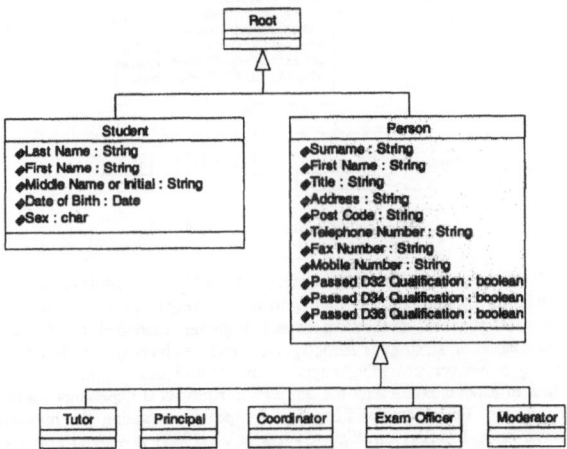

Fig. 6: Database Structure before Evolution

In order to demonstrate the reconfigurability of the instance adaptation strategy in SADES we have employed one of the evolution scenarios from our case studies at Open College of the North West. Fig. 6 shows the database structure prior to evolution (it is assumed that the class hierarchy is single-rooted). The class hierarchy does not conform to good OO design principles as the class *Student* is not a subclass of the class *Person*. Fig. 7 shows the structure to be adopted to conform to good practice. In this structure the class *Student* becomes a subclass of the class *Person*. The class *Person* defines attributes common to both student and staff objects. A non-leaf class *Staff* is introduced to capture attributes specific to staff objects. In order to simplify the description, the modification of the class *Person* in the evolution scenario is used for describing the SADES instance adaptation strategy. For further simplification attributes defined by subclasses are not considered in the objects associated with *Person*. This simplification is syntactically and semantically correct as *Person* is not an abstract class and can be instantiated directly.

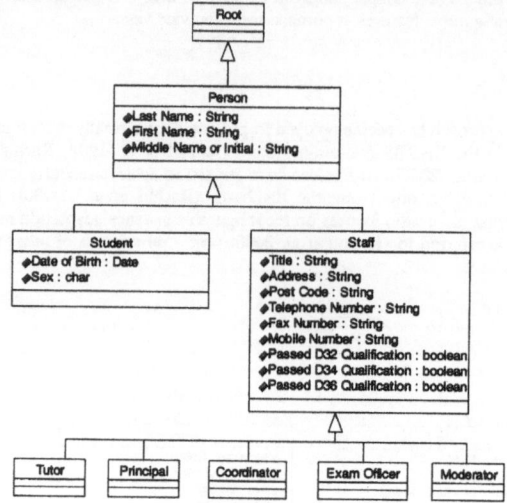

Fig. 7: Database Structure after Evolution

As shown in fig. 8 the instance adaptation strategy and adaptation routines in SADES are separated from the schema manager and class versions respectively using aspects (the aspects are specified using a general-purpose, declarative aspect language modelled on AspectJ (Xerox 2000)). The instance adaptation strategy is reconfigurable and can be dynamically woven into the schema manager using a weaver providing support for compile-time, run-time and persistent aspects. The selection of aspects containing the adaptation routines is dependent on the instance adaptation strategy chosen. For example, from fig. 8 aspects containing the handlers will be woven only when the error handlers strategy (Skarra et al. 1986) is woven into the SADES schema manager. If the aspect containing the error-handlers strategy is exchanged with the one containing the update/backdate methods strategy (Monk et al. 1993), the aspects containing the handlers will be exchanged with those containing the update/backdate methods. Note that the choice of instance adaptation strategies is not limited to error-handlers and update/backdate methods. Other instance adaptation strategies can be employed as shown in fig. 8.

Separating the instance adaptation code into aspects allows reconfiguration of the instance adaptation strategy and adaptation routines without posing maintenance problems for the schema manager or existing class versions. The changes are local to the aspect and are propagated to the class versions through dynamic weaving. This makes it possible to reconfigure the instance adaptation strategy for specific evolution scenarios such as performing or simulating an *information preserving* move of attributes across classes or class versions. For example, in fig. 8, the backdate method for objects associated with *Person_V2* can test whether the object being associated with *Person_V1* is a *Staff* object. If this is the case the attributes *Title, Address*, etc. can take on the values of the attributes in the *Staff* object. This is a customisation of the update/backdate methods strategy employed by CLOSQL and makes it possible to simulate the *move attribute primitive* not available in the SADES evolution taxonomy.

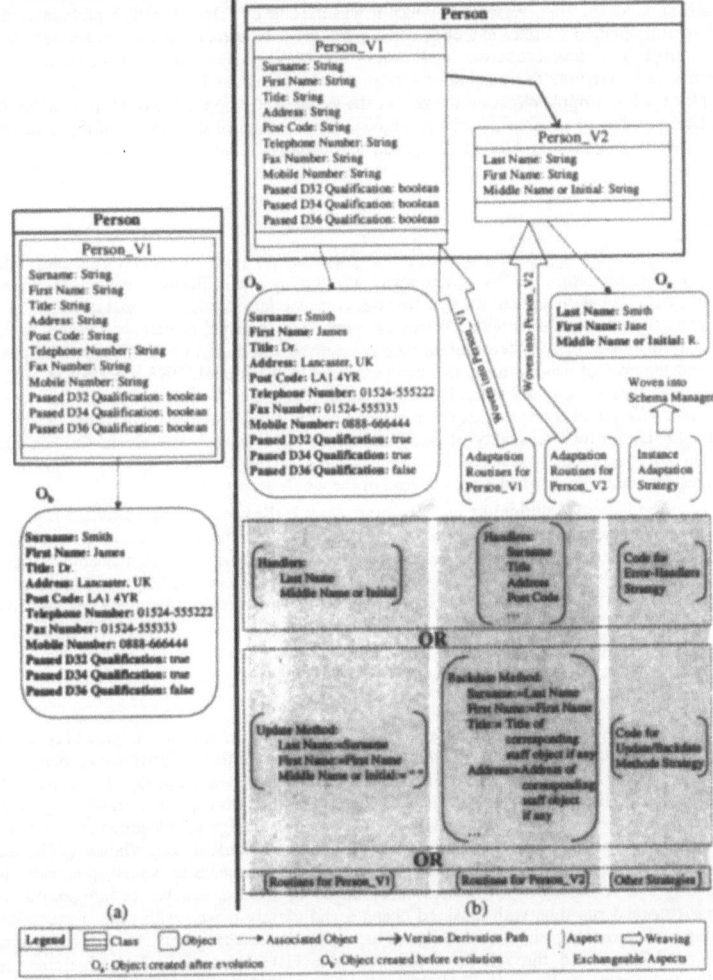

Fig. 8: Instance adaptation in SADES (a) Before evolution (b) After evolution

The high degree of reconfigurability in the SADES instance adaptation strategy is in direct contrast with existing evolution systems such as ENCORE (Skarra et al. 1986) and CLOSQL (Monk et al. 1993). These systems introduce the adaptation code directly into the class versions upon evolution. Often, the same adaptation routines are introduced into a number of class versions. Consequently, if the behaviour of a routine needs to be changed maintenance has to be performed on all the class versions in which it was introduced. There is a high probability that a number of adaptation routines in a class version will never be invoked as only newer applications will attempt to access properties and methods unavailable for objects associated with the particular class version. The adaptation strategy is spread across the system and adoption of a new strategy has a ripple effect on the rest of the system and triggers the need for changes to all or a large number of versions of existing classes. A more detailed description of the dynamically reconfigurable instance adaptation strategy can be found in (Rashid et al. 2000a).

5. Open Issues

The reconfigurability approach proposed in this paper heavily relies on weaver efficiency. One of the key research issues is the development of correct and efficient weaving mechanisms. Efficiency is particularly critical for dynamic weaving as it introduces additional overhead at run-time and can be feasible only with efficient weavers. AOP research, to date, has mainly focussed on the development of AOP techniques, their correctness and design issues for aspect languages. Different lifetimes of aspects have also been explored (Kenens et al. 1998, Kiczales et al. 1997, Rashid et al. 2000b, Rashid 2000a). However, the development of efficient weavers has not been considered. We are of the view that efficiency and correctness of weavers will be the determining factors for commercial feasibility of AOP and hence need extensive research. One interesting solution worth exploring is *selective weaving* (Rashid et al. 2000a): weaving only the modified or previously unwoven parts of an aspect instead of the whole aspect itself.

Another issue identified during the course of our work is the need for parameterised aspects. At present this is not supported by aspect languages. If aspect parameterisation is available the aspects encapsulating reconfigurable features can be more generic and maintainable. An aspect can be parameterised by classes in which it is to be woven, hence, making the join points and crosscuts generic. Special *weave parameters* can be used to provide a generic reconfiguration mechanism during dynamic weaving.

6. Conclusions and Future Work

This paper has proposed the use of aspects to achieve a high degree of reconfigurability in object database management systems. The novelty of the work lies in the cost-effective reconfiguration mechanism localising changes to reconfigurable features and automatically propagating them during weaving. It was argued that similar reconfigurations are expensive in existing systems because reconfigurable features are closely woven with non-configurable features and each other. This code tangling is a direct effect of the trade-off between modularity and efficiency. The use of aspects to separate reconfigurable features provides a mechanism which preserves both modularity and efficiency. The features encapsulated by aspects can be reconfigured at both compile-time and run-time with localised changes and closely woven with other features using weaving tools providing support for different aspect lifetimes. The effectiveness of the approach has been demonstrated through its application to achieve dynamically reconfigurable, cost-effective instance adaptation in the SADES evolution system. Our work in the future will focus on the open issues identified in section 5. We will explore the development of efficient weaving mechanisms in order to reduce the overhead associated with such a highly reconfigurable architecture especially at run-time. We will also investigate the syntax and semantics of aspect parameterisation and its potential to make the reconfiguration mechanism more generic.

Acknowledgements. The work presented in this paper is supported by EPSRC grant GR/R08612: AspOEv - An Aspect-Oriented Evolution Framework for Object-Oriented Databases. The authors would also like to thank the Open College of the North West, UK for providing opportunities for database evolution case studies.

References

(Aksit et al. 1998):   M. Aksit, B. Tekinerdogan, *Aspect-Oriented Programming using Composition Filters*, Proceedings of the AOP Workshop at ECOOP '98, 1998

(Boellert 1999):   K. Boellert, *On Weaving Aspects*, Proceedings of the AOP Workshop at ECOOP '99, 1999

(Brown et al. 1996):   A. W. Brown, K. C. Wallnau, *Engineering of Component-Based Systems*, Component-Based Software Engineering, IEEE Computer Society Press, 1996, pp. 7-15

(Gamma et al. 1995):   E. Gamma, et al., *Design Patterns - Elements of Reusable Object-Oriented Software*, Addison Wesley, c1995

(Guzenda 2000):   L. Guzenda, *Objectivity/DB - A High Performance Object Database Architecture*, Invited Talk, Workshop on High Performance Object Databases, Cardiff, UK, July 2000

(Harrison et al. 1993):   W. Harrison, H. Ossher, *Subject-Oriented Programming (A Critique of Pure Objects)*, Proceedings of OOPSLA 1993, ACM SIGPLAN Notices, Vol. 28, No. 10, Oct. 1993, pp. 411-428

(IBM 2000):   IBM Research, USA, *Multi-dimensional Separation of Concerns using Hyperspaces*, http://www.research.ibm.com/hyperspace/

(Kenens et al. 1998):   P. Kenens, et al., *An AOP Case with Static and Dynamic Aspects*, Proceedings of the AOP Workshop at ECOOP '98, 1998

(Kersten et al. 1999):   M. A. Kersten, G. C. Murphy, *Atlas: A Case Study in Building a Web-based Learning Environment using Aspect-oriented Programming*, Proceedings of OOPSLA 1999, ACM SIGPLAN Notices, Vol. 34, No. 10, Oct. 1999, pp. 340-352

(Kiczales et al. 1997):   G. Kiczales, J. Lamping, A. Mendhekar, C. Maeda, C. Lopes, J. Loingtier, J. Irwin, *Aspect-Oriented Programming*, Proceedings of ECOOP '97, LNCS 1241, pp. 220-242

(Lieberherr 2000):   K. J. Lieberherr, *Demeter*, http://www.ccs.neu.edu/research/demeter/index.html

(McCann 2000):   J. McCann, *Component-based Operating Systems and their Implications for Database Architectures*, Invited Talk, Workshop on High Performance Object Databases, Cardiff, UK, July 2000

(Mezini et al. 1998):   M. Mezini, K. J. Lieberherr, *Adaptive Plug-and-Play Components for Evolutionary Software Development*, Proceedings of OOPSLA 1998, ACM SIGPLAN Notices, Vol. 33, No. 10, Oct. 1998, pp.97-116

(Monk et al. 1993):   S. Monk, I. Sommerville, *Schema Evolution in OODBs Using Class Versioning*, SIGMOD Record, Vol. 22, No. 3, Sept. 1993, pp. 16-22

(Pulvermueller et al. 1999):   E. Pulvermueller, H. Klaeren, A. Speck, *Aspects in Distributed Environments*, Proceedings of GCSE 1999, Erfurt, Germany (to be published by Springer-Verlag)

(Rashid et al. 1998):   A. Rashid, P. Sawyer, *Facilitating Virtual Representation of CAD Data through a Learning Based Approach to Conceptual Database Evolution Employing Direct Instance Sharing*, Proceedings of DEXA '98, LNCS 1460, pp. 384-393

(Rashid et al. 1999a):   A. Rashid, P. Sawyer, *Dynamic Relationships in Object Oriented Databases: A Uniform Approach*, Proceedings of DEXA '99, LNCS 1677, pp. 26-35

(Rashid et al. 1999b):   A. Rashid, P. Sawyer, *Transparent Dynamic Database Evolution from Java*, Proceedings of OOPSLA 1999 Workshop on Java and Databases: Persistence Options (extended version to appear in L' Object Journal, Vol. 6, No. 3, November 2000)

(Rashid et al. 2000a):   A. Rashid, P. Sawyer, E. Pulvermueller, *A Flexible Approach for Instance Adaptation during Class Versioning*, Proceedings of ECOOP 2000 OODB Symposium (in print as an LNCS volume by Springer-Verlag)

(Rashid et al. 2000b):   A. Rashid, E. Pulvermueller, *From Object-Oriented to Aspect-Oriented Databases*, Proceedings of DEXA 2000, LNCS1873, pp. 125-134

(Rashid 2000a):   A. Rashid, *On to Aspect Persistence*, To Appear in Proceedings of Net.ObjectDays 2000 Symposium on Generative and Component-Based Software Engineering (GCSE 2000)

(Rashid 2000b):   A. Rashid, *SADES Java API Documentation 1999-2000*, http://www.comp.lancs.ac.uk/computing/users/marash/research/sades/index.html

(Skarra et al. 1986):   A. H. Skarra, S. B. Zdonik, *The Management of Changing Types in an Object-Oriented Database*, Proceedings of the 1st OOPSLA Conference, Sept. 1986, pp. 483-495

(Xerox 2000):   Xerox PARC, USA, *AspectJ Home Page*, http://aspectj.org/

An object oriented approach to represent behavioural knowledge in heterogeneous information systems

Yamine AIT-AMEUR*, Guy PIERRA** and Eric SARDET**

ENSAE-SUPAERO
10 Av E. Belin. BP 4032
31055 Toulouse Cedex 4. France
E-mail : yamine@supaero.fr
Fax: +33 5 62 17 83 45

**LISI-ENSMA*
BP 40109 – Site du Futuroscope
86961 FUTUROSCOPE Cedex FRANCE
Email:{pierra, sardet}@ensma.fr
Fax: +33 5 49 49 80 64

ABSTRACT. *This paper addresses the topic of data and knowledge exchange and sharing in heterogeneous, autonomous and distributed information systems. It shows the maturity of object oriented technology for describing and structuring complex data models. It suggests to use a meta-model which implements a general model whose instances represent particular data models. This meta-model is implemented using an object oriented data modelling language, namely the EXPRESS language. We present two examples of meta-models allowing to exchange Entity-Relationship data models and procedural knowledge. Finally, this paper illustrates the technique we use in order to generate source code, in a target programming language, implementing these data models.*

KEY WORDS: *Data exchange, Data and knowledge sharing, Unified schemas, EXPRESS, meta-programming, procedural knowledge, Meta-data, autonomous and heterogeneous data.*

1. Introduction

The growth of data, the use of INTERNET, the widely organised access to digital data and so on has increased the necessity to suggest formalised models which handle distribution, autonomy and heterogeneity of data. Distribution is the possibility to have the whole or parts of data represented in different places. Autonomy of data is the possibility of accessing these data via different systems. Finally, heterogeneity is the possibility to have different interpretations of data, different hardware or software systems to support data, different query languages for data, different constraints expressed on data. Distribution, autonomy and heterogeneity are the main characteristics which lead researchers to suggest data models like multidabases and federated databases (Chung, 1990)(Landers et. al., 1982)(Pierra , 1992)(Sheth et. al., 1990)(Templeton et. al., 1986). This problem has been addressed in the literature with two points of view: database systems and knowledge based systems.

On the one hand, in database systems, dealing with the management of different information sources has been addressed by federated databases. Federated database management systems, denoted FDBMS, have been defined in order to allow the federation of databases. They are based on the definition of a reference architecture that provides a framework to understand, categorise and compare different architectural options for developing federated database systems. According to (Sheth et. al., 1990) the components of a reference architecture are: data, database, commands (specific actions, e.g., queries), processors (software modules that manipulate commands and data), schemas, and mappings (allowing to map objects of one schema to objects of another schema) (Arens et. Al., 1993)(Barsalou et. Al., 1990)(Bright et. Al., 1994).

However, most of the work achieved in the last decade to describe, formalise and represent reference architectures in federated databases deals with structural and descriptive aspects and fails to address the formalisation of behavioural aspects that are mandatory to formalise commands, processors and mappings in reference architectures of autonomous and heterogeneous information systems.

On the other hand, the second approach for modelling data and knowledge is the one issued from knowledge based systems. Data and knowledge are represented using a knowledge model that is usually based on logic (first order logic) and/or a functional language (like LISP). Several knowledge based systems have been developed. In general, they address a particular engineering area. Sharing, distribution and autonomy of the represented knowledge in these systems remain difficulties to solve. Therefore, several systems have been suggested for integrating such knowledge based systems. They are based on a meta-model approach. The most known meta-model is the one based on the Knowledge Interchange Format (KIF) (Gruber, 1993) that uses LISP as representation language for every form of knowledge. Several systems have been developed on the basis of this format that they share. Moreover, a methodology allowing to describe such models is suggested by KADS (Wielinga et. al., 1992). The obtained systems proved useful for knowledge exploitation and query, but they fail for all the remaining database aspects.

Our approach considers both database and knowledge based systems orientations. It uses the technology issued from both approaches and integrates it in an object oriented approach.

The Parts Library data model, denoted PLib, has been described for exchanging parts libraries between CAD systems (Pierra , 1990) that use a big amount of heterogeneous, autonomous and distributed data. This problem became crucial when parts catalogues have been put on the Web. As followed by (Castano et. Al., 1995)(Castano et. al., 1997) where the domain of application is administrative data, PLib is applied to electronic and mechanical data engineering. Indeed, writing generic models for data and knowledge exchange is possible, but the obtained models become poor since they address several different domains. In the opposite, when data and knowledge models are restricted to particular domain of application, it becomes possible to describe precise data and knowledge models.

The PLib data model has been described in order to allow the capability to exchange complex data between library management systems. It is based on the description of a data meta-model whose instances are particular data models. Its reference architecture is a semantic dictionary where all the characteristics of library management systems are described. Indeed, data, schemas, queries, constraints, domains instances, classes and methods are described.

The PLib data model is completely formalised within the object oriented EXPRESS data modelling language (Bouazza, 1995)(Schenck et.al, 1994) and is, now, widely used in industry. Several tools around this model are developed by software companies and this model has been raised at the international standard level at the ISO (Pierra, 2000)(Zwicker, 2000)(Pierra et.al., 1998)(Wiedmer et. al., 1998) under the number ISO 13584.

Among the features that have been described in the PLib data model, descriptive and structural aspects were easily translated into EXPRESS thanks to the technology offered by object oriented approaches. However, we faced the problem of representing behavioural knowledge like functions, procedures, methods and constraints.

The difficulty was "How to represent functions, procedures, methods and constraints in the same data model within an object oriented data modelling language, EXPRESS, which does not offer the possibility to express formal language processing (grammar processing) ? ".

The goal of this paper is not to present the formal data model associated to PLib. The reader can refer to (Pierra , 1992)(Pierra , 1993)(Pierra , 1997). This paper presents a formal technique that allows to represent procedural and behavioural knowledge in autonomous and heterogeneous information systems. It uses a technique, based on meta-programming, that encodes the representation of programs, procedures, expressions, constraints and so on in a data oriented model. The EXPRESS formal data modelling description language is used as the underlying specification language. A set of meta-data, gathered in an EXPRESS schema, defines all the required expressions. The instantiation of these meta-data allows to represent particular expressions.

This paper is structured as follows. Next section presents the formal object oriented data modelling language EXPRESS. Section 3 reviews the main aspects of the PLib data model and the approach we used to describe this model. Then, in section 4, the meta-programming technique is presented. It consists of describing a set of meta-data, structured in a object oriented way, allowing to encode meta-models. We illustrate the use of this technique on a particular example showing the description of entity/relationship data models. Finally, section 5 presents two examples representing procedural information in the meta-data model. The first one is related to simple expressions and the second one shows a representation of a subset of relational databases through the relational algebra and of the SQL query language. Moreover, this section shows how an interpretation process can be derived from these data models for evaluation and code generation

2. The EXPRESS Language

Describing data models is a major concern of the data management and knowledge management areas. Several formalisms, models and techniques allow to represent data and/or knowledge. For example, UML, OMT and so on are used to represent information systems, while KIF, KADS and so on are techniques for knowledge representation.

The definition of such formalisms for representing information systems requires a set of basic concepts. These concepts are related to structure, description and behaviour.

  – *Structure* defines the organisation of the data in the information system. For example, classification or object orientation or relational databases are ways of structuring information.

  – *Description* is related to the properties of the structured information. It is defined by the set of properties a given description has. Attributes in classes or in relational tables are ways to describe different classes or tables.

  – *Behaviour* gives the information on how the data behave. Behaviour is obtained either by giving a function which shows how data evolve (constructive approach) or by giving constraints on the data to restrict the behaviour to the licit data only.

These three concepts require the definition of a language or any other formalism which allows to handle them. It is highly suitable for this language to be processable. Unfortunately, most of the suggested formalisms allowing to represent data of information systems suffer from the absence of one or two of the previously listed concepts.

Our approach is based on the use of the object oriented data modelling language EXPRESS.

EXPRESS is a normalised language defined in the context of the STEP (STandard for the Exchange of Product model and data) project. It was originally defined to represent data models in the engineering area and it is now widely used for solving several data modelling problems. Moreover, this language can be used for the specification of several applications in computer science areas. The major advantage of this language is the integration of the structural, descriptive and procedural concepts in a common formalism and a common semantics. This integration avoids the use of several models and languages that require putting a bridge over the gap between all the defined models (like in UML, or OMT).

A data model in EXPRESS is represented by a set of schemas that may refer to each other. Each schema contains two parts. The first part is a set of entities that are structured in an object oriented approach (supporting multiple inheritance). The second part is a procedural part that contains procedures, functions and global rules.

2.1 Overview of EXPRESS

This section focuses on the constructions we use in the rest of the paper. More details about the definition of this language can be found in (Bouazza, 1995)(Schenck et.al, 1994).

Firstly, the EXPRESS language focuses on the definition of entities (types) that represent the objects (classes) we want to describe. EXPRESS is type oriented: entity types are defined at compile time and there is no concept of meta-class. Each entity is described by a set of characteristics or properties called attributes. These attributes are characterized by a domain and constraints on these domains. An important aspect of these entities is that they are structured hierarchically possibly using multiple inheritance as in several object oriented languages. This part of the specification describes the structural and the descriptive parts of the domain knowledge.

On the other hand, EXPRESS offers the possibility to describe processes on the data defined in the entities by introducing functions and procedures. These functions are used to define constraints, pre-conditions and post-conditions on the data. They are also used to specify how values of some properties may be derived from values of other properties. This part of the specification describes the procedural part of the domain knowledge.

Finally, in EXPRESS, entities (data) and functions (processes) are embedded in a structure called a *SCHEMA*. These schemas may reference each other allowing a kind of modularity and therefore specification in the large possibilities.

2.2 Entity definition

In EXPRESS, entities are defined in terms of attributes. Indeed, a set of attributes (may be an empty set) is assigned to each entity. Each attribute has a domain (where it takes its values) defining a data type. It can be either a simple domain (like integer, string ...) or a structured domain (like lists, sets, bags ... hard encoded in EXPRESS) or an entity type meaning that an attribute is of type another entity.

We syntactically write:

```
SCHEMA Foo1;
ENTITY A;                      ENTITY B;
 att_A: INTEGER;                att_1: REAL;
INVERSE                         att_2: LIST [0:?] OF STRING;
 att_I: B FOR att_3;            att_3: A;
END_ENTITY;                    END_ENTITY;
END_SCHEMA;
```

Informally, the entity *B* has three attributes: a real, a list of strings and a pointer to another entity *A* which has only one integer attribute. *att_I* is an inverse attribute of entity, *A*, corresponding to the inverse link defined by attribute *att_3* in entity *B*.

Semantically, an entity has a model. In the EXPRESS community, the model is named a physical file. The model consists of a set of entity instances with explicit instance identity. The attribute values are either literal values of the EXPRESS simple or structured built-in types or they are references to other entity instances. Instead of entering into deep semantic details, we give an example of a model (physical file) which can be associated to the previous entity definitions.

Let us consider a particular representation, named instance, of the entity B, where *att_1* evaluates to 4.0, *att_2* is the list ('hello', 'bye') and *att_3* points the particular instance of the entity A where its *att_A* attribute evaluates to 3. Then, the model (physical file) associated to these particular instances of the entities A and B is described by:

```
#  1=A(3);
#  2=B(4.0, ('hello','bye'), #1);
```

2.3 Derived attributes

As it is the case for several object oriented languages, it is possible to describe derived attributes in the entity definitions. For example, we can derive in entity *B2* (assumed to be defined in the same schema *Foo1*) a Boolean attribute stating whether or not the length of the *att_2* list is equal to the integer attribute *att_A* defined in entity *A*. We write:

```
ENTITY B2;
     att_1: REAL;
     att_2: LIST[0:?] OF STRING;
     att_3: A;
DERIVE
     att_4: BOOLEAN := (SELF.att_3\A.att_A
          = SIZEOF(SELF.att_2));
END_ENTITY;
```

where
> 1 - *SELF* is an EXPRESS keyword representing a variable that designates the current entity,
> 2 - '.' is the dot notation to access the attribute of an entity,
> 3 - '\' character allows to access an EXPRESS entity,
> 4 - and *SIZEOF* is an EXPRESS built in function that returns the length of a given aggregate data type.

The derived (computed) attributes do not physically appear in the model (physical file). They are evaluated each time an instance is created.

2.4 Constraining entities

It is possible to limit the allowed population (elements) of the models to those instances that satisfy some stated constraints. EXPRESS uses first order logic which is completely processable since the set of instances (physical file) is finite. Constraints are introduced thanks to the *WHERE* clause of EXPRESS that provides for instance invariant, and thanks to the global *RULE* clause that provides for model invariant.

Let us assume that the allowed values for *att_A* in *A* are [1..10] and that exactly only two instances of entity *A* shall have an attribute value equals to 1. We may write (*QUERY* is a built-in iterator on class):

```
ENTITY A;                        RULE Card FOR A;
     att_A: INTEGER;             WHERE
WHERE                                 SIZEOF(QUERY(inst <* A|
     (SELF.att_A >= 1)                     (inst.att_A=1))) = 2;
          AND                    END_RULE;
     (SELF.att_A <= 10);
END_ENTITY;
```

Derivations and constraints are the only places where functions may occur. They provide the two high level abstraction mechanisms identified as necessary in data driven active databases. Therefore, it is possible to specify formally a global class of problems. Moreover, derivations and constraints are inherited. These features define a set inclusion semantics to the EXPRESS inheritance mechanism.

2.5 Multiple inheritance

Another important feature of the EXPRESS language is the multiple inheritance possibility. This common feature in object oriented languages, is introduced by the *SUPERTYPE* and *SUBTYPE* EXPRESS keywords. The *SUBTYPE* clause occurring in an entity *E'* is followed by the set of entity names representing the superclasses of *E'*. A very specific feature of EXPRESS is that an instance (with the same identity) may belong to several subclasses of an entity type, and that a *SUPERTYPE* may control the *SUBTYPEs* to which each instance shall belong. Let us illustrate, through a small example, how inheritance is represented. An entity *E* is a superclass of entities *E_1*, *E_2* and *E_3*.

```
SCHEMA Foo2;
ENTITY E
   SUPERTYPE OF (E_1, E_2, E_3);
...
END_ENTITY;
```

E_11 is a subclass of *E_1*. It is not declared. *E_2* is a superclass of exactly (*ONEOF*) *E_21*, *E_22* and a subclass of *E*. We write:

```
ENTITY E_1                    ENTITY E_2
   SUBTYPE OF (E);               SUPERTYPE OF(ONEOF(E_21, E_22))
...                              SUBTYPE OF (E);
END_ENTITY;                    END_ENTITY;
```

E_21 is a subclass of both *E_1* and *E_2*, and *E_22* is a subclass of *E_2*.

```
ENTITY E_21                   ENTITY E_22
   SUBTYPE OF (E_1, E_2);        SUBTYPE OF(E_2);
...                              ...
END_ENTITY;                   END_ENTITY;
```

and finally *E_3* is a subclass of *E* without any subclass.

```
ENTITY E_3
   SUBTYPE OF (E);
...
END_ENTITY;
```

2.6 Functions and procedures

As we have seen previously on examples, functions can be used to associate rules to data. These rules may be either derivation or (local or global) constraints. Syntactically, a function is declared in EXPRESS as:

```
FUNCTION F (x: typ_1; y: typ_2): typ_3;
(* Function_Body; *)
END_FUNCTION;
```

The previous declaration has only presented a function interface. It has two parameters (*x* and *y*) of types *typ_1* and *typ_2* respectively. The result is of type *typ_3*. We note that these types can be either built in EXPRESS types, or defined types or defined entities.

Function_Body represents the body of the defined function. Assignment, sequence and control structures (if statements, loops and recursion) can be used in this function body. These features give powerful expression possibilities to the language. Indeed, we get the same expression possibility as other recursive specification languages.

2.7 Built in functions

Several built in functions have been introduced in the EXPRESS language.
We do not review all of them in this paper, but we will present one that is very important and not common in other languages from our point of view: the *TYPEOF* function. It is declared by:

```
FUNCTION TYPEOF(v: generic): SET OF STRING;
   ....
END_FUNCTION;
```

This function returns a set of strings that contains all the names of all the data types to which the parameter belongs to. Each string contains the type name prefixed by the name of the schema where this type is declared or defined. For example, in the schema *Foo2*, if x is a variable of type the entity *E_22*, then *TYPEOF(x) = ['FOO2.E_22','FOO2.E_2','FOO2.E']*. This function enables access, from the rules associated to data, to the structure of the data.

3. The PLib data Meta-model

As we stated in the introduction, PLib is a unified data meta-model which allows to represent data models and data representations for parts libraries in the engineering area. It is mainly used for the managing of electronic and mechanical data and has proved useful for other engineering areas. Up to now, PLib has been implemented in several international industrial projects (ESPRIT-PLUS, ESPRIT-CIREP, IST-MERCI, ...).

The PLib data meta-model structure is based on the definition of a data dictionary which acts as a referential model gathering all the data descriptions and all the instances of the data. This dictionary and the whole data meta-model have been normalised at the ISO level under the ISO 13584 number.

Technically, the meta-model is a set of meta-data that describes data of the following form:

a) *suppliers*: data elements describing suppliers of parts,

b) *classes*: representing parts families. They are provided by suppliers, and are organised through a simple inheritance hierarchy (structural knowledge). For each class, the following items can be associated:

– a *superclass*, is a class describing the parent class allows to represent inheritance of classes and hierarchies of parts,

– *properties*: describing the attributes of the parts families (descriptive knowledge). A type is associated to each property. The properties are divided into three categories: *key properties* (mandatory properties needed to describe a part), *selectable properties* (properties which can be selected by a query) and *derived properties* (properties computed, by derivation functions, from the *key* and *selectable properties*),

– *derivation functions* are expressions (procedural knowledge) that are used to compute the derived properties described before,

– *constraints* are logical expressions that describe logical properties (procedural knowledge) that need to be satisfied by the described part family,

– *tables* contain the values of the properties. They describe the database associated to the part family,

– *documents* as a presentation of the parts families. They are used to describe catalogues on paper or on the Internet, etc.

All the previous characteristics are issued from a deep domain analysis and lead to the description of this model. The complete PLib meta-model is described in the literature (Ait-Ameur et. Al., 1998), (Pierra et.al., 1998), (Wiedmer et. al., 1998). It has been completely described in the EXPRESS language introduced above.

The structural and descriptive parts of the PLib meta-model are classical in object oriented technology. However, we want to focus in this paper on the meta-programming technique that we have put into practice in order to describe, by data (EXPRESS entities), the procedural knowledge related to *derived properties* and *constraints*.

In order to keep this paper in an acceptable length, we only describe a part of the formalisation of the procedural information that allows to encode derived attributes and constraints.

4. Meta-Programming with EXPRESS

Meta-programming is the technique that we use to describe meta-data in the EXPRESS language. It is the process that allows to represent data and/or programs by data in a meta-model. This technique has been completely described in previous papers (Ait-Ameur et. Al., 1995a)(Ait-Ameur et. Al., 1995b). Instead of recalling the theory of the meta-programming technique, let us show an example in next section.

4.1 The entity/relationship (ER) data model

An example of meta-programming is the possibility to describe a meta-model that specifies entity/relationship models (Chen , 1976).

```
SCHEMA Entity_Relationship;

ENTITY Entity_Model;
    its_name: STRING;
    its_attributes: SET[0:?] OF Attribute_Model;
END_ENTITY;
```

This EXPRESS entity describes the basic entity of an E/R model. It is characterized by a name (*its_name* attribute) and a set of attributes (*Attribute_Model*) characterizing properties of the entity (*its_attributes* attribute). Attributes of an *Entity_Model* entity are described by the following EXPRESS entity.

```
ENTITY Attribute_Model;
    its_name: STRING;
    its_type: Attribute_Type_Model;
END_ENTITY;
```

Informally, the *Attribute_Model* EXPRESS entity describes the attributes of the entities in the entity/relationship model. Each attribute is defined by a name that identifies it (*its_name* attribute) and an assigned type (*its_type* attribute). This type is introduced thanks to the *Attribute_Type_Model* EXPRESS entity that defines a type structure for attributes. This type structure is defined in another EXPRESS schema that is imported into the actual schema by the reference mechanism of the EXPRESS language. We do not introduce this type structure in this paper in order to keep it in a reasonable length, but the complete type structure for attributes can be found in (Pierra et.al., 1998)(Wiedmer et. al., 1998).

At this point, we are able to define in our model what a relationship is. It is described by a name, which identifies the relationship, a set of attributes describing the relationship and the set of entities, which are related through this relationship. So, the EXPRESS declaration will be defined as follows:

```
ENTITY Relationship_Model;
     its_name: STRING;
     linked_entities:   SET[2:?] OF Entity_Model;
     its_attributes:    SET[0:?] OF Attribute_Model;
END_ENTITY;
```

We have voluntarily constrained the set of linked entities to contain at least two entities in order to be able to describe several kinds of relationships like unary, binary or n_ary relationships. We can define now a whole entity relationship model to be a set of entities plus a set of relationships. Then, we get:

```
ENTITY Model;
     its_name : String;
     its_entities : SET [1:?] OF Entity_Model;
     its_relations: SET [1:?] OF Relationship_Model;
END_ENTITY;
```

The entity relationship mechanism is now completely described. It is possible to instanciate it to get a representation of any particular entity relationship specification. An example is shown in the following section. Using the meta-specification presented for expressions in section 5, it is possible to specify (and to exchange) all the integrity constraints associated with any particular entity relationship specification.

Moreover, it is possible to write for this model a set of functions that formally describe the different processes we can perform on this model, like deriving relational database schemes from entity relationship models and so on.

4.2 A particular entity/relationship model

Let us describe a particular model starting from the generic one defined previously. Consider a simple model involving two entities: parts and suppliers. Parts are described by their part number and their part name. Suppliers are described by their supplier number, a name and an address. The relationship we are describing is the one named *supply*. It indicates that a supplier supplies a part. It is defined by the supplier number, the part number and the quantity of parts supplied.

The semantic model describing this entity relationship schema is defined by the following physical file. For attributes, we get:

```
#1=Attribute_Model('part_number', # ...)
#2=Attribute_Model('part_name', # ...)
#3=Attribute_Model('quantity', # ...)
#4=Attribute_Model('supplier_number', # ...)
#5=Attribute_Model('address', # ...)
#6=Attribute_Model('name',# ...)
```

The '...' dots describe the type associated to the described attribute type. We have not filled this field because it refers to the type schema for attributes that we have not introduced.

The entities of the model we described, the relationship and the model itself are respectively introduced by:

```
#10=Entity_Model('supplier',[#4,#5,#6]);
#11=Entity_Model('parts',[#1,#2])
#15=Relationship_Model('supply',[#1,#4,#3])
#20=Model('supllier_part',[#10,#11],[#15])
```

The semantic model we have defined through the physical file is the formal representation of the particular entity/relationship model we have previously introduced. This model can be used for different processes.

The previous model suffers from the absence of the possibility to describe procedural knowledge which is mandatory for describing integrity constraints on the entity/relationship data model. This is due to the absence of an EXPRESS data model which is obtained by meta-programming. Such a data model exists. It is described in next section.

5. Representation of the procedural knowledge

As stated above, the problem of representing procedural knowledge is a crucial problem when designing multiple databases or when it is required to transfer programs and constraints or to exchange queries between heterogeneous, distributed and autonomous databases.

In our approach, the problem is solved by considering programs or procedures as data. These data are described thanks to the meta-programming technique. This technique is preferred to formal language based techniques which require the definition of grammar processors.

This section presents the generic model for representing procedural information. The EXPRESS *generic_expressions_schema* schema represents an encoding of a generic expression by a tree, as it is performed in a compiling process. Then, two specializations of this schema are presented. The first one is for simple expressions and the second one represents the relational data model and relational algebra which is used to encode SQL queries.

5.1 An EXPRESS schema for generic expressions

We have chosen to represent expressions like in functional languages and we obtained a schema that covers all the possible expressions in a programming language. However, the structure of this schema exploits object orientation because it is well adapted for specialisation as we will notice in the description of the two particular schemas. This generic schema is presented below.

An expression is modelled to be either a constant (literal), a variable, an unary, a binary or a multiple arity expression.

```
SCHEMA generic_expressions_schema;
ENTITY generic_expression
  ABSTRACT SUPERTYPE OF(ONEOF(
     generic_literal,
     generic_variable,
     unary_generic_expression,
     binary_generic_expression,
     multiple_arity_generic_expression)));
WHERE
    WR1: is_acyclic(SELF);
END_ENTITY;

ENTITY generic_literal
  ABSTRACT SUPERTYPE
  SUBTYPE OF(generic_expression);
END_ENTITY;

ENTITY generic_variable
  ABSTRACT SUPERTYPE
  SUBTYPE OF (generic_expression);
INVERSE
    interpretation :environment FOR syntactic_representation;
END_ENTITY;
```

```
ENTITY variable_semantics
  ABSTRACT SUPERTYPE;
END_ENTITY;

ENTITY environment;
    syntactic_representation: generic_variable;
    semantics: variable_semantics;
END_ENTITY;
```

The *variable_semantics* entity determines the meaning, the semantics or the interpretation of a variable. It is linked, through the *environment* entity, to the *generic_variable* entity.

The underlying structure of an expression is a graph. For soundness purposes, the function *is_acyclic* (see below) ensures that the graph associated to an expression is a direct acyclic graph (DAG). The *used_variables* (see herafter) function collects all the variables occurring in an expression.

```
ENTITY unary_generic_expression
  ABSTRACT SUPERTYPE
  SUBTYPE OF(generic_expression);
    operand: generic_expression;
END_ENTITY;

ENTITY binary_generic_expression
  ABSTRACT SUPERTYPE
  SUBTYPE OF(generic_expression);
    operands: LIST [2:2] OF generic_expression;
END_ENTITY;

ENTITY multiple_arity_generic_expression
  ABSTRACT SUPERTYPE
  SUBTYPE OF(generic_expression);
    operands: LIST [2:?] OF generic_expression;
END_ENTITY;

FUNCTION is_acyclic(arg:generic_expression):
                BOOLEAN;
-- This function returns TRUE when
-- the arg argument denotes a Direct
-- Acyclic Graph
-- else it returns FALSE.
END_FUNCTION; -- is_acyclic

FUNCTION used_variables(arg :generic_expression):
                            SET[0:?] of generic_variable;
-- This function returns the set of generic
-- variables that occur in
-- the arg generic_expression.
END_FUNCTION;
```

This schema has been specialized for several applications issued from programming and data engineering areas. Moreover, this schema, its specializations and its interpretations have been encoded in the JAVA programming language.

Below two specialisations are given.

5.2 Simple expressions

The *expressions_schema* schema, that references the *generic_expressions* schema, represents all the meta-data necessary to encode basic expressions with integer, real, Boolean and string data types. In the following, we only give a restriction of this schema to integer and real expressions.

Specialization is obtained by:

- the inheritance mechanism that allows to describe a new knowledge category,

- the description of constraints (WHERE rules) which define the licit expressions only.

```
SCHEMA expressions_schema;

REFERENCE FROM generic_expressions_schema(
    generic_expression,
    generic_variable,
    generic_literal,
    unary_generic_expression,
    binary_generic_expression,
    multiple_arity_generic_expression);
```

A global *expression* entity gathers all the integer, real, Boolean and string expressions by defining literals, variables, unary, binary and multiple arity expressions by inheritance. We only show the multiplication operator. The other ones can be consulted in (Ait-Ameur et. Al., 1998).

```
ENTITY expression
  ABSTRACT SUPERTYPE OF (ONEOF (
                numeric_expression,
                boolean_expression,
                string_expression))
  SUBTYPE OF (generic_expression);
END_ENTITY;

ENTITY numeric_expression
  ABSTRACT SUPERTYPE OF (ONEOF (
                int_literal,
                real_literal,
                variable,
                unary_numeric_expression,
                binary_numeric_expression,
                multiple_arity_numeric_expression))
  SUBTYPE OF (expression);
END_ENTITY;

ENTITY variable
  ABSTRACT SUPERTYPE OF (ONEOF (
                int_variable,
                real_variable))
  SUBTYPE OF (
                numeric_expression,
                generic_variable);
END_ENTITY;

ENTITY int_literal
  SUBTYPE OF (
                numeric_expression,
                generic_literal);
  the_value: INTEGER;
END_ENTITY;

ENTITY real_literal
  SUBTYPE OF (
```

```
                    numeric_expression,
                    generic_literal);
  the_value: REAL;
END_ENTITY;

ENTITY int_variable
          SUBTYPE OF (variable);
END_ENTITY;

ENTITY real_variable
          SUBTYPE OF (variable);
END_ENTITY;

ENTITY unary_numeric_expression
...
END_ENTITY;

ENTITY binary_numeric_expression
...
END_ENTITY;

ENTITY multiple_arity_numeric_expression
  ABSTRACT SUPERTYPE OF (ONEOF (
                plus_expression,
                mult_expression))
  SUBTYPE OF (
                numeric_expression,
                multiple_arity_generic_expression);
  SELF\multiple_arity_generic_expression.
    operands: LIST [2:?] OF numeric_expression;
END_ENTITY;

ENTITY mult_expression
  SUBTYPE OF (
                multiple_arity_numeric_expression);
...
END_ENTITY;
```

The multiplication operation is carried by the *mult_expression* that is constrained in the *multiple_arity_numeric_expression* to have a list of at least two *numeric_expressions*.

At this level, particular expressions can be obtained by instantiation of the *expressions_schema* schema. The expression $2*\pi*R$ computing the perimeter of a circle of ray R is obtained by the following interpretation of the model presented before. We have voluntarily omitted to precise the semantics associated to the *R* variable. In practice, and for instance in the P-LIB standard, *R* is associated to an attribute of a part thanks to the *variable_semantics* entity. More precisely, *R* could be associated to the ray attribute describing the ray of a circular bearing part. The perimeter attribute of the head of a circle bearing part will be described as a derived property, such a derivation being represented by the following physical file:

```
#1=MULT_EXPRESSION(#2, #3, #4);
#2=INT_LITERAL(2);
#3=REAL_LITERAL(3.14159);
#4=REAL_VARIABLE();
#5=ENVIRONMENT(#4, #6);
#6=VARIABLE_SEMANTICS(...);
```

During the exchange process, the receiving system will read this file and build, by interpretation, the corresponding expression. The interpretation aspects are addressed in section 5.4 of this paper.

5.3 Relational databases

The second instantiation is related to the definition of a referential schema (unified schema) for representing the structure of a relational database, and the query language based on the relational algebra. This representation leads to a language independent representation. So, there is no need to have the native database processor on the receiving database.

5.3.1. Reference to needed elements

The *relational_database_schema* schema references and specializes the *generic_expressions_schema* schema. The *values_schema* contains all the entity values represented by EXPRESS entity instances. This schema is also structured in an object oriented way using the inheritance mechanism.

```
SCHEMA relational_database_schema;

REFERENCE FROM generic_expressions_schema(
                binary_generic_expression,
                generic_expression,
                generic_literal,
                generic_variable,
                multiple_arity_generic_expression,
                unary_generic_expression,
                used_variables,
                variable_semantics);

REFERENCE FROM ISO13584_expressions_schema(expression);

REFERENCE FROM values_schema(
                int_value,
                real_value,
                boolean_value,
                string_value);
```

5.3.2. Representation of the structure of a relational database

A relational database is a set of tables. Each table is identified by the *table_identification* entity.

```
ENTITY relational_database;
        schema_name: STRING;
        the_tables: SET [1:?] OF table_identification;
END_ENTITY;
```

Tables are defined by three entities. The *table_identification* entity identifies a table (reference). The *table_specification* entity describes the specification of a table and gives its structure and the types associated to the columns. Last, the *table_extension* entity gives the content of a table. Each of these two last entities refer to their table identification.

```
ENTITY table_identification
  ABSTRACT SUPERTYPE;
END_ENTITY;
```

```
ENTITY table_specification
  SUPERTYPE OF(RDB_table_specification);
          table_identifier: table_identification;
          column_meaning: LIST[1:?] OF UNIQUE variable_semantics;
          key: SET[1:?] OF variable_semantics;
WHERE
 WR1: SELF.key <= list_to_set(SELF.column_meaning);
 WR2: ...;

END_ENTITY;
```

Here, the constraint rule (or the *WHERE* rule) *WR1* asserts that the set of columns defining the key of the specified table are columns belonging to the described table.

```
ENTITY table_extension
          table_identifier: table_identification;
          content: LIST[1:?] OF UNIQUE simple_column;
WHERE
 WR1: QUERY ( col <* SELF.content | SIZEOF (col.values) <>
                                    SIZEOF(SELF.content[1].values)) = [];

 WR2: ...;
END_ENTITY;
```

The constraint rule *WR1* asserts that each column has the same number of values (same length). Indeed, this definition of tables is based on column description. The *WHERE* rule *WR1* asserts that the lines of the defined table are completely described.

Columns are described on integer, real, Boolean and string types. They are respectively defined by a list of integer, real, Boolean and string values imported from the *values_schema* schema.

```
ENTITY simple_column
  ABSTRACT SUPERTYPE OF (ONEOF(
                int_column,
                real_column,
                boolean_column,
                string_column))
    values: LIST [1:?] OF simple_value;
INVERSE
    belongs_to: table_extension FOR content;
END_ENTITY;

ENTITY int_column
SUBTYPE OF (simple_column);
    SELF\simple_column.values: LIST [1:?] OF integer_value;
END_ENTITY;

ENTITY real_column
...
END_ENTITY;

ENTITY boolean_column
...
END_ENTITY;

ENTITY string_column
...
END_ENTITY;
```

5.3.3. Representation of the relational queries

Having defined the structure of a relational database as a set of tables, it is possible to instanciate the *generic_expressions_schema* schema to describe a query language by expressions on tables. Expressions on tables are described on the basis of the arity of the operators belonging to the set of relational algebra operators.

```
ENTITY table_expression
  ABSTRACT SUPERTYPE OF (ONEOF(
                table_literal,
                table_variable,
                unary_table_expression,
                binary_table_expression,
                multiple_arity_table_expression,
                select_expression))
  SUBTYPE OF (generic_expression);
DERIVE
    its_columns: LIST[1:?] OF variable_semantics:=
                                        collects_columns (SELF);
  the_key: SET[1:?] OF variable_semantics :=
                                        return_key(SELF);
WHERE
 WR1: ...;
END_ENTITY;
```

The *collects_columns* and *return_key* functions compute respectively all the columns and the subset of columns defining the key of the underlying *table_expression*, by traversing the direct acyclic graph representing this expression. These functions are useful to write constraints on tables. Table expressions are defined by specialising unary, binary and multiple-ary generic expressions. All the described operators related to relational algebra can be described by this hierarchy.

```
ENTITY unary_table_expression
  ABSTRACT SUPERTYPE OF (projection_expression)
...
END_ENTITY;

ENTITY binary_table_expression
  ABSTRACT SUPERTYPE OF (ONEOF (
                set_table_expression,
                natural_join_expression))
...
END_ENTITY;

ENTITY multiple_arity_table_expression
  ABSTRACT SUPERTYPE OF (multiple_arity_cartesian_product)
...
END_ENTITY;

ENTITY table_variable
  SUBTYPE OF(table_expression,generic_variable);
    structure: LIST [1:?] OF variable_semantics;
    its_key: SET [1:?] OF variable_semantics;
WHERE
 WR1: SELF.its_key <= list_to_set(SELF.structure);
END_ENTITY;

ENTITY table_literal
  SUBTYPE OF (
```

```
                   table_expression,
                   generic_literal);
     the_value: table_identification;
END_ENTITY;
```

As an example, we present two specialisation: one is a "set" operator and the second is a "relational" operator.

The following entity describes set table expressions, i.e., the tables that are obtained by the union, intersection and difference of two tables.

```
ENTITY set_table_expression
  ABSTRACT SUPERTYPE OF(ONEOF(
                 union_table_expression,
                 intersect_table_expression,
                 difference_table_expression))
  SUBTYPE OF (binary_table_expression);
WHERE
 WR1:SELF\multiple_arity_generic_expression
                    .operands[1]\table_expression.its_columns
                  =
      SELF\multiple_arity_generic_expression
                    .operands[2]\table_expression.its_columns;
END_ENTITY;
```

The assertions *WR1* states that, in order to be a sound set operator, the structure of the two tables shall be the same. Otherwise the operator will not be correctly typed.

The following expression is another particular table expression. It represents the SELECT relational operator. It has two arguments: the table and the filtering condition (that is a Boolean expression of the *expressions_schema* schema) on this table.

```
ENTITY select_expression
SUBTYPE OF (
                 table_expression,
                 binary_generic_expression);
DERIVE
 from_table: generic_expression :=SELF\
                    binary_generic_expression.operands[1];
 condition: generic_expression :=SELF\
                    binary_generic_expression.operands[2];
WHERE
 WR1: 'RELATIONAL_DATABASE_SCHEMA.TABLE_EXPRESSION' IN
             TYPEOF(SELF.from_table);
 WR2:'EXPRESSIONS_SCHEMA.BOOLEAN_EXPRESSION' IN
             TYPEOF(SELF.condition);
 WR3: ...;
 WR4: ...;
END_ENTITY;
...
END_SCHEMA;
```

WR1 and *WR2* state that the first and the second arguments shall respectively be a table expression and a Boolean expression. They use the *TYPEOF* built in EXPRESS function to traverse the inheritance tree corresponding to the operators.

Other entities and assertions are represented in this schema but they are not represented in this paper. This schema has been used in several industrial projects and it proved useful for the exchange of database structures and queries.

5.4 Interpretation

Interpretation is the process of building a procedure that allows to understand (by filtering on the EXPRESS entities) the received instance of a meta-data on the receiving system. It consists in building a program by interpreting the set of received instances of meta-data. It is possible to build, using EXPRESS the corresponding program in the chosen programming language provided that an interpretation schema for this language exists.

But, what is an interpretation schema for a programming language ? Such an interpretation is an EXPRESS schema, obtained by subtyping the entities of the reference schema, which contains particular derived attributes (attributes customised for the receiving system). When these attributes are computed, they allow either the derivation of a statement in a target programming language, or the evaluation of an expression.

As an example, we show, below, the interpretation schema for generating SQL code. Let us consider the *SQL_select_expression* which specializes the *select_expression* of the *relational_database_schema*. It is defined by:

```
SCHEMA SQL_interpretation_schema;
.....
ENTITY SQL_select_expression
  SUBTYPE OF (select_expression);
DERIVE
 SQL_sentence: STRING :=
     'SELECT * FROM '+ SELF\select_expression.from_table
                       \SQL_table_expression.SQL_sentence
    + 'WHERE'
    + SELF\select_expression.condition
                       \SQL_boolean_expression.SQL_sentence;
END_ENTITY;
...
END_SCHEMA;
```

The *SQL_sentence* derived attribute is a string that contains the SQL statement corresponding to the select operator. This attribute is defined for each operator. It allows to produce SQL code.

Notice that another interpretation schema can be described for other query languages. The interpretation schema can be considered either as a local schema allowing to convert a database model into the local language, or a global schema that can be used by several client databases.

This technique offers the possibility to exchange different schemas between different structures. However, it needs the presence of a reference schema which acts as a dictionary and is used as a unifying structure. This is the reason why PLib has been raised at the level of an international standard.

In our approach, interpretation is the process that allows to use a data modelling technique in order to generate code or to evaluate expressions. The originality of this technique is the use of a unique language, namely EXPRESS and the capability to avoid the recourse to traditional techniques issued from formal languages and compiling.

6. Conclusion

Heterogeneous and autonomous information systems have suffered from the lack of representation of procedural knowledge. Most of the work towards the integration of multiple sources of heterogeneous data have failed in representing a common and unified format or schema for encoding either queries or database structures in a language independent format.

In this paper, a formal description technique allowing the representation of procedural knowledge has been described. This approach is totally formalised in the EXPRESS language from both semantics and syntactic point of views. Moreover, it shows the possibility to abstract the representation of the procedural knowledge into a particular neutral representation that encodes a tree representing any language expression.

Two main results can be outlined.

Firstly, the developed approach is an open approach. It allows to enrich the description of other kinds of expressions and therefore of other kinds of database or knowledge base languages. We have also shown that it is possible to interpret the unified schema in any programming or query languages provided that an interpretation schema is defined. This technique has been introduced in the engineering area in the context of industrial projects. These projects aim at exchanging heterogeneous, distributed and autonomous data occurring in the library management systems of CAD systems.

Secondly, the object oriented approach, that has been used to encode both the generic expressions schema, its specicialization schemas and the interpretation schemas has proved useful. Indeed, the hierarchical structure of the entities facilitates schema extension and encapsulation. Therefore, the developed technique provides open systems. This approach is different from the KIF approach based on functional programming (LISP functions and data structures) which provides a flat structure to the data and knowledge models and makes these models hard to manage.

Several open applications of this work appeared during developments. We are currently investigating the possibility of merging document based formalisms like SGML or XML with semantic based formalisms like EXPRESS in order to assist the database administrator during the definition of the different database schemas involved in autonomous and heterogeneous information systems. This approach will increase the readability of EXPRESS schemas.

References

(Ait-Ameur et. Al., 1995a) Ait-Ameur, Y., Besnard, F., Girard, P., Pierra, G., and Potier, J.~C. " Formal Specification and Meta-programming in the EXPRESS Language. International" Conference on Software Engineering and Knowledge Engineering, (1995), KSI Institute in Corporation with ACM Sigsoft and IEEE, pp.~181--189.

(Ait-Ameur et. Al., 1995b) AIT-AMEUR, Y., PIERRA, G., SARDET E., " Using the EXPRESS language for Metaprogramming ", Proc. of the 3rd Interna. Conf. of EXPRESS User Group EUG'95, Grenoble 21-22 Oct. 1995

(Ait-Ameur et. Al., 1998) AIT-AMEUR, Y., WIEDMER, H.U., Eds, " Industrial Automation Systems and Integration, Parts Library, Logical Model of Expressions ", ISO 13584-20, ISO, Geneve, 1998 (88 p.).

(Arens et. Al.,1993) Arens, Y., Chee, C.~Y., HSU, C.-N., and Knoblock, C.~A. " Retrieving and Integrating Data From Multiple Information Sources " International Journal of Intelligent and Cooperative Information Systems 2,2 (1993),127--158.

(Barsalou et. Al., 1990) Barsalou, T., and Wiederhold, G. " Complex Objects for Relational Databases " Computer Aided Design 22, 8 (1990).

(Bouazza, 1995) Bouazza, M. " Le Langage EXPRESS " Hermes, 1995.

(Bright et. Al., 1994) Bright, M., Hurson, A.~R., and Pakzad, S. " Automated Resolution of Semantic Heterogeneity in Multidatabases " ACM Transactions on Database systems 19, 2 (1994), 212--253.

(Castano et. Al., 1995) Castano, S., and De Antonellis, V. " Reference Conceptual Architectures For Re-Engineering Information Systems " International Journal of Cooperative Information Systems 4, 2 (1995), 213--235.

(Castano et. al., 1997) Castano, S., and De Antonellis, V. " Semantic Dictionary Design for Database Interoperability " In 13th International Conference on Data Engineering (1997), IEEE Computer Society Press, pp.~43--54.

(Chen , 1976) Chen, P. P.-S. " The Entity-Relationship Model. Toward a Unified View of Data " ACM Transactions on Database Systems 1, 1 (1976), 9--36.

(Chung, 1990) Chung, C.~W. " Dataplex: An access to Heterogeneous Distributed Databases " Communications of the ACM 33, 1 (1990), 70--80.

(Gruber, 1993) Gruber, T.~R. " Towards Principles for the Design of Ontologies Used for knowledge sharing " In Formal Ontology in Conceptual Analysis and Knowledge Representation (1993), N.~Guarino and R.~Poli, Eds., Kluwer Academic Publisher's.

(Landers et. al., 1982) Landers, T., and Rosenberg, R.~L. " An Overview of Multibase " In Proceedings of the 2nd International symposium on Distributed DatabasesV (1982), North Holland.

(Pierra , 1990) Pierra, G. " An Object Oriented Approach to Ensure Portability of CAD Systems " In EUROGRAPHICSV (1990), pp.~205--214.

(Pierra , 1992) Pierra, G. " Modelling Classes of Pre-existing Components in a CIM Perspective: the ISO 13584 Approach " Revue Internationale de CFAO et d'Inforgraphie 9, 3 (1992), 435--454.

(Pierra , 1993) Pierra, G. " A Multiple Perspective Object Oriented Model for Engineering in Design " In New Advances in Computer Aided Design and Computer Graphics (1993), I.~A. Publishers, Ed., pp.~368--373.

(Pierra , 1997) Pierra, G. " Intelligent Electronic Component Catalogues for Engineering and Manufacturing ", Proc. of the Internat. Symposium on Glogal Engineering Networking, GEN'97, Antwerp, Belgium, April 2-24, Heinz Nixdorf Institute Ed., 1997, pp. 331-352.

(Pierra, 2000) PIERRA, G., Ed., " Industrial Automation Systems and Integration, Parts Library Conceptual Model of Parts Library ", ISO CD 13584-10, National Institute of Standard and Technology, Gaithersburg, MD, USA, 2000. To appear.

(Pierra et.al., 1998) PIERRA, G., AIT-AMEUR, Y., SARDET, E., Eds, " Industrial Automation Systems and Integration, Parts Library, Logical Model of Supplier Library ", ISO DIS 13584-24, ISO,Geneva, 1999 (594 p.)

(Schenck et.al, 1994) Schenck, D., and Wilson, P. " Information Modelling The EXPRESS Way " Oxford University Press, 1994.

(Sheth et. al., 1990) Sheth, A.~P., and Larson, J.~A. " Federated Database Systems for Managing Distributed Heterogeneous, and Autonomous Databases " ACM computing survey 22, 3 (1990), 183--236.

(Templeton et. al., 1986) Templeton, M., Brill, M., Chen, A., and Lund, E." Mermaid: Experiences with Network Operation " In Proceedings of the 2nd International Conference on Data Engineering (1986).

(Wiedmer et. al., 1998) Wiedmer, H., and Pierra, G. " Methodology For Structuring Part Families " ISO-IS 13584-42. ISO Genève, 1998.

(Wielinga et. al., 1992) Wielinga, B.~J., de~Velde, W.~V., Schreiber, A.~T., and Akkermans, J.~M. " The KADS Knowledge Modelling Approach " In Proceedings of the 2nd Japenese Knowledge Aquisition for Knowldge Based Systems (1992), R.~Mizoguchi, H.~Motoda, J.~Boose, B.~Gaines, and R.~Quinlan, Eds., Advanced Research Laboratory Saitama, Japan.

(Zwicker, 2000) Zwicker, E. " Overview and Fundamental Principles " ISO CD 13584-10, National Institute of Standard and Technology, Gaithersburg, MD, USA, 2000. To appear.

ARCHITECTURES, PATTERNS AND VISUALISATION

Janus: Using a Pattern Language to Create Software Architecture

Alan O'Callaghan

Software Technology Research Laboratory
SERC Centre
De Montfort University
The Gateway
LEICESTER LE1 9BH

Tel: +44 116 2551551 x6618
e-mail: aoc@ dmu.ac.uk

Keywords: *software architecture, software patterns, pattern languages, design, migration, ADAPTOR, Janus*

Abstract. *This paper presents the theoretical background to Janus, an ongoing project that has been more fully described elsewhere, that explores the use of software patterns organised in a pattern language, to capture and express the normally tacit and configurational knowledge that is the essence of architectural knowledge. Software development, considered as a professional practice is a design discipline which has been, historically, poorly served by the positivist traditions of Computer Science. Architectural knowledge, as understood in the context of other professional disciplines in which it is utilised, drives design at all levels of scale. The creation of software architectures requires some way of expressing this normally tacit knowledge. The experiences, first of ADAPTOR and now of Janus, strongly suggest that pattern languages may provide just such a vehicle.*

1. Introduction: From ADAPTOR to Janus

There has been a widespread and accelerating interest in software architecture in the last seven or eight years. This has been at least partly prompted by pragmatic issues of scale and distribution following on from the commercial penetration of Object Technology, and the later advances of e-technologies. Significant gains have been made in the recent past in terms of Computer Science's ability to analyse and categorise software systems in terms of their architecture. Shaw and Garlan point out, quite correctly, that the typical box-and-line diagrams that previously passed for 'architectural description' focused on components often to the virtual, and sometimes actual, exclusion of the connectors between them (Shaw 1996). They were therefore underspecified in a number of crucial contexts, notably third-party 'packaged' components, multilanguage systems, legacy systems and, perhaps most critically of all, large-scale real-time embedded systems. Additionally the boxes, lines and the adjacency between boxes lacked semantic consistency between diagrams and sometimes even within the same diagram and ignored the need to structure interface definitions. This points to a minimum of two levels of structure and abstraction that were typically missing: abstractions for connections, and segmentation of interfaces. Architectural Description Languages (ADLs) such as UniCon (Shaw 1995) and ROOM (Selic 1994) now permit the documentation of detailed semantics of components and connectors. A notion of architectural style has been advanced that allows systems to be identified as, for example, 'batch sequential', 'pipes and filters' or some subcategory of 'call-and-return'. However, this increased ability to analyse and describe software structures once they have been built has not been matched in the literature by equivalent advances in how to *create architectures* in the first place.

The Janus project at De Montfort University's Software Technology Research Laboratory (STRL) addresses this issue in a very particular way – using patterns to capture and express 'configurational knowledge'. It emerged originally from work from 1993 onwards on the migration of large-scale legacy systems to Object Technology (O'Callaghan 1999). Such efforts are quintessentially 'architectural' in nature as legacy software systems are restructured to make them more flexible to business and technological change. Codification of the common lessons from projects in five different business areas resulted in the creation of the ADAPTOR pattern language, the acronym standing for "Architecture-Driven And Patterns-based Techniques for Object Re-engineering" (O'Callaghan 1998).

ADAPTOR's approach stood in sharp contrast to traditional re-engineering approaches which rely heavily on formal methods to reverse engineer specifications from existing source code. Instead ADAPTOR stressed an holistic, human-centred approach which placed great store in the use of objects as a "general knowledge capture mechanism" (Graham 1998). Object models which described both the business context and the black-box functionality of the required system were developed first. Only then was existing legacy code examined for suitability in implementing required behaviours. This approach which treated legacy systems as 'living history' rather than as 'archaeology' resulted in its being characterised by at least one outside observer as "not a re-engineering technique at all, but forward engineering that reuses existing legacy components". It was the growing realisation that many ADAPTOR patterns were usable in greenfield development, coupled with a more proactive examination of the ideas of Christopher Alexander and, more generally, theories of architecture in the built environment that led from ADAPTOR to Janus. Whereas ADAPTOR takes an architectural approach to legacy system migration, Janus seeks to establish a pattern language or pattern languages that express a generalised praxis of software architecture. In the sections below we explore the theoretical background to the Janus project.

2. A Critique of the Philosophy of Computer Science

The roots of the research into the analysis of software architecture at Carnegie Mellon University and the Software Engineering Institute (SEI) lie in Mary Shaw's pursuit of a definition of the discipline of software development itself (e.g. Shaw 1990). She opines that the maturity of an engineering discipline is marked by the emergence of a "sufficient scientific basis" to enable a critical mass of science-trained professionals to apply their theory to both the analysis of problems and the synthesis of solutions. Further progress is observed when science becomes a forcing function. She presents, therefore, a model that contends that the emergence of a sound engineering discipline of software depends on the vigorous pursuit of applicable science and then the reduction of that science to an instrumentalist practice. It is in pursuit of this model that ADLs, architectural tools such as AESOP (Shaw 1995), and the notion of architectural style has emerged from Carnegie Mellon. But, notwithstanding these gains, the model itself has been shown in other design disciplines to be problematical.

Donald A. Schön has demonstrated, through his study of professional disciplines such as architecture, town-planning and even psychotherapy that the same model espoused by Shaw, which is both linear ('pure' science first; problem-solving second) and hierarchical (scientific knowledge being rated as superior to mere technical knowledge), is a major hindrance to the development of good practice in the professions (Schön 1983). All such practice is based on "design" which, according to Herbert Simon is "changing existing situations into preferred ones" (Simon 1972). The model of Technical Rationality espoused by Shaw, amongst many others it must be admitted, is rooted in Logical Positivism, a credo long-since abandoned by the majority of philosophers of science (Bernstein 1976). What is true of the major professions appears to be true of software development also. Borenstein (1991), for example, notes that the most interesting part of the process of building software is the human part, its design and its use. "Inasmuch as human-oriented software engineering is the study of this process, it could be argued that it is more properly a branch of anthropology than of mathematical sciences. The study of software creation may, in fact, be grossly misclassified in the academic world today, leading to a distorted overemphasis on formal models and a lack of basic work in collecting raw material that comes, most often, in anecdotal (or at least non-quantative) form" (p.36). Blum (1996,1998), similarly, has called for a redesign of the discipline(s) of Computing Science rejecting the legacy of positivism in favour of a more holistic, design-centred approach.

A common theme amongst these and other critics of the positivist traditions of Computer Science is the discipline's neglect of problem setting[1] as opposed to problem-solving. Blum points out that the program in the computer – the main focus of the discipline historically - is subject to the closed abstractions of mathematics and is, theoretically at least, verifiable against some specification. Indeed the core of interest in the 'program-in-the-computer' is the extent of the difficulty of its construction. But what is in the computer must also exist, on completion, as a 'program-in-the-world' where the one and only test is its usefulness. Its value depends upon its ability to transform the pre-existing situation into which it now inserts itself, both impacting upon and being impacted by that situation. As a result the 'program-in-the-computer' exists in a stable, well-known and formally representable environment, but the very same software as 'the program-in-the-world' is dynamic and incompletely understood.

More than this, the required outcome of the program's intervention (and therefore that of the programmer's) is that the situation now transformed is to one for the better. This demands the destruction of the traditional positivist stance of the Computer Scientist as the 'independent', dispassionate, inquirer distanced from the object of her inquiry who seeks knowledge for knowledge's sake. Successful design, in contrast, requires the engagement of the practitioner as an agent involved in what Schön calls a "reflective conversation with the situation" that starts with a framing of that situation until it turns into a recognisable problem to be solved .

The traditionalist neglect of the problem space in favour of the solution space has been explicitly criticised by various approaches including Client-led Design (see, for example, Stowell 1994) and Jackson's problem frames (Jackson 1995). At the heart of the ADAPTOR pattern language, and now also the Janus project, is the notion that objects permit the modelling of the problem space in such a way as to help drive the software design. Objects are regarded, first and foremost, as behavioural abstractions. In models of the problem space they *capture* the behaviour of key abstractions in the world. In the solution space they *specify* the behaviour of elements of software. Figure 1 illustrates the generic models involved.

---

[1] "Problem setting is a process in which, interactively, we name the things to which we will attend and frame the context in which we will attend to them" (Schön, *op.cit.*, p40)

342

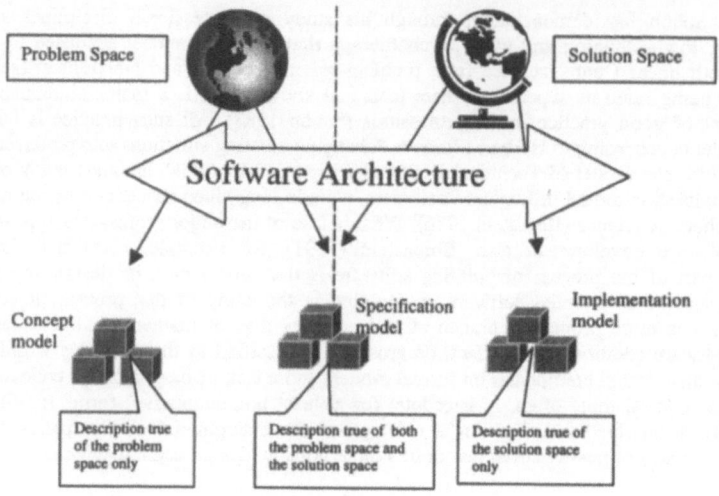

Figure 1: The Role of Software Architecture in Model-driven Development

What is required for both forward and backward traceability between the models is something which sits between the two spaces, looking both to the problem space (to enable proper problem-setting), and towards the solution space to shape the emerging design of the constructable software solution (problem-solving). This Janus[2]-like something is, for us, the Software Architecture. In this notion the Software Architecture is not a separate deliverable. Though clearly strongly relevant to the Specification Model in particular, it is not reducible to it or any other modelling artefact. It is especially not reducible to a high-level description of the gross structure of the system (as per, Bass 1998, for example). We posit that architecture is not separable from any artefact of design but in fact permeates all design decisions, including those of fine detail.

3. Architectural Knowledge

A useful approach to discovering the nature of architecture is to ask the question "What is architectural knowledge?" as opposed to the kind of knowledge required for vernacular design. We are fortunate in being aided in such deliberations by the fact that the Royal Institute of British Architects (RIBA), under the circumstances of political threat to its rights from the deregularition frenzy of the Thatcher Government, itself engaged in a wide-ranging discussion as to the nature of its professional knowledge-base in the 1980's. The record of that discussion is illuminating. Broadly, it concluded that architecture involves:

- Commitment to, and the knowledge required for, advocacy of the client's interests

---

[2] Janus is of course the Roman God who had two faces which could look both ways at once. January, the month which both closes the old year and opens the new year, is named after him.

- 'Design imagination'
- Knowledge of materials, procurement and project management (Duffy 1998)

Hillier (1996) explores the idea of design imagination further and suggests that architectural knowledge is both configurational and, normally, non-discursive (i.e., inherently difficult to talk about). It is configurational because it deals with the complexity of interrelations between spaces that are both structural and social, and difficult to express (except through the designed solution itself) because it deals with ideas for designing with, rather than ideas of designs. In this it is like the unconscious rules we use to form meaningful conversational sentences and phrases on a day-to-day basis, rather than the formal rules of grammar which we might use to deconstruct or analyse such sentences.

Architectural knowledge moves the designer iteratively from a field of possibilities to a constructed actuality in the course of any given design development. It impacts upon design decisions at all levels of scale. It is not scale, but rather the nature of architectural ideas which distinguishes architecture from more routinist design. Such ideas are configurational, typically tacit, acquired 'by doing' or through social and cultural mechanisms and are normally only even attempted to be made explicit when normative rules are compared or contrasted with other, conflicting, such rules (e.g., the comparison of Gothic and Romanesque architectures for cathedrals).

The clear implication that good designers 'know more than they can say' is also a theme of observers as diverse as Chester Barnard (Barnard 1938) and Michael Polyani, who coined the phrase "tacit knowing" (Polyani 1967). If such knowledge is gained, as is suggested, through social and cultural means, then vehicles for expressing design 'best practice' become first class candidates for the accumulation and dissemination of architectural knowledge. In our opinion this is exactly the kind of role that software patterns can play in developing a body of architectural knowledge for software.

4. Patterns and Pattern Languages

Software Patterns are associated with the radical architect of the built environment, Christopher Alexander. In his earliest publication Alexander presents a powerful critique of modern design (Alexander 1964) contrasting the failures of the professional selfconscious process of design with what he called the unselfconscious process by which peasants farmhouses, eskimos' igloos and the huts of the Mousgoum tribespeople of the Cameroon amongst others create their living spaces. In the latter "...the pattern of building operation, the pattern of the building's maintenance, the constraints of the surrounding conditions, and also the pattern of daily life, are fused in the form" (p.31) yet there is no concept of 'design' or 'architecture', let alone separate designers and architects. Each man builds his own house.

Alexander argues that the unselfconscious process has an homeostatic (i.e.,self-organising) structure that produces well-fitting forms even in the face of change, but in the selfconscious process this homeostatic structure has been broken down, making poorly-fitting forms almost inevitable[3]. Although, by definition, there are no explicitly articulated rules for building in the

---

[3] Mature biological systems are homeostatic. Consider how a tree, for example a mighty oak in a wood, is formed. The shape of an individual tree appears well adapted to its environment. The height of the tree is a factor of its competition with neighbouring trees. If used as a windbreak on the edges of farms, it will typically be bent in the direction of the prevailing wind patterns. The number of branches it has depends on the number of leaves it produces

unselfconscious process there is usually a great weight of unspoken, unwritten, implicit rules that are, nevertheless, rigidly maintained by culture and tradition. There are striking parallels here with the discussion of configurational knowledge above. These traditions provide a bedrock of stability, but more than that, a viscosity or resistance to all but the most urgent changes – usually when a form 'fails' in some way. When such changes are required the very simplicity of life itself, and the immediacy of the feedback (since the builder and homeowner are one and the same) mean that the necessary adaption can itself be made immediately, as a 'one-off'. Thus the unselfconscious process is characterised by fast reactions to single 'failures' combined with resistance to all other changes. This allows the process to make a series of minor, incremental adjustments instead of spasmodic global ones. Changes have local impact only, and over a long period of time, the system adjusts "subsystem by subsystem". Since the minor changes happen at a faster rate of change than does the culture, equilibrium is constantly and dynamically re-established after each disturbance.

In the selfconscious process tradition is weakened or becomes non-existent. The feedback loop is lengthened by the distance between the 'user' and the builder. Immediate reaction to failure is not possible because materials are not close to hand. Failures for all these reasons accumulate and require far more drastic action because they have to be dealt with in combination. All the factors which drive the construction process to equilibrium have disappeared in the selfconscious process. Equilibrium, if now reached at all, is unsustainable, not least because of the rate at which culture changes outpaces the rate at which adaptions can be made.

Alexander does not seek a return to primitive forms, but rather a new approach to a modern dilemma: How does the modern designer reacquire the benefits of the slow-moving cultural traditions available to builders in the unselfconscious process? Alexanderian 'theory' is currently expressed in an 11-volume strong literary project Eight of these volumes have been published so far. A common theme of all the books is the rejection of abstract categories of architectural or design principles as being entirely arbitrary. Also rejected is the idea that it is even possible to successfully design "very abstract forms at the big level" (Alexander 1996 p.8). For Alexander architecture gets its highest expression, not at the level of gross structure, but actually in its finest detail, what he calls 'fine structure'. That is to say, the macroscopic clarity of design comes from a consistency, a geometric unity that holds true at all levels of scale. It is not possible for a single mind to envision this recursive structure at all levels in advance of building it. It is in this context that his patterns for the built environment must be understood.

Alexander presents an archetypal pattern language for construction (Alexander 1977). The language is an interconnected network of 253 patterns that encapsulate design best practice at a variety of levels of scale, from the siting of alcoves to the construction of towns and cities. The language is designed to be used collaboratively by all the stakeholders in a development, not just developers. This is premised, in part at least, by the idea that the real experts in buildings are those that live and work in them rather than those that have formally studied architecture or structural engineering. In light of the discussion above we might reinterpret this to say that all of the stakeholders in a design or construction project become partners in problem-setting. The patterns are applied sequentially to the construction itself. Each state change caused by the application of a pattern creates a new context to which the next pattern can be applied. The overall development is an emergent property of the application of the pattern language. The

---

to accommodate local sunshine and rainfall conditions etc. If alone on a hilltop the pattern of growth is normally symmetrical, but if constrained in any way, the tree reflects the constraints in its own growth pattern. The tree's adaptiveness is of course a function of its genetic code. More recently Alexander has talked of his own approach as being a 'genetic' approach and the job of patterns is to instil this genetic code into structures.

language therefore has a generative character: it generates solutions piece-meal from the successive addressing of each individual problem that each of the patterns addresses separately.

In the description of his *Gradual Stiffening* pattern Alexander invites the reader to visualise a 50-year old master carpenter at work. He keeps working, apparently without stopping, until he eventually produces a quality product. The smoothness of his labour comes from the fact that he is making small, sequential, incremental steps such that he can always eliminate a mistake or correct an imperfection with the next step. He compares this with the novice who with a "panic-stricken attention to detail" tries to work out everything in advance, fearful of making an unrecoverable error. Alexander's point is that most modern architecture has the character of the novice's work, not the master craftsman's. Successful construction processes, producing well-fitting forms, come from the postponement of detail design decisions until the building process itself so that the details are fitted into the overall, evolving structure. In this Alexander strikes a common chord with Donald A. Schön whose aforementioned "reflective conversation with the situation" takes the form of a series of what he calls "moves" (i.e., as in a chess game) by the designer, any one of which might result in an unanticipated new situation as a result of the transforming system's "response". This in turn results in a consideration of a new set of moves by the designer. As with Alexander, since it is a concrete state change in the situation which brings forward these moves they cannot be anticipated abstractly in advance of the construction process itself.

5. Generative Architecture

It is against this theoretical background that we are pushing forward the ADAPTOR and Janus project patterns, and against which they will be evaluated. In contrast to the popular view of patterns which, coloured by the high profile exposure of the Gamma catalogue (Gamma 1995), are typically seen as standalone, 'parameterised collaborations', our patterns exist meaningfully only in the context of pattern languages designed to be used to develop software systems through piecemeal growth. They seek to give expression to the configurational and normally non-discursive knowledge that constitutes software architecture by capturing 'best practice' from successful object-oriented developments in terms of providing abstract solutions to the generally recurring problems that emerge through a genuine problem setting process.

ADAPTOR was announced in 1998 as a 'candidate, open, generative pattern language'. It remains, even now within the Janus project which includes experience of a further three 'greenfield' projects in different business areas, a candidate language for two reasons: first, despite the overwhelming success of the projects from which it is drawn ADAPTOR is not comprehensive enough in its coverage or recursed to a sufficient level of detail to be, as yet, truly generative. Secondly, we have different level of confidence in the different patterns with only those having gone through the patterns workshops of the Patterns Movement being regarded as fully mature[4]. Patterns yet to prove themselves in this way are regarded as candidate patterns.

Janus/ADAPTOR is open in a number of senses too. First, like any true language both the language itself and the elements which comprise it are evolvable. Many of the most mature patterns, such as *Get The Model From The People* which was first presented in 1996 at a TelePlop workshop, have gone through numbers of iterations of change. Secondly, following Alexander (Alexander 1977) ADAPTOR's patterns are open abstractions themselves. Since no true pattern provides a complete solution and every time it is applied it delivers different results

---

[4] Some seven patterns have been workshopped at EuroPlop '99 and EuroPlop 2000 (O'Callaghan 1999a, 2000)

(because of different specific contexts to which it is applied), it resists the kind of formalisation that closed abstractions such as rules can be subject to. Finally, and uniquely amongst published software pattern languages ADAPTOR is open because it makes explicit use of other public-domain pattern languages and catalogues, such as Coplien's generative development-process language (Coplien 1995), or the Gamma (Gamma 1995) and Siemens catalogues (Buschmann 1996).

Current patterns in Janus/ADAPTOR include (amongst others):

- *Get The Model From The People*. Requires utilisation of the maintainers of a Legacy system as sources of business information
- *Pay Attention To The Folklore*. Treats the development/maintenance communities as domain experts, even if they don't do so themselves
- *Buffer The System With Scenarios*. Gets the main Business Analysts, marketeers, futurists etc. to roleplay alternative business contexts to the one they bet on in their requirements specifications
- *Shamrock*. Divides a system under development into three loosely coupled 'leaves' – each of which could contain many class categories or packages. The leaves are the conceptual domain (the Problem space objects), the infrastructure domain (Persistence, concurrency etc.) and the interaction domain (GUI's, inter-system protocols etc.)
- *Time-Ordered Coupling*. Clusters classes according to common change rates to accommodate flexibility to change
- *Keeper Of The Flame*. Sets up a role whereby the detailed design decisions can be assured to be in continuity with the architecture. Permits changes to the gross structure if deemed necessary and appropriate.
- *Archetype*. Creates object types to represent the key abstractions discovered in the problem space
- *Semantic Wrapper*. Creates wrappers for legacy code that presents behavioural interfaces of identifiable abstractions to the rest of the system.

Something of the open and generative character aspired to by ADAPTOR can be gained from looking at the typical application of patterns to the early phases of a legacy system migration project. Underpinning ADAPTOR is the model-driven approach described earlier. Problem space models are comprised of object types and the relationships between them which capture the behaviour of key abstractions of the context of the system as well as the system itself. *Archetype* is therefore one of the first patterns used, along with *Get The Model From The People* and *Pay Attention To The Folklore*. At an early stage strategic 'what-if' scenarios are run against this model using *Buffer The System With Scenarios*. *Shamrock* is applied in order to decouple the concept domain object types from the purely system resources needed to deliver them at run-time. The concept domain 'leaf' can then be factored into packages using *Time-Ordered Coupling* to keep types with similar change rates (discovered through the scenario-buffering) together. Coplien's *Conway's Law* is now utilised to design a development organisation that is aligned with the evolving structure of the system. *Code Ownership* (another Coplien pattern) makes sure that every package has someone assigned to it with responsibility for it. An ADAPTOR pattern called *Trackable Component* ensures that these 'code owners' are responsible for publishing the interfaces of their packages that others need to develop to so that they can evolve in a controlled way. The Gamma pattern *Façade* is deployed to enable *A Scaffolding of Interfaces* for the detailed structure of the system. It is at this point that decisions can be made as to which pieces of functionality require new code and which can make use of legacy code. The scaffolding ensures that these decisions, and their implementation consequences, can be dealt with at a rate completely under the control and at the discretion of the development team without fear of runaway ripple effects. For the latter *Semantic Wrapper* is used to interface the old, legacy stuff to the new object-oriented bits.

6. Conclusion

Even with this cursory example we can see how the existing patterns of the Janus project address all of the important issues of architecture (client's needs, conceptual integrity, structure, process and organisation etc.) as well as getting quickly to the heart of the issues of legacy migration. These patterns have already proved, over eight separate projects now, their individual, pragmatic value. The discussion above suggests that pattern languages have an important contribution to play in resolving the historic crisis of software engineering by aiding in the development of a genuine design culture. To the extent that software patterns can capture and articulate the configurational, tacit and normally non-discursive aspects of software development they reflect essential characteristics of Software Architecture. The challenge in the next period is to broaden and deepen the language to its increase its coverage and also the level of detail it addresses. Only then will we be able to say in complete surety that pattern languages for software development can be genuinely generative. The ongoing results are encouraging and, if and when we are able to make such claims it will represent a major breakthrough on the issue of creating software architecture.

References

(Alexander 1964) Alexander, C. 1964. *Notes on the Synthesis of Form*. New York: Oxford University Press

(Alexander 1977) Alexander C., S.Ishikawa, and M.Silverstein with M.Jacobson, I. Fiksdahl-King and S.Angel 1977. *A Pattern Language: Towns, Buildings, Construction*. New York: Oxford University Press

(Alexander 1979) Alexander, C. 1979. *The Timeless Way of Building*. New York: Oxford University Press

(Barnard 1938) Barnard C. 1938. *The Functioning of the Executive*. Cambridge, Mass: Cambridge University Press

(Bass 1998) Bass, L. P.Clements and R. Kazman. 1998. *Software Architecture in Practice*. Reading, Mass: Addison Wesley

(Bernstein 1976) Bernstein R.J. 1976. *The Restructuring of Social and Political Theory*. New York: Harcourt Brace Jovanovich

(Blum 1996) Blum B.I. 1996. *Beyond Programming: To a New Era of Design*. New York: Oxford University Press

(Blum 1998) Blum B.I. 1998. *Software Engineering: A Holistic Approach*. New York: Oxford University Press

(Borenstein 1991) Borenstein. N.S. 1991. *Programming as if People Mattered: Friendly Programs, Software Engineering, and Other Noble Delusions*. Princeton, N.J: Princeton University Press

(Buschmann 1996) Buschmann F., C. Jäkel, R. Meunier, H. Rohnert and M.Stahl 1996. Pattern-Oriented Software Architecture: A System of Patterns. Chichester, England:John Wiley

(Coplien 1995) Coplien J.O. 1995. "A Generative Development-Process Pattern Language" in J.O.Coplien and D.C. Schmidt (eds.) *Pattern Languages of Program Design*. Reading, MA: Addison Wesley

(Duffy 1998) Duffy F. and L Hutton 1998. *Architectural Knowledge: the Idea of a Profession*, London: E. and F.N. Spon.

(Gamma 1995) Gamma E., R.Helm, R. Johnson and J.Vlissides.1995. *Design Patterns* . Reading, MA: Addison Wesley

(Graham 1998) Graham, I. 1998. *Requirements Engineering and Rapid Development*. London, Eng: Addison Wesley

(Hillier 1996) Hillier, B. 1996.*Space is the Machine*. Cambridge, Eng:Cambridge University Press

(Jackson 1995) Jackson M.1995. *Software Requirements and Specifications: A Lexicon of Practice, Principles and Prejudices*. Harlow, Essex: Addison Wesley

(O'Callaghan 1998) O'Callaghan A. ADAPTOR: A Pattern Language for the Re-engineering of Systems to Object Technology. *IEE Colloquium on Software Engineering*. May 1998.

(O'Callaghan 1999) O'Callaghan A. 1999. Migrating Large-Scale Legacy Systems to Component-based and Object Technology: The Evolution of a Pattern Language. *Communications of the AIS*. 2(3) July. http://cais.isworld.org/

(O'Callaghan 1999a) O'Callaghan A. with R.W. Farmer and P. Dai. 1999. *Patterns for Change*. Proceedings of EuroPlop 1999. Irsee, Germany.

(O'Callaghan 2000) O'Callaghan A. 2000. *Patterns for an Architectural Praxis*. Proceedings of EuroPlop 2000. Irsee, Germany.

(Polyani 1967) Polyani M. 1967. *The Tacit Dimension*. New York: Doubleday

(Schön 1983) Schön D.A. 1983. *The Reflective Practitioner*. New York:Basic Books

(Selic 1994) Selic B., G.Gullekson, P.T.Ward, B.Selic and J McGee. 1994. *Real-time Object-Oriented Modeling*. New York: John Wiley & Sons.

(Shaw 1990) Shaw M.1990. Prospects for an Engineering Discipline of Software. *IEEE Software* 7 (6): pp.15-24. November.

(Shaw 1995) Shaw M., R. DeLine, D. V. Klein, T.L. Ross, D.M. Young, and G. Zelesnik.1995. Abstractions for Software Architecture and Tools to Support Them. *IEEE Transactions on Software Engineering*. 21 (4): 314-315. April.

(Shaw 1996) Shaw M. and D. Garlan 1996. *Software Architecture: Perspectives on an Emerging Discipline*. Reading, Mass:Addison Wesley

(Stowell 1994) Stowell, F.A. and D. West. 1994. *Client-led Design: A Systemic Approach to Information System Development*. London: McGraw Hill.

A Probabilistic Model for Classification of Multiple-Record Web Documents

June Tang and Yiu-Kai Ng

Department of Computer Science
Brigham Young University
Provo, Utah 84602, U.S.A.
E-mail:{Junet, ng}@cs.byu.edu   FAX: (801) 378-7775

Abstract

The amount of information available on the World Wide Web, which appear in various Web documents, have been increasing dramatically in recent years. Classification of Web documents is becoming a more significant method for organizing such information. In this paper, we adopt a probabilistic model to classify Web documents into relevant documents and irrelevant documents with respect to an application ontology. Our model is based on the *multivariant statistical analysis* and is different from the conventional probabilistic information retrieval models. The experiments we have conducted using our probabilistic model look promising in terms of classification of multiple-record Web documents.

Keywords: Classification, probabilistic model, object-oriented system, multivariant statistics, application ontologies, ranking function.

1   Introduction

The amount of information available on the World Wide Web has been increasing dramatically in recent years, and keyword-searching and browsing are commonly-used methods for retrieving Web documents of interest. However, keyword-searching often returns either an empty list or a long list of Web documents that a user can not handle, which may include many irrelevant Web documents and exclude many relevant ones with respect to a user query. Browsing the Web is time-consuming process and it often does not locate the desired information. Thus, Classification of Web documents is becoming a more significant method for organizing the huge amount of data available on the Web.

Classification of Web documents can be based on information retrieval (IR) models, such as the Boolean model, the vector space model, and the probabilistic model. Classification of Web documents using these models involve two fundamental issues: (1) the representation of documents and queries and (2) the construction of a ranking function of documents.

The Boolean model is perhaps the best understood IR model due to its simplicity [10]. Because of the *exact matching strategy* and the *document representation scheme*, this model often retrieves either too many or too few documents and is unable to produce ranked outputs.

The vector space model (VSM), on the other hand, ranks documents by using a *similarity matching strategy* [10]. Documents are ranked according to the decreasing values of a similarity measure. Each similarity measure reflects the degree of relevance of its corresponding document with respect to a query. There are various similarity measures (page 202, [10]) and interpretations determined by term weights for document representations (page 205, [10]). VSM, same as the Boolean model, cannot handle any dependent relationships among index terms in a document and query. Hence, they suffer from the problem of oversimplification.

The probabilistic model is an adaptive model based on the Bayes' decision theory. A ranking function, which determines the degree of relevance of a document with respect to a user query, is constructed by relevance feedback, an iterative learning process. The simplest probabilistic information retrieval model is the so-called *binary independence retrieval* (BIR) model [11]. In this model, one assumes that each document in a collection is described by the presence or absence of index terms and is represented by a binary vector

$$x = (x_1, x_2, \cdots, x_n)$$

where $x_i = 0$ (or 1) indicates the absence or presence of the ith $(1 \leq i \leq n)$ index term. In general, it is impossible to calculate the probability of relevance because of the large number of variables involved in the representation of documents comparing with small amount of feedback data available about the relevance of documents [11]. Thus, BIR is hardly applied. The probability of relevance, however, can be estimated under certain assumptions on *independence of terms*. Under the assumption that all terms are mutually, stochastically independent, a ranking function (i.e., a *linear discrimination function*) [11], which is also called the *retrieval status value* (RSV) [5], can be obtained. Assumptions can be made such that pairs, triplets, quadruples, etc., of terms are independent of one another [11]. However, experiments have shown that the gain from the improved independence assumptions does not outweigh the loss from increased estimation errors [5].

A major design issue in probabilistic information retrieval models is to find methods for constructing a ranking function based on probabilities that are both effective and computationally efficient. Some progress has been made in recent research work. [2] propose four models. Two of them are based on the classical probability theory, and the other two are based on a logical technique of evaluating the conditional probability. Fuhr and Buckley [6] introduce a description-oriented probabilistic model for document indexing. In [7], the description-oriented probabilistic indexing approach is adopted to represent Web documents, and documents are categorized using a probabilistic interpretation of the k-nearest neighbor classifier. The average precision of categorization obtained in the experiments, however, is only 26.81%. Wong and Yao [12] develop a unified framework for modeling the retrieval process with probabilistic inference. In general, these models can hardly be applied in real world applications because it is very difficult to estimate their respective probabilities. Various probabilistic information retrieval models are also introduced in a survey article [5].

In this paper, we adopt a probabilistic model to classify Web documents, which is based on the *multivariant statistical analysis*. We apply the model to classify multiple-record Web documents[1], each of which is a sequence of chunks of information related to some entity. Representation of these documents is based on application ontologies [4], which are *object-oriented systems model* instant. We classify Web documents into relevant documents and

---

[1]From now on, whenever we mention (Web) documents, we mean multiple-record Web documents, unless stated otherwise.

irrelevant documents with respect to an application ontology by using a ranking function and a threshold. The construction of the *ranking function* is based on the *multivariant statistical analysis* and involves the estimates of probability distributions of relevance of documents and irrelevance of documents, whereas the *threshold* is determined by a set of training data. The experiments we have performed on the training set of multiple-record Web documents show that the precision of our classification approach is 85%.

This paper is organized as follows. In Section 2, we present a probabilistic model for classifying Web documents, which is based on the multivariant statistical analysis. Evaluation of this model is given in Section 3. In Section 4, we review application ontologies and show how to use them to represent multiple-record Web documents. In section 5, we show the experimental results, and in Section 6 we give a concluding remark.

2 A Probabilistic Model Based on Multivariant Statistical Analysis

In this section, we present a probabilistic model based on multivariant statistical analysis ([1, 8, 9]) for classifying Web documents into two classes, relevant documents and irrelevant documents with respect to a given application ontology. In this paper, we consider two fundamental issues in Web document classification: (1) the representation of documents and (2) the construction of a ranking function for documents.

We assume that all Web documents under consideration are represented by vectors with the same dimension. The vector

$$X = (X_1, X_2, \cdots, X_p)$$

represents a document, which is a vector function from a set of documents to the p-dimensional real vector space, and is called a *vector random variable* in statistics. For a given document d, the value of each $X_i, 1 \leq i \leq p$, is the frequency of occurrence of the corresponding index term (or object instance) in its vector representation. We note that the frequency of occurrence of an index term can be any number, and this implies that the vector random variable X is a *continuous vector random variable*.

We adopt the *multivariant statistical analysis* to construct ranking functions. Let D denote a set of Web documents. Suppose that D is divided into two subsets according to a chosen application ontology A: a set of relevant documents R and another set of irrelevant documents $\bar{R}$ with respect to A, i.e.,

$$D = R \cup \bar{R}.$$

Two *probability density functions*, f_1 and f_2, are associated with the vector random variable X for describing the *probability distributions* of the relevant documents and the irrelevant documents, respectively. Let Ω be the set of all possible values on which the vector random variable X can take. Our goal is to separate Ω into two sets

$$\Omega = \Omega_1 \cup \Omega_2$$

such that a document d is classified as in the relevant set R when the value $x = X(d) \in \Omega_1$, whereas d is classified into the irrelevant set $\bar{R}$ when the value $x = X(d) \in \Omega_2$. However, misclassification often occurs and is associated with a cost. Let $C_{R\bar{R}}$ be the cost when a document in $\bar{R}$ is incorrectly classified as R, and let $C_{\bar{R}R}$ be the cost when a document in R is incorrectly classified as $\bar{R}$. The expected cost of misclassification (ECM) is given by

$$\text{ECM} = C_{RR}P(X \in \Omega_2|R)P(R) + C_{\bar{R}R}P(X \in \Omega_1|\bar{R})P(\bar{R}).$$

Here,

$$P(X \in \Omega_2|R) = \int_{\Omega_2} f_1(x)dx$$

is the probability of misclassification of relevant documents, and

$$P(X \in \Omega_1|\bar{R}) = \int_{\Omega_1} f_2(x)dx$$

is the probability of misclassification of irrelevant documents. Furthermore, $P(R)$ is the probability of relevant documents, and $P(\bar{R})$ is the probability of irrelevant documents such that $P(R) + P(\bar{R}) = 1$.

In order to achieve the best classification results, **ECM** must be minimized. Minimizing **ECM** yields the following classification rule:

Rule 1 (Classification Rule). Ω_1 and Ω_2 that minimize the **ECM** are defined by the value x for which the following inequality hold:

$$\Omega_1 : \frac{f_1(x)}{f_2(x)} \geq \left(\frac{C_{R\bar{R}}}{C_{\bar{R}R}}\right)\left(\frac{P(\bar{R})}{P(R)}\right),$$

$$\Omega_2 : \frac{f_1(x)}{f_2(x)} < \left(\frac{C_{R\bar{R}}}{C_{\bar{R}R}}\right)\left(\frac{P(\bar{R})}{P(R)}\right).$$

The geometric interpretation of this classification rule is that the relevant document vectors and irrelevant document vectors are separated by a *hyper-surface* given by

$$\left\{x \in \Omega : \frac{f_1(x)}{f_2(x)} = threshold = \left(\frac{C_{R\bar{R}}}{C_{\bar{R}R}}\right)\left(\frac{P(\bar{R})}{P(R)}\right)\right\}.$$

In order to apply this classification rule, we must estimate the probability density functions f_1 and f_2. In general, it is very difficult to estimate the probability density functions. A predominant statistical practice always assumes that density functions are *normal* because of their simplicity and reasonably high efficiency across a wide variety of models. Thus, we assume that f_1 and f_2 are *multivariate normal density functions*, the first one associated with mean vector μ_1 and covariance matrix Σ_1 and the second one associated with mean vector μ_2 and covariance matrix Σ_2, i.e., we assume that f_i, $1 \leq i \leq 2$, is of the form:

$$f_i(x) = \frac{1}{(2\pi)^{\frac{p}{2}}|\Sigma_i|^{\frac{1}{2}}}e^{-\frac{1}{2}(x-\mu_i)'\Sigma_i^{-1}(x-\mu_i)},$$

where

$|\Sigma_i|$ is the *determinant* of matrix Σ_i,
$(x - \mu_i)'$ is the *transpose* of $(x - \mu_i)$, and
Σ_i^{-1} is the *inverse matrix* of Σ_i.

Geometrically, the graph of a multivariate normal density function is a *bell-shape* surface, the mean vector is the *center* of the base of the "bell," and the covariant matrix measures the *slope* of the "bell." For relevant Web documents, the mean vector μ_1 is the "center" or "cluster" of the set of relevant documents, and the covariance matrix Σ_1 measures the *spread* of each index term and the association among different index terms.

In this paper, we study only the case when $\Sigma_1 = \Sigma_2 = \Sigma$, which determines the *linear classification rule*. In this case, the probability density $f_i(x)$, $1 \le i \le 2$, is given as

$$f_i(x) = \frac{1}{(2\pi)^{\frac{5}{2}} |\Sigma|^{\frac{1}{2}}} e^{\left[-\frac{1}{2}(x - \mu_i)' \Sigma^{-1}(x - \mu_i) \right]}.$$

Replacing $f_1(x)$ and $f_2(x)$ in Rule 1 by the above functions, we obtain

$$\Omega_1 : e^{\left[-\frac{1}{2}(x - \mu_1)' \Sigma^{-1}(x - \mu_1) + \frac{1}{2}(x - \mu_2)' \Sigma^{-1}(x - \mu_2) \right]} \ge \left(\frac{C_{R\bar{R}}}{C_{\bar{R}R}} \right) \left(\frac{P(\bar{R})}{P(R)} \right),$$

$$\Omega_2 : e^{\left[-\frac{1}{2}(x - \mu_1)' \Sigma^{-1}(x - \mu_1) + \frac{1}{2}(x - \mu_2)' \Sigma^{-1}(x - \mu_2) \right]} < \left(\frac{C_{R\bar{R}}}{C_{\bar{R}R}} \right) \left(\frac{P(\bar{R})}{P(R)} \right).$$

Applying log to both sides of the inequality and then simplifying it, the following rule is established:

Rule 2 (Linear Classification Rule). Document x is classified as relevant if

$$(\mu_1 - \mu_2)' \Sigma^{-1} x - \frac{1}{2}(\mu_1 - \mu_2)' \Sigma^{-1}(\mu_1 + \mu_2) \ge \log \left[\left(\frac{C_{R\bar{R}}}{C_{\bar{R}R}} \right) \left(\frac{P(\bar{R})}{P(R)} \right) \right].$$

Otherwise, x is classified as irrelevant.

We define $g_L(x)$, which is called a *linear discrimination function* or a *linear ranking function*, as

$$g_L(x) = (\mu_1 - \mu_2)' \Sigma^{-1} x - \frac{1}{2}(\mu_1 - \mu_2)' \Sigma^{-1}(\mu_1 + \mu_2).$$

The value of $g_L(x)$ reflects the retrieval status of document x. The quantity

$$\log \left[\left(\frac{C_{R\bar{R}}}{C_{\bar{R}R}} \right) \left(\frac{P(\bar{R})}{P(R)} \right) \right]$$

is a *threshold* for classification. Since the misclassification costs $C_{R\bar{R}}$ and $C_{\bar{R}R}$ and the *prior* probabilities $P(R)$ and $P(\bar{R})$ are very difficult to estimate, in practice a threshold is chosen by using a training set. The geometric interpretation of this linear classification rule is that the relevant document vectors and the irrelevant document vectors are separated by a *hyperplane* given by $g_L(x) = threshold$.

In most practical situations, since we do not know all the documents, the quantities μ_1 and μ_2, and Σ are unknown. However, we can estimate these quantities by using the training set. We show how to use the training set to obtain an approximation of the linear classification rule which we call a *sample linear classification rule*.

Suppose we have n_1 relevant documents

$$x_j, \quad j = 1, 2, \cdots n_1$$

and n_2 irrelevant documents

$$y_j, \quad j = 1, 2, \cdots n_2$$

such that $n_1 + n_2 - 2 \geq p$ and p is the dimension of vector x. From these data, the sample means and covariance matrices are given by

$$\tilde{\mu}_1 = \frac{1}{n_1} \sum_{j=1}^{n_1} x_j, \qquad \tilde{\Sigma}_1 = \frac{1}{n_1-1} \sum_{j=1}^{n_1} (x_j - \tilde{\mu}_1)(x_j - \tilde{\mu}_1)',$$

$$\tilde{\mu}_2 = \frac{1}{n_2} \sum_{j=1}^{n_2} y_j, \qquad \tilde{\Sigma}_2 = \frac{1}{n_2-1} \sum_{j=1}^{n_2} (y_j - \tilde{\mu}_2)(y_j - \tilde{\mu}_2)'.$$

Since we assume that the two density functions have the same covariance matrix Σ, we can combine the sample covariant matrices $\tilde{\Sigma}_1$ and $\tilde{\Sigma}_2$ to derive a single estimation of $\tilde{\Sigma}$, the weighted average, as

$$\tilde{\Sigma} = [\frac{n_1 - 1}{(n_1 - 1) + (n_2 - 1)}]\tilde{\Sigma}_1 + [\frac{n_2 - 1}{(n_1 - 1) + (n_2 - 1)}]\tilde{\Sigma}_2.$$

By replacing the mean μ_i in Rule 2 by the sample mean $\tilde{\mu}_i$ and the covariance matrix Σ by $\tilde{\Sigma}$, we have the sample classification rule.

Rule 3 (Sample Linear Classification Rule). Document x is classified to be relevant if

$$(\tilde{\mu}_1 - \tilde{\mu}_2)'\tilde{\Sigma}^{-1}x - \frac{1}{2}(\tilde{\mu}_1 - \tilde{\mu}_2)'\tilde{\Sigma}^{-1}(\tilde{\mu}_1 + \tilde{\mu}_2) \geq \log\left[\left(\frac{C_{R\bar{R}}}{C_{RR}}\right)\left(\frac{P(\bar{R})}{P(R)}\right)\right].$$

Otherwise, x is classified as irrelevant.

According to Rule 3, we define the sample linear discrimination (or *ranking*) function as

$$\tilde{g}_L(x) = (\tilde{\mu}_1 - \tilde{\mu}_2)'\tilde{\Sigma}^{-1}x - \frac{1}{2}(\tilde{\mu}_1 - \tilde{\mu}_2)'\tilde{\Sigma}^{-1}(\tilde{\mu}_1 + \tilde{\mu}_2).$$

3 Misclassification Probabilities

To evaluate the performance of our classification rules, we calculate their "error rates" or *misclassification probabilities*. Since we do not know all the multiple-record Web documents, the error rates that we compute are determined by the sample classification rules. We estimate the probabilities of misclassification and the precision of classification by a procedure called *Lachenbruch's "holdout" procedure*, and the expected misclassification probabilities are

$$P(\text{irrelevance} \mid \text{relevance}) = \frac{n_{1m}}{n_1}, \quad P(\text{relevance} \mid \text{irrelevance}) = \frac{n_{2m}}{n_2}$$

where

n_1 is the number of relevant documents in the training set T,
n_2 is the number of irrelevant documents in T,
n_{1m} is the number of relevant documents misclassified, and
n_{2m} is the number of irrelevant documents misclassified.

The expected error rate is defined as $Error Rate = \frac{n_{1m}+n_{2m}}{n_1+n_2}$, and the expected precision is defined as $Precision = 1 - Error Rate$.

4 Application Ontology and Representation of Documents

In this section, we review application ontologies [3] and construct representations for multiple-record Web documents.

4.1 Application Ontology

An application ontology is a conceptual model instance that describes a real world application of interest, augmented with semantic data information of constants and context keywords that are defined in the application ontology [3]. An application ontology consists of two components: an *ontological model instance* and *data frames*. The conceptual model adopted by us is the object-oriented systems model (OSM) [3]. An ontological model instance consists of object sets, relationship sets, participation constraints, and generalization/specialization. Figure 1 shows the ontological model instance for the car advertisements application in graphical form, and the entity of interest is Car that is marked by "$\rightarrow \bullet$".

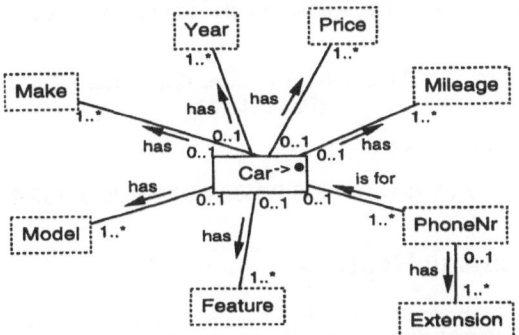

Figure 1: Graphical car advertisement ontology

An OSM *object* can be a person, place, or anything. It can be a physical or conceptual entity. Every OSM object is either *lexical* or *nonlexical*. A lexical object is an object whose representation is considered indistinguishable from the object itself (such as Make and Model in Figure 1). An object whose representation differs from the object itself is nonlexical (such as Car in Figure 1). Objects can be grouped into a set, which is called an *object set* and is denoted by a rectangle that encloses an object set name. Objects in an object set are either lexical or nonlexical. If an object set is lexical, the enclosing rectangle is dashed, and the corresponding set is called a *lexical object set*. If an object set is nonlexical, the enclosing rectangle's edges are solid lines, and the corresponding set is called a *nonlexical object set*.

An OSM *relationship* relates two or more objects. It has a name that describes the relationship. We denote a relationship among n objects by n connected lines, each attached to one of the n objects (such as Car has a Year in Figure 1). Relationships of the same type are grouped into a set which is called a *relationship set*. Binary relationship sets are specified by a *verb phrase* and a reading-direction *arrow*. N-ary relationships have a diamond and a full description name that includes the names of its connected object sets.

A *participation constraint* specifies the minimum and maximum number of times an object in an object set may participate in a relationship set. For example, the "1..*" near Mileage in Figure 1 denotes that a mileage must associate with at least one car.

4.2 Representation of Multiple-Record Web Documents

In this section, we show how to use an application ontology to represent multiple-record Web documents. Given an application ontology, we use a vector random variable $X = (X_1, X_2, \cdots, X_p)$ to represent each document under consideration. The names of the coordinates in X are the object-set names extracted from the application ontology. The value of each X_i, $1 \leq i \leq p$, of a document d is the frequency of occurrence of the corresponding object in d. We construct a document vector for a multiple-record Web document based on the car advertisements application ontology as

$$(Year, Make, Model, Mileage, Price, Feature, PhoneNr).$$

The value of each component is the *frequency of occurrence* of the object in a multiple-record Web document. For example, let's consider a multiple-record Web document d on car advertisements with a total of 60 records and the number of occurrences of each object is given by

(Year; 62), (Make; 58), (Model; 48), (Mileage; 12), (Price; 58), (Feature; 49), and (PhoneNr; 33).

Hence, the vector representation of d is

$$(62, 58, 48, 12, 58, 49, 33)/60 = (1.0333, 0.9667, 0.8000, 0.2000, 0.9667, 0.8167, 0.5500).$$

5 Experimental Results

We apply the classification rules introduced in Section 2 to a training set and a testing set of multiple-record Web documents on car advertisements. The training set contains 20 relevant documents and 20 irrelevant documents, whereas the testing set contains 10 relevant documents and 20 irrelevant documents. We use the training set to compute the coefficients of the linear ranking function and determine thresholds. Hereafter, we apply the testing set to evaluate our results. Table 1 show the results obtained by using the linear ranking function $\tilde{g}_L(x)$ and the Vector Space Model (VSM). The results indicate that the *linear classification rule* performs better than VSM. Following the Lachenbruch's "holdout" procedure, we obtained the linear discriminate function $\tilde{g}_L(x)$ which yielded the precision = 85%, whereas the precision for the Vector Space Model is 77.5%.

6 Conclusions

In this paper, we present a probabilistic model to classify multiple-record Web documents into classes: the class of relevant documents and another class of irrelevant documents with respect to a particular application ontology. Our model is based on the *multivariant statistical analysis*, and the experimental results are better than ones obtained by the Vector Space Model. It shows that our probabilistic model is a promising model. Furthermore, our approach can be extended to classify multiple-record Web documents into several classes.

Relevant Web Documents — Irrelevant Web Documents

Doc	$\tilde{g}_L(x)$	Rel	VSM	Rel	Doc	$\tilde{g}_L(x)$	Rel	VSM	Rel	Doc	$\tilde{g}_L(x)$	Rel	VSM	Rel
d_1	-1.07	no	0.93	yes	d_{11}	-2.97	no	0.54	no	d_{21}	-3.20	no	0.46	no
d_2	-0.41	no	0.79	yes	d_{12}	-5.46	no	0.42	no	d_{22}	-1.20	no	0.75	yes
d_3	0.93	yes	0.88	yes	d_{13}	-3.27	no	0.55	no	d_{23}	-5.85	no	0.37	no
d_4	2.13	yes	0.98	yes	d_{14}	-4.35	no	0.45	no	d_{24}	-3.63	no	0.83	yes
d_5	3.21	yes	0.88	yes	d_{15}	-4.64	no	0.46	no	d_{25}	-5.12	no	0.50	no
d_6	2.64	yes	0.93	yes	d_{16}	-4.43	no	0.45	no	d_{26}	5.28	yes	0.56	no
d_7	3.08	yes	0.94	yes	d_{17}	-1.96	no	0.52	no	d_{27}	-0.32	no	0.77	yes
d_8	3.52	yes	0.96	yes	d_{18}	-3.42	no	0.53	no	d_{28}	-0.41	no	0.62	yes
d_9	-1.54	no	0.88	yes	d_{19}	-5.66	no	0.32	no	d_{29}	3.74	yes	0.66	yes
d_{10}	3.23	yes	0.99	yes	d_{20}	-4.05	no	0.46	no	d_{30}	7.85	yes	0.87	yes

Table 1: Results on the testing set, where *Rel* stands for "relevance"

References

[1] Anderson, T. W. *An Introduction to Multivariate Statistical Methods*. John Wiley, New York, 1984.

[2] Crestani, F. and van Rijsbergen, C. J. *A Study of Probability Kinetmatics in Information Retrieval*. ACM Trans. Inf. Syst. 16(3), 225-255, 1998.

[3] Embley, D. W. *Object Database Development: Concepts and Principles*. Addison Wesley Longman, 1998.

[4] Embley, D. W., Campbell, D. M., Jiang, Y., Liddle, S. W., Lonsdale,D. W., Ng, Y.-K., and Smith, R. D. *Conceptual-Model-Based Data Extraction from Multiple-Record Web Pages*, Journal of Data and Knowledge Engineering. 31(3), 227-251, 1999.

[5] Fuhr, N. *The Probabilistic Models in Information Retrieval*. Comput. J. 35(3), 243-255, June 1992.

[6] Fuhr, N. and Buckley, C. *A Probabilistic Learning Approach for Document Indexing*. ACM Trans. Inf. Syst. 9(3), 223-248, 1991.

[7] Növert, N., Lalmas, M., and Fuhr, N. *A Probabilistic Description-Oriented Approach for Categorising Web Documents*. Preprint, 1999.

[8] Johnson, R. A. and Wichern, D. W. *Applied Multivariante Statistical Analysis*. Prentice-Hall Inc., New Jersey, 1998.

[9] Kendall, M. G. *Multivariate Analysis*. Hafner Press, New York, 1975.

[10] Salton, G. and McGill, M. J. *Introduction to Modern Information Retrieval*, McGraw-Hill, New York, 1983.

[11] van Rijsbergen, C. J. *Information Retrieval*. Butterworths, London, U. K., 1979.

[12] Wong, S. K. M. and Yao, Y. Y.] *On Modeling Information Retrieval with Probabilistic Inference*. ACM Trans. Inf. Syst. 13(1), 38-68, 1995.

Constructing Language Processors using Object-Oriented Techniques

David Basanta , Cándida Luengo, Raul Izquierdo, J. Emilio Labra, and J. Manuel Cueva

Department of Computer Science
University of Oviedo
Calvo Sotelo, s/n, 33007 Oviedo- SPAIN
E-mail: basanta@ieee.org, {candi,ric,labra,cueva}@lsi.uniovi.es   FAX: 34-8 5103354

ABSTRACT. *Language processors are not only important for the construction of compilers and interpreters but also for an increasing number of applications that relay on XML parsers like e-commerce software or grammar checkers like word processors.*
Compiler construction tools have proven to be very useful for programmers and language designers although traditional tools have not seen much improvement in recent years. What is more important, those tools have bypassed the object-oriented revolution. This is particularly unfortunate because compilers, being complex systems, would definitely benefit from the modularity and code reuse that object orientation allows.
In this paper, an object-oriented framework generator called O2C2 is presented. The tool has the potential to improve the quality of compiler construction by introducing the concept of frameworks in the field of compilers and language processors.

KEY WORDS: *Compiler, Object-Oriented techniques, Framework, Pattern, YACC, JavaCC, ANTLR, SableCC, O2C2*

1. Introduction

From the 1970s on, compilers are developed with the help of scanner and parser generators, YACC (Johnson, 1975) being the most popular of them. However few things have changed since the first tools, also called compiler compilers, were introduced. These tools have a number of problems in the way they operate and in the way that the analysers they generate are designed.

In this paper, we present a tool called **O2C2** (Object Oriented Compiler Compiler) that brings into the world of compiler compilers some of the advancements that have appeared in computer science in the last two decades.

The paper is organised as follows. In section 2 we describe several problems with traditional compiler construction tools. In section 3 we study how object oriented techniques could help solving those problems. In section 4 we explain other features. In section 5 we discuss related work. In section 6 we describe future work and in section 7 some conclusions are presented.

2. Drawbacks of compiler construction tools

Classical tools used in the construction of language processors, like Lex (Lesk, 1975) and YACC

(Johnson, 1975) and versions of these tools ported to Java like Jlex (Berk, 2000) and CUP (Hudson, 2000) present a number of problems:

- They read a specification that contains both the grammar of the language and the actions associated with each alternative of an element in the grammar. This is fundamental flaw due to its lack of modularity.

- Action code embedded in parsers is very difficult to debug. The source of this difficulty is the abstraction required to understand the operation of a table-based LALR parser.

- It is necessary both to compile the specification file and the resulting code to find errors.

- The lack of support for Abstract Syntax Trees (ASTs) makes it difficult for developers to write multiple-pass language processors for complex grammars.

Other tools like JavaCC (Sun, 2000) and ANTLR (Megelang, 2000) that are widely used today, generate parsers for Java applications. Some *drawbacks* of using these tools are:

- The specifications tend to become huge and debugging actions involve the following steps: writing action code, compiling the specification file, compiling the resulting code, executing the resulting program, locating the errors and looking back in the specification file for the related erroneous action code.

- The flexibility of predicates could generate a very high cost in performance.

- Syntactic and semantic predicates are an integral part of the resulting grammar. This obscures the grammar.

- The responsibility of keeping the specification and the generated code synchronized is left to the programmer.

3. Applying object-oriented techniques in compiler construction. O2C2

Compilers are expected to work with a source text through a series of stages and that makes it easy to think about procedural techniques.

A **framework** is a reusable design of all or part of a software system described by a set of abstract classes and the way that instances of those classes collaborate (Roberts *et al., 1997*). This means that we can develop a set of classes designed to work together and with other external classes.

It is easy to see how frameworks could be used to improve the process of developing language processors and compilers. A framework can reduce the cost of development by making easier to reuse the design and the code in a well-defined domain such as language processor development. Unfortunately this is not true, compilers operate in a number of stages that are common, but the differences between languages are so important that it is impractical to design a framework for language processors.

Another approach has been taken to develop O2C2 so those problems could be addressed. A well-defined set of classes is necessary in a framework in order to achieve a level of consistency between the different software applications that could be using that framework. On the other hand, a sufficient level of flexibility is also a must because otherwise the compiler would not adapt to the language it is designed for.

The aim of O2C2 is to help developers create recursive descent parsers by generating a specific black-box framework from a given syntactic specification of the language. This framework will complement a white-box framework that is common for all the frameworks that O2C2 will generate.

O2C2 generated classes are organised around a framework that represents an AST (Abstract Syntax Tree). This AST's nodes will be strictly typed so the data cannot be corrupted which helps reducing debugging time.

3.1. The framework generator

The best way to achieve a valid solution was to design a tool to create frameworks. That is, given a grammatical specification of the language whose compiler or processor we want to build, the tool should generate a framework tailored exclusively for that language. The user should use the classes to compose a parser and create some new classes to give a semantic meaning to the language processor.

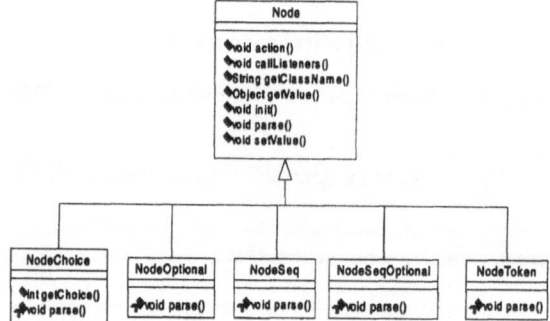

Figure 1: Core Framework in UML notation

3.2. The root framework

Each time O2C2 creates a new framework, it doesn't need to begin from zero, O2C2 relays on the O2C2-RT (O2C2 Run Time). O2C2-RT is the core of the framework (as shown in figure 1) and it allows a level of consistency between the language processors of different languages.

Node is the root of every framework. When an O2C2-based analyser is used, a syntax tree is generated so any token found in the input automatically becomes an instance of a class that inherits from Node. Node also has methods that are common in every node in the AST.

The rest of the classes are designed to work with the different elements that could appear in a grammar expressed in EBNF notation. For instance, a subclass of **NodeChoice** is created to treat each of the alternatives that a non-terminal element in the grammar could have.

NodeOptional is the super class of all the classes that treat the elements of the grammar whose appearance is not mandatory.

NodeSeq's subclasses represent a sequence of elements of the grammar; let them be terminals, non-terminals or EBNF elements that will be discussed later.

NodeSeqOptional is very similar in concept to NodeSeq but this time the existence of the sequence of grammatical elements is just optional.

NodeToken doesn't have subclasses. Its mission is to read the terminals of the syntax tree created by the parser at run-time.

The implementation of the *parse()* method is the main difference between the different subclasses of **Node**.

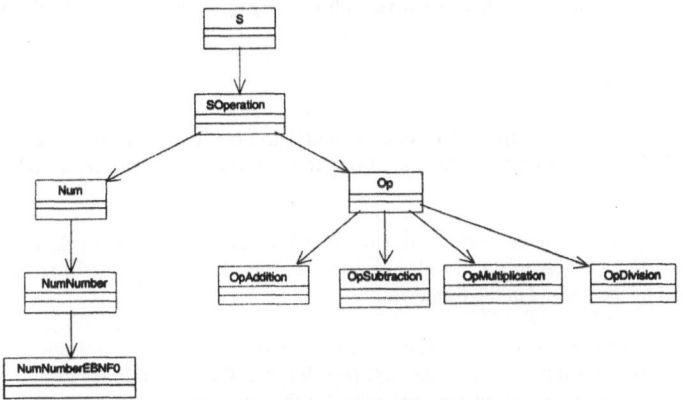

Figure 2: Object diagram in UML

3.3. The grammar-specific classes

With the framework just described, it would be difficult to build a compiler, or at least, it wouldn't be a significant advantage to use the framework. But O2C2 is not only a framework, it is, a framework generator. With these classes and the framework, the user can obtain a working parser.

As an example, consider the following grammar.

```
<S>    ::= "Operation" <Num> <Op> <Num> ;
<Op>   ::= "Addition" + | "Subtraction" - | "Multiplication" * | "Division" / ;
<Num>  ::= "Number" DIGIT {DIGIT} ;
```

The diagram of figure 2 shows that for each element of the grammar a class is generated. For instance, each non-terminal generates a class whose name is the same as the non-terminal. Each alternative that belongs to a non-terminal generates a class whose name is a composition of the name of the non-terminal and the name of the alternative. Of course, all these classes are descendants from the interfaces and classes that compose the core framework.

S is a subclass of *NodeChoice*. On the other hand **SOperation** is a subclass of *NodeSeq*, which means that to parse *SOperation* we first have to parse **num** (two times) and **Op**.

NumNumberEBNF0 is a subclass of *NodeSeqOptional* and its name comes from the fact that there is an EBNF repetition that occupies the first position in the alternative called *Number* that belongs to the non-terminal called *Num*. The only EBNF element is *{DIGIT}*, so what this class will do when invoked is parse while there is a *DIGIT* to be read at the input.

This diagram also represents the calling dependencies between the different classes generated from the grammar provided by the user of O2C2. The process of parsing a source text whose structure follows a grammar previously defined means calling the *parse()* method of the first class in the object diagram, in the previous example this was class S. From this class, the parser continues calling the *parse()* method of class **SOperation** all the way down to a class that calls a *NodeToken*.

3.4. Adding user code to the parser

O2C2 not only provides a core framework and generates classes to complement it; it has some utility classes so when O2C2 finishes its work the user already has a working analyser ready to be compiled.

When a parser generated by O2C2 reduces it an expression, it calls an object provided by the user if there is one. So what the user has to do in order to provide some functionality is to create objects that can be called by the classes in the framework.

This way of adding code to the framework is also known as the **listener pattern,** and it is popular among Java programmers because it is present in the JFC (Fowler, 2000) framework. By using it, O2C2 allows not only the co-existence of classes provided by the user and its own classes but also the communication between both types of classes.

The listener pattern works like this: there are classes that are **event sources** and other classes that are **event listeners.** The former are the classes generated by the O2C2 system, the later are the classes created by the user. The listener classes demonstrate their interest in a specific type of event by subscribing to the classes that generate that event. When an event source class eventually generates an event, it calls a method in all the listener classes that have made a subscription to that event source class.

The analyser generated by O2C2 parses a source text trying to match the input with an element of the grammar. When successful, an event is generated. This event may or may not be interesting to the user. If it is, the user should create a class that registers to this event. In the example of the calculator we can create a class that will be subscribed to events generated by **NumNumber.** This means that every time the parser finds a group of tokens organised as described by the alternative called **Number,** that belongs to the non-terminal called **Num,** then a special method of the user's class, called *performAction()*, will be called. In this method the user can do what she needs, and when it finishes the parsing is resumed.

As opposed to other tools, the user doesn't have to create classes for all the events that can appear in the parsing process. When an event hasn't got a listener subscribed then a default action is performed. This way of doing things frees the user from having to create action code that doesn't provide anything meaningful to the parsing process.

The flexibility of the event delegation approach has many advantages. An object can register or de-register at run-time depending on the circumstances of the source that has already been parsed. A grammar can be used with two or more sets of classes provided by the user. Compilers that work in various passes can be developed easily just registering and de-registering some classes. A group of user classes that deal with the same syntactic structure can be reused effortlessly.

The separation of the grammar specification from the action code means that a change in one of the sides won't affect the other. For example, whenever a change is made to the action code, the specification has to be run through the YACC program and then through the C compiler. In O2C2, when a change is made in the action code, only one class file has to be recompiled. This has the potential to greatly shorten the edit-compile-debug cycle as shown by the diagram of figure 3.

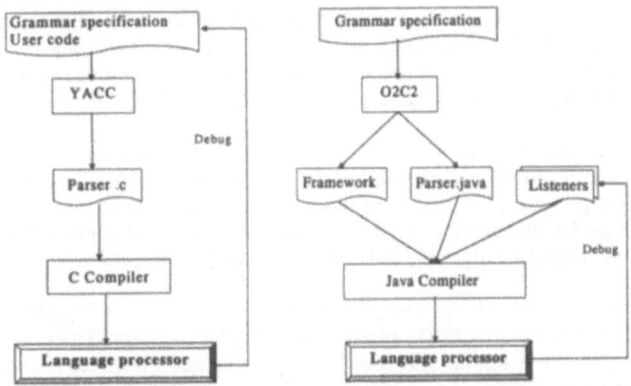

Figure 3: Traditional versus modern Compiler Construction tools

4. Other features of O2C2

O2C2 has evolved over time and is no longer just a tool but a set of tools. Also there are some features that are worth mentioning.

- **Error handling and recovery** uses the same listener pattern. By default, when an O2C2 generated parser finds an error, it displays a meaningful error message and exits, but it is very easy to add extra code that will make the parser fault-tolerant.

- **Action code** in O2C2 is placed in one or more classes that must be created by the users. While this allows a level of modularity that has long-term beneficial effects, lazy users could be not willing to do such an effort. The tool can create skeletons for the listener classes if the user wants it.

- We have developed a small **Graphical User Interface** front-end that makes O2C2 easier to use, more convenient and also more integrated with lexical tool generator.

- We have also created **O2C2Conv**, a version of the O2C2 tool that allows the user to add action code avoiding the need to identify the different elements of the grammar. The user has to add links, that is, quoted words, in the sections of the grammar where she would like her listener classes to be called. Then, the listener classes only have to subscribe to classes whose name is that of the link.

5. Related work

Recently, there have been some attempts to introduce object-oriented techniques in the field of compiler construction. One of the most interesting examples is SableCC (Gagnon et al., 1998).

O2C2 and SableCC have some things in common, beginning with the use of frameworks, but there are also some important differences. O2C2 has a core framework that acts as a run-time and that is present across all parsers that have been generated by O2C2.

SableCC's grammatical specification is bigger because it includes both the lexical and the syntactical specifications while O2C2's specification consists only in the syntactical specification. The reason behind this decision is that we wanted to make O2C2 more modular and let the lexical analysis to specific tools like Jlex (Berk, 2000) or Jflex (Klein , 1999).

The way of integrating user's code is also different. SableCC generates a framework that represents an AST and the user has to build a tree-walker class for it. On the other hand, the framework generated by O2C2 parses a source-text and when it finds something of interest it calls the class or classes generated by the user that have shown interest in that kind of event. We feel that O2C2's approach is more modular, dynamic and flexible than that of SableCC.

People with experience with the SaX API (Megginson, 2000) and XML parser (Apache, 2000), can see some parallelisms between the way O2C2 parsers work and SaX parsers. The event delegation mechanism of O2C2 is present in the JFC (Fowler, 2000) and SaX's interface is also event-based. This means that those people, who already know how to use a SaX parser, also know the basic principles that rule the behaviour of an O2C2- generated parser and therefore should be able to develop their own custom-made parsers in almost no time.

6. Future Work

O2C2 is work in progress. Anyway there are some areas where the authors of O2C2 are now focusing:

- Make O2C2 **language-independent**. Right now, the O2C2 run-time uses Java and the code it generates is in Java too, we plan to make O2C2 able to generate, at least, C++ code.

- **Modular development of programming languages** with the aim of rapidly prototyping domain specific languages (ACM, 2000). This modularity can be achieved separating the language semantics (Gayo et al., 1999) or though the different aspects of the processor (De Moor et al., 1999). It seems a promising area for future research.

7. Conclusions

Compiler construction tools have in most cases failed to take advantage of object oriented techniques. The use of such techniques has the potential to ease the modularity and code reusability. It could also reduce the length of the code written by the programmer, shorten the development time and make the code easier to read and maintain.

The introduction of frameworks and patterns in the field of compiler and language processor construction, will undoubtedly foster the use of object oriented techniques in the same way that frameworks fostered the use of object oriented techniques in the field of graphical user interfaces. This will mean that language processors will appear in more development projects, as they get increasingly easier to develop and maintain.

We feel that O2C2 has the potential to increase the productivity of programmers and the quality of their products as compared with traditional compiler construction tools. At the same time, we think it is easy to learn and most programmers already know the concepts it uses. For all those reasons, we believe that O2C2 could be successfully used with new projects either large or small. We have developed a prototype implementation in Java, which will be available in *http://www.uniovi.es/~oviedo3/*

8. References

(ACM, 2000):   *Proceedings of the USENIX Conference on Domain Specific Languages*, 1999. ACM SIGPLAN vol. 35, 1, January 2000.

(Apache, 2000):   *Apache XML project.* URL: http://xml.apache.org

(Berk, 2000):   E. Berk. *Jlex: A Lexical analyser generator for Java™.* World-Wide Web page URL:http://www.cs.princeton.edu/~appel/modern/java/JLex/

(De Moor et al., 1999):O. De Moor, S. Peyton-Junes, E. Van Wyk. *Aspect Oriented Compilers.* First International Symposium on Generative and Component-Based Software Engineering. LNCS, Springer-Verlag, 1999.

(Fowler, 2000):   Amy Fowler. *A Swing architecture overview. The inside story on JFC Component Design.* . Sun Microsystems. Jun 2000. URL: http://java.sun.com/products/jfc/tsc/articles/architecture/index.html

(Gagnon et al., 1998):E. Gagnon, L. Hendren. *SableCC, an Object-Oriented Compiler Framework.* McGill University, Quebec, Canada. June 1998.

(Gayo et al., 1999):J.E. Labra Gayo, J.M. Cueva Lovelle, M.C. Luengo Díez. *Language Prototyping using modular monadic semantics.* 3rd Latin-American Conference on Functional Programming. Recife, Brasil. March 1999.

(Hudson, 2000):   S.E. Hudson. *CUP parser generator for Java™.* World-Wide Web page URL: http://www.cs.princeton.edu/~appel/modern/java/CUP/

(Johnson, 1975):   S.C. Johnson. *YACC – yet another compiler compiler*. Technical Report Computing Science Technical Report 32, AT&T Bell Laboratories. Murray Hill, N.J.,1975.

(Klein , 1999):   Gerwin Klein. *JFlex user's manua*". URL: http://www.jflex.de. July 1999.

(Lesk, 1975):   M. E. Lesk. *Lex – a lexical analyzer generator*. Technical Report Computing Science Technical Report 39, AT&T Bell Laboratories. Murray Hill, N.J.,1975.

(Megelang, 2000):   Megelang Institute. *ANTLR 2.7.0.* World-Wide Web page URL: http://www.antlr.org/

(Megginson, 2000):David Megginson. *SAX 2.0: The Simple API for XML.* May 2000. URL: http://www.megginson.com/SAX/index.html

(Roberts *et al., 1997*):D. Roberts, R. Ralph Johnson. *Evolving Frameworks: A pattern language for developing object oriented frameworks*. University of Illinois, 1997.

(Sun, 2000):   *JavaCC™.*
URL:http://www.cs.ukc.ac.uk/teaching/resources/java/javacc/DOC/

Architecture as Object Models of Software*

Eyðun Eli Jacobsen

The Maersk Mc-Kinney Moller Institute for Production Technology
University of Southern Denmark/Odense University
DK 5230 Odense M, Denmark
e-mail: jacobsen@mip.sdu.dk

ABSTRACT: Typically, we think of modelling some business domain when we see the word modelling in the context of software — some business domain is not understood and therefore we build models of it to express our understanding of the business domain. In this paper we think of the software domain as the domain that is not understood and therefore we build models of it to express our understanding of the software domain.

We present a model universe that illustrates our view on modelling in general, and we use the model universe and the domains to discuss models of software. Our discussion revolves around the familiar object modelling technique to express of models of software. The object modelling technique is discussed in terms of mechanisms in a special OO language and in terms of UML. We exemplify by representing abstractions such as design patterns in OO software.

We conclude that describing software architecture should be understood as a subdicipline of building models of software, and that OO principles are well-suited for modelling the software domain.

KEYWORDS: Software Architecture, Object Oriented Modelling, Design Patterns

---

1. Introduction

Software is a complex artefact in which many aspects are integrated, or tangled. The complexity of software, which makes software development and evolution difficult, stems from the size of the software together with contemporary ways of building software. Owing to the complexity it is difficult to understand the consequences of changes to the software. Changes to the software may, if they haven't been analysed well, have to be redone when new additions are in line. The complexity of software is a part of the reason for many ad-hoc additions — either the developers don't know that their change is an ad-hoc change (time will tell) or the software developers are aware of the fact, but it will be too difficult or expensive to make the change in a sustainable way.

---

* This research was supported by the Danish National Centre for IT Research, Project No. 74.

Separation of concerns, which is a technique for dealing with complexity, is about treating different concerns in isolation thereafter to integrated in the process of developing software. Separation of concerns is essentially about building models in order to simplify a problem.

Before reasoning about a concern in an effective manner, appropriate concepts must be defined — a set of concepts for conceiving the concern at hand must be formed. Software developers and researchers have discovered many concepts that can be used to get a less complicated understanding of software systems. Examples of such concepts can be found in the many contributions within the field of software architecture, e. g. [Gamma et al., 1995] and [Shaw and Garlan, 1996] (a particular kind of concepts is represented by the field of design patterns [Gamma et al., 1995]). From a separation-of-concerns perspective, research on software architecture can be seen as work on forming concepts for conceiving specific aspects of software. Closely coupled to the work on concept formation is the work on notations for expressing the models that are formed in terms of the newly defined concepts.

In this paper we demonstrate that OO principles are useful for reasoning about architecture, and we illustrate that notations based on object oriented principles can be used to express architectural information. The consequences of using object oriented notations are that a set of objects together with a class model constitute an architectural representation.

Paper Organisation. The remains of this paper is organised as follows: Section 2 presents our overall view on software architecture — this serves as a context for our argument. When discussing models of software we need a general frame of reference for the notion of modelling — this is presented in Section 3. In Section 4 presents the notion of software modelling through a specific kind of models (OO models) and the relationship between the software artefacts and the model artefacts is explored. In Section 5 we discuss how the software modelling ideas fit to UML and we point out how UML should be supported if used according to these ideas. Related Work is described in Section 6, and finally, the conclusion is found in Section 7.

2. Architecture as Models of Software.

Typically, we think of modelling some business domain when we see the word modelling used in the context of software, e. g. some business domain is not understood and therefore we build models of it to express our understanding of the business domain. But in this paper we think of the software domain as the domain that is not understood and therefore we build models of it to express our understanding of the software domain.

As software systems are becoming larger and more complex, developers need to build models of the software in order to reason about the software they construct. In particular, developers need new *kinds* of models that embody new concepts for comprehending the software, because the existing models do not expose all relevant aspects of the software.

The notion of Software Architecture that we use in this paper is described in the following works: [Jacobsen et al., 1999], [Jacobsen, 2000], and [Nowack, 2000]. Central to this view on software architecture are the concepts *software domain* and *development domain*. The inspiration to these concepts are the concepts *problem domain* and *application domain* which are described in [Mathiassen et al., 1993] and in [Mathiassen et al., 2000].

The notions of problem domain and application domain are relative to a user of a software system. We regard the software developer to be a user that uses software development tools in his work. The software domain is the problem domain of the software developer, and the development domain is the application domain of the software developer (Figure 1).

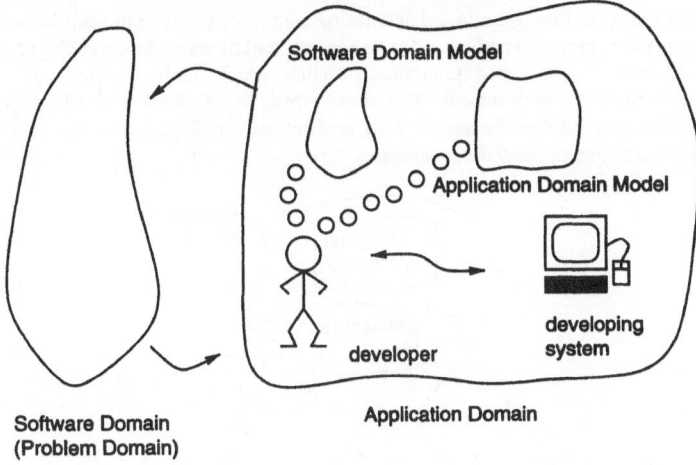

Figure 1: The Problem Domain and the Application Domain for a software developer.

The software domain comprises the software artefacts that are built and used by the developer. The developer's understanding of the software domain, comprises contemporary concepts for comprehending software together with an understanding of the actual system being developed.

The development domain comprises the software development organisation or part of it. The developer's understanding of the application domain, comprises contemporary concepts for comprehending the process in which software development takes place together with an understanding of the actual software development effort.

> We see architecture as abstractions of the software domain and architectural descriptions as models of software.

The phrase "models of software" that we use throughout this paper implies that there exists (or is anticipated) some software in some form such as notations/diagrams. Furthermore there exists other descriptions that contain a model of the software.

When characterising a modelling situation we can consider the modelling perspective and the notation as two essential characteristics. The modelling perspective specifies the aspect of the system to portray in the model, and the notation is the means by which we represent a model. There are many kinds of perspectives and notations. In this paper we focus on one particular type of models, namely object oriented models (in [Jacobsen, 2000] other types of models of software are discussed). The perspective is not coupled to the general OO notation, but in this paper we use a pattern-perspective on the software.

3. Modelling

When human beings interact with some part of their environment, they need to understand their environment in order to have meaningful and desirable interactions with the environment. But the environment is too complex to understand in its entirety, and therefore human beings build models of the environment. A *model* is some familiar structure, which can be used to analyse, to understand, and to control the environment. The model which is a simplification of the environment focuses on and exposes a specific aspect of the environment. In Figure 2 we have illustrated our view on what the notion of *modelling* comprises.

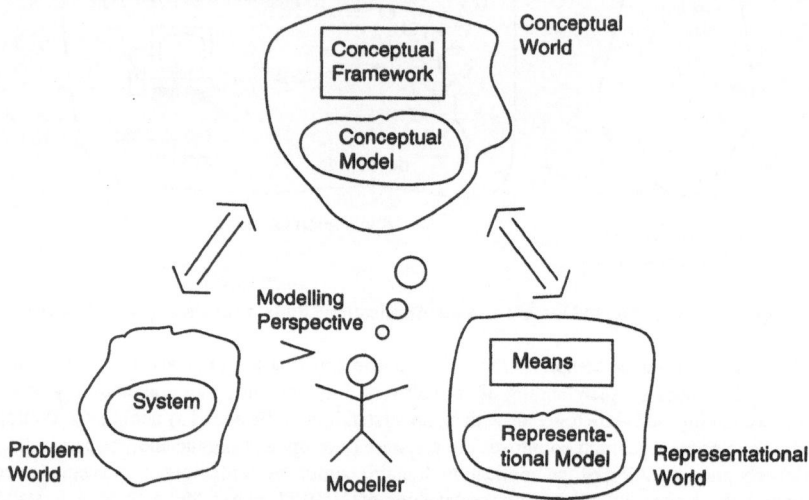

Figure 2: Model Universe

Three worlds are depicted in Figure 2: a *problem world*, which comprises the situation seen as problematical; a *conceptual world*, which comprises the conceptual models of the system and the conceptual framework on which the conceptual model is founded; and a *representational world*, which contains a representation of our conceptual models and the representational means used to form representational models. The conceptual model is a part of a modeller's mind, and it is transient in nature, i. e. the conceptual model is private — restricted to the individual modeller. By forming a representational model the modeller makes the conceptual model explicit and lasting; the representational model is shared in the sense that it is available to other modellers and it can be used as a means in communication between modellers — the original modeller also benefits from a representational model since the modeller can re-create his conceptual model of the system. Furthermore, a representational model is not confined to human interpretation — if it is precise it can also be processed by a computer. In essence, we state:

Modelling = Abstraction + Representation

3.1. OO Modelling

Since we will use OO Modelling principles in later Section we introduce our view on OO modelling here. OO modelling theory (as represented by [Madsen et al., 1993]) states that systems are conceived in terms of *phenomena* and *concepts*. When making a conceptual model of the system the modeller identifies phenomena in the system and he creates mental phenomena in the conceptual world (the modeller's mind). A phenomenon in the conceptual model is a manifestation of the fact that a part of the system is regarded in a specific way. The properties that the modeller associates with the phenomena in the conceptual world are dependent on the modelling perspective, which in turn is determined by the purpose of the model.

The conceptual model, consisting of concepts and phenomena, is the result of an abstraction process ([Madsen et al., 1993] and [Kristensen and Østerbye, 1994]), a process in which phenomena and concepts are interrelated in specific ways. The properties associated with the phenomena in the conceptual world are used to reason about the system. We point out that we do not state anything about *order* in the creative processes in which phenomena and concepts in the conceptual model are created.

The phenomena and the concepts in the conceptual world are represented by objects and classes in the representational model. As for general modelling, the object model (the representational model) helps us to reason about the system being modelled by exposing a specific aspect of the system as properties of the objects in the object model.

Example 3.1: Room Reservation

> Consider a hotel reservation system. The reservation system contains a model of the building; the model contains information about the rooms in the hotel building. A customer asks for a standard-room. The clerk checks the model for a vacancy. An object which models a standard room is found. In order to find the actual room in the building, the customer needs to know where it is, and therefore the object that models the room must contain a reference, e. g. in the form of a room number, to the room. ☐

The example illustrates that an object contains two principally different kinds of information: it contains a reference to the phenomenon it models, and it contains information about the room (the room is a standard-room). The objects that model rooms could have a room-category property which in the above case had to be associated with the value standard-room.

4. Object Models of Software and OO Notations

Below we use the modelling universe and the view on OO modelling presented above to discuss modelling of the software domain.

4.1. OO Models of Software

One particular type of models are object oriented models known from OO programming languages and notations such as UML [OMG, 1999]. OO modelling, which is a general modelling technique, can also be used to build models of software. In Figure 3 we have depicted the modelling universe where the complex artefact that we try to understand is the software. The conceptual framework and the notation are based on object oriented principles (we will return to this Figure in Section 4.2 where we will describe its contents).

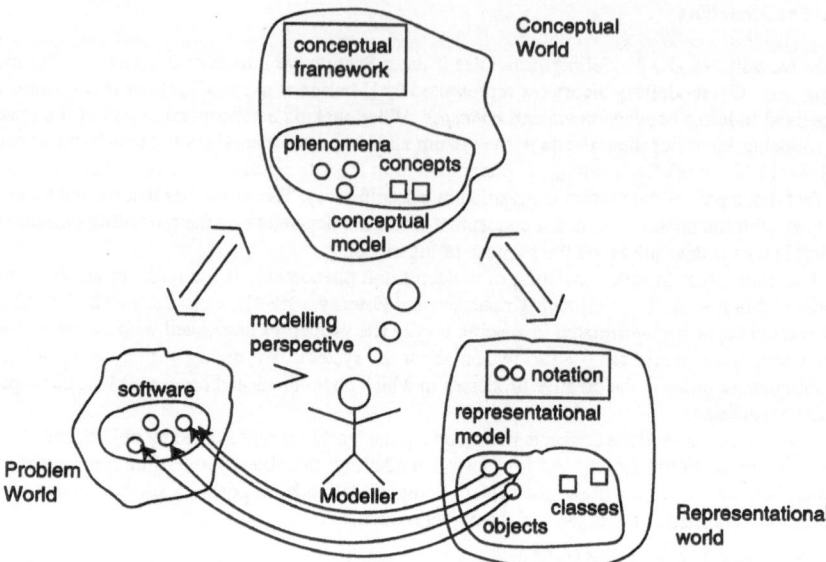

Figure 3: Modelling Software using OO modelling techniques.

Explicit Connections In order to say anything about some software (an artefact) on the basis of a model it is necessary to ensure that the model is a valid model of the software. The relationship between some software and a model of the software can be of various kinds. We mention two kinds: One kind is an informal relationship, which means that human analysis and judgement are needed in order to verify that the model is a valid model of the software. Another kind of relationship is an explicit relationship which means that there are well-defined associations between model elements and elements in the software.

In our work we have focused on explicit connections between the model and the software because we wanted a well-defined relationship and because explicit connections in the form of special references fit well to object oriented modelling.

Example 4.1: Design Patterns

Consider the notion of design patterns [Gamma et al., 1995]. Design patterns are often discussed in the context of being a solution to a problem. Here, we only focus on design patterns as abstractions over OO software. We assume that the system consists of program code in the form of some structured representation.

A design pattern, e. g. STATE, is a general design idea, and it is a concept in conceptual models of programs. A specific instance of the STATE design pattern is an abstraction over a program and it exemplifies the concept STATE design pattern.

To make a representational model of the program with focus on the STATE design pattern we need to describe the design pattern. We will include the three parts of the description. 1) attributes referring to elements in the considered system (elements in the software) over which the design pattern instance is abstracted, 2) attributes referring to related design pattern instances (none in this example), and 3) statements about the elements in the system — this could be that various relations between the elements should hold. □

4.2. OO Modelling Notation

We present a notation that is based upon the principles presented above. The purpose of this is to give the ideas a more concrete and precise form which we then can use to discuss and understand various approaches to building models of software. In particular, we will in Section 5 used these ideas to characterise parts of UML.

The general OO modelling notation is called the Fragment Language ($\mathcal{FL}$). The $\mathcal{FL}$ is not a complete language and as such it is not a contribution per se, but it represents essential mechanisms of a modelling language that can express relations and explicit connection to the software. The $\mathcal{FL}$ should be regarded as exposing principal parts of a notation for expressing models of software — the concrete form of the $\mathcal{FL}$ used here such as textual syntax should not be regarded as an essential aspect of the language.

The $\mathcal{FL}$ describes abstractions by expressing relationships between explicitly selected elements in the software and by using existing descriptions of abstractions. The kind of abstractions that the $\mathcal{FL}$ has been used to describe are exemplified by the work in [Gamma et al., 1995] and in [Pree, 1995].

The $\mathcal{FL}$ is based on OO principles. It is built on concepts that are pendants to the programming language concepts of class, object, inheritance, and attributes. The mechanisms have been derived from a set of experiments on abstraction, constraints, etc. To support the $\mathcal{FL}$ we envision some environment that administers the fragment classes and the fragment objects. The $\mathcal{FL}$ (together with an environment) is a representational means for representing conceptual models of software. Specific fragment classes and fragment objects (within the environment) constitute a representational model of the considered software.

Below we will present key aspects of the $\mathcal{FL}$: class/object distinction, object references, element references, and constraints. This presents our vision of principal ingredients of an object model representing architectural information.

4.2.1. Fragment Classes and Fragment Objects

A representational model based on the $\mathcal{FL}$ contains a set of fragment classes and a set of fragment objects. The fragment classes represent the concept-part of a conceptual model while the fragment objects represent the phenomenon-part of the conceptual model. The considered software is a dynamic entity, and when changes in the considered software are relevant from the given modelling perspective, then this is reflected in the conceptual model by creation and deletion of phenomena.

Concepts in the conceptual model are represented by fragment classes in the representational model. Fragment classes describe fragment objects, i. e. the fragment class lists all the attributes (element attributes and fragment attributes) together with constraints on the element attributes that a fragment object should have. Classes can have virtual attributes and they can be organised in inheritance hierarchies to model concept specialisation, but we will not treat this further in this paper (see [Jacobsen, 2000] for details).

A fragment object is a representation of a phenomenon in the conceptual model, and therefore a fragment object must represent every relevant aspect of a phenomenon. The two domains of relationships relevant for phenomena (relationships in the conceptual model and relations between the conceptual model and the considered software) are represented in fragment objects. The relationships relevant to a phenomenon are represented by values in the fragment object. Fragment objects hold two kinds of values, namely *element references* and *fragment object references*. Below we briefly describe these two kinds of values.

4.2.2. Element References

An element reference is a value by which we refer to an element. The phenomena and concepts in the conceptual model are related to the elements in considered software, and element references are used to capture this relationship.

The reason for having element references in the fragment objects is that the relationship between elements in the considered system and the phenomena in the conceptual model is not obvious. From tangible elements in the software (the considered system), intangible elements are created in the conceptual model as a result of the conceptualisation process. The element references are a way of relating the intangible phenomena in the conceptual model to elements in the software.

Element references are values of attributes which we call *element attributes*. The element attributes are qualified by the type of element it should reference. We must make some assumptions about how the considered system is represented, before the discussion about qualifications of the element attributes. Here it satisfies to assume that classes, methods, and attributes make up the software (cf. [Jacobsen, 2000]). Below we briefly exemplify the notion of element attributes by describing parts of the metapatterns in [Pree, 1995].

Example 4.2: Template and Hook Fragment Classes.

> We describe the two basic fragment classes template and hook which are being used in the description of the individual metapatterns. Each metapattern is a specific arrangement of the template class and the hook class in relation to each other. Note that a 'class' denotes a class in some software; a 'class node' denotes an element in the software representation, and 'a fragment class' denotes a named description in the $\mathcal{FL}$. When describing a metapattern we will relate the two basic fragment classes as dictated by the pattern.

> The template and the hook fragment classes are identical with the exception of the name of their attributes. The fragment classes contain two element attributes, one referencing a class node and one referencing a method node. In the template fragment class the attribute tmethod is associated with the word part-of, which means that the tmethod attribute can only reference method nodes in the software representation that are part of the class node which is being referenced by the tclass attribute. Similarly for the hook fragment class. For the moment we will rely on the intuition and the associated descriptive text behind constraints like part-of. In this paper we do not consider the aspect of what to do if a constraint is not satisfied.

```
template: fragment class {
```

```
      element attributes
         tclass: <class>      // reference to class node
         tmethod: <method> part-of tclass
   }

hook: fragment class {
      element attributes
         hclass: <class>
         hmethod: <method> part-of hclass
   }
```

□

4.2.3. Fragment Object References

Fragment objects can contain a number of fragment object references. These references are used to represent aggregation and association relationships with other fragment objects. The references are called *Fragment Object References* and they are values of *fragment attributes*. Fragment attributes are qualified by a fragment class which means that the attribute can only hold references to instances of its qualification fragment class or its subclasses.

Below we illustrate how a fragment class that describes a metapattern is composed out of one instance of the template fragment class and one instance of the hook fragment class.

Example 4.3: 1:1 Connection Metapattern.

This example uses the template and the hook fragment classes from the example above.

In the 1:1 CONNECTION metapattern the template class references the hook class and there is no inheritance relationship between the classes. The basic fragment class template does not contain any element attribute that represents the reference between the template class and the hook class, so this must be added. We add an element attribute tref to the fragment class in which the two fragment instances are placed.

```
1:1 Connection: fragment class {
      fragment attributes
         ti: template       // reference to template object
         hi: hook           // reference to hook object
      element attributes
         tref: <attribute> part-of ti.tclass
                            qualified-by hi.hclass

   }
```

The added attribute must reference an <attribute> node which is contained in the <class> node referenced by the tclass attribute of the ti fragment object — this is what is stated with the part-of keyword. Furthermore the qualification of the <attribute> node referred to by tref must be the class referred to by the hi.hclass attribute.

By instantiating in the same context one hook fragment object and one instance of the template fragment class and relating the objects to each other (by adding an attribute whose constraints are expressed in term of ti and hi) we have expressed the 1:1 CONNECTION metapattern. We can only assign nodes in the software representation to the attributes of an object of the 1:1 Connection fragment class such that the <attribute> node referenced by the tref element attribute has as qualification the <class> node referenced by the hi.hclass attribute.

The template fragment class does not describe any details about on the <method> node, i. e. nothing is specified about the node other than it should be part-of of the <class> node referred to by the tclass attribute.

An instance of this metapattern is illustrated in Figure 7 in Section 5.2 where we discuss UML. □

4.3. *Supporting Models of Software*

As indicated above, managing classes and objects that model the software requires much work. There is a need for a developing environment that manages the class and object models. This involves presenting the classes and objects in an appropriate way, and checking consistency of the object model, e. g. checking that the constraints specified in the classes satisfied. Such a developing environment should support the developer in investigating the software both on the model level and on the program level — the developer should be able to see how the model level and the program level are related.

5. Modelling Software Using UML

In this Section we discuss how the ideas in the previous Section relate to technologies such as UML. UML is a standard notation for describing software systems, and therefore it is interesting to investigate how UML can be used to express models of software. In this Section we investigate this aspect of UML through its class diagrams, object diagrams, and collaboration diagrams.

The traditional use of the class and object diagrams in UML is to model some business domain. The class diagrams are used to express how concepts from the business domain are related and to specify the objects in the software system to be built. Object diagrams are used to show examples of how objects in the software system will be related, and collaboration diagrams are used to show how object roles interact and are related. Pattern Structure, which are parametrised collaboration diagrams, are used to express design patterns. We will discuss the characteristics of UML through two examples. We will use UML in two different ways to express the metapattern discussed in Section 4.

5.1. *Using Pattern Structure*

A collaboration diagram in UML expresses a number of roles, their associations, and interactions among the roles. A collaboration diagram can be parametrised which means that it becomes a template. Parametrised collaborations are used to capture design patterns and actual usages of collaborations are used to express instances of design patterns, i. e. emphasis is put on the behavioural aspects of software when using Pattern Structure since it is based on collaborations. When using a parametrised collaboration, the model elements in the surrounding diagram are bound to the collaboration's model elements that are parameters.

Although a class diagram contains the features and relationships expressed in a collaboration it does not mean that the collaboration is a redundant description. Rather, the collaboration expresses new information by relating selected features and relations and by giving them a name.

The only notation related to parametrised collaborations is *instance*-level notation, i. e. the notation is used to express an application of a collaboration. In other words, there is no notation for a parametrised collaboration at the *type*-level. This reflects that the collaboration concept as an abstraction is relatively undeveloped (compared to the notion of classes and objects) — only vague descriptions of how collaborations can be related are found in the UML specification [OMG, 1999].

We conclude that pattern structure in UML is best suited to situations where behaviour is the interesting aspect, and where the underlying collaboration is defined in terms of the basic model elements (such as Classifier Roles and Association Roles) and not related to other collaborations.

We use the 1:1 CONNECTION metapattern to illustrate collaborations. In Figure 5 we illustrate the application of the collaboration in Figure 4. We assume that there is a constraint that states that the classes being bound to the application of the collaboration must not be related by generalisation. Comparing the notion of Pattern Structure to the notion of fragment object references and element references from Section 4.2, we observe that element references correspond to the binding relations between classes and the application of a collaboration. Element references were used to connect the model to the software, and this is precisely what the bindings do — here the class diagram corresponds to the software and the collaboration applications correspond to the model of the software. But nothing in Figure 5 corresponds to fragment object references (which were used to relate entities in the model). This is, as said above, because there is only one collaboration and it is not related to other collaborations.

Figure 4: The 1:1 CONNECTION metapattern expressed as a Collaboration Diagram.

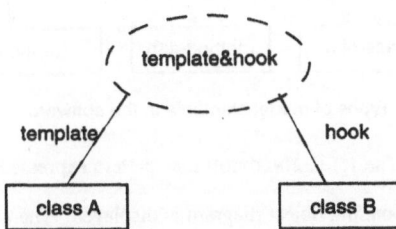

Figure 5: An application of the collaboration that captures an instance of the 1:1 CONNECTION metapattern.

378

5.2. Using Class & Object Diagrams

Above we have discussed a feature of UML that was intended to express models of software. Below we focus on using basic class and object notation in UML to describe models of software. The class diagram and the object diagram in UML are typically used to express a model of some business domain. The class diagrams describes how concepts from the domain are related, and the object diagram is used to describe examples of object relations.

A class model is good for reasoning about the concepts in the domain, but in order to comprehend an actual part of a domain we need an object model that models the specific phenomena in the domain Such an object model, or object universe, exists in the running software system.

Example 5.1: 1_1 Connection metapattern in UML

In Figure 6 we have illustrated a simple class model of the 1:1 CONNECTION metapattern. The classes are interrelated and they also specify references to the types of elements in the software. The classes ending with "-elm" are classes that model various types of elements in the software representation. These classes correspond to the classes in the metamodel layer of the four level metamodelling architecture of UML [OMG, 1999, p. 2-5]. The class 1_1 Connection is defined as a composition (aggregation) of the two classes template and hook.

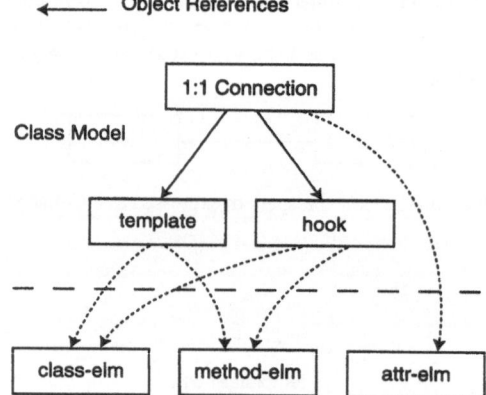

Figure 6: The 1:1 CONNECTION metapattern expressed in UML.

In Figure 7 a corresponding object diagram is displayed. The actual software being modelled consists of the classes A and B, and the model consists of the objects a1_1, aTemplate, and aHook. The model is associated with the software through element references.

□

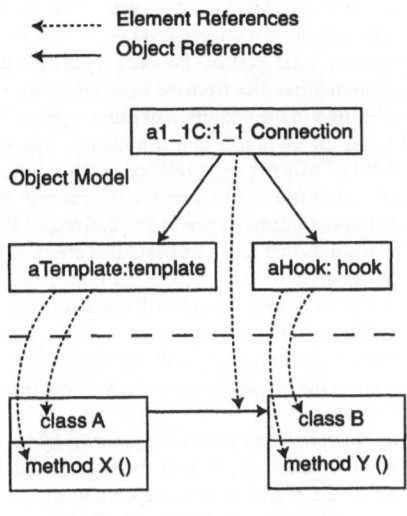

Figure 7: An instance of the 1:1 CONNECTION metapattern expressed in UML.

UML is intended to assist the developer in analysing and building a software system. When modelling a business domain the class model serves a medium for communication between the user (domain expert) and the developer and as a foundation for building the actual system. Therefore the class model in UML is important for the developer. The class model is used to express properties and relationship between concepts in the domain. Object diagrams are used as examples of how actual object relations and behaviours could occur. But the object model that reflects the state of the business domain exists as a object universe in the running software system. The object model is important for the user in his work since it is through the object model that the user administers or controls the business domain. The actual object universe is of no interest to the developer.

Now consider the situation where the class and object notations from UML are used to model some software, e. g. to express which design patterns or metapatterns are instantiated in the software. A class model of the patterns is important since it expresses relations and properties of the patterns. The object model is important, because now the developer is interested in the state of the domain — the domain is the software domain and in this example its state covers which patterns are instantiated. In other words, the object universe is important, because it reflects the patterns that the developer sees in the software. Since the object universe is important, the means for modelling patterns must have strong support for phenomenon-level modelling. OO Modelling languages with a run-time environment for managing object universes have strong support for instance-level modelling, but it implies that a run-time must be present. This implies that only using UML's class diagram is insufficient for exposing the patterns that are applied in the software.

To sum up on using UML as a notation for expressing pattern-like abstractions over software we make the following observations. There are two kinds of notations to use. The first one is

Pattern Structure which is a phenomenon-level notation that is based on collaboration diagrams. The Pattern Structure notation is weak at the concept-level — there is no explicit notation on types of Pattern Structure and it is vague on what relations between types of Pattern Structure. In essence, it is possible to define named Pattern Structures from the basic elements, but the composite element (the pattern structure) can not be used in the definition of other types of Pattern Structure.

The other kind of notations is the class and object notation. The class notation is good for reasoning about the concept-level of patterns since relations such as association, aggregation, and specialisation can be used to comprehend and to describe the concept-level. The object notation can be used to express which pattern instances are in the software. But, there are some issues associated with this. If the abstractions that are to be described are relatively stable, then it makes sense to draw an object diagram on paper or using a tool. The object diagram will display an object model that will be a valid model of the software and it will not need to change that often. But if the abstractions are relatively unstable, e. g. the pattern instances in the software under development, then an object diagram that is maintained manually will not be of much value since it will need to change often, and therefore the benefits of the object model will not outweigh the effort that must go into updating the object diagram.

Finally, if we choose to use the class and object diagrams in UML for expressing models of some software we must be aware of the fact that it is the object model that captures the actual software architecture. Of course, the object model is specified by a class model, but the class model only specifies the kinds of object models that are possible. In other words, the class model models the concepts that are used to conceive the software and the object model models the actual conception of the software.

6. Related Work

IEEE has a Draft Standard for Architectural Description [IEEE, 1999]. The draft standard discusses architectural descriptions. An architectural description contains a number of views and each view describes aspects of the system that are of concern to one or more stakeholders. A viewpoint describes the concern that is addressed by the view and the viewpoint also determines the languages/notations to be used to describe the view — a view conforms to a viewpoint. Altogether the standard specifies the principal parts of an architectural description and not specific elements such as certain viewpoints or certain stakeholders.

Compared to the points in this paper we note that these works are complementary rather than contradictory. We point out the usefulness of using OO based representations of architectural information — OO based representations provide good support both at the concept level and at the phenomenon level. Our work is thus aimed at the representational means (languages/notations) determined by viewpoints in the draft standard.

In [Shaw and Garlan, 1996] the notions of component and connector are introduced as central concepts in Architectural Description Languages (ADL). ADLs are concerned with describing the architecture — what the various languages mean by architecture varies, but common to them is that they all regard the architecture of a system as "the overall structure of a software system" where a system is composed of a set of components and connectors.

The language Wright [Allen, 1997] is an example of an ADL that used the component and connector notions in [Allen, 1997]. The Wright language describes software architecture in terms of abstract behaviour of components and connectors. The abstract behaviour is expressed in a CSP-like notation. Wright can describe architectural instances (description of individual systems) and architectural styles (description of a family of systems). An architectural instance is described by a configuration which can either be built from scratch or by using an architectural style together with instance specific descriptions. The relationship between an architecture description and the software system it describes is informal. This means that human judgement is needed when considering a specific system in relation to an architecture description.

In [Bass et al., 1998] there are several concepts and models related to architecture. The concepts are related to phases in the development of the software. An architecture is an abstraction of a system. Various kinds of models are related to an architecture — examples include reference models and architectural styles. A reference model expresses a domain specific division of functionality between pieces. An architectural style is a description of component types and connector types, the style specifies a category and architectures. The focus in [Bass et al., 1998] is on the practical issues involved in software engineering and not on notation.

7. Summary

We have presented a modelling perspective on software. The presumptions of this paper were that architecture is a model of software, and that a model describing patterns in OO software describes architectural information.

We have demonstrated that OO thinking is useful for understanding software architecture, in particular the rigorous concept/phenomena distinction provides clarification to the notion of models of software: Models of architecture are phenomenon-level models, models of architecture types are concept-level models. This fundamental observation is used to discuss UML as a notation for describing models of software.

The conclusion on UML is that the notation intended to describe patterns is a phenomena-level notation — it is not developed at the concept-level.

The contribution of this paper include:

- The notion of software architecture is positioned in a modelling universe.

- A demonstration of the usefulness of OO thinking in relation to architectural representation.

- A presentation of the principle parts of an object model of some software.

- A characterization of the suitability of UML to express software models that are based on a pattern-perspective.

Acknowledgements

We thank Palle Nowack and Bent Bruun Kristensen for inspiring and constructive comments.

References

[Allen, 1997] Allen, R. J. (1997). *A Formal Approach to Software Architecture*. PhD thesis, School of Computer Science, Carnegie Mellon University.

[Bass et al., 1998] Bass, L., Clements, P., and Kazman, R. (1998). *Software Architecture in Practice*. The SEI Series in Software Engineering. Addison-Wesley.

[Gamma et al., 1995] Gamma, E., Helm, R., Johnson, R. E., and Vlissides, J. (1995). *Design Patterns Elements of Reusable Object-Oriented Software*. Addison-Wesley.

[IEEE, 1999] IEEE (1999). *Draft Recommended Practice for Architectural Description. IEEE P1471/D5.2*.

[Jacobsen, 2000] Jacobsen, E. E. (2000). *Concepts and Language Mechanisms in Software Modelling*. PhD thesis, The Maersk Mc-Kinney Moeller Institute for Production Technology, University of Southern Denmark.

[Jacobsen et al., 1999] Jacobsen, E. E., Kristensen, B. B., and Nowack, P. (1999). Architecture = Abstractions over Software. In *Proceedings of the 32th International Conference on Technology of Object-Oriented Languages and Systems (TOOLS PACIFIC '99)*, pages 89–99. IEEE Computer Society.

[Kristensen and Østerbye, 1994] Kristensen, B. B. and Østerbye, K. (1994). Conceptual programming. *SIGPLAN Notices*, 29(9).

[Madsen et al., 1993] Madsen, O. L., Møller-Pedersen, B., and Nygaard, K. (1993). *Object-Oriented Programming in the BETA Programming Language*. Addison-Wesley, Reading, Massachusetts.

[Mathiassen et al., 1993] Mathiassen, L., Munk-Madsen, A., Nielsen, P. A., and Stage, J. (1993). *Objektorienteret Analyse*. Marko. In Danish.

[Mathiassen et al., 2000] Mathiassen, L., Munk-Madsen, A., Nielsen, P. A., and Stage, J. (2000). *Object-Oriented Analysis & Design*. Marko.

[Nowack, 2000] Nowack, P. (2000). *Structures and Interactions - Characterizing Object-Oriented Software Architecture*. PhD thesis, The Maersk Mc-Kinney Moeller Institute for Production Technology, University of Southern Denmark.

[OMG, 1999] OMG (1999). *OMG Unified Modeling Language Specification*. Object Management Group, Inc., version 1.3 edition.

[Pree, 1995] Pree, W. (1995). *Design Patterns for Object-Oriented Software Development*. Addison-Wesley, Reading, Massachusetts.

[Shaw and Garlan, 1996] Shaw, M. and Garlan, D. (1996). *Software Architecture (Perspectives on an Emerging Discipline)*. Prentice Hall.

MEASUREMENTS

Gauging the Performance of Object-Oriented Design Metrics

Brian Huston

Systems Engineering Faculty.
Southampton Institute
East Park Terrace, Southampton, SO14 0YN - UK
E-mail: brian.huston@talk21.com

ABSTRACT. *The application of design metrics is intended to highlight the possible misuse of object-oriented concepts such as inheritance and polymorphism, and so lead to more easily maintainable systems. This requires that a given metric be validated, in terms of its general properties and level of predictive power. One aspect of this activity is to examine inter-metric dependencies, and a technique for determining any such elements of metric redundancy is presented. In addition, metric interaction with design patterns is considered, and a method for highlighting incompatibilities between these two approaches to improving software quality is summarised. Initial results suggest that the most quoted metrics in the literature are indeed mainly independent, but that the application of design patterns could cause a tolerance breach for normalised metric scores in certain circumstances.*

KEY WORDS: Software quality, object-orientation, design metrics, metric-pattern interaction

1. Introduction

Quantitative measures give us information about software after it has been written. To aid the design process, however, predictive measures are required. In object oriented design, measures of the amount of coupling in a system, or the structure of an inheritance hierarchy, may give some indication of the future maintainability of a system. Design errors are clearly costly in terms of back-tracking so avoiding them is desirable. The application of design metrics is intended to introduce quality into a system at an earlier stage than may otherwise be the case, providing valuable feedback. Measures such as lines of code may or may not be good indicators of a system property such as maintainability, however such metrics are only available at a later stage in the life cycle. Against this, an early metric will be based on low information and it is therefore more ambitious to say that it is predictive of some finished system property. This then raises the issue of validation.

Validation efforts so far have been undertaken on both theoretical and empirical fronts. The theoretical approach to validation provides an initial filter by removing inconsistent measures, while empirically based efforts aim to prove statistical correlation between metric scores and finished system properties such as defect rate. The theoretical approach has generally relied on evaluating metrics against a set of measurement axioms, which define test conditions for what constitutes a valid measure (Weyuker, 1988; Hitz & Montazeri, 1996). However, a definitive axiom set (sufficient and complete) has yet to be defined, and it may not always be possible to ascertain whether a metric does violate an axiom or not. Indeed, the presence of a violation may indicate that the axiom itself may be anomalous rather than the metric. In the case of empirically based efforts, the sources of variation between software projects tend to confound the goal of producing (and proving) a globally predictive metric suite. Given the profusion of possible systems, empirical studies so far must be seen to represent limited sampling, and taken as a whole seem to produce an excess of (sometimes conflicting) correlations. However, it is clear that without the accumulation of evidence offered by such approaches, the use of design metrics will continue to be limited and arbitrary.

Given these considerations, the work in progress has sought to offer a complementary approach to the validation efforts so far undertaken. The analysis strategy adopted is based on two ideas, namely sample structure generation for discovering inter-metric correlations, and an evaluation of design metric interaction with design patterns.

2. Gauging Inter-Metric Correlations

When attempting to measure any given aspect of an object-oriented design, a number of competing metrics are found to be available for use. For instance, the quality of an inheritance hierarchy may be indicated by measures based on the number of child classes, the ratio of superclasses to subclasses, the average depth in tree and so on. While there is an intuitive feel that there must be some 'overlap' between such metrics, the exact nature of the interaction of their scores remains unclear. If there is a significant correlation between two or more metrics, then redundancy becomes an issue. Moreover, it may be possible that two metrics *m1* and *m2* cannot simultaneously be set within their chosen upper and lower tolerance limits.

One approach used for evaluating a metric is to calculate its score for a number of 'imaginary' structures, and examine how appropriate the returned values are (Henderson-Sellers, 1996). Extending this idea, sample structures can be generated monte carlo style in order to gauge inter metric correlations. The proposed technique for this relies on the adoption of binary matrices to describe design relationships such as inheritance and association.

For instance, a (single) inheritance hierarchy can be denoted by a simple 'class-parent' matrix CP, where $CP_{ij} = 1 \Rightarrow$ class (i) has class (j) as its immediate parent. Of course, invalid forms of CP must be prevented in order to avoid anomalies such as cyclic inheritance. From this base CP matrix, the 'class-ancestor' matrix CA can be calculated as

$$CA = \sum_{i=1}^{NC-1} CP^i \tag{1}$$

where NC is the number of classes. A metric such as average depth in tree (DITµ) is then given by

$$DIT_\mu = \frac{Tr(CA \cdot CA^T)}{NC} \tag{2}$$

where Tr denotes the matrix trace operation. Variation of the inheritance relationship matrix bit pattern then allows for competing metric scores to be generated, and an analysis of inter-metric dependencies to be carried out. A similar approach can be used for elements such as cohesion, coupling and polymorphism.

3. Gauging Metric Interaction with Patterns

The common aim of both design metrics and design patterns is to promote best practice in the formulation of object-oriented designs. Metrics effectively set limits on the extent to which concepts such as inheritance, association and polymorphism should be used. Patterns prescribe certain arrangements of classes which will affect the scores returned by these metrics. If the application of a pattern causes a previously within tolerance metric to exceed its (reasonably set) limits, then the intent of the pattern may be in conflict with the viewpoint behind the metric. In this case either one or the other (or indeed both) may prove to be anomalous. The question then arises as to which metric and pattern combinations could be incompatible, and how to quantify the likelihood of any such discrepancies. It is noted that the specific metrics which will be of interest are those which are normalised, as many patterns imply that simple absolute counts (such as number of classes) will rise (Ververs & Pronk, 1995).

Many structural and behavioral patterns (Gamma et al., 1995) can be framed in terms of their 'dimensional parameters'. One example of this is the Visitor pattern, where the dimensional parameters are seen to be the number of nodes (classes) to be visited, and the number of operations to be performed upon them. Another example is the Bridge pattern, whose scale is determined by the number of abstraction hierarchy classes and the number of specific implementor classes. Given that a corresponding non-pattern form (or 'typical' solution) can be described, these parameters then define the impact that the transformation from non-pattern to pattern will have on the overall system or subsystem being measured.

It is then possible to derive non-pattern to pattern difference equations for specific metrics, so that changes in the metric scores are described as a function of these dimensional parameters. This allows for an evaluation of metric-pattern interaction to be carried out. For example, the change in the 'average methods per class' metric for a standard Visitor non-pattern to pattern conversion can be shown to be

$$\frac{1 + x1 \cdot (2 + x2)}{2 + x1 + x2} - x2 \tag{3}$$

where $x1$ is the number of Visitor nodes and $x2$ is the number of Visitor operations. Given such a metric difference equation, an analysis may then be carried out in two ways. Firstly, scatter plots of scores for non-pattern versus pattern may be produced by randomising the parameters of each part of the difference equation within sensible limits. Secondly, a non-linear optimisation problem subject to constraints can be framed in order to ascertain minimum and maximum score changes. This would identify any circumstances in which the non-pattern to pattern transformation causes a drastic shift in the metric score, so highlighting regions of potential conflict.

Examples of possible scatter plots for non-pattern versus pattern score distributions are shown in Figure 1. For a band-pass metric (i.e. a metric that should have both lower and upper tolerance limits), the most undesirable forms of pattern-metric interaction would be cases ii) and iv). In case ii), there is a reasonable probability that scores which are already excessively high will be increased still further. Similarly, scores at the lower end of the scale may be decreased to an undesirable level. In case iv) this effect is certain, so that the application of the pattern is seen to work in opposition to the viewpoint for the metric. The converse situation is seen in case iii), where an optimum form of interaction is observed. The major benefit here is that scores at the extreme ends of the scale are limited, so that the general effect is to bring them inside a tolerance band. Finally, a pattern may have little or no effect on a given metric. Such a condition results in a scatter plot centred around a gradient of 1, as shown in case i).

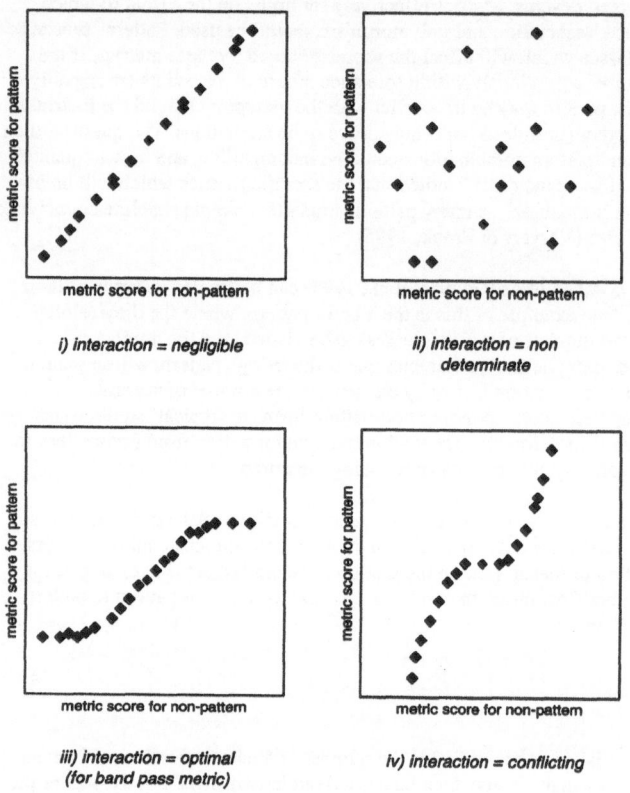

i) interaction = negligible

ii) interaction = non determinate

iii) interaction = optimal (for band pass metric)

iv) interaction = conflicting

Figure 1. Possible forms of metric-pattern interaction

4. A Summary of Results Observed

The primary metrics examined so far have been inheritance based metrics (Chidamber and Kemerer, 1994; Henderson-Sellers, 1996), and the MOOD metric set (Abreu, 1995). An analysis of inter-dependencies between inheritance metrics reveals correlations within certain score ranges, but sufficient divergences elsewhere to rule out redundancy. This is seen to be the case when comparing Reuse Ratio (percentage of system superclasses) to average Depth In Inheritance Tree (DITμ), for example. Other comparisons, such as between Specialisation Ratio (ratio of subclasses to superclasses) and average Number Of Children (NOCμ), display only a negligible correlation. However, indications exist that Reuse Ratio and Specialisation Ratio may well be linked, based on a random population of (30 class) single inheritance hierarchies.

In the case of metric-pattern interaction, a pattern such as Bridge reduces an excessive value for DITμ, and this is desirable in terms of decreasing accumulated complexity in the leaf nodes. However, where the abstraction hierarchy starts with a low score for DITμ, in some circumstances the pattern can reduce this score to an even lower value . This could be a problem if DITμ is treated as a band pass metric with too small a lower tolerance limit. A similar effect holds for NOCμ.

The MOOD metrics of Abreu cover information hiding, inheritance, polymorphism and association. For the Coupling Factor metric (COF), applying the Mediator pattern to a group of classes whose COF value is roughly >= 0.35 starts to reduce the COF score. This accords with the fact that class groups which exhibit low levels of coupling are not intended to have a Mediator pattern applied to them. In the case of inheritance, the State pattern is seen to possibly have a marked effect in reducing Method Inheritance Factor (MIF), where an appreciable number of states and request methods are accompanied by a large number of method overrides. As MIF is regarded as 'band-pass', a lower limit violation is very possible implying that a small lower limit (e.g. 0.1) on MIF must be set to accommodate the pattern.

5. Conclusions

It has been stressed that the collection, and correct interpretation of design metrics has the potential to improve software quality. Design metric values indicate *what* should change about a given design (e.g. reduce coupling, increase depth of inheritance trees). Design patterns represent examples of *how* to change a design. Both metrics and patterns have a rationale behind their use, although this will not prevent either from being applied inappropriately. The indiscriminate application of an unvalidated metric could cause more problems than it solves - however it is not realistic to expect that there will be one definitive study which closes the issue of metric validation. Proving the worth (or otherwise) of design metrics will require an accumulation of evidence, based on both theoretical investigations and empirical studies. The continuing aim of the work discussed is therefore both to reduce the plethora of candidate metrics (by eliminating correlated measures), and to produce a more complete theoretical analysis of metric-pattern interaction. This will lead to a breakdown of whether a given metric is aligned with, is neutral to, or is opposed to each element in a set of established pattern structures, in much the same way as has been done for measurement axioms. Beyond this, empirical studies which consider refactorings of actual systems to incorporate pattern structures, and provide an analysis of before and after metric scores, are suggested for future research.

References:

(Abreu et al., 1995):   Abreu, F.B., Esteves, R., Goulao, M. *The Design of Eiffel Programs: Quantitive Evaluation Using the MOOD Metrics.* Technical Report, INESC, Lisbon, Portugal.

(Basili et al., 1996):   Basili, V.R., Briand, L.C., Melo, W.L. *A Validation of Object-Oriented Design Metrics as Quality Indicators.* IEEE Transactions On Software Engineering, 22(10), pages 751--760.

(Binkley & Schach, 1996):   Binkley, A.B. and Schach, S.R. *A comparison of sixteen quality metrics for object-oriented design.* Information Processing Letters, 58, pages 271--275.

(Brown et al., 1998): Brown, W.J., Malveau, R.C., McCormick, H.W., Mowbray, T.J. *AntiPatterns*. New York: John Wiley & Sons.

(Chidamber & Kemerer, 1994): Chidamber, S. and Kemerer, C. *A metrics suite for object-oriented design*. IEEE Transactions On Software Engineering, 20(6), pages 476--493.

(Chung & Lee, 1992): Chi-Ming Chung and Ming-Chi Lee. *Inheritance-Based Metric for Complexity Analysis in Object-Oriented Design*. Journal of Information Science and Engineering, 8(3), pages 431--437.

(Etzkorn et al., 1998): Etzkorn, L., Davis, C., Li, W. *A Practical Look at the Lack of Cohesion in Methods Metric*. Journal of Object Oriented Programming, 11(5), pages 27--34.

(Gamma et al., 1995): Gamma, E., Helm, R., Johnson, R., Vlissides, J. *Design Patterns: Elements of Reusable Design*. Reading, Massachusetts: Addison-Wesley.

(Harrison & Counsell, 1998): Harrison, R. and Counsell, S.J. *An Evaluation of the MOOD Set of Object-Oriented Software Metrics*. IEEE Transactions on Software Engineering, 24(6), pages 491—496.

(Henderson-Sellers, 1996): Henderson-Sellers, B. *Object-Oriented Metrics: Measures of Complexity*. New Jersey: Prentice Hall, pages 143--146.

(Hitz & Montazeri, 1996): Hitz, M. and Montazeri, B. *Chidamber and Kemerer's Metrics Suite: A Measurement Theory Perspective*. IEEE Transactions On Software Engineering, 22(4), pages 267--271.

(Huston, 2000): Huston, B. *An Assessment of the MOOD Metric Scores under Design Pattern Usage*. Proc. Emerging Issues in Computer and Systems Sciences, Stockholm University, Sept 2000.

(Lorenz & Kidd, 1994): Lorenz, M. and Kidd J. *Object-Oriented Software Metrics*. Prentice Hall.

(Shepperd & Ince, 1993): Shepperd, M. and Ince, D. *Derivation and Validation of Software Metrics*. Oxford: Oxford Science Publications.

(Tegarden et al., 1995): Tegarden, D.P., Sheetz, S.D., Monarchi, D.E. *A software complexity model of object-oriented systems*. Decision Support Systems, 13, pages 241--262.

(Ververs & Pronk, 1995): Ververs, F. and Pronk, C. *On the Interaction between Metrics and Patterns*. Proc. OOIS '95 Dublin, pages 303--314.

(Weyuker, 1988): Weyuker, E. *Evaluating software complexity measures*. IEEE Transactions on Software Engineering, 14(9), pages 1357--1365.

(Whitmire, 1997): Whitmire, S. *Object-Oriented Design Measurement*. John Wiley & Sons.

Defining Complexity Metrics for Object-Relational Databases

Coral Calero, Mario Piattini, Marcela Genero

Departamento de Informática
Universidad de Castilla-La Mancha
Ronda Calatrava, 5
13071 Ciudad Real (Spain)
email: {ccalero, mpiattin, mgenero}@inf-cr.uclm. Fax: +34 926295300

ABSTRACT . *New Object-Relational Databases Management Systems (ORDBMSs) are replacing existing relational ones. In spite of the high expressiveness, application systems built upon ORDBMS are more complex and difficult to maintain due to the mixing of both paradigms, the relational and the object-oriented. All these reasons made necessary to dispose on metrics for measuring the complexity of this kind of databases and controlling its correct design. However, not always it is easy to propose correct metrics. This paper describes the method used by the authors for proposing metrics and the process of feedback needed for obtaining them in a correct way.*

KEY WORDS: *Object-relational databases, metrics, complexity*

1. Introduction

We are witnessing important advances in database technology; a new ``generation'' of DBMS (Database Management System) is coming out, among which object-relational ones (e.g. Oracle 8, Informix Dynamic Server, DB2) stand out. Object-relational databases will replace relational systems to become the next great wave of databases (Stonebraker and Brown, 1999). This kind of DBMSs supports a more complex data model having a stronger influence on the overall application maintenance effort. Taking into account that software maintenance is the most expensive stage in the software industry, it is very important to have maintainability metrics for this new kind of databases.

Maintainability is achieved by three factors: understandability, modifiability and testability, which in turn are influenced by complexity (Li and Chen, 1987). We must be conscious, however, that a general complexity measure is "the impossible holy grail" (Fenton, 1994). Henderson-Sellers (1996) distinguishes three types of complexity: computational, psychological and representational, and for psychological complexity three components are considered: problem complexity, human cognitive factors and product complexity. The last one is our focus.

In the next section we summarize the features of object-relational databases. In section 3, we describe the used method for proposing metrics. Metrics definition and refinement are presented in section 4. Finally, section 5 summarizes the paper and draws our conclusions.

2. Object-Relational databases

Object-relational databases combine traditional database characteristics (data model, recovery, security, concurrency, high-level language, etc.) with object-oriented principles (e.g. encapsulation, generalization, aggregation, polymorphism, ...). These products offer the possibility of defining classes or abstract data types, in addition to tables, primary and foreign keys and constraints[1], as relational databases.

Besides, generalization hierarchies can be defined between classes (super and subclasses) and between tables, subtables and supertables. Table attributes can be defined in a simple domain, e.g. CHAR(25), or in a user-defined class as complex number or image, In figure 1 an example based on the presented in (Cannan, 1999) is shown.

```
CREATE TABLE house(              CREATE TYPE address AS(
idhouse INTEGER,                 street CHAR(30),
price INTEGER,                   city CHAR(20),
rooms INTEGER,                   state CHAR(2),
size DECIMAL (8,2),              zip INTEGER) NOT FINAL;
location address,
desc text,                       CREATE TYPE employee AS(
front_view bitmap,               name CHAR(40),
document doc,                    base_salary DECIMAL(9,2),
seller employee,                 bonus DECIMAL(9,2))
PRIMARY KEY(idhouse));           INSTANTIABLE  NOT FINAL
                                 METHOD      salary()      RETURNS
CREATE TABLE person(             DECIMAL(9,2);
id INTEGER,
myhouse INTEGER,                 CREATE METHOD salary() FOR employee
PRIMARY KEY (id),                BEGIN
FOREIGN KEY (myhouse) REFERENCES house);   ...
                                 END;
```

Figure 1. Example of table definition in SQL:1999

3. Used method

As we have said previously, our goal is to define metrics for controlling object-relational databases maintainability. But metrics definition must be done in a methodological way, it is necessary to follow a number of steps for ensure the reliability of the proposed metrics. Figure 2 presents the method we apply for the metrics proposal (Calero et al., 2001).

---

[1] In this first approximation constraints are not considered for measure purposes.

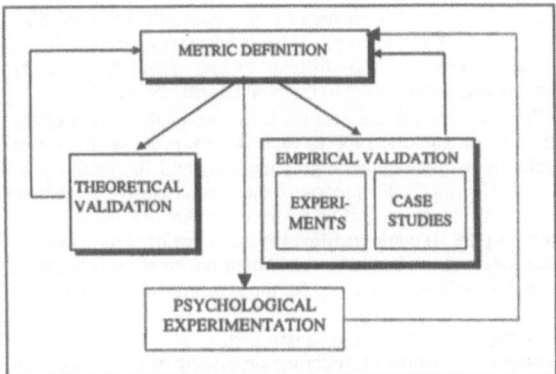

Figure 2. Steps followed in the definition and validation of the database metrics

In this figure we have four main activities:

- **Metrics definition.** The first step is the proposal of metrics. Although this step could look simple, it is necessary to take care on defining the metrics. This definition must be made taking into account the specific characteristics of the database we want to measure and the experience of database designers and administrators with these databases.
- **Theoretical validation.** The second step is the formal validation of the metrics. The formal validation help us to know when and how applying the metrics. There are two main tendencies in metrics validation: the frameworks based on axiomatic approaches and the ones based on the measurement theory. The goal of the first ones is merely definitional by defining formally desirable properties for measures for a given software attribute, so axioms must be used as guidelines for the definition of a measure. The most well-known frameworks of this type are those proposed by Weyuker (1988), Briand et al. (1996) and Morasca and Briand (1997). Software metrics axioms sets have been developed without a consensus and sometimes without a common understanding of the data to which they apply. The main goal of axiomatisation in software metrics research is the clarification of concepts to ensure that new metrics are in some sense valid. However, if an axiom set cannot itself be shown to be fit for purpose, it cannot be used to validate metrics. We cannot tell whether a measure that does not satisfy the axioms has failed because it is not a measure of the class defined by the set of axioms (e.g. complexity, length...) or because the axiom set is inappropriate. Since the goal of axiomatisation in software metrics research is primarily definitional, with the aim of providing a standard against which to validate software metrics, it is not so obvious that the risks outweigh the benefits (Kitchenham y Stell, 1997). The measurement theory-based frameworks (such as Zuse, 1998 or Withmire, 1998) specify a general framework in which measures should be defined. The strength of measurement theory is the formulation of empirical conditions from which we can derive hypothesis of reality.
- **Empirical validation.** The goal of this step is to prove the practical utility of the proposed metrics. There are a lot of ways to made it but basically we can divide the empirical validation in two: experimentation and case studies. The experimentation is usually made using controlled experiments and the case studies usually work with real data. Both of them are necessary, the controlled experiments for having a first approach and the case studies for making the results stronger. In both

cases, the results are analyzed using either statistics tests or advanced techniques as C4.5 a machine learning algorithm, and RoC a robust Bayesian classifier and so on. Also is necessary the experiment replication because the isolate results of an experiment it is difficult to understand how widely applicable the results are and, thus, to assess the true contribution to the field (Basili, 1999).

- **Psychological explanation.** Ideally we will be able to explain also the influence of the values of the metrics from a psychological point of view. Some authors, such as Siau (1999), propose the use of cognitive psychology as a reference discipline in the engineering of methods and the studying of information modeling. Cant et al. (1995) and Klemola(2000) propose the use of cognitive models to define object-oriented complexity metrics. In this sense, cognitive psychology theories (such as the Adaptive Control of Thought (ACT), Anderson (1983)) could justified the influence of certain metrics in the database understandability. The knowledge of the limitation of human information processing capacity could also be helpful in establishing threshold in the metrics for the assuring database quality.

As we can see in figure 2, the process of defining and validating database metrics is evolutionary and iterative. As a result of the feedback metrics could be redefined of discarded depending of the theoretical, empirical or psychological validations.

4. Metrics for object-relational databases

4.1. First definition of our metrics

Taking into account the characteristics of an object-relational schema, we proposed three metrics:

Size of a Schema(SS)
We define the size of a schema as the sum of the size of the tables of the schema:

$$SS = \sum_{i=1}^{NT} TS_i \qquad \text{being NT the number of tables in the schema}$$

We define the table size (TS) as the sum of the total size of the simple columns (TSSC) and the total size of the complex columns (TSCC) in the table:

$$TS = TSSC + TSCC$$

We consider that all simple columns have a size equal to one, and then the TSSC metric is equal to the number of simple columns in the table (NSA).

$$TSSC = NSA$$

And the TSCC is defined as the sum of each complex column size (CCS):

$$TSCC = \sum_{i=1}^{NCC} CCS_i \qquad \text{being NCC the number of complex columns in the table.}$$

The value for CCS is obtained as the "size of the hierarchy (formed by the class and its ancestors)" above which the column is defined and may be defined as the sum of each class size in the hierarchy (SC):

$$CCS = \sum_{i=1}^{NCH} SC_i \qquad \text{being NCH the number of classes in the hierarchy.}$$

The size of a class is defined as:

$$SC = \frac{SAC + SMC}{NHC}$$

being SAC the sum of the size attributes of the class, SMC the size methods of the class and NHC the number of hierarchies to which the class pertain.

The attributes of a class may also be simple or complex, then the SAC is defined as the sum of the simple attributes size (SAS, that have size equal to one like simple attributes) and the complex attributes size (CAS) in the class.

$$SAC = SAS + CAS$$

And the SMC is calculated with the version of the cyclomatic complexity given by [12]:

$$SMC = \sum_{i=1}^{NMC} V_i(G) \qquad \text{being NMC the number of methods in the class}$$

Complexity of References Between Tables

In object-relational databases, other characteristics of relational databases are preserved, the most important of which is referential integrity. We propose to use two metrics for referential integrity (Calero et al., 1999):

- Depth of Relational Tree (DRT) is defined as the longest referential path between tables in the schema database

- Referential Degree (RD) is defined as the number of foreign keys in the schema database:

$$RD = \sum_{i=1}^{NT} NFK_i \qquad \text{being NT the number of tables in the schema.}$$

4.2. First empirical validation of our metrics

Once we had the metrics defined based on the specific characteristics of the object-relational databases, we made a proof with a small set of people for assuring that the metrics were correctly designed.

We designed an example with an object-relational table. This table had five columns, two of them were simple columns and three of them were complex columns (two of these three were defined above the same class hierarchy and the other column above another class hierarchy).

People must to calculate the size of each column and we recorded the time needed for each subject of the team. Finally we calculated the average time needed for each column and we observed that they weren't differences between the time expended to calculate the time of the simple columns but it was a big difference between the average of the time needed to calculate the size of the complex columns that shared the class hierarchy. When the persons calculated the size the first time they expended more time than the second time.

We thought about these results and we ended that perhaps it was more easy to calculate the value of the class hierarchy once they knew the hierarchy. So we decided to reflect this fact in the metric definition dividing the size of the class hierarchy between the number of columns that used it.

4.3. Debugging of the SS metric definition

The final definition of the SS metrics is:

We define the size of a schema in the same way:

$$SS = \sum_{i=1}^{NT} TS_i$$

and the table size (TS) also as the first time:

$$TS = TSSC + TSCC$$

Also the TSSC and the TSCC have the same expression:

$$TSSC = NSA$$

$$TSCC = \sum_{i=1}^{NCC} CCS_i$$

But now, the value for CCS is obtained as:

$$CCS = \frac{SHC}{NCU}$$

Being SHC the "size of the hierarchy (formed by the class and its antecessors)" above which the column is defined and NCU is the number of columns defined above this hierarchy. This expression is used to reflect the fact detected in the proof.

The SHC may be defined as the sum of each class size in the hierarchy (SC):

$$SHC = \sum_{i=1}^{NCH} SC_i \qquad \text{being NCH the number of classes in the hierarchy.}$$

And the rest of the metrics have the same definition than before.

4.4. Example of our metrics

We present the values for the different metrics for the example presented in figure 1. Let us assume that all methods have a cylomatic complexity equal to 1 and all the large objects (LOBs) have also a size equal to one. In table 1, we present the value of each user defined type size.

Name Class	SAS	CAS	SAC	SMC	SC
address	4	0	4	0	4
employee	3	0	3	1	4

Table 1. Size values of the classes

The value for TSSC is given by the four simple columns of the table house. The value for TSCC is given by the four complex attributes with size equal to one (desc, front_view and document) plus the size of the complex column location plus the size of the complex columns address. So, we obtain the next values for the rest of metrics and finally for the table size:

$$CCS_{address} = \frac{4}{1} = 4 \qquad\qquad TSSC = 4$$

$$CCS_{employee} = \frac{4}{1} = 4 \qquad\qquad TSCC = 3 + 4 + 4 = 12$$

$$TS_{house} = 12 + 4 = 16 \qquad TS_{person} = 2$$

$$SS = 16 + 2 = 18$$

DRT=1 and RD=1

4.5. Formal verification of the metrics

Once the metric definition was made and refined we were able to made the formal verification of the metrics. In table 2 we present the results of the formal verification of our metrics in two formal frameworks: the formal framework proposed by Briand et al. (1996) as an example of axiomatic approach and the Zuse's formal framework (Zuse, 1998) which is based on measurement theory. In Piattini et al. (1998) and Calero et al. (1999) it is possible to find a complete explanation of Briand et al and Zuse formal frameworks and the formal verification of the metrics respectively.

	BRIAND ET AL(1996)	ZUSE(1998)
SS	SIZE	ABOVE THE ORDINAL
TS	SIZE	ABOVE THE ORDINAL
RD	COMPLEXITY	ABOVE THE ORDINAL
DRT	LENGTH	ABOVE THE ORDINAL

Table 2. Summary of metrics formal validation

4.6. Empirical validation

We prepared an experiment for validating empirically our metrics. In Piattini et al (2000) it is possible to find the complete experiment developed.

The experiment was developed in order to evaluate whether the proposed measures can be used as indicators for estimating the maintainability of an OR database. Five object-relational databases were used in this experiment with the average of 10 relations per database (ranging from 6 to 13). The people were given a form, which include for each table, a triplet of values to compute using the corresponding schema. These values are those of three measures TS, DRT and RD. Our idea is that to compute these measures, we need to understand the subschema (objects and relations) defined by the concerned table. A table (and then the corresponding subschema) is easy to understand if (almost) all the people find the right values of the metrics in a limited time (2 minutes per table).

To analyze the usefulness of the metrics proposed, we used two techniques: C4.5 (Quinlan, 1993), a machine learning algorithms and RoC (Ramoni and Sebastiani, 1999), a robust Bayesian classifier

From both techniques we find out that the table size metric (TS) is a good indicator for the maintainability of a table. The depth of the referential tree metric (DRT) is also presented as an indicator by C4.5 and the referential degree metric (RD) does not seem to have a real impact on the maintainability of a table.

5. Conclusions

Object-relational database management systems are replacing simpler relational ones. One of the main consequences of this change will be the stronger weight of the ORDBMSs in software systems maintainability.

It is necessary to dispose on metrics for controlling the complexity of this kind of databases. For obtaining good metrics is necessary to follow a set of steps. The method that we use for defining metrics is composed by the definition of the metrics, the formal verification, and the empirical validation of the metrics proposed. All these steps are related making a loop between the different steps. This loop means that a feedback could be necessary for obtaining good metrics.

In this paper we present the feedback, derived from an empirical validation, made in one of the proposed metrics for object-relational databases. From this empirical validation, we detected an error in the definition of a metric and its redefinition was necessary.

With this paper, we want to point up that the proposal of metrics for object-relational databases is not so easy that it seems and it is necessary to be careful in the definition.

Acknowledgement

This research is part of the MANTICA project, partially supported by the CICYT and the European Union (CICYT-1FD97-0168) and by the CALIDAT project carried out by Cronos Ibérica (supported by the Consejería de Educación de la Comunidad de Madrid, Nr. 09/0013/1999).

References

(Anderson, 1983)   Anderson, J.R. (1983). The Architecture of Cognition. Cambridge, MA: Harvard University Press.

(Basili et al., 1999)   Basili, V.R., Shull, F. and Lanubille, F. (1999), Building Knowledge through families of experiments, IEEE Transactions on Software Engineering, July/August, Nr. 4. Pp. 456-473.

(Briand et al., 1996)   Briand, L.C., Morasca, S. And Basili, V. (1996). Property-based software engineering measurement. IEEE Transactions on Software Engineering, Vol.22(1). pp. 68-85.

(Calero et al., 1999)   Calero, C., Piattini, M., Ruiz, F. and Polo, M. (1999).Validation of metrics for Object-Relational Databases, International Workshop on Quantitative Approaches in Object-Oriented Software Engineering (ECOOP99), (Lisbon ,Portugal. June 1999), 14-18.

(Calero et al., 2001)   Calero, C., Piattini, M. and Genero, M (2001), Metrics for controlling database complexity, Accepted chapter for the book Developing quality complex database systems: practices, techniques and technologies.

(Cannan, 1999)   Cannan, S.J. (1999), The New SQL Standard Good, Bad or Simply Ugly, Jornadas de Ingeniería del Software y Bases de Datos (JISBD99), Cáceres, Spain, November 1999.

(Cant et al., 1995)   Cant, S., Jeffrey, D.R. and Henderson-Sellers, B., (1995), A conceptual model of cognitive complexity of elements of the programming process, Inf. Software Technolofy, 37(7), 351-362.

(Fenton, 1994)   Fenton, N. (1994).Software Measurement: A Necessary Scientific Basis. IEEE Transactions on Software Engineering, 20(3): 199-206.

(Henderson-Sellers, 1996) Henderson-Sellers, B. (1996). Object-oriented Metrics - Measures of complexity. (Upper Saddle River, New Jersey). Prentice-Hall,

(Kitchenham et al., 1997) Kitchenham, B. and Stell, J.G. (1997). The danger of using axioms in software metrics. IEE Proc.-Softw. Eng. Vol.144, No 5-6, October-December, pp 279-285

(Klemola, 2000)   Klemola, T. (2000) A cognitive model for complexity metrics, ECOOP'2000, Cannes, 13 June.

(Li et al., 1987)   Li, H.F. and Chen, W.K. (1987) An empirical study of software metrics. IEEE Trans. on Software Engineering, 13 (6): 679-708.

(Morasca et al., 1997)   Morasca, S. and Briand, L.C. (1997). Towards a Theoretical Framework for measuring software attributes. Proceeding of the Fourth International, Software Metrics Symposium, 119-126.

(Piattini et al., 1998)   Piattini, M., Calero, C., Polo, M. and Ruiz, F. (1998). Maintainability in Object-Relational Databases. . Proc of The European Software Measurement Conference FESMA 98, Antwerp, May 6-8, Coombes, Van Huysduynen and Peeters (eds.). pp. 223-230.

(Piattini et al., 2000)   Piattini, M., Calero, C., Sahraoui, H. and Lounis, H. (2000) An empirical study with object-relational database metrics, ECOOP'2000, Cannes, 13 June.

(Quinlan, 1993)   Quinlan, J.R., C4.5: Programs for Machine Learning, (1993), Morgan Kaufmann Publishers.

(Ramoni et al., 1999)   Ramoni, M. and Sebastiani, P. (1999). Bayesian methods for intelligent data analysis. In M. Berthold and D.J. Hand, editors, An Introduction to Intelligent Data Analysis, (New York). Springer.

(Siau, 1999)   Siau, K. (1999). Information Modeling and Method Engineering: A

400

Psychological Perspective. Journal of Database Management 10 (4), 44-50.

(Stonebraker et al., 1999)   Stonebraker, M. and Brown, P. (1999) Object-Relational DBMSs tracking the next great wave, (California), Morgan Kauffman Publishers.

(Weyuker, 1988)   Weyuker, E.J. (1988). Evaluating software complexity measures. IEEE Transactions on   Software Engineering Vol.14(9). pp. 1357-1365.

Whitmire, S.A. (1997), Object Oriented Design Measurement, Ed. Wiley.

(Zuse, 1998)   Zuse, H. (1998). A Framework of Software Measurement. Berlin, Walter de Gruyter.

Measuring the Effect of Refactoring

Richard Pitt and Andy Carmichael

Object UK Ltd,
Bank House, High Road, Southampton SO16 2HZ - UK
E-mail:{richard.pitt, andy.carmichael}@objectuk.co.uk   Fax: +44 23 8039 9991

ABSTRACT. *This paper reports a work in progress, a research project being carried out at Object UK, to measure the effect of refactoring. As part of the project a refactoring tool is being developed using the Feature Driven Development (FDD) management process. On each timebox of the project, a suite of metrics is being collected to monitor (a) the amount of refactoring being carried out during development and (b) the effectiveness of the design changes. Once the project is completed, the data will be analysed for measures to indicate the success or otherwise of refactoring. The tools and methodology will then be available to apply to larger scale development projects.*

KEY WORDS: *refactoring, metrics, design, methodology, Feature Driven Development*

1. Background – the role of refactoring

To refactor code is to change its design without changing its observable behaviour. This is achieved by applying refactorings. A refactoring can be thought of as a well-defined and well-understood procedure for introducing a behaviour-preserving change into a software system and a number of such refactorings have been catalogued by Fowler (Fowler, 1999).

Refactoring is gaining recognition as a technique for improving the design of an existing system. There is a need to quantify the value of these design changes since, as there is no change in the system's behaviour, they apparently add no immediate business benefit. This paper discusses how metrics may be used to aid this quantification.

There can be no doubt that since the beginning of software development, programmers have sometimes felt the need to "tidy up" their code by applying changes that do not change behaviour. In the development of object-oriented systems, it was probably the Smalltalk development community that first formalised some of these activities into recognised refactorings (Roberts, 1996).

A more universal issue in software development is that of reuse, arguably the most important motivation for the rise of object-oriented technologies in the 1980's. Reuse is also a strong motivation for the development of refactoring techniques (Opdyke, 1992).

Object-oriented technologies also promised flexibility – the second major motivation for refactoring. Refactoring can be used to increase the plasticity of the design, possibly after previous changes to the functionality of the system have made the design brittle. Maintaining a flexible design is essential to lightweight, iterative development processes, such as FDD (Coad,

1999) and eXtreme Programming (XP) (Beck, 1999), which require changes to the software to be continually integrated and tested.

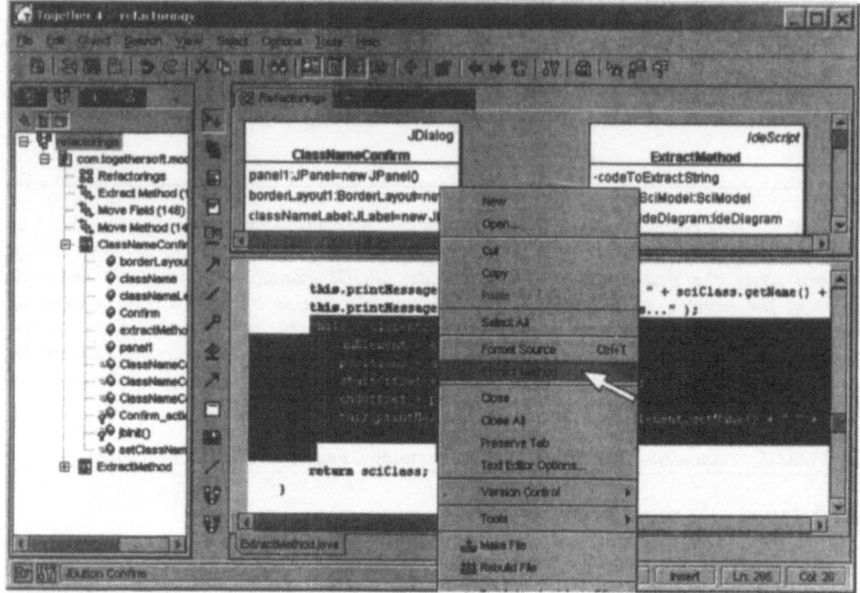

Figure 1 Prototype of the user interface to the Extract Method refactoring

Another development in object-oriented technology is the definition of design patterns (Gamma, 1995). These have become increasingly significant as they become part of the designer's vocabulary. Patterns may also provide a higher level of abstraction – increasing the granularity of design. Refactorings have much in common with patterns – both are formalised, catalogued and categorised by consensus and cooperation. A refactoring can be defined when a developer becomes aware of a common problem (e.g. a section of code needs to be extracted to become a new method) and formalises the steps taken to make the corresponding changes to the code.

Refactoring can be at a high level or low level. Opdyke focused on refactoring complete frameworks (Opdyke, 1992) by identifying transformations which could be proved to be behaviour preserving. Although Tokuda and Batory found that formal proof of even simple transformations involved considerable effort to automate, the value of refactoring from an engineering viewpoint was high (Tokuda, 1999). Fowler has catalogued a number of refactorings so that, as with design patterns, they can become part of a designers day to day development practice (Fowler, 1999), and this catalogue was a primary source for the current work.

2. Metrics – possible approaches

The first software metric to be widely used was the measurement of the number of lines of code. We can characterise this type of approach as the enumeration of concrete elements of a system (referred to here as "concrete metrics"). Other examples of concrete metrics are *Maximum (or average) size of operations*, or *Depth of inheritance hierarchy*. These metrics allow people to make quantitative comparisons between systems and then proceed to make links between these measures and desirable design characteristics. Lorenz and Kidd, for example, suggest a link between the degree of object orientation of code and the number of lines of code per method (Lorenz, 1994). They assert that if the lines of code per method is high, then the system is less object-oriented.

Although concrete metrics allow people to make quantitative comparisons between systems they do not actually give qualitative advice concerning which of alternative designs is "better". An alternative approach is to derive "abstract metrics" to quantify theoretically desirable design qualities, for example high cohesion and loose coupling. McCabe's measurement of cyclomatic complexity is a good example of this (McCabe, 1976), as is Halstead's definition of programme difficulty or effort (Halstead, 1977). These metrics are of course calculated using concrete statistics about the system.

Another example of the effort to derive abstract metrics from theoretically desirable design qualities is given by Martin (Martin, 1995). He notes that components that are to be reusable should be stable, and models instability using dependency statistics:
afferent couplings (Ca) - the number of classes outside the given category that *depend on* classes within it;
efferent couplings (Ce) - the number of classes outside the given category that *are depended on by* classes within it.
Then instability (I) is measured as:

$$I = \frac{Ce}{(Ca + Ce)}.$$

$I = 0$ represents maximum stability (no efferent couplings), which is desirable for reusable components and roots of class hierarchies.
$I = 1$ represents maximum instability (no afferent couplings), which is desirable for an application specific class at the leaf of a class hierarchy.

Having identified the two extremes, Martin also suggests there may be intermediate values that are desirable for different categories of classes falling between the extremes of 0 and 1.

In a project carried out in 1998/99 (TROOP, 1999), certain design patterns, as described by Gamma *et al.* (Gamma, 1995), were introduced into a large code base. The motivation for this was the premise that systems designed using patterns are easier to understand – the granularity of the design is coarser. At the start of the TROOP work, none of the 272 classes in the system were part of a design pattern. Nine months later 15% of the classes were playing a role in one or more design patterns. This was found to decrease the overhead of communication between developers, and make it easier for new workers to understand the whole system.

It is interesting to note that patterns are an example of "best practice" – they represent a solution that has been demonstrated valid by experience (Gamma, 1995). The use of patterns, however, does not guarantee the quality of the design. It is the suitability of the patterns that matters. The metrics derived in the TROOP experiment tell us how many classes were playing a role in a pattern, and also that the use of patterns improved the development process, but they do not inform us as to how effective each pattern was in solving a particular problem. It is these effectiveness metrics that are sought in the current project.

3. Measuring refactoring in this project

The product being developed in the current project is a small module to automate the Extract Method refactoring (Fowler, 1999), which will be integrated in TogetherSoft's Together® development tool (TogetherSoft, 2000). The API of Together is being used to implement the module. A prototype of the user-interface to the tool is shown in figure 1.

The scope of the project is quite limited in size and scope but it is hoped that the approach used can be scaled up to much larger, multi-developer projects. The module will be produced in a series of iterations, delivering features in short timeboxes. There is no code base to begin with, so there is no scope for refactoring an existing system, however as the design progresses. data will be generated to record the use of refactoring during the development . The advantage to be gained from refactoring will thus be measured in the evolving design.

We are using a simple routine for profiling the software at the end of each iteration. The software is version controlled after the delivery of each feature and the suite of metrics is used to capture a profile of the design. Subsequent analysis will seek to quantify the relationships between the metrics and the evolving design. Thus one aim of the project is to profile a design as it progresses, and analyse the data for links between the metrics measured and the success of refactoring. It is hoped that lessons will be learned about the usefulness of metrics as indicators of both the need for refactoring and its success. Appendix 1 lists the forty metrics that can easily be collected in the Together® metrics suite which we are using for data capture. We have characterised them as either concrete metrics, or abstract.

The measurements made will be related to the cost of refactoring. This is necessary because in order to evaluate the gains attributable to refactoring, the cost incurred must be taken into account. The time spent refactoring is the main cost. This will be measured by defining all development work in one of two modes:
adding new features;
refactoring (in order to facilitate the addition of new features or clean up after).
Being disciplined about the difference between refactoring and adding new features is encouraged by Beck (Beck, 1999). It has a secondary usefulness here in distinguishing the cost of adding new features from the cost of refactoring.

The metrics will be analysed for evidence of other costs. Fowler points out that it is much easier to teach the "how" of refactoring than the "when" (Fowler, 1999). It may be that refactoring in one direction causes desirable design characteristics to be lost in another. The profile of metrics will be analysed for indicators of these negative effects. This could be an area where metrics lend support to developers who are learning to refactor.

In addition to our investigation of refactoring, we are proposing this as a low-cost technique for the collection and analysis of metrics. Others may adopt this approach, building a record of development from which numerical values can be drawn in the light of hindsight and experience. Where best practice is identified, the data can be checked for indicators that could be used in a predictive manner in future work.

4. Conclusion

We have discussed the need for data to support refactoring decisions and given a broad characterisation of two approaches to defining metrics as either "concrete" or "abstract". As well as implementing a tool for applying a particular refactoring, we are using the small-scale development project itself to trial a method for quantifying the cost of refactoring and measuring its effect on design through a set of commonly used metrics. Analysis of the data may provide retrospective insight into the use of metrics to aid refactoring decisions. The methodology and tools may also be applied to larger scale projects in future to examine the value of refactoring larger systems.

REFERENCES

(Beck, 1999)   Beck, K. *Extreme Programming – Embrace Change* Addison-Wesley 1999

(Bieman, 1996)   Bieman J   "Metric Development for OO Software" in *Software Measurement* International Thompson Computer Press 1996

(Coad, 1999)   Coad P, E Lefebvre, J DeLuca   *Java Modelling in Colour with UML* Prentice Hall 1999

(Fowler, 1999)   Fowler, M. *Refactoring, improving the design of existing code* Addison-Wesley 1999

(Gamma, 1995)   Gamma, E., R. Helm, R. Johnson, and J. Vlissides. *Design Patterns: Elements of reusable Object-Oriented Software* Addison-Wesley 1995

(Halstead, 1977)   Halstead M. H. *Elements of Software Science* Elsevier 1977

(Lorenz, 1994)   Lorenz, M. and J. Kidd   Object-Oriented Software Metrics – A Practical Guide Prentice-Hall 1994

(Martin, 1995)   Martin R. OO design quality metrics: An analysis of dependencies, *ROAD 2(3)* SIGS Publications New York 1995.

(McCabe, 1976)   McCabe T. J. A Complexity Measure *IEEE Trans. Software Engineering*, SE-2(4):308-320, 1976

(Opdyke, 1992)   Opdyke, W. *Refactoring object-oriented frameworks* PhD diss., University of Illinois at Urbana-Champaign. (Also available as Technical Report UIUCDCS-R-92-1759, Department of Computer Science, University of Illinois at Urbana-Champaign)

(Roberts, 1996)   Roberts, D., J. Brant and R. Johnson "A Refactoring Tool for Smalltalk" In *The Theory and Practice of Object Systems, Special issue on software reengineering Engineering* John Wiley 1996

(TogetherSoft, 2000) TogetherSoft LLC: www.togethersoft.com

(Tokuda, 1999)   Tokuda, L and D Batory   Automating three modes of evolution for object-oriented Software Architectures. In *Proceedings, COOTS'99* 1999

(TROOP, 1999)   TROOP Consortium   *Transformation of Object Oriented design using design Patterns – Final Report.* CAS Software AG 1999

APPENDIX 1 – Metrics being collected

The following metrics will be gathered on the project using the Together metrics suite (TogetherSoft 2000).

Concrete metrics

operation	MNOL – Maximum Number of Levels MNOP – Maximum Number of Parameters MSOO – Maximum Size of Operation
class	LOC – Lines of Code NOA – Number of Attributes NOO – Number of Operations NOIS – Number of Import Statements NOM – Number of Members CR – Comment Ratio TCR – True Comment Ratio CC – Cyclomatic Complexity
relationships between classes	PpubM – Percentage of Public Members PPkgM – Percentage of Package Members POPriv – Percentage of Private Members PprotM – Percentage of Protected Members NORM – Number of Remote Methods RFC – Response for Class CBO – Coupling between Objects DAC – Data Abstraction Coupling FO – Fanout
inheritance	NOOM – Number of Overridden Methods NOAM – Number of Added Methods RFC – Response for Class DOIH – Depth of Inheritance Hierarchy NOCC – Number of Child Classes
other	NOC – Number of Classes

Abstract metrics

relationships between operations	LOCOM1 – Lack of Cohesion of Methods 1 LOCOM2 – Lack of Cohesion of Methods 2 LOCOM3 – Lack of Cohesion of Methods 3
internal structure of classes	AC – Attribute Complexity WMPC1 – Weighted Methods per Class 1 WMPC2 – Weighted Methods per Class 2 CC – Cyclomatic Complexity

Model Engineering for Distributed O-O Component Testing

Sita Ramakrishnan, Heinz Schmidt
School of Computer Science and Software Engineering
Monash University, Melbourne, Victoria 3145, Australia
email: {sitar,hws}@csse.monash.edu.au

Abstract

A model engineering approach is used in developing a testing method called VISWAS for the validation of distributed systems to test for safety and liveness properties. The VISWAS method is an integrated testing method, which incorporates a test environment with software modelling and automatic test sequence generation. This paper describes the three layered test architecture model of VISWAS, which includes a distributed architecture model (Ken-Gate model), a method (UML, OCL) and techniques (with Temporal Logic and TLA), to develop a tool for automatic test sequence generation.

Keywords

Distributed Component Testing, Metamodel, Model Engineering, UML, OCL, Temporal Logic of Action

1 Introduction

Model Engineering allows a systematic process for the definition of specification and design of O-O systems to meet system requirements. The model engineering approach provides a first-class status to models and model elements, similar to the first-class status associated to objects in the first and second generation O-O methods. The representation of a model itself requires the use of a notation, underpinned by a rigorous definition, which usually starts with a metamodel. In the main stream modelling language, UML, the metamodel and the notation together make up the *modelling language*. The semantic details for the various modelling levels in UML can be specified using the UML meta model and its companion object constraint language, OCL. Such a metamodel-driven modelling is also termed an ontology-driven modelling, and is different from the earlier themes of second generation O-O methods, namely of defining an analysis, a design or a programming notation in the O-O paradigm.

An ontology closely corresponds to the definition of a meta-model and contains concepts and relations that are relevant to the modelling task as described by Bezivin (1998). An ontology defines what should be extracted (filtered) from the system in order to build a given model of a system. A given ontology usually has three levels of details: definitional layer, assertional layer and a toolbox layer. The definitional layer contains basic concepts and relations; the assertional layer contains axioms that apply to the basic concepts and relations; and the toolbox layer contains pragmatical information. Bezivin (1998) considers the three layers of details in UML models as the UML meta-model level, the OCL level and the graphical notation level.

In this paper, we consider the modelling requirements for the specification based testing of distributed systems. Concurrent and distributed systems require specification languages that can express information about the temporal ordering of a series of actions. Therefore, concurrent distributed systems need models with constructs that can unambiguously express temporal events and actions in order to use this information as part of a testing process.

The ontology-driven modelling and the Unified Modeling Language (UML) metamodel structure that make up the new model engineering approach has been applied in developing a testing method called *VISWAS*. This paper describes a three layered architectural model using the model engineering approach, and highlights the additional requirements that need to be specified to take the critical dimension of time into account in modelling distributed systems.

2 Ontology-Driven Modelling For Viswas

The specification and testing of distributed reactive systems require the consideration of their temporal aspects as well as the structural and behavioural aspects in developing precise models. However, temporal properties and relations, as expressed in linear temporal logic and temporal logic of action are not available in the UML models and its companion language, OCL. These limitations in UML/OCL models are overcome by proposing extensions to the modeling language and following an ontology-driven modelling approach to precisely describe the concepts and their relations that exist in a distributed and concurrent system.

The ontology-driven modelling approach for *VISWAS* has a three layered architecture (Figure 1) to facilitate the development of detailed models for implementation and testing of concurrent and distributed O-O components. The three layers as shown in Figure 1 from the model engineering view point are:

1. Representational layer - to model the given concurrent and distributed system to be tested,

2. Assertional layer - to capture the safety and liveness properties of the given system for testing, and

3. Tool layer - to automate test sequence generation.

The three layered model is used to generate test sequences for testing an interoperable distributed software system.

3 Representational Layer

The representational layer has been chosen to be a distributed architectural model, which supports interoperability and addresses testability aspects of concurrent and distributed software systems. As part of this layer, an implementation model is also derived from the static architectural model to represent the distributed software system under test. Industry standard interoperable tools and languages, such as CORBA/JAVA IDL and Java, are used in the implementation model for the software system under test as shown in Figure 2. The interoperable distributed generic model of Ken-Gate software architecture by Schmidt (1995) forms the representational layer. A specific Ken-Gate model is derived from the generic model for building an implementation of the system under test. An extended version of the UML state chart is produced from the Ken Gate architectural model by incorporating

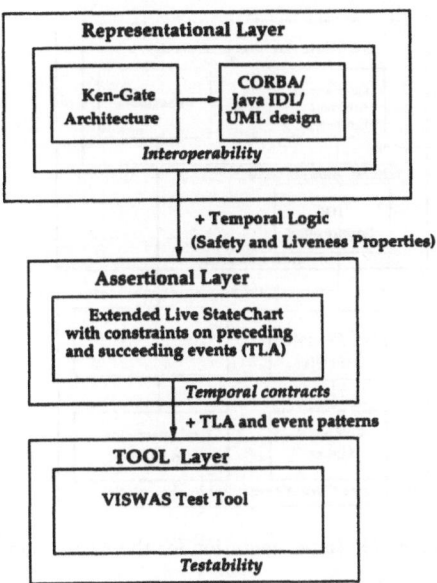

Figure 1. Modelling Layers in Viswas Test Method

critical aspects of saefty and liveness properties, which form the elements of the assertional layer in the *VISWAS* method.

UML is a general purpose visual modelling language used to specify, visualize, construct, and document the artifacts of software systems (Booch, Rumbaugh, and Jacobson 1999). The abstract syntax in UML is provided as a subset of UML, with UML structural diagrams to present the UML metamodel, its metaclasses, relationships, and constraints. The abstract syntax is used in the representational layer for describing the state model and message sequence diagrams.

The Ken-Gate model is an interoperable distributed architectural model with concurrency protocol interfaces required for modelling distributed systems. However, temporal constraints need to be added to the architectural model for generating test sequences for testing distributed systems.

A Ken-Gate model can be described from three view points: i) a distributed hierarchial architecture, ii) concurrent interface definitions that deal with coordination and synchronization, and iii) computation. Concurrent objects are represented using these three abstractions: kens, gates and rules. Kens capture the notion of a loosely coupled distributed architecture made up of relatively independent, cohesive components. Kens are course-grained objects composed of finer grained interdependent objects. Kens are guarded by synchronization constraints. These constraints are not part of the implementation code but of the interface of the callee class, and can be used to encapsulate access policies. Gates are the interface objects that connect kens. Gates control ken's entrance and coordinate objects' entry and exit, and act as guardians of kens. Mutual exclusion is achievable by associating a lock to each ken. A called method proceeds with the execution only if all its entry conditions are satisfied, including hold and guard rules, and thus guarantees exclusion with other conflict-

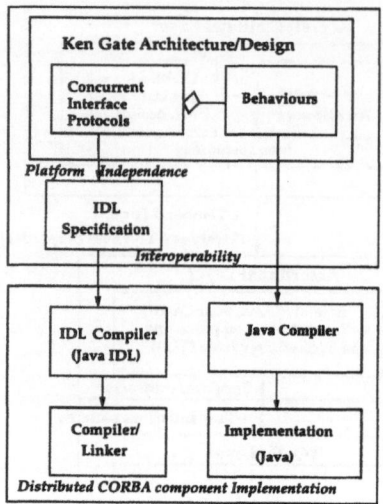

Figure 2. Interoperable Implementation for the Representation Layer

ing methods. Kens generalise Hoare monitors by using a pattern of related gates, leading to composite objects or component architecture. Several gates can share future conditions, which then take the role of *monitor condition variables*.

The concurrency interface protocols, conformance and correctness constraints discussed above, extend the design by contract (Meyer 1988) and form the foundation for deriving a test method for distributed component testing. The interface definitions expose the interaction constraints and component object's distribution.

An extended state chart, called *Live State Chart*, is derived from the Ken-Gate model to show temporal details of the interface definitions of a concurrent distributed component such as mutual exclusions and interaction constraints.

4 Assertional Layer

The Assertional layer is used to represent the dynamic software model with state machines and message sequence charts (MSCs). As part of the dynamic model, temporal properties must be included explicitly in order to capture the safety and liveness requirements for distributed component testing. The well-formed rules of the models and constraints in UML are expressed in object constraint language (OCL). Methods such as the UML (Booch, Rumbaugh, and Jacobson 1999) and OPEN (Graham, Henderson-Sellers, and Younessi 1997) dynamic models currently do not support any temporal operators in OCL. Hence OCL has been extended with temporal logic operators in MSCs. Temporal logic of action (TLA) formalism has been applied to state machines. As shown in Figure 1, temporal operators, safety and liveness properties of TLA are added to the UML state machine to produce an extended state chart with constraints on preceding and succeeding events. These constraints together with the extended design by contract from the distributed architectural model represent the temporal contracts that are modelled as part of validating an interoperable distributed system. From the Ken-Gate model, the assertional layer is derived for including the temporal contracts of components.

The temporal logic operators have been used to extend UML/OCL to show the liveness properties of *guarantee* and *response* in MSCs. The temporal properties that specify program properties have been classified by Manna and Pnueli (1992) into *safety, guarantee, obligation, response, persistence,* and *reactivity.* All these temporal properties except the *safety* property exhibit liveness characteristics. The rationale for adding temporal logic to OCL, and extensions to message sequence charts for modelling the safety and liveness properties of a distributed component have been discussed in an earlier paper by the author (Ramakrishnan and McGregor 1999).

Temporal Logic of Action (TLA) are considered for extending UML state charts by including safety and liveness properties, and making the charts test ready. Lamport's temporal logic of actions (TLA) (Lamport 1994) is a logic of actions for specifying and reasoning about concurrent systems and algorithms. TLA, unlike some other temporal logic formalisms, is very close to the description of state machines (Lamport 1994). A component specification is described in TLA as a state machine and consists of an initial condition, next state relation and fairness requirements, which ensure that certain actions actually occur. An action includes defined actions (safety) and desired actions (liveness) (Ladkin 1997).

Fairness means that if a certain operation is possible, it will eventually be executed by the program. For concurrent algorithms, fairness requirements can be expressed in terms of weak fairness and strong fairness conditions. Weak fairness asserts that *eventually* an operation must either be executed or be impossible to execute, may be for a brief period of time. Strong fairness asserts that an operation is either *eventually* executed, or its execution is infinitely often impossible. Infinitely often impossible is interpreted as not infinitely possible, and that means *eventually* always impossible.

Writing the temporal part of a specification requires specifying liveness properties and choosing fairness conditions. Since TLA is very close to the description of state machines and a component is specified in TLA as a state machine with preceding and succeeding events with fairness condition, some of these TLA notions have been applied to extend UML state charts with liveness properties. TLA applied to the extended state chart forms the assertional (temporal contract) layer in the three layered model of the *VISWAS* method. Temporal action propagation ($\mathcal{TAP}$) sequences have been derived using TLA's *always, never, eventually true* and *eventually false* properties, and included in the extended version of the state chart called *Live State Chart* with $\mathcal{TAP}$ sequences.

The assertional layer provides the constraints, which need to be included in the representational layer of the state chart, to consider the critical aspects of safety and liveness properties of concurrent distributed systems.

5 Tool Layer

The tool layer is used to represent the testing tool requirement for automating distributed test sequence generation. The tool layer also supports the testability needs of a distributed software system. The extended live state chart with its temporal contracts and event patterns are fed to the tool layer to generate a *functional test sequence generator.* The temporal contracts and event patterns take important safety properties such as mutual exclusion, absence of deadlock with *always* and *never*, and liveness properties such as *eventually enabled* into account.

The tool layer represents the layer that draws on the information from the dynamic state machine meta model to build a test tool. The test tool is based on extended notions of design by contract for interface protocols for distributed components and temporal properties such as safety and liveness. The tool layer contains tools for managing the testing process, which includes a test tool for automating the test generation process and a test environment for conformance checking against the system under test. The advantages of using model engineering is illustrated next with an elaboration of the test sequence generation phase and the test environment in the *VISWAS* method.

6 Test Environment in the context of Model Engineering

Model engineering facilitates the clear separation of (testing) requirements, constraints (rules) to be satisfied by the requirement model and the pragmatic solution (tool) layer.

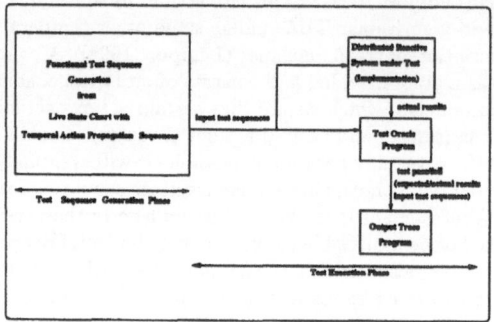

Figure 3. Testing Environment

The essential (core) requirements of the testing environment and the test sequence generation phase (Figure 3 and 4) considered are: the specification model to be fed to the JavaCC tools in the context of a Grammar, creation of a *functional test sequence generator* tool, and a system under test for testing against the input test sequences. The rest of the infrastructure such as the test oracle and the output trace programs are required to provide a fully functional automated specification tool.

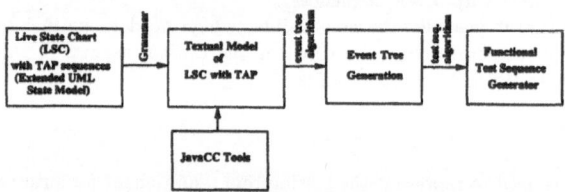

Figure 4. Test Sequences Generation Phase

The *Live State Chart* is an extended version of the visual dynamic UML state model. A textual extended BNF notation has been used to provide a Grammar for the *Live State Chart*. The UML metamodel has been used to provide a textual description for the *Live State Chart*. The *Live State Chart* of the distributed reactive component has been transformed into an event tree using JavaCC tools. A prototype tool for the automated test sequence generation has been implemented from the event tree of the *Live State Chart*.

7 Summary

Model engineering which is becoming an essential part of software engineering process has been used to develop a testing method, *VISWAS*, for testing distributed systems. The *VISWAS* model uses three layers which are: a representational layer to model the given concurrent and distributed system to be tested; an assertional layer to capture the safety and liveness properties of the given system for tesing; and a tool layer to automate test sequence generation. We have overcome the limitations of current UML/OCL models by extending the UML state model and MSC to include the critical aspects of safety and liveness properties of distributed systems. These critical properties are contained in the *Live State Chart* with temporal action propagation ($\mathcal{TAP}$) sequences in the three layered architecture.

Acknowledgement: The authors gratefully acknowledge the technical support provided by Mr Dean Thompson, ph.D student in the School of CSSE in producing the final camera ready version using latex.

References

Bezivin, J. (1998). Who is Afraid of Ontologies? In *CDIF Workshop OOPSLA98*, *http://www.metamodel.com/oopsla98-cdif-workshop/bezivin1/ cited Sep 99*.

Booch, G., J. Rumbaugh, and I. Jacobson (1999). *The Unified Modeling Language User Guide*. Addison-Wesley.

Graham, I., B. Henderson-Sellers, and H. Younessi (1997). *The OPEN Process Specification*. Addison-Wesley Longman Ltd.

Ladkin, P. (1997, June). A Tutorial on TLA Verification. *Technical Report, Universitat Bielefeld, Germany*, 1–69.

Lamport, L. (1994, May). The Temporal Logic of Actions. *ACM Transactions on Programming Languages and Systems 16(3)*, 872–923.

Manna, Z. and A. Pnueli (1992). *The Temporal Logic of Reactive and Concurrent Systems*. Springer-Verlag.

Meyer, B. (1988). *Object-oriented Software Construction*. Prentice-Hall.

Ramakrishnan, S. and J. D. McGregor (1999, May). Extending OCL to support Temporal Operators. In *Workshop on Testing Distributed Component-based Systems held in conjunction with the 21st International Conference on S.E.*

Schmidt, H. (1995). Reasoning about concurrent objects. *Technical-Report TR95/11, Dept. Software Development, Monash University*.

Early metrics for object oriented information systems

Marcela Genero [1], Mª Esperanza Manso[2], Mario Piattini [1], Francisco García[3]

[1] *Department of Computer Science- University of Castilla-La Mancha*
Tel. (+34) 926 29 53 00 Ext. 3715 – Fax (+34) 926 29 53 54
Ciudad Real – Spain
{mgenero, mpiattin}@inf-cr.uclm.es

[2] *Department of Computer Science - University of Valladolid*
Tel. (+34) 983 42 30 00 – Fax 983 42 36 71
Valladolid – Spain
manso@infor.uva.es

[3] *Department of Computer Science and Automatic - University of Salamanca*
Tlf: +34-923-294400 ext. 1302 Fax: +34-923-294514
Salamanca – Spain
fgarcia@gugu.usal.es

ABSTRACT. *The quality of object oriented information systems (OOIS) depends greatly on the decisions taken at the initial phases of their development. In a typical object oriented information systems development a class diagram is first built. Class diagrams lay the foundation for all later design work. So, their quality heavily affects on the product that will be ultimately implemented. Even though the appearance of the Unified Modelling Language (UML) as a standard of modelling OOIS have provided a great contribution towards building quality OOIS, it is not enough. Early availability of metrics is a key factor in the successful management of OOIS development. The goal of this work is to propose a set of metrics in order to assess the complexity of UML class diagrams. We also put the proposed metrics under empirical validation in order to provide empirical support to their practical significance and usefulness.*

Keywords. quality in object oriented information systems, object oriented metrics, class diagrams complexity, UML class diagrams

1. Introduction

A widely accepted principle in software engineering is that quality of a software product should be assured in the early phases of its life cycle. In a typical OOIS design at the early phases, a class diagram is first built. Class diagrams lay the foundation for all later design work. So, their quality can have a significant impact on the quality of the system which is ultimately implemented. Improving the quality of class, will therefore be a major step towards the quality improvement of the system development.

The appearance of UML (Object Management Group, 1999), as standard OO modelling language, should contribute to this. Even though, we have to be aware that a standard modelling language, can only give us syntax and semantics to work with, but it cannot tell us whether a "good" model has been produced. Naturally, even when language is mastered, there is no guarantee that the models produced will be good. Therefore, it is necessary to assess their quality.

Quality is a multidimensional concept, composed of different characteristics such as functionality, reliability, usability, efficiency, maintainability and portability (ISO 9126, 1999). However, the definition of the different characteristics that compose the concept of "quality" is not enough on its own in order to ensure quality in practice as people will generally make different interpretations of the same concept. Software measurement plays and important role in this sense because metrics provide a valuable and objective insight into specific ways of enhancing each of the software quality characteristics. Measurement data can be gathered and analysed using various quality models to assess current product quality, to predict future quality, and to drive quality improvement initiatives (Tian, 1999).

Most the external quality attributes proposed in the ISO 9126 (1999), such as maintainability, reliability, etc. can only be measured late in the OOIS life cycle. So it is necessary to find early indicators of such qualities based, for example, on the structural properties of class diagrams (Briand, 1999b).

Early availability of measures is a key factor in the successful management of software development, since it allows for (Briand et al., 1999a):

1. the early detection of problems in the artifacts produced in the initial phases of the life cycle (specification and design documents) and, therefore, reduction of the cost of change-late identification and correction of the problems are much more costly than early ones;
2. better software quality monitoring from the early phases of the life cycle;
3. quantitative comparison of techniques and empirical refinement of the processes to which there are applied;
4. more accurate planning of resource allocation, based upon the predicted quality of the system and its constitutent parts.

Within the field of software engineering a plethora of metrics have been proposed for measuring OO software products, even though most of them are related on products obtained from advanced design and implementation phases (Chidamber and Kemerer, 1994, Lorenz and Kidd, 1994; Brito e Abreu and Melo, 1996; Henderson-Sellers, 1996). Genero et al. (1999) have proposed some metrics for measuring OMT class diagrams. Few works have been done specifically about measures applied to UML class diagrams (Marchesi, 1998; Genero et al., 2000).

The goal of this work is to propose a set of metrics in order to measure the complexity of UML class diagrams (section 2) focusing specially in the different UML relationships, such as associations, aggregations, generalisations and dependencies. We also put the proposed metrics under empirical validation in order to provide empirical support to their practical significance and usefulness (section 3). Lastly, section 4 summarises the paper, draws our conclusions, and presents future trends in metrics for object modelling using UML.

2. A proposal of metrics for UML class diagrams

In this section we will propose a set of closed-ended metrics (Lethbridge, 1998) for assessing the complexity of UML class diagrams at the initial phase of the OOIS life cycle. A closed-ended metric is where measurements can only fall within a particular range, and where it is impossible for them to fall outside that range (most of our metrics fall in the range [0,1]). As the aim of this work is simplify class diagrams as much as possible, our goal will be minimise the metric values. We consider the worth case value when the metric value tends to 1, and the best case when the metric value tends to 0.

All of the proposed metrics measure the complexity of class diagrams due to relationships. UML allows to define the following kinds of relationships: associations, aggregations, generalisations and dependencies.

2.1 ASvsC metric

The Associations vs. Classes metric measures the relation that exists between the number of associations and the number of classes in an UML class diagram. It is based on M_{RPROP} metric proposed by Lethbridge (1998). We define this metric as follows:

$$ASvsC = \left(\frac{N^{AS}}{N^{AS} + N^C} \right)^2$$	N^{AS} is the number of associations in an UML class diagram. N^C is the number of classes in an UML class diagram. Where $N^{AS} + N^C > 0$.

2.2 AGvsC metric

The Aggregations vs. Classes metric measures the relation that exists between the number of aggregations and the number of classes in an UML class diagram. We define this metric as follows:

$$AGvsC = \left(\frac{N^{AG}}{N^{AG} + N^C} \right)^2$$	N^{AG} is the number of aggregations in an UML class diagram. N^C is the number of classes in an UML class diagram. Where $N^{AG} + N^C > 0$.

We consider as the number of aggregations each level of aggregation hierarchies , ie. each symbol $\Diamond$ in the class diagram.

2.3 DEPvsC Metric

The Dependencies vs. Classes metric measures the relation that exists between the number of dependencies and the number of classes in an UML class diagram. We define this metric as follows:

$$DEPvsC = \left(\frac{N^{DEP}}{N^{DEP} + N^C} \right)^2$$	N^{DEP} is the number of dependencies in an UML class diagram. N^C is the number of classes in an UML class diagram. Where $N^{DEP} + N^C > 0$.

2.4 GEvsC metric

The Generalisations vs. Classes metric measures the relation that exists between the number of generalisations and the number of classes in an UML class diagram. We define this metric as follows:

$$GEvsC = \left(\frac{N^{GE}}{N^{GE} + N^C} \right)^2$$	N^{GE} is the number of generalisations in an UML class diagram. N^C is the number of classes in an UML class diagram. Where $N^{GE} + N^C > 0$.

We consider as the number of generalisations each level of generalisation hierarchies, ie. each symbol

$\triangle$ in the class diagram

2.5 M_{GH} metric

The goal of Generalisation Hierarchy metric is to evaluate the complexity of class diagrams due to generalisation hierarchies. For this we take into account some of the factors that influence in the hierarchy structure (number of classes, number of levels and the use of multiple inheritance).

We define this metric as follow:

1. If the class diagram has no generalisation hierarchies: $M_{GH} = 0$

2. If the class diagram has generalisation hierarchies, M_{GH} is defined as: $M_{GH} = \sum_{i=1}^{n} CJ_i$, where CJ_i is the complexity of the ith generalisation hierarchy and n is the number of generalisation hierarchy within a class diagram

In order to calculate CJ_i we combine two factors: The first factor is the number of classes that are leaves of the hierarchy. This factor called $FLEAF_i$, is calculated thus: $FLEAF_i = \dfrac{N_i^{LEAF}}{N_i^C}$, where N_i^{LEAF} is the number of leaf classes in the ith generalisation hierarchy and N_i^C is the number of classes in the ith hierarchy.

Figure 1 shows different generalisation hierarchies with their values of $FLEAF_i$. $FLEAF_i$ approaches to 0.5 when the generalisation hierarchy is a binary tree (figure 1, parts c and d). It approaches zero in the ridiculous case of a unary "tree" with just a single superclass-subclass chain (figure 1, part b). And it approaches one if every superclass is an immediate subclass of the root class (part a).
On its own, $FLEAF_i$ has the undesirable property that for a very shallow hierarchy (e.g. just two or three levels) with a high branching factor it gives a measurement that is unreasonably high, from a subjective standpoint (part a of fig. 1 illustrate this). To correct this problem with $FLEAF_i$, an additional factor is used in the calculation of CJ_i, : the average number of direct and indirect superclasses per non-root class $ALLSUP_i$ (the root class of the generalisation hierarchy is not counted since it cannot have parents). This second factor is related to hierarchy depth but depends to some extent on the amount of multiple inheritance.

CJ_i is thus calculated using the following formula: $CJ_i = FLEAF_i - \dfrac{FLEAF_i}{ALLSUP_i}$

418

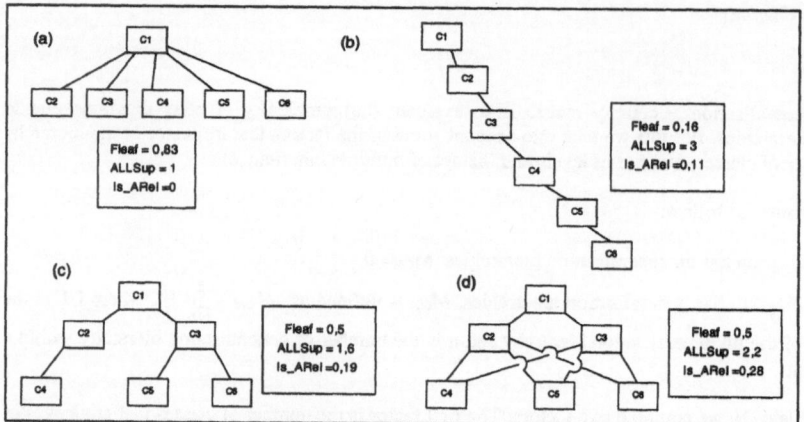

Figure 1. Examples of generalisation hierarchies

2.6 M_{MI} metric

Multiple Inheritance metric measures the complexity of generalisation hierarchies due to multiple inheritance.

M_{MI} is defined thus:

1. If the class diagram has no generalisation hierarchies $M_{MI}= 0$

2. If the class diagram has generalisation hierarchies M_{MI} is defined as follows: $M_{MI} = \sum_{i=1}^{n} CMI_i$, where
   CMI_i is the complexity of multiple inheritance of the ith generalisation hierarchy, and n is the number of generalisation hierarchies within a class diagram.

   $CJHM_i$ measures the ratio of extra parents (more than one) of each class. It is defined thus: $CMI_i = \dfrac{N_i^{EX}}{N_i^C}$,

where N_i^{EX} is the number of extra parents of the ith class, and N_i^C is the number of classes in such generalisation hierarchy.

2.7 AvsC metric

The Attributes vs. Classes metric measures the relation that exists between the number of attributes and the number of classes in an UML class diagram.

We define this metric as follows:

| $AvsC = \left(\dfrac{N^A}{N^A + N^C} \right)^2$ | N^A is the number of attributes in an UML class diagram. N^C is the number of classes in an UML class diagram. Where $N^A + N^C > 0$. |

2.8 MEvsC metric

The Methods vs. Classes metric measures the relation that exists between the number of methods and the number of classes in an UML class diagram.

We define this metric as follows:

| $MEvsC = \left(\dfrac{N^{ME}}{N^{ME} + N^C} \right)^2$ | N^{ME} is the number of methods in an UML class diagram. N^C is the number of classes in an UML class diagram. Where $N^{ME} + N^C > 0$. |

3. Our metrics in practice

The software measures have an important role on management and qualification of OOIS, at the initial phase of their life cycle. Nevertheless, it is well known that the definition of new metrics is not enough to cover this purpose. Another fundamental aspect in this aim rests on the empirical validation and correct interpretation of the observed measures (Fenton, 1994; Zuse, 1998). According to this purpose we have studied the behaviour of the proposed metrics in a set of assets (reusable software elements) stored in the GIRO repository.

The GIRO repository was founding as part of a research work on reuse, and it includes assets coming from different stages of software development and from various software paradigms, basically object oriented and classical (García, 2000).

3.1 Data collection and analysis

For the moment, the supplier of GIRO repository is the membership of GIRO and students from the University of Valladolid, who are developing their final project in Computer Technical Engineering. The asset measured belong to three product lines: 7 of Image (I), 7 of Disabled (D) and 13 of Optic (O). All of them were developed following the OO paradigm and UML, using the RATIONAL ROSE case tool; DELPHY was the implementation language.

To each asset we calculate the proposed metrics. Each asset has those values as part of its quality documentation.

The methodology followed in this research is thus:

1. Extract relevant information from a summary of data.
2. Analyse the data in order to find differences between product lines.
   The null hypotheses to test is: H^1o: *there is no difference between metric X in line1 and metric X in line2*

Where X is each of the eight selected metrics, and line1 and line2 are each of the three product lines. As result, we have 24 test.

3. Analyse this data in order to study relations between metrics.

The null hypotheses to test are H^2o and H^3o:

H^2o: metric X is no correlated with Y in the product line1.

Where X and Y are each of the eight selected metrics, and line1 is each of the three product lines. As result we have 84 test.

H^3o: metric X is no correlated with Y in all product lines.

Where X and Y are each of the eight selected metrics, as result we have 28 test.

Really, the number of test analysed was smaller, because there were a set of metrics without enough observed values. We have used the Mann-Whitney test to compare medians and Spearman correlation test to study relationships (Siegel, 1985), which are suitable statistical analysis techniques to study ordinal metrics

3.2 Metric summary

Table 1 shows the observed percentiles by product line and globally. The legends D, I, O, G mean Disabled, Image, Optic and Globally, and each cell shows the 25, 50 and 75 percentiles. The metrics with higher Percentiles are AvsC and MEvsC, so attributes and methods can introduce the biggest complexity in the design. Considering the box-and-whisker plots, only AvsC could have a symmetric distribution in Optic line. The N-ary metric has not observed values.

	asset count	ASvsC	N-ary	AGvsC	GEvsC	DEPvsC	AvsC	MEvsC	M_{GH}
D	7	0.0513	0	0	0	0.0400	**0.2430**	**0.6277**	0
		0.1600	0	0	0	0.0865	**0.4440**	**0.6766**	0
		0.1805	0	0	0	0.1029	**0.5070**	**0.7212**	0
I	7	0.0073	0	0.0004	0.0598	0	**0.4970**	**0.6488**	0.1925
		0.0076	0	0.0021	0.0625	0	**0.5710**	**0.6877**	0.385
		0.1738	0	0.0323	0.0625	0	**0.6860**	**0.7606**	0.385
O	13	0.0400	0	0	0.1185	0	**0.5870**	**0.6400**	0
		0.0625	0	0	0.1503	0	**0.6400**	**0.6655**	0
		0.1111	0	0.0083	0.1600	0	**0.7380**	**0.6694**	0
G	27	0.0083	0	0	0.0587	0	**0.4970**	**0.6463**	0
		0.0494	0	0	0.0625	0	**0.5710**	**0.6694**	0.0550
		0.1111	0	0.0052	0.1503	0.0400	**0.6690**	**0.7137**	0.3850

Table 1 Percentiles

3.3 Set of metrics which can differentiate between products lines

We test H^1o hypothesis to study the behaviour of the metrics by product lines in order to find significative differences. If a metric have different behaviour in two product lines then, it must be considered in future researches.

The sample is small (7 D products, 7 I products and 13 O products), but even so can detect some tracks. The hypothesis is that there is no difference between each pair of medians:

H^1o: Median X(line1) = Median X(line2)

"-" There are few observations						
	ASvsC	AGvsC	GEvsC	DEPvsC	AvsC	MEvsC	M$_{GH}$
I/D	**0.0087**	-	0.9350	-	0.2013	0.7983	-
I/O	**0.0383**	**0.0066**	-	-	**0.0383**	0.4273	-
D/O	0.1303	-	-	-	**0.0015**	0.5253	-

Table 2. P-Value (p) of Mann-Whitney Test

Considering Table 2, we can conclude that:

– The ASvsC can differentiate between product lines I and D.
– Furthermore I is different of O, when ASvsC, AGvsC and AvsC are considered.
– The AvsC can differentiate between product lines D and O.

3.4 Relationships among metrics

Every metric considered should quantify a distinct feature of the software products. To achieve this goal they need to be independent from each other, we can express the hypothesis H^2o and H^3o as: $r_{xy}= 0$

Tables 3, 4 and 5 summarise the results achieved applying the Spearman correlation test. The cells contain the p-value and the Spearman correlation coefficient. If there are insufficient observations the cell contains "-".

From table 3, we can conclude that MEvsC could have positive correlation with AGvsC(p= 0.0326) and DEPvsC(p=0.0663) in product line I.

From table 4, we have not observed any correlation in product line D, (p > 0.1 in all cases).

From table 5, we can conclude that GEvsC could have negative correlation with MEvsC(p= 0.0154) in the product line O.

When we studied the metric dependency in all the sample (n = 27) we only observed positive correlation between ASvsC and DEPvsC (p =0.0598), the relationships detected into product lines disappeared.

Image	ASvsC	AGvsC	GEvsC	DEPvsC	AvsC	MEvsC
ASvsC		0.7875	0.95815	-	0.7575	0.40187
		-0.1101	-0.0263		7	-0.3424
					-01261	
AGvsC			0.1945	-	0.1089	**0.0326**
			-0.6489		0.6547	**0.8729**
GEvsC				-	0.4727	0.8375
					0.3591	-0.1026
DEPvsC					-	-
AvsC						**0.0663**
						0.7500

Table 3. Matrix of Spearman correlation in product line Image

Disabled	ASvsC	AGvsC	GEvsC	DEPvsC	AvsC	MEvsC
ASvsC		-	-	0.6274	0.1154	0.7931
				0.1982	0.6429	0.1071
AGvsC			-	-	-	-
GEvsC				-	-	-
DEPvsC					0.3316	0.7575
					0.3964	0.1261
AvsC						0.7931
						-0.1071

Table 4 Matrix of Spearman correlation in product line Disabled

Optic	ASvsC	AGvsC	GEvsC	DEPvsC	AvsC	MEvsC
ASvsC		0.2413	0.8493	-	0.2156	0.1507
		0.3354	-0.0633		0.3574	0.4148
AGvsC			0.8067	-	0.16193	0.9068
			-0.0815		-0.4038	-0.0338
GEvsC				-	0.5828	**0.0154**
					0.1831	**-0.8074**
DEPvsC					-	-
AvsC						0.7366
						-0.0971

Table 5. Matrix of Spearman correlation in product line Optic

In conclusion, the complexity metrics ASvsC, AGvsC and AvsC could have different behaviour by product lines, so if we ignore it we can have confounding (Kleinbaum, 1987). Furthermore, some metrics, such as MEvsC wtih AGvsC, AvsC and GEvsC could be correlated in different product lines, and so we must consider this relationship in future models. We cannot forget that the sample is small, so the conclusions must be corroborated with other larger samples.

4. Conclusions and future work

Due to the growing complexity of OOIS, continuous attention to and assessment of object models are necessary to produce quality software systems. The fact that UML has emerged is a great step forward in object modelling. Even though this does not guarantee the quality of the models produced through the IS life cycle. Therefore, it is necessary to have metrics in order to evaluate their quality from the early phases in the OOIS development process.

In this work we have presented a set of metrics for assessing the complexity of UML class diagrams, obtained at early phases of the OOIS life cycle. It is widely accepted that the greater complex an UML class diagram, the greater complex the OOIS which is finally implemented, and therefore more effort is needed to develop and maintain it. So that the proposed metrics could be very fruitful, because they will allow OOIS designers to assess the complexity of their designs, and compare between design alternatives, from the early phases of OOIS life cycle.

As in other aspects of Software Engineering, proposing techniques and metrics is not enough, validation is critical to the success of software measurement (Kitchenham et al., 1995; Fenton and Pflegeer, 1997; Schneidewind, 1992; Basili et al.,1999). It is also necessary for them under theoretical and empirical validation, in order to assure their utility. Furthermore, it is important to understand their behaviour in order to define suitable models and appropriate design of the experiments (Montgomery, 1991, Kleinbaum et al., 1987), i.e. the quality model changes if we need consider blocks (product lines in this case), or if we have variables which are not independent (MEvsC and AGvsC).

With regard to empirical validation, we are carrying out some experimentation not only with controlled experiments but also with "real" cases taken from some enterprises, with the objective of assessing these metrics as predictors of maintenance efforts, and therefore, determine whether they can be used as early quality indicators.

In future work, we will focus our research on measuring other quality factors like those proposed in the ISO 9126 (1999), which not only tackle class diagrams, but also evaluate other UML diagrams, such as use-case diagrams, state diagrams, etc. To our knowledge, few works have been done towards measuring dynamic and functional models (Derr, 1995; Poels, 1999; Poels 2000). As is quoted in (Brito e Abreu et al., 1999) this is an area which lacks in depth investigation. In addition further empirical validation of the proposed metrics is needed to research their usefulness in the development software process. Furthermore we need a sample bigger to confirm the tracks find in this study and a quality model which includes a set of interest variables.

We will extend our metric, called MANTICA (created to measures data models), in order to provide support for collecting, analysing and visualising metric values applied to UML class diagrams.

Acknowledgements

This research is part of the MANTICA project, partially supported by CICYT and the European Union (1FD97-0168), and MENHIR project, supported by CICYT TIC97-0593-C05-05.

References

(Basili et al., 1999):   V. Basili, F. Shull and F. Lanubile. *Building knowledge through families of experiments.* IEEE Transactions on Software Engineering, 25(4), pages 435--437, 1999.

(Briand et al., 1999a):   L. Briand, S. Morasca and V. Basili. *Defining and Validating Measures for Object-Based high-level design.* IEEE Transactions on Software Engineering. 25(5), pages 722--743, 1999.

424

(Briand et al., 1999b):   L. Briand, S. Arisholm, F. Counsell, F. Houdek, F. and Thévenod-Fosse. *Empirical Studies of Object-Oriented Artifacts, Methods, and Processes: State of the Art and Future Directions.* Technical Report IESE 037.99/E, Fraunhofer Institute for Experimental Software Engineering, Kaiserslautern, Germany, 1999.

(Brito e Abreu et al., 1996): F. Brito e Abreu and W. Melo. *Evaluating the Impact of Object-Oriented Design on Software Quality.* Proceedings of 3rd International Metric Symposium, 1996.

(Basili et al., 1999):   V. Basili, F. Shull and F. Lanubile. *Building knowledge through families of experiments.* IEEE Transactions on Software Engineering, 25(4), pages 435-437, 1999.

(Briand et al., 1999a):   L. Briand, S. Morasca and V. Basili. *Defining and Validating Measures for Object-Based high-level design.* IEEE Transactions on Software Engineering. 25(5), pages 722--743, 1999.

(Briand et al., 1999b):   L. Briand, S. Arisholm, F. Counsell, F. Houdek, F. and Thévenod-Fosse. *Empirical Studies of Object-Oriented Artifacts, Methods, and Processes: State of the Art and Future Directions.* Technical Report IESE 037.99/E, Fraunhofer Institute for Experimental Software Engineering, Kaiserslautern, Germany, 1999.

(Brito e Abreu et al., 1996): F. Brito e Abreu and W. Melo. *Evaluating the Impact of Object-Oriented Design on Software Quality.* Proceedings of 3rd International Metric Symposium, 1996.

(Brito e Abreu et al., 1999): F. Brito e Abreu, H. Zuse, H. Sahraoui W. and Melo. *Quantitative Approaches in Object-Oriented Software Engineering.* Object-Oriented technology: ECOOP'99 Workshop Reader, Lecture Notes in Computer Science 1743, Springer-Verlag, pages 326--337, 1999.

(Chidamber et al., 1994):   S. Chidamber and C. Kemerer. *A Metrics Suite for Object Oriented Design.* IEEE Transactions on Software Engineering. 20(6), pages 476--493, 1994.

(Derr, 1995):   K. Derr. *Applying OMT.* SIGS Books, New York, 1995.

(Fenton, 1994):   N. Fenton. *Software Measurement: A Necessary Scientific Basis.* IEEE Transactions on Software Engineering, 20(3), pages 199--206, 1994.

(Fenton et al., 1997):   N. Fenton and S. Pfleeger. *Software Metrics: A Rigorous Approach.* 2nd. edition. London, Chapman & Hall, 1997.

(García, 2000):   F. J. García. *Modelo de Reutilización Soportado por Estructuras Complejas de Reutilización Denominadas Mecanos.* PHD Thesis, University of Salamanca, 2000.

(Genero et al., 1999):   M. Genero, Mª E. Manso, M. Piattini and F. J. García. *Assessing the Quality and the Complexity of OMT Models.* 2nd European Software Measurement Conference - FESMA 99, Amsterdam,The Netherlands, pages 99—109, 1999.

(Generoet al., 2000):   M. Genero, M. Piattini and C. Calero (2000). *Una Propuesta para Medir la Calidad de los Diagramas de Clases en UML.* IDEAS'2000, Cancún,

México, pages 373—384, 2000.

(ISO, 1999): ISO/IEC 9126-1.2. Information technology- Software product quality – Part 1: Quality model, 1999.

(Henderson-Sellers, 1996): B. Henderson-Sellers. *Object-oriented Metrics - Measures of complexity.* Prentice-Hall, Upper Saddle River, New Jersey, 1996.

(Kitchenhan et al., 1995): B. Kitchenham, S. Pflegger and N. Fenton. Towards a Framework for Software Measurement Validation. *IEEE Transactions of Software Engineering,* 21(12), pages 929--943, 1995.

(Kleinbaum et al., 1987): D. Kleinbaum, L. Kupper and K. Muller. *Applied regression analysis and other multivariate methods,* second ed. Duxbury Press, 1987.

(Lethbridge, 1998): Lethbridge, T. *Metrics for Concept-Oriented Knowledge bases.* International Journal of Software Engineering and Knowledge Engineering, 8(2), pages 61—188, 1998.

(Lorenz et al., 1994): M. Lorenz and J. Kidd. *Object-Oriented Software Metrics: A Practical Guide.* Prentice Hall, Englewood Cliffs, New Jersey, 1994.

(Marchesi, 1998): M. Marchesi. *OOA Metrics for the Unified Modeling Language.* Proceedings of the 2nd Euromicro Conference on Software Maintenance and Reengineering, pages 67--73, 1998.

(Montgomery, 1991): D. Montgomery. *Diseño y análisis de experimentos.* Grupo Editorial Iberoamericana, 1991.
(OMG, 1999): Object Management Group. *UML Revision Task Force. OMG Unified Modeling Language Specification, v. 1.3. document ad/99-06-08,* 1999.

(Poels, 1999): G. Poels. *On the use of a Segmentally Additive Proximity Structure to Meausre Object Class Life Cycle Complexity.* Software Measurement : Current Trends in Research and Practice, Deutscher Universitäts Verlag, pages 61-79, 1999.

(Poels, 2000): G. Poels. *On the Measurement of Event-Based Object-Oriented Conceptual Models.* 4th International ECOOP Workshop on Quantitative Approaches in Object-Oriented Software Engineering, June 13, Cannes, France, 2000.

(Schneidewind, 1992): N. Schneidewind. *Methodology For Validating Software Metrics.* IEEE Transactions of Software Engineering, 18(5), pages 410--422, 1992.

(Siegel, 1985): S. Siegel. *Estadística no paramétrica.* Ed. Trillas, 1985.

(Tian, 1999): J. Tian. *Taxonomy and Selection of Quality Measurements and Models.* Proceedings of SEKE'99, The 11th International Conference on Software Engineering & Knowledge Engineering, June 16-19, pages 71--75, 1999.

(Zuse, 1998): H. Zuse. *A Framework of Software Measurement.* Berlin, Walter de Gruyter, 1998.

XML AND CORBA ISSUES II

A View Model for XML Documents

Xavier Baril and Zohra Bellahsène

LIRMM – Laboratoire d'Informatique, de Robotique et de Microélectronique de Montpellier
UMR 5506 CNRS/Université Montpellier II
161 Rue Ada, 34392 Montpellier- France
E-mail:{baril, bella}@lirmm.fr   Fax: +33/0 467 41 85 00

ABSTRACT. *XML is an emergent standard for data representation and exchange on the Web. In this paper, we present a view model for XML based on XML-QL. Views over semistructured data filter data of interest for applications. Furthermore, they provide structure to semistructured data that can be exploited by the query optimiser. A XML view is defined by a query on XML document(s) and returns a XML document that can be handled by any XML browser. In our approach, a DTD validating the view result is generated. Moreover, our view specification language takes into account distribution. Indeed, with our view definition, the user can express which data should be transmitted and materialised.*

KEY WORDS: *XML, View Definition Language, DTD Inference.*

1. Introduction

Data present on the Web is non-structured, or with incomplete, irregular or frequently changed structure. XML is becoming the universal exchange data model on the Web. It has been shown that XML is well appropriate for semistructured data representation. Compared to HTML, XML provides explicit data structuring, and the data presentation is separated from the data content (Abiteboul, 1999).

This paper presents a view model for XML documents. Defining a view mechanism for XML will provide multiple benefits. It would allow restructuring data in order to meet users' needs and requirements. First, as in a classical database system, the view mechanism provides different points of view on the same data, here XML documents. Each point of view corresponds to a specific need of the same document. Furthermore, in the context of unstructured data (i.e., semistructured data), the view mechanism provides means to add a structure to semistructured documents. This structure can be exploited to improve query performance, or to enable application programs to handle easily semistructured documents.

The W3C proposes a language that provides means to restructuring XML documents. This language is XSL (Extensible Stylesheet Language), designed to define stylesheet over XML documents. However, XSL cannot be considered as a view definition language, its expressive power is insufficient.

Some studies addressed the issue of managing XML data (Lahiri et al., 1999, Goldman et al., 1999, Sha et al., 1999). However few of them focused on the view management issue (Abiteboul et al., 1999, Baru et al., 1999). Stanford database group in (Abiteboul et al., 1997a) proposed a view specification language for semistructured data, and focused on the problems caused by the semistructured nature of the data. Serge Abiteboul in (Abiteboul, 1999) discussed the main issues on XML views.

A view model generally relies on a data model and a query language. In this paper, we present a view model for XML documents, and the related data model taking IDREF(S) attributes into account. The query language is a central issue related to the definition of a view model. Our view model is based on a query language close to XML-QL (Deutsch et al., 1999a). Compared to XML-QL our query language adds structure to the view result and provides a DTD validating the result.

The rest of the paper is organised as follows. Section 2 presents the data model. In Section 3, is described the view model that we propose. Section 4 presents related work. In section 5, we conclude and present our future work.

2. Data model

A view model is based essentially on a data model and a query language. XML is only a mark-up language, and we discuss in this section a data model for it.
OEM (Object Exchange Model) (Papakonstantinou et al., 1995) is the de-facto data model for semistructured data, designed for the Lore system (McHugh et al., 1997). Although XML data is semistructured, OEM is not sufficient to describe it. Indeed, order is an important feature that is not provided by OEM. Furthermore, XML syntax provides different links between elements that OEM doesn't support.

We choose a data model strongly inspired from the one defined for XML-QL (Deutsch et al., 1999a). However, our data model supports IDREF(S) attributes defined by the DTD ; this point is not clearly defined in XML-QL. Besides, we choose an ordered data model.

2.1. Ordered data model

XML elements are ordered according to their appearance in the document. We keep this order in our data model. An ordered data model has a richer semantics rather than an unordered one. For instance, let us consider an element paper involving two sub-elements author. With an unordered data model, we can't know who is the first author, and who is the second.

2.2. Identity and elements sharing

To allow element sharing, XML introduces the attribute type ID, which is the element identifier. It binds a unique key with the element. Furthermore, this attribute can be used to identify the node that corresponds to the element in the XML data graph. Attribute type IDREF enables an element to reference another one with its identifier, while type IDREFS enables an element to reference several ones. These attribute types, ID, IDREF(S), must be defined in the DTD of the document. Figure 1 describes an example of XML data, and figure 2 its corresponding DTD. This example describes a database, which contains researchers and departments. A researcher is represented by a firstname, a lastname, and eventually an email and a phone number. A department is represented by a name and eventually several teams. Each researcher, department or team is identified by an ID attribute. The IDREF attributes describe relations between these elements. A researcher contains an IDREF attribute, which points to its department, and eventually attributes, which point to its team and its superior. A department contains an IDREF attribute which point to its director. Finally, the team contains an IDREF attribute which points to the manager.

Our data model takes two kinds of links between elements into account. We can distinguish these two kinds as follows:

- *Composition links,* which express that an element is composed of subelements. This kind of links is implicitly described by the overlap of the elements in the XML document.
- *Reference links,* which express that an element uses another element, which is not a subelement. This kind of links is described by the use of IDREF(S) attributes in the XML document.

```
<?xml version='1.0' standalone='no' ?>
<!-- dtd inclusion -->
<!DOCTYPE bd SYSTEM "bd.dtd" >
<!-- begin of the document -->
<bd>
<!-- researchers -->
<researcher ID="jc" dept="IS" team="db">
        <firstname>Cage</firstname>
        <lastname>Janet</lastname>
        <email>jc@lirmm.fr</email>
</person>
<researcher ID="nc" dept="AI">
        <firstname>Carlson</firstname>
        <lastname>Nick</lastname>
</researcher>
<researcher ID="bj" dept="IS" team="db">
        <firstname>Jones</firstname>
        <lastname>Brian</lastname>
        <email>bjones@lirmm.fr</email>
</researcher>
<researcher ID="jl" dept="AI">
        <firstname>Landry</firstname>
        <lastname>Jenifer</lastname>
</researcher>

<researcher ID="js" dept="IS" team="db"
superior="jc">
        <firstname>Smith</firstname>
        <lastname>James</lastname>
        <email>smith@lirmm.fr</email>
        <phone>8613</phone>
</researcher>
<researcher ID="aw" dept="IS" team="db"
superior="jc">
        <firstname>Williams</firstname>
        <lastname>Alan</lastname>
</researcher>
<!-- departments -->
<department ID="IS" director="bj">
        <name>Information Science</name>
        <team ID="db" name="Databases"
        manager="jc"/>
</department>
<department ID="AI" director="jl">
        <name>Artificial
        Intelligence</name>
</department>
</bd>
<!-- end of the document -->
```

Figure 1. Example of XML data

```
<?xml version='1.0' ?>
<!-- dtd decribing a database about researcher and department -->
<!ELEMENT bd (researcher+,department+) >
<!-- researcher description -->
<!ELEMENT researcher (firstname,lastname,email?,phone?) >
<!ATTLIST researcher ID ID #REQUIRED
                dept IDREF #REQUIRED
                team IDREF #IMPLIED
                superior IDREF #IMPLIED >
<!ELEMENT firstname (#PCDATA) >
<!ELEMENT lastname (#PCDATA) >
<!ELEMENT email (#PCDATA) >
<!ELEMENT phone (#PCDATA) >
<!-- department description -->
<!ELEMENT department (name,team*) >
<!ATTLIST department ID ID #REQUIRED
                director IDREF #REQUIRED >
<!ELEMENT name (#PCDATA) >
<!ELEMENT team EMPTY >
<!ATTLIST team          ID ID #REQUIRED
                name CDATA #REQUIRED
                manager IDREF #REQUIRED >
<!-- end of the dtd -->
```

Figure 2. Example of DTD

2.3. Character data

Only leaf nodes of the XML graph may contain values. It doesn't matter from the database point of view, because all elements are composed of subelement(s) or a character value. But from the document point of view, an element may be composed by subelement(s) and character value(s). Let us consider the following XML example:

```
<a>aa<b>bb</b>aaa<c>cc</c></a>
```

This example is XML well formed, and our data model must be able to represent it. Therefore, we introduce a third kind of link, *character link*, to provide a mapping between an element to a character value.

2.4. XML graph

Our data model represents XML data by a rooted graph, which is labelled and ordered. The graph G is defined as follows.

- G has two kinds of nodes :
  - o Nodes that represent elements of the document. These nodes are labelled with the attributes of the element, except the IDREF(S) attributes. These nodes are ordered.
  - o Nodes that represent character values. These nodes are always leaf nodes and are not labelled.
- G has three kinds of edges :
  - o Edges that represent composition links. These edges are labelled with the elements name.
  - o Edges that represent reference links. These edges are labelled with the name of the IDREF(S) attributes.
  - o Edges that represent character links. These edges are not labelled.
- G has a root node, which represents the root element of the document.

Figure 3 depicts the XML graph corresponding to the XML document described in figure 1. Element nodes are represented by circles. The order of the node is delimited by brackets, and the label of the node is on its line. Character nodes are represented by their values (i.e., string). Composition links are represented by solid arrows with label, reference links by dashed arrows with label and character links by solid arrows without label. Due to space limitations and for a better clarity, we don't represent on the graph all the elements of the document. So "..." means that the element is incompletely defined in the graph.

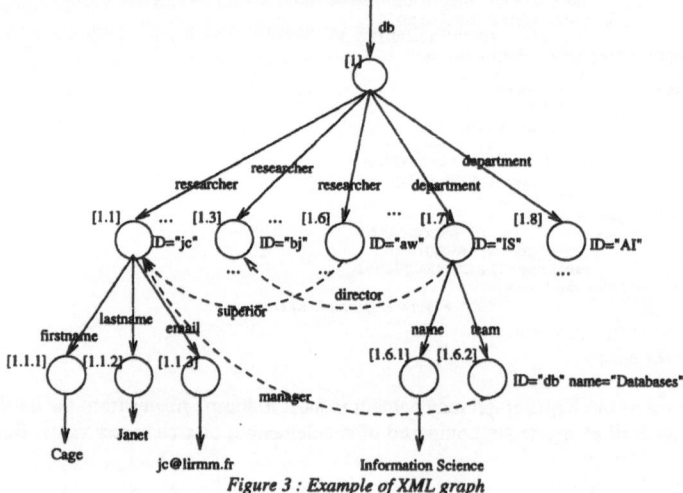

Figure 3 : Example of XML graph

3. The view definition language

In this section, we present first the requirements that motivate the design of our view definition language. Theses requirements are in agreement with those expressed in (Deutsch et al., 1999a) for query languages and for XML views (Abiteboul, 1999).

3.1. Requirements for our language

3.1.1. Closure property

A view defined on XML document(s) should yield an XML document. The closure property enables documents generated by views to be handled by any XML browser. In this way, it allows users and programs use transparently a view or a document.

Lorel (Abiteboul et al., 1997b) doesn't perform this requirement because it produces as result a set of objects. XML-QL (Deutsch et al., 1999a) may return an XML document as result, but it is not mandatory. Moreover, our language ensures that the result is well-formed XML document.

3.1.2. Restructuring possibilities

The view definition language should enable restructuring elements of the source documents. In order to fulfil the programs and users requirements. More precisely, our view model should yield two distinct classes of views:

1. *Select views* that extract existing elements from source document(s).
2. *Composite views* that create new elements or attributes ; an element of the view result doesn't exist in a source document, this element may be created from several elements of the source(s) document(s). Furthermore, aggregation functions (i.e., sum, avg, min, max, count) can be used to define new values for elements or attributes in the view. Moreover, sorting and grouping elements are also provided.

3.1.3. DTD inference

XML documents on which the views are defined can be associated to a DTD but it is not mandatory. In both cases, we can associate a DTD to the view to make it more structured. A DTD (Document Type Definition) describes the structure of a document with a grammar. This DTD should be automatically generated from the query defining the view, and when it is possible, from the sources DTDs.

The generated DTD should be incomplete, it means the DTD describes only partly the structure of the view result. The issue of DTD inference for views or queries was studied in MIX project (Baru et al., 1999). Inferring DTD compromises the expressive power of the view definition language. Compared to XML-QL, our language is less expressive power, but it generates a DTD describing a view result. Providing a DTD associated to the view result is a contribution of our view model, this DTD allows view management optimisation. The DTD can be used to optimise the view storage, or to querying the view.

3.2. Description of the language

3.2.1. View syntax

The syntax of our view definition language is described below. The view definition is composed of three, introduced respectively by the key words CREATE, WHERE and CONSTRUCT. The first part names the view, the second part (WHERE clause) uses XML pattern to match data, and the third part (CONSTRUCT clause) constructs the result with matched data.

```
CREATE [MATERIALIZED] VIEW <view_name> [WITHOUT_REF] AS
WHERE
   (<XML_pattern> IN <XML_document>)+
   (<condition>)*
CONSTUCT
   <result_pattern>
   [GROUP-BY (variable)+]
   [ORDER-BY (variable)+]
```

The first part, introduced by the keyword CREATE VIEW names the view with <view_name>. The optional clause MATERIALIZED allows the user to specify if He/She wants to materialise the view. If so, this means the view query will be executed and the result will be stored. In this way, the user queries can be answered using the MATERIALIZED view without accessing to the source documents. The optional clause WITHOUT_REF enforces the integrity constraint, by deleting IDREF(S) attributes, which don't reference elements of the result. More details about integrity constraint are given below, in subsection 3.2.3.

The WHERE clause matches data by recognising <XML pattern> in a XML_document. An XML pattern contains variable(s) of which names are preceded by $ to distinguish them from string literal. These variables are bound to data in source documents to allow the data matching. A variable can bind to an element, with the clause ELEMENT_AS after the element, or the content of an element, with the clause CONTENT_AS or between the tags of the element.

A <condition> expresses constraint about variables. Furthermore, we can distinguish two kinds of conditions:

- *Simple conditions* that express constraints on the values. These conditions compare variables to values.
- *Complex conditions* that express joins between two XML documents. These conditions compare two variables of different XML patterns.

The CONSTRUCT clause describes the structure of the view result. It uses the variables defined in the WHERE part, and provides structure to the data. This structure generates statically a DTD for the view result.

Finally, like with SQL, it is possible to define view involving GROUP-BY and ORDER-BY clauses. More details are given below, in section 3.2.5.

3.2.2. *Motivating example*

Let us consider the view providing the firstname of researchers who work in the Information Science (IS) department. The view query defining it is given in the figure 4.

```
CREATE VIEW ISResearcher AS
WHERE
   <researcher dept="IS">
        <firstname>$n</firstname>
   </researcher> IN www.lirmm.fr/~baril/xml/bd.xml
CONSTRUCT
   <researcher>$n</researcher>
```
Figure 4 : View definition of ISResearcher

The WHERE clause of the view retrieves researcher elements in the source document. These researcher elements must fulfil some constraints: they must have the dept attribute with "IS" as value, and having the subelement lastname. The variable $n binds to the value of the subelement lastname for the researcher elements which fulfil the previous constraints. The root element of the view uses the view name, and the elements, which match the view query, are nested in the result element.

3.2.3. Integrity of the result

IDREF(S) attributes enable elements sharing in an XML document. However, all elements referenced by IDREF(S) attributes must exist to enforce the validity of the document. This integrity constraint must be enforced in the result of the view. So, when an IDREF(S) attribute is present in the result of the view, its corresponding element(s) must be present in the result too.

Of course, adding to the result elements referenced by the IDREF(S) attributes is costly from the performance point of view. Indeed, this entails the cost to retrieve the elements, and the space cost to store them. To avoid this problem, we introduce the WITHOUT_REF clause in our view definition language, so that the view designer can choose if He/She wants to store the elements referenced by the result elements.

By default, all referenced elements are added to the view result. The view result is composed of two subelements : an element named "result" which contains elements corresponding to the view definition, and an element named "references" which contains elements referenced by those of the result. If the WITHOUT_REF clause is specified, the IDREF(S) attributes are deleted if they don't reference elements, which are in the result.

Example. Let us consider now the view that retrieves the departments. Department elements and subelements contain several IDREF attributes referencing the department director and the team manager. Only the view Department2 involves a WITHOUT_REF clause. The view queries defining them are given in figure 5.

```
CREATE VIEW Department1 AS
WHERE
  <department>
  </department> ELEMENT_AS $d IN www.lirmm.fr/~baril/xml/bd.xml
CONSTUCT
  $d
CREATE VIEW Department2 WITHOUT_REF AS
WHERE
  <department>
  </department> ELEMENT_AS $d IN www.lirmm.fr/~baril/xml/bd.xml
CONSTUCT
  $d
```

Figure 5 : View definitions of Department1 and Department2

These views retrieve department elements in the source document, without particular constraints. View results are given in figure 6. We note that the view Department1 contains a ``references" subelement and view department2 doesn't. Department1 contains IDREF attributes that represent the director of the department and the team manager, and Department2 doesn't. Therefore, the cost of performing the view Department2 is less expensive than the one for view Department1. Besides, its storage cost is less expensive.

```
<Departement1>
  <result>
      <department ID='IS' director='bj'>
          <name>Information Science</name>
          <team ID='db' name='Databases' manager='jc'/>
      </department>
      <department ID='AI' director='jl'>
          <name>Artificial Intelligence</name>
      </departement>
  </result>
```

```
<references>
        <researcher ID="bj" dept="IS" team="db">
                <firstname>Brian</firstname>
                <lastname>Jones</lastname>
        </researcher>
        <researcher ID="jc" dept="IS" team="db">
                <firstname>Janet</firstname>
                <lastname>Cage</lastname>
                <email>dh@lirmm.fr</email>
        </researcher>
        <researcher ID="jl" dept="AI">
                <firstname>Jenifer</firstname>
                <lastname>Landry</lastname>
        </researcher>
</references>
</Departement1>

<Departement2>
  <result>
        <department ID="IS">
                <name>Information Science</name>
                <team ID="db" name="Databases"/>
        </department>
        <department ID="AI">
                <name>Artificial Intelligence</name>
        </departement>
  </result>
</Departement2>
```

Figure 6 : Department1 and Department2 View Result

3.2.4. Implicit and explicit join

Our data model supports IDREF(S) attributes defined by the DTD. As our data model considers an IDREF(S) attribute as a link, we can consider this kind of attributes like subelement(s) of the element containing the attribute. In order to build new elements containing elements referenced by IDREF(S) attributes, our view definition language provides implicit joins.

Example. Let us consider the view, which creates new elements containing the researcher firstname and its associated department name. This view named ResearcherDepartment is defined in figure 7.

```
CREATE VIEW ResearcherDepartment AS
WHERE
  <researcher>
        <firstname>$np</firstname>
        <dept><name>$nd</name></dept>
  </researcher> IN www.lirmm.fr/~baril/xml/bd.xml
CONSTUCT
  <researcher>
        <name>$np</name>
        <dept>$nd</dept>
  </researcher>
```

Figure 7 : View definition with implicit join

In the view ResearcherDepartment, the join is called implicit because it's transparent for the user. The join is expressed by the dept IDREF attribute.

Let us now give an example with an explicit join. The view ResearcherDepartment2 yield the same result as ResearcherDepartment (except for the root element name because the view name is different) using an explicit join. The query defining this view is given in figure 8. The join is called explicit because the user defines a condition to express it. This condition matches the variables $d and $id.

```
CREATE VIEW ResearcherDepartment2 AS
WHERE
  <researcher dept=$d>
        <firstname>$np</firstname>
  </researcher> IN www.lirmm.fr/~baril/xml/bd.xml
  <department ID=$id>
        <name>$nd</name>
  </department> IN www.lirmm.fr/~baril/xml/bd.xml
  $d=$id
CONSTUCT
  <researcher>
        <name>$np</name>
        <dept>$nd</dept>
  </researcher>
```

Figure 8 : View definition with explicit join

3.2.5. Aggregation functions

Our view definition language proposes aggregation functions, as powerful restructuring possibilities. We use a GROUP-BY clause in the CONSTRUCT clause of the view definition to group the content of the variables and allow the use of aggregation functions. Their names are preceded by $, as variable names.

Example. Let us consider the view DepartmentMember that retrieves for each department the number of its members and the list of their firstnames. This view is defined in the figure 9.

```
CREATE VIEW DepartmentMember AS
WHERE
  <researcher dept=$d>
        <firstname>$np</firstname>
  </researcher> IN www.lirmm.fr/~baril/xml/bd.xml
  <department ID=$id>
  </department> IN www.lirmm.fr/~baril/xml/bd.xml
  $d=$id
CONSTUCT
  <department ID=$id size=$count($np)>
        <member>$np</member>
  </department>
  GROUP-BY $id
```

Figure 9 : View definition with aggregation function

This view uses an explicit join to retrieve departments and associated members. The result is group by departments, allowing the use of the $count() aggregation function to count the members of each department. Due to the GROUP-BY clause, each department element contains the list of associated researchers.

3.2.6. DTD inference

As it has been explained in subsection 3.1.3, our view definition language is able to generating a DTD for the view result.
First, the root element of the DTD has the name of the view, and is composed of the "result" element and eventually a "references" element.
Secondly, the structure expressed in the CONSTRUCT part of the view definition is captured to build the DTD.
Thirdly, if a DTD is available for the source document, we eventually add the generated DTD with the definitions of the result elements.

Example. Let us consider the view Department1 (defined figure 5) and its result (figure 6). Our system generates the following DTD (depicted in figure 10) for this view.

```
<!ELEMENT Department1 (result,references*)>
<!ELEMENT result (department*)>
<!ELEMENT department (name,team*) >
<!ATTLIST department ID ID #REQUIRED
                     director IDREF #REQUIRED >
<!ELEMENT name (#PCDATA) >
<!ELEMENT team EMPTY >
<!ATTLIST team       ID ID #REQUIRED
                     name CDATA #REQUIRED
                     manager IDREF #REQUIRED >
<!ELEMENT references (#PCDATA) >
```

Figure 10 : DTD generated for the view Department1

4. Related work

In this section, we present an overview of related work on semistructured and XML data. First, we focus on the management of such data and present some associated query languages. Then, we discuss related work dealing with views on semistructured data.

4.1. Semistructured data management and query language

Lore (McHugh et al., 1997) is the database management system dedicated to semistructured data, which was based on the OEM model. OEM is considered as the de-facto data model for semistructured data, and numerous works about semistrucured data management use it (Sha et al., 1999, Lahiri et al., 1999).

Lorel (Abiteboul et al.,1997b) , the query language of Lore, proposes a `select-from-where` syntax in the spirit of SQL/OQL. Recently, the OEM data model has migrated to an XML data model (Goldman et al., 1999). Lorel, the query language, has migrated too, and exploits XML features not present in OEM. However, the result of a Lorel query is not an XML document, but a set of objects.

Rather than building a new database management system for semistructured data from scratch, another solution consists in using a commercial DBMS. For example, in the Miro-Web project (Sha et al., 1999), semistructured data represented as XML documents are stored in relational tables. The project STORED (Semistructured TO RElational Data) (Deutsch et al., 1999b), proposes an algorithm to compute the mapping from the OEM data model to the relational data model.

As noted in (Abiteboul, 1999), some applications can use both structured data and semistructured data. The Ozone (Lahiri et al., 1999) data model was proposed for managing this kind of hybrid data. In fact, the Ozone data model is an extension of the ODMG data model with an OEM type. A query language that extends OQL for such data has been proposed.

Several propositions of query languages have been done. XML-QL, Lorel, YATL have emerged from the database community, and XQL (Robie et al., 1998) from the document community. Nowadays, there is no standard equivalent to SQL or OQL to query XML data. However, XML-QL (Deutsch et al., 1999a) seems to be a good challenger.

4.2. Semistructured data and views

A view definition language for OEM data has been proposed in (Abiteboul et al., 1997a). The paper focused on the issue of querying views defined on semistructured data. Whereas incremental maintenance of views on semistructured data has been considered in (Abiteboul et al., 1998).

In (Abiteboul, 1999), Serge Abiteboul presents an overview of the main issues concerning XML views, and considers some of his work on views (Abiteboul et al., 1999, Souza et al., 1994). Work reported in (Abiteboul et al., 1999) describes "Active Views" the Web application generator dedicated to electronic commerce.

The MIX (Mediation of Information using XML) (Baru et al., 1999) project proposes a mediator system for XML documents. Members of this project gave some recommendations for an XML view definition language. Their view language called XMAS (XML MAtching and Structuring) and DTD inference issues are discussed. Furthermore, another proposition for defining XML views on relational schemas has been done.

Our proposition attempts to meet the requirements for XML views by S. Abiteboul (Abiteboul, 1999). Our approach is quite different from the one of MIX. MIX is a mediator system using XML as a pivot format. XML documents are generated by wrappers from heterogeneous sources (relational databases, object databases, HTML files). They are all associated with a DTD that is the start point for the query creation with the BBQ interface (Blended Browsing and Querying) (Baru et al., 1999). We propose a view model dealing with a more general class of XML documents. When a DTD is available, we exploit it.

5. Conclusion and future work

This paper describes a view model that is based on an extension of the data model associated to XML-QL taking IDREF(S) attributes into account. Furthermore, several kinds of links between elements : composition links, reference links and character links are considered in our data model.

The view definition language we propose, is based on a query language in the spirit of XML-QL. It enables restructuring XML documents and/or creating new elements. Furthermore, it provides join mechanisms and aggregation functions. Compared to XML-QL, our language yields a structured XML document as view result. This structure is used to generate the DTD validating the view result. Thus, this DTD can be exploited for optimisation purpose.
Moreover, the user can express his preference to materialise the resulting XML document. In this way, the view can be queried without needing to access to the source documents.

We are currently implementing the view model presented in this paper. The code is written in Java, and we use the JAXP API to access XML documents. This API provides classes implementing the DOM interface proposed by W3C.

For improving query performance, views over semistructured data can be MATERIALIZED. Our future work will focus on the selection of views to materialise, given a set of XML views. This problem has been extensively studied for relational model (Bellahsène et al., 2000, Theodoratos et al., 1997), especially in data warehouses. To the best of our knowledge, the issue of selecting XML views to materialise, has not yet been addressed.

References:

(Abiteboul, 1999): S. Abiteboul. *On Views and XML*. In the Proceedings of PODS, In the Proceedings of the Eighteenth Symposium on Principles of Database Systems (PODS), pages 1—9, Philadelphia Pennsylvania, June 1999.

(Abiteboul et al., 1999): S. Abiteboul, B. Amann, S. Cluet, A. Eyal, L. Mignet and T. Milo. *Active Views for Electronic Commerce*. In the Proceedings of the 25ᵗʰ International Conference on Very Large Data Bases, pages 138—149, Edinburgh Scotland, September 1999.

(Abiteboul et al., 1998): S. Abiteboul, J. McHugh, M. Rys, V. Vassalos and J. L. Wiener. *Incremental Maintenance for MATERIALIZED Views over Semistructured Data*. In the Proceedings of the 24ᵗʰ International Conference on Very Large Data Bases, pages 138—149, New York City USA, August 1998.

(Abiteboul et al., 1997a): S. Abiteboul, R. Goldman, V. Vassalos and J. L. Wiener. *Views for Semistructured Data*. In the Proceedings of the International Workshop on Management of Semistructured Data, Tucson USA, May 1997.

(Abiteboul et al., 1997b): S. Abiteboul, D. Quass, J. McHugh, J. Widom and J. L. Wiener. *The Lorel Query Language for Semistructured Data*. In the Proceedings of the International Journal on Digital Librairies, pages 68—88, 1997.

(Baru et al., 1999): C. K. Baru, V. Chu, A. Gupta, B. Ludäescher, R. Marciano, Y. Papakonstantinou and P. Velikhov. *XML-Based Information Mediation with MIX*. In the Proceedings of the Fourth ACM conference on Digital Libraries, pages 214—215, Berkeley USA, August 1999.

(Bellahsène et al., 2000): Z. Bellahsène and P. Marrot, *Materializing a Set of Views: Dynamic Strategies and Performance Evaluation*. In the Proceedings of the International Database Engineering and Applications Symposium, Yokohoma Japan, September 2000.

(Deutsch et al., 1999a): A. Deutsch, M. Fernandez, D. Florescu, A. Levy and D. Suciu. *A Query Language for XML*. In the Proceedings of the 8ᵗʰ International World Wide Web Conference, pages 1155—1169, May 1999.

(Deutsch et al., 1999b): A. Deutsch, M. Fernandez and D. Suciu. *Storing Semistructured Data with STORED*. In the Proceedings of the International Conference on Management of Data, pages 431—442, Philadephia USA, June 1999.

(Goldman et al., 1999): R. Goldman, J. McHugh, D. Quass and J. Widom. *Migrating the Lore Data Model and Query Language*. In the Proceedings of the 2ⁿᵈ International Workshop on the Web and Databases, pages 25—30, Philadephia USA, June 1999.

(Lahiri et al., 1999): T. Lahiri, S. Abiteboul and J. Widom. *Ozone: Integrating Structured and Semistructured Data*. In the Proceedings of the 7ᵗʰ International Conference on Database Programming Languages, pages 25—30, Kinloch Rannoch Scotland, June 1999.

(McHugh et al., 1997): J. McHugh, S. Abiteboul, R. Goldman, D. Quass and J. Widom. *Lore: A Database Management System for Semistructured Data*. In SIGMOD Records, Volume 26, Number 3, pages 54—66, September 1997.

(Papakonstantinou et al., 1995): Y. Papakonstantinou, H. Garcia-Molina and J. Widom. *Object Exchange Across Heterogeneous Informations Sources*. In the Proceedings of the 11ᵗʰ International Conference on Data Engineering, pages 251—260, Taipei Taiwan, March 1995.

(Robie et al., 1998): J. Robie, J. Lapp and D. Schach. *XML Query Language (XQL)*. http://www.w3.org/TandS/QL/QL98/pp/xql.html, 1998.

(Sha et al., 1999): F. Sha, G. Gardarin and L. Nemirovski. *Managing Semistructured Data in Object Relational DBMS*. In the Procceedings of 15èmes Journées Bases de Données Avancées, pages 101—115, Bordeaux France, October 1999.

(Souza et al., 1994): C. Souza, S. Abiteboul and C. Delobel. *Virtual Schemas and Bases*. In the Proceedings of 4th International Conference on Extending Database Technology, pages 81—94, Cambridge United Kingdom, March 1994.

(Theodoratos et al., 1997): D. Theodoratos and T. Sellis. *Data Warehouse Configuration*. In the Proceedings of the 23rd International Conference on Very Large Data Bases, pages 126—135, Athens Greece, August 1997.

Information Monitors: An Architecture Based on XML

George Spanoudakis   Andrea Zisman

City University
Department of Computing
Northampton Square
Phone: +44 020 7477 8346/8413
Fax: +44 020 7477 8587
London EC1V 0HB
{gespan | a.zisman}@soi.city.ac.uk

ABSTRACT. *In this paper we present an approach to allow monitoring of XML documents on the World Wide Web. We describe a distributed information monitoring architecture based on monitor rules. The architecture preserves the autonomy of the participating documents and allows evolution of the system by adding, removing and modifying XML documents. In order to illustrate the approach we present an example in the financial domain.*

KEY WORDS: *Information monitor, information resources, monitor rules, conditions, actions, XML, World Wide Web.*

1. Introduction

In application domains where people need to extract and combine vast amounts of rapidly changing information published in numerous web-sites on a daily (or even more frequent) basis, traditional methods of information retrieval based on browsing and/or search engines become ineffective.

Consider for example private investors who use information published on the World Wide Web to make decisions about their investments. These investors need to access and combine information distributed on different sites. Examples are sites of stockbrokers, sites of newspapers, sites dedicated to the provision of financial information, and sites of companies of which they had or plan to purchase shares. The investors also need to be alerted when new pieces of information, relevant to their investments, become available.

In such settings, people know in advance the information in which they are interested, the sites from where they can access this information, and the ways in which they should combine information and act upon it. People do not need to access information that they have already consulted, unless this information is in disagreement with or related to a newly published piece of information. Therefore, it is necessary to have an effective way to cope with rapid changes of vast amounts of information, happening autonomously at different web-sites.

In order to address the above problem, we propose a system to allow *distributed information monitoring* of documents on the World Wide Web. The approach relies on monitoring and combining information distributed on different resources and alerting the user – or more generally acting on behalf of him/her – when certain conditions regarding this information are satisfied. Our approach assumes information represented in the eXtensible Markup Language (XML (Bray et al.,

1998)), published on different web-sites or dynamically produced by different software applications (referred to as *information resources* in the following).

Our system is based on the use of *monitor rules* to express the interest of users. The monitor rules indicate: (a) which information, stored in the same or different information resources, is relevant to the users and (b) how to act in the presence of changes of this information. The system monitors information resources and acts upon information changes, regarding the monitor rules.

The use of XML as the basis for our approach has been motivated by the increasing popularity of this language as a means for structuring and publishing information on the World Wide Web, as well as for exchanging information between different software applications.

Over the last few years many public and private organisations have formed consortia to define standard types of XML documents for a wide range of application domains. Examples are found in bioinformatics (BIOML, 1999), finance ((FIXML, 1999), (FpML, 1999), (NTM)), mathematics (MathML, 1999), chemistry (CML), and others. In addition, many software vendors have developed frameworks, which support the publication of information content expressed in XML on the World Wide Web such as COCOON project (Apache), and XML support in Active Server Pages (Deitel et al., 1999).

The remainder of the paper is structured as follows. Section 2 describes the architecture of the system with its various components and structures. Section 3 presents the syntax used to express the monitor rules. Section 4 addresses the distributed information monitoring process. Section 5 describes an example to illustrate the approach. Section 6 presents some related work. Finally, section 7 summarises the approach and suggests directions for future work.

2. Architecture

The architecture of the system being proposed is Web-based and allows distributed monitoring of the participating XML documents. It preserves the autonomy of the XML documents being monitored and supports evolution of the system in terms of adding, removing and modifying XML documents, users and monitor rules.

Figure 1 presents the architecture of our approach with its various components. A description of each of the components in terms of their functionality is presented below.

2.1 Information Resources (IR)

The *information resources* (IR) are web-sites composed of different XML documents, which are monitored by the system. Each web-site is related to a company or group of people that want to allow access to their XML documents. Each of the XML documents has an associated Document Type Definition (DTD) (Bray et al., 1998). Documents in the same information resource may have different DTDs.

2.2 User

The participating *users* access the system through the Web. Each user defines the information in which they are interested by describing monitor rules with their respective actions (c.f. Section 3).

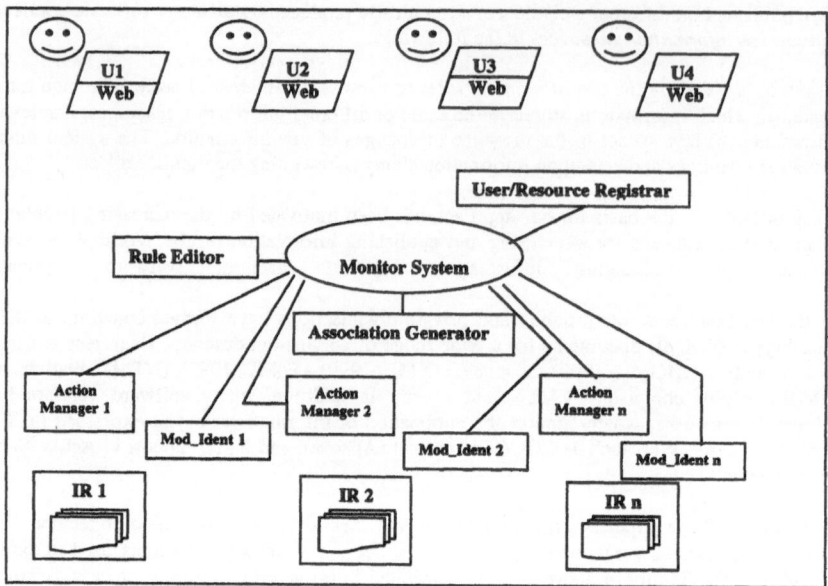

Figure 1: The monitor architecture

2.3 User/Resource Registrar

This component allows the users and information resources to register into the system. After registering into the system, the user can create and edit monitor rules. Each user has distinct 'access rights' for the various information resources.

Each participating information resource has to be registered into the system in order to allow users to define their monitor rules, based on the available information, and to allow the system to monitor its XML documents. The registration of an information resource into the system comprises the specification of its XML documents and their respective DTDs. This information is kept in a special file named *System.xml*. The DTD for this document, *System.dtd*, is presented in Figure 2[1].

The document contains a root element called System, which is composed of any number of IR elements. Each IR element contains a unique identification and an address specified by attributed IR_ID and IR_ADDRESS, respectively. An element IR is composed of any number of DTD_DOC elements. Each DTD_DOC element is composed of any number of XML_DOC elements. A DTD_DOC element is described by a unique identification (DTD_DOC_ID), a name (DTD_DOC_NAME), and an address (DTD_DOC_ADDRESS), for the situation in which the DTD document is located in a different IR. Similarly, a XML_DOC element is described by a unique identification (XML_DOC_ID) and name (XML_DOC_NAME).

---

[1] A description about the syntax of XML is out of the scope of this paper.

```
<!ELEMENT System(IR*)>
<!ELEMENT IR(DTD_DOC*)>
<!ATTLIST IR IR_ID          ID        #REQUIRED
             IR_ADDRESS  CDATA  #REQUIRED>
<!ELEMENT DTD_DOC(XML_DOC*)>
<!ATTLIST DTD_DOC DTD_DOC_ID          ID       #REQUIRED
                  DTD_DOC_NAME     CDATA  #REQUIRED
                  DTD_DOC_ADDRESS  CDATA  #IMPLIED>
<!ELEMENT XML_DOC EMPTY>
<!ATTLIST XML_DOC XML_DOC_ID      ID        #REQUIRED
                  XML_DOC_NAME  CDATA  #REQUIRED>
```

Figure 2: The System.dtd

2.4 Rule Editor

The *rule editor* is a graphical interface, which assists users on creating and editing monitor rules. Before creating a monitor rule, users identify relevant XML documents and their respective DTDs, based on their 'access rights'.

This is executed by either browsing the system and identifying registered information resources, or suggesting new information resources to be added into the system.

The rule editor presents the DTDs of the relevant XML documents to the users. Based on the DTDs, the users define their sets of rules in an interactive way. These rules are expressed in XML and stored in XML documents, called *Uij_Rules.xml*, with i representing a user identification and $j \in N$. The *Uij_Rules.dtd* is presented in Figure 3. The element RuleDoc is composed of any number of MonitorRule elements, and has a unique identification for the user specifying the rule, represented by attribute USER_ID. Element MonitorRule is specified in *MonitorRule.dtd*, presented in section 3, Figure 5.

```
<!ENTITY % monitor_rule.dtd SYSTEM "MonitorRule.dtd">
<!ELEMENT RuleDoc (MonitorRule*)>
<!ATTLIST RuleDoc USER_ID    ID      #REQUIRED>
%monitor_rule.dtd;
```

Figure 3: The Uij_Rule.dtd

2.5 Association Generator

After defining monitor rules and creating *Uij_Rules.xml* documents, it is necessary to keep information about each rule and its associated XML documents to assist with the monitoring process. We propose to store this information in a special file named *Association.xml*, composed of 'extended links', as defined in XLink candidate recommendation (DeRose et al., 2000).

Figure 4 presents the DTD for *Association.xml*, named *Association.dtd*. The DTD is composed of a root element called Association, which contains any number of extended link elements named Rule_assoc_DOC. The extended link contains any number of three different types of 'locators' representing related XML (XML_DOC), DTD (DTD_DOC) and Rule (RULE_DOC) documents.

It also contains any number of 'arc elements' associating the locators. The arc element is called ASSOC.

The *association generator* is responsible for updating *Association.xml* whenever a rule is created, modified, or removed, and whenever a XML document is added to or removed from an information resource. In order to allow distribution of the information monitoring process, various copies of *Association.xml* is replicated through the system. The association generator is responsible for updating all the different copies.

```
<!ELEMENT Association(Rule_assoc_DOC*)>          <!ELEMENT RULE_DOC EMPTY>
<!ELEMENT Rule_assoc_DOC((XML_DOCI            <!ATTLIST RULE_DOC
        DTD_DOCIRULE_DOCIASSOC)*)>                 xmlns:type (locator)      #FIXED "locator"
<!ATTLIST Rule_assoc_DOC                           xmlns:href  CDATA       #REQUIRED
  xmlns:xlink CDATA     #FIXED                     xmlns:role  NMTOKEN #IMPLIED
               href="www.w3.org/199/xlink"         xmlns:title  CDATA      #IMPLIED>
  xmlns:type (extended) #FIXED "extended"       <!ELEMENT ASSOC EMPTY>
  xmlns:role  NMTOKEN #IMPLIED                  <!ATTLIST ASSOC ANY
  xmlns:title  CDATA     #IMPLIED>                 xmlns:type (arc)          #FIXED "arc"
<!ELEMENT XML_DOC EMPTY>                           xmlns:from NMTOKEN #IMPLIED
<!ATTLIST XML_DOC                                  xmlns:to    NMTOKEN #IMPLIED
  xmlns:type (locator)      #FIXED "locator"       xmlns:show (newlreplacelembedlotherlnone)
  xmlns:href  CDATA       #REQUIRED                                        #IMPLIED
  xmlns:role  NMTOKEN #IMPLIED                     xmlns:actuate (onLoadlonRequestlotherl
  xmlns:title  CDATA      #IMPLIED>                                  none) #IMPLIED>
<!ELEMENT DTD_DOC EMPTY>
<!ATTLIST DTD_DOC
  xmlns:type (locator)      #FIXED "locator"
  xmlns:href  CDATA       #REQUIRED
  xmlns:role  NMTOKEN #IMPLIED
  xmlns:title  CDATA      #IMPLIED>
```

Figure 4: The Association.dtd

2.6 Modification Identifier

The *modification identifier* is the component of the system responsible for identifying changes in the XML documents and information resources. In order to avoid centralisation of the monitoring process we use a modification identifier for each participating information resource. Thus, when an existing XML document is modified, or a new XML document is added to an information resource, or an existing XML document is removed from an information resource, the modification identifier notifies *the action manager*. In some cases the association generator is also notified about the changes, in order to update *Association.xml* about links between XML documents and monitor rules (c.f. Section 4).

2.7 Action Manager

The *action manager* is responsible for identifying the monitor rules that are related to modified XML documents and to execute their respective actions. This identification is executed by consulting the *Association.xml* documents. Due to distribution and autonomy issues we use one action manager for each information resource in the system.

3. Monitor Rules

In this section we present the syntax used to express the monitor rules. The monitor rules are described in terms of XML (Bray et al., 1998), XPath (Clark & DeRose, 1999) and XSL (Clark, 1999) syntax. The reasons for using XML, XPath, and XSL are (a) to provide an open and standard way of expressing the rules; (b) to facilitate and standardise the construction and execution of a rule interpreter (action manager); and (c) to facilitate access to and modification of XML documents.

A monitor rule is composed of 3 parts. Part 1 is related to relevant *documents* in various *information resources* to which the rules refer. Part 2 is concerned to *conditions* expressing information in which users are interested, in the various documents and information resources specified in part 1. Part 3 refers to the *actions* that should be taken when a related condition of part 2 is satisfied. An action can be of type "alert", when the user receives an *alert message* notifying that a piece of information has changed, or of type "execute", when part of or an entire XML document has to be modified or created. Note that this XML document can be the document containing the rule, i.e. a monitor rule can be created/modified as a result of an action.

```
<!ELEMENT MonitorRule (IR+,Condition,(LogicalOperator,Condition)*,Action,(LogicalOperator,Action)*)>
<!ATTLIST MonitorRule RULE_ID ID #REQUIRED>
<!ELEMENT IR (DocumentList,XPath)>
<!ATTLIST IR  IR_ID ID  #REQUIRED>
<!ELEMENT DocumentList EMPTY>
<!ATTLIST DocumentList DTD_DOC_ID CDATA  #REQUIRED
                       XML_DOC_ID CDATA  #REQUIRED "all"
                       QUANTIFIER  (foralllexists) #REQUIRED>
<!ELEMENT Condition (Exp,(RelationalOperator,Exp)*)>
<!ATTLIST Condition COND_ID     ID   #REQUIRED>
<!ELEMENT Exp (Quant,(SubExplMathExplAggFuncExp))>
<!ELEMENT Quant EMPTY>
<!ATTLIST Quant VALUE (foralllexists)  #IMPLIED>
<!ELEMENT SubExp(XPath)>
<!ATTLIST SubExp IR_IDREF IDREFS  #REQUIRED>
<!ELEMENT MathExp (MathSubExp,MathematicalOperator,MathSubExp)>
<!ELEMENT MathSubExp (SubExp,(MathematicalOperator,SubExp)*)>
<!ELEMENT AggFuncExp (AggregateFunction,(SubExplMathExp))>
<!ELEMENT XPath  (#PCDATA)>
<!ELEMENT MathematicalOperator EMPTY>
<!ATTLIST MathematicalOperator TYPE (addldiffldivlmult) "add">
<!ELEMENT RelationalOperator EMPTY>
<!ATTLIST RelationalOperator TYPE    (eqlgtlltlgellelneq)  "eq">
<!ELEMENT LogicalOperator EMPTY>
<!ATTLIST LogicalOperator VALUE    (ANDIOR)    "AND">
<!ELEMENT AggregateFunction EMPTY>
<!ATTLIST AggregateFunction TYPE (SumlAvg) #REQUIRED>
<!ELEMENT Action (Assertion*)>
<!ATTLIST Action TYPE           (alertlexecute)  "alert"
                 COND_IDREF   IDREFS   #REQUIRED>
<!ELEMENT Assertion EMPTY>
<!ATTLIST Assertion FUNCTION  (createlremoveladdlnone) "none"
                    XML_DOC_NAME     CDATA  #REQUIRED
                    XML_DOC_ADDRESS CDATA #REQUIRED
                    EXPAssertion        CDATA   #REQUIRED>
```

Figure 5: Monitor rule syntax (MonitorRule.dtd)

In Figure 5 we present the DTD document for the monitor rules, named *MonitorRule.dtd*, containing the syntax for the rules. For each user *i*, the monitor rules are stored in *Uij_Rule.xml*, (j ∈ N). An example of a monitor rule is described in Section 5.

The MonitorRule element is composed of 7 element contents and one attribute. The RULE_ID attribute is a unique identification for each monitor rule in the respective document. The description of the element contents is as follows:

IR – it references different information resources with their relevant XML documents and DTDs. Each information resource has a unique identification represented by attribute IR_ID. The element IR contains elements DocumentList and XPath. These elements are described below:

♦ DocumentList – it describes the different documents in the associated information resource, related to the rule. It is composed of attributes DTD_DOC_ID, referencing the DTD document associated with relevant XML documents; XML_DOC_ID, referencing the relevant XML documents; and QUANTIFIER. The value of XML_DOC_ID can be either a list of XML documents in IR_ID or "all". The latter value means that the conditions associated with the particular IR_ID have to be checked for all XML documents in IR_ID, which conform to the DTD represented in DTD_DOC_ID. The possible values for QUANTIFIER are "forall" and "exists". QUANTIFIER is used to specify when a related Condition has to be satisfied for all documents listed in XML_DOC_ID, or at least one document, respectively.

♦ XPath – it describes XPath expressions (Clark & DeRose, 1999) related to elements in the XML documents for which the conditions in the rule have to be tested.

● Condition – it is composed of a single expression or various expressions associated by relational operators, and a unique identification, represented by attribute COND_ID. The sub-elements composing element Condition are described below:

♦ Exp – it contains a quantifier followed by either a single expression (element SubExp), or a mathematical expression (element MathExp), or an aggregate function expression (element AggFuncExp). The quantifier ("forall", "exists") is represented by element Quant and used to specify when the respective Condition has to be satisfied for all elements resulting from the evaluation of its expressions, or at least one element.

♦ RelationalOperator – it describes a relational operator in attribute TYPE that has to be executed to check the condition.

● SubExp – it is composed of elements of type Xpath or fixed values. It also has references to the IRs containing the documents (attribute IR_IDREF) to which the subexpression needs to be evaluated.

● MathExp – it is composed of mathematical subexpressions (element MathSubExp) associate by mathematical operators (element MathematicalOperator).

♦ MathSubExp – it is composed of one SubExp followed by 0 or more pairs of MathematicalOperator and SubExp, where the MathematicalOperators are of the same type.

♦ MathematicalOperator - it describes a mathematical operator in attribute TYPE that has to be executed to evaluate MathExp, and MathSubExp.

- AggFuncEXp – it is composed of one AggregateFunction followed by either a SubExp or MathExp.

  ◆ AggregateFunction - it describes an aggregate function in attribute TYPE that has to be executed to evaluate AggFuncExp.

- LogicalOperator – this element is concerned to the situation in which the monitor rule is composed of more than one Condition or more than one Action. The element is composed of attribute VALUE, which can have the boolean values "AND" and "OR".

- Action – it is composed of any number of element Assertion, and 2 attributes. Attribute TYPE expresses the kind of action to be executed: "alert" or "execute". In the latter case the information specified by the attributes of element Assertion is executed. Attribute COND_IDREF references related Condition.

- Assertion – it is composed of 4 attributes: FUNCTION, specifies the type of action to be executed; XML_DOC_NAME and XML_DOC_ADDRESS reference the XML document(s) to be created/modified, depending on the FUNCTION; and EXPAssertion, contains XSL expressions to be executed in the XML document(s).

4. Monitoring Process

The process of monitoring XML documents is concerned with the identification of changes in these documents and in the information resources, followed by the execution of the monitor rules. In the next subsections we describe the tasks for each possible situation.

For the description below, consider XML document *xml_docj.xml* in information resource *IR_a*, conforming to *dtd_docj.dtd*. Suppose *mod_ident_a* and *act_mgr_a* the modification identifier and action manager, respectively, associated with *IR-a*.

4.1 Modification of a XML Document

Consider that *xml_docj.xml* has been modified. In this case, *mod_ident_a* identifies that there is a new version of *xml_docj.xml* and sends a message to *act_mgr_a* reporting this fact. After receiving the message, *act_mgr_a* consults document *Association.xml* in order to identify the monitor rules related to *xml_docj.xml*. Note that the rules characterised by "all" XML documents conforming to *dtd_docj.dtd* have also to be identified. In the next step *act_mgr_a* interprets all relevant monitor rules and executes the actions related to the conditions that are satisfied.

4.2 Addition of a New XML Document

Suppose *xml_docj.xml* being added to information resource *IR_a*. After identifying that a new XML document has been added into *IR_a*, *mod_ident_a* sends a message to *act_mgr_a*. After receiving the message, *act_mgr_a* consults *System.xml* to verify if *dtd_docj.dtd* is already participating in the system. There are 2 possibilities:

i. dtd_docj.dtd is already referenced in the system

In this case *act_mgr_a* consults *Association.xml* in order to identify the monitor rules related to all XML documents that conform to *dtd_docj.dtd*. In the next step, *act_mgr_a* interprets all identified rules and executes the actions associated to the conditions that are satisfied. After, *act_mgr_a* updates *System.xml* document, with the information about *xml_docj.xml*, and the multiple copies of *Association.xml*, with the information about the rules related to *xml_docj.xml*.

ii. dtd_docj.dtd is not referenced in the system

In this case *act_mgr_a* updates *System.xml* with the information about the new DTD and XML document.

4.3 Addition of a New XML Document

Suppose *xml_docj.xml* being added to information resource *IR_a*. After identifying that a new XML document has been added into *IR_a*, *mod_ident_a* sends a message to *act_mgr_a*. After receiving the message, *act_mgr_a* consults *System.xml* to verify if *dtd_docj.dtd* is already participating in the system. There are 2 possibilities:

i. dtd_docj.dtd is already referenced in the system

In this case *act_mgr_a* consults *Association.xml* in order to identify the monitor rules related to all XML documents that conform to *dtd_docj.dtd*. In the next step, *act_mgr_a* interprets all identified rules and executes the actions associated to the conditions that are satisfied. After, *act_mgr_a* updates *System.xml* document, with the information about *xml_docj.xml*, and the multiple copies of *Association.xml*, with the information about the rules related to *xml_docj.xml*.

ii. dtd_docj.dtd is not referenced in the system

In this case *act_mgr_a* updates *System.xml* with the information about the new DTD and XML document.

4.4 Removal of a XML Document

Suppose *xml_docj.xml* being removed from information resource *IR_a*. After identifying that XML document has been removed from *IR_a*, *mod_ident_a* sends a message to *act_mgr_a*. After receiving the message, *act_mgr_a* consults *Association.xml* to identify all the rules related to *xml_docj.xml*. In the next step, *act_mgr_a* updates *Association.xml*, relevant monitor rules and *System.xml*.

4.5 Removal of a DTD

Suppose *dtd_docj.dtd* being removed from *IR_a*. In this case *mod_ident_a* identifies this fact and sends a message to *act_mgr_a*. After, *act_mgr_a* consults *System.xml* to identify the related XML documents. In the next steps *act_mgr_a* updates *System.xml*,, consults *Association.xml* to specify rules associated with the identified XML documents and *dtd_docj.dtd*, updates *Association.xml*, and notifies the users of the related rules about the removal of *dtd_docj.dtd*.

```
<RuleDoc   User_ID = "U1">
<MonitorRule Rule_ID = "R1">
<IR   IR_ID ="IR_a">
 <DocumentList   DTD_DOC_ID = "FXSwap"
                 XML_DOC_ID = "all"
                 QUANTIFIER ="exists"> </DocumentList>
 <XPath>root()/child::fpml:FpML/child::fpml:Trade/child::fpml:Product/child::fpswp:FXSwap</XPath>
</IR>
<IR   IR_ID ="IR_b">
 <DocumentList   DTD_DOC_ID = "FXSwap"
                 XML_DOC_ID = "all"
                 QUANTIFIER ="exists"> </DocumentList>
 <XPath>root()/child::fpml:FpML/child::fpml:Trade/child::fpml:Product/child::fpswp:FXSwap</XPath>
</IR>
<Condition COND_ID ="C1">
<Expl IR_IDREF = "IR_a">
<Quant VALUE = "exists"/>
<SubExp> <XPath>./descendant::fxs:settlementDate</XPath> </SubExp>
</Exp>
<RelationalOperator TYPE= "gt"/>
<Exp IR_IDREF = "IR_a">
</QUANT>
<SubExp> <XPath> #2000-09-01</XPath> </SubExp>
</Exp>
</Condition>
<LogicalOperator VALUE = "OR"/>
<Condition COND_ID ="C2">
<Exp IR_IDREF = "IR_b">
<Quant VALUE = "exists"/>
<SubExp> <XPath>./descendant::fxs:settlementDate</XPath> </SubExp>
</Exp>
<RelationalOperator TYPE= "gt"/>
<Exp IR_IDREF = "IR_b">
</QUANT>
<SubExp> <XPath> #2000-09-01 </XPath> </SubExp>
</Exp>
</Condition>
<Action TYPE = "alert"
        COND_IDREF = "C1"/>
<LogicalOperator VALUE = "AND"/>
<Action TYPE = "alert"
        COND_IDREF = "C2"/>
</MonitorRule>
</RuleDoc>
```

Figure 6: An example of U11_Rule.xml

5. An Example

In this section we present an example in the financial domain to illustrate our approach. For the example we use FXSwap.dtd proposed by the Financial product Markup Language (FpML, 1999).

Suppose 2 information resources *IR_a* and *IR_b* with XML documents that conform to FpML DTDs. Consider *IR_a* and *IR_b* related to the sites of 2 branches of a commercial bank called *Controler_Bank*. Suppose user *U1*, the chief risk officer of *Controler_Bank*, wants to be informed of trades that will be settled after *01/09/2000*. Assume *U1* is authorised to know about all trading transactions in *Controler_Bank* and, therefore, he has 'access rights' to *IR_a* and *IR_b*.

The monitor rule is described in *U11_Rule.xml* as presented in Figure 6. In this case, one of the subexpressions of the condition (SubExp) has a fixed value, instead of a specific XPath expression, i.e. *#2000-09-01*.

The described scenario is an example of the addition of new XML documents (c.f. subsection 4.2), which conform to existing DTDs, in the information resources.

Consider a new trade, with *Controler_Bank* as one of the parties, with settlement date *2000-09-12*. Suppose document *New_Trade.xml* related to this trade and added into *IR_a*. In this case the modification identifier associated to *IR_a* identifies the existence of a new XML document and sends a message to the action manager associated to *IR_a*. Upon receiving the message, the action manager executes the tasks described in subsection 4.2, interprets rule R1, and sends an *alert message* to the chief risk officer of *Controler_Bank*.

6. Related Work

The emergence of the XML as a standard for information structuring and publishing on the World Wide Web, triggered work to support information retrieval of XML documents, as described below.

One strand of this work has been concerned with the definition and implementation of query languages for XML documents. Examples are found in XML-QL (DeRose et al., 2000), Lorel (Goldman et al., 1999), and YATL (Cluet et al., 1998). However, none of these languages has been accepted as a standard by the World Wide Web consortium (W3C), which has set up its own working group for defining a query language for XML (W3C, 2000).

Another strand of work has been concerned with the construction of querying engines accessible through APIs to support information retrieval from XML documents, as proposed in XML query engine (Fatdod). In addition, the work regarding indexing schemes used to improve the efficiency of information retrieval from XML documents (Dongwook et al., 1998) (McHugh & Widom, 1999).

Also, numerous commercial systems which combine traditional forms of text-based information retrieval with schemes for retrieving information from structured XML documents have been developed. Examples of such systems are the Ultraseek (Infoseek), InfoGlide XML Similarity Search Engine (InfoGlide), and GoXML (GoXML).

Our scheme for expressing the conditions of the monitor rules is similar to the one used in Lorel (Goldman et al., 1999). In particular, what regards to the use of path expressions, elements treated with no sub-elements as atomic values, and the support for universal and existential quantification. On the other hand, YATL (Cluet et al., 1998) provides a more heavy weight scheme for expressing rules, which determine when and how to integrate information from heterogeneous data sources. These sources include but are not limited to XML documents. The scheme is based on the YAT data model, developed to support the representation of data from those data sources.

To the best of our knowledge most of the above commercial systems focus on information retrieval from XML documents and do not provide a mechanism for constant monitoring of information changes in a specified collection of XML documents. Some of these systems, like the InfoGlide XML Similarity Search Engine (InfoGlide), provide servers with APIs that can be used by user applications. Such servers could be used to construct client applications providing functionality similar to that described in this paper. However, not through the declarative approach that we have advocated here.

7. Conclusion and Future Work

In this paper, we presented a system to allow distributed information monitoring of XML documents on the World Wide Web. The approach preserves the autonomy of the XML documents being monitored and supports evolution of the system.

Our approach is based on monitoring rules, which express information that is relevant to the users. A monitor rule is composed of *conditions* and *actions*. The conditions specify information in which users are interested. The actions refer to the operations that should be taken when the conditions are satisfied.

In order to illustrate our approach we presented an example in the financial domain. However, the approach can be used in other domains where it is important to monitor and be informed of information changes. Examples are found in the health care domain, scientific domain, and e-commerce domain, among others.

Currently our work is at an initial stage, although it builds upon earlier work reported in (Ellmer et al., 2000) (Zisman et al., 2000). In (Ellmer et al., 2000) the authors proposed an approach to allow consistency management of distributed XML documents. The approach relies on rules expressed in XML (Zisman et al., 2000) (called *consistency rules* in that context). A prototype including a consistency rule editor, a consistency rule interpreter, and a consistency link generator has been implemented and tested for examples in the software engineering domain.

At the moment we are developing a prototype to support our monitoring process. We are also building a rule editor to support the construction of the monitor rules and implementing a monitor rule interpreter, together with the action manager and the user/resource registrar.

We plan to experiment and use our approach in large domains. We also intend to investigate the use of schemes for indexing XML documents (Dongwook et al., 1998) (McHugh & Widom, 1999) in the monitoring process. In addition, we are investigating the expressiveness of the monitor rule syntax by exploring different domains. Another aspect that we are investigating is related to the extension of the architecture of the system to allow users to define monitor rules and be informed about relevant information through hand-set devices.

References:

(Adler et al., 2000): S. Adler, A. Berlund, J. Caruso, S. Deach, A. Milowski, S. Parnell, J. Richman, and S. Zilles. Extensible Stylesheet Language (XSL) Version 1.0. Working Draft http://www.w3.org/TR/2000/WD-xsl-20000112, World Wide Web Consortium.

(Apache): Apache XML project. Cocoon. http://xml.apache.org/cocoon/.

(BIOML, 1999): BIOpolymer Markup Language. http://www.bioml.com/BIOML/index.html.

(Bray et al., 1998): T. Bray, J. Paoli, and C.M. Sperberg-McQueen. Extensible Markup Language. Recommendation http://www.w3.org/TR/1998/REC-xml-19980210, World Wide Web Consortium.

(Clark, 1999): J. Clark. XSL Transformations (XSLT) Version 1.0. Recommendation http://www.w3.org/TR/1999/REC-xslt-19991116, World Wide Web Consortium.

(Clark & DeRose, 1999): J. Clark and S. DeRose. XML Path Language (XPath). Recommendation http://www.w3.org/TR/1999/REC-xpath-19991116, World Wide Web Consortium.

(Cluet et al., 1998): S. Cluet, C. Delobel, J. Simeon, and K. Smaga. Your Mediators Need Data Conversion! In Proceedings of ACM-SIGMOD International Conference on Management of Data, 177-188, 1998.

(CML): Chemical Markup Language. http://www.xml-cml.org.

(Deitel et al., 1999): H. Deitel, P. Deitel, and T.R. Nito. Internet and the World Wide Web – How to Program. Prentice Hall, ISBN 0-13-016143-8, 1999.

(DeRose et al., 2000): S. DeRose, E. Maler, D. Orchard, and B. Trafford. XML Linking Language (Xlink) Version 1.0. Candidate Recommendation http://www.w3.org/TR/2000/CR-xlink-20000703, World Wide Web Consortium.

(Deutsch et al., 1999): A. Deutsch, M. Fernandez, D. Florescu, A. Levy, and D. Suciu. A Query Language for XML. In International World Wide Web Conference, 1999. http://www.research.att.com/~mff/files/final.html.

(Dongwook, 1998): S. Dongwook. Structured Querying, Indexing, and Retrieval for SGML/XML Documents. In Proceedings of SGML/XML Japan '98, pp. 199-214.

(DuCharme, 1999): B. DuCharme, XML: The Annotated Specification. Prentice Hall PTR, ISBN: 0-13-082676-6, 1999.

(Ellmer et al., 2000): E. Ellmer, W. Emmerich, A. Finkelstein, D. Smolko, and A. Zisman. Consistency Management of Distributed Documents using XML and Related Technologies *(submitted for publication)*.

(Fatdog, 1999): Fatdog Software, XML Query Engine. http://www.fatdog.com/.

(FIXML, 1999): A Markup Language for the FIX Application Message Layer. http://www.oasis-open.org/cover/fixml.html.

(FpML, 1999): Financial Product Markup Language. http://www.fpml.org/.

(Goldman et al., 1999): R. Goldman, J. McHugh, and J. Widom. From Semistructured Data to XML: Migrating the Lore Data Model and Query Language. Proceedings of the 2nd International Workshop on the Web and Databases (WebDB'99), Philadelphia, Pennsylvania, June 1999.

(GoXML): GoXML, http://www.goxml.com/.

(InfoGlide): The XML Similarity Engine. http://www.infoglide.com/technology/techprod.htm.

(Infoseek): Ultaseek Server v3.1 Release Notes.
        http://software.infoseek.com/products/ultraseek/docs/relnotes_3_1.htm.

(MathML, 1999): Mathematical Markup Language. http://www.w3c.org/Math/.

(McHugh and Widom, 1999): J. McHugh and J. Widom. Query Optimization for XML.
        Proceedings of the Twenty-Fifth International Conference on Very
        Large Data Bases, Edinburgh, Scotland, September 1999.

(NTM): Network Trade Model. Trade Definitions User Guide. http://www.infinity.com.

(OASIS): The XML Cover Pages. http://www.oasis-open.org/cover/sgml-xml.html.

(W3C, 2000): XML Query Requirements, W3C Working Draft 31 January 2000.
        http://www.w3.org/TR/2000/WD-xmlquery-req-20000131, World Wide Web
        Consortium.

(Zisman et al., 2000): A Zisman, W. Emmerich, and A. Finkelstein. Using XML to Build
        Consistency Rules for Distributed Specifications. 10th International
        Workshop on Software Specification and Design (IWSSD), San Diego,
        November, 2000.

A XML Server Architecture
based on Presentation-Abstraction-Control Style

Zaijun Hu

ABB Kommunikations- und Informationsservices GmbH

Kallstadter Strasse 1, D-68309 Mannheim, Germany

E-mail: zaijun.hu@de.abb.com Fax: +49 621 3815111

ABSTRACT. *XML server provides a solution for data exchange, publication and sharing over Internet or Intranet by taking advantage of open, flexible, platform-, vendor-independent Extensible Markup Language (XML). In this paper a kind of XML server architecture based on the presentation-abstraction-control-style (PAC) is presented. The architecture can better address challenges such as adaptability, extensibility, data abstraction, data presentation, and data manipulation that will be faced in developing XML server. The central point of the architecture is design of hierarchically structured cooperating agents that consist of presentation, abstraction and control parts. In this paper we will define the basic structure of the architecture, describe the identified agents and present an implementation of the architecture.*

KEY WORDS: XML, Server, Architecture, Presentation-Abstraction-Control

1. Background

Internet provides a very effective way for broadcasting and sharing information across different platforms. It makes information available anywhere, anytime and to every authorized person. By means of a web browser one can access to, search for and query the required information easily and quickly. HTML or dynamic HTML (DHTML) is used for display information in a web browser on the client side. With the wide use of the Internet a new technology Extensible Markup Language (XML) is developed for describing, modeling, structuring information and the relations among the information elements. The benefits of XML are platform-independence, vendor-independence and programming language independence. It enables easy data description and exchange. Therefore it is being established as a standard that is accepted and driven by major leading Internet solution providers.

2. Introduction

A XML server is a web and/or data server where data is described by means of XML. For a request from a client it returns data in a predefined format such as HTML or DHTML pages that can be displayed and interacted in a web browser directly. It can also generate XML data for data exchange or data integration among different applications and so on. The XML server provides a solution for organizing and structuring data so that data search, query navigation and manipulation become easy and efficient. It also makes multiple views of data possible so that data can be presented in different way for users with different requirements. In order to realize the XML server the following challenges shall be addressed.

Data Abstraction – the data structure, data relation, data type etc. shall be defined and described in XML. The data abstraction is the key part of the XML server. It affects data display for clients and data manipulation.

Data Presentation – the data presentation provides a way for clients or users to view, to access to the information available on the XML server. Good design of data presentation enables easy and efficient access to the information. For the XML server the data presentation shall fully use the structure, rules, types that are defined in the XML data to reach effective information display for the navigation purpose.

Data manipulation – the data manipulation includes data search, navigation and modification.

Performance – the XML shall show satisfied performance in order to attract users to further use of the server.

Adaptability - the change of one local part of the XML server shall not affect the whole server.

The architecture includes the hardware and software aspects. The hardware architecture is the computing infrastructure that consists of computers and networks. But the hardware architecture is not focus of this paper. The software architecture of a XML server is the structure or structures of the system which contain the XML data (usually stored in XML files or in the XML-enabled database), the corresponding software components, the server-side pages which are responsible for generating views and client-side user interaction pages. It defines the structure of the data abstraction, the data presentation, and the data manipulation. The goal of the architecture design is to identify separable parts that comprise the whole system, the externally visible properties and behaviors of those parts and relationships among them. The design of the software architecture of XML server is critical for an easy-to-use and efficient XML server. It is also very important for adaptability. Security is also critical aspect of the software architecture for the XML server. But it is not part of this paper.

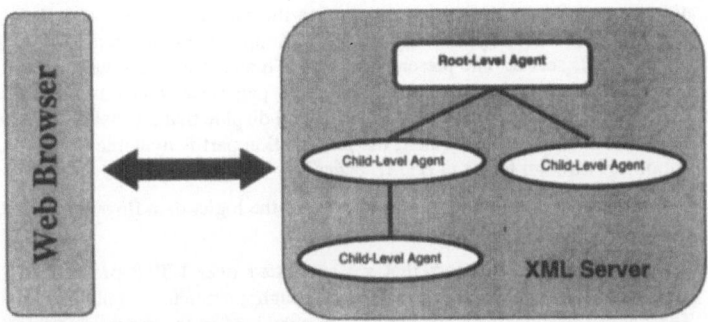

Figure 1 PAC-Architecture

The software architecture with Presentation-Abstraction-Control (PAC) style can be found in many software applications for interactive software system. The detail information on the usual PAC architecture pattern can be found in [1]. We borrow the design concept for the development of the XML server architecture, which provides a solution for the challenges mentioned above.

We will discuss the structure and basic elements of the architecture. We will also demonstrate an implementation of the architecture.

3. Presentation-Abstraction-Control style

The architecture with the presentation-abstraction-control style defines a structure in form of cooperating agents. The agent is the central point of the architecture design. Each agent is responsible for an aspect of functionalities of the whole system and usually consists of three components: presentation, abstraction and control. Such architecture enables division of whole system into parts (agents) and therefore the separate development of individual parts. It also benefits to adaptability and extensibility of the system. Figure 1 illustrates the structure of the PAC-architecture. In this paper we will try to use PAC architecture style to define a software architecture for the XML server that enables the structured and hierarchical presentation and manipulation of the data described or modeled with XML.

In this paper two kinds of agents, the root-level agent and the child-level agent, are identified and shown in figure 1. Each agent comprises three parts: abstraction, control and presentation.

3.1 Root-Level Agent

The root-level agent is responsible for delivering the corresponding response as users access to the XML server using URL address of it. It provides the start page, which for example can include login, registration, overview etc. It is the door to the further content provided by the XML server.

The abstraction part of the root-level agent defines the data model that describes information supplied in the start page of the XML server. It can be, for example, overview information, summary, description of information categories presented by the XML server or guideline etc. The attractive and well-organized information is a very important aspect for building the abstraction part because it has direct influence on the success of the XML server.

The presentation part of the root-level agent specifies the views of data that is defined in the abstraction part. It also provides opportunity for users to input some necessary information that are required by the XML server. The presentation part is realized through one or more than one HTML page that will be transferred to the client. The pages can contain some presentation components that are used for complicated or sophisticated display that a usual HTML page is not capable of. If the user interaction is required the presentation part is dynamic HTML pages. The Input can be submitted through forms in HTML pages.

The control part of the root-level agent is responsible for the logic, data flow control and control flow. It has the following tasks:

- It processes the requests from users that are submitted over HTTP protocol to the XML server. Users can also specify their requests through parameters contained in the URL address. The control part analyzes the parameters contained in the requests and performs the corresponding actions.

- If the presentation part has more than one view the control part is also responsible for coordinating the different views and the communication among views.

- The treatment of multiple users and sessions is also a task of the control part. For example creation and management of the sharable object among multiple users or sessions.

- The control part is also responsible for the performance improvement. Sometimes it is necessary to have cache mechanism for performance improvement. The control part should also implement this function or use the corresponding components and integrate them into the agent.

- The control part of the root level agent also delegates the requests from users to its child-level agent if necessary. It activates the agent on the deeper level to perform the corresponding processing. In this case it is an intermediate between users and the agents on the deeper level.

Figure 2 demonstrates the relation among the tree parts of the root-level agent.

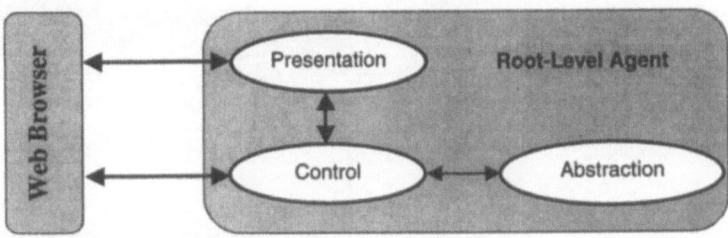

Figure 2 Root-Level Agent

The presentation and control parts of the root-level agent have direct contact to the web browser used by users. The control part receives the requests including parameters specified in URL address. Users can also submit input through forms or interaction components contained in the HTML pages. There is no direct relation between presentation and the abstraction part or between the web browser and the abstraction part of the root-level agent. But to build effective presentation part it is useful to know the internal structure and relations of the abstraction part.

3.2 Child-Level Agent

The child-level agent represents a semantically independent concept of the system. Like the root-level agent. It also comprises three parts: abstraction, presentation and control. The functions of the three parts are the same as those of the root-level-agent.

The abstraction part represents semantically independent information or data. It could be a category, more concrete information that users are directly interested, and a coupled group of information etc. It defines the basic information atoms, the relationship among them and the structure. The abstraction part of the child-level agent should be semantically or logically related to the one of its parent. In this way we build a hierarchical structure of the abstraction parts for different abstraction levels. Dependent on complexity and complication of the information, that should be abstracted or modeled, it is usually useful to introduce one or more than one meta layer for describing information. The meta-layer represents the types, relations and structures of data. Because XML is very suitable for describing structure, relation, hierarchy, types of information it will be used to model the abstraction part.

The presentation part of the child-level agent has the similar responsibilities to the one of the root-level agent. In the presentation design the relation to the parent-level shall be taken into account.

Besides the functions mentioned for the root-agent the control part of the child-level also builds bridge between the current child-level agent and its parent as well as relation between it and its child. If the presentation part has more than one view and each view is complicated it is probably necessary to build the control component for each view for manipulation of the view. Figure 3 shows a root-level agent with a child-level agent.

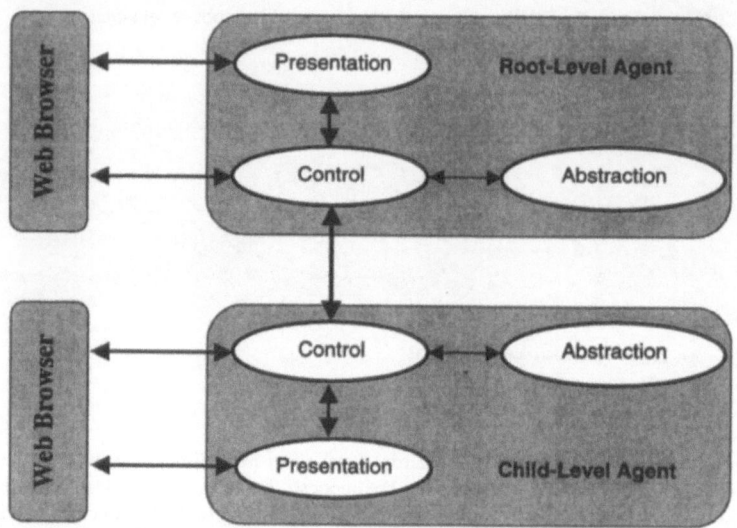

Figure 3 Relation between Root-level and Child-level Agents

4. Implementation

We have explained the XML server architecture with the Presentation-Abstraction-Control style. The key element of the architecture is the agent that consists of presentation, abstraction and control parts. The important characteristic of the architecture is the hierarchical structure. Each agent is associated to a node of the hierarchy. In the following we will present an implementation of such a architecture.

4.1 Three-tier environment

Because XML server is a web and/or a data server we will use the usual and popular three-tier structure as the implementation environment for the design of the XML server architecture. The three-tier structure consists of front-end for user interaction, middle-tier for the application-specific logic and backend for the model repository. The middle-tier and the backend tier can physically be located on the same machine or on the separate machines.

4.1.1 Backend-tier

The backend tier is the storage that stores the data described with XML. The abstraction parts of the agents will be realized in this tier. The backend design is extremely important for the whole system. The following points have to be considered in the design of the tier.

Storage form

The way of how data shall be stored must be decided. Should data be kept in a database or can be organized in the file system? If the data is stored in a database it is convenient that the database has XML support. That means, the database can either export or import XML data or it is like a XML DOM object that accepts the normal XML object operations. The database solution requires usually either the expensive development work or license fee of existing commercial products. The database solution is suitable for the large amount of data and high performance. Another alternative is using the file system to manage XML data. In this case XML data is organized in many XML files. In contrast to the database solution the file system method is relatively simple and reasonably priced. In this paper we choose the file system solution for the implementation of the PAC-architecture. But the management of the XML files has to be realized. The storage form has direct influence on the design and implementation of other tiers and parts such as presentation and control ones.

Information classification

Information classification is about classifying information into a group of information categories. Each category represents a semantically independent information unit or concept. For example an information system for a bookstore contains categories such as history, entertainment, sport, travel, computer science and so on. The information classification has direct impact on the organization of XML data. The number of the XML files to be built is proportional to the number of categories. The more categories there are, the more complex the system is. Therefore an optimal classification is important for the final realization of the system.

Information hierarchy

The information classification is division of information into some parallel groups according to content. The groups are independent of each other. In another word the information classification is about the horizontal structuring of information. No layer is created or defined through the classification. Information hierarchy defines layers or levels that structure information vertically. Each layer is conceptually or semantically the superset of its descendants. Just as the information classification it is also important for the information hierarchy to find an optimal depth or the number of layers. Through the information classification and hierarchy we build a information tree that can be best described with XML.

Information type

The information type describes a group of the common characteristic shared by a set or collection of information elements. For example a book has author, title, publication date, ISBN number etc. Book can be defined as a type that can be used for describing book instances. A type represents not only the common attributes of information elements but also associates a set of operations to it. The type also defines structure of data and relationships among elements. For example: which elements are child elements of others, the sequence in which the child elements can appear and the number of the child elements. The introduction of types into data simplifies the data query, search and presentation. Another benefit of the type is to enable standardization of data description so that data exchange and data sharing become easier. The type also enables the validation of data. A set of types that are introduced to data builds the type system of data. In the XML server we use XML schema to define the type system of data because XML schema is itself XML and uses XML syntax and rules.

Well XML schema files defines types of the data and XML instance files contain data itself.

One question to be answered is the organization of XML schema files and the relation between XML schema files and XML instance files. Shall we have one big XML schema file for the XML server or shall we have more than one XML schema files? Shall a set of XML instance file share one XML schema file? Or each XML instance file owns its own schema file.

In the figure 4 four variations for the relations among the XML schema files and XML instance files are illustrated.

M:1 - Relation - in this case many XML instance files share one XML schema file. The advantage of such variation is that it is easy to keep types consistent throughout the whole XML

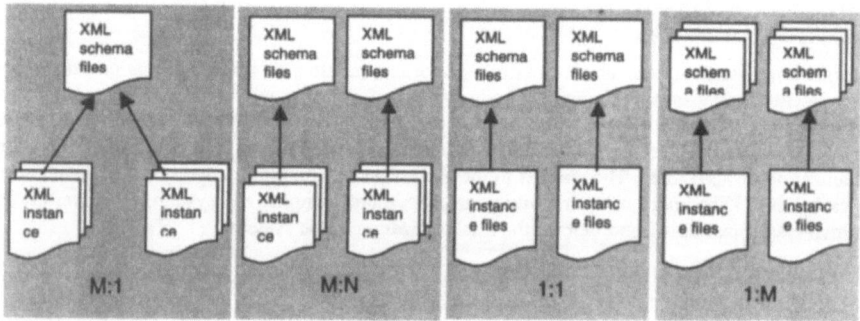

Figure 4 Relation between XML schema file and XML instance file

instance files. The changes in the XML schema file forces adaptation of all XML instance files to keep those files validate. That leads to simultaneous actions undertaken by different persons if different persons are involved in developing the XML instance files. Therefore the efficient coordination is required. But this is sometimes impossible if human resources are already allocated to other tasks. Another drawback of such variation is that the XML schema is usually large and the performance will be influenced negatively.

1:1 – Relation - in this variation each XML instance file owns a XML schema that describes the types used in the XML instance file. The benefit of the implementation is that the development of each XML instance file is independent of others so that the coordination cost can be kept low. But on the other hand this variation will sometimes leads to the inconsistent problem.

1:M – Relation - the variation means that a XML instance file can be bound to many XML schema files. That is usual case for a XML instance file. The relation enables a XML instance file to use more than one type system defined in different XML schema files. The development of XML schema files can be carried out separately. The relation usually appears in combination

M:N – Relation - the variation enables some XML instance files to share the same XML schema. This is a compromise of the M:1 and 1:1 relations. Because it could overcome the drawbacks of M:1 and 1:1 variations. Therefore it could be the best choice.

Directory structure in the file system

As mentioned earlier we have chosen the file system as the storage form. That means the modeled data are stored in XML instance files. The organization of XML schema files and instance files will be realized through the directory structure provided by the operating system.

The directory structure fully depends on the information tree structure. Each directory corresponds to a node in the information tree and has at least one XML instance file. But not every node in the information tree is associated to a directory. A directory with the XML files contained under the directory represents a subtree in the information tree structure. Figure 5

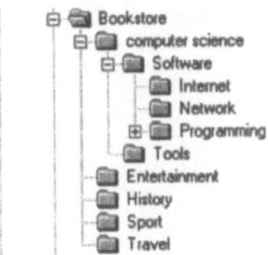

Figure 5 Directory Structure

shows an example of a directory structure.

If the abstraction part and other parts of agent are located at the same machine the directory structure can also be used for organizing other parts of the agents.

4.1.2 Middle-tier

As mentioned above the architecture with PAC-style consists of three parts: data abstraction, data presentation and control. The three parts can be distributed on the different machines. In the section 4.1.1 we have explained the part of the data abstraction. Here we will present an implementation where the parts for the data presentation and control are located at the middle tier and on the same machine.

Presentation

The data presentation is about design of the client-side display of the data described in the data abstraction part. It also deals with the user interaction such as user inputs, manipulation of the client-side display performed by users. The key question here is how to use the structure, relationship, hierarchy defined in the data abstraction to generate the client-side presentation efficiently.

Unlike HTML XML does not predefine display properties for specific elements. XSL (Extensible Stylesheet Language) is designed for that purpose. Therefore XSL best understands the structure, hierarchy, relationship, and types defined with XML. XSL enables the separation of data modeling and data presentation so that the development of data model and data display can

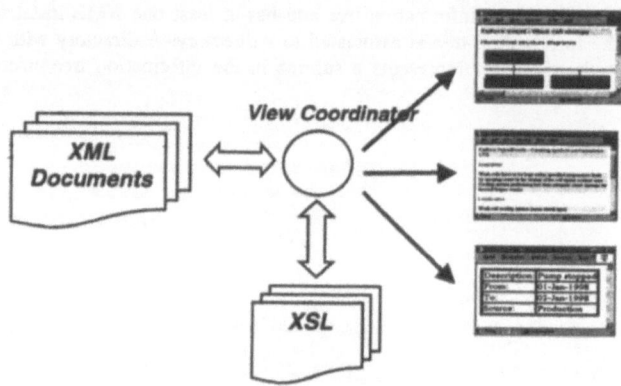

Figure 6 Data Presentation with XSL

developed independently. Another advantage of XSL is that XSL uses the same syntax as XML and it can also contain script language such as JScript. XSL can be used to describe different rules for data display so that multiple views of data can be realized. Figure 6 illustrates the principle of using XSL for the presentation of XML data. In figure 6 three views are created. Each view is realized through a XSL file that is loaded and used to transform XML data to HTML elements displayed in the web browser. The view coordinator, that is a component of the control part, is responsible for this task.

Controller (Control Part of Agent)

The control part is responsible for the dynamic aspect of the XML server, such as control flow, application logic, data exchange, message transfer, request delegation etc. The control parts of agents on different levels are also subject to the structure, hierarchy defined in the XML data. The implementation of the control part of the agent depends on which one of the two distribution variations is chosen: server-side variation or client-side variation.

- *Server-side variation*

The XML server-side variation means XML data/documents including XSL documents are hold on the server machine. No XML documents are downloaded or transferred to the clients. The control parts of agents (controller) are also located on the server machine at runtime. The client

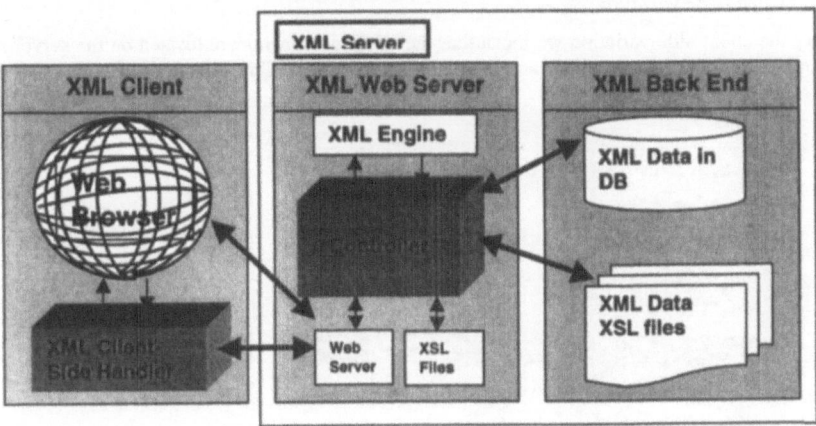

Figure 7 Server-side variation

can only see the HTML data converted from the corresponding XML data. The advantage of this variation is that the client can use any browser that support HTML to access the XML server. There is no need for the client-side XML support for processing XML documents [3]. Therefore the implementation of the manipulation of XML documents does not depend on the web browser used by the XML client. Another benefit of the architecture is the performance for one-time access. It is not necessary to download all XML documents to the client side, which are not required by the XML client. That will reduce the network load and improve the performance for one-time access. But on the other hand the variation will increase the network traffic because each user interaction that requires processing of XML documents is performed on the server machine. Therefore compromise shall be found for the optimal realization. The figure 7 illustrates the XML server-side variation.

In our implementation the XML client uses the web browser to access the XML server that consists of the XML web server and XML backend. The client-side handler deals with the manipulation of the HTML documents generated by the XML server and the user interaction with the XML server. The controller uses XML engine to manipulate XML documents. The XML engine is a XML parser component.

In the server-side variation the controller is realized with the server page that contains the server-side script and can be executed on the server. ASP (Active Server Page) is an example of the server page. The server page is responsible for loading XML data, transforming XML data into HTML page containing the corresponding client-side script by using XSL files. It also analyzes the requests from users or clients and performs actions according to the result of analysis. The communication between agents on the different levels is also undertaken by the control part (controller) of the agents. Other functions of the control part mentioned earlier are implemented in one or more than one server page. It is also possible to establish a special server page for handling a view created by a XSL file.

- *Client-side variation*

By the client-side variation we mean that the XML documents are located on the server machine and downloaded to the client and processed on the client side as users access the XML server.

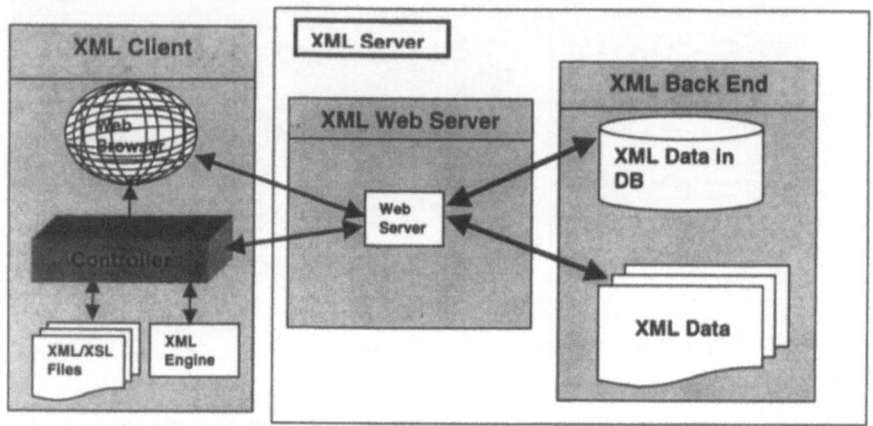

Figure 8 client-side variation

The advantage of the variation is that the network traffic can be reduced. Because the manipulation of the XML documents is performed on the client side it is not dependent on the server performance. The drawback of the variation is that the web browser deployed on the client side can affect the implementation of the manipulation of XML documents. Another disadvantage is that all XML documents have to be downloaded once to the client. It will takes long time for a big XML document. Figure 8 shows the client-side variation.

In comparison to the server-side variation the control parts of the agents are transferred to the client side at runtime. The processing of XML documents is performed on the client side. The XML web server is reduced to the usual web server that is responsible for delivering the HTML or XML/XSL documents required by users. The controller downloaded to the client side is also responsible for the client-side handling of user interaction.

In the client-side variation the control parts of the agents on the different levels are implemented through usual HTML pages containing client-side script that deals with user interaction and manipulation of HTML documents. Because of this implementation the client-side variation can not analyze or process the parameter contained in the URL address so that it is impossible for users to parameterize their requests. All possible user interactions are predefined by the system. Users do not have opportunities to program the XML server for some special cases. That is less flexible in comparison to the server-side variation. The connection between agents on different levels is simply the hyperlink in the case of the client-side variation.

Agent Hierarchy and Organization

We have presented a directory structure for organizing data abstraction. The same directory structure is also used for the management of agent hierarchy. Each directory contains not only XML data but also the control part and the presentation part that are implemented through server pages and XSL files. That means, each directory represents an agent that consists of data abstraction, data presentation, and control. Figure 9 demonstrates an example of teh directory structure that can be used for managing agent hierarchy. To store images and scripts that are needed for the agent two subdirectories are established, one is /images and another is /scripts.

5. Conclusion

In this paper we have presented an XML server architecture with the presenation-abstraction-control style. The architecture is characterized through cooperative agents that consist of three parts: presentation, abstraction and control. The agents are organized in a hierarchical structure defined in the XML data that are located on the server, should be manipulated and displayed in a web browser on the clinet side. The architecture enables easy extensibility and separate development of different parts of data modeling, presentation and application logic. It addresses the challenges faced in establishing the XML server.

6. Reference

[1]   F. Buschmann "Pattern-Oriented Software Architecture. A System of Pattern" Jon Wiley & Sons, Ltd, 1996

[2]   L. Bass: "Software Architecture in Practice" Addison Wesley Longman, Inc.

[3]   H. Behme "XML in der Praxis" Addison Wesley Longman Inc.

[4]   T. Bray; J. Paoli; C.M. Sperberg-McQueen; E. Maler:Extensible Markup Language(XML) 1.0 2000, http://www.w3.org/TR/2000/REC-xml-20001006.htm

[5]   Design Issue. http://www.w3.org/DesignIssues/Overview.html

[6]   R. Anderson; C. Blexrud, A. Chiareli; D. Denault; A. Homer; D. Esposito, B. Francis, M. Gibbs, B. Kropog, C.Mcqueen; G. Reilly; S. Robinson; J. Schenken; D. Sonderegger; D. Sussman: "Professional Active Server Page 3.0", Wrox Press, 1999

AUTHOR INDEX